# AUDITING

# THE IRWIN SERIES IN UNDERGRADUATE ACCOUNTING

**Hermanson, Turner, Plunkett and Walker**
Computerized Accounting with Peachtree

**Hermanson, Strawser, and Strawser**
Auditing Theory and Practice
*Sixth Edition*

**Holt, Grinnaker and Broome**
Principles Disk

**Hopson and Meyer**
Income Tax Fundamentals for 1993 Tax Returns,
*1994 Edition*

**Hoyle**
Advanced Accounting
*Fourth Edition*

**Jesser**
Integrated Accounting for Microcomputers

**Koerber**
College Accounting
*Revised Edition*

**Larson and Miller**
Fundamental Accounting Principles
*Thirteenth Edition*

**Larson and Miller**
Financial Accounting
*Fifth Edition*

**Larson, Spoede and Miller**
Principles of Financial and Manageral Accounting

**Maher and Deakin**
Cost Accounting
*Fourth Edition*

**Marshall**
A Survey of Accounting: What the Numbers Mean
*Second Edition*

**Miller and Redding**
The FASB: The People, the Process and the Politics
*Third Edition*

**Mueller, Gernon and Meek**
International Accounting
*Third Edition*

**Pany and Whittington**
Auditing

**Pratt and Kulsrud**
Individual Taxation
*1995 Edition*

**Pratt and Kulsrud**
Corporate, Partnership, Estate and Gift Taxation
*1995 Edition*

**Pratt and Kulsrud**
Federal Taxation
*1995 Edition*

**Rayburn**
Cost Accounting: Using a Cost Management Approach
*Fifth Edition*

**Anthony and Reece**
Accounting Principles
*Seventh Edition*

**Anthony and Reece**
Accounting: Texts and Cases
*Ninth Edition*

**Robertson**
Auditing
*Seventh Edition*

**Schroeder and Zlatkovich**
Survey of Accounting

**Short**
Fundamentals of Financial Accounting
*Seventh Edition*

**Smith and Wiggins**
Readings and Problems in Accounting Information Systems

**Whittington, Pany, Meigs and Meigs**
Principles of Auditing
*Tenth Edition*

# AUDITING

◆

KURT PANY
ARIZONA STATE UNIVERSITY

O. RAY WHITTINGTON
SAN DIEGO STATE UNIVERSITY

**IRWIN**

Burr Ridge, Illinois
Boston, Massachusetts
Sydney, Australia

Cover image: ''Stream,'' 3-D computer image. Copyright © 1991 by Char Davies, courtesy of Char Davies/ SOFTIMAGE Inc. (Montreal, Canada).

Senior sponsoring editor:   *Ron Regis*
Developmental editor:       *Cheryl D. Wilson*
Marketing manager:          *Cindy L. Ledwith*
Project editor:             *Rita McMullen*
Production manager:         *Diane Palmer*
Art coordinator:            *Mark Malloy*
Art studio:                 *David Corona Design*
Compositor:                 *The Clarinda Company*
Typeface:                   *10/12 Times Roman*
Printer:                    *R. R. Donnelley & Sons Company*

**Library of Congress Cataloging–in–Publication Data**

Pany, Kurt.
    Auditing / Kurt Pany, O. Ray Whittington,
        p.      cm.
    Includes index.
    ISBN 0-256-11637-7 (alk. paper)
    1. Auditing.  2. Auditor's reports.   I. Whittington, Ray, date
. II. Title.
HF5667.P344   1994
657'.45—dc20                                    93–4070

*Printed in the United States of America*
1 2 3 4 5 6 7 8 9 0  DOC  0 9 8 7 6 5 4 3

# PREFACE

This first edition of *Auditing* introduces and describes the rapidly changing audit function. Written in a clear and understandable manner, it is appropriate for students who have not had significant audit experience. The text's approach is to integrate auditing material with that obtained by students in previous courses in accounting systems and in financial and managerial accounting.

*Auditing* is well suited for the introductory one-semester or one-quarter course. Alternatively, key chapters may be covered in greater detail in a first course, with other chapters being included in a subsequent auditing course. One way to divide the information is to cover in a second course the second sampling chapter (Chapter 11), cycles other than the revenue cycle (Chapters 14 through 17) and other responsibilities (Chapters 19 and 20). In this manner, the first course would include professional responsibilities, design of an audit, the fundamentals of audit sampling, and extensive coverage of the revenue cycle.

While the text stresses accounting systems with computerized applications throughout, it recognizes the reality that most accounting systems are not computerized or manual, but are composed of a combination of computerized and manual subsystems. Accordingly, the text illustrates these types of systems.

## ORGANIZATION OF TEXT

*Auditing* is divided into five parts:

| Part | Title | Chapters |
|------|-------|----------|
| I | Professional Responsibilities | 1–5 |
| II | The Design of Audits | 6–8 |
| III | Technology and Sampling Approaches | 9–11 |
| IV | Testing Controls and Performing Substantive Tests | 12–18 |
| V | Other Responsibilities | 19–20 |

Because the chapters are written to stand alone (with the exceptions of Chapter 10 and 13 on sampling and the revenue cycle, respectively), various combinations and ordering of chapters may be used.

Part I — Professional Responsibilities.    The opening chapters discuss the role and professional responsibilities of the auditors. Rather than focus only on audits of financial statements, the discussion in the first chapter covers the broad concepts of the attest function and focuses on how audits of financial statements relate to that function. Chapter 2 covers the professional standards that provide the overall measures of performance for audits and various other types of attest engagements. Chapter 3, on audit reports, presents the various reporting responsibilities when audits of financial statements are performed. Chapter 4 discusses ethical standards and emphasizes emerging and controversial issues that illustrate the need for judgment in evaluating situations that might impair the auditors' independence. An up-to-date description of the legal liability of auditors in the 1990s is presented in Chapter 5.

Part II — The Design of Audits.    Chapter 6 presents the audit risk model with its components of inherent risk, control risk, and detection risk. It also describes the nature of audit evidence and includes an integrated discussion of the relationships among audit risk, financial statement assertions, evidence about inherent and control risk, and evidence to restrict detection risk. These relationships are emphasized throughout the remainder of the text. Chapter 7 discusses the major factors to be considered in planning the audit, with an emphasis on the critical aspect of assessing risk. Chapter 8 presents information on internal control structures and on the manner in which auditors consider internal control in planning the audit and in assessing control risk.

Part III — Technology and Sampling Approaches.    Chapter 9, on internal control in a computer system, has been structured around the most recent professional pronouncements that directly incorporate consideration of computerized controls into the internal control structure. While all of the procedural chapters of the text incorporate discussions of accounting systems with computerized operations, Chapter 9 emphasizes the auditors' consideration of computerized internal control systems ranging in sophistication from those using a single microcomputer to those using complex, networked mainframe computers. Chapters 10 and 11 provide an easy-to-understand discussion of audit sampling, both statistical and nonstatistical. Chapter 10, which many instructors may consider sufficient topical coverage of the area, includes discussions of overall concepts, attributes sampling, and the essentials of variables sampling. Chapter 11 presents the details of various sampling techniques that are used for substantive testing.

Part IV — Testing Controls and Performing Substantive Tests.    Information on testing controls and performing substantive tests may be structured in several ways, including by account or by transaction cycle. This text provides a cycles-based approach that attempts to capture the essence of Statement on Auditing Standards (SAS) 55 on internal control and the earlier SAS 31 on evidential matter. Since SAS 55 requires auditors to assess control risk by assertion, the text deals directly with assertions and avoids the intermediate stage of "internal control" objectives. Chapter 12 on the auditors' consideration of internal control for the revenue cycle illustrates a computerized system similar to those one might expect to encounter in practice. The illustration is described in detail so students with the limited background in systems and computers that many accounting majors currently receive can understand it. The inclusion of detailed systems flowcharts in Chapter 12 facilitates very detailed coverage of the cycle. Alternatively, the flowcharts may be quickly reviewed, with increased emphasis on the broader concepts being addressed. Chapter 13 presents the material on substantive tests of the revenue cycle accounts, including sales, receivables, and cash. Chapters 14 through 17 provide similar discussions for the other accounting cycles. Finally, Chapter 18 includes information about auditing the operations of the company and completing the audit.

Part V—Other Responsibilities.    Chapter 19 presents a discussion of other attest and nonattest services provided by certified public accountants. Chapter 20, on internal, operational, and compliance auditing, describes the professional standards of internal auditors, the purpose and nature of operational audits, and various types of compliance audit engagements. Compliance auditing continues to gain importance as auditors receive increasing requests from Congress and regulatory agencies to audit for compliance for laws and regulations, especially those relating to the use of taxpayers' funds.

# FEATURES OF THIS TEXT

This text includes a variety of features to enhance the learning experience:

**Chapter Objectives** provide a concise presentation of each chapter's most important concepts.

**Keystone Computers & Networks, Inc.** is the text's **Illustrative Audit Case.** It is based on an actual company and begins in the planning chapter (Chapter 7). It continues in Chapters 12, 13, and 18 (case only). The case both illustrates audit methods and provides realistic, thought-provoking case exercises. Although each portion of the case is designed to stand alone, if used in combination, the case will help the student develop problem-solving activities in planning (Chapter 7), internal control (Chapter 12), testing account balances (Chapter 13) and completing the audit (Chapter 18). Besides incorporating the use of computerized accounting applications, the case also integrates the fundamentals of audit sampling from Chapters 10 and 11.

**Illustrative Cases** use actual business and accounting examples to illustrate key chapter concepts. The cases are boxed and appear throughout the text.

**International Auditing Standards** are discussed as appropriate. These standards are becoming increasingly significant as countries attempt to create international markets for securities.

**Key Terms Introduced or Emphasized** is a glossary of each chapter's most important terms. The terms are boldface within the chapter and are defined at the end of the chapter. Placing the definitions at the end of each chapter allows the student to quickly find the meaning of unfamiliar terms while reading the material. The glossary also serves as an excellent review tool and helps the student see how well he or she understands the major ideas presented.

Illustrations, tables, and flowcharts are used throughout to enhance and clarify the presentation. Chapter Summaries recap the most important information presented in the chapter.

## END-OF-CHAPTER PROBLEM MATERIAL

A combination of questions carefully selected to address each chapter's objectives have been written by the authors and adapted from various professional examinations. The questions at the end of each chapter are segregated as follows: Group I—Review Questions, Group II—Questions Requiring Analysis, Group III—Problems, Group IV—Research and Discussion Cases, and Group V—Audit Case Exercises.

The Review Questions are closely related to the material in the chapter and provide a convenient means of determining whether students have grasped the major concepts and details contained in that chapter.

The Questions Requiring Analysis call for thoughtful consideration of realistic auditing situations and the application of generally accepted auditing standards. A number of these Group II questions are taken from CPA and other professional examinations, and others describe real-world audit situations. These questions, generally shorter than those in Group III, tend to stress value judgments and conflicting opinions.

Many of the Group III Problems have been drawn from CPA and CIA examinations. In selecting these problems, consideration was given to ones appearing in recent professional exams. However, older questions are included when they are superior to others available.

## RESEARCH AND DISCUSSION CASES

These cases involve controversial situations that do not lend themselves to clear-cut answers. Students are required to research appropriate auditing and accounting literature and to then apply critical thinking skills to logically formulate and justify their personal positions on the issues involved in each case. The cases acquaint students with the professional literature, develop research and communication skills, and demonstrate that several diverse, yet defensible, positions may be argued persuasively in a given situation.

## AUDIT CASE EXERCISES

These exercises all pertain to the text's continuing integrated case, Keystone Computers & Networks, Inc. While each exercise may stand alone, when used in combination these case exercises lead the students from the original planning of an audit through the process of performing tests of controls and substantive tests to evaluating the audit results. Audit Case Exercises are included in Chapters 7, 12, 13 and 18.

# REFERENCES TO AUTHORITATIVE SOURCES

Numerous references are made to the pronouncements of the American Institute of Certified Public Accountants (AICPA), the Institute of Internal Auditors (IIA), the Financial Accounting Standards Board, the Governmental Accounting Standards Board, and the Securities and Exchange Commission. The cooperation of the AICPA and the IIA in permitting the use of their published materials and of questions from the CPA and CIA examinations brings to an auditing text an element of authority not otherwise available.

# SUPPLEMENTS

A **Study Guide,** written by the text's authors, enables students to review text material and to test their understanding. The guide includes a summary of each chapter's highlights and an abundance of objective questions and exercises. Since the guide includes answers to the questions and exercises, it provides immediate feedback to students.

Our **Instructor's Lecture Guide** includes topical outlines of each chapter, the authors' personal comments on each chapter, and numerous instructional aids, including transparency masters. The **Solutions Manual** includes thorough and up-to-date solutions to the text's questions, problems, and exercises. The **Test Bank** includes both original questions and problems, and questions adapted from various professional examinations.

**Computest3** is the computerized version of the test bank. This advanced-feature test generator allows the adding and editing of questions; saves and reloads tests; creates up to 99 versions of each test; attaches graphics to questions and answers; imports and exports ASCII files; and permits the section of questions based on type, level of difficulty, or keyword. Computest3 provides password protection of saved tests and question databases and can run on a network. It is available on 5.25 and 3.5 disks.

**Teaching Transparencies** feature new illustrations as well as selected exhibits from the text.

# CONTRIBUTIONS BY OTHERS

We express our sincere thanks to the many professors, practitioners, and governmental regulators who have offered helpful suggestions for this text. Especially helpful were the advice and suggestions of the following reviewers:

Professor Michael D. Akers
Marquette University

Professor Lawrence P. Kalbers
John Carroll University

Professor Darlene R. Kausch
University of Akron

We also appreciate the insightful suggestions of Walton Conn, a Practice Fellow at the AICPA and manager for KPMG Peat Marwick.

Kurt Pany

O. Ray Whittington

# CONTENTS IN BRIEF

# CONTENTS

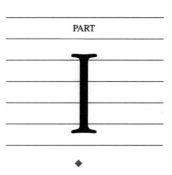

PART

I

◆

# PROFESSIONAL RESPONSIBILITIES

# THE ROLE OF THE AUDITOR IN THE AMERICAN ECONOMY

## CHAPTER OBJECTIVES

After studying this chapter, you should be able to:

- Discuss the nature of the attest function.

- Describe the nature of financial statement audits.

- Explain why audits are demanded by society.

- Contrast the various types of audits and types of auditors.

- Describe how CPA firms are typically organized and the responsibilities of auditors at the various levels in the organization.

- Discuss the effects that the major organizations have had on the accounting profession.

D ependable information is essential to the very existence of our society. The investor making a decision to buy or sell securities, the banker deciding whether to approve a loan, the government in obtaining revenue based on income tax returns, all are relying upon information provided by others. In many of these situations, the goals of the providers of information run directly counter to those of the users of the information. Implicit in this line of reasoning is recognition of the social need for independent auditors—individuals of professional competence and integrity who can tell us whether the information on which we rely constitutes a fair picture of what is really going on.

Our purpose in this chapter is to make clear the nature of independent audits and the auditing profession. We begin with a discussion of the broader concept of an *attest engagement,* of which audits of financial statements are an important type. Another goal of this chapter is to summarize the influence exerted on the public accounting profession by the American Institute of Certified Public Accountants (AICPA), the Financial Accounting Standards Board (FASB), the Governmental Accounting Standards Board (GASB), and the Securities and Exchange Commission (SEC). We will also explore types of audits other than the examination of financial statements and note the impact of the Institute of Internal Auditors (IIA) and the General Accounting Office (GAO). Finally, we will examine other types of professional services and the nature and organization of CPA firms.

## WHAT IS THE ATTEST FUNCTION?

To *attest* to information means to provide assurance as to its reliability. More formally, the AICPA has defined an **attest engagement** as one in which:

> a practitioner is engaged to issue or does issue a written communication that expresses a conclusion about the reliability of a written assertion that is the responsibility of another party.

A financial statement audit is, by far, the most common type of attest engagement. However, CPAs attest to the reliability of a wide range of other types of information, including financial forecasts, internal control, compliance with laws and regulations, and advertising claims.

---

◆ ILLUSTRATIVE CASE ◆

CPAs have attested to the assertion that a supermarket chain in Phoenix has the lowest overall prices in that city. The CPAs selected a sample of approximately 1,000 items and compared the prices to those of the various other major supermarkets. Representatives of the supermarket chain stated that the credibility added by the CPAs has helped to convince consumers that the chain's prices are indeed the lowest.

---

The nature of the attest function is essentially the same, regardless of the information being examined. Figure 1–1 describes the attest function, which begins with an **assertion** by management; for example, "the company's financial statements are prepared following **generally accepted accounting principles** (GAAP)." The CPAs gather evidence that

Figure 1–1    The Attest Function

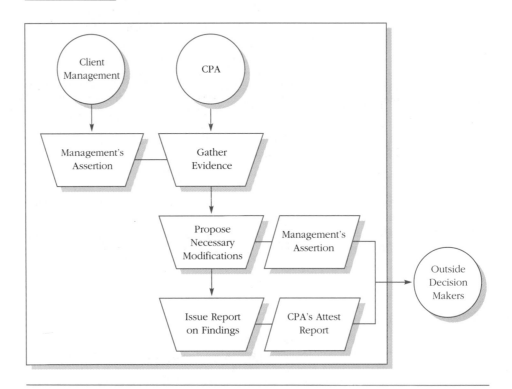

enables them to provide assurance on the accuracy of management's assertion. Then, they issue a report summarizing their findings.

The amount of evidence obtained by the CPAs and the content of the attest report depend on the nature of the engagement. The standards of the AICPA recognize three forms of attestation engagements—examinations, reviews, and the performance of agreed-upon procedures. An **examination,** referred to as an audit when it involves financial statements, provides the highest form of assurance that CPAs provide about management's assertion. In an examination, the CPAs select from all available evidence a combination that limits to a low level the risk that they will not find a *material misstatement* of the assertion. A **review** is substantially less in scope of procedures than an examination, and is designed to lend only a limited, or moderate, amount of assurance about the assertion. If an examination or review does not meet the client's needs, the CPAs and a specified user of the information may mutually decide on specific **agreed-upon procedures** that the CPAs will perform. Then, the CPAs will issue a report to the specified user that describes their procedures and findings.

Throughout this chapter, we will focus primarily on the attest function as it relates to an audit of financial statements. Other types of attest services are discussed in Chapters 19 and 20.

# WHAT IS A FINANCIAL STATEMENT AUDIT?

In a financial statement audit the auditors undertake to gather evidence and provide a high level of assurance that the financial statements follow generally accepted accounting principles, or some other appropriate basis of accounting. An audit involves searching and verifying the accounting records and examining other evidence supporting those financial statements. By obtaining an understanding of the company's internal control, inspecting documents, observing assets, making inquiries within and outside the company, and performing other auditing procedures, the auditors will gather the evidence necessary to issue an audit report. That audit report states that it is the auditors' opinion that the financial statements follow generally accepted accounting principles. The flowchart in Figure 1–2 illustrates an audit of financial statements.

**Figure 1–2   Audit of Financial Statements**

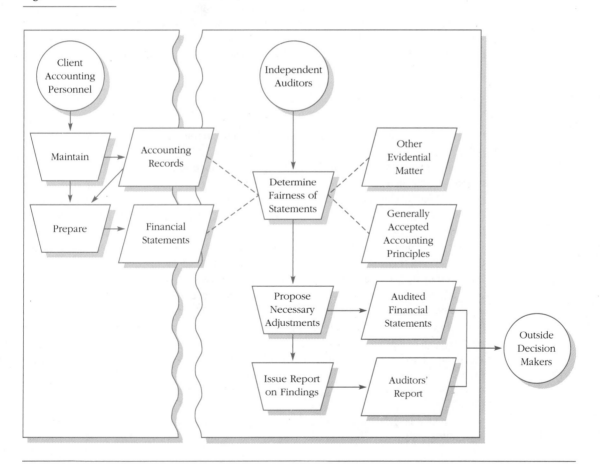

The evidence gathered by the auditors focuses on whether the financial statements are presented in accordance with generally accepted accounting principles. More specifically, an audit addresses management's assertions that the assets listed in the balance sheet really exist, that the company has title to the assets, and that the valuations assigned to the assets have been established in conformity with generally accepted accounting principles. Evidence is gathered to show that the balance sheet contains *all the liabilities* of the company; otherwise the balance sheet might be grossly misleading because certain important liabilities had been accidentally or deliberately omitted. Similarly, the auditors gather evidence about the income statement. They demand evidence that the reported sales really occurred, that the goods were actually shipped to customers, and that the recorded costs and expenses are applicable to the current period and that all expenses have been recognized. Only if sufficient evidence is gathered in support of all of these significant assertions can the auditors conclude that the financial statements are presented in accordance with generally accepted accounting principles.

The procedures comprising an audit vary considerably from one engagement to the next. Many of the procedures appropriate to the audit of a small retail store would not be appropriate for the audit of a giant manufacturing corporation such as General Motors. Auditors perform audits of all types of businesses, and of governmental and nonprofit organizations as well. Banks and breweries, factories and stores, colleges and churches, school districts and labor unions—all are regularly visited by auditors. The selection of the procedures best suited to each audit requires the exercise of professional skill and judgment.

## What Creates the Demand for Audits?

Good accounting and financial reporting aid society in allocating resources in an efficient manner. A primary goal is to allocate limited capital resources to the production of those goods and services for which demand is great. Economic resources are attracted to the industries, the geographic areas, and the organizational entities that are shown by accounting measurements to be capable of using the resources to the best advantage. Inadequate accounting and reporting, on the other hand, conceal waste and inefficiency, thereby preventing an efficient allocation of economic resources.

The contribution of the independent auditor is to give *credibility* to information. Credibility, in this usage, means that the information can be believed; that is, it can be relied upon by outsiders, such as stockholders, creditors, government regulators, and other interested third parties. These third parties use the information to make various economic decisions, for example, decisions about whether to invest in the organization. These economic decisions are made under conditions of uncertainty; there is always a risk that the decision maker will select the wrong alternative and incur a significant loss. The credibility added to the information by auditors actually reduces the decision maker's risk. To be more precise, the auditors reduce **information risk,** which is the risk that the financial information used to make a decision is materially misstated.

Audited financial statements are the accepted means by which business corporations report financial information on their operating results and financial position. The word *audited,* when applied to financial statements, means that the balance sheet, statements of income and retained earnings, and statement of cash flows are accompanied by an audit report prepared by independent public accountants, expressing their professional opinion as to the fairness of the company's financial statements.

Financial statements prepared by management and transmitted to outsiders without first being audited by independent accountants leave a credibility gap. In reporting on its own administration of the business, management can hardly be expected to be entirely impartial and unbiased, any more than a football coach could be expected to serve as both coach and official referee in the same game. Independent auditors have no material personal or financial interest in the business; their reports can be expected to be impartial and free from bias.

Unaudited financial statements may have been honestly, but carelessly, prepared. Liabilities may have been overlooked and omitted from the balance sheet. Assets may have been overstated as a result of arithmetical errors or due to a lack of knowledge of generally accepted accounting principles. Net income may have been exaggerated because revenue expenditures were capitalized or because sales transactions were recorded in advance of delivery dates.

Finally, there is the possibility that unaudited financial statements have been deliberately falsified in order to conceal theft and **fraud** or as a means of inducing the reader to invest in the business or to extend credit. Although deliberate falsification of financial statements is not common, it does occur and can cause disastrous losses to persons who make decisions based upon such misleading statements.

For all of these reasons (accidental errors, lack of knowledge of accounting principles, unintentional bias, and deliberate falsification) financial statements may depart from generally accepted accounting principles. Unaudited financial statements are much less reliable than statements that have been audited by independent auditors.

Illustrating the Demand for Auditing.   A decision by a bank loan officer about whether to make a loan to a business can be used to illustrate the demand for auditing. Since the bank's objective in making the loan is to earn an appropriate rate of interest and to collect the principal of the loan at maturity, the loan officer is usually making two related decisions: (1) whether to make the loan at all and (2) what rate of interest adequately compensates the bank for the level of risk assumed. The loan officer will make these decisions based on a careful study of the company's financial statements along with other information. Therefore, the risk assumed by the bank actually has two aspects:

1.  **Business risk.**   The risk that the company will not be able to make the interest payments and repay the principal of the loan, because of economic conditions or poor management decisions. Business risk is assessed by considering factors such as the financial position of the company, the nature of its operations, the characteristics of the industry in which it operates, and the quality and integrity of its management.

2.  **Information risk.**   The risk that the information used to assess business risk is not accurate. Information risk includes the possibility that the financial statements might contain material departures from generally accepted accounting principles.

While auditing has no direct effect on business risk, it can significantly affect the level of information risk.[1] If the loan officer has assurance from the auditors that the company's financial statements are prepared in accordance with generally accepted accounting principles, he will have more confidence in his assessment of business risk. In addition, periodic audits performed after the loan has been made provide the loan officer with a way of monitoring management performance and compliance with the various loan provisions. By reducing information risk, the auditors reduce the overall risk to the bank; the company is more likely to obtain the loan and it will be made at a lower rate of interest. Therefore, management of the company has an incentive to provide audited financial statements to the loan officer to obtain the loan and to get the best possible interest rate.

A major portion of our economy is characterized by large corporate organizations that have gathered capital from millions of investors and that control economic resources spread throughout the country or even throughout the world. Top management in the corporate headquarters is often remote from the operations of company plants and branches and must rely on financial statements and other reports to control the corporation's resources. In brief, the decision makers in a large corporation cannot obtain much information on a firsthand basis. They must rely on information provided by lower-level management, and this fact creates a risk of receiving unreliable information. As in the case of the loan officer, auditing can reduce the risk of poor management decisions by reducing information risk and by monitoring the performance of management at every level within the organization.

The millions of individuals who have entrusted their savings to corporations by investing in securities rely upon annual and quarterly financial statements for investment decisions and for assurance that their invested funds are being used honestly and efficiently. Even greater numbers of people entrust their savings to banks, insurance companies, and pension funds, which in turn invest the money in corporate securities. Thus, directly or indirectly, almost everyone has a financial stake in corporate enterprises, and the public interest demands prompt, *reliable* financial reporting on the operations and the financial health of publicly owned corporations.

Various regulatory agencies also demand audit services. As an example, consider the income tax reporting system in our country. The information provided on tax returns is provided by taxpayers and may be biased because of the self-interest of the providers. The government attempts to compensate for this inherent weakness through verification by audits carried out by agents of the Internal Revenue Service.

## Major Auditing Developments of the 20th Century

Although the objectives and concepts that guide present-day audits were almost unknown in the early years of the 20th century, audits of one type or another have been made throughout the recorded history of commerce and government finance. The original meaning of the word *auditor* was "one who hears" and was appropriate to the era during which governmental accounting records were approved only after a public reading in which the

---

[1]Although auditing itself does not directly affect business risk, operating recommendations that auditors typically make during the course of an audit may improve management decisions and, therefore, reduce business risk.

accounts were read aloud. From medieval times on through the Industrial Revolution, audits were made to determine whether persons in positions of official responsibility in government and commerce were acting and reporting in an honest manner.

During the Industrial Revolution, as manufacturing concerns grew in size, their owners began to use the services of hired managers. With this separation of the ownership and management groups, the absentee owners turned increasingly to auditors to protect themselves against the danger of unintentional errors as well as fraud committed by managers and employees. Bankers were the primary outside users of financial reports (usually only balance sheets), and they were also concerned with whether the reports were distorted by errors or fraud. Before 1900, consistent with this primary objective to detect errors and fraud, audits often included a study of all, or almost all, recorded transactions.

In the first half of the 20th century, the direction of audit work tended to move away from fraud detection toward a new goal of determining whether financial statements gave a full and fair picture of financial position, operating results, and changes in financial position. This shift in emphasis was a response to the increasing number of shareholders and the corresponding increased size of corporate entities. In addition to the new shareholders, auditors became more responsible to governmental agencies, stock exchanges representing these new investors, as well as to other parties who might rely upon the financial information. No longer were bankers the only important outside users of audited financial data. The fairness of reported earnings became of prime importance.

As large-scale corporate entities developed rapidly in both Great Britain and the United States, auditors began to sample selected transactions, rather than study all transactions. Auditors and business managers gradually came to accept the proposition that careful examination of relatively few transactions selected at random would give a cost-effective, reliable indication of the accuracy of other similar transactions.

In addition to sampling, auditors became aware of the importance of effective internal control. A company's internal control consists of the policies and procedures established to provide reasonable assurance that the objectives of the company will be achieved, including the objective of preparing accurate financial statements. Auditors found that by studying the client's internal control they could identify areas of strength as well as areas of weakness. *The stronger the internal control, the less testing of financial statement account balances required by the auditors.* For any account or any phase of financial operations in which controls were weak, the auditors learned that they must expand the nature and extent of their tests of the account balance.

With the increased reliance upon sampling and internal control, professional standards began to emphasize limitations on auditors' ability to detect fraud. The profession recognized that audits designed to discover fraud would be too costly. Good internal control and surety bonds were recognized as better fraud protection techniques than audits.

Beginning in the 1960s, the detection of large-scale fraud assumed a larger role in the audit process. Professional standards began to use the term *irregularities* to describe fraudulent financial reporting (also called management fraud) and misappropriation of assets (also called defalcations). This shift in emphasis to taking a greater responsibility for the detection of irregularities resulted from (1) a dramatic increase in congressional pressure to assume more responsibility for large-scale frauds, (2) a number of successful lawsuits claiming that management fraud had improperly gone undetected by the independent auditors, and (3) a belief by public accountants that audits should be expected to detect material irregularities.

The increasing use of sophisticated computer systems has not altered the auditor's responsibility for detecting errors and irregularities. The nature of audit procedures has been affected, however, as auditors have been required to develop new approaches to testing internal control and account balances.

In the late 1980s and early 1990s, the billions of dollars in federal funds that were required to "bail out" the savings and loan industry caused a movement toward increased regulation of federally insured financial institutions. Congress and regulatory agencies believed that the key to preventing similar problems in other types of organizations was the enactment of effective laws and regulations. Auditors were asked to assume increasing responsibility for performing tests of compliance with these laws and regulations. In addition, the Federal Deposit Improvement Act of 1991 was adopted. This law, among other things, requires management of large financial institutions to have their auditors attest to the effectiveness of assertions by management about the effectiveness of the institution's internal controls over financial reporting.

Many of the ideas mentioned in this brief historical sketch of the development of auditing will be analyzed in detail in later sections of this book. Our purpose at this point is merely to orient ourselves with a quick overall look at some of the major auditing developments of the 20th century:

1.  A shift in emphasis to the determination of fairness in financial statements.
2.  Increased responsibility of the auditor to third parties, such as governmental agencies, stock exchanges, and an investing public numbered in the millions.
3.  A change in auditing method from detailed examination of individual transactions to use of sampling techniques, including statistical sampling.
4.  Recognition of the need to consider the effectiveness of internal control as a guide to the direction and amount of testing and sampling to be performed.
5.  Development of new auditing procedures applicable to electronic data processing systems, and use of the computer as an auditing tool.
6.  Recognition of the need for auditors to find means of protecting themselves from the current wave of litigation.
7.  An increase in demand for prompt disclosure of both favorable and unfavorable information concerning any publicly owned company.
8.  Increased demand for attestation to compliance with laws and regulations by all types of organizations.
9.  Demand for attestation by auditors to assertions by management about the organization's internal control structure.

## Types of Audits

Audits are often viewed as falling into three major types: (1) audits of financial statements, (2) compliance audits, and (3) operational audits.

### Audits of Financial Statements.

The **audit of financial statements** (which is our primary concern) ordinarily covers the balance sheet and the related statements of income, retained earnings, and cash flows. The goal is to determine whether these statements have been prepared in conformity with generally accepted accounting principles. Financial statement audits are normally performed by firms of certified public accountants; users of auditors' reports include management, investors, bankers, creditors, financial analysts, and government agencies.

Compliance Audits.  The performance of a **compliance audit** is dependent upon the existence of verifiable data and of recognized criteria or standards, such as established laws and regulations, or an organization's policies and procedures. A familiar example is the audit of an income tax return by an auditor of the Internal Revenue Service (IRS). Such audits seek to determine whether a tax return is in compliance with tax laws and IRS regulations. The findings of the IRS auditors are transmitted to the taxpayer by means of the IRS auditor's report.

Another example of a compliance audit is the periodic bank examination conducted on a surprise basis by bank examiners employed by the Federal Deposit Insurance Corporation and the state banking departments. These audits measure compliance with banking laws and regulations and with traditional standards of sound banking practice.

Many state and local governmental entities and nonprofit organizations that receive financial assistance from the federal government must arrange for compliance audits under the Single Audit Act of 1984 or OMB Circular A–133. Such audits are designed to determine whether the financial assistance is spent in accordance with applicable laws and regulations. Compliance audits are described in greater detail in Chapter 20.

Operational Audits.  An **operational audit** is a study of a specific unit of an organization for the purpose of measuring its performance. The operations of the receiving department of a manufacturing company, for example, may be evaluated in terms of its *effectiveness,* that is, its success in meeting its stated goals and responsibilities. Performance is also judged in terms of *efficiency,* that is, success in using to its best advantage the resources available to the department. Because the criteria for effectiveness and efficiency are not as clearly established as are generally accepted accounting principles and many laws and regulations, an operational audit tends to require more subjective judgment than do audits of financial statements or compliance audits. For example, quantifiable criteria often must be developed by the auditors to be used to measure the effectiveness or efficiency of the department. Operational auditing is discussed in detail in Chapter 20.

## Types of Auditors

In addition to the audit of financial statements by certified public accountants, other professional groups carry on large-scale auditing programs. Among these other well-known types of auditors are internal auditors, auditors of the General Accounting Office, and internal revenue agents.

Internal Auditing.  Nearly every large corporation maintains an internal auditing staff. Internal auditors are also employed extensively by governmental and nonprofit organizations. A principal goal of the internal auditors is to investigate and appraise the effectiveness with which the various organizational units of the company are carrying out their assigned functions. Much attention is given by internal auditors to the study and appraisal of internal control.

The internal auditing staff often reports to an audit committee of the board of directors, and also to the president or another high executive. This strategic placement high in the organizational structure helps ensure that the internal auditors will have ready access to all units of the organization, and that their recommendations will be given prompt attention by department heads. It is imperative that the internal auditors be independent of the department heads and other line executives whose work they review. Thus, it would generally not be desirable for the internal auditing staff to be under the authority of the chief accountant. Regardless of their reporting level, however, the internal auditors are not independent in the same sense as the independent auditors. The internal auditors are employees of the organization in which they work, subject to the restraints inherent in the employer-employee relationship.

A large part of the work of the internal auditors consists of operational audits; in addition, they may conduct numerous compliance audits. The number and kind of investigative projects varies from year to year. Unlike the CPAs, who are committed to verify each significant item in the annual financial statements, the internal auditors are not obligated to repeat their audits on an annual basis.

The Institute of Internal Auditors (IIA) is the international organization of internal auditors. It has developed various standards relating to internal auditing and it administers the certified internal auditor (CIA) examination. Chapter 20 provides further discussion of internal auditing and of the CIA exam.

General Accounting Office.   Congress has long had its own auditing staff, headed by the comptroller general and known as the General Accounting Office, or GAO. The work of GAO auditors includes both compliance audits and operational audits. These assignments include audits of government agencies to determine that spending programs follow the intent of Congress and operational audits to evaluate the effectiveness and efficiency of selected government programs. GAO auditors also conduct examinations of corporations holding government contracts to verify that contract payments by the government have been proper.

The enormous size of many of the federal agencies has caused the GAO to stress the development of computer auditing techniques and statistical sampling plans. Its pioneering in these areas has led to the recognition of the GAO as a sophisticated professional auditing staff.

Internal Revenue Agents.   The Internal Revenue Service is responsible for enforcement of the federal tax laws. Its agents conduct compliance audits of the income tax returns of individuals and corporations to determine that income has been computed and taxes paid as required by federal law. Although IRS audits include some simple individual tax returns that can be completed in an hour or so in an IRS office, they also include field audits of the nation's largest corporations and involve highly complex tax issues.

# THE PUBLIC ACCOUNTING PROFESSION

In recognition of the public trust afforded to public accountants, each state recognizes public accountancy as a profession and issues the certificate of **Certified Public Accoun-**

**tant.** The CPA certificate is a symbol of technical competence. This official recognition by the state is comparable to that accorded to the legal, medical, and other professions.

The licensing of CPAs by the states reflects a belief that the public interest will be protected by an official identification of competent professional accountants who offer their services to the public. Although CPAs provide various types of services, including tax, consulting, and accounting services which are also provided by non-CPAs, the various states generally restrict performance of audits of financial statements to CPAs. It is this performance of the attest function on financial statements that is most unique to CPAs.

## American Institute of Certified Public Accountants

At the very heart of the public accounting profession is the AICPA, a voluntary national organization of more than 300,000 CPAs. Four of the major areas of the AICPA's work are of particular interest to students of auditing. These are:

1. Establishing standards and rules to guide CPAs in their conduct of professional services.
2. Carrying on a continuous program of research and publication.
3. Promoting continuing professional education.
4. Contributing to the profession's system of self-regulation.

### Establishing Standards.

The AICPA has assigned to its Auditing Standards Board (ASB) responsibility for issuing official pronouncements on auditing matters. A most important series of pronouncements on auditing by the Auditing Standards Board is entitled *Statements on Auditing Standards* (SASs). Chapter 2 will consider how CPA firms utilize SASs in every audit engagement.

The AICPA also issues *Statements on Standards for Attestation Engagements* (SSAEs). These statements provide CPAs with guidance for attesting to information other than financial statements, such as financial forecasts. Chapter 2 also provides a description of the SSAEs.

The Accounting and Review Services Committee of the AICPA establishes standards for reporting on financial statements when the CPAs' role is to compile or review the financial statements rather than to perform an independent audit. The series of pronouncements by this committee is called *Statements on Standards for Accounting and Review Services* (SSARs). These SSARs provide guidance for the many sensitive situations in which a CPA firm is in some way associated with the financial statements of a nonpublic company and, therefore, needs to make clear the extent of the responsibility that the CPA firm assumes for the fairness of the statements. SSARs are discussed more fully in Chapter 19.

### Research and Publication.

In addition to the professional standards indicated above, the AICPA maintains a research staff and issues additional technical guidance. Many accounting students are familiar with the *Journal of Accountancy,* published monthly. Another AICPA monthly journal is *The Tax Advisor*. Publications bearing directly on auditing include:

Industry Audit and Accounting Guides. These guides cover various industries, including, for example, *Audits of Casinos.*

Auditing Procedure Studies. This series is intended to keep auditors informed of new developments and advances in auditing procedures.

A number of other AICPA publications bear directly on accounting issues, including:

Accounting Research Bulletins. These 51 bulletins, issued over a period of 15 years, were one of the earliest efforts to develop greater uniformity of accounting practice.

Opinions of the Accounting Principles Board. These 31 opinions were issued by the predecessor group of the FASB.

Accounting Research Studies. The results of studies of accounting methods are described in these publications.

Statements of Position of the Accounting Standards Division. These statements express the AICPA's position on the appropriate method of accounting for particular events or transactions.

Accounting Trends & Techniques. This is an annual study of current reporting practices of a large number of corporations.

Continuing Professional Education.    Another important activity of the AICPA is the development of a continuing professional education program. Continuing education is a necessity for CPAs to remain knowledgeable about the unending stream of changes in accounting principles, tax law, auditing, computers, and consulting services. Continuing education programs are offered by the AICPA, state societies, and by other professional organizations. State laws require CPAs to participate in continuing education programs as a condition for license renewal.

Self-Regulation.    It is a tribute to the public accounting profession's system of self-regulation that Congress has not elected to enact legislation to regulate the profession. However, the profession has not been free from criticism. Over the years, various congressional committees have threatened to intercede, usually as a result of some highly publicized financial failure. The profession's system of self-regulation has had to be responsive to changes in the legislative, economic, and legal environment. The AICPA has contributed significantly to this regulatory process by developing regulatory mechanisms that apply to both individual CPAs and CPA firms.

Regulation of Individual CPAs.    The membership of the AICPA has adopted ethical rules for CPAs in the form of a goal-oriented *Code of Professional Conduct*. This ethical code sets forth positively stated principles on which CPAs can make decisions about appropriate conduct. The AICPA *Code of Professional Conduct* is described completely in Chapter 4.

A desire for effective self-regulation also is apparent in the new requirements for membership in the AICPA, which include the following:

1. Members in public practice must practice with a firm enrolled in an approved practice (peer) review program.
2. Members must obtain continuing education: 120 hours every three years for members in public practice and 90 hours every three years for other members.

In addition to these membership requirements that apply currently, after the year 2000, applicants for AICPA membership must have 150 semester hours of college education, including a bachelor's degree from an accredited college or university.

Regulation of CPA Firms.   The AICPA also has a division in which the members are CPA firms, rather than individual CPAs. The *Division for CPA Firms* was created for the purpose of improving the quality of practice in CPA firms of all sizes. The division actually has two sections: the Private Companies Practice Section and the SEC Practice Section. Membership is voluntary; a CPA firm may join either, or both, sections. Once a CPA firm joins one of the sections, it is subject to the membership requirements of that section, which include mandatory peer review.

A *peer review* occurs when a CPA firm arranges for a critical review of its practices by another CPA firm. Such an external review clearly offers a more objective evaluation of the quality of performance than could be made by self-review. The purpose of this concept is to encourage rigorous adherence to the AICPA's quality control standards. Quality control standards and the peer review process are discussed in detail in Chapter 2.

The AICPA — In Perspective.   Throughout its existence, the AICPA has contributed enormously to the evolution of generally accepted accounting principles as well as to the development of professional standards. The many technical divisions and committees of the Institute (such as the Auditing Standards Board) provide a means of focusing the collective experience and ability of the profession on current problems. Governmental agencies such as the Securities and Exchange Commission and the General Accounting Office continually seek the advice and cooperation of the Institute in developing laws and regulations relating to accounting and auditing matters.

## The CPA Examination

The CPA examination is a uniform national examination prepared and graded by the American Institute of Certified Public Accountants. It is given twice each year, in May and November. Although the preparation and grading of the examination are in the hands of the AICPA, the issuance of CPA certificates is a function of each state or territory. Passing the CPA examination does not, in itself, entitle the candidate to a CPA certificate; most states require up to two years of professional experience before a certificate will be awarded. Each state also determines the educational qualifications and other criteria to be met by its citizens who wish to take the examination. Some states require a separate additional examination on professional ethics or other topics.

The CPA examination is essentially an academic one; in most states, candidates are not required to have any work experience to sit for the examination. In the opinion of the authors, the ideal time to take the examination is immediately after the completion of a comprehensive program of accounting courses in a college or university. The new CPA examination extends over two days and has four parts: Financial Accounting and Reporting — Business Enterprises; Accounting and Reporting — Taxation, Managerial, Governmental, and Not-For-Profit Organizations; Auditing; and Business Law and Professional Responsibilities.

Over the years only about 10 percent of the candidates taking the examination have passed all four parts on their first attempt. Of the candidates who hold a university degree with a major in accounting, the percentage passing two or more parts on the first attempt is somewhat higher. In other words, admission to the examination is relatively easy, but passing the examination is difficult.

The compilation of the questions and problems included in this textbook involved a review of all CPA examinations of the past 10 years and the selection of representative questions and problems. Use of this material is with the consent of the American Institute of Certified Public Accountants. Many other problems and questions (not from CPA examinations) are also included with each chapter.

## Financial Accounting Standards Board

Auditors must determine whether financial statements are prepared in conformity with generally accepted accounting principles. The AICPA has designated the Financial Accounting Standards Board as the body with power to set forth these principles for entities other than state and local governments. Thus, *FASB Statements,* exposure drafts, public hearings, and research projects are all of major concern to the public accounting profession.

The structure, history, and pronouncements of the FASB (and its predecessor, the Accounting Principles Board) are appropriately covered in introductory, intermediate, and advanced accounting courses.

## Governmental Accounting Standards Board

The Governmental Accounting Standards Board (GASB) was established in 1984 to establish and improve standards of financial accounting for state and local government entities. The operational structure of the GASB is similar to that of the FASB. Auditors of state and local government entities, such as cities and school districts, look to the GASB pronouncements for the appropriate accounting principles.

## Securities and Exchange Commission

The SEC is an agency of the U.S. government. It administers the Securities Act of 1933, the Securities Exchange Act of 1934, and other legislation concerning securities and financial matters. The function of the SEC is to protect investors and the public by requiring full disclosure of financial information by companies offering securities for sale to the public. A second objective is to prevent misrepresentation, deceit, or other fraud in the sale of securities.

The term *registration statement* is an important one in any discussion of the impact of the SEC on accounting practice. To *register* securities means to qualify them for sale to the public by filing with the SEC financial statements and other data in a form acceptable to the Commission. A registration statement contains *audited financial statements,* including balance sheets for a two-year period and income statements and statements of cash flows for a three-year period.

The legislation creating the SEC made the Commission responsible for determining whether the financial statements presented to it reflect proper application of accounting principles. To aid the Commission in discharging this responsibility, the Securities Acts provide for an examination and report by an *independent* public accountant. Thus, from its beginning, the Securities and Exchange Commission has been a major user of audited financial statements and has exercised great influence upon the development of accounting principles, the strengthening of auditing standards, and upon the concept of auditor independence.

Protection of investors, of course, requires that the public have available the information contained in a registration statement concerning a proposed issue of securities. The issuing company is therefore required to deliver to prospective buyers of securities a *prospectus,* or selling circular, from the registration statement. The registration of securities does not insure investors against loss; the SEC does not pass on the merit of securities. There is in fact only one purpose of registration: to provide disclosure of the important facts so that the investor has available all pertinent information on which to base an intelligent decision on whether to buy a given security. If the SEC believes that a given registration statement does not meet its standards of disclosure, it may require amendment of the statement or may issue a stop order preventing sale of the securities.

To improve the quality of the financial statements filed with it and the professional standards of the independent accountants who report on these statements, the SEC has adopted a basic accounting regulation known as *Regulation S-X* and entitled *Form and Content of Financial Statements*. Between 1937 and 1982, the SEC issued 307 *Accounting Series Releases* (ASRs) addressing various accounting and auditing issues. In 1982 the series was replaced by two series—*Financial Reporting Releases* and *Accounting and Auditing Enforcement Releases*. *Financial Reporting Releases* present the SEC's current views on financial reporting and auditing issues. *Accounting and Auditing Enforcement Releases* summarize enforcement activities against auditors when the SEC has found deficiencies in the auditors' work.

## Other Types of Professional Services

In addition to auditing, CPA firms offer other types of services to their clients, including tax services, consulting services, accounting and review services, and personal financial planning. CPA firms tend to specialize in particular types of services depending on their size and the expertise of their personnel.

Tax Services.   Tax services that are performed by CPA firms fall into two broad categories: compliance work and tax planning. Compliance work involves preparing the federal, state, and local tax returns of corporations, partnerships, individuals, and estates and trusts. Tax planning, on the other hand, involves consulting with clients on how to structure their business affairs to legally minimize the amount and postpone the payment of their taxes.

Consulting Services.   CPA firms offer a variety of services that are designed to improve the effectiveness and efficiency of their clients' operations. Initially, these services developed as a natural extension of the audit, and primarily involved consulting on accounting and internal control systems. In recent years, CPA firms have expanded by offering a host of services that tend to be more operational in nature. Examples are developing strategic planning models and management information systems and performing executive search services.

### Accounting and Review Services.

Audits are expensive. For a small business, the cost of an audit will run into the thousands of dollars; for large corporations, the cost may exceed a million dollars. The most common reason for a small business to incur the cost of an audit is the influence exerted by a bank that insists upon audited financial statements as a condition for granting a bank loan. If a small business is not in need of a significant amount of bank credit, the cost of an audit may exceed its benefits.

An alternative is to retain a CPA firm to perform other services, such as the compilation or review of financial statements. To compile financial statements means to prepare them; this service is often rendered when the client does not have accounting personnel capable of preparing statements. The CPA firm issues a compilation report on the financial statements that provides *no assurance* that the statements are presented fairly in accordance with generally accepted accounting principles.

A review of financial statements by a CPA firm is substantially less in scope than an audit and is designed to provide *limited assurance* on the credibility of the statements. It stresses inquiries by the CPA and comparison of amounts in the statements to comparable financial and nonfinancial data. These comparisons, which are referred to as analytical procedures, are useful in bringing to light possible misstatements of financial statement amounts. Compilations and reviews are discussed in Chapter 19.

### Personal Financial Planning.

CPA firms also may advise individuals on their personal financial affairs. For example, a CPA firm may review a client's investment portfolio and evaluate whether the nature of the investments meets the client's financial objectives. The CPA firm might also advise the client on the nature and amount of insurance coverage that is appropriate. The AICPA offers the designation "Personal Financial Specialist" to CPAs that satisfy certain experience requirements and pass a one-day examination on personal financial planning topics, such as income tax planning, risk management planning, investment planning, retirement planning, and estate planning.

## Organization of the Public Accounting Profession

Many CPA firms are organized as either sole practitioners or partnerships. A CPA may also practice as a member of a professional corporation or, in a number of states, as a limited liability company (LLC).

*Professional corporations* differ from traditional corporations in a number of respects. For example, all shareholders and directors of a professional corporation must be engaged in the practice of public accounting. In addition, shareholders and directors of the professional corporation may be held personally liable for the corporation's actions, although they may choose to carry liability insurance to cover damages caused by negligent actions. *Limited liability companies* are similar to professional corporations, but they provide for the protection of the personal assets of any shareholders or partners not directly involved in providing services on engagements resulting in litigation.

In comparison with a sole proprietorship, forms of practice that have multiple owners offer several advantages. When two or more CPAs join forces, the opportunity for specialization is increased, and the scope of services offered to clients may be expanded.

CPA firms range in size from 1 person to over 20,000 on the professional staff. In terms of size, CPA firms are often grouped into the following four categories:

Local Firms.   Local firms typically have one or two offices, include only one CPA or a few CPAs as partners, and serve clients in a single city or area. These firms often emphasize income tax, consulting, and accounting services. Auditing is usually only a small part of the practice, and tends to involve small business concerns that find need for audited financial statements to support applications for bank loans.

Regional Firms.   Many local firms have become regional firms by opening additional offices in neighboring cities or states and increasing the number of professional staff. Merger with other local firms is often a route to regional status. This growth is often accompanied by an increase in the amount of auditing as compared to other services.

National Firms.   CPA firms with offices in most major cities in the United States are called national firms. These firms may operate internationally as well, either with their own offices or through affiliations with firms in other countries.

Big 6 Firms.   Often in the news are the large international CPA firms. Until 1989, there were eight of these firms. However, mergers have reduced them to the "Big 6." Since only a very large CPA firm has sufficient staff and resources to audit a giant corporation, these firms audit nearly all of the largest American corporations. Although these firms offer a wide range of services, auditing represents a large, if not the largest, share of their work. Annual revenue of an international firm is in the billions of dollars. In alphabetical order, the six firms are Arthur Andersen & Co.; Coopers & Lybrand; Deloitte & Touche; Ernst & Young; KPMG Peat Marwick; and Price Waterhouse.

## Responsibilities of the Professional Staff

Human resources—the competence, judgment, and integrity of personnel—represent the greatest asset of any public accounting firm. The professional staff of a typical public accounting firm includes partners, managers, senior accountants, and staff assistants.

Partners.   The principal responsibility of the partner is to maintain contacts with clients. These contacts include discussing with clients the objectives and scope of the audit work, resolving controversies that may arise as to how items are to be presented in the financial statements, and attending the client's stockholders' meetings to answer any questions regarding the financial statements or the auditors' report. Other responsibilities of the partner include recruiting new staff members, general supervision of the professional staff, reviewing audit working papers, and signing the audit reports.

Specialization by each partner in a different area of the firm's practice is often advantageous. One partner, for example, may become expert in tax matters and head the firm's tax department; another may specialize in SEC registrations; and a third may devote full time to design and installation of data processing systems.

The partnership level in a public accounting firm is comparable to that of top management in an industrial organization. Executives at this level are concerned with the long-run well-being of the organization and of the community it serves. They should and do contribute important amounts of time to civic, professional, and educational activities in the community. Participation in the state society of certified public accountants and in the AICPA is, of course, a requisite if the partners are to do their share in building the profession. Contribution of their specialized skills and professional judgment to leadership of civic organizations is equally necessary in developing the economic and social environment in which business and professional accomplishment is possible.

An important aspect of partners' active participation in various business and civic organizations is the prestige and recognition that may come to their firms. Many clients select a particular public accounting firm because they have come to know and respect one of the firm's partners. Thus, partners who are widely known and highly regarded within the community may be a significant factor in attracting business to the firm.

Managers.   In large public accounting firms, managers or supervisors perform many of the duties that would be discharged by partners in smaller firms. A manager may be responsible for supervising two or more concurrent audit engagements. This supervisory work includes reviewing the audit working papers and discussing with the audit staff and with the client any accounting or auditing problems that may arise during the engagement. The manager is responsible for determining the audit procedures applicable to specific audits and for maintaining uniform standards of fieldwork. Often, managers have the administrative duties of compiling and collecting the firm's billings to clients.

Familiarity with tax laws and with SEC regulations, as well as a broad and current knowledge of accounting theory and practice, are essential qualifications for a successful manager. Like the partner, the audit manager may specialize in specific industries or other areas of the firm's practice.

Senior Auditors.   The senior or "in charge" auditor is an individual qualified to assume responsibility for planning and conducting an audit and drafting the audit report, subject to review and approval by the manager and partner. In conducting the audit, the senior will delegate most audit tasks to assistants based on an appraisal of each assistant's ability to perform particular phases of the work. A well-qualified university graduate with a formal education in accounting may progress from staff assistant to senior auditor within two or three years, or even less.

One of the major responsibilities of the senior is on-the-job staff training. When assigning work to staff assistants, the senior should make clear the end objectives of the particular audit operation. By assigning assistants a wide variety of audit tasks and by providing constructive criticism of the assistants' work, the senior should try to make each audit a significant learning experience for the staff assistants.

Reviewing working papers shortly after they are completed is another duty of the senior in charge of an audit. This enables the senior to control the progress of the work and to ascertain that each phase of the engagement is adequately covered. At the conclusion of the field work, the senior will make a final review, tracing all items from individual working papers to the financial statements.

The senior will also maintain a continuous record of the hours devoted by all members of the staff to the various phases of the examination. In addition to maintaining uniform professional standards of field work, the senior is responsible for preventing the accumulation of excessive staff-hours on inconsequential matters and for completing the entire engagement within the budgeted time, if possible.

Staff Assistants.   The first position of a college graduate entering the public accounting profession is that of a staff assistant. Staff assistants usually encounter a variety of assignments that fully utilize their capacity for analysis and growth. Of course some routine work must be done in every audit engagement, but college graduates with thorough training in accounting need have no fear of being assigned for long to extensive routine procedures when they enter the field of public accounting. Most firms are anxious to increase the assigned responsibility to younger staff members as rapidly as they are able to assume it. In recent years, the demand for accounting services has been so high as to create a situation in which every incentive has existed for rapid development of promising assistants.

The audit staff members of all public accounting firms attend training programs that are either developed "in house" or sponsored by professional organizations. One of the most attractive features of the public accounting profession is the richness and variety of experience acquired even by the beginning staff member. Because of the high quality of the experience gained by certified public accountants as they move from one audit engagement to another, many business concerns select individuals from the public accounting field to fill such executive positions as controller or treasurer.

## Professional Development for CPA Firm Personnel

A major problem in public accounting is keeping abreast of current developments within the profession. New business practices; new pronouncements by the Auditing Standards Board, the SEC, the FASB, and the GASB; and changes in the tax laws are only a few of the factors that require members of the profession continually to update their technical knowledge.

A CPA firm must make certain that the professional staff remains continuously up to date on technical issues. To assist in this updating process, most large public accounting firms maintain a separate professional development section.

Professional development sections offer a wide range of seminars and educational programs to personnel of the firm. The curriculum of each program is especially designed to suit the needs and responsibilities of participants. Partners may attend programs focusing on the firm's policies on audit quality control or means of minimizing exposure to lawsuits; on the other hand, programs designed for staff assistants may cover audit procedures or use of the firm's microcomputers. In addition to offering educational programs, the professional development section usually publishes a monthly newsletter or journal for distribution to personnel of the CPA firm and other interested persons.

Many public accounting firms that are too small to maintain their own professional development departments have banded together into associations of CPA firms. These associations organize educational programs, distribute information on technical issues, and engage in other professional activities that are designed to meet the needs of their members. Since the cost of the association's professional activities are shared by all members, the firms are provided with many of the benefits of having their own professional development department at a fraction of the cost.

## Seasonal Fluctuations in Public Accounting Work

One of the traditional disadvantages of the public accounting profession has been the concentration of work during the "busy season" from December through April, followed by a period of slack demand during the summer months. This seasonal trend is caused by the fact that many companies keep their records on a calendar-year basis and require auditing services immediately after the December 31 closing of the accounts. Another important factor is the spring deadline for filing of federal income tax returns.

Auditors often work a considerable number of hours of overtime during the busy season. Some public accounting firms pay their staff a premium for overtime hours. Other firms allow their staff to accumulate the overtime in an "overtime bank" and to "withdraw" these hours in the form of additional vacation time during the less busy times of the year.

## Relationships with Clients

The wide-ranging scope of public accountants' activities today demands that CPAs be interested and well informed on economic trends, political developments, and other topics that play a significant part in business and social contacts. Although an in-depth knowledge of accounting is a most important qualification of the CPA, an ability to meet people easily and to gain their confidence and goodwill may be no less important in achieving success in the profession of public accounting. The ability to work effectively with clients will be enhanced by a sincere interest in their problems and by a relaxed and cordial manner.

The question of the auditors' independence inevitably arises in considering the advisability of social activities with clients. The partner in today's public accounting firm may play golf or tennis with the executives of client companies and other business associates. These relationships actually may make it easier to resolve differences of opinions that arise during the audit, if the client has learned to know and respect the partner. This mutual understanding need not prevent the CPA from standing firm on matters of accounting principle. This is perhaps the "moment of truth" for the practitioners of a profession.

However, the CPA must always remember that the concept of independence embodies an *appearance* of independence. This appearance of independence may be impaired if an auditor becomes excessively involved in social activities with clients. For example, if a CPA frequently attends lavish parties held by a client or dates an officer or employee of a client corporation, the question might be raised as to whether the CPA will appear independent to outsiders. This dilemma is but one illustration of the continual need for judgment and perspective on the part of an auditor.

## ◆ CHAPTER SUMMARY

This chapter explored the nature of the attest function, independent audits, and the auditing profession. To summarize:

1. A primary reason for the development of the public accounting profession is the attest function. When CPAs attest to information they issue a report with a conclusion about the reliability of a written assertion by management. In the case of financial statement audits, the audit report most frequently includes an opinion about whether management's financial statements conform to generally accepted accounting principles.

2. CPAs perform three different types of attestation engagements, including examinations, reviews, and agreed-upon procedures. When financial statements are examined, the engagement is called an audit.

3. Since audits involve examinations of financial information by independent experts, they increase the credibility of the information contained in the statements. Decision makers both within and outside the organization can use audited financial information with confidence that it is not likely to be materially misstated. Audits reduce information risk and, therefore, they reduce the overall risk of making various types of economic decisions.

4. The nature and emphasis of auditing has changed over the years. Auditing began with the objective of detecting fraud by examination of all, or most, business transactions. Today the objective of an audit is to attest to the fairness of the financial statements. Because of the large size of business organizations, audits necessarily involve the use of sampling techniques based on the auditors' consideration of the organization's internal controls. Auditors also are being asked to assume more responsibility for attesting to compliance with laws and regulations, and to the effectiveness of internal controls.

5. The auditing profession is much broader than auditors involved in public accounting; it also includes internal auditors and various governmental auditors, such as auditors of the General Accounting Office and the Internal Revenue Service.

6. Various professional and regulatory organizations have a significant influence on the auditing profession, including the American Institute of Certified Public Accountants, the Financial Accounting Standards Board, the Governmental Accounting Standards Board, the Securities and Exchange Commission, and the Institute of Internal Auditors.

7. In addition to performing attestation engagements, CPA firms offer tax services, consulting services, and accounting and review services. CPA firms range in size from sole practitioners to the large international firms referred to as the "Big 6" firms. The professional staff of a typical medium-to-large CPA firm includes partners, managers, senior accountants, and staff assistants.

# ◆ KEY TERMS INTRODUCED OR EMPHASIZED IN CHAPTER 1

**Agreed-upon procedures engagement**    An attest engagement in which the CPAs agree to perform procedures for a specified party and issue a report that is restricted to use by that party.

**American Institute of Certified Public Accountants (AICPA)**    The national professional organization of CPAs engaged in promoting high professional standards to ensure that CPAs serve the public interest.

**Assertion**    A representation or declaration, typically made by the management of an entity.

**Attest engagement**    An engagement in which a practitioner is engaged to express a conclusion about the reliability of an assertion that is the responsibility of another party (generally management).

**Audit of financial statements**    An examination designed to provide the highest level of assurance that CPAs provide that the financial statements follow generally accepted accounting principles, or another acceptable basis of accounting.

**Business risk**    The risk that a company will not be able to meet its financial obligations because of economic conditions or poor management decisions.

**Certified public accountant**    A person licensed by the state to practice public accounting as a profession, based on having passed the Uniform CPA Examination and having met certain educational and experience requirements.

**Compilation of financial statements**    Presenting in the form of financial statements information that is the representation of management without undertaking to express any assurance on the statements.

**Compliance audit**    An audit to measure the compliance of the organization with some established criteria; for example, laws and regulations.

**CPA examination**    A uniform examination administered twice a year by the American Institute of Certified Public Accountants for state boards of accountancy to enable them to issue CPA licenses. The examination covers the topics of accounting and reporting, auditing, and professional responsibilities.

**Examination**    An attest engagement designed to provide the highest level of assurance that CPAs provide on an assertion. An examination of financial statements is referred to as an audit.

**Fraud**    Misrepresentation by a person of a material fact, known by that person to be untrue or made with reckless indifference as to whether the fact is true, with intent to deceive and with the result that another party is injured.

**Generally accepted accounting principles (GAAP)**    Concepts or standards established by such authoritative bodies as the Accounting Principles Board (APB), the FASB, and the GASB and accepted by the accounting profession as essential to proper financial reporting.

**Information risk**    The risk that the information used to assess business risk is not accurate. Auditing can directly reduce information risk, but not business risk.

**Operational audit**    An analysis of a department or other unit of a business or governmental organization to measure the effectiveness and efficiency of operations.

**Review**    An engagement designed to lend only a limited degree of assurance relating to an assertion. As discussed in further detail in Chapter 19, the procedures performed are generally limited to inquiries and analytical procedures.

**Securities and Exchange Commission (SEC)**    A government agency authorized to regulate companies seeking approval to issue securities for sale to the public.

**Statements on Auditing Standards (SASs)**   A series of statements issued by the Auditing Standards Board of the AICPA. These statements are considered to be interpretations of generally accepted auditing standards.

# ◆ GROUP I: REVIEW QUESTIONS

1-1   The attest function is said to be the principal reason for the existence of a public accounting profession. What is meant by attesting to a client's financial statements?

1-2   What is the most common type of attest engagement? What is most frequently being "asserted" by management on this type of engagement?

1-3   What is the principal use and significance of an audit report to a large corporation with securities listed on a stock exchange? To a small family-owned enterprise?

1-4   Describe several business situations that would create a need for a report by an independent public accountant concerning the fairness of a company's financial statements.

1-5   Explain the following statement: One contribution of the independent auditor is to give *credibility* to financial statements.

1-6   The overall risk of the investment in a business includes both business risk and information risk. Contrast these two types of risk. Which one is most directly affected by the auditors?

1-7   Contrast the objectives of auditing at the beginning of this century with the objectives of auditing today.

1-8   What does an operational audit try to measure? Does an operational audit involve more or fewer subjective judgments than a compliance audit or an audit of financial statements? Explain. To whom is the report usually directed after completion of an operational audit?

1-9   Distinguish between a compliance audit and an operational audit.

1-10   CPA firms are sometimes grouped into categories of local firms, regional firms, and national firms. Explain briefly the characteristics of each. Include in your answer the types of services stressed in each group.

1-11   How does the role of the Securities and Exchange Commission differ from that of the AICPA?

1-12   Describe briefly the function of the General Accounting Office.

1-13   List two of the more important contributions to auditing literature by the American Institute of Certified Public Accountants.

1-14   Apart from auditing, what other professional services are offered by CPA firms?

1-15   Describe the various levels or grades of accounting personnel in a large public accounting firm.

1-16   Distinguish between the responsibilities of a senior auditor and a staff assistant.

1-17   List three of the more important responsibilities of a partner in a public accounting firm.

1-18   Is an *independent status* possible or desirable for internal auditors as compared with the independence of a CPA firm? Explain.

1-19   Spacecraft, Inc. is a large corporation audited regularly by a CPA firm and also maintaining an internal auditing staff. Explain briefly how the relationship of the CPA firm to Spacecraft differs from the relationship of the internal auditing staff to Spacecraft.

1-20   What is meant by a *peer review* in public accounting?

1-21   What are the advantages of organizing a CPA firm as a partnership rather than a sole proprietorship?

1-22   How does a professional corporation differ from the traditional corporation?

# ◆ GROUP II: QUESTIONS REQUIRING ANALYSIS

1-23   A corporation is contemplating issuing debenture bonds to a group of investors.

*Required:*   *a.*   Explain how independent audits of the corporation's financial statements facilitate this transaction.

   *b.*   Describe the likely effects on the transaction if the corporation decides not to obtain independent audits of the corporation's financial statements.

1-24   Evaluate the following quotation: "Every business, large or small, should have an annual audit by a CPA firm. To forgo an audit because of its cost is false economy."

1-25   The self-interest of the provider of financial information (whether an individual or a business entity) often runs directly counter to the interests of the user of the information.

*Required:*   *a.*   Give an example of such opposing interests.

   *b.*   What may be done to compensate for the possible bias existing because of the self-interest of the individual or business entity providing the financial information?

1-26   The role of the auditor in the American economy has changed over the years in response to changes in our economic and political institutions. Consequently, the nature of an audit today is quite different from that of an audit performed in the year 1900. Classify the following phrases into two groups: (1) phrases more applicable to an audit performed in 1900 and (2) phrases more applicable to an audit performed today.

   *a.*   Complete review of all transactions.
   *b.*   Assessment of internal control.
   *c.*   Auditors' attention concentrated on balance sheet.
   *d.*   Emphasis upon use of sampling techniques.
   *e.*   Determination of fairness of financial statements.
   *f.*   Audit procedures to prevent or detect fraud on the part of all employees and managers.
   *g.*   Registration statement.
   *h.*   Fairness of reported earnings per share.
   *i.*   Influence of stock exchanges and the investing public upon use of independent auditors.
   *j.*   Generally accepted auditing standards.
   *k.*   Bankers and short-term creditors as principal users of audit reports.
   *l.*   Pressure for more disclosure.
   *m.*   Auditing for compliance with laws and regulations.

1-27   Select the best answer for each of the following items and give reasons for your choice.

   *a.*   Which of the following has primary responsibility for the fairness of the representations made in financial statements?
      (1)   Client's management.
      (2)   Independent auditor.
      (3)   Audit committee.
      (4)   AICPA.

   *b.*   The most important benefit of having an annual audit by a CPA firm is to:

      (1) Provide assurance to investors and other outsiders that the financial statements are dependable.

      (2) Enable officers and directors to avoid personal responsibility for any misstatements in the financial statements.

      (3) Meet the requirements of government agencies.

      (4) Provide assurance that illegal acts, if any exist, will be brought to light.

   *c.* Which of these organizations is designated to issue attestation standards?

      (1) American Institute of Certified Public Accountants.

      (2) Governmental Accounting Standards Board.

      (3) Financial Accounting Standards Board.

      (4) General Accounting Office.

   *d.* Governmental auditing, in addition to including audits of financial statements, often includes audits of efficiency, effectiveness, and:

      (1) Adequacy.

      (2) Evaluation.

      (3) Accuracy.

      (4) Compliance.

   *e.* In general, internal auditors' independence will be greatest when they report directly to the:

      (1) Financial vice president.

      (2) Corporate controller.

      (3) Audit committee of the board of directors.

      (4) Corporate stockholders.

   *f.* Operational audits often have an objective of determining whether an entity's:

      (1) Internal control structure is adequately operating as designed.

      (2) Operational information is in accordance with generally accepted governmental auditing standards.

      (3) Financial statements present fairly the results of operations.

      (4) Specific operating units are functioning efficiently and effectively.

                                                             (AICPA, adapted)

# ◆ GROUP III: PROBLEMS

**1-28** For the purposes of this problem, you are to assume the existence of five types of auditors: CPA, GAO, IRS, bank examiner, and internal auditor. Also assume that the work of these various auditors can be grouped into five classifications: audits of financial statements, compliance audits, operational audits, accounting services, and consulting services.

    For each of the following topics, you are to state the type of auditor most probably involved. Also identify the topic with one of the above classes of work.

    You should organize your answer in a three-column format as follows: Column 1, list the number of the topic; Column 2, list the type of auditor involved; and Column 3, list the class of work.

   1. Financial statements of a small business to be submitted to a bank in support of a loan application.

   2. Financial statements of a large bank listed on the New York Stock Exchange to be distributed to stockholders.

   3. Review of the management directive stating the goals and responsibilities of a corporation's mail-handling department.

4.  Review of costs and accomplishments of a military research program carried on within the Air Force to determine whether the program was cost effective.

5.  Examination on a surprise basis of Midtown State Bank. Emphasis placed on verification of cash, marketable securities, and loans receivable and on consistent observation of the banking code.

6.  Analysis of the accounting system of a small business with the objective of making recommendations concerning installation of a computer-based system.

7.  Determination of fairness of financial statements for public distribution by a corporation that has a professional level internal auditing staff.

8.  Review of the activities of the receiving department of a large manufacturing company, with special attention to efficiency of materials inspection and promptness of reports issued.

9.  Review of tax return of corporate president to determine whether charitable contributions are adequately substantiated.

10. Review of daily attendance during spring term at Blue Ridge Consolidated School District to ascertain whether payments received from the state were substantiated by pupil-day data, and whether disbursements by the District were within authorized limits.

11. Review of transactions of government agency to determine whether disbursements under Payment-In-Kind program of U.S. Department of Agriculture followed the intent of Congress.

12. Compilation of quarterly financial statements for a small business that does not have any accounting personnel capable of preparing financial statements.

1-29   Listed below are 10 publications in the fields of auditing and accounting.

1.  *Statements on Auditing Standards* (SASs).
2.  The *Journal of Accountancy*.
3.  *Regulation S-X, Form and Content of Financial Statements*.
4.  *Statements on Standards for Accounting and Review Services* (SSARSs).
5.  *Financial Reporting Releases* (FRR).
6.  Accounting and Reporting Standards for Corporate Financial Statements.
7.  Accounting and Reporting Standards for Governmental Entities.
8.  *Industry Audit and Accounting Guides*.
9.  *Auditing Procedure Studies*.
10. *The Tax Advisor*.

The list of organizations shown below includes the sponsors or publishers of the above 10 publications.

(a)  Accounting Principles Board (APB).
(b)  Securities and Exchange Commission (SEC).
(c)  American Institute of Certified Public Accountants (AICPA).
(d)  Financial Accounting Standards Board (FASB).
(e)  Internal Revenue Service (IRS).
(f)  General Accounting Office (GAO).
(g)  Governmental Accounting Standards Board (GASB).

*Required:*  You are to identify the sponsoring organization for each of the 10 publications. (Some of the organizations may not have a publication in this list.) Organize your answer in a two-column format. In the left-hand column, list the number and name of each publication in the order shown above. In the right-hand column, list the identifying letter and the abbreviation of the sponsoring organization. For example, on line 1, list (1) *Statements on Auditing Standards* in the left column and (2) AICPA in the right column.

1-30   Each auditing term (or organizational name) in Column One below bears a close relationship to a term in Column Two.

| **Column One** | **Column Two** |
|---|---|
| 1. Quality control. | *a.* Compliance audit. |
| 2. Operational audit. | *b.* Attest function. |
| 3. Internal control. | *c.* Material information. |
| 4. General Accounting Office. | *d.* Credibility. |
| 5. Disclosure. | *e.* Peer review. |
| 6. Major reason for development of public accounting profession. | *f.* Registration statement. |
| | *g.* Accounting service. |
| 7. Internal Revenue Service. | *h.* Measurement of effectiveness and efficiency of a unit of an organization. |
| 8. Securities and Exchange Commission. | |
| 9. Audited financial statements. | *i.* Basis for sampling and testing. |
| 10. Compilation of financial statements. | *j.* Auditing staff reporting to Congress. |

*Required:* You are to identify the most closely related terms in Columns One and Two. Organize your answer in a two-column format by copying the numbers and terms in Column One as given. Then, rearrange the sequence of terms in Column Two so that each line of your schedule will contain two closely related terms.

1-31 Feller, the sole owner of a small hardware business, has been told that the business should have financial statements audited by an independent CPA. Feller, having some bookkeeping experience, has personally prepared the company's financial statements and does not understand why such statements should be audited by a CPA. Feller discussed the matter with Farber, a CPA, and asked Farber to explain why an audit is considered important.

*Required:*   *a.* Describe the objectives of an independent audit.

         *b.* Identify five ways in which an independent audit may be beneficial to Feller.

1-32 Will Williams, a college senior, has begun the interviewing process. He has discovered a great variety of organizations in search of "accounting majors." He finds that various CPA firms, corporations, the General Accounting Office, and the Internal Revenue Service are all interviewing candidates at his school.

    He has come to you and asked for your advice. He has suggested that although he has had only one class session of auditing, he already realizes that it is going to be a great course. But, he also especially enjoyed his tax and accounting systems courses.

*Required:* Compare and contrast his possibilities with CPA firms, corporations, the General Accounting Office, and the Internal Revenue Service if he wishes to emphasize the following areas of expertise.

         *a.* Taxation.

         *b.* Auditing.

         *c.* Systems design.

For example, first compare and contrast his likely responsibilities with each of the above organizations if he chooses to emphasize taxation.

1-33 In a discussion between Peters and Ferrel, two auditing students, Peters made the following statement:

    "A CPA is a professional person who is licensed by the state for the purpose of providing an independent expert opinion on the fairness of financial statements. To maintain an attitude of mental independence and objectivity in all phases of audit work, it is advisable that the CPA not fraternize with client personnel. The CPA should be courteous but reserved and dignified at all times. Indulging in social contacts with clients outside of business hours will make it more difficult to be firm and objective if the CPA finds evidence of fraud or of unsound accounting practices."

Ferrel replied as follows:

"You are 50 years behind the times, Peters. An auditor and a client are both human beings. The auditor needs the cooperation of the client to do a good job; you're much more likely to get cooperation if you're relaxed and friendly rather than being cold and impersonal. Having a few beers or going to a football game with a client won't keep the CPA from being independent. It will make the working relationship a lot more comfortable, and will probably cause the client to recommend the CPA to other business people who need auditing services. In other words, the approach you're recommending should be called 'How to Avoid Friends and Alienate Clients.' I will admit, though, that with so many women entering public accounting and other women holding executive positions in business, a few complications may arise when auditor-client relations get pretty relaxed."

Evaluate the opposing views expressed by Peters and Ferrel.

## ◆ RESEARCH AND DISCUSSION CASE

1-34    Smith & Co., a local Dallas CPA firm, is incorporated as a professional corporation, with three shareholders, all CPAs. The shareholders have developed a combination of marketing, software, and professional expertise which has allowed them to perform the accounting service of compiling individuals' personal financial statements in an extremely efficient manner.

The three shareholders are interested in "going national" with their accounting service, but currently lack the capital necessary to expand to other cities. They are currently considering the possibility of obtaining outside capital as a way to expand their business by offering their firm's services to individuals in other markets. They estimate that by raising $4,000,000 of capital they could open and staff 15 offices within the next 12 months.

In a recent meeting of the three shareholders, the possibility of raising the capital through incorporation as a traditional corporation and thereby selling stock to the public was discussed. The original three shareholders would retain 51 percent of the total stock which would be traded "over-the-counter." The only work performed through the new corporation would be the compilation of individuals' financial statements.

Subsequently, the shareholders were dismayed to learn that states do not generally allow CPAs to practice as a traditional corporation. Also, those states that do allow "limited liability companies" generally require that shareholders be involved in public accounting. Only by establishing a separate organization not held out as a CPA firm will the current three shareholders be allowed to follow their expansion plan.

Required:   a.  Summarize the arguments for allowing CPA firms to sell ownership interests to individuals not in public accounting through incorporation as a traditional corporation.
   b.  Summarize the arguments in favor of restricting CPA firm ownership to those involved in public accounting.
   c.  Express your personal opinion as to whether ownership of public accounting firms should be restricted to individuals involved in public accounting.

## ◆ SUGGESTED REFERENCES

AICPA, *Professional Standards, Volume 2,* Commerce Clearing House, Section ET 505 (*Code of Professional Conduct,* Rule 505).

Appropriate chapters from other accounting and business textbooks that discuss the advantages of the corporate form of business.

# 2

# PROFESSIONAL STANDARDS

After studying this chapter, you should be able to:

- Identify the 10 generally accepted auditing standards.
- Describe the authoritative status of the *Statements on Auditing Standards*.
- Discuss the auditors' responsibility for detecting errors, irregularities, and illegal acts.
- Explain the key elements of the auditors' standard report.
- Discuss the other types of reports that are issued by auditors.
- Describe the attestation standards.
- Describe the quality control standards and their purposes.
- Explain the status of international auditing standards.

Standards are established to measure the quality of performance of individuals and organizations. Standards relating to the accounting profession concern themselves both with the CPA's professional qualities, and with the judgment exercised by CPAs in the performance of their professional engagements.

Our purpose in this chapter is to make clear the nature of generally accepted auditing standards, attestation standards, and quality control standards. In our discussion of the generally accepted auditing standards, we consider in detail the nature of the independent auditors' report—that brief but important document that emerges as the end product of an audit engagement. It is the auditors' report that gives credibility to a set of financial statements and makes them acceptable to investors, bankers, government, and other users.

# GENERALLY ACCEPTED AUDITING STANDARDS (GAAS)

The existence of generally accepted auditing standards is evidence that auditors are very concerned with the maintenance of a uniformly high quality of audit work by all independent public accountants. If every certified public accountant has adequate technical training and performs audits with skill, care, and professional judgment, the prestige of the profession will rise, and the public will attribute more and more significance to the auditors' opinion attached to financial statements.

What are the standards developed by the public accounting profession? The AICPA has set forth the basic framework in the following 10 **generally accepted auditing standards.**

---

**General Standards**

1. The audit is to be performed by a person or persons having adequate *technical training* and *proficiency* as an auditor.
2. In all matters relating to the assignment, an *independence in mental attitude* is to be maintained by the auditor or auditors.
3. *Due professional care* is to be exercised in the performance of the audit and the preparation of the report.

**Standards of Field Work**

1. The work is to be *adequately planned* and assistants, if any, are to be *properly supervised.*
2. A *sufficient understanding of the internal control structure* is to be obtained to plan the audit and to determine the nature, timing, and extent of tests to be performed.
3. *Sufficient competent evidential matter* is to be obtained through inspection, observation, inquiries, and confirmations to afford a reasonable basis for an opinion regarding the financial statements under audit.

**Standards of Reporting**

1. The report shall state *whether* the financial statements are presented in accordance with *generally accepted accounting principles.*

*(continued)*

> 2. The report shall identify those circumstances in which such principles have *not* been *consistently observed* in the current period in relation to the preceding period.
> 3. *Informative disclosures* in the financial statements are to be regarded as reasonably adequate *unless otherwise stated in the report.*
> 4. The report shall either contain an *expression of opinion* regarding the financial statements, taken as a whole, or an assertion to the effect that an opinion cannot be expressed. When an overall opinion cannot be expressed, the reasons therefor should be stated. In all cases where an auditor's name is associated with financial statements, the report should contain a clear-cut indication of the *character of the auditor's work* if any, and the *degree of responsibility* the auditor is taking. [Emphasis added.]

## Application of Auditing Standards

The 10 standards set forth by the American Institute of Certified Public Accountants include such subjective terms of measurement as *"adequate* planning," *"sufficient* understanding of the internal control structure," *"sufficient competent* evidential matter," and *"adequate* disclosure." To decide under the circumstances of each audit engagement what is adequate, sufficient, and competent requires the exercise of professional judgment. Auditing cannot be reduced to rote; the exercise of judgment by the auditor is vital at numerous points in every engagement. However, the formulation and publication of carefully worded auditing standards are of immense aid in raising the quality of audit work, even though these standards require professional judgment in their application.

## Training and Proficiency

How does the independent auditor achieve the "adequate technical training and proficiency" required by the first general standard? This requirement is usually interpreted to mean college or university education in accounting and auditing, substantial public accounting experience, ability to design procedures suitable for computer-based accounting systems, and participation in continuing education programs. A technical knowledge of the industry in which the client operates is also part of the personal qualifications of the auditor. It follows that a CPA firm must not accept an audit engagement without first determining that members of its staff have the technical training and proficiency needed to function effectively in the particular industry.

## Independence

An opinion by an independent public accountant as to the fairness of a company's financial statements is of no value unless the accountant is truly independent. Consequently, the auditing standard that states "in all matters relating to the assignment an independence in mental attitude is to be maintained by the auditor" is perhaps the most essential factor in the existence of a public accounting profession.

If auditors owned shares of stock in a company that they audited, or if they served as members of the board of directors, they might subconsciously be biased in the performance of auditing duties. A CPA should therefore avoid any relationship with a client that would cause an outsider who had knowledge of all the facts to doubt the CPA's independence. It is not enough that CPAs be independent; they must conduct themselves in such a manner that informed members of the public will have no reason to doubt their independence.

## Due Professional Care

The third general standard requires due professional care in the conduct of the audit and in the preparation of the audit report. This standard requires the auditors to carry out every step of the audit engagement in an alert and diligent manner. Full compliance with this standard would rule out any negligent acts or material omissions by the auditors. Of course, auditors, as well as members of other professions, inevitably make occasional errors in judgment.

## Standards of Field Work—Accumulating and Evaluating Evidence

The three standards of field work relate to accumulating and evaluating evidence sufficient for the auditors to express an opinion on the financial statements. One major type of evidence is the client's internal control. By understanding and testing the **internal control structure,** the auditors can assess whether the structure offers assurance that the financial statements will be free from material errors and irregularities. A second major type of evidence consists of information that substantiates the amounts on the financial statements being audited. Examples of such evidence include written confirmations from outsiders and firsthand observation of assets by the auditors. The gathering and evaluating of evidence lies at the very heart of the audit process and is a continuing theme throughout this textbook.

## Adequate Planning and Supervision

Adequate planning is essential to a satisfactory audit. Some portions of the examination can be performed prior to the end of the year under audit; some information may be compiled by the client's staff and made available for the auditors' review. The appropriate number of audit staff of various levels of skill and the time required of each need to be determined in advance of field work. These are but a few of the elements of planning the audit.

Most of the field work of an audit is carried out by staff members with limited experience. The key to successful use of relatively new staff members is close supervision at every level. This concept extends from providing a specific written audit program to staff members all the way to an overall review of the work by the partner in charge of the engagement.

## Sufficient Understanding of Internal Control

An effective internal control structure provides strong assurance that the client's records are dependable and that its assets are protected. When the auditors find this type of strong internal control, the quantity of other evidence required is much less than if controls were weak. Thus, the auditors' assessment of internal control has great impact on the length and nature of the audit process.

## Sufficient Competent Evidential Matter

The third standard of field work requires that the auditors gather sufficient competent evidence to have a basis for expressing an opinion on the financial statements. The term *competent* refers to the quality of the evidence; some forms of evidence are stronger and more convincing than others. In Chapter 6, we shall explore at length the meaning of this standard.

## Standards of Reporting

The four reporting standards establish some specific directives for preparation of the auditors' report. The report must specifically state whether the financial statements are in conformity with generally accepted accounting principles. The report must contain an opinion on the financial statements as a whole, or must disclaim an opinion. **Consistency** in the application of generally accepted accounting principles and adequate informative disclosure in the financial statements is to be assumed unless the audit report states otherwise. These basic reporting standards are considered more fully in Chapters 3 and 19.

## Statements on Auditing Standards (SASs)

Statements on Auditing Standards are serially numbered pronouncements issued by the Auditing Standards Board (ASB). The first in the series, *SAS 1,* is a codification of 54 *Statements* previously issued over many years by the Committee on Auditing Procedure, a predecessor of the ASB. Since *SAS 1* was released in 1972, many additional statements on specific topics have been issued to provide more detailed guidance than is available from the 10 generally accepted auditing standards.

The SASs are considered to be *interpretations* of the 10 generally accepted auditing standards discussed earlier in this chapter. They are the most authoritative references that auditors can utilize to resolve problems encountered during an audit. The term *auditing standards* is often used in practice to refer to the SASs, to the 10 generally accepted auditing standards, or to both.

The authoritative status of the SASs, as interpretations of generally accepted auditing standards, is derived from the AICPA *Code of Professional Conduct* (Rule 202). The Code requires auditors to adhere to these pronouncements. A CPA firm must be prepared to justify any departure from the SASs, a task not to be taken lightly.

The SASs, although more detailed and specific than the generally accepted auditing standards, do not usually prescribe specific auditing procedures to be followed. For more detailed, but less authoritative guidelines on specific audit problems, auditors can refer to *Industry Audit and Accounting Guides* and *Auditing Procedure Studies,* various technical studies published by the AICPA, auditing textbooks, and articles in professional journals, such as the *Journal of Accountancy* and *The CPA Journal.*

The 10 basic concepts embodied in generally accepted auditing standards and the role of the SASs are summarized in Figure 2–1. Keep in mind, however, that compliance with the SASs does not represent an ideal level of audit performance, but rather a *minimum standard* for all audit engagements.

**Figure 2–1    Summary of the 10 Generally Accepted Auditing Standards**

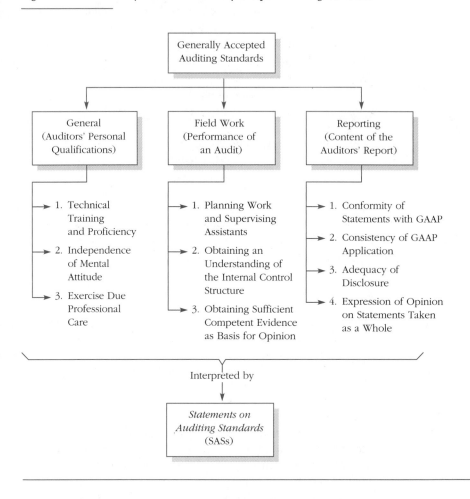

Throughout this textbook, we will be making references to individual SASs. Each SAS is identified under two numbering systems: the original SAS number and an AU number. The SAS numbering system organizes the SASs by date of issue, whereas the AU numbering system organizes them by topic. Thus, *Statement on Auditing Standards 11,* "Using the Work of a Specialist," is identified as *SAS 11* and AU 336. The AU numbering system is used in the AICPA *Codification of Statements on Auditing Standards* and also in the AICPA *Professional Standards, Volume 1,* published annually by Commerce Clearing House (4025 West Peterson Avenue, Chicago, Illinois 60646).

## THE AUDITORS' RESPONSIBILITY FOR DETECTING MISSTATEMENTS

For financial statements to be in accordance with generally accepted accounting principles, they must be free from material misstatements. Therefore, auditors have a responsibility to detect various types of material misstatements, including errors, irregularities, and those caused by certain illegal acts. The profession's views on these responsibilities are presented in *SAS 53* (AU 316), "The Auditor's Responsibility to Detect and Report Errors and Irregularities," and *SAS 54* (AU 317), "Illegal Acts by Clients."

Errors and Irregularities.   *SAS 53* (AU 316) defines the term **errors** as unintentional mistakes or omissions in financial statements, including mistakes in the application of accounting principles. **Irregularities,** on the other hand, is a term used to describe intentional misstatements of financial statements (management fraud) and theft of assets (employee fraud). Throughout this text, we will use the terms irregularities and fraud interchangeably.

The auditors are required to assess the risk that errors and irregularities have occurred affecting the client's financial records. Based on that assessment, they design their audit to provide *reasonable assurance* of detecting errors and irregularities that are *material* to the financial statements. In doing so, the auditors must exercise due care in planning, performing, and evaluating the results of their audit procedures. They also must exercise the proper degree of *professional skepticism* by not assuming unquestioned honesty on the part of management.

An audit provides reasonable assurance of detecting a material misstatement of the financial statements, not absolute assurance. A properly designed and executed audit may not detect certain material misstatements, especially irregularities that involve forgery or collusion among client personnel. Audits providing absolute assurance of detecting material misstatement of financial statements would be far too costly.

Illegal Acts by Clients.   Laws and regulations vary in their relation to the client's financial statements. Certain laws have a direct effect on the financial statement amounts and are considered on every audit. An example is the income tax law which affects the amount of income tax expense in the financial statements of most clients. The auditors' responsibility for detecting violations of these laws is greater than their responsibility to detect illegal acts arising from laws that only indirectly affect the client's financial statements, such as violations of antitrust laws.

As explained in *SAS 54* (AU 317) an audit carried out in accordance with generally accepted auditing standards should be designed to provide reasonable assurance of detecting illegal acts having a material *direct* effect on the determination of financial statement amounts—this is the same responsibility the auditors have for material errors and irregularities. An audit does *not* generally provide a basis for detecting violations of laws or regulations which have an *indirect* effect on financial statement amounts. However, the media and the public sometimes tend to blame auditors when illegal acts by a client company are not brought to light during an audit. Only those persons who understand the scope and limitations of an audit realize that audits by their very nature cannot be relied on to detect all types of illegal acts by the client. Of course, audit procedures such as reading minutes of the board of directors and inquiring of management and the client's attorney may result in the discovery of certain indirect illegal acts. Also, the auditors are alert throughout their audit for information that raises a question regarding the possibility of illegal acts, such as transactions that are unauthorized or improperly recorded, investigations by governmental agencies, and excessive or unusual payments.

Under no circumstances should the auditors condone or ignore actions they *know* to be dishonest or illegal. This does not mean that the auditors should report such acts to governmental authorities; it means that they should not permit their firm's name to be associated with financial statements that are misleading or that conceal morally indefensible actions by a client.

If the auditors have knowledge of dishonest or clearly illegal actions by a client, they should attempt to assess the impact of the actions on the financial statements. This usually requires consulting legal counsel or another specialist. The auditors should also discuss the situation with top management and notify the audit committee of the board of directors so that proper action can be taken, including making any necessary disclosures or adjustments to the financial statements. If the client fails to take appropriate corrective action, the auditors should withdraw from the engagement. This action on the part of the auditors makes clear that they will not be associated in any way with dishonorable or illegal activities.

# THE AUDITORS' REPORT

The end product of an audit of a business entity is a report expressing the auditors' opinion on the client's financial statements. In 1988 the Auditing Standards Board made a number of changes in the profession's reporting standards. The auditors' **standard unqualified report** (as illustrated on the next page) that resulted from these changes consists of three paragraphs. The first paragraph clarifies the responsibilities of management and the auditors and is referred to as the *introductory paragraph*. The second paragraph, which describes the nature of the audit, is called the *scope paragraph;* the final paragraph, the *opinion paragraph,* is a concise statement of the auditors' opinion based on the audit.

The auditors' report is addressed to the person or persons who retained the auditors; in the case of corporations, the selection of an auditing firm is usually made by the board of directors and ratified by the stockholders.

## The Introductory Paragraph of the Auditors' Report

To gain a full understanding of the introductory paragraph of the auditors' report we need to emphasize the following two points:

1.  **The client company is primarily responsible for the financial statements.**   The management of a company has the responsibility of maintaining adequate accounting records and of preparing proper financial statements for the use of stockholders and creditors. Even though the financial statements are sometimes constructed and printed in the auditors' office, primary responsibility for the statements remains with management.

The auditors' product is their report. It is a separate document from the client's financial statements, although the two are closely related and transmitted together to stockholders and to creditors.

---

INDEPENDENT AUDITORS' REPORT

To the Board of Directors and Stockholders
XYZ Company:

We have audited the accompanying balance sheet of XYZ Company as of December 31, 19X1, and the related statements of income, retained earnings, and cash flows for the year then ended. These financial statements are the responsibility of the Company's management. Our responsibility is to express an opinion on these financial statements based on our audit.

We conducted our audit in accordance with generally accepted auditing standards. Those standards require that we plan and perform the audit to obtain reasonable assurance about whether the financial statements are free of material misstatement. An audit includes examining, on a test basis, evidence supporting the amounts and disclosures in the financial statements. An audit also includes assessing the accounting principles used and significant estimates made by management, as well as evaluating the overall financial statement presentation. We believe that our audit provides a reasonable basis for our opinion.

In our opinion, the financial statements referred to above present fairly, in all material respects, the financial position of XYZ Company as of December 31, 19X1, and the results of its operations and its cash flows for the year then ended in conformity with generally accepted accounting principles.

Los Angeles, Calif.                                    *Blue, Gray & Company*

                                                       Certified Public Accountants
                                                       February 26, 19X2

---

Once we recognize that the financial statements are the statements of the company and not of the auditors, we realize that the auditors have no right to make changes in the financial statements. What action then should the auditors take if they do not agree with the presentation of a material item in the balance sheet or income statement? Assume, for example, that the allowance for doubtful accounts is not sufficient (in the auditors' opinion) to cover the probable collection losses in the accounts receivable.

The auditors will first discuss the problem with management and point out why they believe the valuation allowance to be inadequate. If management agrees to increase the allowance for doubtful accounts, an adjusting entry will be made for that purpose, and the problem is solved. If management is not convinced by the auditors' arguments and declines to increase the doubtful accounts allowance, the auditors will probably **qualify** their opinion by stating in the report that the financial statements reflect fairly the company's financial position and operating results, *except for the effects of not providing an adequate provision for doubtful account losses.* Usually such issues are satisfactorily disposed of in discussions between the auditors and the client, and a qualification of the auditors' opinion is avoided. A full consideration of the use of qualifications in the auditors' report is presented in Chapter 3.

**2.    The auditors render a report on the financial statements, not on the accounting records.**    The primary purpose of an audit is to provide assurance to the users of the financial statements that these statements are reliable. Auditors do not express an opinion on the client's accounting records. The auditors' investigation of financial statement items includes reference to the client's accounting records, but is not limited to these records. An audit includes observation of tangible assets, inspection of such documents as purchase orders and contracts, and the gathering of evidence from outsiders (such as banks, customers, and suppliers), as well as analysis of the client's accounting records.

It is true that a principal means of establishing the validity of a balance sheet and income statement is to trace the statement figures to the accounting records and back through the records to the original evidence of transactions. However, the auditors' use of the accounting records is only a means to an end—and merely a part of the audit. It is, therefore, appropriate for the auditors to state in their report that they have made an audit of the *financial statements* rather than to say that they have made an audit of the accounting records.

## The Scope Paragraph of the Auditors' Report

The scope paragraph describes the nature of the CPAs' audit. It states that the audit was conducted in accordance with generally accepted auditing standards and points out that while an audit is meant to obtain *reasonable assurance* that the financial statements are free of material misstatement, the procedures are applied on a test basis. Thus, an audit cannot provide *absolute assurance* that the financial statements are free from material misstatement; the auditors do, however, believe the procedures performed provide a reasonable basis for their opinion.

## The Opinion Paragraph of the Auditors' Report

The opinion paragraph consists of only one sentence, which is restated here with certain significant phrases shown in italics:

---

*In our opinion,* the financial statements referred to above *present fairly, in all material respects,* the financial position of XYZ Company as of December 31, 19X1, and the results of its operations and its cash flows for the year then ended in conformity with *generally accepted accounting principles.*

---

Each of the italicized phrases has a special significance. The first phrase, "in our opinion," makes clear that the auditors are expressing nothing more than an informed opinion; they are not guaranteeing or certifying that the statements are accurate, correct, or true. In an earlier period of public accounting, the wording of the audit report contained the phrase "We certify that . . . ," but this expression was discontinued on the grounds that it was misleading. To "certify" implies a positive assurance of accuracy, which an audit simply does not provide.

The auditors cannot guarantee the correctness of the financial statements because the statements include many estimates, not absolute facts. Furthermore, the auditors do not make a complete and detailed examination of all transactions. Their audit is limited to a program of tests that leaves the possibility of some misstatements going undetected. Because of limitations inherent in the accounting process and because of practical limitations of time and cost in performing an audit, the auditors' work culminates in the expression of an opinion and not in the issuance of a guarantee of accuracy. The growth of public accounting and the increased confidence placed in audited statements by all sectors of the economy indicate that the auditors' opinion is usually sufficient assurance that the statements may be relied upon.

The Financial Statements "Present Fairly, in All Material Respects . . ."   Since many of the items in financial statements cannot be measured exactly, the auditors cannot say that the statements present exactly or correctly the financial position or operating results. The meaning of "present fairly" as used in the context of the auditors' report has been much discussed in court cases and in auditing literature. Some accountants believed that financial statements were fair if they conformed to GAAP; others insisted that fairness was a distinct concept, broader than mere compliance with GAAP. This discussion led to the issuance by the Auditing Standards Board of *SAS 69* (AU 411), "The Meaning of 'Present Fairly in Conformity with Generally Accepted Accounting Principles' in the Independent Auditor's Report." In the opinion of the authors, the essence of *SAS 69* is to equate the quality of *presenting fairly* with that of *not being misleading*. Financial statements must not be so presented as to lead users to conclusions that a company and its independent auditors know are unsound or unlikely.

What Is "Material"?   Auditors cannot issue an unqualified opinion on financial statements that contain material deficiencies. The term *material* may be defined as "sufficiently important to influence decisions made by reasonable users of financial statements." In the audit of a small client—such as a condominium property owners' association—$1,000 might be considered material. On the other hand, in the audit of an IBM or a General Motors, an amount of $1 million might be considered to be immaterial.

In practice, one of the most significant elements of professional judgment is the ability to draw the line between material and immaterial departures from generally accepted accounting practices. The auditor who raises objections over immaterial items will soon lose the respect of both clients and associates. On the other hand, the auditor who fails to identify and disclose material deficiencies in financial statements may be liable for the losses of those who rely upon the audited statements. In short, applying the concept of materiality is one of the most complex problems faced by auditors.

Materiality depends upon both the *dollar amount* and the *nature of the item*. For example, a $500,000 error in the balance of the Cash account is far more important than a $500,000 error in the balance of Accumulated Depreciation. If a corporation sells assets to a member of top management and then buys the assets back at a higher price, this *related party transaction* warrants disclosure even though the dollar amounts are not large in relation to the financial statements as a whole. The reason for requiring disclosure of such a transaction—that is, the possibility of management impropriety—is based more on the nature of the transaction than upon the dollar amount.

Adequate Informative Disclosure. If financial statements are to present fairly, in all material respects, the financial position and operating results of a company, there must be adequate disclosure of all essential information. A financial statement may be misleading if it does not give a complete picture. For example, if an extraordinary item arising from an uninsured flood loss of plant and equipment were combined with operating income and not clearly identified, the reader might be misled as to the earning power of the company.

## Generally Accepted Accounting Principles (GAAP)

In our study of the main ideas contained in the auditors' report, the next key phrase to be considered is "generally accepted accounting principles." The wording of the audit report implies that generally accepted accounting principles represent a concept well known to CPAs and sophisticated users of financial statements. However, no official list of accounting principles exists, and a satisfactory concise definition is yet to be developed.

When evaluating whether a particular accounting principle used by a client is generally accepted, the auditors may refer to a variety of sources, from *Statements* of the FASB and the GASB to articles in accounting journals. The auditors look to these references to determine whether or not there is *substantial authoritative support* for the principle. Figure 2–2 illustrates the relative authority of sources of generally accepted accounting principles from the category with highest authority to that with the least. As illustrated, the pronouncements that contain generally accepted accounting principles are different for state and local governments than they are for businesses and other types of entities.

In situations in which there is a conflict between the accounting treatment suggested by pronouncements from two different categories, the pronouncement from the higher category should be followed. For example, authoritative body pronouncements prevail over pronouncements of other experts and widely recognized practices and pronouncements. When there is a conflict within a category, the auditors should select the accounting principle that most clearly reflects the *economic substance* of the particular transaction.

## Other Types of Auditors' Reports

The form of auditors' report discussed in this chapter is called a *standard unqualified opinion*. An unqualified opinion denotes that the audit was adequate in scope and that the financial statements present fairly the financial position, results of operations, and cash flows in conformity with generally accepted accounting principles. Under these circumstances, the auditors are taking *no exceptions* and inserting *no qualifications* in the report.

An unqualified opinion is the type of report the client wants and also the type auditors prefer to issue. In some audits, however, the circumstances do not permit the auditors to give their unqualified opinion on the financial statements. As alternatives to an unqualified opinion, auditors may issue a **qualified opinion,** an **adverse opinion,** or a **disclaimer of opinion.** In some situations, the auditors also include additional *"explanatory language"* in the report.

The auditors issue a *qualified opinion* on financial statements when there is some limitation on their audit, or when one or more items in the financial statements are not

## Figure 2-2

| | Category | Nongovernmental Entities | State and Local Governments |
|---|---|---|---|
| a. | Authoritative body pronouncements | FASB *Statements* and *Interpretations* APB *Opinions* AICPA *Accounting Research Bulletins* | GASB *Statements* and *Interpretations* FASB and AICPA pronouncements made applicable by a GASB *Statement* or *Interpretation* |
| b. | Pronouncements of bodies composed of expert accountants, exposed for public comment | FASB *Technical Bulletins* AICPA *Industry Audit and Accounting Guides* and *Statements of Position* (cleared by FASB) | GASB *Technical Bulletins* AICPA *Industry Audit and Accounting Guides* and *Statements of Position* (cleared by GASB) |
| c. | Pronouncements of bodies composed of expert accountants, *not* exposed for public comment | *Consensus Positions of the FASB Emerging Issues Task Force* AICPA *Practice Bulletins* (cleared by FASB) | *Consensus Positions of the GASB Emerging Issues Task Force* AICPA *Practice Bulletins* (cleared by GASB) |
| d. | Widely recognized practices and pronouncements | FASB staff *"Questions and Answers"* AICPA *Accounting Interpretations* Widely accepted industry practices | GASB staff *"Questions and Answers"* Widely accepted industry practices |
| e. | Other accounting literature | FASB *Concepts Statements* APB *Statements* AICPA *Issues Papers* and *Technical Practice Aids* International Accounting Standards Committee *Statements* GASB *Statements, Interpretations,* and *Technical Bulletins* Pronouncements of other professional associations or regulatory agencies Accounting textbooks, handbooks, and articles | GASB *Concepts Statements* Pronouncements in (a) through (d) of nongovernmental hierarchy not specifically made applicable APB *Statements* FASB *Concepts Statements* AICPA *Issues Papers* and *Technical Practice Aids* International Accounting Standards Committee *Statements* Pronouncements of other professional associations or regulatory agencies Accounting textbooks, handbooks, and articles |

Source: *SAS 69* (AU 411), "The Meaning of 'Present Fairly in Conformity with Generally Accepted Accounting Principles' in the Independent Auditor's Report."

presented in accordance with generally accepted accounting principles. The limitation or exception must be significant but not so material as to overshadow an overall opinion on the financial statements.

An *adverse opinion* states that the financial statements are not fairly presented. In practice an adverse opinion is rare, because it would be of little use to the client. If the financial statements contain such material departures from generally accepted accounting

## Figure 2–3   AICPA Attestation Standards

**General Standards**

1.  The engagement shall be performed by a practitioner or practitioners with adequate technical training and proficiency in the attest function.
2.  The engagement shall be performed by a practitioner or practitioners having adequate knowledge in the subject matter of the assertion.
3.  The practitioner shall perform an engagement only if he or she has reason to believe that the following two conditions exist:
    a.  The assertion is capable of evaluation against reasonable criteria that either have been established by a recognized body or are stated in the presentation of the assertion in a sufficiently clear and comprehensive manner for a knowledgeable reader to be able to understand them.
    b.  The assertion is capable of reasonably consistent estimation or measurement using such criteria.
4.  In all matters relating to the engagement, an independence in mental attitude shall be maintained by the practitioner or practitioners.
5.  Due professional care shall be exercised in the performance of the engagement.

**Standards of Field Work**

1.  The work shall be adequately planned and assistants, if any, shall be properly supervised.
2.  Sufficient evidence shall be obtained to provide a reasonable basis for the conclusion that is expressed in the report.

**Standards of Reporting**

1.  The report shall identify the assertion being reported on and state the character of the engagement.
2.  The report shall state the practitioner's conclusion about whether the assertion is presented in conformity with the established or stated criteria against which it was measured.
3.  The report shall state all of the practitioner's significant reservations about the engagement and the presentation of the assertion.
4.  The report on an engagement to evaluate an assertion that has been prepared in conformity with agreed-upon criteria or on an engagement to apply agreed-upon procedures should contain a statement limiting its use to the parties who have agreed upon such criteria or procedures.

principles as to warrant an adverse opinion, this situation will be discussed among the auditors and the client's management. The management probably will agree to make the changes necessary to avoid an adverse opinion or will decide to terminate the audit engagement and thus avoid paying additional audit fees.

The auditors will issue a *disclaimer of opinion* if they are unable to determine the overall fairness of the financial statements. This type of report results from very significant limitations in the scope of the auditors' examination or limitations that are imposed by the client.

When a qualified, adverse, or disclaimer of opinion is issued on the financial statements, *explanatory language* is added to the report describing the matter of concern. In certain other circumstances, explanatory language may be added to what remains an unqualified opinion. For example, it is important for users of financial statements to be informed of matters such as material uncertainties that may affect the financial statements, changes in accounting principles in relation to the prior year, or the fact that another audit firm is responsible for a significant portion of the audit. In circumstances such as these, although the opinion may remain unqualified, the overall wording of the report itself deviates from the wording of the standard unqualified report.

## THE ATTESTATION STANDARDS

The generally accepted auditing standards were passed by the accounting profession to provide guidance for the performance of audits of historical financial statements. The expansion of the attestation function has led the accounting profession to develop more general attestation standards. These attestation standards, presented as Figure 2–3, are meant to serve as a general framework and set boundaries for the attest function. The relationship of the attestation standards to other professional standards is illustrated in Figure 2–4.

As illustrated, the attestation standards provide a general framework for standards on the second level; they *do not* supersede any of the other standards. As a practical matter, the attestation standards relate most directly to other attest engagements which are not covered by specific authoritative standards; for example, attest engagements related to assertions about the internal controls included in computer software.

Figure 2–4    Relationship of Attestation Standards to Other Professional Standards

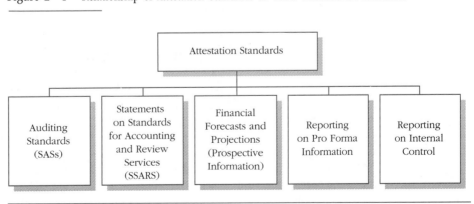

# QUALITY CONTROL IN CPA FIRMS

A CPA firm should establish adequate quality control policies and procedures to provide reasonable assurance that it follows professional standards on every engagement. To provide CPA firms with guidance in establishing quality control policies, the AICPA has issued *Statements on Quality Control Standards 1* (QC 10), "System of Quality Control for a CPA Firm," which identifies nine "elements" of quality control. The elements of quality control may be regarded as the *areas* in which the AICPA considers it desirable for a CPA firm to establish quality control procedures.

The AICPA does not require specific quality control procedures. In fact, it states that the specific procedures should depend upon the size of the firm, the number of offices, and the nature of the firm's practice. Thus, the quality control procedures employed by a 200-office international firm will differ considerably from those employed by a single-office firm that audits only small businesses. Technically, the AICPA's *Statements on Quality Control Standards 1* applies only to auditing, attestation, and accounting services for which professional standards have been established by the AICPA. As a practical matter, however, every CPA firm should have quality control procedures applicable to *every aspect of its practice*. In the broad sense, the concept of "quality control" means that CPA firms should establish controls to provide assurance that they meet their responsibilities to their clients and to the public.

Figure 2–5 indicates the nine areas in which the AICPA has indicated that quality control procedures are appropriate. In addition, the table explains the basic objective to be achieved in each area and provides an example of a procedure that a CPA firm might implement as a step toward achieving the objective.

## Division for CPA Firms

The AICPA took another step toward establishing quality control standards within the profession with the formation of the AICPA Division for CPA Firms. This action represented a positive response to certain congressional committees and other critics of the profession's system of self-regulation. Prior to forming the Division, CPAs joined the AICPA only as individuals; no mechanism existed for enforcing professional standards for CPA firms. In the Division for CPA Firms, membership is granted to CPA firms, not to individual CPAs.

The Division for CPA Firms actually includes two separate sections, the *SEC Practice Section* and the *Private Companies Practice Section*. CPA firms voluntarily join either or both sections based on the type of clients that they serve. Both sections require member firms to establish and maintain an adequate system of quality control and adhere to certain membership requirements. For example, the SEC Practice Section requires audit partners on SEC audit clients to be rotated at least every seven years. Audit engagements for such clients must be subjected to review by a second partner. Members of the SEC Practice Section are also prohibited from performing certain consulting services for SEC clients, including executive recruiting activities. Regular *peer reviews* and mandatory continuing education for firm personnel (120 hours every three years) are part of the membership requirements of both firm sections.

Figure 2-5   Elements of Quality Control

| Element of Quality Control | Basic Objective | Example of Procedure |
| --- | --- | --- |
| Independence | Firm personnel should meet the independence requirements of the AICPA *Code of Professional Conduct* | An investigation is made to determine the firm's independence before accepting a new audit client |
| Assigning personnel to engagements | Work should be performed by personnel with appropriate technical training and proficiency | Periodic meetings of audit managers are held to assign staff to upcoming jobs |
| Consultation | Advice should be sought from appropriate sources to help resolve complex problems | A "technical center" is maintained by a large CPA firm to provide research and consulting services to any practice office in the firm |
| Supervision | Personnel should be properly supervised | Working papers are reviewed by the manager and any deficiencies are discussed with the preparer |
| Hiring | New employees should possess the characteristics and qualifications to handle their jobs | Prospective employees are interviewed by both the personnel partner and by a technical partner in the area in which they will work |
| Professional development | Personnel should continue to expand their knowledge as required to meet their responsibilities | Each professional must annually receive at least 40 hours of continuing education |
| Advancement | Persons promoted should be qualified to assume their new responsibilities | Professionals are evaluated by their supervisors at the end of each engagement; the evaluations are placed in their personnel files |
| Acceptance and continuation of clients | Care should be taken to avoid association with clients lacking in integrity | Background information is gathered on all prospective audit clients and is discussed at a partners' meeting before accepting the client |
| Inspection | Controls should exist to provide reasonable assurance that established quality control procedures are being effectively applied | A quality control partner periodically tests the application of quality control procedures |

The executive committees of the two sections have the power to sanction member firms for substandard performance. These sanctions may include additional education requirements for firm personnel, special peer reviews, fines, and suspension or expulsion from the Division.

## The Public Oversight Board

A vital aspect of the profession's system of self-regulation is the Public Oversight Board, which is made up of prominent individuals who are not members of the accounting profession. The board oversees the activities of the SEC Practice Section and can intervene when the members of the Board think that the public's interest is not being served. Periodic reports inform the SEC and Congress about the activities of the Public Oversight Board.

## Peer Reviews

An important feature of the AICPA Division for Firms is the mandatory peer reviews that are required periodically of members of both sections. Every three years, member firms must subject their practice to a peer review. A peer review involves a study of the adequacy of the firm's established quality control policies and tests to determine the extent of the firm's compliance with these policies. In large part, these tests consist of a review of working paper files and reports for selected engagements. These engagements are evaluated for compliance with established quality control policies and professional standards.

The reviewers also examine many internal records of the CPA firm. They are especially interested in records concerning the promotions of employees, continuing education of firm personnel, staffing of engagements, client acceptance, and the employment of professional personnel. Based on the reviewers' study and tests of the quality controls, they issue a report that includes an opinion as to the adequacy of the reviewed firm's quality control system. Suggestions for improvement to the system are outlined in a "letter of comments" issued by the reviewers to the reviewed firm.

# INTERNATIONAL ACCOUNTING AND AUDITING STANDARDS

Auditing standards are currently determined on a country-by-country basis. However, as securities markets around the world are becoming more multinational, a need has developed for common auditing standards. The International Federation of Accountants (IFAC) is a worldwide organization of national accounting bodies (e.g., the AICPA) of approximately 80 countries, established to help foster a coordinated worldwide accounting profession with harmonized standards. One of its committees, the International Auditing Practices Committee (IAPC) issues *International Auditing Guidelines* that provide procedural and reporting guidance to auditors.

The pronouncements of the IAPC do not override the national auditing standards of its members. Rather they are meant to foster the development of consistent worldwide professional standards. Members from countries that do not have such standards are encouraged to adopt IAPC standards; members from countries that already have such standards are encouraged to compare them to IAPC standards and to seek to eliminate any material inconsistencies.

The international auditing standards setting process is at an early stage of development. Yet, one might expect rapid progress as multinational securities offerings and stock markets develop. Ultimately, we may find an audit in conformity with IAPC standards to be acceptable for multinational securities offerings in all of the participating nations.

The International Audit Report.   The reporting guidance of the IAPC is similar to that included in U.S. standards. However, the report itself is somewhat different, as illustrated below:

---

### INDEPENDENT AUDITORS' REPORT TO THE
### SHAREHOLDERS OF ABC COMPANY

We have audited the accompanying balance sheet of ABC Company as of December 31, 19X8, and the related statements of income, and cash flows for the year then ended. These financial statements are the responsibility of the Company's management. Our responsibility is to express an opinion on these financial statements based on our audit.

We conducted our audit in accordance with International Standards on Auditing. Those Standards require that we plan and perform the audit to obtain reasonable assurance about whether the financial statements are free of material misstatement. An audit includes examining, on a test basis, evidence supporting the amounts and disclosures in the financial statements. An audit also includes assessing the accounting principles used and significant estimates made by management, as well as evaluating the overall financial statement presentation. We believe that our audit provides a reasonable basis for our opinion.

In our opinion, the financial statements present fairly, in all material respects, the financial position of ABC Company as of December 31, 19X8, and the results of its operations and its cash flows for the year then ended in accordance with International Accounting Standards.

February 17, 19X9
Los Angeles, California, USA

*Robert Blue*
*Blue, Gray & Company*

---

The international report includes several differences when compared to the U.S. report. First, the auditors have several reporting options. For example, instead of indicating that the financial statements "present fairly, in all material respects," the auditors may substitute the phrase "give a true and fair view," as is contained in the auditors' report in the United Kingdom. Also, the report may indicate that the financial statements comply with the country's relevant statutes or laws. The report may be signed using the personal name of the auditor, the firm, or both—as is done in the above illustration. In addition, the inclusion of the city in which the auditors maintain an office is a required part of the international report.

## ◆ CHAPTER SUMMARY

This chapter described the nature of the generally accepted auditing standards, the attestation standards, and quality control standards. To summarize:

1.  The 10 generally accepted auditing standards were adopted by the profession to provide a measure of quality for audits. These standards are divided into three types: general standards, standards of field work, and standards of reporting. All audits must be performed in accordance with generally accepted auditing standards.

2.  An audit provides reasonable assurance of detecting material misstatements of the financial statements (both errors and irregularities) and illegal acts that have a direct and material effect on the determination of financial statement amounts. Although an audit does not provide reasonable assurance of detecting illegal acts that have only an indirect effect on the financial statements, the auditors remain alert for such acts. If illegal acts are discovered, regardless of their type, the auditors must carefully evaluate their effects on the financial statements.

3.  The attestation standards were adopted to provide a general framework for the attest function, and to set boundaries for these types of engagements. Similar to the generally accepted auditing standards, the 11 attestation standards are structured as general standards, standards of field work, and standards of reporting.

4.  CPA firms establish quality control systems to ensure that all professional engagements are performed in accordance with applicable professional standards. The AICPA's Quality Control Standards provide guidance in developing these systems. To ensure that their quality control systems are adequate and operating effectively, CPA firms may arrange to have their practices peer reviewed by other CPAs. Obtaining periodic peer reviews is a requirement for membership in the AICPA.

5.  Future auditing standards are expected to be developed on an international basis. Currently, the International Auditing Practices Committee issues pronouncements designed to foster the development of consistent worldwide auditing standards.

## ◆ KEY TERMS INTRODUCED OR EMPHASIZED IN CHAPTER 2

**Adequate disclosure**   All essential information as required by generally accepted accounting principles (or some other appropriate basis of accounting) is included in the financial statements.

**Adverse opinion**   An opinion issued by the auditors that the financial statements they have audited *do not present fairly* the financial position, results of operation, or cash flows in conformity with generally accepted accounting principles.

**Auditors' standard report**   A very precise document designed to communicate exactly the character and limitations of the responsibility being assumed by the auditors; in standard form, the report consists of an introductory paragraph, a scope paragraph, and an opinion paragraph.

**Consistency**   The concept of using the same accounting principles from year to year so that the successive financial statements issued by a business entity will be comparable.

**Disclaimer of opinion**   A form of report in which the auditors state that they do not express an opinion on the financial statements; it should include a separate paragraph stating the auditors' reasons for disclaiming an opinion and also disclosing any reservations they may have concerning the financial statements.

**Division for CPA Firms**   A division of the AICPA providing a mechanism to regulate CPA firms. Firms may voluntarily join either or both sections: the SEC Practice Section and the Private Companies Practice Section.

**Error**   An unintentional misstatement of financial statements or omission of an amount or a disclosure.

**Generally accepted auditing standards (GAAS)**   A set of 10 standards adopted by the AICPA and binding on its members—designed to ensure the quality of the auditors' work.

**Illegal Acts**   Violations of laws or governmental regulations.

**Independence**   A most important auditing standard, which prohibits CPAs from expressing an opinion on financial statements of an enterprise unless they are independent with respect to such enterprise; independence is impaired by a direct financial interest, service as an officer or trustee, certain loans to or from the enterprise, and various other relationships.

**Internal control structure**   A company's control environment, accounting system, and control policies and procedures that are established to provide reasonable assurance that the company's objectives will be achieved. Such objectives include: (1) safeguarding its resources from waste, fraud and inefficiency; (2) promoting accuracy and reliability in accounting and operating data; (3) encouraging compliance with company policy; and (4) judging the efficiency of operations in all divisions of the business.

**International Auditing Practices Committee (IAPC)**   A committee of the International Federation of Accountants, established to issue standards on auditing and reporting practices to improve the degree of uniformity of auditing practices and related services throughout the world.

**International Federation of Accountants**   A worldwide organization of national accounting bodies to help foster a coordinated worldwide accounting profession with harmonized standards.

**Irregularity**   An intentional misstatement of financial statements or omission of an amount or a disclosure.

**Peer review**   The study and evaluation of a CPA firm's quality control policies and procedures by another CPA firm or a team of qualified CPAs.

**Public Oversight Board**   An independent group of prominent nonaccountants who monitor the activities of the SEC Practice Section to provide assurance that the section is serving the public's interest.

**Qualified opinion**   The appropriate form of audit report when there is a limitation in the scope of the audit or when the financial statements depart from GAAP significantly enough to require mention in the auditors' report, but not so materially as to necessitate disclaiming an opinion or expressing an adverse opinion.

**Quality control standards**   Standards for establishing quality control policies and procedures that provide reasonable assurance that all of a CPA firm's engagements are conducted in accordance with applicable professional standards.

**Unqualified opinion**   The form of audit report issued when the examination was adequate in scope and the auditors believe that the financial statements present fairly the financial position, operating results, and cash flows in conformity with generally accepted accounting principles.

---

## ◆ GROUP I: REVIEW QUESTIONS

2-1   What is the difference between generally accepted accounting principles (GAAP) and generally accepted auditing standards (GAAS)? Give an example of a generally accepted accounting principle and an example of a generally accepted auditing standard falling under the subhead of *general standards*.

2-2   The generally accepted auditing standards established by the AICPA list first the requirement that "the examination is to be performed by a person or persons having adequate technical training and proficiency as an auditor." What would be the usual avenues for an individual to meet these personal qualifications?

2-3   What relationship exists between generally accepted auditing standards (GAAS) and the Statements on Auditing Standards (SASs)?

2-4   The first SAS issued was substantially larger and different in coverage from all the following ones. What explains this difference?

2-5   Do the attestation standards supersede any of the generally accepted auditing standards? Explain.

2-6   You are to evaluate the following quotation:
      "If a CPA firm completes an examination of Adam Company's financial statements following generally accepted auditing standards and is satisfied with the results of the audit, an *unqualified* audit report may be issued. On the other hand, if no audit is performed of the current year's financial statements, but the CPA firm has performed satisfactory audits in prior years, has confidence in the management of the company, and makes a quick review of the current year's financial statements, a qualified report may be issued."
      Do you agree? Give reasons to support your answer.

2-7   Pike Company has had an annual audit performed by the same firm of certified public accountants for many years. The financial statements and copies of the audit report are distributed to stockholders each year shortly after completion of the audit. Who is primarily responsible for the fairness of these financial statements? Explain.

2-8   Draft the standard form of audit report commonly issued after a satisfactory audit of a client's financial statements.

2-9   Davis & Co., Certified Public Accountants, after completing an audit of Samson Company decided that it would be unable to issue an unqualified opinion. What circumstances might explain this decision?

2-10  State the principal assertions made by the auditors in the opinion paragraph of the auditors' standard report.

2-11  Alan Weston, CPA, completed an audit of Kirsten Manufacturing Company and issued an unqualified audit report. What does this tell us about the extent of the auditing procedures included in the audit?

2-12  What is a "material" amount from the perspective of auditors? Give an example of how that amount may differ based on the nature of the item.

2-13  When a CPA firm completes an audit of a business and issues a report, does it express an opinion on the client's accounting records, financial statements, or both? Give reasons.

2-14  A CPA firm does not guarantee the financial soundness of a client when it renders an opinion on financial statements, nor does the CPA firm guarantee the absolute accuracy of the statements. Yet the CPA firm's opinion is respected and accepted. What is expected of the CPA firm in order to merit such confidence?

2-15  List the five categories of generally accepted accounting principles. Explain how the auditors determine the appropriate principle when there is a conflict between sources in two of the categories.

2-16  If a CPA firm has performed a thorough professional audit of a client's financial statements, should it not be able to issue a report dealing with facts rather than the mere expression of an opinion? Explain.

2-17   What is the meaning of *quality control* and *peer review* as these terms relate to the operation of a CPA firm? Is peer review mandatory? Explain.

2-18   What has the AICPA done to help ensure adequate quality control by CPA firms?

2-19   Explain the basic objective of establishing quality control procedures in the following areas:
  *a.*   Consultation.
  *b.*   Acceptance and continuation of clients.
  *c.*   Inspection.

2-20   Does the AICPA's *Statement of Quality Control Standards 1* require every CPA firm to implement similar quality control procedures? Explain.

2-21   What is the Public Oversight Board? What is its purpose?

2-22   Your CPA firm has been requested to perform a peer review of the firm of William & Stafford. What is involved in the performance of such an engagement? Discuss.

2-23   Explain briefly the auditors' responsibility for detecting illegal acts by clients.

2-24   Distinguish between management fraud and employee fraud.

2-25   What is the International Auditing Practices Committee? What is the purpose of its pronouncements? Do these pronouncements establish standards which override a member nation's auditing standards?

2-26   Briefly describe three differences between an international audit report and one based on the U.S. reporting standards.

---

# ◆ GROUP II: QUESTIONS REQUIRING ANALYSIS

2-27   Reed, CPA, accepted an engagement to audit the financial statements of Smith Company. Reed's discussions with Smith's new management and the predecessor auditor indicated the possibility that Smith's financial statements may be misstated due to the possible occurrence of errors, irregularities, and illegal acts.

*Required:*   *a.*   Identify and describe Reed's responsibilities to detect Smith's errors and irregularities. Do *not* identify specific audit procedures.
  *b.*   Describe Reed's responsibilities to detect Smith's material illegal acts. Do *not* identify specific audit procedures.
  *c.*   Identify and describe Reed's responsibilities to report Smith's illegal acts.

(AICPA, adapted)

2-28   An attitude of independence is a most essential element of an audit by a firm of certified public accountants. Describe several situations in which the CPA firm might find it somewhat difficult to maintain this independent point of view.

2-29   Jane Lee, a director of a large corporation with many stockholders and lines of credit with several banks, suggested that the corporation appoint as controller John Madison, a certified public accountant on the staff of the auditing firm that had made annual audits of the corporation for many years. Lee expressed the opinion that this move would effect a considerable saving in professional fees because annual audits would no longer be needed. She proposed to give the controller, if appointed, an internal auditing staff to carry on such continuing investigations of accounting data as appeared necessary. Evaluate this proposal.

2-30   Select the best answer for each of the following items and give reasons for your choice.
  *a.*   The three generally accepted auditing standards classified as standards of field work may be summarized as:

      (1)   The need to maintain an independence in mental attitude throughout the audit.

      (2)   The criteria for audit planning and evidence-gathering.

      (3)   The criteria for the content of the auditors' report on financial statements.

      (4)   The competence, independence, and professional care to be exerted while performing the audit.

*b.* A basic objective of a CPA firm is to provide professional services that conform with professional standards. Reasonable assurance of achieving this basic objective is provided through:

      (1)   Compliance with generally accepted reporting standards.

      (2)   A system of quality control.

      (3)   A system of peer review.

      (4)   Continuing professional education.

*c.* Which of the following is *not* explicitly included in an unqualified standard audit report?

      (1)   The CPA's opinion that the financial statements comply with generally accepted accounting principles.

      (2)   That generally accepted auditing standards were followed during the audit.

      (3)   That the internal control structure of the client was satisfactory.

      (4)   The subjects of the audit.

*d.* The general group of the generally accepted auditing standards requires that:

      (1)   The auditors maintain an independent mental attitude.

      (2)   The audit be conducted in conformity with generally accepted accounting principles.

      (3)   Assistants, if any, be properly supervised.

      (4)   The auditor obtain an understanding of the internal control structure.

*e.* Which quality control standard would *most* likely be satisfied when a CPA firm maintains records indicating which partners or employees of the firm were previously employed by the CPA firm's clients?

      (1)   Professional relationship.

      (2)   Supervision.

      (3)   Independence.

      (4)   Advancement.

*f.* An "external peer review" is most likely to be performed by:

      (1)   Employees and partners of the firm who are *not* associated with the audits being reviewed.

      (2)   Audit review staff of the Securities and Exchange Commission.

      (3)   Audit review staff of the American Institute of Certified Public Accountants.

      (4)   Employees and partners of another CPA firm.

(AICPA, adapted)

# ◆ GROUP III: PROBLEMS

2-31   Joe Rezzo, a college student majoring in accounting, helped finance his education with a part-time job maintaining all accounting records for a small business, White Company, located near the campus. Upon graduation, Rezzo passed the CPA examination and joined the audit staff of a national CPA firm. However, he continued to perform all accounting work for White Company during his "leisure time." Two years later, Rezzo received his CPA certificate and decided to give up his part-time work with White Company. He notified White that he would no longer be available after preparing the year-end financial statements.

      On January 7, Rezzo delivered the annual financial statements as his final act for White Company. The owner then made the following request: "Joe, I am applying for a substantial bank loan, and the bank loan officer insists upon getting audited financial statements to support my loan application. You are now a CPA, and you know everything that's happened in this company and everything that's included in these financial statements, and you know they give a fair picture. I would appreciate it if you would write out the standard audit report and attach it to the financial statements. Then I'll be able to get some fast action on my loan application.''

*Required:*   *a.*   Would Rezzo be justified in complying with White's request for an auditor's opinion? Explain.

*b.*   If you think Rezzo should issue the audit report, do you think he should first perform an audit of the company despite his detailed knowledge of the company's affairs? Explain.

*c.*   If White had requested an audit by the national CPA firm for which Rezzo worked, would it have been reasonable for that firm to accept and to assign Rezzo to perform the audit? Explain.

2-32   The following audit report is deficient in several respects.

---

**To Whom It May Concern:**

We have examined the accounting records of Garland Corporation for the year ended June 30, 19X1. We counted the cash and marketable securities, studied the accounting methods in use (which were consistently followed throughout the year), and made tests of the ledger accounts for assets and liabilities. The internal control structure contained no weaknesses.

In our opinion the accompanying balance sheet and related income statement present correctly the financial condition of the Corporation at June 30, 19X1.

The accounting records of Garland Corporation are maintained in accordance with accounting principles generally observed throughout the industry. Our examination was made in accordance with generally accepted auditing standards, and we certify the records and financial statements without qualification.

---

*Required:*   You are to criticize the report systematically from beginning to end, considering each sentence in turn. Use a separate paragraph with identifying heading for each point, as for example, Paragraph 1, Sentence 1. You may also wish to make comments on the overall contents of each paragraph and upon any omissions. Give reasons to support your views. After completing this critical review of the report, draft a revised report, on the assumption that your examination was adequate in all respects and disclosed no significant deficiencies.

2-33   Bart James, a partner in the CPA firm of James and Day, received the following memorandum from John Gray, president of Gray Manufacturing Corporation, an audit client of many years.

---

Dear Bart:

I have a new type of engagement for you. You are familiar with how much time and money we have been spending in installing equipment to eliminate the air and water pollution caused by our manufacturing plant. We have changed our production process to reduce discharge of gases; we have changed to more expensive fuel sources with less pollution potential; and we have discontinued some products because we couldn't produce them without causing considerable pollution.

*(continued)*

---

I don't think the stockholders and the public are aware of the efforts we have made, and I want to inform them of our accomplishments in avoiding danger to the environment. We will devote a major part of our annual report to this topic, stressing that our company is the leader of the entire industry in combating pollution. To make this publicity more convincing, I would like to retain your firm to study what we have done and to attest as independent accountants that our operations are the best in the industry as far as preventing pollution is concerned.

To justify your statement, you are welcome to investigate every aspect of our operations as fully as you wish. We will pay for your services at your regular audit rates and will publish your "pollution opinion" in our annual report to stockholders immediately following some pictures and discussion of our special equipment and processes for preventing industrial pollution. We may put this section of the annual report in a separate cover and distribute it free to the public. Please let me know at once if this engagement is acceptable to you.

*Required:*   Put yourself in Bart James's position and write a reply to this client's request. Indicate clearly whether you are willing to accept the engagement and explain your attitude toward this proposed extension of the auditor's attest function. (In drafting your letter, keep in mind that Gray is a valued audit client whose goodwill you want to maintain.)

2-34   John Clinton, owner of Clinton Company, applied for a bank loan and was informed by the banker that audited financial statements of the business must be submitted before the bank could consider the loan application. Clinton then retained Arthur Jones, CPA, to perform an audit. Clinton informed Jones that audited financial statements were required by the bank and that the audit must be completed within three weeks. Clinton also promised to pay Jones a fixed fee plus a bonus if the bank approved the loan. Jones agreed and accepted the engagement.

The first step taken by Jones was to hire two accounting students to conduct the audit. He spent several hours telling them exactly what to do. Jones told the students not to spend time reviewing internal controls but instead to concentrate on proving the mathematical accuracy of the ledger accounts and summarizing the data in the accounting records that support Clinton Company's financial statements. The students followed Jones's instructions and after two weeks gave Jones the financial statements that did not include any notes. Jones reviewed the statements and prepared an unqualified audit report. The report, however, did not refer to generally accepted accounting principles.

*Required:*   List on the left side of the sheet of paper the generally accepted auditing standards that were violated by Jones, and indicate how the actions of Jones resulted in a failure to comply with each standard. Organize your answer as follows:

| *Generally Accepted Auditing Standards* | *Actions by Jones Resulting in Failure to Comply with Generally Accepted Auditing Standards* |
|---|---|
| General standards<br>(1)  The examination is to be performed by a person or persons having adequate technical training and proficiency as an auditor. | (1) |

2-35   The business activities of Casa Royale, Inc. consist of the administration and maintenance of approximately 400 condominiums and common property owned by individuals in a suburban residential development. Revenue consists of monthly fees collected from each condominium owner, plus some miscellaneous revenue. The principal expenses are property taxes and maintenance of all the buildings, shrubbery, swimming pools, lakes, parking lots, and other facilities. The furniture, fixtures, and equipment owned by the corporation and used to perform its maintenance functions represent about 25 percent of its total assets of $400,000.

The corporation retained Howard Smith, CPA, to perform an audit of its financial statements for the current year and received from him the following audit report.

---

**Independent Auditors' Report**

Board of Governors
Casa Royale, Inc.

I have audited the accompanying balance sheet of Casa Royale, Inc. as of December 31, 19X1, and the related statements of income, retained earnings, and cash flows for the year then ended. These financial statements are the responsibility of the Company's management. My responsibility is to express an opinion on these financial statements based on my audit.

I conducted my audit in accordance with generally accepted auditing standards. Those standards require that I plan and perform the audit to obtain reasonable assurance about whether the financial statements are free of material misstatement. An audit includes examining, on a test basis, evidence supporting the amounts and disclosures in the financial statements. An audit also includes assessing the accounting principles used and significant estimates made by management, as well as evaluating the overall financial statement presentation. I believe that my audit provides a reasonable basis for my opinion.

As further amplified in Note 3 to the financial statements, my engagement did not include an examination of records relating to furniture, fixtures, equipment, or other assets indicated on the balance sheet.

In my opinion, except for the effect of such adjustments, if any, as might have been determined to be necessary had I been able to examine evidence regarding plant assets, the financial statements referred to above present fairly, in all material respects, the financial position of Casa Royale, Inc. as of December 31, 19X1, and the results of its operations and its cash flows for the year then ended in conformity with generally accepted accounting principles.

*Howard Smith, CPA*

---

The note to the financial statements referred to in the audit report read as follows: "The equipment necessary for administration and maintenance was acquired in various years going back as far as the origin of the Corporation 10 years ago. Therefore, the records do not lend themselves readily to application of standard auditing procedures and are not included in our engagement of independent auditors. The equipment is being depreciated using the straight-line method over various estimated useful lives."

*Required:*  a.   What type of audit report did the CPA issue? Was this the appropriate type of report under the circumstances? Explain.

b.   What contradiction, if any, exists between the scope paragraph of the audit report and the note to the financial statements? Do you consider the note to be a reasonable statement? Why or why not?

  *c.*  Did the omission of the examination of plant assets from the audit engagement have any bearing on the evidence needed by the auditor in order to express an opinion on the income statement? Explain fully.

## ◆ GROUP IV: RESEARCH AND DISCUSSION CASE

2-36  Enormo Corporation is a large multinational audit client of your CPA firm. One of Enormo's subsidiaries, Ultro, Ltd., is a successful electronics assembly company that operates in a small Caribbean country. The country in which Ultro operates has very strict laws governing the transfer of funds to other countries. Violations of these laws may result in fines or the expropriation of the assets of the company.

  During the current year, you discover that $50,000 worth of foreign currency was smuggled out of the Caribbean country by one of Ultro's employees and deposited in one of Enormo's bank accounts. Ultro's management generated the funds by selling company automobiles, which were fully depreciated on Ultro's books, to company employees.

  You are concerned about this illegal act committed by Ultro's management and decide to discuss the matter with Enormo's management and the company's legal counsel. Enormo's management and board of directors seemed to be unconcerned with the matter and expressed the opinion that you were making far too much of a situation involving an immaterial dollar amount. They also believe that it is unnecessary to take any steps to prevent Ultro's management from engaging in illegal activities in the future. Enormo's legal counsel indicated that the probability was remote that such an illegal act would ever be discovered, and that if discovery occurred, it would probably result in a fine that would not be material to the client's consolidated financial statements.

  Your CPA firm is ready to issue its opinion on Enormo's consolidated financial statements for the current year, and you are trying to decide on the appropriate course of action regarding the illegal act.

*Required:*  *a.*  Discuss the implications of this illegal act by Ultro's management.

  *b.*  Describe the courses of action that are available to your CPA firm regarding this matter.

  *c.*  State your opinion as to the course of action that is appropriate. Explain.

## ◆ SUGGESTED REFERENCES

AICPA, *Professional Standards, Volume 2,* Commerce Clearing House, *Statements on Quality Control Standards,* Section QC 10.

AICPA, *Statement on Auditing Standards No. 53,* "The Auditor's Responsibility to Detect and Report Errors and Irregularities" (New York, 1988) AU 316.

AICPA, *Statement on Auditing Standards No. 54,* "Illegal Acts by Clients" (New York, 1988) AU 317.

*FASB Statement No. 5,* "Accounting for Contingencies," pars. 8–12.

# AUDITORS' REPORTS

## CHAPTER OBJECTIVES

After studying this chapter, you should be able to:

- Describe the standard audit report.

- Explain the circumstances that result in inclusion of additional explanatory language in an unqualified audit report.

- Discuss how materiality affects the consideration of the type of audit report to be issued.

- Identify the circumstances that may result in qualified opinions, adverse opinions, and disclaimers of opinion.

- Describe the auditors' responsibilities for reporting on comparative financial statements.

E xpressing an independent and expert opinion on the fairness of financial statements is the most frequently performed attestation service rendered by the public accounting profession. The fourth standard of reporting states:

> The [auditors'] report shall either contain an *expression of opinion* regarding the financial statements, taken as a whole, or an assertion to the effect that an opinion cannot be expressed. When an overall opinion cannot be expressed, the reasons therefor should be stated. In all cases where an auditor's name is associated with financial statements, the report should contain a clear-cut indication of the *character of the auditor's work,* if any, and the *degree of responsibility the auditor is taking.* [Emphasis added.]

In Chapter 2, we saw that the auditors' standard report meets this standard by (*a*) stating that the auditors' examination was performed in conformity with generally accepted auditing standards and (*b*) expressing an opinion that the client's financial statements are presented fairly in conformity with generally accepted accounting principles. However, if there are material deficiencies in the client's financial statements or limitations in the auditors' examination, or if there are other unusual conditions about which the readers of the financial statements should be informed, auditors *cannot* issue the standard report. Instead, they must carefully modify their report to make these problems or conditions known to users of the audited financial statements.

In this chapter, we shall discuss the different types of reports that auditors may issue in order to indicate clearly the character of their work and the degree of responsibility they are taking.

## Financial Statements

The reporting phase of an audit begins when the independent auditors have completed their field work and they have proposed any necessary adjustments to the client. Before drafting their report, the auditors must review the client-prepared financial statements for form and content, or draft the financial statements on behalf of the client.

The financial statements on which the independent auditors customarily report are the balance sheet, the income statement, the statement of retained earnings, and the statement of cash flows. Often, the statement of retained earnings is combined with the income statement. In some cases, the retained earnings statement may be expanded to a statement of stockholders' equity. Financial statements generally are presented in comparative form for the current year and the preceding year and are accompanied by explanatory notes. The financial statements for a parent corporation usually are consolidated with those of the subsidiaries.

## Financial Statement Disclosures

The purpose of notes to financial statements is to achieve adequate disclosure when information in the financial statements proper is insufficient to attain this objective. Although the notes, like the financial statements themselves, are representations of the client, the independent auditors generally assist in drafting the notes. The writing of notes to financial statements is a challenging task because complex issues must be summarized in a clear and concise manner. Adequate disclosure in the notes to the financial statements is necessary for the auditors to issue an unqualified opinion on the financial statements.

The Financial Accounting Standards Board, the Government Accounting Standards Board, and the Securities and Exchange Commission have issued numerous pronouncements that have added extensive disclosure requirements. Examples of note disclosure requirements that have become a part of the basic financial statements include the disclosure of significant accounting policies, accounting changes, loss contingencies, and lease and pension information.

In addition to the note disclosures that are part of the basic financial statements, many clients are required by the FASB, the GASB, or the SEC to present *supplementary information*. Such information, while not a required part of the basic financial statements, is required to be presented as unaudited supplementary schedules accompanying the financial statements. As an example, certain companies are required to disclose selected interim financial data with their annual financial statements.

In evaluating financial reporting disclosures, the auditors should keep in mind that disclosures are meant to supplement the information in the financial statements and not to *correct* improper financial statement presentation. Thus, a note or supplementary schedule, no matter how skillfully drafted, does not compensate for the erroneous presentation of an item in the financial statements.

## The Auditors' Standard Report

For convenient reference, the auditors' standard unqualified report, which was introduced and discussed in Chapter 2, is presented on page 62.

Before continuing, let us mention a few details about this report. It has a title that includes the word "independent." The first paragraph is referred to as the **introductory paragraph.** It clearly indicates that (1) the financial statements have been audited, (2) the financial statements are the responsibility of management, and (3) the auditors' responsibility is to express an opinion on them. The second paragraph, which describes the nature of an audit, is called the **scope paragraph.** Finally, the **opinion paragraph** presents the auditors' opinion on whether the financial statements are in conformity with generally accepted accounting principles.

Notice that the report is signed with the name of the CPA firm, not the name of an individual partner in the firm. This signature stresses that it is the *firm,* not an individual, that takes responsibility for the auditors' report. If the CPA performing the audit is an individual practitioner, the report will be signed with the CPA's personal signature. In addition, a sole practitioner should use the word *I* instead of *we* in the auditors' report.

Also notice the date under the signature. This date is normally the **last day of field work**—that is, the date upon which the auditors conclude their investigative procedures. This date is quite significant, because the auditors have a responsibility to perform procedures to that date to search for any subsequent events that may affect the fairness of the client's financial statements.

An unqualified auditors' report may be issued only when the following conditions have been met:

1. The financial statements are presented in conformity with *generally accepted accounting principles,* including adequate disclosure.
2. The audit was performed in accordance with generally accepted auditing standards, including no significant *scope limitations* preventing the auditors from gathering the evidence necessary to support their opinion.

---

INDEPENDENT AUDITORS' REPORT

To the Board of Directors and Stockholders
XYZ Company:

We have audited the accompanying balance sheet of XYZ Company as of December 31, 19XX, and the related statements of income, retained earnings, and cash flows for the year then ended. These financial statements are the responsibility of the Company's management. Our responsibility is to express an opinion on these financial statements based on our audit.

We conducted our audit in accordance with generally accepted auditing standards. Those standards require that we plan and perform the audit to obtain reasonable assurance about whether the financial statements are free of material misstatement. An audit includes examining, on a test basis, evidence supporting the amounts and disclosures in the financial statements. An audit also includes assessing the accounting principles used and significant estimates made by management, as well as evaluating the overall financial statement presentation. We believe that our audit provides a reasonable basis for our opinion.

In our opinion, the financial statements referred to above present fairly, in all material respects, the financial position of XYZ Company as of December 31, 19XX, and the results of its operations and its cash flows for the year then ended in conformity with generally accepted accounting principles.

*Blue, Gray & Company*

Los Angeles, Calif.

Certified Public Accountants
February 26, 19XY

---

When considered material, departure from either of these conditions results in a situation in which a report that is other than unqualified is required. Additionally, when certain other conditions exist, the auditors add *explanatory language* to the standard report, but still express an *unqualified opinion.*

## EXPRESSION OF AN OPINION

The auditors' options when expressing an opinion on financial statements may be summarized as follows:

1. *An unqualified opinion—standard report.* This report represents a "clean opinion" and may be issued when the two conditions listed above have been met, and when no conditions requiring explanatory language exist.

2. *An unqualified opinion—with explanatory language added to report.*   This is an audit report with an unqualified opinion and explanatory language resulting from certain circumstances. Examples of such circumstances are those in which other auditors have performed a portion of the audit, or when major uncertainties exist with respect to the company being audited.

3. *A qualified opinion.*   A qualified opinion is basically a positive opinion. It asserts that the financial statements, viewed as a whole, are not misleading. Qualified reports are issued when the financial statements depart materially from generally accepted accounting principles, or limitations are placed on the scope of the auditors' procedures. The problems, while material, *do not overshadow the overall fairness of the statements.*

4. *An adverse opinion.*   This is a *negative opinion,* asserting that the financial statements *are not* a fair presentation. Auditors will issue an adverse opinion when the deficiencies in the financial statements are *so significant* that the financial statements taken as a whole are misleading. All significant reasons for the issuance of an adverse opinion should be set forth in an explanatory paragraph.

5. *A disclaimer of opinion.*   A disclaimer of opinion means that due to a significant scope restriction (or very major uncertainties), the auditors *were unable to form an opinion* on the fairness of the financial statements. A disclaimer is neither a positive nor a negative opinion—it simply means that the auditors do not have an adequate basis for expressing an opinion.

## Materiality

Auditors must qualify their report whenever there are *material* deficiencies in the client's financial statements; when the deficiencies are *immaterial,* an unqualified report may be issued. Accordingly, auditors must exercise professional judgment to evaluate the materiality of any such departures. At this stage of the audit, the auditors can consider both the *quantitative* and *qualitative* effects of the deficiencies. For example, a related-party transaction of a relatively small amount may be considered to be material.

Auditors are required to issue an adverse opinion when the deficiencies in financial statements are *"so significant"* that a qualified opinion would be inappropriate. A qualified opinion is considered *insufficient* when the deficiencies in financial statements are so material that they *overshadow the fairness of the financial statements viewed as a whole.* For example, misstatements that make an insolvent business appear to be solvent would be considered sufficiently material as to overshadow the fairness of the statements viewed as a whole.

The distinction between problems that are material but do not overshadow the fairness of the statements and those problems that do overshadow the fairness of the statements is again a matter of professional judgment. In our following discussions, it will not be practical to present sufficient detail for readers to make these judgments. Therefore, we will use the term **material** to describe problems sufficient to require qualification of the auditors' report, but which do not overshadow the fairness of the statements. Problems overshadowing the fairness of the statements will be described as *"very material"* or as causing the statements to be *"substantially misleading."*

## The Unqualified Report

Auditors express an unqualified opinion on the client's financial statements when they have no material exceptions as to the fairness of the application of accounting principles, and there have been no unresolved restrictions on the scope of their engagement. The unqualified opinion is, of course, the most desirable report from the client's point of view. The client usually will make any necessary adjustments to the statements to enable the auditors to issue this type of opinion.

## Explanatory Language Added to the Unqualified Opinion

Under certain circumstances auditors add explanatory language to the standard report, even when issuing an unqualified opinion. Adding the additional language *is not regarded as a qualification* because it does *not lessen* the auditors' reporting responsibility for the financial statements. Rather, the language merely *draws attention* to a significant situation. Auditors add explanatory language to an unqualified opinion to indicate a division of responsibility with another CPA firm, to refer to an uncertainty that could have a material impact on the financial statements, to indicate an inconsistency in the application of accounting principles, to emphasize a matter, and to justify a departure from officially recognized accounting principles.

### Reliance upon Other Auditors.

On occasion it may be necessary for the principal auditors of a company to rely upon another CPA firm to perform a portion of the audit work. The most common situation in which CPAs rely upon the work of other auditors is in the audit of consolidated entities. If certain subsidiaries have been audited by other CPA firms, the auditors of the parent company will usually decide to rely upon the work of these other CPAs rather than conduct another examination of the subsidiaries.

When more than one CPA firm participates in an engagement, the auditors' report is issued by the **principal auditors**—that is, by the CPA firm that did the majority of the audit work and has an overall understanding of the financial statements. The principal auditors have two basic alternatives in wording their report:

**1. Make no reference to the other auditors.** If the principal auditors *make no reference* in their report to the portions of the engagement performed by other CPAs, the principal auditors *assume full responsibility* for the other auditors' work. This approach is usually followed when the other CPA firm is well known, or when the principal auditors hired the other auditors. When no reference is made, the principal auditors should consider visiting the other auditors, reviewing the other auditors' audit programs and working papers, or performing additional audit procedures. If the principal auditors elect to make no reference, they may issue the standard auditors' report with no additional wording.

**2. Make reference to the other auditors.** Making reference to the work done by other auditors *divides* the responsibility for the engagement *among the participating CPA firms*. This type of report is called a **shared responsibility opinion,** even though it is signed only by the principal auditors. A shared responsibility opinion is usually issued when the other auditors were engaged by the client, rather than by the principal auditors.

A shared responsibility opinion should indicate the portion of the engagement performed by the other auditors. A typical shared responsibility opinion is illustrated below, with emphasis on the special wording added to the standard report:

---

### INDEPENDENT AUDITORS' REPORT

To the Board of Directors and Stockholders
XYZ Company:

We have audited the consolidated balance sheet of XYZ Company as of December 31, 19XX, and the related statements of income, retained earnings, and cash flows for the year then ended. These financial statements are the responsibility of the Company's management. Our responsibility is to express an opinion on these financial statements based on our audit. *We did not audit the financial statements of Sub Company, a wholly owned subsidiary, which statements reflect total assets of $ _____ as of December 31, 19XX and total revenues of $ _____ for the year then ended. These statements were audited by other auditors whose report has been furnished to us, and our opinion, insofar as it relates to the amounts included for Sub Company, is based solely on the report of the other auditors.*

We conducted our audit in accordance with generally accepted auditing standards. Those standards require that we plan and perform the audit to obtain reasonable assurance about whether the financial statements are free of material misstatement. An audit includes examining, on a test basis, evidence supporting the amounts and disclosures in the financial statements. An audit also includes assessing the accounting principles used and significant estimates made by management, as well as evaluating the overall financial statement presentation. We believe that our audit *and the report of other auditors* provide a reasonable basis for our opinion.

In our opinion, *based on our audit and the report of other auditors,* the consolidated financial statements referred to above present fairly, in all material respects, the financial position of XYZ Company as of December 31, 19XX, and the results of its operations and its cash flows for the year then ended in conformity with generally accepted accounting principles.

Los Angeles, Calif.                               *Blue, Gray & Company*

Certified Public Accountants
February 26, 19XY

---

The additional wording found in a shared responsibility opinion is not a qualification, as it does not lessen the auditors' collective responsibility for the fairness of the statements. Rather, the report merely divides this responsibility between two or more CPA firms.[1]

What if the other auditors qualify their report on a particular subsidiary? The principal auditors *do not necessarily have to qualify their shared responsibility report*. The shared responsibility report focuses upon the consolidated entity, which may involve a very different level of materiality than does the subsidiary examined by the other auditors. To determine whether a qualification is in order, the principal auditors must evaluate the materiality of the matter in relation to the consolidated financial statements.

---

[1]Another acceptable, although less frequently used, option allows the principal auditor to obtain permission of the other auditor to explicitly use that auditor's name in the audit report. In such circumstances the other auditor's report must also be presented with that of the principal auditor.

Whether or not the principal auditors plan to make reference to the work of the other auditor, they should make inquiries concerning the other auditors' *professional reputation* and *independence*. Inquiries concerning the other auditors' reputation might be made of the AICPA, other practitioners, or bankers. A letter should also be obtained from the other auditors stating that they are aware of the use of their report and that they meet the AICPA's and, for publicly traded clients, the SEC's standards of independence.

Principal auditors are never *forced* to rely on the work of other auditors. Instead, they may insist upon *personally* auditing any aspect of the client's operations. If the client refuses to permit them to do so, the auditors may regard this action as a **scope limitation** and, depending upon materiality, issue a qualified report or a disclaimer of opinion. As a practical matter, qualified opinions are seldom issued for this reason. Satisfactory arrangements as to who will audit the various aspects of a client's business normally will be worked out before the audit begins.

Uncertainties.    Substantial uncertainty as to the outcome of a contingency affecting the client's financial statements may require the auditors to add an explanatory paragraph to their audit report to indicate the existence of the uncertainty. In accordance with *FASB Statement No. 5,* contingencies that are probable and can be reasonably estimated should be accrued in the financial statements. Failure to do so would be a departure from generally accepted accounting principles that leads to a qualified or an adverse opinion by the auditors. It is when the contingency is not *susceptible of reasonable estimation* that the auditors should consider adding an explanatory paragraph to their unqualified opinion, based on the materiality of the contingency and the probability of unfavorable outcome. When a material loss is probable, but management is unable to estimate it, the auditors should add an explanatory paragraph to their unqualified report. When the loss is reasonably possible, the auditors *should consider* the need for an explanatory paragraph; as the magnitude of the amount of the loss and the likelihood of its occurrence increase, the auditors are more likely to add such a paragraph.

A modification of the report for an uncertainty is appropriate when the client has properly disclosed contingencies in conformity with FASB *Statement No. 5.* If such disclosures have not been made, a *departure from generally accepted accounting principles* also exists, and a qualified or an adverse opinion may be appropriate. Finally, no explanatory paragraph is required for a loss with a remote likelihood of occurrence since FASB *Statement No. 5* does not require disclosure of such contingent losses.

---

◆  ILLUSTRATIVE CASE  ◆

The auditors of a company that produced asbestos-containing products modified their report for the uncertainty pertaining to claims arising due to products sold 10 (and more) years earlier. The uncertainty pertained to (1) the future outcome of legal proceedings currently filed and expected to be filed in the future against the company in numerous courts, and (2) uncertainty relating to the results of the company's suits against its

*(continued)*

> insurers who have disputed liability under various company insurance policies. The company's financial statements suggested that many years may pass before the problems are finally resolved and before their impact, "if any," on the company's financial position can be determined.

The standard report modified for uncertainty includes a fourth paragraph following the opinion paragraph that describes the uncertainty. The following is an example of such a paragraph:

> As discussed in Note X to the financial statements, the Company is currently a defendant in a number of legal proceedings and may in the future be a defendant in additional, related proceedings expected to be filed alleging damages due to products sold in the past. The Company has filed a legal action against its insurers who have disputed liability under various company insurance policies. The ultimate outcome of the current and expected future lawsuits cannot presently be determined. Accordingly, no provision for any liability that may result upon adjudication has been made in the accompanying financial statements.

Historically, uncertainties have resulted in reports that were qualified "subject to" the outcome of the uncertainty. Currently, the reports contain explanatory paragraphs, but they are unqualified.

Question about a Company's Going-Concern Status.   A special type of significant uncertainty concerns the ability of a client company to continue as a going concern. Under generally accepted accounting principles, both assets and liabilities are recorded and classified on the assumption that the company will continue to operate. Assets, for example, may be presented at amounts that are significantly greater than their liquidation values.

SAS 59 (AU 341), "The Auditor's Consideration of an Entity's Ability to Continue as a Going Concern," describes the auditors' responsibilities for evaluating an entity's ability to continue as a going concern. Although the auditors are not required to perform procedures specifically related to the going-concern assumption, they must evaluate the results of the normal procedures performed in planning, gathering evidential matter, and completing the audit. Conditions that may cause the auditors to question the going-concern assumption include negative cash flows from operations, defaults on loan agreements, adverse financial ratios, work stoppages, and legal proceedings. When such conditions or events are identified, the auditors should gather clarifying information and consider whether management's plans for dealing with the conditions are likely to negate the problem. If, after evaluating all the information and management's plans, a substantial doubt still exists about the company's ability to continue as a going concern for a period of one year from the balance sheet date, the auditors should modify their report by adding a final paragraph such as the following:

> The accompanying financial statements have been prepared assuming that XYZ Company will continue as a going concern. As discussed in Note X to the financial statements, XYZ Company has suffered recurring losses from operations and has a net capital deficiency that raises substantial doubt about the entity's ability to continue as a going concern. Management's plans in regard to these matters are also described in Note X. The financial statements do not include any adjustments that might result from the outcome of this uncertainty.

GAAP Not Consistently Applied.    If a client company makes a change in accounting principle (including a change in the reporting entity), the nature of, justification for, and effect of the change are reported in a note to the financial statements for the period in which the change was made. Any such change having a material effect upon the financial statements will also require modification of the auditors' report, even though the auditors are in full agreement with the change. Changes in accounting estimates need not be reported in the auditors' report.

Changes from one generally accepted accounting principle to another generally accepted accounting principle, when justified, do not result in qualification of the auditors' report. The report is merely modified to highlight the lack of consistent application of acceptable accounting principles. Of course, if the client elects to change to an unacceptable accounting principle, the auditors should qualify their report for lack of conformity with generally accepted accounting principles, or issue an adverse opinion. A report modified for a change to an acceptable accounting principle includes an additional paragraph following the opinion paragraph, such as the one illustrated below:

> As discussed in Note 2 to the financial statements, XYZ Company changed its method of computing depreciation in 19X2.

In the preceding example, Note 2 to the financial statements would describe the nature and justification for the change in method of computing depreciation, as well as the effects on the financial statements.

Emphasis of a Matter.    Auditors also may issue an unqualified opinion that departs from the wording of the standard report in order to emphasize some element within the client's financial statements. For example, the auditors may add an additional paragraph to their unqualified opinion calling attention to a significant related-party transaction described in a note to the financial statements. The paragraph may either precede or follow the opinion paragraph.

Justified Departures from Officially Recognized Accounting Principles.    FASB and GASB *Statements and Interpretations* and APB *Opinions* have the status of authoritative body pronouncements. They represent the highest level of generally accepted accounting principles. In unusual circumstances, however, auditors may consider it appropriate for the financial statements to depart from these pronouncements in order to achieve the more important objective of a fair presentation. In such cases, the CPAs may still issue an unqualified report, but they must disclose the departure in an explanatory paragraph, either before or after the opinion paragraph. Such reports are sometimes called ''203 reports,'' because Rule 203 of the AICPA *Code of Professional Conduct* officially recognizes these standards. The *Code of Professional Conduct* is discussed in the next chapter.

## Qualified Opinions

A qualified opinion expresses the auditors' reservations about fair presentation in some areas of the financial statements. The opinion states that *except for* the effects of some deficiency in the financial statements, or some limitation in the scope of the auditors' examination, *the financial statements are presented fairly*. All qualified reports include a *separate explanatory paragraph* before the opinion paragraph disclosing the reasons for the qualification. The opinion paragraph of a qualified report includes the appropriate qualifying language and a reference to the explanatory paragraph.

The materiality of the exception governs the use of the qualified opinion. The exception must be sufficiently significant to warrant mentioning in the auditors' report, but it must not be so significant as to necessitate a disclaimer of opinion or an adverse opinion. Consequently, the propriety of a qualified opinion in the event of a significant exception is a matter for careful professional judgment by the auditors.

### Departure from a Generally Accepted Accounting Principle.  The auditors sometimes do not agree with the accounting principles used in preparing the financial statements. Usually, when the auditors' objections are carefully explained, the client will agree to change the statements in an acceptable manner. If the client does not agree to make the suggested changes, the auditors will be forced to qualify their opinion (or if the exception is very material, to issue an adverse opinion). When the report is qualified, the introductory and scope paragraphs of the standard report are unaffected. The modification involves adding an explanatory paragraph following the scope paragraph and qualifying the opinion paragraph. The **qualifying language** used in the opinion paragraph always begins with the term *except for*. Following is an example of the explanatory and opinion paragraphs of an audit report qualified for a departure from generally accepted accounting principles.

---

The Company has excluded from property and debt in the accompanying balance sheet certain lease obligations that, in our opinion, should be capitalized in order to conform with generally accepted accounting principles. If these lease obligations were capitalized, property would be increased by $_____, long-term debt by $_____, and retained earnings by $ _____ as of December 31, 19XX, and net income and earnings per share would be increased (decreased) by $ _____ and $_____, respectively, for the year then ended.

In our opinion, *except for the effects of not capitalizing lease obligations, as discussed in the preceding paragraph,* the financial statements referred to above present fairly, in all material respects, the financial position of XYZ Company as of December 31, 19XX, and the results of its operations and its cash flows for the year then ended in conformity with generally accepted accounting principles.

---

The third standard of reporting addresses a particular type of departure from generally accepted accounting principles—inadequate disclosures—and states that:

> Informative disclosures in the financial statements are to be regarded as reasonably adequate unless otherwise stated in the [auditors'] report.

Thus, auditors may need to issue a qualified or adverse opinion if they consider the disclosure in the client's financial statements to be inadequate.

*SAS 32* (AU 431), "Adequacy of Disclosure in Financial Statements," requires auditors to include the omitted disclosure in an additional paragraph of their auditors' report, if it is practicable to do so. The word *practicable* in this context means that the information can reasonably be obtained and that its inclusion in the report would not cast the auditors in the role of the preparer of the information. For example, the omission by the client of a statement of cash flows would not cause the auditors to include such a statement in their report.

Obviously a client who is reluctant to make a particular disclosure would rather make the disclosure in a note than have it highlighted in the auditors' report. Therefore, very few auditors' reports actually are qualified because of inadequate disclosure. Instead, the requirements of *SAS 32* usually convince the client to include the necessary disclosure among the notes to the financial statements.

Scope Limitations.   Limitations in the scope of the auditors' examination arise when the auditors are unable to perform an essential audit procedure. Limitations may be due either to circumstances surrounding the audit (for example, the auditors were engaged too late in the year to observe the client's beginning inventory[2]) or due to the client (for example, the client refuses to allow the auditors to send confirmations).

When a circumstance-imposed scope limitation is involved, the auditors attempt to perform alternative procedures to gather sufficient competent evidential matter. If such evidential matter is collected and the auditors believe that it is sufficient, an unqualified opinion may be issued. In situations in which alternative procedures do not provide sufficient evidence, the auditors will either qualify the opinion to reflect the scope limitation or disclaim an opinion. The qualifying language and the explanatory paragraph that distinguish the qualified report from the auditors' standard report are emphasized below.

> *Except as discussed in the following paragraph,* we conducted our audit in accordance with generally accepted auditing standards. Those standards require that we plan and perform the audit to obtain reasonable assurance about whether the financial statements are free of
>
> *(continued)*

---

[2]Note that even though this may be the "fault" of the client, it is considered a circumstance-imposed limitation because the client is not refusing to allow the auditor to perform a procedure which is possible to perform.

material misstatement. An audit includes examining, on a test basis, evidence supporting the amounts and disclosures in the financial statements. An audit also includes assessing the accounting principles used and significant estimates made by management, as well as evaluating the overall financial statement presentation. We believe that our audit provides a reasonable basis for our opinion.

*We were unable to obtain audited financial statements supporting the Company's investment in a foreign affiliate stated at $_____, or its equity in earnings of that affiliate of $_____, which is included in net income, as described in Note 8 to the financial statements; nor were we able to satisfy ourselves as to the carrying value of the investment in the foreign affiliate or the equity in earnings by other auditing procedures.*

In our opinion, *except for the effects of such adjustments, if any, as might have been determined to be necessary had we been able to examine evidence regarding the foreign affiliate investment and earnings,* the financial statements referred to above present fairly, in all material respects, the financial position of XYZ Company as of December 31, 19XX, and the results of its operations and its cash flows for the year then ended in conformity with generally accepted accounting principles.

If a circumstance-imposed scope limitation affects a "very material" portion of the financial statements or if the client imposes a significant limitation, a qualified opinion would normally be considered inappropriate, and the auditors should issue a disclaimer of opinion.

## Two or More Qualifications

An auditors' report may be qualified for two or more situations. For example, the report may be qualified because of both a scope limitation and a separate problem involving accounting principles. The wording of such a report would include the appropriate qualifying language and explanatory paragraphs for both types of qualifications.

When there are several situations requiring the qualification of an opinion, the auditors should consider the cumulative effects of these problems. If the effect of the problems is to overshadow the fairness of the statements viewed as a whole or to prevent the auditors from forming an overall opinion, a qualified opinion would be inappropriate. In such cases, the auditors should issue either an adverse opinion or a disclaimer of opinion, depending upon the circumstances.

## Adverse Opinions

An adverse opinion is the opposite of an unqualified opinion; it is an opinion that the financial statements *do not* present fairly the financial position, results of operations, and cash flows of the client, in conformity with generally accepted accounting principles. When the auditors express an adverse opinion, they must have accumulated sufficient evidence to support their unfavorable opinion.

The auditors should express an adverse opinion if the statements are so lacking in fairness that a qualified opinion would not be warning enough. Whenever the auditors issue an adverse opinion, they should disclose in a separate paragraph of their report the reasons for the adverse opinion and the principal effects on the financial statements of the matters causing the adverse opinion, if the effects can be determined.

Thus, an audit report that expresses an adverse opinion generally includes standard introductory and scope paragraphs, one or more explanatory paragraphs preceding the opinion paragraph and describing the reasons for the adverse opinion, and an opinion paragraph. Because the reasons for an adverse opinion are usually lengthy and complex, we illustrate only the opinion paragraph below:

> In our opinion, because of the effects of the matters discussed in the preceding paragraph, the financial statements referred to above do not present fairly, in conformity with generally accepted accounting principles, the financial position of XYZ Company as of December 31, 19X5, or the results of its operations or its cash flows for the year then ended.

Adverse opinions are rare because most clients follow the recommendations of the independent auditors with respect to fair presentation of financial statements. One possible source of adverse opinions is the actions of regulatory agencies that require organizations to use accounting practices that are not in accordance with generally accepted accounting principles.

## Disclaimer of Opinion

A disclaimer of opinion is *no opinion*. In an audit engagement, a disclaimer is required when substantial scope restrictions or other conditions preclude the auditors' compliance with generally accepted auditing standards.

### Substantial Circumstance-Imposed Scope Restrictions.
If a scope restriction is so severe that a qualified opinion is inappropriate, the auditors should issue a disclaimer of opinion. This might happen, for example, if the auditors were engaged after year-end and the client did not take a physical inventory. A disclaimer issued because of a scope limitation will omit the scope paragraph of the standard report and will include an explanatory paragraph describing the scope limitation in its place. The wording of the opinion paragraph will change considerably, because the auditors are *not expressing an opinion*—rather, they are saying that *they have no opinion*. A disclaimer of opinion is illustrated below:

> *We were engaged* to audit the accompanying balance sheet of XYZ Company as of December 31, 19X2, and the related statements of income, retained earnings, and cash flows for the year then ended. These financial statements are the responsibility of the Company's management.
>
> *The Company did not make a count of its physical inventory, stated in the accompanying financial statements at $ _____ as of December 31, 19X2. Further, evidence supporting the*
> *(continued)*

> *cost of property and equipment acquired prior to December 31, 19X1, is no longer available. The Company's records do not permit the application of other auditing procedures to inventories or property and equipment.*
>
> *Since the Company did not take physical inventories and we were not able to apply other auditing procedures to satisfy ourselves as to inventory quantities and the cost of property and equipment, the scope of our work was not sufficient to enable us to express, and we do not express, an opinion on these financial statements.*

Disclaimers of opinion because of scope restrictions are relatively rare. The auditors should be able to foresee these types of problems in the planning stage of the engagement. The client usually will not want to incur the cost of an audit if it is apparent from the start that the auditors must issue a disclaimer of opinion.

Scope Restrictions Imposed by the Client.   The professional standards state that when client-imposed restrictions significantly limit the scope of the audit, the auditor generally should disclaim an opinion on the financial statements. Two reasons exist for this requirement. First, a disclaimer is relatively useless to the client. Therefore, the fact that the auditors may have to issue a disclaimer is a substantial deterrent to the client imposing any scope restrictions in the first place. Second, a client who imposes scope restrictions upon the auditors apparently has something to hide. An audit must be undertaken with an atmosphere of trust and cooperation. If the client is attempting to conceal information, no audit can ensure that all of the problems have been brought to light.

Disclaimer because of Uncertainty.   An unqualified opinion with an explanatory paragraph is generally appropriate for a material uncertainty that is described adequately in notes to the client's financial statements. However, the standards allow the issuance of a *disclaimer of opinion* because of a material uncertainty, including one about the company's ability to continue as a going concern.

Other Disclaimers Issued by CPAs.   In this section, we have discussed only those disclaimers of opinion issued in *audit* engagements. CPA firms issue disclaimers of opinion in many other types of engagements; these disclaimers are dealt with in Chapter 19.

Disclaimers Are Not Alternatives to Adverse Opinions.   A disclaimer can *only* be issued when the auditors do not have sufficient information to form an opinion on the financial statements. If the auditors have *already formed a negative opinion,* the disclaimer *cannot* be used as a way to avoid expressing an adverse opinion. In fact, even when auditors issue a disclaimer of opinion, they should express in explanatory paragraphs of their report *any reservations* they have concerning the financial statements. These reservations include any material exceptions as to generally accepted accounting principles, including disclosure. In short, the issuance of a disclaimer *can never be used to avoid warning financial statement users about problems that the auditors know to exist in the financial statements.*

## Summary of Auditors' Reports

Figure 3–1 summarizes the types of auditors' reports that should be issued under different conditions. Figure 3–2 summarizes the format and the modifying language found in each of the different reports.

## Different Opinions on Different Statements

The fourth standard of reporting states that the auditors shall express an opinion on the financial statements "taken as a whole." This phrase may apply to an entire set of financial statements, or to an individual financial statement, such as a balance sheet. Thus, it is acceptable for the auditors to express an unqualified opinion on one of the financial statements while expressing a qualified, adverse, or disclaimer of opinion on the others.

One circumstance in which this may occur is when the auditors are retained *after* the client has taken its *beginning* inventory. In this case, the auditors can satisfy themselves as to the amounts in the year-end balance sheet, but may not be able to satisfy themselves as to the statements of income, retained earnings, and cash flows. However, the auditors

Figure 3–1   Summary of Appropriate Auditors' Reports

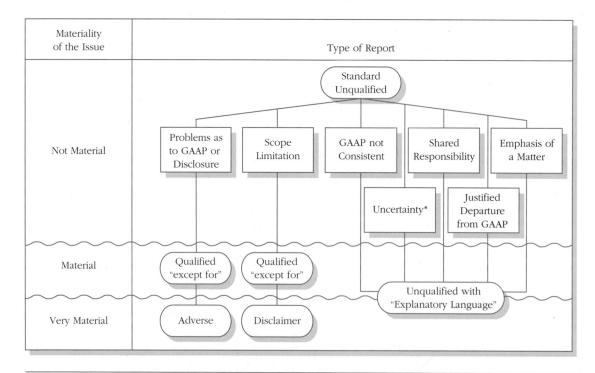

*Including uncertainty about the ability to continue as a going concern. The auditors are not precluded from issuing disclaimers in these situations.

Figure 3-2

| Type of Report | Modifications Required in the Auditors' Report: | | |
| --- | --- | --- | --- |
| | **Introductory or Scope Paragraph** | **Explanatory Paragraph** | **Opinion Paragraph** |
| **Unqualified Reports:** | | | |
| Shared responsibility opinions | Describe work of other auditors (in introductory paragraph) | None | ". . . based on our audit and the report of other auditors . . ." |
| Uncertainty, including those about the going concern* | None | Describe uncertainty | None |
| GAAP not consistently applied | None | Describe change in accounting principle | None |
| Emphasis of a matter | None | Describe matter | None |
| Justified departure from official GAAP | None | Describe departure | None |
| **Qualified Opinions:** | | | |
| Exception as to GAAP, including disclosure | None | Describe departure or make disclosure | ". . . except for (the problem) the financial statements present fairly . . ." |
| Scope restriction | "Except as explained in the following paragraph . . ." (in scope paragraph) | Describe scope restriction | ". . . except for the effects of such adjustments as might have been determined to be necessary . . . the financial statements present fairly . . ." |
| **Adverse Opinion:** | | | |
| Very material exception as to GAAP | None | Describe substantial reasons for adverse opinion | ". . . the financial statements do not present fairly . . ." |
| **Disclaimer of Opinion:** | | | |
| Scope restriction (client imposed or very material) | "We were engaged . . ." and omit "Our responsibility . . ." (in introductory paragraph) Omit scope paragraph | Describe scope restriction and any reservations | ". . . we do not express an opinion on the financial statements" |

*The auditors may decide to issue a disclaimer in this situation.

may be able to perform a useful service by issuing an unqualified opinion on the balance sheet and a disclaimer of opinion on the other financial statements.

## Comparative Financial Statements in Audit Reports

The AICPA has long supported the presentation of comparative financial statements for a series of accounting periods in annual or interim reports to shareholders. Comparative statements show changes and trends in the financial position and operating results of a company over an extended period, and thus are more useful to investors and creditors than are financial statements for a single period.

When comparative financial statements are presented by the client company, the auditors' report should cover the current year's financial statements as well as those for prior periods if their firm has audited them. Publicly owned companies include in their annual reports the balance sheets for each of the last two years, and the related statements of income, retained earnings, and cash flows for each of the last three years. The auditors report on all of these statements. An unqualified report on two-year comparative financial statements is illustrated below:

---

INDEPENDENT AUDITORS' REPORT

To the Board of Directors and Stockholders
XYZ Company:

We have audited the accompanying balance sheets of XYZ Company as of December 31, 19X1, and 19X0, and the related statements of income, retained earnings, and cash flows for the two years then ended. These financial statements are the responsibility of the Company's management. Our responsibility is to express an opinion on these financial statements based on our audits.

We conducted our audits in accordance with generally accepted auditing standards. Those standards require that we plan and perform the audit to obtain reasonable assurance about whether the financial statements are free of material misstatement. An audit includes examining, on a test basis, evidence supporting the amounts and disclosures in the financial statements. An audit also includes assessing the accounting principles used and significant estimates made by management, as well as evaluating the overall financial statement presentation. We believe that our audits provide a reasonable basis for our opinion.

In our opinion, the financial statements referred to above present fairly, in all material respects, the financial position of XYZ Company as of December 31, 19X1, and 19X0, and the results of its operations and its cash flows for the years then ended in conformity with generally accepted accounting principles.

---

The auditors may express different opinions on the financial statements of different years. In addition, auditors should update their reports for all prior periods presented for comparative purposes. *Updating* the report means either to re-express the opinion originally issued or, depending upon the circumstances, to issue a different opinion from that originally issued. A different opinion on the prior-period financial statements may be warranted because new information may come to light that causes the auditors to alter their original opinion. For example, the client may revise previously issued financial statements to correct a deficiency, indicating that a qualified opinion is no longer needed.

If the financial statements of prior comparative periods were unaudited, this fact should be stated on the applicable financial statements and the auditors' report should include a disclaimer of opinion on those financial statements.

If prior-period financial statements were audited by another CPA firm, the successor CPA's opinion will cover only the year(s) the successor has audited. For the prior financial statements, there are two reporting options. First, the predecessor's report may be reissued by that CPA firm bearing its original date. Alternatively, the successor auditors may indicate in the introductory paragraph of their report that (1) the prior-period statements were audited by another auditor, (2) the date and type of report issued by the other auditor, and (3) if that report was other than standard, the reasons therefor. The successor should specifically describe any explanatory language included in the previous auditor's report.

An example of the introductory paragraph of a report in which another CPA firm's report on the prior year was qualified but not presented in the current year is illustrated below, with the explanatory language emphasized.

---

We have audited the balance sheet of XYZ Company as of December 31, 19X2, and the related statements of income, retained earnings, and cash flows for the year then ended. These financial statements are the responsibility of the Company's management. Our responsibility is to express an opinion based on our audit. *The financial statements of XYZ Company for the year ended December 31, 19X1, were audited by other auditors whose opinion, dated March 1, 19X2, on those statements was qualified as being presented fairly except for the effects on the 19X1 statements of the adjustments pertaining to the valuation of inventory, as discussed in Note X to the financial statements.*

---

## Reports to the SEC

Most publicly owned corporations are subject to the financial reporting requirements of the federal securities laws, administered by the Securities and Exchange Commission (SEC). Many of the reports, or *forms,* filed with the SEC include audited financial statements for one or more years. Among the most important of these forms are the following:

1. **Forms S-1 through S-18.**   These forms are the "registration statements" for companies planning to issue securities to the public.
2. **Form 8-K.**   This is a "current report" filed for any month in which significant events occur for a company subject to the Securities Exchange Act of 1934. If the

significant event is a business combination, audited financial statements of the acquired company often are required in the current report. An 8-K report is also used to notify the SEC of a change in auditors.

3. **Form 10-Q.**   This form is filed quarterly with the SEC by publicly owned companies. It contains unaudited financial information. The companies' auditors may perform reviews of this information, but their work is substantially less in scope than an audit.

4. **Form 10-K.**   This report is filed annually with the SEC by publicly owned companies. The report includes audited financial statements and other detailed financial information.

Auditors dealing with these reports should be well versed on the requirements of each form, as well as in the provisions of the SEC's Regulation S-X, which governs the form and content of financial statements filed with the various forms.

The SEC has the power to enforce a high quality of audit work on financial statements submitted to it. The federal securities laws provide both civil and criminal penalties for any person, including auditors, responsible for misrepresentations of fact in audited statements filed with the SEC. The auditors' legal liability under the federal securities acts is discussed in Chapter 5.

## ◆ CHAPTER SUMMARY

This chapter explained the different types of reports that auditors issue to indicate the character of their examination and the degree of responsibility they are taking. To summarize:

1. The auditors' report should be viewed as a very carefully structured technical communication expressed in specialized terminology. The auditors' standard unqualified report includes an introductory paragraph, clarifying the responsibilities of management and the auditors; a scope paragraph, describing the nature of the audit; and an opinion paragraph, summarizing the auditors' opinion based on the audit. The report has a title that includes the word "independent," is addressed to the company whose financial statements are being audited or to its board of directors or stockholders, and is signed with the name of the CPA firm.

2. The auditors' alternatives when expressing an opinion are a standard unqualified opinion, an unqualified opinion with explanatory language, a qualified opinion, an adverse opinion, and a disclaimer of opinion. Figure 3–2 provides details on the appropriate modifications required for each of these types of reports.

3. When a client presents comparative financial statements for one or more prior periods with the current-period financial statements, the auditors should make certain that all periods are covered by an audit report. Audit reports on prior periods should be updated based on any new information that might affect the auditors' opinion. When predecessor auditors examined the prior-period financial statements, the successor auditors may summarize the predecessor auditors' opinion in the current-year audit

report, or the client may arrange to have the predecessor auditors reissue their audit report.

4.  Auditors of publicly held corporations must understand the various reporting requirements of the Securities and Exchange Commission (SEC). The reports filed with the SEC must be in accordance with Regulation S-X, which governs the form and content of the corporation's financial statements.

## ◆ KEY TERMS INTRODUCED OR EMPHASIZED IN CHAPTER 3

**Accounting change**  A change in an accounting principle, in an accounting estimate, or in the reporting entity. Changes in accounting principles and reporting entities result in an explanatory paragraph being added to the auditors' report.

**Adverse opinion**  An opinion that the financial statements *do not* fairly present financial position, results of operations, and cash flows, in conformity with generally accepted accounting principles.

**Disclaimer of opinion**  A form of report in which the auditors state that they do not express an opinion on the financial statements.

**Explanatory paragraph**  A paragraph inserted in an auditors' report to explain a matter or to describe the reasons for giving an opinion that is other than unqualified.

**Introductory paragraph**  The paragraph of the auditors' report in which the auditors indicate that they have audited the financial statements and that the financial statements are the responsibility of management.

**Last day of field work**  The day upon which the auditors conclude their investigative procedures on a particular audit.

**Material**  Being of substantial importance. Significant enough to affect evaluations or decisions by users of financial statements. Information that should be disclosed in order for the financial statements to constitute a fair presentation. It involves both quantitative and qualitative criteria.

**Opinion paragraph**  The paragraph of an auditors' report that communicates the degree of responsibility that the auditors are taking for the financial statements.

**Principal auditors**  Auditors who use the work and reports of other independent CPAs who have audited the financial statements of one or more subsidiaries, branches, or other segments of the principal auditors' client.

**Qualified opinion**  A modification of the auditors' standard report, employing an *except for* clause to limit the auditors' opinion on the financial statements. A qualified opinion indicates that except for some limitation on the scope of the examination or some departure from generally accepted accounting principles, the financial statements are fairly presented.

**Qualifying language**  Language inserted in the opinion paragraph, and sometimes in the scope paragraph, to express the auditors' reservations about some aspect of the client's financial statements.

**Scope limitation**  A restriction that prevents the auditors from being able to apply all of the audit procedures that they consider necessary under the circumstances. Scope limitations may be client imposed or may be imposed by other circumstances.

**Scope paragraph**  The paragraph of an auditors' report in which the auditors describe the character of their audit.

**Shared responsibility opinion**  An auditors' report in which the principal auditors decide to share responsibility with other auditors who audited some segment of the client's business. The sharing of responsibility is done by making reference to the other auditors. Making reference is not, in itself, a qualification of the auditors' report.

**Standard report**   The "standard wording" of an unqualified auditors' report, not including such modifications as emphasis of a matter, a material uncertainty, a change in accounting principle, departures from official GAAP, or a shared responsibility opinion.

**Unqualified opinion**   An opinion that the financial statements present fairly financial position, results of operations, and cash flows, in conformity with generally accepted accounting principles.

---

## ◆ GROUP I: REVIEW QUESTIONS

3-1   Comment on the following: "If the financial statements contain a material departure from generally accepted accounting principles, the auditors may decide to add an explanatory paragraph to the audit report and, given that the information is included in that paragraph, issue an unqualified opinion on the financial statements."

3-2   Name the three paragraphs of the standard audit report.

3-3   What is the function of notes to financial statements?

3-4   What basic conditions must be met before auditors can issue an unqualified auditors' report?

3-5   Identify the basic types of opinions that an auditor may issue and explain when each is appropriate.

3-6   Howard Green is a partner with Cary, Loeb, & Co. On February 20, Green completed the audit of Baker Manufacturing for the year ended last December 31. It is now March 1, and Green is about to sign the auditors' report. How should Green sign and date the report?

3-7   What is meant by the term *qualifying language* in an auditors' report?

3-8   Is a shared responsibility opinion a qualified opinion? Explain.

3-9   Explain three situations in which the wording of an *unqualified* opinion might depart from the auditors' standard report.

3-10   The auditors do not believe that certain lease obligations have been reflected in conformity with generally accepted accounting principles in the client's financial statements. What type of opinion should the auditors issue if they decide that the exceptions are immaterial? Material? Very material?

3-11   Can the client change a set of financial statements to receive an unqualified opinion instead of an opinion qualified as to disclosure? Can the client change the financial statements to avoid a report modified because of uncertainty? Explain.

3-12   Why are adverse opinions rare?

3-13   What type of report should auditors issue when the client has imposed significant scope limitations?

3-14   The auditors know that the client's accounting for deferred income taxes is not in accordance with generally accepted accounting principles, but because of a very significant scope limitation they have not been able to form an opinion on the financial statements taken as a whole. What type of report should they issue?

3-15   Only one type of qualified opinion has qualifying language in both the scope paragraph and the opinion paragraph. What is the reason for this type of qualification?

3-16   Assume that CPAs are attesting to comparative financial statements. Can the CPAs express differing opinions on the financial statements of two successive years?

3-17   Assume that CPAs are attesting to comparative financial statements. Can the CPAs change their report on the prior year's statements?

3-18   Wade Corporation has been your audit client for several years. At the beginning of the current year, the company changed its method of inventory valuation from average cost to LIFO. The change, which had been under consideration for some time, was in your opinion a logical and proper step for the company to take. What effect, if any, will this situation have on your audit report for the current year?

3-19   Describe the reports containing audited financial statements customarily filed by a company subject to the reporting requirements of the SEC.

# ◆ GROUP II: QUESTIONS REQUIRING ANALYSIS

3-20   What type of audit report (unqualified opinion, qualified opinion, adverse opinion, disclaimer of opinion) should the auditors *generally* issue in each of the following situations? Explain.
   a.   Client-imposed restrictions limit significantly the scope of the auditors' procedures.
   b.   The auditors decide to make reference to the report of another CPA firm as a basis, in part, for the auditors' opinion.
   c.   The auditors believe that the financial statements have been presented in conformity with generally accepted accounting principles in all respects other than those contingent on the outcome of a material uncertainty.

3-21   The following statement is representative of attitudes and opinions sometimes encountered by CPAs in their professional practices: ''It is important to read the notes to financial statements, even though they often are presented in technical language and are incomprehensible. The auditors may reduce their exposure to third-party liability by stating something in the notes that contradicts completely what they have presented in the balance sheet or income statement.''

*Required:*   Evaluate the above statement and indicate:
   a.   Areas of agreement with the statement, if any.
   b.   Areas of misconception, incompleteness, or fallacious reasoning included in the statement, if any.

(AICPA, adapted)

3-22   Rowe & Myers are the principal auditors of Dunbar Electronics. During the audit, Rowe & Myers engaged Jones & Abbot, a Canadian public accounting firm, to audit Dunbar's wholly owned Canadian subsidiary.

*Required:*   a.   Must Rowe & Myers make reference to the other auditors in their audit report? Explain.
   b.   Assume that Jones & Abbot issued a qualified report on the Canadian subsidiary. Must Rowe & Myers include the same qualification in their report on Dunbar Electronics?

3-23   Lando Corporation is a domestic company with two wholly owned domestic subsidiaries. Michaels, CPA, has been engaged to audit the financial statements of the parent company and one of the subsidiaries and to act as the principal auditor. Thomas, CPA, has audited the financial statements of the other subsidiary whose operations are material in relation to the consolidated financial statements.

   The work performed by Michaels is sufficient for Michaels to serve as the principal auditor and to report as such on the financial statements. Michaels has not yet decided whether to make reference to the audit made by Thomas.

*Required:*     *a.*    There are certain required audit procedures that Michaels should perform with respect to the audit made by Thomas, whether or not Michaels decides to make reference to Thomas in Michaels' auditors' report. What are these audit procedures?

         *b.*    What are the reporting requirements with which Michaels must comply if Michaels decides to make reference to the audit of Thomas?

(AICPA, adapted)

3-24    While performing your audit of Williams Paper Company, you discover evidence that indicates that Williams may not have the ability to continue as a going concern.

*Required:*    *a.*    Discuss the types of information that may indicate a going-concern problem.

         *b.*    Explain the auditors' reporting obligation in such situations.

3-25    Select the best answer for each of the following and explain fully the reason for your selection:

     *a.*    A material departure from generally accepted accounting principles will result in auditor consideration of:

       (1)    Whether to issue an adverse opinion rather than a disclaimer of opinion.

       (2)    Whether to issue a disclaimer of opinion rather than an "except for" opinion.

       (3)    Whether to issue an adverse opinion rather than an "except for" opinion.

       (4)    Nothing, because none of these opinions is applicable to this type of exception.

     *b.*    The auditors' report should be dated as of the date the:

       (1)    Report is delivered to the client.

       (2)    Field work is completed.

       (3)    Fiscal period under audit ends.

       (4)    Review of the working papers is completed.

     *c.*    In the report of the principal auditor, reference to the fact that a portion of the audit was made by another auditor is:

       (1)    Not to be construed as a qualification, but rather as a division of responsibility between the two CPA firms.

       (2)    Not in accordance with generally accepted auditing standards.

       (3)    A qualification that lessens the collective responsibility of both CPA firms.

       (4)    An example of a dual opinion requiring the signatures of both auditors.

     *d.*    Assume that the opinion paragraph of an auditor's report begins as follows: "With the explanation given in note 6, the financial statements referred to above present fairly . . . ." This is:

       (1)    An unqualified opinion.

       (2)    A disclaimer of opinion.

       (3)    An "except for" opinion.

       (4)    An improper type of reporting.

     *e.*    The auditor who wishes to indicate that the entity has significant transactions with related parties should disclose this fact in:

       (1)    An explanatory paragraph to the auditors' report.

       (2)    An explanatory footnote to the financial statements.

       (3)    The body of the financial statements.

       (4)    The "summary of significant accounting policies" section of the financial statements.

     *f.*    When restrictions that significantly limit the scope of the audit are imposed by the client, the auditor should generally issue which of the following opinions?

       (1)    Qualified.

       (2)    Disclaimer.

       (3)    Adverse.

       (4)    Unqualified.

(AICPA, adapted)

# ◆ GROUP III: PROBLEMS

3-26   The auditors' report below was drafted by a staff accountant of Williams & Co., CPAs, at the completion of the audit of the financial statements of Lenz Corporation for the year ended March 31, 19X9. It was submitted to the engagement partner, who reviewed matters thoroughly and properly concluded that Lenz's disclosures concerning its ability to continue as a going concern for a reasonable period of time were adequate.

---

### INDEPENDENT AUDITORS' REPORT

To the Board of Directors of Lenz Corporation:

We have audited the accompanying balance sheet of Lenz Corporation, as of March 31, 19X9, and the related financial statements for the year then ended. Our responsibility is to express an opinion on these financial statements based on our audit. We conducted our audit in accordance with standards that require that we plan and perform the audit to obtain reasonable assurance about whether the financial statements are in conformity with generally accepted accounting principles. An audit includes examining, on a test basis, evidence supporting the amounts and disclosures in the financial statements. An audit also includes assessing the accounting principles used and significant estimates made by management.

The accompanying financial statements have been prepared assuming that the Company will continue as a going concern. As discussed in Note X to the financial statements, the Company has suffered recurring losses from operations and has a net capital deficiency that raises substantial doubt about its ability to continue as a going concern. We believe that management's plans in regard to these matters, which are also described in Note X, will permit the Company to continue as a going concern beyond a reasonable period of time. The financial statements do not include any adjustments that might result from the outcome of this uncertainty.

In our opinion, subject to the effect on the financial statements of such adjustments, if any, as might have been required had the outcome of the uncertainty referred to in the preceding paragraph been known, the financial statements referred to above present fairly, in all material respects, the financial position of Lenz Corporation and the results of its operations and its cash flows in conformity with generally accepted accounting principles applied on a basis consistent with that of the preceding year.

*only state if not consistently applied*

Williams & Co., CPAs

April 28, 19X9

---

*Required:*   Identify the deficiencies contained in the auditors' report as drafted by the staff accountant. Group the deficiencies by paragraph.

3-27   Sturdy Corporation owns and operates a large office building in a desirable section of New York City's financial center. For many years, the management of Sturdy Corporation has modified the presentation of their financial statements by:
1.   Reflecting a write-up to appraisal values in the building accounts.
2.   Accounting for depreciation expense on the basis of such valuations.

Wyley, CPA, was asked to audit the financial statements of Sturdy Corporation for the year ended December 31, 19X3. After completing the audit, Wyley concluded that, consistent with prior years, an adverse opinion would have to be expressed because of the materiality of the deviation from the historical-cost principle.

*Required:*   *a.*   Describe in detail the appropriate content of the explanatory paragraph of the auditors' report on the financial statements of Sturdy Corporation for the year ended December 31, 19X3. *Do not discuss deferred taxes.*

*b.*   Write a draft of the opinion paragraph of the auditors' report on the financial statements of Sturdy Corporation for the year ended December 31, 19X3.

3-28   What type of auditors' report would be issued in each of the following cases? Justify your choice.

*a.*   Bowles Company is engaged in a hazardous trade and cannot obtain insurance coverage from any source. A material portion of the company's assets could be destroyed by a serious accident.

*b.*   Draves Company owns substantial properties that have appreciated significantly in value since the date of purchase. The properties were appraised and are reported in the balance sheet at the appraised values with full disclosure. The CPAs believe that the appraised values reported in the balance sheet reasonably estimate the assets' current values.

*c.*   The CPA firm is auditing the financial statements that are to be included in the annual report to the stockholders of Eagle Company, a regulated company. Eagle's financial statements are prepared as prescribed by a regulatory agency of the U.S. government, and some items are not presented in accordance with generally accepted accounting principles. The amounts involved are somewhat material and are adequately disclosed in notes to the financial statements.

*d.*   London Company has material investments in stocks of subsidiary companies. Stocks of the subsidiary companies are not actively traded in the market, and the CPA firm's engagement does not extend to any subsidiary company. The CPA firm is able to determine that all investments are carried at original cost, and the auditors have no reason to suspect that the amounts are not stated fairly.

*e.*   Slade Company has material investments in stocks of subsidiary companies. Stocks of the subsidiary companies are actively traded in the market, but the CPA firm's engagement does not extend to any subsidiary company. Management insists that all investments shall be carried at original costs, and the CPA firm is satisfied that the original costs are accurate. The CPA firm believes that the client will never ultimately realize a substantial portion of the investments, and the client has fully disclosed the facts in notes to the financial statements.

(AICPA, adapted)

3-29   Roscoe and Jones, CPAs, have completed the audit of the financial statements of Excelsior Corporation as of, and for, the year ended December 31, 1994. Roscoe also audited and reported on the Excelsior financial statements for the prior year. Roscoe drafted the following report for 1994.

---

We have audited the accompanying balance sheet of Excelsior Corporation Inc. as of December 31, 1994, and the related statements of income and retained earnings for the year then ended. These financial statements are the responsibility of the Company's management. Our responsibility is to express an opinion on these financial statements based on our audit.

We conducted our audit in accordance with generally accepted auditing standards. Those standards require that we plan and perform the audit to obtain reasonable assurance about

*(continued)*

whether the financial statements are free of material misstatement. An audit includes examining, on a test basis, evidence supporting the amounts and disclosures in the financial statements. An audit also includes assessing the accounting principles used and significant estimates made by management, as well as evaluating the overall financial statement presentation. We believe that our audit provides a reasonable basis for our opinion.

In our opinion, the financial statements referred to above present fairly, in all material respects, the financial position of Excelsior Corporation as of December 31, 1994, and the results of its operations for the year then ended in conformity with generally accepted accounting principles, applied on a basis consistent with that of the preceding year.

Roscoe & Jones, CPAs
March 15, 1995

*Other information:*
(1) Excelsior is presenting comparative financial statements.
(2) Excelsior does not wish to present a statement of cash flows for either year.
(3) During 1994, Excelsior changed its method of accounting for long-term construction contracts and properly reflected the effect of the change in the current year's financial statements and restated the prior year's statements. Roscoe is satisfied with Excelsior's justification for making the change. The change is discussed in note 12.
(4) Roscoe was unable to perform normal accounts receivable confirmation procedures, but alternate procedures were used to satisfy Roscoe as to the validity of the receivables.
(5) Excelsior Corporation is the defendant in litigation, the outcome of which is highly uncertain. If the case is settled in favor of the plaintiff, Excelsior will be required to pay a substantial amount of cash that might require the sale of certain fixed assets. The litigation and the possible effects have been properly disclosed in note 11.
(6) Excelsior issued debentures on January 31, 1993, in the amount of $10 million. The funds obtained from the issuance were used to finance the expansion of plant facilities. The debenture agreement restricts the payment of future cash dividends to earnings after December 31, 1993. Excelsior declined to disclose this essential data in the notes to the financial statements.

*Required:* Consider all facts given, and rewrite the auditors' report in acceptable and complete format, incorporating any necessary departures from the standard report. Do not discuss the draft of Roscoe's report, but identify and explain any items included in *"Other information"* that need not be part of the auditors' report.

(AICPA, adapted)

3-30 Various types of accounting changes can affect the second reporting standard of the generally accepted auditing standards. This standard addresses whether accounting principles have been consistently observed in the current period in relation to the preceding period.

Assume that the following list describes changes that have a material effect on a client's financial statements for the current year.
(1) A change from the completed-contract method to the percentage-of-completion method of accounting for long-term construction-type contracts.
(2) A change in the estimated service lives of previously recorded plant assets based on newly acquired information.
(3) Correction of a mathematical error in inventory pricing made in a prior period.
(4) A change from prime costing to full absorption costing for inventory valuation.

(5) A change from presentation of financial statements of individual companies to presentation of consolidated financial statements.

(6) A change from deferring and amortizing preproduction costs to recording such costs as an expense when incurred because future benefits of the costs have become doubtful. The new accounting method was adopted in recognition of the change in estimated future benefits.

(7) A change to including the employer's share of FICA taxes as "Retirement benefits" on the income statement from including it with "Other taxes."

(8) A change from the FIFO method of inventory pricing to the LIFO method of inventory pricing.

*Required:*    Identify the type of change described in each item above; state whether any modification is required in the auditors' report as it relates to the second standard of reporting; and state whether the prior year's financial statements should be restated when presented in comparative form with the current year's statements. Organize your answer sheet as shown on the following page.

For example, a change from the LIFO method of inventory pricing to FIFO method of inventory pricing would appear as shown.

| Item No. | Type of Change | Should Auditors' Report Be Modified? | Should Prior Year's Statements Be Restated? |
|----------|----------------|--------------------------------------|---------------------------------------------|
| Example | An accounting change from one generally accepted accounting principle to another generally accepted accounting principle. | Yes | Yes |

(AICPA, adapted)

3-31    Brown & Brown, CPAs, was engaged by the board of directors of Cook Industries, Inc. to audit Cook's calendar year 19X8 financial statements. The following report was drafted by an audit assistant at the completion of the engagement. It was submitted to Brown, the engagement partner, for review on March 7, 19X9, the date of the completion of field work. Brown has reviewed matters thoroughly and properly concluded that an adverse opinion was appropriate.

Brown also became aware of a March 14, 19X9 subsequent event which the client has properly disclosed in the notes to the financial statements. Brown wants responsibility for subsequent events to be limited to the specific event referred to in the applicable note to the client's financial statements.

The financial statements of Cook Industries, Inc. for the calendar year 19X7 were audited by predecessor auditors who also expressed an adverse opinion and have not reissued their report. The financial statements for 19X7 and 19X8 are presented in comparative form.

---

To the President of Cook Industries, Inc.:

We have audited the accompanying balance sheet of Cook Industries, Inc. as of December 31, 19X8, and the related statements of income, retained earnings, and cash flows for the year then ended. These financial statements are the responsibility of the Company's management. Our responsibility is to express an opinion on these financial statements based on our audit. As discussed in Note K to the financial statements, the Company has properly disclosed a subsequent event dated March 14, 19X9.

*(continued)*

We conducted our audit in accordance with generally accepted auditing standards. Those standards require that we plan and perform the audit to obtain reasonable assurance about whether the financial statements are free of material misstatement. An audit includes examining, on a test basis, evidence supporting the amounts and disclosures in the financial statements. An audit also includes assessing the accounting principles used and significant estimates made by management, as well as evaluating the overall financial statement presentation. We believe that our audit provides a reasonable basis for our opinion.

In our opinion, except for the matters discussed in the first and the final paragraphs of this report, the financial statements referred to above present fairly, in all material respects, the financial position of Cook Industries, Inc. as of December 31, 19X8, and the results of its operations and its cash flows for the year then ended in conformity with generally accepted accounting principles applied on a basis consistent with that of the preceding year.

As discussed in Note G to the financial statements, the Company carries its property and equipment at appraisal values, and provides depreciation on the basis of such values. Further, the company does not provide for income taxes with respect to differences between financial income and taxable income arising because of the use, for income tax purposes, of the installment method of reporting gross profit from certain types of sales. We believe that these appraisal values are reasonable.

Brown & Brown, CPAs
March 7, 19X9

*Required:*   Identify the deficiencies in the draft of the proposed report. Do *not* redraft the report or discuss corrections.

(AICPA, adapted)

3-32   Your client, Quaid Company, requests your assistance in rewriting the note presented below, to make it clearer and more concise.

*Note 6.* The indenture relating to the long-term debt contains certain provisions regarding the maintenance of working capital, the payment of dividends, and the purchase of the company's capital stock. The most restrictive of these provisions requires that: (*a*) working capital will be maintained at not less than $4,500,000; (*b*) the company cannot pay cash dividends or purchase its capital stock, if after it has done so, working capital is less than $5,000,000; and (*c*) cash dividends paid since January 1, 1992, plus the excess of capital stock purchased over the proceeds of stock sold during the same period, cannot exceed 70 percent of net earnings (since January 1, 1992) plus $250,000. At December 31, 1994, $2,441,291 of retained earnings were available for the payment of dividends under this last provision, as follows:

| | |
|---|---:|
| Net earnings since January 1, 1992 | $5,478,127 |
| 70 percent of above | $3,834,688 |
| Additional amount available under indenture | 250,000 |
| | 4,084,688 |
| Cash dividends paid since January 1, 1992 | 1,643,397 |
| Retained earnings available December 31, 1994 | $2,441,291 |

*Required:*   Rewrite the note in accordance with your client's instructions.

3-33   On September 30, 1994, White & Co., CPAs, was engaged to audit the consolidated financial statements of National Motors, Inc. for the year ended December 31, 1994. The consolidated financial statements of National had not been audited the prior year. National's inadequate inventory records precluded White from forming an opinion as to the proper or consistent application of generally accepted accounting principles to inventory balances on January 1, 1994. Therefore, White decided not to express an opinion on the results of operations for the year ended December 31, 1994. National decided not to present comparative financial statements.

Rapid Parts Company, a consolidated subsidiary of National, was audited for the year ended December 31, 1994, by Green & Co., CPAs. Green completed its field work on February 28, 1995, and submitted an unqualified opinion on Rapid's financial statements on March 7, 1995. Rapid's statements reflect total assets and revenues of $7,000,000 and $8,000,000, respectively, of the consolidated totals of National. White decided not to assume responsibility for the work of Green. Green's report on Rapid does not accompany National's consolidated statements.

White completed its field work on March 28, 1995, and submitted its auditors' report to National on April 4, 1995.

Required:   Prepare White & Company's auditors' report on the consolidated financial statements of National Motors, Inc.

# ◆ GROUP IV: RESEARCH AND DISCUSSION CASE

3-34   Your firm audits Metropolitan Power Supply (MPS). The issue under consideration is the treatment in the company's financial statements of $700 million in capitalized construction costs relating to Eagle Mountain, a partially completed nuclear power plant.

Seven years ago, MPS began construction of Eagle Mountain, with an original cost estimate of $400 million and completion expected within five years. Cost overruns were enormous, and construction has been repeatedly delayed by litigation initiated by the antinuclear lobby. At present, the project is little more than 50 percent complete, and construction has been halted because MPS does not have the funds to continue.

If Eagle Mountain is ultimately completed, the state utilities commission will determine the extent to which MPS may recover its construction costs through its rate structure. The commission's rulings are difficult to predict, but it is quite possible that the commission will not allow MPS to include all of the Eagle Mountain construction costs in its "rate base." If Eagle Mountain were abandoned today, none of the construction costs would be recoverable. The related write-off would amount to over 70 percent of MPS's stockholders' equity, but the company would survive.

MPS's management, however, remains committed to the completion of the Eagle Mountain facility. Management has obtained authorization from the company's stockholders to issue $500 million in bonds and additional shares of common stock to finance completion of the project. If MPS incurs this additional debt and is still not able to make Eagle Mountain fully operational, it is doubtful that the company can avoid bankruptcy. In short, management has elected to gamble—all of its chips are riding on Eagle Mountain.

Required:   a.   Discuss the arguments for and against the auditors insisting that MPS begin expensing some portion of the construction costs rather than continuing to accumulate an ever-increasing asset. Indicate the position you would take as the auditor.

b.   Discuss whether the auditors should modify their report because of uncertainty as to whether or not MPS can remain a going concern. Indicate the type of opinion that you would issue. (You need not limit yourself to a "going-concern" modification.)

# ◆ SUGGESTED REFERENCES

*Part a:*

*FASB Statement No. 19,* ''Financial Accounting and Reporting by Oil and Gas Producing Companies,'' paragraphs 15, 28.

*FASB Statement No. 5,* ''Accounting for Contingencies,'' paragraph 31.

*Part b:*

*Statement on Auditing Standards No. 59,* ''The Auditor's Consideration of an Entity's Ability to Continue as a Going Concern'' (New York, 1988) AU 341.

*Statement on Auditing Standards No. 58,* ''The Auditor's Standard Report'' (New York, 1988) AU 508.

# PROFESSIONAL ETHICS

## CHAPTER OBJECTIVES

After studying this chapter, you should be able to:

- Describe the reasons that professions establish professional ethics.

- Identify the two parts of the AICPA *Code of Professional Conduct*.

- Discuss the Principles section of the AICPA *Code of Professional Conduct*.

- Describe each of the Rules contained in the AICPA *Code of Professional Conduct*.

- Explain the concept of independence and identify circumstances in which independence is impaired.

- Discuss *The Institute of Internal Auditors Code of Ethics*.

# The Need for Professional Ethics

All recognized professions have developed codes of professional ethics. The fundamental purpose of such codes is to provide members with guidelines for maintaining a professional attitude and conducting themselves in a manner that will enhance the professional stature of their discipline.

To understand the importance of a code of ethics to public accountants and other professionals, one must understand the nature of a profession as opposed to other vocations. There is no universally accepted definition of what constitutes a profession; yet, for generations, certain types of activities have been recognized as professions while others have not. Medicine, law, engineering, architecture, and theology are examples of disciplines long accorded professional status. Public accounting is a relative newcomer to the ranks of the professions, but it has achieved widespread recognition in recent decades.

All of the recognized **professions** have several common characteristics. The most important of these characteristics are *(a)* a responsibility to serve the public, *(b)* a complex body of knowledge, *(c)* standards of admission to the profession, and *(d)* a need for public confidence. Let us briefly discuss these characteristics as they apply to public accounting.

Responsibility to Serve the Public.   The certified public accountant is a representative of the public—creditors, stockholders, consumers, employees, and others—in the financial reporting process. The role of the independent auditor is to ensure that financial statements are *fair to all parties* and not biased to benefit one group at the expense of another. This responsibility to serve the public interest must be a basic motivation for the professional.

There is a saying in public accounting that "the public is our only client." This expression is an oversimplification, since the entity being audited pays the auditor's fee and is, in fact, the client. Yet the saying conveys an ideal that is essential to the long-run professional status of public accounting. Public accountants must maintain a high degree of independence from their clients if they are to be of service to the larger community. Independence is perhaps the most important concept embodied in public accounting's *Code of Professional Conduct*.

Complex Body of Knowledge.   Any practitioner or student of accounting has only to look at the abundance of authoritative pronouncements governing financial reports to realize that accounting is a complex body of knowledge. One reason why such pronouncements continue to proliferate is that accounting must reflect what is taking place in an increasingly complex environment. As the environment changes—such as the trend toward business reorganizations in the 1980s—accounting principles and auditing practices must adapt. The continual growth in the "common body of knowledge" for practicing accountants has led the AICPA to enact continuing education requirements for CPAs. The need for technical competence and familiarity with current standards of practice is embodied in the *Code of Professional Conduct*.

Standards of Admission to the Profession.   Attaining a license to practice as a certified public accountant requires an individual to meet minimum standards for education and experience. The individual must also pass the uniform CPA examination showing mastery of the body of knowledge described above. Once licensed, certified public accountants must adhere to the ethics of the profession or risk disciplinary action.

Need for Public Confidence.    Physicians, lawyers, certified public accountants, and all other professionals must have the confidence of the public to be successful. To the CPA, however, public confidence is of special significance. The CPA's product is credibility. Without public confidence in the attestor, the attest function serves no useful purpose.

Professional ethics in public accounting as in other professions have developed gradually and are still in a process of change as the practice of public accounting itself changes. Often new concepts are added as a result of unfortunate incidents that reflect unfavorably upon the profession, although not specific violations of existing standards.

## Professional Ethics in Public Accounting

Careless work or lack of integrity on the part of any CPA is a reflection upon the entire profession. Consequently, the members of the public accounting profession have acted in unison through the American Institute of Certified Public Accountants to devise a code of conduct. This code provides practical guidance to the individual member in maintaining a professional attitude. In addition, this code gives assurance to clients and to the public that the profession intends to maintain high standards and to enforce compliance by individual members.

Evidence that public accounting has achieved the status of a profession is found in the willingness of its members to accept voluntarily standards of conduct more rigorous than those imposed by law. These standards of conduct set forth the basic responsibilities of CPAs to the public, clients, and fellow practitioners. To be effective, a body of professional ethics must be attainable and enforceable; it must consist not merely of abstract ideals but of attainable goals and practical working rules that can be enforced.

In the short run, the restraints imposed on the individual CPA by a body of professional ethics may sometimes appear to constitute a hardship. From a long-run point of view, however, it is clear that the individual practitioner, the profession as a whole, and the public all benefit from the existence of a well-defined body of professional ethics.

## THE AICPA *CODE OF PROFESSIONAL CONDUCT*

The AICPA *Code of Professional Conduct* was restructured by vote of the membership in November 1987. Developing the new code represents a positive response by the profession to the rapidly changing environment of public accounting. It is designed to provide a framework for expanding professional services and responding to other changes in the profession, such as the increasingly competitive environment.

The restructured *Code of Professional Conduct* consists of two sections. The first section, the **Principles,** is a goal-oriented, positively stated discussion of the profession's responsibilities to the public, clients, and fellow practitioners. The Principles provide the framework for the Rules, the second section of the Code. The **Rules** are enforceable applications of the Principles. They define acceptable behavior and identify sources of authority for performance standards.

To provide guidelines for the scope and application of the Rules, the AICPA issues **Interpretations.** Senior Technical Committees of the AICPA, such as the Auditing

## Figure 4-1    AICPA Professional Ethics

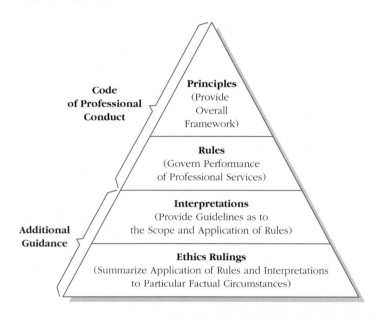

Standards Board, interpret the Rules applying to their area of responsibility; the Professional Ethics Executive Committee issues interpretations that apply to all professional activities. The AICPA also issues **Ethics Rulings** which explain the application of the Rules and Interpretations to specific factual circumstances involving professional ethics. Figure 4-1 summarizes the relationships among the Principles, Rules, Interpretations, and Ethics Rulings.

A portion of the Principles section of the *Code of Professional Conduct* is quoted below, followed by a presentation and analysis of the section of the Code that includes the Rules.

### SECTION I—PRINCIPLES[1]

#### Preamble

Membership in the American Institute of Certified Public Accountants is voluntary. By accepting membership, a certified public accountant assumes an obligation of self-discipline above and beyond the requirements of laws and regulations.

These Principles of the *Code of Professional Conduct* of the American Institute of Certified Public Accountants express the profession's recognition of its responsibilities to the public, to clients, and to colleagues. They guide members in the performance of their professional responsibilities and express the basic tenets of ethical and professional conduct. The Principles call for an unswerving commitment to honorable behavior, even at the sacrifice of personal advantage.

---

[1]Copyright by the American Institute of Certified Public Accountants, Inc.

### Article I
### Responsibilities

*In carrying out their responsibilities as professionals, members should exercise sensitive professional and moral judgments in all their activities.*

As professionals, certified public accountants perform an essential role in society. Consistent with that role, members of the American Institute of Certified Public Accountants have responsibilities to all those who use their professional services. Members also have a continuing responsibility to cooperate with each other to improve the art of accounting, maintain the public's confidence, and carry out the profession's special responsibilities for self-governance. The collective efforts of all members are required to maintain and enhance the traditions of the profession.

### Article II
### The Public Interest

*Members should accept the obligation to act in a way that will serve the public interest, honor the public trust, and demonstrate commitment to professionalism.*

A distinguishing mark of a profession is acceptance of its responsibility to the public. The accounting profession's public consists of clients, credit grantors, governments, employers, investors, the business and financial community, and others who rely on the objectivity and integrity of certified public accountants to maintain the orderly functioning of commerce. This reliance imposes a public interest responsibility on certified public accountants. The public interest is defined as the collective well-being of the community of people and institutions the profession serves.

In discharging their professional responsibilities, members may encounter conflicting pressures from among each of those groups. In resolving those conflicts, members should act with integrity, guided by the precept that when members fulfill their responsibility to the public, clients' and employers' interests are best served.

Those who rely on certified public accountants expect them to discharge their responsibilities with integrity, objectivity, due professional care, and a genuine interest in serving the public. They are expected to provide quality services, enter into fee arrangements, and offer a range of services—all in a manner that demonstrates a level of professionalism consistent with these Principles of the *Code of Professional Conduct*.

All who accept membership in the American Institute of Certified Public Accountants commit themselves to honor the public trust. In return for the faith that the public reposes in them, members should seek continually to demonstrate their dedication to professional excellence.

### Article III
### Integrity

*To maintain and broaden public confidence, members should perform all professional responsibilities with the highest sense of integrity.*

### Article IV
### Objectivity and Independence

*A member should maintain objectivity and be free of conflicts of interest in discharging professional responsibilities. A member in public practice should be independent in fact and appearance when providing auditing and other attestation services.*

### Article V
### Due Care

*A member should observe the profession's technical and ethical standards, strive continually to improve competence and the quality of services, and discharge professional responsibility to the best of the member's ability.*

**Article VI**
**Scope and Nature of Services**

*A member in public practice should observe the Principles of the Code of Professional Conduct in determining the scope and nature of services to be provided.*

Each of these Principles should be considered by members in determining whether or not to provide specific services in individual circumstances. In some instances, they may represent an overall constraint on the nonaudit services that might be offered to a specific client. No hard-and-fast rules can be developed to help members reach these judgments, but they must be satisfied that they are meeting the spirit of the Principles in this regard.

In order to accomplish this, members should—

* Practice in firms that have in place internal quality-control procedures to ensure that services are competently delivered and adequately supervised.

* Determine, in their individual judgments, whether the scope and nature of other services provided to an audit client would create a conflict of interest in the performance of the audit function for that client.

* Assess, in their individual judgments, whether an activity is consistent with their role as professionals (for example, is such activity a reasonable extension or variation of existing services offered by the member or others in the profession?).

### SECTION II—RULES

**Applicability**

*The bylaws of the American Institute of Certified Public Accountants require that members adhere to the Rules of the Code of Professional Conduct. Members must be prepared to justify departures from these Rules.*

Figure 4–2 is a complete listing of the Rules, which are presented and analyzed below.

---

Figure 4–2   The Rules of the AICPA *Code of Professional Conduct*

| Rule | Title |
|------|-------|
| *101* | Independence |
| *102* | Integrity and Objectivity |
| *201* | General Standards |
| *202* | Compliance with Standards |
| *203* | Accounting Principles |
| *301* | Confidential Client Information |
| *302* | Contingent Fees |
| *501* | Acts Discreditable |
| *502* | Advertising and Other Forms of Solicitation |
| *503* | Commissions and Referral Fees |
| *504* | (Deleted) |
| *505* | Form of Organization and Name |

## Rule 101 — Independence

*A member in public practice shall be independent in the performance of professional services as required by standards promulgated by bodies designated by Council.*

Interpretation 101–1 of the Code contains examples of transactions, interests, and relationships which result in a lack of independence in appearance. Specifically, the interpretation states that independence will be considered impaired if:

A.  During the period of a professional engagement or at the time of expressing an opinion, a member or a member's firm:
  1. Had or was committed to acquire any direct or material indirect financial interest in the enterprise.
  2. Was a trustee of any trust or executor or administrator of any estate if such trust or estate had or was committed to acquire any direct or material indirect financial interest in the enterprise.
  3. Had any joint, closely held business investment with the enterprise or with any officer, director, or principal stockholders thereof that was material in relation to the member's net worth or to the net worth of the member's firm.
  4. Had any loan to or from the enterprise or any officer, director, or principal stockholder of the enterprise, except as specifically permitted in Interpretation 101–5.[2]

B.  During the period covered by the financial statements, during the period of the professional engagement, or at the time of expressing an opinion, a member or a member's firm:
  1. Was connected with the enterprise as a promoter, underwriter, or voting trustee, a director or officer or in any capacity equivalent to that of a member of management or of an employee.
  2. Was a trustee for any pension or profit-sharing trust of the enterprise.

The above examples are not intended to be all-inclusive.

## Analysis of Independence

The first Rule of Conduct is concerned with the vital issue of the auditors' independence. Two distinct ideas are involved in the concept of independence. First, the CPAs must in fact be independent of any enterprises they audit. *Independence in fact* refers to the CPAs' ability to maintain an objective and impartial mental attitude throughout the engagement. Second, the relationships between the CPAs and their clients must be such that the accountants will *appear independent* to third parties. If the attest function is to lend

---

[2]Interpretation 101–5 allows certain loans from financial institution clients. Those loans include (1) automobile loans and leases collateralized by the automobile, (2) loans of the surrender value under an terms of an insurance policy, (3) borrowings fully collateralized by cash deposits at the same financial institution (e.g., "passbook loans"), and (4) credit cards and cash advances on checking accounts up to $5,000. In addition, certain "grandfathered loans," outstanding when the interpretation was issued, are allowed (e.g., a home mortgage with a financial institution that subsequently becomes an audit client); these loans must be current as to all terms and may not be renegotiated.

credibility to financial statements, it is essential that readers of those statements *perceive* the CPAs as being objective and impartial.

### Applicability of the Independence Rule.

The independence rule does not apply to all services performed by public accountants. CPAs perform a host of services in which the client is the major beneficiary, such as management consulting, tax, and accounting services. In performing these services, the CPAs are not attesting to information for third parties, and *observance of the independence rule is not required.* Of course, the independence rule applies to auditing, but it also applies to all other attestation services, such as reviews of financial statements, examinations of financial forecasts, and the application of agreed-upon procedures to financial information. Our comments below regarding independence when performing audits apply equally to CPAs when they are performing any attestation service.

### Independence of Partners and Staff.

Must all employees of a CPA firm be independent of the client? No, the term *a member or a member's firm* as used in Interpretation 101–1 applies to (1) *all* partners (or stockholders) in the firm, (2) all managerial employees[3] *assigned to an office* that significantly participates in the engagement, and (3) all professional staff *personally participating* in the engagement. Thus, the independence of a large CPA firm is not necessarily impaired merely because one employee of the firm is not independent of the client. If the employee does not have managerial responsibilities, the problem can be resolved easily by assigning the employee to other engagements. If the employee does have managerial responsibilities, it will be necessary to transfer the employee to an office of the firm that is not significantly involved with the audit engagement.

### Financial Interests in Audit Clients.

Naturally, outsiders will question the auditors' impartiality if the auditors have a financial interest in the client's business. When a CPA firm acquires a new audit client,[4] all of the firm's partners, and the other professional staff indicated in the preceding section must be independent of the client. By disposing of such investments, the auditors avoid a challenge to their independence in dealing with the new client company.

### Direct and Indirect Financial Interests.

Interpretation 101–1 makes a distinction between direct and indirect financial interests. Any **direct financial interest** in an audit client impairs audit independence. A direct financial interest includes an investment in the client, such as owning capital stock and providing loans.

An auditor may have an **indirect interest** in an audit client if the investment is not material to the CPA's net worth. This distinction enables auditors to invest in companies or in mutual funds, which in turn may hold minor interests in audit clients.

---

[3]Loosely translated, the term **managerial employee** refers to professional staff at the rank of "manager" or above. Staff auditors, often called "assistants" and "seniors," are not "managerial employees."

[4]The period for which independence is required starts when the audit begins, and ends when the professional relationship has been terminated.

---

**◆ ILLUSTRATIVE CASE ◆**

John Bates, a partner in the CPA firm of Reynolds and Co., owns shares in a regulated mutual investment fund, which in turn holds shares of stock in audit clients of Reynolds and Co. The CPA firm inquired of the AICPA Professional Ethics Division whether this financial interest by Bates affected the firm's independence.

The response was that this indirect interest would not normally impair the independence of the CPA firm, because investment decisions are made only by the mutual fund's management. However, if the portfolio of the mutual fund were heavily invested in securities of a client of Reynolds and Co., the indirect interest could become material to Bates and thereby impair the independence of the CPA firm.

---

Past Employment with the Client.    Independence problems from financial interests, which are described in the first part of Interpretation 101–1, can be remedied simply by disposing of the financial interest before the engagement commences. This is not true of relationships described in part B of that Interpretation. CPAs who previously were employed by the client in a management capacity must disassociate themselves from that client and must not participate in audits of any periods during which they were employed by the client. The firm remains independent of the client (even if the individual is a partner), but the individual is not.

Interests of a CPA's Relatives.    Another question that often arises in discussions of independence may be stated as follows: How is independence affected by a financial interest or business position held by a relative of a CPA? The answer depends on the *closeness* of the family relationship and on whether the CPA works in a firm office that participates in the audit.

As a general rule, the financial interests and business relationships of a CPA's *spouse and dependents* (including relatives supported by the CPA) are attributed *directly to the CPA*. Accordingly, if the CPA's spouse owns even one share of a client's stock, the situation is evaluated as if the CPA owned the stock. That individual's independence is impaired. Is the firm's independence also impaired? Firm independence depends upon our earlier discussion of independence of partners and staff—independence is not impaired unless that individual is a partner, a managerial employee assigned to an office that significantly participates in the engagement, or a professional staff member who personally participates in the audit.

Certain business positions held by a spouse or a dependent are treated somewhat more leniently than the above general rule. Neither the individual's nor the firm's independence is impaired solely because of the employment of the CPA's spouse or dependent with an audit client, as long as the relative's position does not involve exercising **significant influence** over the client's operating, financial, or accounting policies.[5] However, if a

---

[5]Significant influence includes, for example, serving as an executive, operating, financial, or accounting officer, as a board of directors member, or as an underwriter for the client.

Figure 4-3    Effects of Relative Business and Financial Interests on Auditor Independence*

| Relative | General Rule | Major Exceptions |
|---|---|---|
| Spouse and dependents | Independence rules same as for CPA | Independence not impaired if relative is an employee of client, as long as the relative is not in a position of significant influence, and is not in an audit-sensitive position |
| Close relatives | Independence impaired when close relative has (1) a position of significant influence, (2) an audit-sensitive position, or (3) a material financial interest of which the CPA is aware | Partners may be transferred to another office if the problem involves (1); other professional staff and partners with a situation involving (2) or (3) must not be allowed to work on the engagement |
| Other relatives | Normally, no effect on independence | Independence may be impaired when circumstances (e.g., business and personal relationships) would lead a reasonable person to question the CPA's independence |

*This table applies to (1) all partners in the firm, (2) all managerial employees assigned to an office that significantly participates in the engagement, and (3) all professional staff personally participating in the engagement.

CPA's spouse or dependent is employed by the client in an audit-sensitive position[6] that CPA should not participate in the engagement.

Independence may also be impaired by financial interests or business relationships of other *close relatives,* such as parents, grandparents, parents-in-law, brothers, sisters, nondependent children, grandchildren, and their respective spouses. However, the financial interests of these relatives are not attributed directly to the CPA, and independence is impaired only by investments of which the CPA is aware that are material to the relative's net worth. None of the CPAs participating in the engagement can have a close relative that (1) has a material financial interest in the client of which the CPA is aware or (2) is employed by the client in a position of *significant influence* or an *audit-sensitive* position. In addition, a partner that has a close relative employed in a position of significant influence cannot be assigned to an office that significantly participates in the engagement. To avoid an impairment of independence, it is sometimes necessary to transfer a partner to an office that does not participate in a particular engagement.

Impairment of independence does not result from a business or financial interest of other relatives of a CPA, unless there are close personal or financial ties between the CPA and the relative. Figure 4-3 provides a brief summary of these complex independence requirements for relatives. But, staff members with potential problems should consult their firm's policies, as well as Independence *Interpretation 101-9* on family relationships.

Other Situations that May Impair Independence.   It is impossible to describe all the situations that impair the appearance of independence. Interpretations and Ethics Rulings are issued regularly describing the application of Rule 101 to new situations. For example,

---

[6]Examples of audit-sensitive positions include cashier, internal auditor, general accounting clerk, purchasing agent, or inventory warehouse supervisor.

rulings have been issued regarding cohabitation, past-due audit fees, gifts from clients, and client-auditor litigation.

A CPA's relationship with a cohabitant may be equivalent to that of a spouse. To assess the effects of such a relationship on independence, the CPA should consider the cohabitant's ability to act independently, and whether a reasonable person aware of all the facts would consider the relationship to be equivalent to that with a spouse. If so, the ethical restrictions apply.

If fees owed by a client to a CPA firm become long overdue, it may appear that the CPAs' prospects for collection depend upon the nature of the auditors' report on the current financial statements. Thus, independence is considered impaired if fees for professional services rendered in prior years have not been collected before issuance of the auditors' report for the current year.

An outsider may question the independence of a CPA firm in situations in which a partner or employee accepts an expensive gift from a client. It would appear that special considerations might be tied to the acceptance of the gift, and the auditor might not act with complete impartiality. To avoid this implication of a lack of independence, auditors should decline all but token gifts from audit clients.

Litigation involving the auditors and the client may also affect the independence of auditors. The relationship between the auditors and client management must be characterized by complete candor and full disclosure. A relationship with these characteristics may not exist when litigation places the auditors and client management in an adversary position. Auditors in litigation, or potential litigation, with a client must evaluate the situation to determine whether the significance of the litigation affects the client's confidence in the auditors or the auditors' objectivity.

Independence as Defined by the SEC.    A discussion of professional ethics would be incomplete without considering the important role played by the Securities and Exchange Commission. A principal aim of the Commission throughout its existence has been the improvement of auditing standards and the establishment of high levels of professional conduct by the independent public accountants practicing before the Commission.

The laws administered by the SEC require that financial statements be audited by certified public accountants. The Commission has established its own standards on auditor independence to supplement those of the AICPA. The following was adopted as part of Rule 2–01 of *Regulation S-X:*

---

The Commission will not recognize any certified public accountant . . . as independent who is not in fact independent. For example, an accountant will be considered not independent with respect to any person . . . (1) in which, during the period of his professional engagement to examine the financial statements being reported on or at the date of his report, he or his firm or a member thereof had, or was committed to acquire, any direct financial

*(continued)*

interest or any material indirect financial interest; or (2) with which, during the period of his professional engagement to examine the financial statements being reported on, at the date of his report or during the period covered by the financial statements, he or his firm or a member thereof was connected as a promoter, underwriter, voting trustee, director, officer, or employee. . . . For the purposes of Rule 2–01 the term "member" means all partners in the firm and all professional employees participating in the audit or located in an office of the firm participating in a significant portion of the audit.

In applying this rule to specific cases, the SEC has held that the public accountant was not independent in the following situations, among others:

1. A partner in an accounting firm also acted as legal counsel for the audit client.
2. An accounting firm performed the month-end accounting work of the audit client, including the making of adjusting and closing entries for the general ledger.
3. A partner of an accounting firm that audited a wholly owned subsidiary company invested in a nominal amount of stock of the subsidiary's nonclient parent company.

Independence When the Auditors Perform Accounting Services.   One difference between the concept of independence required by the SEC and that set forth in the AICPA *Code of Professional Conduct* relates to auditors who perform accounting services for a client. Can CPAs who post the general ledger, make closing entries, and maintain subsidiary records also serve as independent auditors for the company? The SEC answer is no; the CPAs are not independent under these circumstances. The auditors should be outsiders who review the work performed by the client's accounting employees. If independent auditors perform the original accounting work, they cannot maintain the posture of an outside critic. In *Financial Reporting Releases, Sec. 602,* the SEC states: "The Commission is of the opinion that an accountant cannot objectively audit books and records which he has maintained for a client."

The AICPA, on the other hand, has often considered the propriety of combining the performance of manual or automated accounting services with the conduct of an independent audit for a client but has not opposed the practice as damaging to the auditor's independence. As long as the client takes responsibility for the financial statements and the auditors perform their engagement in accordance with generally accepted auditing standards, the AICPA indicates that independence is not impaired. Of course, the accounting services cannot include executing transactions or performance of any other management function. If the AICPA ruled that independence is impaired whenever the auditors perform accounting services, such a ruling would no doubt be a blow to many small public accounting firms with practices including considerable write-up work and occasional audits for write-up clients.

> ◆ ILLUSTRATIVE CASE ◆
>
> The SEC found in one famous case (*In the Matter of Interstate Hosiery Mills, Inc.*, 4 SEC 706, 717 [1939]) that a staff member of the CPA firm had been maintaining the accounting records of a client; the financial statements had been falsified, and the audit staff member was responsible for the falsification. Clearly the dual role of internal accountant and independent auditor played by this individual had resulted in defeating the purpose of the audit.

**Does Rendering of Consulting Services Impair the Auditors' Independence?**    A problem to be considered in rendering consulting services is the possible threat to the auditors' independence when auditing and a variety of such services are performed for the same client. Can a public accounting firm that renders extensive *consulting services* for a client still maintain the independent status so essential in an audit and in the expression of an opinion on the client's financial statements?

A CPA who becomes a part-time controller for a client and assumes a *decision-making role* in the client's affairs is not in a position to make an independent audit of the financial statements. On the other hand, public accounting firms have long been rendering certain purely *advisory* services to management while continuing to perform audits in an independent manner that serves the public interest. Advisory services can generally be distinguished from management proper; the work of the consultant or adviser consists of such functions as conducting special studies and investigations, making suggestions to management, pointing out the existence of weaknesses, outlining various alternative corrective measures, and making recommendations.

**Independence—A Matter of Degree.**    The concept of independence is not absolute; no auditors can claim *complete* independence of a client. Rather, independence is relative—a matter of degree. As long as the auditors work closely with client management and are paid fees by their clients, complete independence can be considered merely an ideal. Auditors must strive for the greatest degree of independence consistent with their environment.

Recent developments have served to increase the auditor's independence in dealings with management. One of these developments is the widespread adoption of **audit committees** by corporations. Members of these audit committees are selected from the company's board of directors. Ideally, audit committee members are outside directors; that is, board members who are not also officers of the company. The functions of the audit committee include appointing and discharging the independent auditors, determining the scope of the auditors' services, reviewing audit findings, and resolving conflicts between the auditors and management.

## Rule 102—Integrity and Objectivity

> *In the performance of any professional service, a member shall maintain objectivity and integrity, shall be free of conflicts of interest, and shall not knowingly misrepresent facts or subordinate his or her judgment to others.*

## Analysis of Integrity and Objectivity

Rule 102 applies to all members of the AICPA and all services provided by CPAs. It recognizes that clients, employers, or others may at times attempt to influence the judgment of CPAs on professional matters. To maintain the confidence and respect of the public, CPAs must never subordinate their professional judgments to others.

It is often difficult to determine if an individual has "knowingly misrepresented facts." Thus in evaluating whether a CPA has violated that part of Rule 102, we must look to whether or not, based on the circumstances, the CPA *should have known* of the misrepresentation. A ruling that a CPA violated Rule 102 is most commonly based upon evidence that the auditors should have been knowledgeable of the facts.

## Rule 201 — General Standards

*A member shall comply with the following standards and with any interpretations thereof by bodies designated by Council.*

A. *Professional Competence. Undertake only those professional services that the member or the member's firm can reasonably expect to be completed with professional competence.*

B. *Due Professional Care. Exercise due professional care in the performance of professional services.*

C. *Planning and Supervision. Adequately plan and supervise the performance of professional services.*

D. *Sufficient Relevant Data. Obtain sufficient relevant data to afford a reasonable basis for conclusions or recommendations in relation to any professional services performed.*

## Analysis of General Standards

In addition to performing audits, CPAs also provide accounting, review, tax, and consulting services. Clients and the general public expect these services to be performed with competence and professional care. Therefore, the general standards of Rule 201 apply to *all CPA services.*

## Rule 202 — Compliance with Standards

*A member who performs auditing, review, compilation, management consulting, tax, or other professional services shall comply with standards promulgated by bodies designated by Council.*

## Analysis of Compliance with Standards

Rule 202 requires CPAs to adhere to professional standards issued by other technical bodies. To date, the Council of the AICPA has recognized five bodies and given them authority for the following performance standards:

| Technical Body | Authority | Performance Standards |
|---|---|---|
| Auditing Standards Board (ASB) | Prescribe auditing standards and responsibilities with respect to standards for disclosure of supplementary information outside the financial statements | *Statements on Auditing Standards* |
| Management Consulting Services Executive Committee (MCSEC) | Prescribe standards for management advisory services | *Statements on Standards for Consulting Services* |
| Accounting and Review Services Committee (ARSC) | Prescribe standards for unaudited financial information services for nonpublic companies | *Statements on Standards for Accounting and Review Services* |
| ASB, MCSEC, and ARSC | Prescribe attestation standards in their areas | *Statements on Standards for Attestation Engagements* |
| Financial Accounting Standards Board and Governmental Accounting Standards Board* | Prescribe disclosure standards for supplementary information outside the financial statements | *Statements of Financial Accounting Standards, Statements of Governmental Accounting Standards,* and related *Interpretations* |

*Rule 203 gives these bodies authority for accounting standards.

CPAs must become familiar with such statements and apply them to their engagements. To violate standards prescribed by these bodies is to violate Rule 202 of the Code.

Professional Standards for Consulting Services.   As indicated above, the AICPA's Management Consulting Services Executive Committee is authorized to issue *Statements on Standards for Consulting Services* to provide practitioners with authoritative guidance on providing consulting services to their clients. Consulting services are broadly defined by these standards to include virtually all services other than auditing and attestation services, accounting and review services, and tax services. To the general standards contained in Rule 201, these standards add the following additional requirements for these types of engagements:

1. *Client interest*. The practitioner should strive to meet the objectives of the client while maintaining integrity and objectivity.
2. *Understanding with client*. The practitioner should establish a written or oral understanding with the client about the nature, scope, and limitations of the consulting engagement.
3. *Communication with client*. The practitioner should inform the client of *(a)* any conflicts of interest that may occur with respect to the engagement, *(b)* any significant

reservations about the scope or benefits of the engagement, and *(c)* all significant findings or events.

## Rule 203—Accounting Principles

*A member shall not (1) express an opinion or state affirmatively that the financial statements or other financial data of any entity are presented in conformity with generally accepted accounting principles or (2) state that he or she is not aware of any material modifications that should be made to such statements or data in order for them to be in conformity with generally accepted accounting principles, if such statements or data contain any departure from an accounting principle promulgated by bodies designated by Council to establish such principles that has a material effect on the statements or data taken as a whole. If, however, the statements or data contain such a departure and the member can demonstrate that due to unusual circumstances the financial statements or data would otherwise have been misleading, the member can comply with the rule by describing the departure, its approximate effects, if practicable, and the reasons why compliance with the principle would result in a misleading statement.*

## Analysis of Accounting Principles

Rule 203 recognizes the authority of certain designated bodies to issue accounting principles. Under this rule, the AICPA has designated the *Statements* and *Interpretations* of the Financial Accounting Standards Board and the Governmental Accounting Standards Board as primary sources of generally accepted accounting principles. CPAs should not issue an unqualified opinion on a set of financial statements that materially depart from one of these pronouncements, except in the *rare* situation in which application of the pronouncement would result in misleading financial statements.

## Rule 301—Confidential Client Information

*A member in public practice shall not disclose any confidential client information without the specific consent of the client.*

   *This rule shall not be construed (1) to relieve a member of the member's professional obligations under rules 202 and 203, (2) to affect in any way the member's obligation to comply with a validly issued and enforceable subpoena or summons, (3) to prohibit review of a member's professional practice under AICPA or state CPA society authorization, or (4) to preclude a member from initiating a complaint with or responding to any inquiry made by a recognized investigative or disciplinary body.*

   *Members of a recognized investigative or disciplinary body and professional practice reviewers shall not use to their own advantage or disclose any member's confidential client information that comes to their attention in carrying out their official responsibilities. However, this prohibition shall not restrict the exchange of information with a recognized investigative or disciplinary body or affect, in any way, compliance with a validly issued and enforceable subpoena or summons.*

## Analysis of Confidential Client Information

Rule 301 stresses the confidential nature of information obtained by CPAs from their clients. The nature of accountants' work makes it necessary for them to have access to their clients' most confidential financial affairs. Independent accountants may thus gain insider knowledge of impending business combinations, proposed financing, prospective stock splits or dividend changes, contracts being negotiated, and other confidential information that, if disclosed or otherwise improperly used, could bring the accountants quick monetary profits. Of course, the client would be financially injured, as well as embarrassed, if the CPAs were to "leak" such information. Any loose talk by independent public accountants concerning the affairs of their clients would immediately brand them as lacking in professional ethics. On the other hand, the confidential relationship between the CPA and the client is *never* a justification for the CPA to cooperate in any deceitful act. The personal integrity of the CPA is essential to the performance of the attest function.

Confidentiality versus Privileged Communications.   The communications between CPAs and their clients are confidential, but they are not *privileged* under common law, as are communications with attorneys, clergymen, or physicians. The difference is that disclosure of legally privileged communications cannot be required by a subpoena or court order. Thus, auditors may be compelled to disclose their communications with clients in certain types of court proceedings. Some individual states, however, have adopted statutes providing that public accountants cannot be required by the state courts to give evidence gained in confidence from clients. Such state laws, however, do not apply to federal courts.

## Rule 302 — Contingent Fees

*A member in public practice shall not:*

1. *Perform for a contingent fee any professional services for, or receive such a fee from a client for whom the member or the member's firm performs:*
   a. *An audit or review of a financial statement; or*
   b. *A compilation of a financial statement when the member expects, or reasonably might expect, that a third party will use the financial statement and the member's compilation report does not disclose a lack of independence; or*
   c. *An examination of prospective financial information; or*
2. *Prepare an original or amended tax return or claim for a tax refund for a contingent fee for any client.*

   *The prohibition in (1) above applies during the period in which the member or the member's firm is engaged to perform any of the services listed above and the period covered by any historical financial statements involved in any such listed services.*

*Except as stated in the next sentence, a contingent fee is a fee established for the performance of any service pursuant to an arrangement in which no fee will be charged unless a specified finding or result is attained, or in which the amount of the fee is otherwise dependent upon the finding or result of such service. Solely for purposes of this rule, fees are not regarded as being contingent if fixed by courts or other public authorities, or, in tax matters, if determined based on the results of judicial proceedings or the findings of governmental agencies.*

*A member's fees may vary depending, for example, on the complexity of services rendered.*

## Analysis of Contingent Fees

An accountant is prohibited by Rule 302 from providing services on a contingent fee basis in certain circumstances. A CPA may not receive a contingent fee for the preparation of original or amended tax returns or claims for tax refunds. Preparation of a tax return includes giving advice on how particular items should be handled on the return. Also, no contingent fee engagements are allowed for *any* services performed for a client that also engages that CPA firm to perform financial statement audits, reviews or certain compilations, or examinations of prospective information. For example, consulting services may not be performed for a contingent fee for an audit client of the CPA firm.

The CPAs may perform services for contingent fees for clients for which none of the services listed in Rule 302 are performed. Consider a CPA firm with a prospective new client whose management requests assistance in redesigning its cash disbursements system. In such circumstances, if none of the listed services are provided for that client, the CPAs may perform the service for a contingent fee. For example, the CPAs may redesign the disbursements system and receive a fee that is contingent on the amount of cost savings realized by the client in processing future cash disbursements. The CPAs' fee might be, for example, 25 percent of the next four years' cost savings.

The contingent fee rule is the result of a consent agreement the AICPA entered into with the Federal Trade Commission—previously all fees considered contingent had been prohibited. Reviews and compilations of financial statements, and examinations of prospective information are discussed in detail in Chapter 19.

## Rule 501—Acts Discreditable

*A member shall not commit an act discreditable to the profession.*

## Analysis of Acts Discreditable

Rule 501 gives the AICPA the authority to discipline those members who act in a manner damaging to the reputation of the profession. The rule is not specific as to what constitutes a discreditable act; it is subject to interpretation. In the past, such acts as signing a false or misleading opinion or statement, committing a felony, and engaging in discriminatory employment practices have been interpreted to be violations of Rule 501.

One interesting practice that has been interpreted to be discreditable is failure to return client records. These situations generally arise when the CPAs have been discharged and not paid for their services. To refuse to return a client's ledger is clearly wrong, but what if the CPA retains working papers needed by the client? To enforce collection of a fee, some CPAs have refused to allow the client or the successor CPAs access to their working papers. Since the working papers are the CPAs' property, this is a legitimate business practice, not a violation of Rule 501. However, CPAs should be aware that when working papers provide the only support for entries in the client's financial records, those working papers should be made available to the client after the CPAs' fees have been paid.

## Rule 502—Advertising and Other Forms of Solicitation

*A member in public practice shall not seek to obtain clients by advertising or other forms of solicitations in a manner that is false, misleading, or deceptive. Solicitation by the use of coercion, overreaching, or harassing conduct is prohibited.*

## Analysis of Advertising and Other Forms of Solicitation

Until 1978, advertising by CPAs was strictly forbidden by the AICPA Rules. Most certified public accountants considered advertising in any form to be unprofessional. However, this prohibition was dropped because it was deemed a possible violation of the federal antitrust laws. Members of the public accounting profession may now advertise their services so long as the advertising is not false, misleading, or deceptive. Unethical advertising includes advertising that creates unjustified expectations of favorable results or indicates an ability to influence a court or other official body.

Acceptable advertising is that which is informative and based upon verifiable fact. Indications of the types of services offered, certificates and degrees of members of the firm, and fees for services are all acceptable forms of advertising.

## Rule 503—Commissions and Referral Fees

1. *Prohibited commissions.   A member in public practice shall not for a commission recommend or refer to a client any product or service, or for a commission recommend or refer any product or service to be supplied by a client, or receive a commission, when the member or the member's firm also performs for that client:*
   a. *An audit or review of a financial statement.*
   b. *A compilation of a financial statement when the member expects, or reasonably might expect, that a third party will use the financial statement and the member's compilation report does not disclose a lack of independence.*
   c. *An examination of prospective financial information.*
      *This prohibition applies during the period in which the member is engaged to perform any of the services listed above and the period covered by any historical financial statements involved in such listed services.*
2. *Disclosure of permitted commissions.   A member in public practice who is not prohibited by this rule from performing services for or receiving a commission and who is paid or expects to be paid a commission shall disclose that fact to any person or entity to whom the member recommends or refers a product or service to which the commission relates.*
3. *Referral fees.   Any member who accepts a referral fee for recommending or referring any service of a CPA to any person or entity or who pays a referral fee to obtain a client shall disclose such acceptance or payment to the client.*

## Analysis of Commissions and Referral Fees

Clients look to their CPAs for advice on the purchase of products and services, including services from other CPAs. Historically, CPAs have been prohibited from accepting a commission from the providers of such products and services. The consent agreement between the AICPA and the Federal Trade Commission, mentioned under Rule 302, allows CPAs to accept such commissions provided that they inform the client and do not provide any of the prohibited services. For example, CPAs that do not perform financial statement audits, reviews, or certain compilations or examinations of prospective information for a client, may receive commissions for purchasing and selling securities for that client, provided they disclose the existence of the commissions to the client.

## Rule 505—Form of Organization and Name

*A member may practice public accounting in a form of organization permitted by state law or regulation whose characteristics conform to resolutions of Council.*

*A member shall not practice public accounting under a firm name that is misleading. Names of one or more past owners may be included in the firm name of a successor organization. Also, an owner surviving the death or withdrawal of all other owners may continue to practice under a name which includes the name of past owners for up to two years after becoming a sole practitioner.*

*A firm may not designate itself as "Members of the American Institute of Certified Public Accountants" unless all of its owners are members of the Institute.*

## Analysis of Form of Organization and Name

In 1991, the membership of the AICPA voted to modify the *Code of Professional Conduct* to allow CPAs to practice in any legal business form. The revised Rule 505 allows CPAs to practice as professional corporations, limited liability companies (previously prohibited), partnerships, or sole practitioners.

Many state laws, as well as the *Code of Professional Conduct,* allow CPAs to form professional corporations. Professional corporations have certain tax advantages not available to partnerships, such as tax deductibility of pension and profit-sharing plans. The shareholders of professional corporations retain liability for acts of the corporation, regardless of whether they participated in the engagement resulting in the liability. Besides providing for financial liability, all corporate stock must be owned and control over professional matters must rest with individuals authorized to practice public accounting.

Currently, a number of states allow CPAs to practice in the form of a limited liability company. Although similar to professional corporations in many ways, limited liability companies protect the personal assets of any partner or shareholder not directly involved in providing services on engagements resulting in liability. Over the coming years one might expect more states to allow CPAs to form such limited liability companies to shield the personal assets of partners not involved on an engagement.

---

◆ ILLUSTRATIVE CASE ◆

Large malpractice lawsuits and economic conditions resulted in the 1990 bankruptcy of Leventhol & Horwath, the seventh largest CPA firm in the United States. Not only did the partners lose their investment in the firm, they found themselves personally liable for a portion of the partnership liabilities.

Previous versions of Rule 505 prohibited public accountants from practicing under a name that was fictitious or indicated a specialization. Because this prohibition was sensitive to antitrust attack, the revised Rule 505 allows fictitious names so long as they are not false, misleading, or deceptive. An example of a misleading firm name is where a partner surviving the withdrawal of all other partners continues to practice under the partnership name for longer than a two-year period. It is misleading for a sole practitioner to practice in a partnership name.

## The CPA as Tax Adviser—Ethical Problems

What is the responsibility of the CPA in serving as tax adviser? The CPA has a primary responsibility to the client; that is, to see that the client pays the proper amount of tax and no more. In the role of tax adviser, the certified public accountant may properly resolve questionable issues in favor of the client; the CPA is not obliged to maintain the posture of independence required in audit work. However, CPAs must adhere to the same standards of objectivity and integrity in tax work as in all other professional activities. Any departure from these standards on a tax engagement would surely destroy the reputation of certified public accountants in performing their work as independent auditors.

A second responsibility of CPAs on tax engagements is to the public, whose interests are represented by the government—more specifically by the Internal Revenue Service. To meet this responsibility, CPAs must observe the preparer's declaration on the tax returns they prepare. The declaration requires the preparer to state that the return is "true, correct, and complete . . . based on all information of which the preparer has any knowledge." To comply with this declaration, what steps must the CPA firm take to acquire knowledge relating to the tax return? The firm is not required to make an audit; knowledge of the return may be limited to information supplied to the firm by the client. However, if this information appears unreasonable or contradictory, the CPAs are obligated to make sufficient investigation to resolve these issues. Information that appears plausible to a layman might appear unreasonable to CPAs, since they are experts in evaluating financial data. CPAs are not obligated to investigate any and all information provided by the taxpayer, but they cannot ignore clues that cast doubt on the accuracy of these data.

In addition to being guided by the declaration on the tax return, CPAs should look to a series of pronouncements issued by the AICPA, entitled *Statements on Responsibilities in Tax Practice*. These statements address such questions as: Under what circumstances should a CPA sign the preparer's declaration on a tax return? What is the CPA's responsibility for errors in previously filed returns? Should CPAs disclose the taking of positions that differ from IRS interpretations of the tax code? The purpose of this series is to provide guidance to CPAs, and the statements are not directly enforceable under the *Code of Professional Conduct*.

## Enforcement of Professional Ethics

The AICPA and the state societies of CPAs have established a joint ethics enforcement plan. Under the plan, complaints about a CPA's conduct are first referred to the Professional Ethics Division of the AICPA for investigation. If the Professional Ethics Division finds the complaint to be valid, it may take several courses of action. For minor violations, the Division may take direct remedial action, such as requiring the member to get additional continuing education. More serious violations are turned over to the joint trial board for a hearing. If found guilty, the offending member may be censured, suspended from membership for up to two years, or expelled permanently from the AICPA. Although expulsion from the AICPA would not in itself cause the loss of a CPA's license, the damage to the CPA's professional reputation would be very substantial.

The provisions of the AICPA Rules have been used as a model by the boards of accountancy throughout the country to develop the ethical standards in their states. Thus, revocation of the CPA's license to practice also is a possible consequence of violation of the AICPA ethical standards.

# ETHICS FOR INTERNAL AUDITORS

Internal auditors, acting through their national organization, the Institute of Internal Auditors, have developed their own code of professional ethics. *The Institute of Internal Auditors Code of Ethics* is organized with an Introduction, an Interpretation of Principles, and 11 Articles. The Articles primarily address internal auditors' obligations to their employers, but they also include provisions that prescribe honesty, objectivity, competence, and morality in the practice of the internal auditing profession. Violation of the articles could result in revocation of the auditor's membership in the Institute of Internal Auditors or forfeiture of the auditor's "Certified Internal Auditor" designation. *The Institute of Internal Auditors Code of Ethics* is reproduced below.

## THE INSTITUTE OF INTERNAL AUDITORS CODE OF ETHICS

PURPOSE: A distinguishing mark of a profession is acceptance by its members of responsibility to the interests of those it serves. Members of The Institute of Internal Auditors (Members) and Certified Internal Auditors (CIAs) must maintain high standards of conduct in order to effectively discharge this responsibility. The Institute of Internal Auditors (Institute) adopts this *Code of Ethics* for Members and CIAs.

APPLICABILITY: This *Code of Ethics* is applicable to all Members and CIAs. Membership in The Institute and acceptance of the "Certified Internal Auditor" designation are voluntary actions. By acceptance, Members and CIAs assume an obligation of self-discipline above and beyond the requirements of laws and regulations.

The standards of conduct set forth in this *Code of Ethics* provide basic principles in the practice of internal auditing. Members and CIAs should realize that their individual judgment is required in the application of these principles.

CIAs shall use the "Certified Internal Auditor" designation with discretion and in a dignified manner, fully aware of what the designation denotes. The designation shall also be used in a manner consistent with all statutory requirements.

Members who are judged by the Board of Directors of The Institute to be in violation of the standards of conduct of the *Code of Ethics* shall be subject to forfeiture of their membership in The Institute. CIAs who are similarly judged also shall be subject to forfeiture of the "Certified Internal Auditor" designation.

## STANDARDS OF CONDUCT

I.  Members and CIAs shall exercise honesty, objectivity, and diligence in the performance of their duties and responsibilities.

II.  Members and CIAs shall exhibit loyalty in all matters pertaining to the affairs of their organization or to whomever they may be rendering a service. However, Members and CIAs shall not knowingly be a party to any illegal or improper activity.

III. Members and CIAs shall not knowingly engage in acts or activities which are discreditable to the profession of internal auditing or to their organization.

IV.  Members and CIAs shall refrain from entering into any activity which may be in conflict with the interest of their organization or which would prejudice their ability to carry out objectively their duties and responsibilities.

V.   Members and CIAs shall not accept anything of value from an employee, client, customer, supplier, or business associate of their organization which would impair or be presumed to impair their professional judgment.

VI.  Members and CIAs shall undertake only those services which they can reasonably expect to complete with professional competence.

VII. Members and CIAs shall adopt suitable means to comply with the *Standards for the Professional Practice of Internal Auditing*.

VIII. Members and CIAs shall be prudent in the use of information acquired in the course of their duties. They shall not use confidential information for any personal gain nor in any manner which would be contrary to law or detrimental to the welfare of their organization.

IX.  Members and CIAs, when reporting on the results of their work, shall reveal all material facts known to them which, if not revealed, could either distort reports of operations under review or conceal unlawful practices.

X.   Members and CIAs shall continually strive for improvement in their proficiency, and in the effectiveness and quality of their service.

XI.  Members and CIAs, in the practice of their profession, shall be ever mindful of their obligation to maintain the high standards of competence, morality, and dignity promulgated by The Institute. Members shall abide by the *Bylaws* and uphold the objectives of The Institute.

---

## ◆ CHAPTER SUMMARY

This chapter explained the need for professionals to adhere to high standards of professional conduct, and described the details of the codes of ethics that apply to both external and internal auditors. To summarize:

1.  Among the characteristics common to recognized professions are *(a)* acknowledgment of a responsibility to serve the public, *(b)* existence of a complex body of knowledge, *(c)* standards of admission to the profession, and *(d)* a need for public confidence.

2.  The membership of the AICPA has adopted a *Code of Professional Conduct,* consisting of two sections—Principles and Rules. In addition, the AICPA issues *Interpretations* and *Ethics Rulings* to provide further guidance on appropriate ethical conduct.

3.  Independence is required when CPAs perform audits and other types of attest engagements. Interpretation 101–1 provides guidance on various financial and business relationships that may impair a CPA's independence. That standard prohibits all direct financial interests in a client, as well as material indirect financial interests. The independence standards apply to all partners, all managerial employees assigned to an

office that significantly participates in an engagement, and all professional staff personally participating in the engagement.

4. The Rules of the AICPA *Code of Professional Conduct* set forth the professional standards that must be followed by CPAs when performing various types of professional services. For example, Rule 202 requires auditors to adhere to generally accepted auditing standards, as interpreted by *Statements on Auditing Standards*. Accounting standards of the FASB and the GASB are enforced by Rule 203.

5. In performing an audit, the auditors have access to the details of the client's most confidential information. If the auditors disclosed this information, they might damage their clients' businesses. Therefore, CPAs are required to maintain a strict confidentiality relationship with their clients.

6. CPAs generally may accept engagements for contingent fees and receive commissions for referrals, but only if the CPAs do not also provide certain attestation or compilation services for the client.

7. A CPA firm may practice public accounting in any form of organization permitted by state law or regulation, including as a sole practitioner, partnership, professional corporation, or limited liability company.

8. The *Code of Ethics* of the Institute of Internal Auditors primarily addresses internal auditors' obligations to their employees, but it also includes provisions requiring honesty, objectivity, competence, and morality in the practice of internal auditing.

## ◆ KEY TERMS INTRODUCED OR EMPHASIZED IN CHAPTER 4

**Audit committee**   A committee of a corporation's board of directors that engages independent auditors, reviews audit findings, monitors activities of the internal auditing staff, and intervenes in any disputes between management and the independent auditors. Preferably, members of the audit committee are outside directors, that is, members of the board of directors who do not also serve as corporate officers.

**Audit-sensitive position**   A position in which the activities are normally an element of, or subject to, significant internal controls. Examples include cashier, internal auditor, general accounting clerk, purchasing agent, or inventory warehouse supervisor.

**Direct financial interest**   A personal investment under the direct control of the investor. The *Code of Professional Conduct* prohibits CPAs from having any direct financial interests in their audit clients. Investments made by a CPA's spouse or dependent child also are regarded as direct financial interests of the CPA.

**Ethics Rulings**   Pronouncements of the AICPA that explain the application of Rules and Interpretations of the *Code of Professional Conduct* to specific factual circumstances involving professional ethics.

**Independence**   A most important Rule of Conduct that prohibits CPAs from performing attestation services for an enterprise unless they are independent with respect to such enterprise; independence is impaired by a financial interest, service as an officer or trustee, loans to or from the enterprise, and various other relationships.

**Indirect financial interest**   An investment in which the specific investment decisions are not under the direct control of the investor. An example is an investment in a professionally managed mutual fund. The *Code of Professional Conduct* allows CPAs to have indirect financial interests in audit clients, as long as the investment is not material in relation to the CPA's net worth.

**Interpretations of Rules**   Guidelines issued by the AICPA for the scope and application of the Rules of Conduct.

**Managerial employee**   A professional employee who either has a position generally similar to that of a partner or has a management position. Loosely translated, the term refers to professional staff at the rank of ''manager'' or above.

**Principles of the Code**   The part of the AICPA *Code of Professional Conduct* that expresses the profession's responsibilities to the public, clients, and colleagues, and provides a framework for the Rules.

**Profession**   An activity that involves a responsibility to serve the public, has a complex body of knowledge, has standards for admission, and has a need for public confidence.

**Prospective financial information**   Presentations of future financial position, results of operations, or cash flows. Such presentations are often referred to as financial forecasts or projections.

**Rules**   A group of enforceable ethical standards included in the AICPA *Code of Professional Conduct*.

**Significant influence (over the operating, financial, or accounting policies of an entity)**   Examples of positions that are able to exert significant influence include serving as an executive, operating, financial or accounting officer, as a board of directors member, or as an underwriter for the client.

## ◆ GROUP I: REVIEW QUESTIONS

4-1  What is the basic purpose of a code of ethics for a profession?

4-2  Briefly describe the two parts of the AICPA *Code of Professional Conduct*.

4-3  In Chapter 2, the 10 generally accepted auditing standards were discussed. How does the AICPA *Code of Professional Conduct* relate, if at all, to these 10 generally accepted auditing standards?

4-4  Explain how a CPA might have an indirect financial interest in an audit client. Does the AICPA *Code of Professional Conduct* prohibit such interests?

4-5  Identify the circumstances under which a CPA may *not* perform professional services on a contingent fee basis?

4-6  Bill Scott works as a manager in the Phoenix office of an international CPA firm. His father has just taken a position as a purchasing agent for one of the CPA firm's Phoenix clients. Has Bill's independence been impaired with respect to this audit client? Has the CPA firm's independence been impaired if Bill does not work on the audit?

4-7  Three months ago, a national CPA firm hired Greg Scott to work as a staff auditor in its New York office. Yesterday Scott's father was hired to be the chief financial officer of one of the CPA firm's New York clients. Has the independence of the CPA firm with respect to this client been impaired?

4-8  Sara Kole, CPA, has been requested by the president of Noyes Company, a closely held corporation and audit client, to cosign Noyes Company checks with the Noyes treasurer when the president is away on business trips. Would Kole violate the AICPA *Code of Professional Conduct* if she accepted this request? Explain.

4-9  Sandy Schultz, CPA, has performed a consulting services job in which she made recommendations which ultimately resulted in one of her audit clients purchasing a computer manufactured by the AMZ Computer Corporation. Shortly thereafter, Ms. Schultz was surprised when she received a $1,000 unsolicited commission from AMZ Computer Corporation. Would acceptance of this commission violate the AICPA *Code of Professional Conduct?* Explain.

4-10   How do the positions of the SEC and the AICPA differ with respect to the independence of a CPA who performs routine accounting services for a client?

4-11   What bodies are given authority to issue performance standards under Rule 202 of the AICPA *Code of Professional Conduct?* What authoritative standards does each body issue?

4-12   Arthur Brown is a CPA who often serves as an expert witness in court cases. Is it proper for Brown to receive compensation in a damage suit based on the amount awarded to the plaintiff? Discuss.

4-13   Laura Clark, wife of Jon Clark, CPA, is a life insurance agent. May Jon Clark refer audit clients needing officer life insurance to Laura Clark or to another life insurance agent who will share a commission with Laura Clark? Explain.

4-14   Must a CPA maintain independence and an impartial mental attitude when preparing a client's income tax return? Explain.

4-15   In what organizational forms may CPAs practice public accounting?

4-16   Comment on the following: When performing a consulting engagement for a client, a CPA may perform any services that the client requests.

4-17   In preparing a client's income tax return, a CPA feels that certain expenses are unreasonably high and probably are overstated. Explain the CPA's responsibilities in this situation.

4-18   "Since internal auditors are employees, they have no ethical responsibilities to others beyond their employers." Comment on this statement.

# ◆ GROUP II: QUESTIONS REQUIRING ANALYSIS

4-19   Sally Adams, CPA, is an auditor with a large CPA firm. Her husband, Steve Adams, plans to accept a position as controller of Coast Corporation, an audit client of Sally's firm. Comment upon whether the CPA firm's independence will be impaired assuming that Sally Adams is:
   *a.*   A senior in the CPA firm.
   *b.*   A partner in the CPA firm.

4-20   Tracy Smith, CPA, is in charge of the audit of Olympic Fashions, Inc. Seven young members of the CPA firm's professional staff are working with Smith on this engagement, and several of the young auditors are avid skiers. Olympic Fashions owns two condominiums in Aspen, Colorado, which it uses primarily to entertain clients. The controller of Olympic Fashions has told Smith that she and any of her audit staff are welcome to use the condominiums at no charge any time that they are not already in use. How should Smith respond to this offer? Explain.

4-21   Harris Fell, CPA and member of the AICPA, was engaged to audit the financial statements of Wilson Corporation. Fell had half-completed the audit when he had a dispute with the management of Wilson Corporation and was discharged. Hal Compton, CPA, was promptly engaged to replace Fell. Wilson Corporation did not compensate Fell for his work to date; therefore, Fell refused to allow Wilson Corporation's management to examine his working papers. Certain of the working papers consisted of adjusting journal entries and supporting analysis. Wilson Corporation's management had no other source of this information. Did Fell violate the AICPA *Code of Professional Conduct?* Explain fully.

4-22   Select the best answer for each of the following. Explain the reasons for your selection.
  *a.* In which of the following situations would a CPA firm have violated the AICPA *Code of Professional Conduct* in determining its fee?
   (1) A fee is based on whether or not the CPA firm's audit report leads to the approval of the client's application for bank financing.
   (2) A fee is to be established at a later date by the Bankruptcy Court.
   (3) A fee is based upon the nature of the engagement rather than upon the actual time spent on the engagement.
   (4) A fee is based on the fee charged by the client's former auditors.
  *b.* According to the AICPA's ethical standards, an auditor would be considered independent in which of the following instances?
   (1) The auditor's checking account, which is fully insured by the Federal Deposit Insurance Corporation, is held at a client financial institution.
   (2) A managerial employee of the auditor donates service as vice president of a charitable organization that is a client.
   (3) The client owes the auditor fees for this and last year's annual audits.
   (4) The auditor's five year old son owns stock in a client.
  *c.* Which of the following is implied when a CPA signs the preparer's declaration on a federal income tax return?
   (1) The return is not misleading based on all information of which the CPA has knowledge.
   (2) The return is prepared in accordance with generally accepted accounting principles.
   (3) The CPA has audited the return.
   (4) The CPA maintained an impartial mental attitude while preparing the return.
  *d.* The AICPA *Code of Professional Conduct* states that a CPA shall not disclose any confidential information obtained in the course of a professional engagement except with the consent of the client. This rule may preclude a CPA from responding to an inquiry made by:
   (1) An investigative body of a state CPA society.
   (2) The trial board of the AICPA.
   (3) A CPA-shareholder of the client corporation.
   (4) An AICPA voluntary quality review body.
  *e.* Pursuant to the AICPA rules of conduct, if a partner in a two-member partnership dies, the surviving partner may continue to practice as an individual under the existing firm title which includes the deceased partner's name:
   (1) For a period of time *not* to exceed five years.
   (2) For a period of time *not* to exceed two years.
   (3) Indefinitely.
   (4) Until the partnership payout to the deceased partner's estate is terminated.
  *f.* Bill Adams, CPA, accepted the audit engagement of Kelly Company. During the audit, Adams became aware of his lack of competence required for the engagement. What should Adams do?
   (1) Disclaim an opinion.
   (2) Issue an adverse opinion.
   (3) Suggest that Kelly Company engage another CPA to perform the audit.
   (4) Rely on the competence of client personnel.

(AICPA, adapted)

# ◆ GROUP III: PROBLEMS

4-23  The firm of McGraw and West, CPAs, has two offices, one in Phoenix and one in San Diego. The firm has audited the Cameron Corporation out of its Phoenix office for the past five years. For each of the following independent cases which occurred during the year under audit, indicate whether the independence of either (1) the firm or (2) the CPA involved would be impaired.

   *a.* Mary McGraw, a partner in the San Diego office, fell wildly in love with Bill Smith, the treasurer for Cameron Corporation. They were married in Las Vegas. During the week McGraw still lives in San Diego and works in that office, while Bill Smith lives in Phoenix, working for Cameron. On weekends they commute to their home in Yuma. Mary does not participate in the engagement.

   *b.* Jim West is the father of Will West, a Phoenix partner. Jim West has a material investment in Cameron. Will West is unaware of his father's investment, but does participate in the engagement.

   *c.* Bill Johnson, a senior in the San Diego office, has a material investment in the capital stock of Cameron. He does not participate in the engagement.

   *d.* Sandra Steversen, a staff assistant in the Phoenix office, works on the Cameron audit. Her uncle works as the chief accounting officer for Cameron.

4-24  Donald Westerman is president of Westerman Corporation, a manufacturer of kitchen cabinets. He has been approached by Darlene Zabish, a partner with Zabish and Co., CPAs, who suggests that her firm can design a payroll system for Westerman which will either save his corporation money, or be free. More specifically, Ms. Zabish proposes to design a payroll system for Westerman on a contingent fee basis. She suggests that her firm's fee will be 25 percent of the savings in payroll for each of the next four years. After four years Westerman will be able to keep all future savings. Westerman Corporation's payroll system costs currently are approximately $200,000 annually, and the corporation has not previously been a client of Zabish.

   Westerman discussed this offer with his current CPA, Bill Zabrinski, whose firm annually audits Westerman Corporation's financial statements. Zabrinski states that this is a relatively simple task, and that he would be willing to provide the service for $30,000.

*Required:*  *a.* Would either Zabish or Zabrinski violate the AICPA *Code of Professional Conduct* by offering to provide these services? Explain.

   *b.* Now assume that Westerman has indicated to Zabrinski that he was leaning toward accepting Zabish's offer. Zabrinski then offered to provide the service for 15 percent of Westerman's savings for the next three years. Would performing the engagement in accordance with the terms of this offer violate the AICPA *Code of Professional Conduct?* Explain.

4-25  James Daleiden, CPA, is interested in expanding his practice through acquisition of new clients. For each of the following independent cases, indicate whether Daleiden would violate the AICPA *Code of Professional Conduct* by engaging in the suggested practice and explain why. If more information is needed to arrive at a final determination indicate the nature of such information.

   *a.* Daleiden wishes to form a professional corporation and use the name AAAAAAAA the CPAs, so as to obtain the first ad in the yellow pages of the telephone book.

   *b.* Daleiden wishes to prepare a one page "flyer" which he will have his son stuff on the windshields of each car at the Pleasant Valley shopping mall. The "flyer" will outline the services provided by Daleiden's firm and will include a $50 off coupon for services provided on the first visit.

   *c.* Daleiden has a thorough knowledge of the tax law. He has a number of acquaintances who prepare their own tax returns. He proposes to offer to review these returns before they are filed with the Internal Revenue Service. For this review, he will charge no fee unless he is able to identify legal tax savings opportunities. He proposes to charge each individual one third of the tax savings he is able to identify.

d. Daleiden and his associates audit a number of municipalities. He proposes to contact other CPAs and inform them of his interest in obtaining more of these types of audits. He offers a $500 "finder's fee" to CPAs who forward business to him.

4-26  The firm of Bell & Greer, CPAs, has been asked to audit Trek Corporation for the year ended December 31, Year 5. Bell & Greer has two offices: one in Los Angeles and the other in Newport Beach. Trek Corporation would be audited by the Los Angeles office. For each of the following independent cases, indicate whether Bell & Greer would be independent with respect to Trek Corporation and explain why.

a. A partner in the Los Angeles office of Bell & Greer has been a long-time personal friend of the chief executive officer of Trek Corporation.

b. The former controller of Trek Corporation became a partner in the Newport Beach office of Bell & Greer on March 15, Year 5, resigning from Trek Corporation on that date.

c. A managerial employee in the Newport Beach office of Bell & Greer is the son of the treasurer of Trek Corporation.

d. A partner in the Newport office of Bell & Greer jointly owns a cattle ranch in Montana with one of the directors of Trek Corporation. The value of the investment is material to both parties.

e. Trek Corporation has not yet paid Bell & Greer for professional services rendered in Year 4. This fee is substantial in amount and is now 15 months past due.

4-27  Roland Company, a retail store, has utilized your services as independent auditor for several years. During the current year, the company opened a new store, and in the course of your annual audit, you verify the cost of the fixtures installed in the new store by examining purchase orders, invoices, and other documents. This review brings to light an understated invoice nearly a year old in which a clerical error by the supplier, Western Showcase, Inc. caused the total of the invoice to read $28,893.62 when it should have read $82,893.62. The invoice was paid immediately upon receipt without any notice of the error, and subsequent statements and correspondence from Western Showcase, Inc. showed that the account with Roland Company had been paid in full. Assume that the amount in question is material in relation to the financial position of both companies.

*Required:*  a. What action should you take in this situation?

b. If the client should decline to take any action in the matter, would you insist that the unpaid amount of $54,000 be included in the liabilities shown on the balance sheet as a condition necessary to your issuance of an unqualified audit report?

c. Assuming that you were later retained to make an audit of Western Showcase, Inc., would you utilize the information gained in your examination of Roland Company to initiate a reopening of the account with that company?

4-28  Auditors must not only appear to be independent; they must also be independent in fact.

*Required:*  a. Explain the concept of an "auditor's independence" as it applies to third-party reliance upon financial statements.

b. (1)  What determines whether or not an auditor is independent in fact?

  (2)  What determines whether or not an auditor appears to be independent?

c. Explain how an auditor may be independent in fact but not appear to be independent.

d. Would Joe Marks, a CPA, be considered independent for an audit of the financial statements of a:

    (1)   Church for which he is serving as treasurer without compensation? Explain.

    (2)   Women's club for which his wife is serving as treasurer-accountant if he is not to receive a fee for the audit? Explain.

**4-29**   An audit client, March Corporation, requested that John Day, CPA, conduct a feasibility study to advise management of the best way the corporation can use electronic data processing equipment and which computer, if any, best meets the corporation's requirements. Day is technically competent in this area and accepts the engagement. Upon completion of Day's study the corporation accepts his suggestions and installs the computer and related equipment that he recommended.

*Required:*   *a.*   Discuss the effect that acceptance of this consulting services engagement would have upon John Day's independence in expressing an opinion on the financial statements of March Corporation.

    *b.*   A local company printing data processing forms customarily offers a commission for recommending it as a supplier. The client is aware of the commission offer and suggests that Day accept it. Would it be proper for Day to accept the commission with the client's approval? Discuss.

**4-30**   Thomas Gilbert and Susan Bradley formed a professional corporation called "Financial Services Inc.—A Professional Corporation," each taking 50 percent of the authorized common stock. Gilbert is a CPA and a member of the AICPA. Bradley is a CPCU (Chartered Property Casualty Underwriter). The corporation performs auditing and tax services under Gilbert's direction and insurance services under Bradley's supervision.

    One of the corporation's first audit clients was Grandtime Company. Grandtime had total assets of $600,000 and total liabilities of $270,000. In the course of his examination, Gilbert found that Grandtime's building with a carrying value of $240,000 was pledged as collateral for a 10-year-term note in the amount of $200,000. The client's financial statements did not mention that the building was pledged as collateral for the 10-year-term note. However, as the failure to disclose the lien did not affect either the value of the assets or the amount of the liabilities, and his examination was satisfactory in all other respects, Gilbert rendered an unqualified opinion on Grandtime's financial statements. About two months after the date of his opinion, Gilbert learned that an insurance company was planning to loan Grandtime $150,000 in the form of a first-mortgage note on the building. Realizing that the insurance company was unaware of the existing lien on the building, Gilbert had Bradley notify the insurance company of the fact that Grandtime's building was pledged as collateral for a term note.

    Shortly after the events described above, Gilbert was charged with several violations of professional ethics.

*Required:*   Identify and discuss at least four ethical implications of those acts by Gilbert that were in violation of the AICPA *Code of Professional Conduct*.

---

## ◆ GROUP IV: RESEARCH AND DISCUSSION CASE

**4-31**   You are the Partner-in-Charge of a large metropolitan office of a regional CPA firm. Two members of your professional staff have come to you to discuss problems that may affect the firm's independence. Neither of these situations has been specifically answered by the AICPA Professional Ethics Division. Therefore, you must reach your own conclusions as to what to advise your staff members, and what actions, if any, are to be taken by the firm.

    *Case 1:* Don Moore, a partner in the firm, has recently moved into a condominium which he shares with his girlfriend, Joan Scott. Moore owns the condominium and pays all of the expenses relating to its maintenance. Otherwise, the two are self-supporting. Scott is a stockbroker, and recently she has started acquiring shares in one of the audit clients of this office of the CPA firm. The shares are held in Scott's name. At present, the shares are not material in relation to her net worth.

*Case 2:* Mary Reed, a new staff auditor with no managerial responsibilities in the firm, has recently separated from her husband. Mary has filed for divorce, but the divorce cannot become final for at least five months. The property settlement is being bitterly contested. Mary's husband has always resented her professional career and has just used community property to acquire one share of common stock in each of the publicly owned companies audited by the office in which Mary works.

*Required:*   For each case, you are to:

a.  Set forth arguments indicating that the firm's independence has *not* been impaired.
b.  Set forth arguments indicating that the firm's independence has been impaired.
c.  Express your personal opinion. Identify those arguments from parts *(a)* or *(b)* that you found most persuasive. If you believe that the firm's independence has been impaired, make suggestions as to how the problem might be resolved.

## ◆ SUGGESTED REFERENCE

AICPA, *Professional Standards, Volume 2,* Commerce Clearing House, Section ET 101. (*Code of Professional Conduct,* Rule 101).

# LEGAL LIABILITY OF AUDITORS

## CHAPTER OBJECTIVES

After studying this chapter, you should be able to:

* Define the major legal concepts that relate to auditors' liability.

* Distinguish between auditors' liability under common law and their liability under statutory law.

* Explain the factors that must be proven by clients and third parties to be successful in actions against the auditors under common law and the auditors' defenses.

* Contrast liability under the Securities Act of 1933 and the Securities Exchange Act of 1934.

* Describe accountants' legal liability for accounting and review services.

W e live in an era of litigation, in which persons with real or fancied grievances are likely to take their complaints to court. In this environment, investors and creditors who suffer financial reversals find auditors, as well as attorneys and corporate directors, tempting targets for lawsuits alleging professional "malpractice." Auditors must approach every engagement with the prospect that they may be required to defend their work in court. Even if the court finds in favor of the auditors, the costs of defending a legal action can be astronomical. As a result, the cost of professional liability insurance has escalated at an alarming rate.

Costs are not the only concern in this area; lawsuits can be extremely damaging to a professional's reputation. In extreme cases, the auditors may even be tried criminally for malpractice. Every man and woman considering a career in public accounting should be aware of the legal liability inherent in the practice of this profession.

## Unique Vulnerability of Accountants to Lawsuits

The potential liability of CPAs to persons who might be injured as a result of improper professional practice greatly exceeds that of physicians or any other group of professionals. A reason for this is the large potential number of injured parties. If a physician or an attorney is negligent, the injured party usually consists only of the professional's patient or client. If a CPA is negligent in expressing an opinion on financial statements, literally millions of investors may sustain losses.

---

**♦ ILLUSTRATIVE CASE ♦**

The severity of the legal liability problem facing the accounting profession may be viewed from several different perspectives. First, the chairman of one of the "Big 6" CPA firms estimates that "Big 6" firms are currently spending approximately 10 percent of their revenues from audit and accounting services on litigation costs and settlements. This amount is more than $55,000 per partner per year.

As a further indication, the chairman of another "Big 6" firm describes a lawsuit which went to trial against his firm for an audit with fees of approximately $20,000. Although the firm successfully defended itself in court, the cost of defending the firm was approximately $6 million.

Finally, a vice president of a major insurance company stated in *The Wall Street Journal* that his company no longer is willing to insure accounting firms for liability. The company continues to insure engineers, architects, attorneys, physicians, and surgeons. "The risks aren't as great," the vice president observed.

---

Juries have awarded amounts in excess of $200 million to parties in several lawsuits against CPA firms. While these lawsuits represent the extreme examples that were eventually resolved for lessor amounts, the amounts paid exceeded the limits of the CPA firms' professional liability insurance.

# Definition of Terms

Discussion of auditors' liability is best prefaced by a definition of some of the common terms of business law. Among these are the following:

**Negligence,** also referred to as **ordinary** or **simple negligence,** is violation of a legal duty to exercise a degree of care that an ordinary prudent person would exercise under similar circumstances. For the CPA, negligence is failure to perform a duty in accordance with applicable standards. For practical purposes, negligence may be viewed as "failure to exercise due professional care."

**Gross negligence** is the lack of even slight care, indicative of a **reckless disregard** for one's professional responsibilities. Substantial failures on the part of an auditor to comply with generally accepted auditing standards might be interpreted as gross negligence.

**Fraud** is defined as misrepresentation by a person of a material fact, known by that person to be untrue or made with reckless indifference as to whether the fact is true, with the intention of deceiving the other party and with the result that the other party is injured. Rule 102 of the AICPA's *Code of Professional Conduct* (discussed in Chapter 4) states that a member of the AICPA shall not knowingly misrepresent facts. A CPA found to have violated this provision of Rule 102 might be sued for fraud by the client or another injured party.

**Constructive fraud** differs from fraud as defined above in that constructive fraud does not involve a misrepresentation with intent to deceive. Gross negligence on the part of an auditor has been interpreted by the courts as constructive fraud.

*Privity* is the relationship between parties to a contract. A CPA firm is in privity with the client it is serving, as well as with any third-party beneficiary.

A **third-party beneficiary** is a person—not the promisor or promisee—who is named in a contract or intended by the contracting parties to have definite rights and benefits under the contract. For example, if Warren & Co., CPAs, is engaged to examine the financial statements of Arthur Company and to send a copy of its audit report to Third National Bank as support for a loan, the bank is a third-party beneficiary under the contract between Warren & Co. and Arthur Company.

An *engagement letter* is the written contract summarizing the contractual relationships between auditor and client. The engagement letter typically specifies the scope of professional services to be rendered, expected completion dates, and the basis for determination of the CPAs' fee. Engagement letters will be discussed more fully in Chapter 7.

*Breach of contract* is failure of one or both parties to a contract to perform in accordance with the contract's provisions. A CPA firm might be sued for breach of contract, for example, if the firm failed to perform the engagement in accordance with the engagement letter. Negligence on the part of the CPAs also constitutes breach of contract.

*Proximate cause* exists when damage to another is directly attributable to a wrongdoer's act. The issue of proximate cause may be raised as a defense in litigation. Even though a CPA firm might have been negligent in rendering services, it will not be liable for the *plaintiff's* loss if its negligence was not the proximate cause of the loss.

The *plaintiff* is the party claiming damages and bringing suit against the *defendant.*

*Contributory negligence* is negligence on the part of the plaintiff that has contributed to his or her having incurred a loss. Contributory negligence may be used as a defense, because the court may limit or bar recovery by a plaintiff whose own negligence contributed to the loss.

*Comparative negligence* is a concept used by certain courts to allocate damages between negligent parties based on the degree to which each party is at fault.

**Common law** is unwritten law that has developed through court decisions; it represents judicial interpretation of a society's concept of fairness. For example, the right to sue a person for fraud is a common-law right.

**Statutory law** is law that has been adopted by a governmental unit, such as the federal government. CPAs must concern themselves particularly with the federal securities acts and state blue-sky laws. These laws regulate the issuance and trading of securities.

## Litigation Placed in Perspective

As we discuss auditors' liability for negligence, gross negligence, and fraud, there may be a tendency to conclude that CPAs are often careless in rendering professional services. This is simply not the case. The overwhelming majority of engagements are completed successfully by CPAs without any allegations of improper conduct. However, in any endeavor as complex as auditing, it is inevitable that some mistakes will be made. Any large CPA firm that performs thousands of audits will, at one time or another, find that it has issued an unqualified report on financial statements that were, in some respect, misleading. Also, investors who have sustained large losses become desperate to recover their losses by any means possible. Thus, if bringing suit against a company's CPAs offers even the most remote chance of recovery, the injured parties are likely to initiate legal action.

CPAs must recognize occasional allegations of misconduct as a fact of life. Some of the lawsuits brought against CPAs will be frivolous—desperate attempts by plaintiffs to recover their losses. Others will have some basis in fact—judgmental errors made by the CPAs during the engagement. No matter how careful CPAs are, any CPA firm may find itself as a defendant in litigation.

An injured party may elect to bring suit against auditors under common law or, if applicable statutes exist, under statutory law. When there is a choice, the plaintiff will select the form of suit that has the best prospects for success. Since the federal Securities Acts allow class-action lawsuits, in which an entire class of investors becomes the plaintiff in a single legal action, and hold auditors to very strict standards, most lawsuits against auditors by stockholders or bondholders in publicly owned corporations are brought under these statutes.

Notice in our definitions of terms that *negligence, gross negligence,* and *fraud* each represent different *degrees of improper performance* by the CPAs. The extent to which the CPAs' services are found to be improper determines the parties to whom the CPAs are liable for losses proximately caused by their improper actions. Liability may arise from improper performance on any type of engagement—an audit, tax services, accounting services, or consulting services. However, CPAs are *never liable to any party* if they perform their services with *due professional care*. Having exercised due professional care is a *complete defense* against any charge of improper conduct.

# AUDITORS' LIABILITY TO THEIR CLIENTS UNDER COMMON LAW

When CPAs take on any type of engagement, they are obliged to render due professional care. This obligation exists whether or not it is specifically set forth in the written contract with the client. Thus, CPAs are liable to their clients under common law for any losses proximately caused by the CPAs' *failure to render due professional care*. In short, *ordinary negligence* is a sufficient degree of misconduct to make CPAs liable for damages caused to their clients.

Auditors' liability to clients most often arises from a failure to uncover an embezzlement or defalcation being perpetrated against the client by client employees. A client who has sustained such losses may allege that the auditors were negligent in not uncovering the scheme and sue the auditors for the amount of the loss. The key factor in determining whether the auditors are liable is *not* just whether the auditors failed to uncover fraud. Rather, the issue is whether this failure *stems from the auditors' negligence*.

In Chapter 2 we discussed the auditor's responsibility for detecting **errors** and **irregularities.** Auditors must design their audits to provide *reasonable assurance* of detecting errors and irregularities that are material to the financial statements. In doing so, they must exercise due care and professional skepticism in planning, performing, and evaluating the results of audit procedures.

These requirements *do not imply* that auditors were negligent whenever errors or irregularities are later found to exist in audited financial statements. An audit has certain limitations; it does not involve a complete and detailed examination of all records and transactions. To do so would entail a prohibitive cost, which would certainly not be warranted under ordinary business conditions. There can never be absolute assurance that errors or irregularities do not exist among the transactions not included in the CPAs' test. Also, the possibility exists that the documents have been so skillfully forged, or other irregularities so expertly concealed, that the application of normal auditing techniques would not reveal the irregularities. When a CPA firm's audit *has been made in accordance with generally accepted auditing standards,* the firm *should not be held liable* for failure to detect the existence of errors or irregularities.

## Lawsuits by Clients

To obtain a judgment against its auditors, an injured client must prove that it sustained a loss as a result of the auditors' negligence. As defendants, the auditors can refute this claim by showing that either (1) they were not negligent in the performance of their duties, or (2) their negligence was not the proximate cause of the client's loss. Demonstrating *contributory negligence* by the client is one means of showing that the auditors' negligence was not the cause (or sole cause) of the client's loss. In some jurisdictions, a defense of contributory negligence will entirely eliminate the auditors' liability to their client. In others, the concept of *comparative negligence* is used to allocate damages between the client and the auditors based on the extent to which each is at fault.

---

◆ ILLUSTRATIVE CASE ◆

Calvert Roth, CPA, has audited the financial statements of Metro Bank for the last five years. At the conclusion of each audit, Roth has suggested improvements in Metro Bank's internal controls over consumer loans. However, Metro's management failed to make the recommended improvements in internal controls. Recently, it was discovered that Harold Kay, a loan officer, had embezzled funds through the creation of fictitious consumer loans. Metro Bank filed suit against Roth for negligence in the performance of his audits. By means of expert testimony by other CPAs, it was established that Roth had been negligent in the performance of the last two audits. The court concluded that if Roth had performed his audit work adequately, there was a reasonable chance that the defalcations would have been detected. However, the court also concluded that Metro Bank's management was negligent in not carrying out the suggested improvements in internal control. Following the principle of *comparative negligence,* management of the bank was found to be 80 percent at fault, and Roth was found to be 20 percent at fault. Thus, Roth was held liable for only 20 percent of the losses of Metro Bank.

---

# AUDITORS' COMMON-LAW LIABILITY TO THIRD PARTIES

Clients have recourse against auditors for damages caused by an improper audit because of rights under their contract with the auditors. But what about the many third parties who rely upon audited financial statements? How may these parties recover their losses from auditors who have performed an improper audit?

Legal actions under common law require the plaintiffs to bear most of the burden of affirmative proof. Thus, a third party seeking damages from a CPA firm must prove that it sustained loss, that the party relied upon audited financial statements that were misleading, that this reliance was the proximate cause of its losses, and that the auditors were guilty of a certain degree of negligence. The auditors named as defendants in a common-law action are in the position of having to refute the charges brought by the plaintiffs.

The degree of negligence required to establish the auditors' liability to third parties under common law varies from one jurisdiction (e.g., state) to another. Three general approaches may be used to summarize auditors' liability to third parties under common law in the various state courts—*Ultramares, Restatement of Torts,* and *Rosenblum.*

## *Ultramares* Approach

The most widely cited common-law **precedent** stems from the landmark case, **Ultramares v. Touche & Co.** (1931). In this case, the defendant CPAs issued an unqualified opinion on the balance sheet of a company engaged in the importation and sale of rubber. On the basis of the CPAs' opinion, Ultramares, a factor, made several loans to the company. Shortly thereafter, the company was declared bankrupt, and Ultramares sued the CPAs for ordinary negligence. The New York Court of Appeals (the state's highest court) ruled that the CPAs should be held liable for *ordinary negligence* only to their client and any third party (beneficiary) specifically identified as a user of the CPAs' report. The court went on to indicate that the auditors should be held liable to *unidentified* third-party users of the audit report for *gross negligence or fraud*. In the *Ultramares* case, the audit was performed "primarily for the benefit" of the client; Ultramares was not specifically identified as a user of the audit report. Therefore, to recover its losses, Ultramares would have been required to prove that the CPAs were grossly negligent in performing their audits. The case eventually was settled out of court, with no determination as to whether the auditors had been grossly negligent.

The *Ultramares* precedent has been reaffirmed and interpreted in many subsequent cases. These cases have clarified the conditions necessary for parties to be considered to be *third-party beneficiaries* of the audit. For example, the New York Court of Appeals upheld and interpreted the *Ultramares* precedent in the case of **Credit Alliance Corp. v. Arthur Andersen & Co.** (1985). The court stated that before the auditors may be held liable for ordinary negligence to a third party: (1) the auditors must have *been aware* that the financial statements were to be used for a particular purpose by a *known party or parties,* and (2) *some action* by the auditors must indicate that knowledge. The Ultramares approach to third-party liability is often called the *privity approach* to auditor liability.

## Restatement of Torts Approach

The principle of auditor liability for ordinary negligence to a limited class of foreseen third parties is supported by the American Law Institute's *Second Restatement of the Law of Torts,* which guides many court common-law rulings. The *Restatement of Torts* approach, also referred to as the foreseen third-party approach, expands the auditors' liability for ordinary negligence to include third parties of a limited class of known or intended users of the audited financial statements. *The specific identity of these third parties need not be known to the CPA.* The courts in many states have followed this principle, including a court in Rhode Island in the leading case of *Rusch Factors, Inc.* v. *Levin* (1968). In that case, the CPAs were found liable for ordinary negligence to a third party that subsequently provided financing to the audit client. The third party had *not* been specifically identified to the CPAs, although they were aware that the financial statements were to be used to help obtain the financing.

---

◆ ILLUSTRATIVE CASE ◆

Dianne Holiday, CPA, performed the audit of Lyman Corporation for the year ended December 31. Holiday was aware that Lyman intended to use the audit report to obtain a bank loan. However, no specific bank was identified to Holiday. After the report was issued, Lyman obtained loans from the First National Bank and Dime Box State Bank. Also, Wallace Manufacturing Co. relied on Holiday's opinion in providing trade credit to Lyman. If the court applied the principles contained in the *Second Restatement of the Law*

*(continued)*

of Torts, Holiday could be held liable to First National and Dime Box if she were found guilty of ordinary negligence in the performance of her audit. The banks form a limited class of third parties who could be foreseen to rely on the audit report. Wallace Manufacturing Co., on the other hand, would have to prove *gross negligence* on the part of Holiday to recover its losses. The audit was not performed for the use of trade creditors; therefore, Wallace would not be considered a part of a limited class of foreseen parties.

## *Rosenblum* Approach

In 1983, the New Jersey Supreme Court rejected both the *Ultramares* and *Restatement of Torts* approaches and established a very different standard in the case of **Rosenblum v. Adler.** In this case, the defendant CPAs issued an unqualified report on the financial statements of Giant Stores Corporation which showed the corporation to be profitable. In reliance upon these statements, Rosenblum sold a catalog showroom business to Giant in exchange for shares of Giant's stock. Shortly afterward, Giant filed for bankruptcy and the stock became worthless. Rosenblum sued Giant's CPAs, alleging ordinary negligence. The case was dismissed by the trial court, on the premise that the CPAs were not liable to unidentified third parties for ordinary negligence. However, the New Jersey Supreme Court reversed the lower court, finding that CPAs *can* be held liable for ordinary negligence to any third party the auditors could "reasonably foresee" as recipients of the statements for routine business purposes. This approach, also referred to as the foreseeable third-party approach, has the potential effect of expanding CPA liability to third parties whose purposes are totally unknown to the CPAs.

Common-law cases are decided, in large part, by reference to established precedents—that is, past decisions. The *Ultramares, Restatement of Torts,* and *Rosenblum* approaches create conflicting precedents as to which third parties can hold the auditors liable for ordinary negligence. Variants of each of these approaches exist in the various states. Presumably, courts within New York and New Jersey will adhere to the standard established by their respective highest courts. The standard likely to be applied in other jurisdictions, however, is less certain. The *Rosenblum* approach, which has subsequently been embraced by courts in other states, has certainly opened the door to auditors being held liable under common law to virtually all third parties for ordinary negligence.

## LABILITY TO THIRD PARTIES UNDER STATUTORY LAW

Statutory law is written law, created by state or federal legislative bodies. Most states have "blue-sky" laws, which regulate the issuance and trading of securities within the state. The two most important federal laws relating to auditors' liability are the **Securities Act of 1933** (1933 Act) and the **Securities Exchange Act of 1934** (1934 Act). Surprisingly, CPAs must also be concerned with the application of the Racketeer Influenced and Corrupt Organizations Act (RICO). Even though our discussion of statutory law will be limited to these three federal acts, CPAs need to be familiar with the other laws administered by the SEC, and the "blue-sky" laws in those states in which their clients sell securities.

Courts have much less discretion in deciding statutory cases than common-law cases. Common law is unwritten and evolves from court decisions. In deciding a common-law case, a court may even depart from past decisions and create a new legal precedent, as was done in *Rosenblum* v. *Adler*. In deciding a statutory case, however, the court interprets the law exactly as it is written.

# Securities Act of 1933

The 1933 Act requires a company intending to offer its securities for sale to the public to first file a **registration statement** with the SEC.[1] This registration statement includes audited financial statements, and numerous other disclosures. The 1933 Act states that both the company filing the registration statement and its auditors may be held liable to the initial purchasers of the securities in the event that the registration statement is found to contain material misstatements or omissions.[2] The wording of Section 11(a) of the Act on this point is as follows:

> In case any part of the registration statement, when such part became effective, contained an untrue statement of a material fact or omitted to state a material fact required to be stated therein or necessary to make the statements therein not misleading, any person acquiring such security (unless it is proved that at the time of such acquisition he knew of such untruth or omission) may . . . sue . . .

**Plaintiffs' Rights under the 1933 Act.**   The 1933 Act offers protection to only a limited group of investors—those who initially purchase a security (stock or bond) offered for sale to the public. For those investors, however, the 1933 Act shifts much of the burden of proof from the plaintiff to the defendant. The plaintiffs (security purchasers) need only prove that (1) they sustained a loss and (2) the registration statement was misleading. They *need not* prove that they relied upon the registration or that the auditors were negligent.[3]

**Auditors' Defenses under the 1933 Act.**   If auditors are to avoid liability for the plaintiffs' losses, they generally must affirmatively prove that (1) they conducted the audit with **due diligence,** (2) the plaintiffs' losses were not caused by misstated financial statements, or (3) the plaintiff knew of the financial statement misstatement when the securities were purchased.[4]

---

[1]The 1933 Act requires registration statements to be filed by any company that will offer securities for sale to the public through the mails or interstate commerce. There are certain exceptions, for example, for charitable institutions and other not-for-profit organizations, and for offerings of small dollar amounts.

[2]The auditors are liable for misstatements or omissions in only those portions of the registration statement covered by their audit and report.

[3]An exception exists in that the plaintiff must prove reliance when the security was purchased at least 12 months after the effective date of the registration statement.

[4]Action must be brought against the auditors within one year from discovery of the false statement or omission or, if earlier, within three years after the security was offered to the public.

As a practical matter, it is the due diligence defense which auditors often raise. Section 11 of the act states that the auditors are not liable if they

> had, after reasonable investigation, reasonable ground to believe and did believe, at the time . . . the registration statement became effective, that the statements therein were true and that there was no omission to state a material fact. . . .

Stated in approximate terms, the auditors must prove that they were not negligent. The 1933 Act establishes the highest level of auditor responsibility for justifying their performance. Not only are the auditors liable for losses caused by acts of ordinary negligence, but they must *prove their innocence* rather than merely refute the accusations of the plaintiffs.

*Escott* v. *BarChris Construction Corporation.*  A significant case involving auditors' liability under the Securities Act of 1933 was the *BarChris* case. *Escott* v. *BarChris Construction Corporation,* 283 F. Supp. 643 (1968), was an action under Section 11 of the Securities Act of 1933 undertaken by purchasers of BarChris's registered debentures against the directors, underwriters, and independent auditors of BarChris. Subsequent to issuance of the debentures, BarChris, a builder of bowling alleys, became bankrupt. The plaintiffs claimed that the registration statement for the debentures contained materially false statements and material omissions; the defendants all countered with the due diligence defense. The court found that the registration statement (Form S-1) was false and misleading and that with a few exceptions none of the defendants had established their due diligence defense. The court also found that the CPA firm had failed to comply with generally accepted auditing standards. The court was especially critical of the CPA firm's conduct of the S-1 review, so called because it is an investigation carried out by the CPA firm some time after completion of the audit, but just prior to the effective date of the registration statement filed with the SEC. In an S-1 review, the CPAs look for any evidence arising since their audit that indicates that the registration statement is misleading as filed. The court criticized the CPA firm for performing too limited a review and with being "too easily satisfied with glib answers by management" to inquiries.

## Securities Exchange Act of 1934

The 1934 Act requires all companies under SEC jurisdiction to file audited financial statements with the SEC.[5] The act also creates potential liability for the filing company and its auditors to anyone who buys or sells the company's securities in the event that these annual statements are found to be misleading. Remember that the 1933 Act creates liability only to those investors who originally purchase the security at a public offering. The 1934 Act expands coverage to subsequent purchasers and sellers of the stock. The two primary liability sections of the act are Sections 10 and 18.

---

[5]Companies under SEC jurisdiction include those (1) whose securities are listed on a national stock exchange, or (2) with equity securities traded on the over-the-counter market, and total assets exceeding $5 million and 500 or more stockholders.

Section 10, with Rule 10b-5 promulgated by the SEC under Section 10(b) of the act reads as follows:

> It shall be unlawful for any person, directly or indirectly, by the use of any means or instrumentality of interstate commerce or of the mails, or of any national securities exchange . . .
>
>   (1) to employ any device, scheme, or artifice to defraud,
>   (2) to make any untrue statement of a material fact or to omit to state a material fact necessary in order to make the statements . . . not misleading, or
>   (3) to engage in any act, practice, or course of business which operates or would operate as a fraud or deceit upon any person, in connection with the purchase or sale of any security.

Section 18(a) of the 1934 Act, which relates to misstated financial statements, provides for liability to:

> . . . any person (not knowing that such statement was false or misleading) who, in reliance upon such statement, shall have purchased or sold a security at a price which was affected by such statement, for damages by such reliance, *unless the person sued shall prove that he acted in good faith* and had no knowledge that such statement was false or misleading. [Emphasis added.]

Plaintiffs Rights under the 1934 Act.   The 1934 Act offers protection to both original and subsequent purchasers and sellers of securities. Under both Sections 10 and 18 the plaintiffs (security purchasers and sellers) must prove that (1) they sustained a loss, (2) the financial statements were misleading, and (3) they relied upon the financial statements. Section 10(b) and Rule 10b-5, as interpreted by the landmark *Hochfelder* v. *Ernst* case, requires that the plaintiffs prove **scienter** (intent to deceive, manipulate, or defraud) on the part of the auditors. Section 18(a) states that plaintiffs may recover from defendants who are unable to prove that they "acted in good faith."

Auditors' Defenses under the 1934 Act.   The auditors' primary defense under Section 10 is that scienter does not exist. That is, they will attempt to refute charges that they have performed the audit with the intent to deceive, manipulate, or defraud. Under Section 18, the auditors may avoid liability by proving "good faith," which they will normally be able to establish unless they have been guilty of gross negligence or fraud. In addition, to avoid liability for the plaintiffs' losses under either Section 10 or 18, the auditors may establish that the losses were caused by other factors.

*Hochfelder* v. *Ernst*.   As indicated above, this case was a landmark case for auditor liability under the Securities Exchange of 1934. The suit was brought by a group of investors against the CPA firm that for 21 years had audited the financial statements of First Securities Company of Chicago, a small brokerage firm. The president of First

Securities, who was also its majority stockholder, committed suicide, leaving a note stating that the firm was insolvent and disclosing a fraud that he had perpetrated upon several investors. The president had persuaded the investors to mail him their personal checks, the funds from which he was to invest in escrow accounts yielding high returns to the investors. There were no such escrow accounts in the accounting records of First Securities Company; instead, the president diverted the investors' checks to his own use immediately upon receipt.

The investors filed suit under SEC Rule 10b-5 (and the related Securities Exchange Act of 1934 Section 10[b]) against the CPA firm, charging it with *ordinary negligence,* and thus with responsibility for the investors' losses in the fraud. The plaintiffs did *not accuse the CPA firm of fraud or intentional misconduct.*

The basis for the plaintiffs' charge of negligence was that the CPA firm failed to discover a weakness in First Securities Company's internal control that enabled the company's president to carry on the fraud. The control weakness, called the "mail rule," was the president's policy that *only he* could open mail addressed to him at First Securities, or addressed to First Securities to his attention. (It is common practice at financial institutions for *all* incoming mail to be opened in the mailroom, in part to avoid the possibility of employees' perpetrating some type of fraud.)

The U.S. district court which heard the case dismissed it, holding that there was no issue of material fact as to whether the CPA firm had conducted its audits of First Securities in accordance with generally accepted auditing standards. The U.S. Court of Appeals reversed the district court and ruled that the CPA firm was liable for damages for aiding and abetting the First Securities president's fraud because the CPA firm had breached its duty of inquiry and disclosure regarding the First Securities internal control weakness.

The U.S. Supreme Court reversed the court of appeals, deciding that an action for damages under Section 10(b) of the 1934 Act and the related SEC Rule 10b-5 was not warranted in the absence of *scienter* on the auditors' part. In the Court's opinion, Mr. Justice Powell wrote:

> The words "manipulative or deceptive" used in conjunction with "device or contrivance" strongly suggest that (Section) 10(b) was intended to proscribe knowing or intentional misconduct.
>
> \*   \*   \*   \*   \*
>
> When a statute speaks so specifically in terms of manipulation and deception, and of implementing devices and contrivances—the commonly understood terminology of intentional wrongdoing—and when its history reflects no more expansive intent, we are quite unwilling to extend the scope of the statute to negligent conduct.

## Comparison of the 1933 and 1934 Acts

The 1933 Act holds the auditors to a higher standard of performance than does the 1934 Act, but its protection is offered to fewer third parties. The 1933 Act offers recourse only to the *initial* purchasers of securities, whereas the 1934 Act offers recourse to *any* person buying or selling the securities at a later date.

The 1933 Act holds the auditors liable for acts of *ordinary negligence*. Following the *Hochfelder* decision, the 1934 Act creates liability for gross negligence and fraud, but not for ordinary negligence.

In comparison to common law, both of the federal Securities Acts shift significant burdens of proof from the plaintiffs to the defendants. However, some differences exist between the defendant's burden under the 1933 and 1934 Acts. Under the 1933 Act, plaintiffs *need not prove reliance* upon the audited financial statements; it is left to the defendant to show that misstatements in the financial statements were not the proximate cause of the plaintiffs' losses. The 1934 Act, however, generally requires plaintiffs to prove that they relied upon the misleading statements.

Next, both acts place the burden of proving adequate performance on the defendants. The 1933 Act requires the auditors to prove "due diligence"—that is, that they were *not negligent*. The 1934 Act is more lenient in that the CPAs must only prove that they "acted in good faith," meaning that they were *not grossly negligent*. The "good faith" defense is considerably easier to establish than is "due diligence."

## The Racketeer Influenced and Corrupt Organizations Act

In 1970, Congress enacted the Racketeer Influenced and Corrupt Organizations Act (RICO) to be a potent weapon against mobsters and racketeers who were influencing legitimate business. A discussion of RICO would appear to be out of place in a discussion of legal liability of auditors. However, the act broadly defines the term *racketeering activities* to include crimes such as mail fraud and fraud in the sale of securities. In prior years, these provisions have been used successfully in a small number of cases against CPAs in which it could be shown that the CPAs knew, or perhaps should have known, of material misstatements of financial statements when the problems were indicative of a pattern of improper activity. A primary concern with the RICO act is the provision that allows triple damages in civil cases brought under the act.

The recent favorable ruling by the U.S. Supreme Court in the case of *Reves* v. *Ernst & Young* has relieved some of the concern. In that case, the court decided that the accountants cannot be held liable under the RICO act unless they actually participated in the operation or management of the organization.

## Auditors' Civil Liability: A Summary

The auditors' civil liability under common law and under the federal Securities Acts is summarized in Figure 5–1. Notice that under certain circumstances auditors may be held liable to any third party—not just to clients—for losses attributable to acts of ordinary negligence. In common-law cases brought by third parties, the extent of the auditors' liability may vary depending upon the state (jurisdiction) in which the suit is filed.

## Auditors' Criminal Liability under the Securities Acts

Both the Securities Act of 1933 and the Securities Exchange Act of 1934 include provisions for *criminal charges* against CPAs who willfully (knowingly) allow misstatements in SEC filings. These provisions are found in Section 24 of the Securities Act of 1933 and Section 32(a) of the Securities Exchange Act of 1934. In addition, in extreme cases CPAs

**Figure 5–1**   Summary of Auditors' Civil Liability

| Plaintiff (Injured Party) | Suit Brought Under | Burden of Proof for: | |
|---|---|---|---|
| | | **Plaintiff** | **Defendant Auditor** |
| Client | Common law | Loss<br>Auditor negligence<br>Reliance on auditors' representations<br>Proximate cause | None[a] (unless defense is based on proving contributory negligence on the part of the plaintiff) |
| Third-party beneficiary | Common law | Loss<br>Auditor negligence<br>Reliance on auditors' report<br>Proximate cause | None[a] (unless defense is based on proving other causes for the plaintiff's losses) |
| Limited class of foreseen third parties | Common law | Loss<br>Auditor negligence<br>or<br>Auditor gross negligence[b]<br>Reliance on auditors' report<br>Proximate cause | None[a] (unless defense is based on proving other causes for the plaintiff's losses) |
| Other foreseeable third parties | Common law | Loss<br>Auditor negligence<br>or<br>Auditor gross negligence [c]<br>Reliance on auditors' reports<br>Proximate cause | None[a] (unless defense is based on proving other causes for the plaintiff's losses) |
| Initial purchaser of security in a public company | Securities Act of 1933 | Loss<br>Financial statements were misleading | Due diligence<br>and/or<br>Not proximate cause (loss caused by other factors) |
| Any purchaser or seller of a security in a public company | Securities Exchange Act of 1934 | Loss<br>Financial statements were misleading<br>Reliance on statements<br>Scienter by auditor (Section 10) | Acted in good faith (Section 18)<br>and/or<br>Not proximate cause (loss caused by other factors) |

[a]Under common law, the entire burden of proof is borne by the plaintiff, as the defendant is presumed innocent until proven guilty. The defendant will actively participate in the case, however, by introducing evidence to refute the plaintiff's allegations.
[b]In states that have adopted the *Ultramares* approach to auditor liability to third parties.
[c]In states that have adopted the *Ultramares* approach or the *Restatement of Torts* approach to auditor liability to third parties.

can be prosecuted under the criminal provisions of the Racketeer Influenced and Corrupt Organizations Act.

The *Continental Vending Machine Corporation* case was accompanied by a celebrated criminal case involving three members of the CPA firm that audited Continental's financial statements. The criminal charges rocked the profession, because there was no intent to defraud on the part of the CPAs; they were convicted of criminal fraud on the basis of gross negligence. The verdict of guilty was affirmed by a U.S. Court of Appeals, and the U.S. Supreme Court refused to review the case. The three CPAs were later pardoned by the president of the United States.

The principal facts of the *Continental Vending* case (*United States* v. *Simon,* 425 F.2d 796 [1969]) are as follows. The U.S. government's case of fraud against the three CPAs hinged upon a note to Continental's audited financial statements, which read:

---

The amount receivable from Valley Commercial Corp. (an affiliated company of which . . . [Continental's president] is an officer, director, and stockholder) bears interest at 12 percent a year. Such amount, less the balance of the notes payable to that company, is secured by the assignment to the Company of Valley's equity in certain marketable securities. As of . . . [the date of the auditors' report] . . . the amount of such equity at current market quotations exceeded the net amount receivable.

---

The note did not disclose—and the auditors were aware—that the affiliated company had loaned approximately that same amount to Continental's president. The president was unable to repay the affiliate, which was unable to repay Continental. In addition, most of the collateral furnished by the president was stock and convertible debentures of Continental itself.

The auditors' defense in this case was that the note complied with existing generally accepted accounting principles. Eight "leaders of the profession" testified as expert witnesses that the note was consistent with generally accepted accounting principles and the audit was performed in accordance with generally accepted auditing standards. However, the judge rejected this argument and instructed the jury to evaluate whether the financial statements were "fairly presented" without reference to generally accepted accounting principles. The finding by the jury that the balance sheet did not present fairly Continental's financial position led to conviction of the three CPAs.

Because the *Continental Vending* case involved both criminal and civil proceedings, it has significant implications for the public accounting profession. Not only is civil liability an ever-present hazard for CPAs, but criminal charges may also be involved.

## The SEC's Regulation of Accountants

The SEC has issued rules for the appearance and practice of CPAs, attorneys, and others before the Commission under the statutes it administers. Rule of Practice 2(e), giving the SEC the power of suspension and disbarment, has the following wording:

---

The Commission may deny, temporarily or permanently, the privilege of appearing or practicing before it in any way to any person who is found by the Commission . . . (1) not to possess the requisite qualifications to represent others, or (2) to be lacking in character or integrity or to have engaged in unethical or improper professional conduct.

---

On occasion, the Commission has taken punitive action against public accounting firms when it has found the audit work deficient with regard to financial statements filed with the Commission. These actions against public accounting firms usually arise when a listed corporation encounters financial difficulties and it later appears that misleading financial statements had served to conceal for a time the losses being incurred by the company. In recent years, the SEC has taken action against CPA firms by the use of consent decrees in which the CPAs have agreed to certain penalties or restrictions. For example, a CPA firm may agree under pressure from the SEC not to accept new SEC clients during a specified period and to permit a review of its practice.

## Accountants' Liability for Accounting and Review Services

Up to this point, we have emphasized the liability of CPA firms when they are associated with audited financial statements. In addition, CPAs may perform many accounting services, such as write-up work and **compilations** of unaudited financial statements. These services differ from audits in that the CPAs neither perform the investigative procedures involved in an audit nor do they issue an auditors' opinion as to the fairness of the financial information.

The term *compilation* refers to the *preparation* of financial statements based upon information provided to the CPA by the client (or the client's representatives). A compilation is *not intended to lend any assurance* to any party that the CPA has determined the information to be reliable. A **review** consists of *limited* investigative procedures, *substantially less in scope than an audit,* designed to provide users of the unaudited financial statements with a *limited* degree of assurance as to the statements' reliability. Compilations and reviews are discussed in Chapter 19.

Do CPAs associated with unaudited financial statements have any potential legal liability? The answer is *yes.* The CPAs, acting as *accountants* rather than as *auditors,* still have a liability to their client to exercise due professional care. In addition, they still may be liable under common law for losses to third parties attributable to the accountants' ordinary or gross negligence.

### Accountants or Auditors?

Accountants or Auditors?    When CPAs are associated with unaudited financial statements, a possibility exists that the client or third parties may misinterpret the extent of their services and believe that the accountants actually are acting as auditors.

The risks to CPA firms engaged in the preparation of unaudited financial statements were brought sharply into focus by the *1136 Tenants' Corporation* v. *Rothenberg* case. In this common-law case, an incorporated apartment cooperative, which was owned by its shareholder-tenants and managed by a separate realty agent, orally retained a CPA firm for a period of 17 months to perform certain services, including the preparation of financial statements for the cooperative. The CPA firm's fee was to be only $600 per year.

The CPA firm submitted financial statements of the corporation for one full year and the first six months of the following year. The financial statements bore the notation "subject to comments in letter of transmittal." The referenced letter of transmittal read in part:

> Pursuant to our engagement, we have reviewed and summarized the statements of your managing agent and other data submitted to us by . . . [the agent], pertaining to 1136 Tenants' Corporation. . . .
>
> The following statements were prepared from the books and records of the Corporation. No independent verifications were undertaken thereon. . . .

The client corporation later sued the CPA firm for damages totaling $174,000 for the CPAs' alleged failure to discover defalcations of the corporation's funds committed by the managing agent. The client contended that the CPAs had been retained to render all necessary accounting *and auditing* services for it. The CPAs maintained they had been engaged to do write-up work only, although a working paper they had prepared supporting accrued expenses payable in the balance sheet included an entry for "audit expense."

The New York state trial court ruled in favor of the plaintiff in this common-law case, as did the Appellate Court of New York. The latter found that the CPAs' working papers indicated that the CPAs had examined the client's bank statements, invoices, and bills, and had made notations in their working papers concerning "missing invoices." The New York Court of Appeals affirmed the decision.

In summary, the court held the CPAs liable because it found that they had led their client to believe that they were performing an audit. Consequently, the courts held the CPAs responsible for performing their work in accordance with generally accepted auditing standards, which they clearly had not done. More importantly, however, the court also concluded that the CPAs had a duty to follow up on significant problems (the missing invoices) uncovered during their engagement. Thus, it is probable that the CPA firm would have been held liable to its client *even if the court had recognized that the firm was not performing an audit*. Whenever CPAs encounter evidence that their client may be sustaining a loss through embezzlement or other irregularities, they should warn the client immediately.

There are several lessons for CPA firms in the *1136 Tenants' Corporation* case:

1.  CPAs who prepare unaudited financial statements should adhere closely to Rules of Conduct 102 and 202 of the AICPA's *Code of Professional Conduct*. Rule 102 states that a CPA shall not knowingly misrepresent facts, and Rule 202 requires a CPA firm to comply with professional standards, including standards for accounting and review services. The actions of the CPA firm described in the preceding paragraph might be construed as violating both rules.

2.  Engagement letters are as essential for accounting and review services as they are for independent audits. Oral arrangements for accounting and review services are of scant assistance when there is a dispute as to the nature of the services to be rendered by the CPA firm to the client.

3.  A CPA engaged to perform *accounting* or *review* services should be alert for, and follow up on, such unusual items as missing invoices. As professionals, CPAs are bound to exercise *due professional care*, even though their engagements do not include independent audits of the client's financial statements.

4.  CPAs should report on financial statements clearly and concisely, using as far as possible the standardized language set forth in *Statements on Auditing Standards* and *Statements on Standards for Accounting and Review Services*. Reports should indicate the nature of the services rendered and the degree of responsibility being assumed by the CPA firm.

## The CPAs' Posture in the Age of Litigation

In addition to the preceding court cases, numerous other actions against CPAs, under both common law and the Securities Acts, are pending trial. It is apparent that lawsuits will continue to plague the public accounting profession, as they have the legal and medical professions. The question thus is: What should be the CPAs' reaction to this age of litigation?

In the opinion of the authors, positive actions helpful to CPAs in withstanding threats of possible lawsuits include the following:

1.  Greater emphasis upon compliance with the public accounting profession's generally accepted auditing standards and *Code of Professional Conduct*. Close analysis of the court cases and other actions described in this chapter discloses numerous instances in which the auditors appear not to have complied fully with one or more auditing standards and Rules of Conduct.

2.  Retaining legal counsel that is familiar with CPAs' legal liability. The CPAs should thoroughly discuss all potentially dangerous situations with their legal counsel and should carefully consider their counsel's advice.

3.  Maintenance of adequate liability insurance coverage. Although liability insurance coverage should not be considered a substitute for the CPAs' compliance with the preceding recommendations, public accountants must protect themselves against possible financial losses from lawsuits. Adequate liability insurance is essential.

4.  Thorough investigation of prospective clients. As indicated in preceding sections of this chapter, many court cases involving CPAs have been accompanied by criminal charges against top management of the CPAs' clients. CPAs should use great care in screening prospective clients to avoid the risks involved in professional relationships with the criminally inclined.

5.  Obtaining a thorough knowledge of the client's business. One of the major causes of audit failures has been a lack of understanding by auditors of the client's business and of industry practices.

6.  Use of engagement letters for all professional services. Controversies over what services are to be rendered by a CPA can be minimized by a clearly written contract describing the agreed-upon services. Engagement letters are discussed in Chapter 7.

7.  In planning engagements, carefully assessing the probability of errors and irregularities in the client's financial statements. Exercise special care when the client has material weaknesses in internal control.

8.  Exercising extreme care in audits of clients in financial difficulties or with a high degree of business risk. Creditors and shareholders of companies that are insolvent or in bankruptcy are likely to seek scapegoats to blame for their losses. As the court

cases described in this chapter demonstrate, litigation involving CPAs tends to center around auditing of clients who later become bankrupt.

## ◆ CHAPTER SUMMARY

This chapter described the legal liability of auditors, emphasizing liability under both common law and statutory law. To summarize:

1. Under common law, auditors are liable to their clients for failure to exercise due professional care. Accordingly, ordinary negligence is a sufficient degree of misconduct to hold CPAs liable for damages caused to their clients.

2. Auditors' liability to third parties under common law varies from state to state. Three general approaches have been adopted—*Ultramares, Restatement of Torts,* and *Rosenblum.* Under the *Ultramares* approach, CPAs are held liable for ordinary negligence only to third-party beneficiaries. Other third parties must prove gross negligence on the part of the auditors. Under the *Restatement of Torts* approach, liability for ordinary negligence to third parties is extended to include any limited class of parties that could be foreseen to rely upon the financial statements. The *Rosenblum* approach extends the auditors' liability for ordinary negligence even further to include any third party the auditors could reasonably foresee as recipients of the financial statements.

3. Auditors may also be held liable to third parties under the federal securities laws, which allow class action lawsuits by purchasers or sellers of a company's securities. The Securities Act of 1933 is unique in that most of the burden of proof in litigation is shifted to the auditors.

4. CPAs are also subject to criminal prosecution for violation of various statutes. In several cases, including the *Continental Vending* case, auditors have been convicted of criminal fraud because they were grossly negligent in performing an audit.

5. To protect themselves from the liability crisis of today, auditors strive to adhere to a high level of professional performance. They also attempt to avoid engagements which have very high risk of litigation.

## ◆ KEY TERMS INTRODUCED OR EMPHASIZED IN CHAPTER 5*

**Common law**   Unwritten legal principles developed through court decisions.

**Compilation of financial statements**   The preparation of financial statements by CPAs based on representations of management, with the expression of no assurance concerning the statements' compliance with generally accepted accounting principles.

**Constructive fraud**   Performing duties with such recklessness that persons believing the duties to have been completed carefully are being misled. Differs from fraud in that constructive fraud does not involve knowledge of misrepresentations within the financial statements.

---

*Note: The first portion of this chapter defines a number of other legal concepts. A number of those terms are not repeated in this glossary.

***Credit Alliance Corp. v. Arthur Andersen & Co.***   A common-law decision by the New York Court of Appeals (New York's highest court) stating that auditors must demonstrate knowledge of reliance on the financial statements by a third party for a particular purpose to be held liable for ordinary negligence to that party. Basically, upheld the *Ultramares* v. *Touche* rule.

**Due diligence**   A CPA firm's contention that its audit work was adequate to support its opinion on financial statements included in a registration statement filed with the SEC under the Securities Act of 1933.

**Error**   An unintentional misstatement of financial statements or omission of an amount or a disclosure.

**Fraud**   Misrepresentation by a person of a material fact, known by that person to be untrue or made with reckless indifference as to whether the fact is true, with intent to deceive and with the result that another party is injured.

**Gross negligence**   Reckless disregard for professional responsibilities.

***Hochfelder v. Ernst***   A landmark case in which the U.S. Supreme Court decided that auditors could not be held liable under the Securities Exchange Act of 1934 for ordinary negligence.

**Irregularity**   An intentional misstatement of financial statements or omission of an amount or a disclosure.

**Negligence**   Violation of a legal duty to exercise a degree of care that an ordinarily prudent person would exercise under similar circumstances.

**Precedent**   A legal principle that evolves from a common-law court decision and then serves as a standard for future decisions in similar cases.

**Registration statement**   A document including audited financial statements that must be filed with the SEC by any company intending to sell its securities to the public through the mails or interstate commerce. The Securities Act of 1933 provides liability to security purchasers for material misrepresentations in registration statements.

**Restatement of Law of Torts**   A summary of tort liability, which when applied to auditor common-law liability, expands auditors' liability for ordinary negligence to include third parties of a limited class of known or intended users of the audited financial statements. Conflicts with the precedent established by the *Ultramares* approach and the *Rosenblum* approach to legal liability.

**Review of financial statements**   The performance of limited investigative procedures that are substantially less in scope than an audit made in accordance with generally accepted auditing standards. The procedures provide the CPAs with a basis to provide *limited* assurance that the financial statements are in accordance with generally accepted accounting principles.

***Rosenblum v. Adler***   A common-law decision by the New Jersey Supreme Court that holds CPAs liable for acts of ordinary negligence to ''reasonably foreseeable third parties'' not in privity of contract. Conflicts with the precedents established in both the *Ultramares* and *Rosenblum* approaches to liability.

**Scienter**   Intent to deceive, manipulate, or defraud. The U.S. Supreme Court held in the *Hochfelder* case that scienter must be proved for the auditors to be held liable under the Securities Exchange Act of 1934.

**Securities Act of 1933**   A federal securities statute covering registration statements for securities to be sold to the public. The Act requires auditors to exercise ''due diligence,'' and creates both civil and criminal penalties for misrepresentation.

**Securities Exchange Act of 1934**   A federal securities statute requiring public companies to file annual audited financial statements with the SEC. The Act requires auditors to ''act in good faith,'' and creates civil and criminal penalties for misrepresentation.

**Statutory law**   Written law created by state or federal legislative bodies.

**Third-party beneficiary**   A person, not the auditors or their client, who is named in a contract (or known to the contracting parties) with the intention that such person should have definite rights and benefits under the contract.

**Ultramares v. Touche & Co.**   A common-law decision by the New York Court of Appeals (New York's highest court) stating that auditors are liable to third parties not in privity of contract for acts of fraud or gross negligence, but not for ordinary negligence. Conflicts with precedents established by the *Restatement of Torts* and *Rosenblum* approaches.

## ◆ GROUP I: REVIEW QUESTIONS

5-1   Distinguish between common law and statutory law.

5-2   Explain why the potential liability of CPAs for professional "malpractice" exceeds that of physicians or other professionals.

5-3   What is meant by the term *privity?* How does privity affect the auditor's liability under common law?

5-4   Distinguish between ordinary negligence and gross negligence within the context of a CPA's work.

5-5   Define the term *third-party beneficiary*.

5-6   Briefly describe the differences in liability to third parties under the *Ultramares* and the *Restatement of Torts* approaches to CPA liability.

5-7   Briefly describe the different common-law precedents set by the *Ultramares* v. *Touche* case and the *Rosenblum* v. *Adler* case.

5-8   What landmark case was embraced by the court in the case of *Credit Alliance Corp.* v. *Arthur Andersen & Co.?* Identify the two factors that the court stated must be proved for the auditors to be held liable for ordinary negligence to a third party.

5-9   Compare auditors' common-law liability to clients and third-party beneficiaries with their common-law liability to other third parties.

5-10   Compare the rights of plaintiffs under common law with the rights of persons who purchase securities registered under the Securities Act of 1933 and sustain losses. In your answer emphasize the issue of who must bear the burden of proof.

5-11   State briefly a major distinction between the Securities Act of 1933 and the Securities Exchange Act of 1934 with respect to the type of transactions regulated.

5-12   Why was the *Hochfelder* v. *Ernst* decision considered a "victory" for the accounting profession?

5-13   How was the *Continental Vending* case unusual with respect to penalties levied against auditors?

5-14   Why did Congress enact the Racketeer Influenced and Corrupt Organizations Act? Why has it been of concern to CPAs? What recent development has reduced this concern?

5-15   How does the SEC regulate CPAs who appear and practice before the commission?

5-16   In the *1136 Tenants' Corporation* case, what was the essential difference in the way the client and the CPAs viewed the work to be done in the engagement?

5-17   Comment on the following statement: While engagement letters are useful for audit engagements, they are not necessary for compilation and review engagements.

5-18  Rogers and Green, CPAs, admit they failed substantially to follow generally accepted auditing standards in their audit of Martin Corporation. "We were overworked and understaffed and never should have accepted the engagement," said Rogers. Does this situation constitute fraud on the part of the CPA firm? Explain.

5-19  Assume that in a particular audit the CPAs were negligent but not grossly negligent. Indicate whether they would be "Liable" or "Not liable" for the following losses proximately caused by their negligence:

a. Loss sustained by client; suit brought under common law.

b. Loss sustained by trade creditor, not in privity of contract; suit brought in a state court that adheres to the *Ultramares* v. *Touche* precedent.

c. Loss sustained by a bank known to the auditors to be relying on the financial statements for a loan; suit brought in a state court that adheres to the *Credit Alliance* v. *Arthur Andersen* precedent.

d. Losses to stockholders purchasing shares at a public offering; suit brought under Securities Act of 1933.

e. Loss sustained by a bank named as a third-party beneficiary in the engagement letter; suit brought under common law.

f. Loss sustained by a lender not in privity of contract; suit brought in a state court that adheres to the *Rosenblum* v. *Adler* precedent.

g. Losses sustained by stockholders; suit brought under Sections 18(a) and 10(b) of the Securities Exchange Act of 1934.

---

## ◆ GROUP II: QUESTIONS REQUIRING ANALYSIS

5-20  Jensen, Inc. filed suit against a CPA firm, alleging that the auditors' negligence was responsible for failure to disclose a large defalcation that had been in process for several years. The CPA firm responded that it may have been negligent, but that Jensen, Inc. was really to blame because it had completely ignored the CPA firm's repeated recommendations for improvements in the internal control structure.

If the CPA firm was negligent, is it responsible for the loss sustained by the client? Does the failure by Jensen, Inc. to follow the CPAs' recommendation for better internal controls have any bearing on the question of liability? Explain.

5-21  The CPA firm of Hanson and Brown was expanding very rapidly. Consequently, it hired several staff assistants, including James Small. Subsequently, the partners of the firm became dissatisfied with Small's production and warned him that they would be forced to discharge him unless his output increased significantly.

At that time Small was engaged in audits of several clients. He decided that to avoid being fired, he would reduce or omit entirely some of the required auditing procedures listed in audit programs prepared by the partners. One of the CPA firm's non-SEC clients, Newell Corporation, was in serious financial difficulty and had adjusted several of its accounts being examined by Small to appear financially sound. Small prepared fictitious working papers in his home at night to support purported completion of auditing procedures assigned to him, although he in fact did not examine the Newell adjusting entries. The CPA firm rendered an unqualified opinion on Newell's financial statements, which were grossly misstated. Several creditors, relying upon the audited financial statements, subsequently extended large sums of money to Newell Corporation.

*Required:*  Would the CPA firm be liable to the creditors who extended the money in reliance on the erroneous financial statements if Newell Corporation should fail to pay the creditors? Explain.

5-22 Match these important cases with the appropriate legal precedent or implication.

*Case*

_____ a. *Hochfelder* v. *Ernst*
_____ b. *Escott* v. *BarChris Construction Corp.*
_____ c. *Credit Alliance* v. *Arthur Andersen & Co.*
_____ d. *Ultramares* v. *Touche & Co.*
_____ e. *Rosenblum* v. *Adler*
_____ f. *Rusch Factors, Inc.* v. *Levin*
_____ g. *United States* v. *Simon (Continental Vending)*

*Legal Precedent or Implication*

1. A landmark case establishing that auditors should be held liable to third parties not in privity of contract for gross negligence, but not for ordinary negligence.
2. A case in which the court used the guidance of the *Second Restatement of the Law of Torts* to decide the auditors' liability to third parties under common law.
3. A landmark case in which the auditors were held liable under Section 11 of the Securities Act of 1933.
4. A case in which auditors were held liable for criminal negligence.
5. A case that established that auditors should not be held liable under the Securities Exchange Act of 1934 unless there was intent to deceive.
6. A case that established the precedent that auditors should be held liable under common law for ordinary negligence to all foreseeable third parties.
7. A common-law case in which the court held that auditors should be held liable for ordinary negligence only to third parties they know will use the financial statements for a particular purpose.

5-23 Susan Harris is a new assistant auditor with the CPA firm of Sparks, Watts, and Wilcox, CPAs. On her third audit assignment, Harris examined the documentation underlying 60 disbursements as a test of controls over purchasing, receiving, vouchers payable, and cash disbursement procedures. In the process, she found five disbursements for the purchase of materials with no receiving reports in the documentation. She noted the exceptions in her working papers and called them to the attention of the senior auditor. Relying on prior experience with the client, the senior auditor disregarded Harris' comments, and nothing further was done about the exceptions.

Subsequently, it was learned that one of the client's purchasing agents and a member of its accounting department were engaged in a fraudulent scheme whereby they diverted the receipt of materials to a public warehouse while sending the invoices to the client. When the client discovered the fraud, the conspirators had obtained approximately $700,000, of which $500,000 was after the completion of the audit.

*Required:* Discuss the legal implications and liabilities to Sparks, Watts, and Wilcox as a result of the above facts.

(AICPA, adapted)

5-24 Gordon & Moore, CPAs, were the auditors of Fox & Company, a brokerage firm. Gordon & Moore examined and reported on the financial statements of Fox, which were filed with the Securities and Exchange Commission.

Several of Fox's customers were swindled by a fraudulent scheme perpetrated by two key officers of the company. The facts establish that Gordon & Moore were negligent, but not reckless or grossly negligent, in the conduct of the audit, and neither participated in the fraudulent scheme nor knew of its existence.

The customers are suing Gordon & Moore under the antifraud provisions of Section 10(b) and Rule 10b-5 of the Securities Exchange Act of 1934 for aiding and abetting the fraudulent scheme of the officers. The customers' suit for fraud is predicated exclusively on the negligence of the auditors in failing to conduct a proper audit, thereby failing to discover the fraudulent scheme.

*Required:*    Answer the following, setting forth reasons for any conclusions stated.

    *a.*    What is the probable outcome of the lawsuit? Explain.

    *b.*    What other theory of liability might the customers have asserted?

(AICPA, adapted)

5-25    Wanda Young, doing business as Wanda Young Fashions, engaged the CPA partnership of Scott & Green to audit her financial statements. During the audit, Scott & Green discovered certain irregularities that would have indicated to a reasonably prudent auditor that James Smith, the chief accountant, might be engaged in a fraud. However, Scott & Green, not having been engaged to discover defalcations, submitted an unqualified opinion in its report and did not mention the potential defalcation problem.

*Required:*    What are the legal implications of the above facts as they relate to the relationship between Scott & Green and Wanda Young? Explain.

5-26    Select the best answer for each of the following questions and explain the reasons for your choice.

    *a.*    If a CPA recklessly performs an audit, the CPA will be liable to third parties who were unknown and not foreseeable to the CPA for:

        (1)    Strict liability for all damages incurred.

        (2)    Gross negligence.

        (3)    Either ordinary or gross negligence.

        (4)    Breach of contract.

    *b.*    A CPA issued an unqualified opinion on the financial statements of a company that sold common stock in a public offering subject to the Securities Act of 1933. Based on a misstatement in the financial statements, the CPA is being sued by an investor who purchased shares of this public offering. Which of the following represents a viable defense?

        (1)    The investor has *not* proven fraud or negligence by the CPA.

        (2)    The investor did *not* actually rely upon the false statement.

        (3)    The CPA detected the false statement after the audit date.

        (4)    The false statement is immaterial in the overall context of the financial statements.

    *c.*    Which of the following elements is necessary to hold a CPA liable to a *client?*

        (1)    Acted with scienter or guilty knowledge.

        (2)    Was not independent of the client.

        (3)    Failed to exercise due care.

        (4)    Did not use an engagement letter.

    *d.*    Which statement best expresses the factors that purchasers of securities registered under the Securities Act of 1933 need prove to recover losses from the auditors?

        (1)    The purchasers of securities must prove ordinary negligence by the auditors and reliance on the audited financial statements.

        (2)    The purchasers of securities must prove that the financial statements were misleading and that they relied on them to purchase the securities.

        (3)    The purchasers of securities must prove that the financial statements were misleading; then, the burden of proof is shifted to the auditors to show that the audit was performed with ''due diligence.''

        (4)    The purchasers of securities must prove that the financial statements were misleading and the auditors were negligent.

    *e.*    The most significant result of the *Continental Vending* case was that it:

        (1)    Created a more general awareness of the possibility of auditor criminal prosecution.

(2)  Extended the auditor's responsibility to all information included in registration statements.

(3)  Defined the CPA's responsibilities for unaudited financial statements.

(4)  Established a precedent for auditors being held liable to third parties under common law for ordinary negligence.

    *f.*  The *1136 Tenants'* case was important because of its emphasis upon the legal liability of the CPA when associated with:

(1)  A review of annual statements.

(2)  Unaudited financial statements.

(3)  An audit resulting in a disclaimer of opinion.

(4)  Letters for underwriters.

(AICPA, adapted)

5-27  For several years, the CPA firm of Carter, Reed, & Co. has audited Cobra Corporation, a closely held manufacturing company that is not under SEC jurisdiction. Cobra is now planning to ''go public,'' issuing common shares to the public and using the proceeds to finance growth. The planned stock offering would put the company under the jurisdiction of the SEC.

*Required:*  Discuss the reasons why the CPA firm's potential legal liability with respect to this client will increase substantially if the company ''goes public.''

5-28  Dandy Container Corporation engaged the accounting firm of Adams and Adams to audit financial statements to be used in connection with an interstate public offering of securities. The audit was completed, and an unqualified opinion was expressed on the financial statements that were submitted to the Securities and Exchange Commission along with the registration statement. Two hundred thousand shares of Dandy Container common stock were offered to the public at $11 a share. Eight months later the stock fell to $2 a share when it was disclosed that several large loans to two ''paper'' corporations owned by one of the directors were worthless. The loans were secured by the stock of the borrowing corporations, which was owned by the director. These facts were not disclosed in the financial statements. The director involved and the two corporations are insolvent.

*Required:*  State whether each of the following statements is true or false, and explain why.

    *a.*  The Securities Act of 1933 applies to the above-described public offering of securities.

    *b.*  The accounting firm has potential liability to any person who acquired the stock.

    *c.*  An insider who had knowledge of all the facts regarding the loans to the two paper corporations could nevertheless recover from the accounting firm.

    *d.*  In court, investors who bought shares in Dandy Container need only show that they sustained a loss and that failure to explain the nature of the loans in question constituted a false statement or misleading omission in the financial statements.

    *e.*  The accountants could avoid liability if they could show they were not negligent.

    *f.*  The accountants could avoid or reduce the damages asserted against them if they could establish that the drop in the stock's market price was due in whole or in part to other causes.

    *g.*  The Securities and Exchange Commission would defend any action brought against the accountants in that the SEC examined and approved the registration statement.

## ◆ GROUP III: PROBLEMS

5-29  Risk Capital Limited, a publicly held Delaware corporation, was considering the purchase of a substantial amount of the treasury stock held by Florida Sunshine Corporation, a closely held corporation. Initial discussions with the Florida Sunshine Corporation began late in 199X.

Wilson and Wyatt, CPAs, Florida Sunshine's public accountants, regularly prepared quarterly and annual unaudited financial statements. The most recently prepared unaudited financial statements were for the fiscal year ended September 30, 199X.

On November 15, 199X, after protracted negotiations, Risk Capital agreed to purchase 100,000 shares of no-par, Class A treasury stock of Florida Sunshine at $12.50 per share. However, Risk Capital insisted upon audited statements for the calendar year 199X. The contract specifically provided: "Risk Capital shall have the right to rescind the purchase of said stock if the audited financial statements of Florida Sunshine for calendar year 199X show a material adverse change in the financial position of the Corporation."

At the request of Florida Sunshine, Wilson and Wyatt audited the company's financial statements for the year ended December 31, 199X. The December 31, 199X, audited financial statements furnished to Florida Sunshine by Wilson and Wyatt showed no material adverse change from the September 30, 199X, unaudited statements. Risk Capital relied upon the audited statements and purchased the treasury stock of Florida Sunshine. It was subsequently discovered that as of the balance sheet date, the audited statements contained several misstatements and that in fact there had been a material adverse change in the financial position of the corporation. Florida Sunshine has become insolvent, and Risk Capital will lose virtually its entire investment.

Risk Capital seeks recovery against Wilson and Wyatt.

*Required:*   *a.*   Discuss each of the theories of liability that Risk Capital will probably assert as its basis for recovery.

*b.*   Assuming that only ordinary negligence by Wilson and Wyatt is proven, will Risk Capital prevail? State yes or no and explain.

5-30   Cragsmore & Company, a medium-sized partnership of CPAs, was engaged by Marlowe Manufacturing, Inc., a closely held corporation, to audit its financial statements for the year ended December 31, 199X.

Before preparing the audit report, William Cragsmore, a partner, and Joan Willmore, a staff senior, reviewed the disclosures necessary in the notes to the financial statements. One note involved the terms, costs, and obligations of a lease between Marlowe and Acme Leasing Company.

Willmore suggested that the note disclose the following: "Acme Leasing Company is owned by persons who have a 35 percent interest in the capital stock and who are officers of Marlowe Manufacturing, Inc."

On Cragsmore's recommendation, this was revised by substituting "minority shareholders" for "persons who have a 35 percent interest in the capital stock and who are officers."

The audit report and financial statements were forwarded to Marlowe Manufacturing for review. The officer-shareholders of Marlowe who also owned Acme Leasing objected to the revised wording and insisted that the note be changed to describe the relationship between Acme and Marlowe as merely one of affiliation. Cragsmore acceded to this request.

The audit report was issued on this basis with an unqualified opinion. But the working papers included the drafts that showed the changes in the wording of the note.

Subsequent to delivery of the audit report, Marlowe suffered a substantial uninsured fire loss and was forced into bankruptcy. The failure of Marlowe to carry any fire insurance coverage was not noted in the financial statements.

*Required:*   What legal problems for Cragsmore & Company are suggested by these facts? Discuss.

(AICPA, adapted)

5-31   After Commuter Airlines was forced into bankruptcy, the company's stockholders brought suit against Thomas & Ross, the company's independent auditors. Three independent assumptions concerning this litigation are listed below:

*Independent*      *a.*   Commuter Airlines is not under SEC jurisdiction. The plaintiff's suit is brought under
*Assumptions:*            common law in a state court that adheres to the *Ultramares* doctrine of auditors' liability.

            *b.*   Commuter Airlines had recently issued its publicly held securities. The stockholders' suit is
               brought in federal court under the Securities Act of 1933.

            *c.*   Commuter Airlines is under SEC jurisdiction. The stockholders' suit is brought in federal
               court alleging violations of Sections 18(a) and 10(b) of the Securities Exchange Act of 1934.

*Required:*   Under each of the independent assumptions, separately explain (1) the allegations that must be
proven in court by the plaintiffs, and (2) any defenses for which the auditors must bear the burden
of proof if they are to avoid or reduce their liability.

5-32   Meglow Corporation, a closely held manufacturer of dresses and blouses, sought a loan from
Busch Factors. Busch had previously extended $50,000 credit to Meglow but refused to lend any
additional money without obtaining copies of Meglow's audited financial statements.

     Meglow contacted the CPA firm of Seavers & Dean to perform the audit. In arranging for the
audit, Meglow clearly indicated that its purpose was to satisfy Busch Factors as to the corporation's sound financial condition and to obtain an additional loan of $100,000. Seavers & Dean
accepted the engagement, performed the audit in a negligent manner, and rendered an unqualified
opinion. If an adequate audit had been performed, the financial statements would have been found
to be misleading.

     Meglow submitted the audited financial statements to Busch Factors and obtained an addi-
tional loan of $70,000. Busch refused to lend more than that amount. After several other factors
also refused, Meglow finally was able to persuade Maxwell Department Stores, one of its
customers, to lend the additional $30,000. Maxwell relied upon the financial statements audited
by Seavers & Dean.

     Meglow is now in bankruptcy, and Busch seeks to collect from Seavers & Dean the $120,000
it loaned Meglow. Maxwell seeks to recover from Seavers & Dean the $30,000 it loaned
Meglow.

*Required:*   *a.*   Will Busch recover? Explain.

            *b.*   Will Maxwell recover? Explain.

5-33   Mark Williams, CPA, was engaged by Jackson Financial Development Company to audit the
financial statements of Apex Construction Company, a small closely held corporation. Williams
was told when he was engaged that Jackson Financial needed reliable financial statements that
would be used to determine whether or not to purchase a substantial amount of Apex Construction's convertible debentures at the price asked by the estate of one of Apex's former directors.

     Williams performed his audit in a negligent manner. As a result of his negligence, he failed
to discover substantial defalcations by Carl Brown, the Apex controller. Jackson Financial
purchased the debentures, but it would not have done so if the defalcations had been discovered.
After discovery of the fraud, Jackson Financial promptly sold them for the highest price offered
in the market at a $70,000 loss.

*Required:*   *a.*   What liability does Williams have to Jackson Financial? Explain.

            *b.*   If Apex Construction also sues Williams for negligence, what are the probable legal defenses
Williams's attorney would raise? Explain.

            *c.*   Will the negligence of Mark Williams, CPA, as described above prevent him from recov-
ering on a liability insurance policy covering the practice of his profession? Explain.

5-34   Charles Worthington, the founding and senior partner of a successful and respected CPA firm,
was a highly competent practitioner who always emphasized high professional standards. One of
the policies of the firm was that all reports by members or staff be submitted to Worthington for
review.

Recently, Arthur Craft, a junior partner in the firm, received a phone call from Herbert Flack, a close personal friend. Flack informed Craft that he, his family, and some friends were planning to create a corporation to engage in various land development ventures; that various members of the family are presently in a partnership (Flack Ventures), which holds some land and other assets; and that the partnership would contribute all of its assets to the new corporation and the corporation would assume the liabilities of the partnership.

Flack asked Craft to prepare a balance sheet of the partnership that he could show to members of his family, who were in the partnership, and to friends, to determine whether they might have an interest in joining in the formation and financing of the new corporation. Flack said he had the partnership general ledger in front of him and proceeded to read to Craft the names of the accounts and their balances at the end of the latest month. Craft took the notes he made during the telephone conversation with Flack, classified and organized the data into a conventional balance sheet, and had his secretary type the balance sheet and an accompanying letter on firm stationery. He did not consult Worthington on this matter or submit this work to him for review.

The transmittal letter stated: ''We have reviewed the books and records of Flack Ventures, a partnership, and have prepared the attached balance sheet at March 31, 199X. We did not perform an audit in conformity with generally accepted auditing standards, and therefore do not express an opinion on the accompanying balance sheet.'' The balance sheet was prominently marked ''unaudited.'' Craft signed the letter and instructed his secretary to send it to Flack.

*Required:*    What legal problems are suggested by these facts? Explain.

5-35   The limitations on professional responsibilities of CPAs when they are associated with unaudited financial statements are often misunderstood. These misunderstandings can be reduced substantially if CPAs carefully follow professional pronouncements in the course of their work and take other appropriate measures.

*Required:*    The following list describes four situations CPAs may encounter in their association with and preparation of unaudited financial statements. Briefly discuss the extent of the CPAs' responsibilities and, if appropriate, the actions to be taken to minimize misunderstandings. Identify your answers to correspond with the letters in the following list.

*a.*    A CPA was engaged by telephone to perform accounting work including the compilation of financial statements. His client believes that the CPA has been engaged to audit the financial statements and examine the records accordingly.

*b.*    A group of business executives who own a farm managed by an independent agent engage Linda Lopez, a CPA, to compile quarterly unaudited financial statements for them. The CPA compiles the financial statements from information given to her by the independent agent. Subsequently, the business executives find the statements were inaccurate because their independent agent was embezzling funds. The executives refuse to pay the CPA's fee and blame her for allowing the situation to go undetected, contending that she should not have relied on representations from the independent agent.

*c.*    In comparing the trial balance with the general ledger, a CPA finds an account labeled Audit Fees in which the client has accumulated the CPA's quarterly billings for accounting services including the compilation of quarterly unaudited financial statements.

*d.*    To determine appropriate account classification, John Day, CPA, reviewed a number of the client's invoices. He noted in his working papers that some invoices were missing but did nothing further because he thought they did not affect the unaudited financial statements he was compiling. When the client subsequently discovered that invoices were missing, he contended that the CPA should not have ignored the missing invoices when compiling the financial statements and had a responsibility to at least inform him that they were missing.

# ◆ GROUP IV: RESEARCH AND DISCUSSION CASE

(5-36) You are a partner in the Denver office of a national CPA firm. During the audit of Mountain Resources, you learn that this audit client is negotiating to sell some of its unproved oil and gas properties to SuperFund, a large investment company. SuperFund is an audit client of your New York office.

Mountain Resources acquired these properties several years ago at a cost of $15 million. The company drilled several exploratory wells but found no developable resources. Last year, you and Mountain Resources agreed that the value of these unproved properties had been "impaired" as defined in paragraph 28 of *FASB 19*. The company wrote the carrying value of the properties down to an estimated realizable value of $9 million and recognized a $6 million loss. You concurred with this treatment and issued an unqualified auditors' report on the company's financial statements.

You are now amazed to learn that the sales price for these properties being discussed by Mountain Resources and SuperFund is $42 million. You cannot understand why SuperFund would pay such a high price and you wonder what representations Mountain Resources may have made to SuperFund concerning these properties. The management of Mountain Resources declines to discuss the details of the negotiations with you, calling them "quite delicate" and correctly pointing out that the future sale of these properties will not affect the financial statements currently under audit.

*Required:*   a.   Summarize the arguments for advising SuperFund (through your New York office) that you consider the properties grossly overpriced at $42 million.

b.   Summarize the arguments for remaining silent and not offering any advice to SuperFund on this matter.

c.   Express your personal opinion as to the course of action you should take. Indicate which arguments from parts *(a)* or *(b)* most influenced your decision.

# ◆ SUGGESTED REFERENCES

AICPA, *Professional Standards, Volume 2*, Commerce Clearing House, Section ET 301 (*Code of Professional Conduct*, Rule 301).

AICPA, *Statement on Auditing Standards No. 53*, "The Auditor's Responsibility to Detect and Report Errors and Irregularities" (New York, 1988) AU 316.

AICPA, *Statement on Auditing Standards No. 54*, "Illegal Acts by Clients" (New York, 1988) AU 317.

*FASB Statement No. 19*, "Financial Accounting and Reporting by Oil and Gas Producing Companies," pars. 15, 28, and 208.

# II

# THE DESIGN OF AUDITS

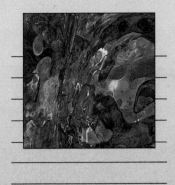

# AUDIT EVIDENCE AND DOCUMENTATION

CHAPTER OBJECTIVES

After studying this chapter, you should be able to:

- Explain the relationship between evidence and audit risk.
- Identify and explain the components of audit risk.
- Distinguish between the concepts of competence and sufficiency as they apply to audit evidence.
- Describe the types of procedures used to obtain audit evidence.
- Explain the characteristics of accounts with high inherent risk.
- List and describe types of evidence used to restrict detection risk.
- Describe the auditors' approach to auditing accounting estimates.
- Describe the functions of audit working papers.
- Discuss the factors that affect the auditors' judgment as to the quantity, types, and content of working papers.
- Describe the types of working papers, and the way they are organized.

D uring financial statement audits, the auditors gather and evaluate evidence to form an opinion on whether financial statements follow the appropriate criteria, usually generally accepted accounting principles. Enough evidence must be gathered to provide an adequate basis for the auditors' opinion on the financial statements. This evidence is collected and the work documented in the auditors' working papers.

# THE RELATIONSHIP OF EVIDENCE TO AUDIT RISK

The term **audit risk** refers to the possibility that the auditors may unknowingly fail to appropriately modify their opinion on financial statements that are materially misstated. Audit risk is reduced by gathering evidence—the more evidence gathered the less audit risk assumed. Obviously, one way to gather additional evidence is to increase the extent of the audit procedures. However, additional evidence may also be obtained by selecting a more effective audit procedure or by performing the procedures closer to the balance sheet date. In Chapter 5, we examined the consequences of issuing an unqualified audit opinion on financial statements that are materially misstated. These situations almost always result in accusations of negligence on the part of the auditors. Therefore, auditors must gather sufficient evidence to reduce audit risk to a low level in every audit. This concept is reflected in the third standard of field work that states:

> **Sufficient competent evidential matter** is to be obtained through inspection, observation, inquiries, and confirmations to afford a reasonable basis for an opinion regarding the financial statements under audit. [Emphasis added.]

## Financial Statement Assertions

Audit procedures are designed to obtain evidence about the assertions of management that are embodied in the financial statements. When the auditors have gathered sufficient audit evidence about each material financial statement assertion, they have gathered sufficient evidence to support their opinion. These financial statement assertions are summarized in *SAS 31* (AU 326), "Evidential Matter," as:

1. *Existence or occurrence*—assets, liabilities, and owners' equity reflected in the financial statements exist; the recorded transactions have occurred.

2. *Completeness*—all transactions, assets, liabilities, and owners' equity that should be presented in the financial statements are included.

3. *Rights and obligations*—the client has rights to assets and obligations to pay liabilities that are included in the financial statements.

4. *Valuation or allocation*—assets, liabilities, owners' equity, revenues, and expenses are presented at amounts that are determined in accordance with generally accepted accounting principles.

5. *Presentation and disclosure*—accounts are described and classified in the financial statements in accordance with generally accepted accounting principles, and all material disclosures are provided.

## Audit Risk at the Assertion Level

Since an audit involves gathering evidence for each material financial statement assertion, audit risk can also be examined at that level. For each financial statement account, *audit risk* is the possibility that (1) a material misstatement in an assertion about the account has occurred, and (2) the auditors do not detect the misstatement. The risk of occurrence of a material misstatement may be separated into two components—inherent risk and control risk. **Inherent risk** refers to the possibility of a material misstatement occurring in an assertion assuming no related internal controls, and **control risk** is the risk that the material misstatement will not be prevented or detected on a timely basis by the company's internal control structure. The risk that the auditors will not detect the misstatement with their audit procedures is called **detection risk.** That is, detection risk is the risk that the auditors' procedures will lead them to conclude that a material misstatement does *not* exist in an assertion when in fact such misstatement does exist.

## Measuring Audit Risk

In practice the various components of audit risk are not typically quantified. Instead, the auditors usually use qualitative categories, such as low, medium, and high risk. However, from the discussion in *SAS 47* (AU 312), "Audit Risk and Materiality in Conducting an Audit," the following formula may be developed to illustrate the relationship between audit risk, inherent risk, control risk, and detection risk:

$$AR = IR \times CR \times DR$$

where:

    $AR$ = Audit risk
    $IR$  = Inherent risk
    $CR$ = Control risk
    $DR$ = Detection risk

To illustrate the measurement of audit risk, assume that the auditors have assessed inherent risk for a particular assertion at 50 percent and control risk at 40 percent. In addition, they have performed audit procedures that they believe have a 20 percent risk of failing to detect a material misstatement in the assertion. The audit risk for the assertion may be computed as follows:

$$AR = IR \times CR \times DR$$
$$= .50 \times .40 \times .20$$
$$= .04$$

Thus, the auditors face a 4 percent audit risk that material misstatement has evaded both the client's internal controls and the auditors' procedures.

# SUFFICIENT COMPETENT EVIDENTIAL MATTER

What constitutes "sufficient competent evidential matter"? This question arises repeatedly when planning and performing every audit. When CPAs are accused of negligence in the performance of an audit, the answer to this question will often determine their innocence or guilt. To provide auditors with guidelines for answering this question, the Auditing Standards Board has issued *SAS 31* (AU 326) specifically addressing the nature, competence, and sufficiency of audit evidence.

## Nature of Evidential Matter

**Evidential matter** is *any information that corroborates or refutes* an assertion. The evidential matter supporting the assertions in a company's financial statements consists of the underlying accounting data and all corroborating information available to the auditors. Auditors use a variety of audit procedures to obtain corroborating information. These procedures will be discussed in detail as they apply to specific accounts in Chapters 12 through 18. Here we will briefly present the most common types of audit procedures.

*Physical examination* means to view physical evidence of an asset. For example, the auditors might physically examine plant, equipment, or inventory items to obtain evidence as to their existence or condition.

*Confirmation* is the process of obtaining and evaluating a response from a debtor, creditor, or other party in reply to a request for information about a particular item affecting the financial statements. Most frequently, confirmation requests (and responses) are in a written form.

*Comparison* is the process of agreeing or contrasting two different sources of information. Auditors often use comparison to test information at various stages of processing within the accounting system. In describing this process, we will distinguish between tracing and vouching.

*Tracing* is the process of establishing the completeness of transaction processing by following a transaction forward through the accounting records. For example, the auditors may trace from a source document to the subsequent recorded transaction.

*Vouching* is the process of establishing the occurrence or valuation of recorded transactions by following a transaction back to supporting documents from a subsequent processing step. For example, the auditors may select recorded purchase transactions in the purchases journal and vouch them to supporting evidence such as invoices, paid checks, and receiving reports. The direction of testing for vouching is the reverse of that used for tracing. Vouching is also referred to as "tracing back."

*Reperformance* is the process of repeating a client activity. For example, the auditors may recalculate depreciation, or reperform a bank account reconciliation. Other examples of reperformance include footing, cross-footing, and extending. *Footing* is the process of proving the totals of a vertical column of figures, such as the total of daily sales for the month from the sales journal. *Cross-footing,* on the other hand, is the process of proving the total of a horizontal row. An example of cross-footing is determining that withholdings plus net pay is equal to gross pay for an employee in the payroll journal. *Extending* is the process of recomputing by multiplication. To extend the client's inventory listing is to multiply the quantities in units by the cost per unit. The resultant product is the extension.

*Observation* is the process of viewing a client activity. For example, the auditors may observe the application of internal control procedures such as the client's inventory-taking procedures. The distinction between physical examination and observation is that for observation to be performed an activity must be involved. Thus, while physical examination and observation both may involve inventory, observation would require a client activity (e.g., counting) to be occurring. In practice, the term observation is sometimes used to refer to both types of procedures.

*Inspection* involves a reading or point-by-point review of a document or record. For example, the auditors may inspect a loan agreement. The terms *examine, review, read,* and *scan* are often used to describe applications of the inspection technique.

*Reconciliations* are used to establish agreement between two sets of independently maintained but related records. Thus, the ledger account for Cash in Bank is reconciled with the bank statement, and the home office record of shipments to a branch office is reconciled with the record of receipts maintained by the branch.

*Inquiries* are questions directed toward appropriate client personnel. The responses to the questions may be oral or in writing. An example of the inquiry technique is the auditors' questioning of the client's controller about the segregation of duties for cash receipts. The term *inquiry* is also sometimes used to refer to the technique of questioning parties outside the organization. For example, a letter of audit inquiry may be sent to the client's lawyer.

*Analytical procedures* are evaluations of financial information made by a study of expected relationships among financial and nonfinancial data. For example, analytical procedures might involve comparison of the client's financial ratios for the year under audit with those of prior years.

## Competence—A Relative Term

The competence of evidential matter refers to its *reliability*. To be competent, evidence must be both *relevant* and *valid*. For evidence to be relevant, it must apply to the audit objective being tested. The validity of evidence is dependent on the circumstances in which it is obtained. While this makes generalizations difficult, the following factors *generally* affect the validity of evidential matter:

1. When auditors obtain evidence from independent sources *outside of the client company,* it provides greater assurance of reliability than that secured solely within the company.

2. The more effective the *internal control,* the greater the reliability of the accounting records and other internally generated documents.

3. Evidence obtained *directly* by the auditors through physical examination, observation, computation, and inspection is more persuasive than information obtained indirectly, or secondhand.

In addition, the competence of evidential matter is increased when the auditors are able to obtain additional information to support the original evidence. Thus, several pieces of related evidence may form a package of evidence that has greater competence than do any of the pieces viewed individually.

## Sufficiency—A Matter of Judgment

The term *sufficient* relates to the *quantity* of evidence the auditors should obtain. The amount of evidential matter that is considered sufficient to support the auditors' opinion is a matter of professional judgment. However, the following considerations may be useful in evaluating the sufficiency of audit evidence.

1. The amount of evidence that is sufficient in a specific situation varies inversely with the competence of the evidence available. Thus, the more competent the evidential matter, the less the amount of evidence that is needed to support the auditors' opinion.

2. The need for evidential matter is closely related to the concept of materiality. The more material a financial statement amount, the greater the need for competent evidential matter. Conversely, little or no evidence is needed to support items that are not material.

3. The risk that the financial statements may be materially misstated varies from one engagement to the next, depending upon such factors as the client's financial condition, line of business, internal control structure, and the integrity of management. As the risk of material misstatement associated with a particular engagement increases, the auditors should require more evidence to support their opinion. In some audit engagements the auditors are aware in advance that fraud is suspected and that the accounting records may include fictitious or altered entries. Perhaps the auditors have been engaged because of a dispute between partners or because of dissatisfaction on the part of stockholders with the existing management. The risk involved in such engagements will cause the auditors to assign different weight to various types of evidence than they otherwise would.

# TYPES OF AUDIT EVIDENCE

When conducting audits, the auditors gather a combination of many types of evidence to adequately restrict audit risk. As described above, audit risk at the account balance level has three components—inherent risk, control risk, and detection risk. The evidence that the auditors gather pertaining to each of these risks differs. As a starting point, it is helpful to recognize that while the auditors gather evidence to assess inherent and control risk, they gather evidence to restrict detection risk to the appropriate level. Therefore, detection risk is the only risk that is completely a function of the sufficiency of the evidence gathered through the auditors' procedures.

## Evidence about Inherent Risk

Just as the level of risk differs for various audits, it also differs for various accounts within a given audit. *Inherent risk,* the risk of material misstatement before considering internal control, is one source of this difference.

The very nature of some accounts makes the inherent risk of misstatement of those accounts greater than for others. Assume that in a given business the balance of the Cash account amounts to only one tenth that of the Buildings account. Does this relationship indicate that the auditors should spend only one tenth as much time in the verification of cash as in the verification of the buildings? Cash is much more susceptible to error or theft than are buildings, and the great number of cash transactions affords an opportunity for errors to be well hidden. The amount of time devoted to the verification of cash balances and of cash transactions during the year will generally be much greater in proportion to the dollar amounts involved than will be necessary for assets such as buildings.

The auditors assess inherent risk for an audit by considering factors such as the nature of the financial statement accounts, the complexity of the transactions going through the accounts, and any misstatements detected in prior year audits.

## Evidence about Control Risk

It is not practical for the auditors to examine every invoice, check, or other piece of documentary evidence. To do so would make an audit far too expensive. The solution lies in a study of the methods and procedures by which the company controls its accounting processes. If these procedures are well designed and consistently followed, the financial statements will be accurate and complete. An effective internal control structure promotes reliability in the accounting data. Errors are quickly and automatically brought to light by the built-in proofs and cross-checks that are inherent in the system.

To obtain an understanding of the client's internal controls and to determine whether these procedures are designed and operating effectively, the auditors use a combination of inquiry, inspection, observation and reperformance procedures performed during the current year, as well as any knowledge obtained from previous audits. If the auditors find that the client company has designed effective internal control for a particular account and that the prescribed practices are being consistently followed in day-to-day operations, they will assess control risk for the related assertions to be low, and thereby accept a higher level of detection risk. Thus, the effectiveness of the client's internal control is a major factor in determining how much evidence the auditors will gather to restrict detection risk.

## Evidence That Restricts Detection Risk

A primary portion of the time on all audits is devoted to performing procedures that restrict detection risk—the risk that the auditors' procedures will fail to detect a material misstatement of the financial statements. The *major* types of evidence that are gathered to restrict detection risk may be summarized as follows:

1. Physical evidence. ( "most reliable" - per Brody)
2. Documentary evidence.
    a. Documentary evidence created outside the client organization and transmitted directly to the auditors.
    b. Documentary evidence created outside the client organization and held by the client.
    c. Documentary evidence created and held within the client organization.

3.   Accounting records.
4.   Analytical procedures.   *planning / substantive tests / overall review*
5.   Computations.
6.   Evidence provided by specialists.
7.   Oral evidence.
8.   Client representation letters.

1.   Physical Evidence.   Actual physical examination provides the best evidence of the existence of certain assets. The existence of property and equipment, such as automobiles, buildings, office equipment, and factory machinery, may be established by physical examination. Similarly, the amount of cash on hand is verified by counting; and inventories are observed and counted.

At first thought, it might seem that physical examination of an asset would be conclusive verification for all assertions relating to the account; but this is often not true. For example, if the cash on hand to be counted by the auditors includes checks received from customers, counting provides no assurance with respect to the valuation of the account—the checks may prove to be uncollectible when deposited. There is also the possibility that one or more worthless checks may have been created deliberately by a dishonest employee as a means of concealing from the auditors the existence of a cash shortage.

The observation of the client's count of inventory may also leave some important questions unanswered. The quality and condition of merchandise or of goods in process are vital in determining their salability. If the goods counted by the auditors contain hidden defects or are obsolete, a mere counting of units does not substantiate their balance sheet valuation. CPAs should be alert to any clues that raise a doubt as to the quality or condition of inventories. Also, they occasionally may need to arrange for independent specialists to provide information on quality or condition of inventories.

---

◆   ILLUSTRATIVE CASE   ◆

During the observation of the physical inventory of a company manufacturing semiconductors—small chips of photographically etched silicon that channel electricity along microscopic pathways—one of the auditors counted semiconductors purportedly worth several hundred thousand dollars. He then asked why apparently identical appearing semiconductors on another wall were not being counted. The client informed him that these semiconductors were defective and could not be sold. To the auditor, the defective semiconductors were identical in appearance with those included in the count. Shortly thereafter the auditor entered academics.

---

In the case of plant and equipment, the auditors' physical examination verifies the existence of the asset, but gives no proof of ownership. A fleet of automobiles used by salespeople and company executives, for example, might be leased rather than owned—or if owned might be subject to a mortgage. Also, physical examination does not substantiate the cost of the plant assets.

In summary, physical examination provides evidence as to the *existence* of certain assets, but generally needs to be supplemented by other types of evidence to determine the ownership, proper valuation, and condition of these assets. For some types of assets, such as accounts receivable or intangible assets, even the existence of the asset cannot be verified through physical evidence.

2.   Documentary Evidence.   An important type of evidence relied upon by auditors consists of documents. The worth of a document as evidence depends in part upon whether it was created within the company (e.g., a sales invoice) or came from outside the company (e.g., a vendor's invoice). Some documents created within the company (checks, for example) are sent outside the organization for endorsement and processing; because of this critical review by outsiders, these documents are regarded as very reliable evidence.

In appraising the reliability of documentary evidence, the auditors should consider whether the document is of a type that could easily be forged or created in its entirety by a dishonest employee. A stock certificate evidencing an investment in marketable securities is usually elaborately engraved and would be most difficult to falsify. On the other hand, a note receivable may be created by anyone in a moment merely by filling in the blank spaces in one of the standard note forms available at any office supply store.

Documentary Evidence Created outside the Client Organization and Transmitted Directly to the Auditors.   The most reliable documentary evidence consists of documents created by independent parties outside the client's organization and transmitted directly to the auditors without passing through the client's hands. For example, in the verification of accounts receivable, the customer is requested by the client to write directly to the auditors to confirm the amount owed to the auditors' client.

As indicated in *SAS 67* (AU 330), "The Confirmation Process," confirmation requests to third parties can address any of the assertions about a particular financial statement amount. However, they do not address all assertions equally well. Confirmations are generally effective at addressing the assertion of existence of the items, but less effective at addressing completeness and the appropriate valuation of the amounts. For example, while a returned account receivable confirmation provides reliable evidence about the existence of an obligation, it does not address whether the debtor can pay the obligation.

To ensure the reliability of the confirmation process, the auditors should carefully design the confirmation requests to seek the appropriate information and make it easy for the recipient to provide a meaningful response. Also, the auditors should consider whether it is necessary to specifically address the confirmation request to an individual in the outside organization that has access to the information being confirmed.

To make sure that the confirmation reply comes directly to the auditors and not to the client, the auditors will enclose with the confirmation request a return envelope addressed to the auditors' office. If the replies were addressed to the auditors at the client's place of business, an opportunity would exist for someone in the client's organization to intercept the returned confirmation and alter the information reported, or even destroy the letter.

Another type of document created outside the client's organization and transmitted directly to the auditors is a letter from the client's attorney describing any pending litigation. Again, the client requests the attorney to furnish the information directly to the auditors in an envelope addressed to the auditors' office, and the auditors mail the request.

**Documentary Evidence Created outside the Client Organization and Held by the Client.** Many of the externally created documents referred to by the auditors will be in the client's possession. Examples include bank statements, vendors' invoices and statements, property tax bills, notes receivable, contracts, customers' purchase orders, and stock and bond certificates. In deciding how much reliance to place upon this type of evidence, the auditors should consider whether the document is of a type that could be easily created or altered by someone in the client's employ. The auditors should be particularly cautious in accepting as evidence photo copies of documents or documents that have been altered in any way. The auditors cannot afford to overlook the possibility that an alteration on a document may have been made deliberately to misstate the facts and to mislead auditors or others who relied upon the document.

In pointing out the possibility that externally created documents in the client's possession *might* have been forged or altered, it is not intended to discredit this type of evidence. Externally created documents in the possession of the client are used extensively by auditors and are considered, in general, as a stronger type of evidence than documents created by the client.

**Documentary Evidence Created and Held within the Client Organization.** No doubt the most dependable single piece of documentary evidence created within the client's organization is a paid check. The check bears the endorsement of the payee and a perforation or stamp indicating payment by the bank. Because of this review and processing of a check by outsiders, the auditors will usually look upon a paid check as a strong type of evidence. The paid check may be viewed as evidence that an asset was acquired at a given cost, or as a proof that a liability was paid or an expense incurred.

Most documents created within the client organization represent a lower quality of evidence than a paid check because they circulate only within the company and do not receive critical review by an outsider. Examples of internally created documents that do not leave the client's possession are sales invoices, shipping notices, purchase orders, receiving reports, and credit memoranda. Of course, the original copy of a sales invoice or purchase order is sent to the customer or supplier, but the copy available for the auditors' inspection has not left the client's possession.

The degree of reliance to be placed on documents created and used only within the organization depends on the effectiveness of the internal control. If the accounting procedures are so designed that a document prepared by one person must be critically reviewed by another, and if all documents are serially numbered and all numbers in the series accounted for, these documents may represent reasonably good evidence. Adequate internal control will also provide for extensive segregation of duties so that no one employee handles a transaction from beginning to end. An employee who maintains records or creates documents, such as credit memoranda, should not have access to cash. Under these conditions there is no incentive for an employee to falsify a document, since the employee creating documents does not have custody of assets.

On the other hand, if internal control is weak, the auditors cannot place as much reliance on documentary evidence created within the organization and not reviewed by outsiders. If an employee is authorized to create documents such as sales invoices and credit memoranda and also has access to cash, an incentive exists to falsify documents to conceal a theft. If documents are not controlled by serial numbers, the possibility arises that the auditors are not being given access to all documents or that duplicates are being used to support fictitious transactions. There is the danger not only of fictitious documents created to cover theft by an employee, but also the possibility, however remote, that management is purposely presenting misleading financial statements and has prepared false supporting documents for the purpose of deceiving the auditors.

### 3.   Accounting Records as Evidence.

When auditors attempt to verify an amount in the financial statements by tracing it back through the accounting records, they will ordinarily carry this process through the ledgers to the journals and vouch the item to such basic documentary evidence as a paid check, invoice, or other source documents. To some extent, however, the ledger accounts and the journals constitute worthwhile evidence in themselves.

The dependability of ledgers and journals as evidence is indicated by the extent of internal control covering their preparation. Whenever possible, subsidiary ledgers for receivables, payables, and plant equipment should be maintained by persons not responsible for the general ledger. All general journal entries should be approved in writing by the controller or other official. If ledgers and journals are produced by an electronic data processing system, various computer controls should be in effect. When controls of this type exist and the records appear to be well maintained, the auditors may regard the ledgers and journals as affording some support for the financial statements.

In addition to journals and ledgers, other accounting records providing evidential matter for independent auditors include sales summaries, trial balances, interim financial statements, and operating and financial reports prepared for management.

### 4.   Analytical Procedures.

Analytical procedures involve evaluations of financial statement information by a study of relationships among financial and nonfinancial data. *SAS 56* (AU 329), "Analytical Procedures," provides guidance and examples of applications of these procedures.

Essentially, the process of performing analytical procedures consists of four steps:

1.   Develop an expectation of an account balance.
2.   Determine the amount of difference from the expectation that can be accepted without investigation.
3.   Compare the company's account balance with the expected account balance.
4.   Investigate significant deviations from the expected account balance.

Techniques used in performing analytical procedures range in sophistication from straightforward comparisons and ratios to complex models involving many relationships and data from many previous years. Examples of analytical procedures include comparisons of revenue and expense amounts for the current year to those of prior periods, to industry averages, to budgeted levels, and to relevant nonfinancial data, such as units produced or hours of direct labor. A more sophisticated analytical procedure might involve the development of a multiple regression model to estimate the amount of sales for the year using economic and industry data. In addition, analytical procedures may involve computations of percentage relationships of various items in the financial statements, such as gross profit percentages. When the relationships turn out as expected, auditors are provided with evidence that the data being reviewed are free from material error. On the other hand, unusual fluctuations in these relationships may indicate serious problems in the financial statements and should be investigated fully by the auditors.

---

◆ ILLUSTRATIVE CASE ◆

In performing analytical procedures for a marine supply store, the auditors noticed that uncollectible accounts expense, which normally had been running about 1 percent of net sales for several years, had increased in the current year to 4 percent of net sales. This significant variation caused the auditors to make a careful investigation of all accounts written off during the year and those presently past due. Most of the uncollectible accounts examined were found to be fictitious, and the cashier-bookkeeper then admitted that he had created those accounts to cover up his abstraction of cash receipts.

---

Comparisons with Industry Averages.   Average statistics for various industries are available through such sources as Dun & Bradstreet's *Key Business Ratios* and Robert Morris Associates' *Annual Statement Studies*. Such averages provide a potentially rich source of information for analytical procedures. Comparisons with industry statistics may alert auditors to classification errors, improper applications of accounting principles, or other errors in specific items in the client's financial statements. In addition, these comparisons may highlight the client's strengths and weaknesses relative to similar companies, thus providing the auditors with a basis for making constructive recommendations to the client.

Problems are encountered when using industry averages for analytical procedures because of a lack of comparability among companies and inability to obtain current industry data. Other companies in the same industry may be larger or smaller, engage in other lines of business that affect their ratios, or use different accounting methods than does the auditors' client. In addition, the time required to assemble industry averages creates a situation in which the most recent averages are always a year or so old. Thus, auditors should carefully consider the extent of comparability and timeliness of the data before drawing conclusions based upon comparisons with industry averages.

Comparisons with Internal Client Data.   Every audit client generates internal information that may be used in performing analytical procedures. Forecasts, production reports, and monthly performance reports are but a few data sources that may be expected to bear predictable relationships to financial statement amounts. In establishing these relationships, auditors may use dollar amounts, physical quantities, ratios, or percentages. Separate relationships may be computed for each division or product line.

*Trend analysis* is a technique for identifying consistent patterns in the relationships of data from successive time periods. For example, a review of the client's sales for the past three years might reveal a consistent growth rate of about 7 percent. This information would assist the auditors in evaluating the reasonableness of the sales reported in the client's income statement for the current year.

Figure 6–1    Potential Problems Disclosed by Analytical Procedures

| Analytical Procedure | Potential Problems |
|---|---|
| 1. Comparison of inventory levels for the current year to that of prior years. | Misstatement of inventory; inventory obsolescence problem. |
| 2. Comparison of research and development expense to the budgeted amount. | Misclassification of research and development expenses. |
| 3. Comparison of accounts receivable turnover for the current year to that of prior years. | Misstatement of sales or accounts receivable; misstatement of the allowance for uncollectible accounts. |
| 4. Comparison of the client's gross profit percentage to published industry averages. | Misstatement of sales and accounts receivable; misstatement of cost of goods sold and inventory. |
| 5. Comparison of production records in units to sales. | Misstatement of sales; misstatement of inventory. |
| 6. Comparison of interest expense to the average outstanding balance of interest-bearing debt. | Understatement of liabilities; misstatement of interest expense. |

Timing of Analytical Procedures.    Analytical procedures are used at various times throughout the audit. They are useful in the early *planning* stage for assisting in planning the nature, timing, and extent of other audit procedures and directing the auditors' attention to areas requiring special investigation. Some of the problems that may be brought to light by the application of specific analytical procedures are illustrated in Figure 6–1. Analytical procedures also may be applied during the audit as **substantive tests** to provide evidence as to the reasonableness of specific account balances. Finally, analytical procedures are performed at the end of the engagement as a *final overall review* of the audited figures. This last application provides assurance that the auditors have not "failed to see the forest because of the trees." *SAS 56* (AU 329) requires the performance of analytical procedures: (1) during the planning stage of the audit, and (2) as a final overall review near the completion.

The quality or competence of evidence obtained from analytical procedures depends upon the strength of the relationships among the data being compared, and the accuracy of the data. Analytical procedures usually may be performed quickly and inexpensively (often on a microcomputer using audit software).

5.   Computations.    Another form of audit evidence consists of computations made independently by the auditors to prove the arithmetical accuracy of the client's records. Computations differ from analytical procedures. Analytical procedures involve the analysis of plausible relationships among financial data, whereas computations simply verify mathematical processes. In its simplest form, an auditor's computation might consist of footing a column of figures in a sales journal or in a ledger account to prove the column total.

Independent computations may be used to prove the accuracy of such client calculations as earnings per share, depreciation expense, allowance for uncollectible accounts, revenue recognized on a percentage-of-completion basis, and provisions for federal and state income taxes. The computation of a client's liability for postretirement benefits involves actuarial assumptions and computations beyond an auditor's area of expertise. Therefore, auditors usually rely on the services of an actuary to compute this liability.

6.  Evidence Provided by Specialists.   We have pointed out that CPAs may not be experts in such technical tasks as judging the quality of a client's inventory or making the actuarial computations to verify liabilities for postretirement benefits. Other phases of an audit in which CPAs lack the special qualifications necessary to determine the fairness of the client's representations include assessing the probable outcome of pending litigation and estimating the number of barrels of oil in an underground oil field.

In *SAS 11* (AU 336), "Using the Work of a Specialist," the AICPA recognized the necessity for CPAs to consult with experts, when appropriate, as a means of gathering competent audit evidence. *SAS 11* defines a **specialist** as a person or firm possessing special skill or knowledge in a field other than accounting or auditing, giving as examples actuaries, appraisers, attorneys, engineers, and geologists. It is desirable that the specialist consulted by the auditors be unrelated to the client; however, it is acceptable for the specialist to have an existing relationship with the client. For example, the most logical specialist to consult regarding pending litigation would be the client's legal counsel. In any event, the auditors are responsible for ascertaining the professional qualifications and reputation of the specialist consulted.

Auditors cannot accept a specialist's findings blindly; they must obtain an understanding of the methods or assumptions used by the specialist and test accounting data furnished to the specialist by the client. The CPAs may accept the specialist's findings as competent audit evidence unless their tests cause them to believe the findings are unreasonable. However, the auditors should not refer to the specialist in their audit report unless the specialist's findings are not consistent with the representations in the financial statements causing the auditors to qualify their opinion.

7.  Oral Evidence.   Throughout their examination the auditors will ask a great many questions of the officers and employees of the client's organization. These questions cover an endless range of topics—the location of records and documents, the reasons underlying an unusual accounting procedure, the probabilities of collecting a long-past-due account receivable.

The answers auditors receive to these questions constitute another type of evidence. Generally, oral evidence is not sufficient in itself, but it may be useful in disclosing situations that require investigation or in corroborating other forms of evidence. For example, after making a careful analysis of all past-due accounts receivable, an auditor will normally discuss with the credit manager the prospects for collection of accounts considered doubtful. If the opinions of the credit manager are in accordance with the estimates of uncollectible accounts that have been made independently by the auditor, this oral evidence will constitute significant support for the conclusions reached. In repeat audits of a business, the auditor will be in a better position to evaluate the opinions of the credit manager based on how well the manager's estimates in prior years have worked out.

8.  Client Representation Letter.   At the conclusion of the examination, auditors obtain from the client a written **representation letter** summarizing the most important oral representations made during the engagement. Many specific items are included in this representation letter. For example, management usually represents that all liabilities known to exist are reflected in the financial statements. Most of the representations fall into the following broad categories:

1.  All accounting records, financial data, and minutes of directors' meetings have been made available to the auditors.

2.  The financial statements are complete and prepared in conformity with generally accepted accounting principles.

3.  All items requiring disclosure (such as loss contingencies, illegal acts, and related party transactions) have been properly disclosed.

*SAS 19* (AU 333), "Client Representations," requires auditors to obtain a representation letter on every engagement and provides suggestions as to its form and content. These letters are dated as of the last day of field work and usually are signed by both the client's chief executive officer and chief financial officer.

A client representation letter is a low grade of audit evidence and *should never be used as a substitute for performing other audit procedures*. The financial statements already constitute written representations by the client; hence, a representation letter does little more than assert that the original representations were correct.

---

### ◆ ILLUSTRATIVE CASE ◆

The income statement of National Student Marketing Corporation (NSMC) included total gains of $370,000 from the sale of two subsidiary companies to employees of the subsidiaries. Consideration for the sales was notes receivable collateralized by 7,700 shares of NSMC stock. Because both subsidiaries had been operating at substantial losses, NSMC's independent auditors obtained written representations from three officers of NSMC that there were no indemnification or repurchase commitments given to the purchasers.

The SEC criticized the auditors for relying too heavily on management representations regarding the sales. The SEC considered the sales to be sham transactions that would have been brought to light had the auditors sufficiently extended their auditing procedures. NSMC had executed various side agreements to assume all risks of ownership after the "sale" of one subsidiary, and had agreed to make cash contributions and guarantee a bank line of credit after the "sale" of the other subsidiary. Further, the NSMC stock collateralizing the notes receivable had been given to the subsidiaries' "purchasers" by officers of NSMC.

---

Although representation letters are not a substitute for other necessary auditing procedures, they do serve several important audit purposes. One purpose is to *remind the client officers of their primary and personal responsibility for the financial statements*.

~~client officers of their primary and personal responsibility for the financial statements~~. Another purpose is to document in the audit working papers the client's responses to the many questions asked by the auditors during the engagement. Also, a representation by management may be the only evidence available with respect to management's *future intentions*. For example, whether maturing debt is classified as a current or a long-term liability may depend upon whether management has both the ability and the *intention* to refinance the debt.

## Evidence about Accounting Estimates

The auditors must be especially careful in considering financial statement accounts that are affected by estimates made by management (often referred to as accounting estimates), particularly those for which a wide range of accounting methods are considered acceptable. Examples of accounting estimates include allowances for loan losses and obsolete inventory, and estimates of warranty liabilities. Making accounting estimates is management's responsibility, and such estimates are generally more susceptible to material misstatement than financial statement amounts which are more certain in amount. *SAS 57* (AU 342), "Auditing Accounting Estimates," requires the auditors to determine that *(a)* all necessary estimates have been developed, *(b)* the accounting estimates are reasonable, and *(c)* the accounting estimates are properly accounted for and disclosed.

Determining whether all necessary estimates have been developed and accounted for properly (steps *[a]* and *[c]*) requires a knowledge of the client's business and the applicable generally accepted accounting principles. When evaluating the reasonableness of accounting estimates (step *[b]*), the auditors may use one or more of the following three basic approaches:

1. Reviewing and testing management's process of developing the estimates—this will often involve evaluating the reasonableness of the steps performed by management.

2. Independently developing an estimate of the amount to compare to management's estimate.

3. Reviewing subsequent events or transactions bearing on the estimate, such as actual payments of an estimated amount made subsequent to year-end.

---

◆ ILLUSTRATIVE CASE ◆

The financial difficulties of the savings and loan industry during the late 1980s and early 1990s present a good example of the potential risk to CPAs presented by accounting estimates. A number of savings and loans organizations ran into financial difficulties due in large part to making loans which subsequently proved to be uncollectible.

One savings and loan organization which made over $1 billion in real estate loans during the late 1980s originally estimated its required loan loss reserve to be $11 million. Subsequently, the Federal Deposit Insurance Corporation (FDIC) alleged that those loans resulted in losses of $450 million. Shortly thereafter, the FDIC filed a lawsuit against the CPA firm that had audited the savings and loan organization.

The wide range of potential accounting methods complicates transactions involving accounting estimates. Pensions, leases, and long-term construction contracts are just a few examples of transactions with complex accounting methods that vary depending on the nature of the agreements and the specific circumstances. It is the auditors' responsibility to evaluate whether the accounting rules followed are appropriate in the circumstances. While it sounds so basic as to almost be trivial, it is essential that the auditors understand the transactions in which their clients are involved. In practice, this requirement is onerous since the auditors may be involved in a variety of audits, requiring knowledge of a host of different accounting methods and estimates.

## The Cost of Obtaining Evidence

CPAs can no more disregard the cost of alternative auditing procedures than a store manager can disregard a difference in the costs of competing brands of merchandise. Cost is not the primary factor influencing the auditors in deciding what evidence should be obtained, but cost is always an important consideration.

The cost factor may preclude gathering the strongest possible form of evidence and necessitate the substitution of other forms of evidence that are of lesser quality, yet still satisfactory. For example, assume that the auditors find that the client has a large note receivable from a customer. What evidence should the auditors obtain to be satisfied that the note is authentic and will be paid at maturity? One alternative is for the auditors to correspond directly with the customer and obtain written confirmation of the amount, maturity date, and other terms of the note. This confirmation is evidence that the customer issued the note and regards it as a valid obligation. Second, the auditors might test the collectibility of the note by obtaining a credit report on the customer from Dun & Bradstreet, Inc., or from a local credit association. They might also obtain copies of the customer's most recent financial statements accompanied, if possible, by the opinion of an independent CPA. To carry our illustration to an extreme, the auditors might obtain permission to make an audit of the financial statements of the customer. The cost of conducting this separate audit could amount to more than the note receivable the auditors wished to verify.

The point of this illustration is that auditors *do not* always insist upon obtaining the strongest possible evidence. They do insist upon obtaining evidence that is sufficient under the circumstances. The greater the risk of material misstatement of the item to be verified, the stronger the evidence required by the auditors, and the greater the cost they may be willing to incur in obtaining it.

# EVIDENCE FOR RELATED PARTY TRANSACTIONS

How should auditors react if a corporation buys a parcel of real estate from one of its executive officers at an obviously excessive price? This situation illustrates the problems that may arise for auditors when the client company enters into **related party transactions.** The term *related parties* refers to the client entity and any other party with which the client may deal where one party has the ability to influence the other to the extent that one party to the transaction may not pursue its own separate interests. Examples of related parties include officers, directors, principal owners, and members of their immediate families; and affiliated companies, such as subsidiaries. A related party transaction is any transaction between the company and these parties (except for normal compensation arrangements, expense allowances, and similar transactions arising in the ordinary course of business). Since transactions with related parties are not conducted at arm's length, the auditors should be aware that the *economic substance* of these transactions may differ from their form.

The primary concern of the auditors is that material related party transactions are *adequately disclosed* in the client's financial statements or the related notes.[1] Disclosure of related party transactions should include: the nature of the relationship; a description of the transactions, including dollar amounts; and amounts due to and from related parties, together with terms and manner of settlement.

*SAS 45* (AU 334), "Omnibus Statement on Auditing Standards," suggests guidelines for identifying related parties and related party transactions. Common methods of identifying related parties include making inquiries of management and reviewing SEC filings, stockholders' listings, and conflict-of-interest statements obtained by the client from its executives. A list of all known related parties should be prepared at the beginning of the audit so that the audit staff may be alert for related party transactions throughout the engagement. This list is retained in the auditors' permanent file for reference and updating in successive engagements. As they perform the audit, the auditors will be alert for transactions with these parties and any transactions with unusual terms that might be indicative of related party negotiations.

# DOCUMENTATION

**Working papers** are the connecting link between the client's accounting records and the auditors' report. They document all of the work performed by the auditors and provide the justification for the auditors' report. The sufficient, competent evidential matter required by the third field work standard must be clearly documented in the auditors' working papers.

Some working papers take the form of bank reconciliations or analyses of ledger accounts; others may consist of photocopies of **minutes** of directors' meetings; still others might be organization charts or flowcharts of the client's internal control structure. Working trial balances, audit programs, internal control questionnaires, letters of representation obtained from the client and from the client's legal counsel, returned confirmation forms—all of these schedules, lists, notes, and documents are part of the auditors' working papers.

Thus, the term *audit working papers* is quite comprehensive. Remember that the partner who signs the auditors' report did not personally perform most of the audit procedures. The partner's opinion was developed primarily by reviewing the working papers prepared by the audit staff. Therefore, the working papers must include adequate support *for expressing an opinion on the fairness of the client's financial statements*.

---

[1]*FASB Statement 57*, "Related Party Disclosures," contains requirements for disclosure of related party transactions.

Most large CPA firms send new staff assistants to special training schools to learn the firm's working paper "techniques." Of course, no one standard set of working papers is suitable for all engagements. As auditors move from one client to another they encounter different business operations and different kinds of accounting records and internal controls. It follows that the auditors must tailor the form and content of their working papers to fit the circumstances of each engagement.

## Functions of Working Papers

Audit working papers assist auditors in several major ways: they *(a)* provide a means of assigning and coordinating audit work; *(b)* aid seniors, managers, and partners in supervising and reviewing the work; *(c)* provide the support for the auditors' report; *(d)* document the auditors' compliance with the generally accepted auditing standards relating to field work; and *(e)* aid in planning and conducting future audits of the client. In addition, working papers provide information useful in rendering additional professional services, such as preparing income tax returns, making recommendations for improving internal control, and providing consulting services.

### Assigning and Coordinating Audit Work.

Most audits are a joint effort. Several auditors, perhaps even several different offices of a CPA firm, usually are involved in each engagement. The work of these different auditors is coordinated through the audit working papers. Work may be conveniently delegated by assigning different assistants responsibility for completing different working papers. The senior auditor might fill in the column headings on a working paper and enter one or two sample transactions, requesting that a staff assistant complete the paper. In this manner, a senior can initiate and supervise the work of several assistants simultaneously.

Often it is not possible to complete all of the work on an account at one time. For example, cash on hand may be counted at the balance sheet date, but confirmations of bank balances may not be received until a week or so later. As each step in the verification of the client's cash balance is completed, a working paper is filed, to be expanded and updated as additional information is obtained. Thus, the audit work on a given account might be started early in the engagement by one assistant and completed later by another.

### Supervising and Reviewing the Work of Assistants.

As working papers are completed by staff assistants, they are *reviewed* by the senior running the job. If the senior finds any shortcomings in an assistant's work, the senior will write "review notes" to the assistant explaining how the working papers should be revised. Once the senior is satisfied with the working paper, it will be passed on to the manager, who will perform a similar review. If the manager has any questions or finds any problems, the working paper is again returned to the audit staff with the manager's review notes. After the manager is satisfied that the working paper documents complete and thorough audit work, the working paper is reviewed by one or more partners. This process of successive levels of review helps to ensure that work of the audit staff is carefully reviewed and supervised. As each review is completed, the reviewer "signs off" by initialing the working paper.

Support for the Report.   The working papers must contain adequate evidence and documentation to convince the partner on the engagement that it is appropriate for the CPA firm to issue a particular type of opinion on the client's financial statements. The partner knows that some risk always exists that investors may sustain losses and bring a lawsuit against the CPAs alleging an improper audit. Therefore, the partner will want to be certain that the auditors' report is supported and justified by the evidence contained in the working papers.

Compliance with the Three Standards of Field Work.   As discussed in Chapter 5, auditors may find themselves liable for losses sustained by financial statement users if the audit was not performed in accordance with generally accepted auditing standards. The working papers are the principal means by which auditors can demonstrate their compliance with the standards of field work. Thus, the working papers should document adequate planning and proper supervision of assistants (the first standard of field work), a proper understanding of internal control (second standard), and the gathering of sufficient competent evidential matter to afford a reasonable basis for the opinion (third standard).

Planning and Conducting the Next Audit.   The working papers from the previous audit of a particular client provide a wealth of information that is useful in planning and conducting the next audit. For example, the prior year's working papers show how much time was required to perform the audit, provide insight into the client's internal control structure, and refresh the auditors' memory of any special problems encountered during the engagement. In addition, some working papers, such as the substantiation of land, bonds payable, or capital stock may be updated from one year to the next with very little effort. Finally, working papers from the previous audit may be used as a starting point for designing current-year working papers. But the auditors must determine that the design is still appropriate and should try to improve upon it.

## Confidential Nature of Working Papers

To conduct a satisfactory audit, the auditors must be given unrestricted access to all information about the client's business. Much of this information is confidential, such as the profit margins on individual products, tentative plans for business combinations with other companies, and the salaries of officers and key employees. Officers of the client company would not be willing to make available to the auditors information that is carefully guarded from competitors, employees, and others unless they could rely on the auditors maintaining a professional silence on these matters.

Much of the information gained in confidence by the auditors is recorded in their working papers; consequently, the working papers are confidential in nature. The AICPA *Code of Professional Conduct,* discussed in Chapter 4, includes a rule that generally prohibits a member in public practice from disclosing confidential information.

Under normal circumstances, auditors think of confidential information as being information that must not be divulged *outside* of the client organization. But the confidential nature of information in the auditors' working papers has another dimension—it often must not be divulged *within* the client organization. If, for example, the client does not want certain employees to know the levels of executive salaries, the auditors obviously should not defeat this policy by exposing their working papers to unauthorized client personnel. Also, the working papers may identify particular accounts, branches, or time periods to be tested by the auditors; to permit the client's employees to learn of these in advance would weaken the significance of the tests.

Since audit working papers are highly confidential, they must be safeguarded at all times. Safeguarding working papers usually means keeping them locked in a file cabinet or an audit case during lunch and after working hours.

## Ownership of Audit Working Papers

Audit working papers are the *property of the auditors,* not of the client. At no time does the client have the right to demand access to the auditors' working papers. After the audit, the working papers are retained by the auditors.

Clients may sometimes find it helpful to refer to information from the auditors' working papers from prior years. Auditors usually are willing to provide this information, but their working papers should not be regarded as a substitute for the client's own accounting records.

## Working Papers and Auditors' Liability

The auditors' working papers are the principal record of the extent of the procedures applied and evidence gathered during the audit. If the auditors, after completing an engagement, are charged with negligence, their audit working papers will be a major factor in refuting or substantiating the charge. Working papers, if not properly prepared, are as likely to injure the auditors as to protect them.

If a lawsuit is brought against the auditors, the plaintiffs will subpoena the auditors' working papers and analyze them in great detail, looking for contradictions, omissions, or any evidence of carelessness or fraud. This possibility suggests the need for public accounting firms to make their own critical review of the working papers at the end of each engagement. During this review, the auditors should bear in mind that any unexplained contradictory statements, or evidence that is not consistent with the conclusions finally reached, may be used at a later date to support a charge of improper auditing.

Differences of Opinion.   On occasion, inconsistencies will arise in the working papers because different members of the audit staff—say, a senior and the engagement partner—will reach different conclusions on some complex auditing or accounting issue. In such cases, the disagreeing auditors should discuss the matter to see if they can reach agreement. If they are able to do so, the working papers should be revised to reflect their common opinion. If they are not able to reach agreement, the opinion of the partner-in-charge of the engagement will prevail with respect to the content of the auditors' report. However, all other members of the audit team have the right to document in the working papers *their disagreement* with the ultimate decision. In the event that a staff person elects to document his or her disagreement, the partner-in-charge obviously should be extremely thorough in documenting the rationale underlying the firm's ultimate decision in a carefully written memorandum.

# Types of Working Papers

Since the audit working papers document a variety of information gathered by the auditors, there are numerous types of papers. However, there are certain general categories into which most working papers may be grouped; these are: (1) audit administrative working papers; (2) working trial balance and lead schedules; (3) adjusting journal entries and reclassification entries; (4) supporting schedules, analyses, reconciliations, and computational working papers; and (5) corroborating documents.

*Audit Administrative Working Papers.*   Auditing is a sophisticated activity requiring planning, supervision, control, and coordination. Certain working papers are specifically designed to aid the auditors in the planning and administration of engagements. These working papers include audit plans and programs, internal control questionnaires and flowcharts, engagement letters, and time budgets. Memoranda of the planning process and significant discussions with client management are also considered **administrative working papers.**

*Working Trial Balance.*   The **working trial balance** is a schedule listing the balances of the accounts in the general ledger for the current and previous year, and also providing columns for the auditors' proposed adjustments and reclassifications and for the final amounts that will appear in the financial statements. A working trial balance is the "backbone" of the entire set of audit working papers; it is the key schedule that controls and summarizes all supporting papers. This type of working paper may appear as shown below when audit software is used.

```
PROCESS COMPANY, INC.                                    PREPARED BY ATT
WORKING TRIAL BALANCE                                    REVIEWED BY RBS
FOR THE PERIOD ENDED DECEMBER 31, 19X5
                                                                    Page 1
```

| | | PRIOR PERIOD BALANCE 12/31/X4 | UNADJUSTED TRIAL BALANCE DR (CR) | | ADJUSTMENTS | BALANCE SHEET | |
| | | | | | | | |
| ACCOUNT # | ACCOUNT NAME | | | REF # | DR (CR) | DR | CR |
|---|---|---|---|---|---|---|---|
| 1001.01 | CASH | 398,743 | 481,413.00 | | | 481,413 | |
| 1010.01 | SHORT TERM INVESTMENTS | | 167,890.00 | | | 167,890 | |
| 1040.01 | ACCOUNTS RECEIVABLE | 2,053,914 | 2,298,722.00 | | | 2,298,722 | |
| 1045.01 | ALLOWANCE FOR BAD DEBTS | (45,325) | (56,984.00) | AJE-11 | (10,456.00) | | 67,440 |
| 1050.01 | INVENTORIES | 2,567,665 | 2,701,814.00 | AJE-12 | (129,799.00) | 2,572,015 | |

In many audits, the client furnishes the auditors with a working trial balance after all normal end-of-period journal entries have been posted. Before accepting the trial balance for their working papers, the auditors should compare the amounts to the general ledger to determine that the trial balance is prepared accurately.

Lead Schedules.    Separate **lead schedules** (also called *grouping sheets* or *summary schedules*) are set up to combine similar general ledger accounts, the total of which appears on the working trial balance as a single amount. For example, a lead schedule for Cash might combine the following general ledger accounts: Petty Cash, $500; General bank account, $196,240; Factory Payroll bank account, $500; and Dividend bank account, $1,000. Similar lead schedules would be set up for Accounts Receivable, Inventories, Stockholders' Equity, Net Sales, and for other balance sheet or income statement captions.

Adjusting Journal Entries and Reclassification Entries.    During the course of an audit engagement, the auditors may discover various types of misstatements in the client's financial statements and accounting records. These misstatements may be large or small in amount; they may arise from the omission of transactions or from the use of incorrect amounts; or they may result from improper classification or **cutoff,** or from misinterpretation of transactions. Generally, these misstatements are accidental errors; however, the auditors may discover irregularities in the accounting records.

To correct **material** errors or irregularities discovered in the financial statements and accounting records, the auditors draft **adjusting journal entries** (AJEs), which they recommend for entry in the client's accounting records. In addition, the auditors develop **reclassification journal entries** (RJEs) for items that, although correctly recorded in the accounting records, must be reclassified for fair presentation in the client's financial statements. For example, accounts receivable with large credit balances should be *reclassified* as a liability in the balance sheet. Reclassification entries affect only the financial statement presentation; therefore, they are *not recorded* in the client's accounting records. Reclassification entries appear only on accounting worksheets.

Supporting Schedules.    Although all types of working papers may loosely be called schedules, auditors prefer to use this term to describe a listing of the elements or details comprising the balance in an asset or liability account at a specific date. Thus, a list of amounts owed to vendors making up the balance of the Trade Accounts Payable account is properly described as a *schedule*.

Analysis of a Ledger Account.    An **analysis** of a ledger account is another common type of audit working paper. The purpose of an analysis is to show on one paper *all changes* in an asset, liability, equity, revenue, or expense account during the period covered by the audit. If a number of the changes are individually immaterial, they may be recorded as a single item in the analysis working paper. Account analyses are most useful in substantiating those accounts affected by relatively few transactions during the year. Examples include plant asset accounts, long-term debt accounts, capital stock accounts, and retained earnings.

To analyze a ledger account, the auditors first list the beginning balance and indicate the nature of the items comprising this balance. Next, the auditors list and investigate the nature of all debits and credits to the account during the period. These entries, when combined with the beginning balance, produce a figure representing the balance in the account as of the audit date. If any misstatements or omissions of importance are detected during this analysis of the account, the necessary adjusting journal entry approved by the client is entered on the working paper to produce the adjusted balance required for the financial statements.

Reconciliations.   Frequently, auditors wish to prove the relationship between amounts obtained from different sources. When they do so, they obtain or prepare working papers known as reconciliations. These reconciliations provide evidence as to the accuracy of one or both of the amounts and are important to the audit of many accounts, including cash, accounts receivable, and inventories.

Computational Working Papers.   Another type of supporting working paper is the computational working paper. The auditors' approach to verifying certain types of accounts and other figures is to make an independent computation and compare their results with the amounts shown by the client's records. Examples of amounts that might be verified by computation are interest expense, depreciation, payroll taxes, income taxes, pension liabilities, and earnings per share.

Corroborating Documents.   Auditing is not limited to the examination of financial records, and working papers are not confined to schedules and analyses. During the course of an audit, the auditors may gather much purely expository material to substantiate their report. One common example is copies of minutes of directors' and stockholders' meetings. Other examples include copies of articles of incorporation and bylaws; copies of important contracts, bond indentures, and mortgages; memoranda pertaining to examination of records; audit confirmations; and representation letters from the client and from the client's legal counsel.

## Organization of the Working Papers

The auditors usually maintain two files of working papers for each client: (1) current files for every completed audit and (2) a permanent file of relatively unchanging data. The current file (as for the 1995 audit) pertains solely to that year's audit; the permanent file contains such things as copies of the articles of incorporation, which are of continuing audit interest.

The Current Files.   The auditors' report for a particular year is supported by the working papers contained in the current files. Many CPA firms have found it useful to organize the current files around the arrangement of the accounts in the client's financial statements. The administrative working papers usually begin the current files, including a draft of the financial statements and the auditors' report. These working papers are followed by the working trial balance and the adjusting and reclassification entries. The remaining portion of the current files consists of working papers supporting the balances and other representations in the client's financial statements. It begins with working papers for each asset account and continues with papers for liabilities, owners' equity accounts, and revenue and expense accounts.

Each working paper in a file is assigned an index number, and information is tied together through a system of cross-referencing. In this way, a reviewer may trace back amounts on the working trial balance to the supporting working papers. Figure 6–2

## Figure 6–2   Organization of the Current Files

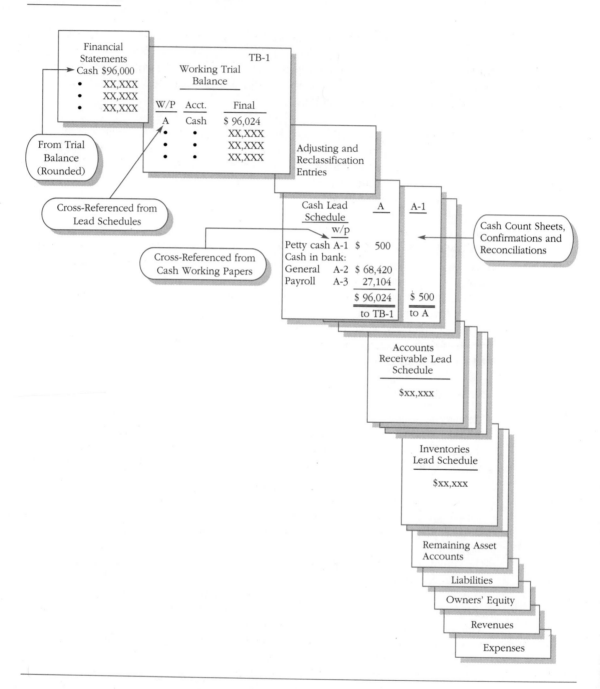

illustrates a system of cross-referencing and a typical arrangement of the current files after the administrative working papers.

The Permanent File.   The **permanent file** serves three purposes: (1) to refresh the auditors' memories on items applicable over a period of many years; (2) to provide for new staff members a quick summary of the policies and organization of the client; and (3) to preserve working papers on items that show relatively few or no changes, thus eliminating the necessity for their preparation year after year.

Much of the information contained in the permanent file is gathered during the course of the first audit of a client's records. A considerable portion of the time spent on a first audit is devoted to gathering and appraising background information, such as copies of articles of incorporation and bylaws, leases, patent agreements, pension plans, labor contracts, long-term construction contracts, known related parties, charts of accounts, and prior years' tax returns.

Analyses of accounts that show few changes over a period of years are also included in the permanent file. These accounts may include land, buildings, accumulated depreciation, long-term investments, long-term liabilities, capital stock, and other owners' equity accounts. The initial investigation of these accounts must often include the transactions of many years. But once these historical analyses have been brought up to date, the work required in subsequent examinations will be limited to a review of the current year's transactions in these accounts. In this respect, the permanent file is a timesaving device because current changes in such accounts need only be added to the permanent papers without reappearing in the current working papers. Adequate cross-referencing in the working papers, of course, should be provided to show where in the permanent file such information is to be found.

## Guidelines for Preparation of Working Papers

We will now summarize in a few short paragraphs our basic guidelines for preparing working papers that will meet current professional standards.

A separate, properly identified working paper should be prepared for each topic. Proper identification of a working paper is accomplished by a heading that includes the name of the client company, a clear description of the information presented, and the applicable date or the period covered. If the working paper was prepared by the client's staff, it should be labeled ''PBC'' (prepared by client) and appropriately tested.

Complete and specific identification of documents examined, employees interviewed, and sites visited is essential for good working paper practice. The preparer of a working paper should date and sign or initial the working paper; the signatures or initials of the senior, manager, or partner who reviewed the working paper should also appear on the paper.

Working papers should be appropriately referenced and cross-referenced to the working trial balance or relevant lead schedule. Where reference is necessary between working papers, there must be adequate cross-referencing.

The nature of verification work performed by the auditors should be clearly indicated on each working paper. A review of paid purchase invoices, for example, might be supplemented by inspection of the related purchase orders and receiving documents to substantiate the authenticity of the invoices examined; a description of this verification procedure should be included on the working paper. As audit working papers are prepared, the auditors will use several different symbols to identify specific steps in the work performed. These symbols, or **tick marks,** provide a very concise means of indicating the auditing procedures applied to particular amounts. Whenever tick marks are employed, they must be accompanied by a legend explaining their meaning.

The working papers should include comments by the auditors indicating their conclusions on each aspect of the work. In other words, the auditors should clearly express the opinion they have formed as a result of having performed the auditing procedures summarized in the working paper. Figure 6–3 illustrates such a conclusion related to the audit of the allowance for uncollectible accounts, along with other aspects of a properly prepared working paper.

## Computer-Generated Working Papers

Traditionally working papers have been prepared in pencil on columnar paper. Today, many working papers are prepared on portable personal computers carried by the auditors to the work site. When an adjustment is entered on computer-based working papers, it appears instantly on the appropriate lead schedules, the adjustments schedule, and the working trial balance. The necessary cross-references are automatically entered on each schedule. If the adjustment affects taxable income, the income tax expense account and the tax liability are automatically adjusted using the client's marginal tax rate. In addition, all of the subtotals, column totals, and cross-footings in the working papers are instantly adjusted.

When working papers are maintained manually, all of these entries and changes must be made by hand with a pencil, an eraser, and a calculator. With a personal computer, an adjustment that might take a half hour or more to "push through" manual working papers can be entered in a few seconds. Thus, personal computers have taken much of the "pencil pushing" and the "number crunching" out of working paper preparation.

## The Review of Audit Working Papers

Working papers are reviewed at every supervisory level of a CPA firm. Senior auditors review the working papers of staff assistants; managers review all working papers prepared by staff assistants and by senior auditors; the partner in charge of the engagement reviews the entire set of working papers. Many CPA firms also require a review by a second partner.

### What Do the Reviewers Look for?    All reviewers look to see that the working papers properly document the audit. However, there are differences in the nature of the reviews. The senior's review is the most technical, and it generally is performed promptly after the completion of the individual working paper. Seniors look primarily to see that the staff assistant has performed the audit procedures properly and that the assistant's findings and conclusions are clearly expressed.

Figure 6–3  Preparation of a Working Paper

Working Paper
Heading

Reviewer's Initials
and Date

Preparer's Initials
and Date

Index

Maine Company, Inc.
Allowances for Uncollectable Accounts
March 31, 19X3

V.M.A.
May 6, X3

C-5
B. J.D.
April 24, X3

Balance per ledger, Mar. 31, X2                                    22 881 75 ✗

Deduct: Write-offs during fiscal 19X3
        June 18, X2   Morgan Desk Co              6 581 44 n
        Feb. 12, X3   Baker Cabinet Co.           8 041 60  14 623 04
                                                             8 258 71

"Tick Mark"
Symbols

Add: Provision for year ended Mar. 31, X3 based on
     aged trial balance of trade accounts
     receivable at Mar. 31, X3                                       6 589 81

Balance per ledger, Mar. 31, X23                                    14 848 52 ✗

        A.J.E. 7 – to increase allowances based on
        tests of collectibility and analytical
        procedures on C-6                                            5 151 48  to TB-5-2

Adjusting Entry
Cross-Referenced to
Adjusting Entries
Working Papers
(below)

Explanation of
Audit Work
Performed

Adjusted balance Mar. 31, X3                                        20,000 00
                                                                      f
                                                                     to C

        f   Footed
        n   Examined Controller's authorization for write-off.
        ✗   agreed to general ledger.
            Based on the results of the tests of collectibility
            and analytical procedures on C-6, the adjusted balance
            of the allowance for uncollectible accounts, appears to be
            adequate to value the accounts receivable
            at net realizable value.
                                            B. J.D.
                                            V.M.A.

Cross-Referenced to
Accounts Receivable
Lead Schedule

Auditors'
Conclusion

Maine Company, Inc
Adjusting Journal Entries
March 31, 19X3

TB-5-2
V. M. A
4/26/X3

| Working Paper Reference | Account No. | Account Title and Explanation ⑦ | Dr. | Cr. |
|---|---|---|---|---|
| C-5 | 524 | Uncollectible Accounts Expenses | 5 151 48 | |
| | 126 | Allowance for Uncollectible Accounts | | 5 151 48 |
| | | To increase the allowance for uncollectible accounts to amount considered necessary based on test work performed. | | |

The reviews by managers and partners are often performed near the *end* of the engagement, when the reviewer may examine at one time the entire set of working papers. These reviewers are primarily interested in determining that the audit was performed in accordance with generally accepted auditing standards and that the working papers properly support the auditors' report that will be issued on the financial statements. There are several advantages to reviewing all of the working papers at once. The reviewer can determine that the working papers "tie together"—that is, that amounts are properly carried forward from one working paper to another. As we mentioned earlier in the chapter, these reviewers should look critically for any inconsistencies, omissions, or "loose ends" that might later support a plaintiff's allegations of improper auditing. In addition, the reviewer should consider whether the various immaterial discrepancies that were passed without adjustment might *cumulatively* have a material effect upon the financial statements.

The purposes of a *second partner review* are to provide assurance that all of the CPA firm's in-house *quality control policies* have been complied with, as well as to provide a "second opinion" that the audit was performed in accordance with generally accepted auditing standards. The second partner review, sometimes called a *cold review,* usually is performed by a partner with no personal or professional ties to the audit client. Multioffice CPA firms sometimes bring in a partner from another office to perform the second partner review. Not until all of these reviewers have "signed off" on the audit working papers is the CPA firm's name signed to the auditors' report.

## ◆ CHAPTER SUMMARY

This chapter focuses on the concept of sufficient competent evidential matter, and the manner in which this evidence is documented in the audit working papers. To summarize:

1.  The third standard of field work requires the auditors to obtain sufficient competent evidential matter to support their audit opinion. To be competent, evidence must be both relevant and valid. In general, evidence is considered more valid when it is *(a)* obtained from independent sources outside of the client organization, *(b)* generated from an accounting system that has effective internal controls, or *(c)* obtained directly by the auditors, rather than from a secondary source. The auditors use professional judgment to determine the amount of evidence that is sufficient to support their opinion.

2.  Evidence is gathered by the auditors to reduce audit risk, which is the risk of failing to modify their opinion on financial statements that are materially misstated. Since financial statements consist of a series of assertions by management, the auditors must obtain sufficient competent evidential matter about each material financial statement assertion.

3.  At the individual account balance level, audit risk consists of (1) the risk that a material misstatement in an assertion has occurred (composed of inherent risk and control risk), and (2) the risk that the auditors do not detect the misstatement (detection risk). Audit evidence is gathered by the auditors to assess both inherent and control risk, and to restrict detection risk.

4. Auditors must be especially careful in considering financial statement accounts that are affected by estimates made by management, such as the allowance for doubtful accounts. The inherent risk of these types of accounts is generally much greater than for other financial statement accounts.

5. Working papers are the connecting link between the client's accounting records and the auditors' report. They are the property of the auditors, and are designed to assist the auditors in coordinating and reviewing the audit work, provide support for the audit report, document the auditors' compliance with the generally accepted auditing standards, and facilitate future audits of the client.

## ◆ KEY TERMS INTRODUCED OR EMPHASIZED IN CHAPTER 6*

**Adjusting journal entry**   A journal entry drafted by the auditors to correct a misstatement discovered in the financial statements and accounting records.

**Administrative working papers**   Working papers specifically designed to help the auditors in planning and administration of the engagement, such as audit programs, internal control questionnaires and flowcharts, time budgets, and engagement memoranda.

**Analysis**   A working paper showing all changes in an asset, liability, equity, revenue, or expense account during the period covered by the audit.

**Audit risk**   The risk that the auditors may unknowingly fail to appropriately modify their opinion on financial statements that are materially misstated.

**Competence**   The competence of evidential matter relates to its quality. To be competent, evidence must be both valid and relevant.

**Control risk**   The risk that a material misstatement that could occur in an account will not be prevented or detected on a timely basis by internal control.

**Corroborating documents**   Documents and memoranda included in the working papers that substantiate representations contained in the client's financial statements. These working papers include audit confirmations, lawyers' letters, copies of contracts, copies of minutes of directors' and stockholders' meetings, and representation letters from the client's management.

**Cutoff**   The process of determining that transactions occurring near the balance sheet date are assigned to the proper accounting period.

**Detection risk**   The risk that the auditors' procedures will lead them to conclude that a financial statement assertion is not materially misstated, when in fact such misstatement does exist.

**Evidential matter**   Any information that corroborates or refutes the auditors' premise that the financial statements present fairly the client's financial position and operating results.

**Inherent risk**   The risk of material misstatement of a financial statement assertion, assuming there were no related internal controls.

**Lead schedule**   A working paper with columnar headings similar to those in a working trial balance, set up to combine similar ledger accounts the total of which appears in the working trial balance as a single amount.

---

*Note: The first portion of this chapter defines a number of audit procedures. Those terms are not repeated in this glossary.

**Material**    Of substantial importance. Significant enough to affect evaluations or decisions by users of financial statements. Information that should be disclosed in order that financial statements constitute a fair presentation. Involves both qualitative and quantitative considerations.

**Minutes book**    A formal record of the issues discussed and actions taken in meetings of stockholders and of the board of directors.

**Permanent file**    A file of working papers containing relatively unchanging data, such as copies of articles of incorporation and bylaws, copies of minutes of directors', stockholders', and committee meetings, and analyses of such ledger accounts as land and retained earnings.

**Reclassification entry**    A working paper entry drafted by the auditors to assure fair presentation of the client's financial statements, such as an entry to transfer accounts receivable credit balances to the current liabilities section of the client's balance sheet. Since reclassification entries do not correct misstatements in the client company's accounting records, they are not posted to the client's ledger accounts.

**Related party transaction**    A transaction in which one party has the ability to influence significantly the management or operating policies of the other party, to the extent that one of the transacting parties might be prevented from pursuing fully its own separate interests.

**Representation letter**    A single letter or separate letters prepared by officers of the client company at the auditors' request setting forth certain representations about the company's financial position or operations.

**Specialist**    A person or firm possessing special skill or knowledge in a field other than accounting or auditing, such as an actuary.

**Substantive tests**    Tests of account balances and transactions designed to detect any material misstatements in the financial statements.

**Sufficient**    Sufficient evidential matter is a measure of the quantity of the evidence.

**Tick mark**    A symbol used in working papers by the auditor to indicate a specific step in the work performed. Whenever tick marks are used, they must be accompanied by a legend explaining their meaning.

**Working papers**    Papers that document the evidence gathered by auditors to show the work they have done, the methods and procedures they have followed, and the conclusions they have developed in an audit of financial statements or other type of engagement.

**Working trial balance**    A working paper that lists the balances of accounts in the general ledger for the current and the previous year and also provides columns for the auditors' adjustments and reclassifications and for the final amounts that will appear in the financial statements.

---

## ◆ GROUP I: REVIEW QUESTIONS

6-1    In a conversation with you, Mark Rogers, CPA, claims that both the *sufficiency* and the *competence* of audit evidence are a matter of judgment in every audit. Do you agree? Explain.

6-2    Describe the relationship between detection risk and audit risk.

6-3    Define inherent risk. Can the auditors reduce inherent risk by performing audit procedures?

6-4    Distinguish between the components of audit risk that the auditors gather evidence to assess versus the component of audit risk that they collect evidence to restrict.

6-5    ''The best means of verification of cash, inventory, office equipment, and nearly all other assets is a physical count of the units; only a physical count gives the auditors complete assurance as to the accuracy of the amounts listed on the balance sheet.'' Evaluate this statement.

6-6    As part of the verification of accounts receivable as of the balance sheet date, the auditors might inspect copies of sales invoices. Similarly, as part of the verification of accounts payable, the auditors might inspect purchase invoices. Which of these two types of invoices do you think represents the stronger type of evidence? Why?

6-7    In verifying the asset accounts Notes Receivable and Marketable Securities, the auditors examined all notes receivable and all stock certificates. Which of these documents represents the stronger type of evidence? Why?

6-8    When in the course of an audit might the auditor find it useful to apply analytical procedures?

6-9    List and briefly describe the three approaches to auditing accounting estimates that are included in a client's financial statements.

6-10   Give at least four examples of *specialists* whose findings might provide competent evidence for the independent auditors.

6-11   What are the major purposes of obtaining representation letters from audit clients?

6-12   ''In deciding upon the type of evidence to be gathered in support of a given item on the financial statements, the auditors should not be influenced by the differences in cost of obtaining alternative forms of evidence.'' Do you agree? Explain.

6-13   The cost of an audit might be significantly reduced if the auditors relied upon a representation letter from the client instead of observing the physical counting of inventory. Would this use of a representation letter be an acceptable means of reducing the cost of an audit?

6-14   What are *related party transactions?*

6-15   What disclosures should be made in the financial statements regarding material related party transactions?

6-16   Evaluate the following statement: ''Identifying related parties and obtaining a client representation letter are two required audit procedures normally performed on the last day of field work.''

6-17   What are the major functions of audit working papers?

6-18   Why are the prior year's audit working papers a useful reference to staff assistants during the current audit?

6-19   Why are the final figures from the prior year's audit included in a working trial balance or lead schedules? Explain.

6-20   Should the working trial balance prepared by the auditors include revenue and expense accounts if the balances of these accounts for the audit year have been closed into retained earnings prior to the auditors' arrival? Explain.

6-21   Explain the meaning of the term *permanent file* as used in connection with audit working papers. What kinds of information are usually included in the permanent file?

6-22   List the major types of audit working papers and give a brief explanation of each. For example, one type of audit working paper is an account analysis. This working paper shows the changes that occurred in a given account during the period under audit. By analyzing an account, the auditors determine its nature and content.

6-23   List several rules to be observed in the preparation of working papers that will reflect current professional practice.

6-24   In their review of audit working papers, what do managers and partners look for?

6-25   Should the auditors prepare adjusting journal entries to correct all errors they discover in the accounting records for the year under audit? Explain.

6-26    "Audit working papers are the property of the auditors, who may destroy the papers, sell them, or give them away." Criticize this quotation.

6-27    Describe a situation in which a set of audit working papers might be used by third parties to support a charge of gross negligence against the auditors.

6-28    "I have finished my testing of footings of the cash journals," said the assistant auditor to the senior auditor. "Shall I state in the working papers the periods for which I verified footings, or should I just list the totals of the receipts and disbursements I have proved to be correct?" Prepare an answer to the assistant's question, stressing the reasoning involved.

6-29    What is the purpose of a "second partner review"? What should be the extent of the second partner's association with the engagement being reviewed?

6-30    What is the nature of the working papers used by the auditors to summarize the audit work performed on the accounting records?

# ◆ GROUP II: QUESTIONS REQUIRING ANALYSIS

6-31    In an audit of financial statements, the auditors gather various types of evidential matter. List eight major types of evidence and provide a procedural example of each.

6-32    Analytical procedures are extremely useful in the initial audit planning stage.

*Required:*    a.    Explain why analytical procedures are considered substantive tests.
b.    Explain how analytical procedures are useful in the initial audit planning stage.
c.    Should analytical procedures be applied at any other stages of the audit process? Explain.
d.    List several types of comparisons a CPA might make in performing analytical procedures.

6-33    When analytical procedures disclose unexpected changes in financial relationships relative to prior years, the auditors consider the possible reasons for the changes. Give several possible reasons for the following significant changes in relationships:
a.    The rate of inventory turnover (ratio of cost of goods sold to average inventory) has declined from the prior year's rate.
b.    The number of days' sales in accounts receivable has increased over the prior year.

6-34    Comment on the competence of each of the following examples of audit evidence. Arrange your answer in the form of a separate paragraph for each item. Explain fully the reasoning employed in judging the competence of each item.
a.    Copies of client's sales invoices.
b.    Auditors' independent computation of earnings per share.
c.    Paid checks returned with a bank statement.
d.    Response from customer of client addressed to auditors' office confirming amount owed to client at balance sheet date.
e.    Representation letter by controller of client company stating that all liabilities of which she has knowledge are reflected in the company's accounts.

6-35    Financial statements contain five broad assertions about the accounts included in the statements.

*Required:*    a.    Identify who makes these assertions.
b.    List and describe each of the assertions.

6-36    One of the assets of Vista Corporation is 6,000 acres of land in a remote area of the Arizona desert. The land is held as a long-term investment and is carried in the accounting records at a cost of $200 per acre. A recent topographical map prepared by the U.S. Soil Conservation Service shows the land to be nearly flat with no standing bodies of water. The land is accessible only by aircraft or four-wheel-drive vehicles. Evaluate the merits of the auditors personally physically examining this land as a means of obtaining audit evidence.

6-37  Auditors are required on every engagement to obtain a representation letter from the client.

*Required:*  a.  What are the objectives of the client's representation letter?
        b.  Who should prepare and sign the client's representation letter?
        c.  When should the client's representation letter be obtained?

6-38  What would you accept as satisfactory documentary evidence in support of entries in the following?
        a.  Sales journal.
        b.  Sales returns journal.
        c.  Voucher or invoice register.
        d.  Payroll journal.
        e.  Check register.

6-39  Marion Watson & Co., CPAs, are planning their audit procedures for their tests of the valuation of inventories of East Coast Manufacturing Co. The auditors on the engagement have assessed inherent risk and control risk for valuation of inventories at 100 percent and 50 percent, respectively.

*Required:*  a.  Calculate the appropriate level of detection risk for the audit of this assertion, given that the auditors wish to control audit risk for the assertion at 3 percent.
        b.  Calculate the appropriate level of detection risk for the audit of this assertion, given that the auditors wish to control audit risk for the assertion at 5 percent.

6-40  Select the best answer for each of the following questions. Explain the reasons for your selection.
        a.  As part of their examination, auditors obtain a representation letter from their client. Which of the following is *not* a valid purpose of such a letter?
            (1)  To increase the efficiency of the audit by eliminating the need for other audit procedures.
            (2)  To remind the client's management of its primary responsibility for the financial statements.
            (3)  To document in the audit working papers the client's responses to certain verbal inquiries made by the auditors during the engagement.
            (4)  To provide evidence in those areas dependent upon management's future intentions.
        b.  Which of the following statements best describes why auditors investigate related party transactions?
            (1)  Related party transactions generally are illegal acts.
            (2)  The substance of related party transactions may differ from their form.
            (3)  All related party transactions must be eliminated as a step in preparing consolidated financial statements.
            (4)  Related party transactions are a form of management fraud.
        c.  Of the following, which is the *least* persuasive type of audit evidence?
            (1)  Confirmations mailed by outsiders to the auditors.
            (2)  Correspondence between the auditors and suppliers.
            (3)  Copies of sales invoices inspected by the auditors.
            (4)  Canceled checks returned in the year-end bank statement directly to the client.

d. Analytical procedures are most likely to detect:
   (1) Weaknesses of a material nature in internal control.
   (2) Unusual transactions.
   (3) Noncompliance with prescribed control procedures.
   (4) Improper separation of accounting and other financial duties.
e. A primary purpose of the audit working papers is to:
   (1) Aid the auditors in adequately planning their work.
   (2) Provide a point of reference for future audit engagements.
   (3) Support the underlying concepts included in the preparation of the basic financial statements.
   (4) Support the auditors' opinion.
f. A difference of opinion concerning accounting and auditing matters relative to a particular phase of the audit arises between an assistant auditor and the auditor responsible for the engagement. After appropriate consultation, the assistant auditor asks to be disassociated from the resolution of the matter. The working papers would probably:
   (1) Remain silent on the matter since it is an internal matter of the auditing firm.
   (2) Note that the assistant auditor is completely dissociated from responsibility for the auditor's opinion.
   (3) Document the additional work required, since all disagreements of this type will require expanded substantive testing.
   (4) Document the assistant auditor's position, and how the difference of opinion was resolved.

6-41 An important part of every audit of financial statements is the preparation of audit working papers.

*Required:* a. Discuss the relationship of audit working papers to each of the standards of field work.
b. You are instructing an inexperienced staff assistant on her first auditing assignment. She is to examine an account. An analysis of the account has been prepared by the client for inclusion in the audit working papers. Prepare a list of the comments, commentaries, and notations that the staff assistant should make or have made on the account analysis to provide an adequate working paper as evidence of her examination. (Do not include a description of auditing procedures applicable to the account.)

(AICPA, adapted)

6-42 The preparation of working papers is an integral part of the auditors' examination of financial statements. On a recurring engagement the auditors review the working papers from their prior audit while planning the current examination to determine the papers' usefulness for the current engagement.

*Required:* a. (1) What are the purposes or functions of audit working papers?
   (2) What records of the auditors may be included in audit working papers?
b. What factors affect the auditors' judgment of the type and content of the working papers for a particular engagement?
c. To comply with generally accepted auditing standards, the auditors include certain evidence in their working papers, for example, ''evidence that the engagement was planned and work of assistants was supervised and reviewed.'' What other evidence should the auditors include in audit working papers to comply with generally accepted auditing standards?

(AICPA, adapted)

6-43 ''Working papers should contain facts and nothing but facts,'' said student A. ''Not at all,'' replied student B. ''The audit working papers may also include expressions of opinion. Facts are not always available to settle all issues.'' ''In my opinion,'' said student C, ''a mixture of facts and opinions in the audit working papers would be most confusing if the papers were produced as a means of supporting the auditors' position when their report has been challenged.'' Evaluate the issues underlying these arguments.

 At 12 o'clock, when the plant whistle sounded, George Green, an assistant auditor, had his desk completely covered with various types of working papers. Green stopped work immediately, but not wanting to leave the desk with such a disorderly appearance he took a few minutes to sort the papers into proper order, place them in a neat pile, and weight them down with a heavy ash tray. He then departed for lunch. The auditor-in-charge, who had been observing what was going on, was critical of the assistant's actions. What do you think was the basis for criticism by the auditor-in-charge?

# ◆ GROUP III: PROBLEMS

6-45   Assume that the auditors find serious weaknesses in the internal control of Oak Canyon, Inc., a producer and distributor of fine wines. Would these internal control weaknesses cause the auditors to rely more or less upon each of the following types of evidence during their audit of Oak Canyon?
   *a.*   Documents created and used only within the organization.
   *b.*   Physical evidence.
   *c.*   Evidence provided by specialists.
   *d.*   Analytical procedures.
   *e.*   Accounting records.

*Required:*   For each of the above five items, state your conclusion and explain fully the underlying reasoning.

6-46   The financial statements of Wayne Company indicate that large amounts of notes payable to banks were retired during the period under audit. Evaluate the reliability of each of the following types of evidence supporting these transactions:
   *a.*   Debit entries in the Notes Payable account.
   *b.*   Entries in the check register.
   *c.*   Paid checks.
   *d.*   Notes payable bearing bank perforation stamp PAID and the date of payment.
   *e.*   Statement by client's treasurer that notes had been paid at maturity.
   *f.*   Letter received by auditors directly from bank stating that no indebtedness on part of client existed as of the balance sheet date.

6-47   During your examination of the accounts receivable of Hope Ranch, a new client, you notice that one account is much larger than the rest, and you therefore decide to examine the evidence supporting this customer's account. Comment on the relative reliability and adequacy of the following types of evidence:
   *a.*   Computer printout from accounts receivable subsidiary ledger.
   *b.*   Copies of sales invoices in amount of the receivable.
   *c.*   Purchase orders received from customer.
   *d.*   Shipping documents describing the articles sold.
   *e.*   Letter received by client from customer acknowledging the correctness of the receivable in the amount shown on client's accounting records.
   *f.*   Letter received by auditors directly from customer acknowledging the correctness of the amount shown as receivable on client's accounting records.

6-48   Criticize the working paper below that you are reviewing as senior auditor on the December 31, 1993, audit of Pratt Company.

|  |  |  |
|---|---|---|
| *Pratt Company* | | |
| *Cash* | | *E-2* |
| *Per bank* | | *44,874.50* ✓ |
| *Deposit in transit* | | *837.50* ✓ |
| *Bank charges* | | *2.80* |
| | | *45,714.80* |
| *Outstanding checks* | | |
| | *46.40* | |
| | *10.00* | |
| | *30.00* | |
| | *1,013.60* ✓ | |
| | *1,200.00* ✓ | |
| | *10.00* | |
| | *25.00* ✓ | |
| | *15.00* ✓ | |
| | *50.00* ✓ | |
| | *1,002.00* ✓ | *3,402.00* |
| *Per ledger* | | *42,312.80* ✓ |
| | | |
| ✓ - *Verified* | | |
| | | |
| *R.G.H.* | | |
| *1-15-94* | | |

6-49   One of the practical problems confronting the auditors is that of determining whether adjusting journal entries or other corrective actions are warranted for misstatements, omissions, and inconsistencies. The following items were noted by the auditors during their year-end audit of a small manufacturing partnership having net sales of approximately $1.6 million; net income of approximately $40,000; total assets of nearly $2 million; and total partners' capital of $300,000.

   (1)   Proceeds of $250 from the sale of fully depreciated office equipment were credited to Miscellaneous Revenue rather than to Gain and Loss on Sale of Equipment, a ledger account that had not been used for several years.

   (2)   The Trade Accounts Receivable control account showed a balance of $79,600. The individual accounts comprising this balance included three with credit balances of $320, $19, and $250, respectively.

   (3)   Several debits and credits to general ledger accounts had been made directly without use of journal entries. The amounts involved did not exceed $500.

   (4)   Credit memoranda were not serially numbered or signed, but a file of duplicates was maintained.

(5) General journal entries did not include explanations for any but unusual transactions.

(6) Posting references were occasionally omitted from entries in general ledger accounts.

(7) An expenditure of $200 for automobile repairs was recorded as a December expense, although shown by the invoice to be a November charge.

(8) The auditors' count of petty cash disclosed a shortage of $20.

(9) Expenditures for advertising amounting to $8,000 were charged to the Advertising Expense account; other advertising expenses amounting to $3,000 had been charged to Miscellaneous Expense.

(10) On September 12, the client borrowed $288,000 from First Bank by signing a 120-day note payable in the face amount of $300,000. The note matures on January 10. The client's accountant had charged the entire $12,000 interest included in the face amount of the note to the interest expense of the current year. He stated that he did not consider deferring part of the interest to the following year to be warranted by the dollar amounts involved.

*Required:*   You are to state clearly the position the auditors should take with respect to each of the above items during the course of an annual audit. If adjusting journal entries are necessary, include them in your solution.

---

## ◆ GROUP IV: RESEARCH AND DISCUSSION CASE

6-50   You are the partner on the audit of Datasave, Inc., a small publicly held corporation that manufactures high-speed tape drives for the computer industry. The audit of Datasave had been progressing satisfactorily until you were about a month away from issuing your opinion. Suddenly, and quite mysteriously, Carl Wagner, the financial vice president, resigned. John Ross, who had been a manager with a large CPA firm, was quickly hired to replace Wagner. Although the change in Datasave's chief financial officer caused some disruption, the audit was completed on a timely basis.

As the last step in the audit process, you have the representation letter prepared for signing. You wanted the letter to be signed by William Cox, the president; Robert Star, the controller; and Wagner, who occasionally came to the company's offices to resolve matters regarding his past compensation. The signatures of Cox and Star were obtained, and you approached Wagner for his signature. In response to your request, Wagner replied, "I no longer am employed with this crazy company. Why should I take any responsibility for the financial statements?" Despite your attempts to persuade him, Wagner refused to sign the letter. Wagner also refused to discuss the reasons for his resignation, other than to say the reasons were personal.

When you discussed the problem of Wagner's refusal to sign with Cox, he indicated that there was no problem because Ross would sign the letter. You see this as a possible solution, but you are aware that Ross knows very little about the financial statements for the year under audit. Also, you are still somewhat concerned about the reasons for Wagner's resignation.

*Required:*   *a.*   Describe fully the alternatives that are available to you in this situation.

*b.*   Express your personal opinion as to the appropriate course of action and provide reasoning to support your opinion.

---

## ◆ SUGGESTED REFERENCES

AICPA, *Statement on Auditing Standards No. 19*, "Client Representations," (New York, 1977) AU 333.

AICPA, *Statement on Auditing Standards No. 58*, "Reports on Audited Financial Statements," (New York, 1988) AU 508.

# PLANNING THE AUDIT; DESIGNING AUDIT PROGRAMS

## CHAPTER OBJECTIVES

After studying this chapter, you should be able to:

- Identify the factors considered by auditors in accepting new clients.

- Explain a CPA's responsibilities when planning an audit.

- Describe the manner in which an audit is affected by the auditors' assessment of audit risk and materiality.

- Distinguish between the systems portion of the audit program and the substantive test part.

- Describe the general objectives of audit programs for asset accounts.

- Explain how the general objectives of audit programs are used to develop the specific objectives that are then used to determine the audit procedures to be applied to an account.

- Discuss the major steps in the audit process.

H ow do auditors determine whether a prospective client is reputable? After accepting an audit client how do auditors go about planning the engagement and preparing the initial audit program? When one considers the potential legal liability involved, it becomes obvious that auditors do not merely accept a new audit client and then arrive at the client's premises to ''start auditing.'' The first standard of field work states:

> The work is to be *adequately planned,* and assistants, if any, are to be *properly supervised.* [Emphasis added.]

The concept of adequate planning includes investigating a prospective client before deciding whether to accept the engagement, obtaining an understanding of the client's business operations, and developing an overall strategy to organize, coordinate, and schedule the activities of the audit staff. Although much planning is done before beginning the actual audit field work, the planning process continues throughout the engagement. Whenever a problem is encountered during the audit, the auditors must plan their response to the situation. This chapter describes this dynamic process of planning the audit, beginning with the acceptance of a client and proceeding through the design of the audit program. It also provides an overview of the entire audit.

## CLIENT ACCEPTANCE

Public accounting is a competitive profession, and most CPA firms are anxious to obtain new clients. However, a CPA firm's principal product is its reputation for credibility. No auditor can afford to be associated with clients who are engaging in management fraud or other misleading practices.

The continuing wave of litigation involving auditors underscores the need for CPA firms to develop quality control policies for investigating prospective clients *before accepting an engagement.* The CPAs should investigate the history of the prospective client, including such matters as the identities and reputations of the directors, officers, and major stockholders.

---

◆ ILLUSTRATIVE CASE ◆

ZZZZ Best Co. was a carpet cleaning company started in 1981 by Barry Minkow, a 15-year-old high school student. Although the company experienced significant growth during the period 1983 through 1985, it was not fast enough for Minkow. He hired several officers with criminal records and conceived a plan to restore damaged buildings for insurance companies. A number of multimillion-dollar restoration contracts were supposedly undertaken that later were found to be completely fictitious. Minkow attempted to cover up the scheme by spending several million dollars to lease a building

*(continued)*

and make it appear to be a legitimate restoration project when the CPAs insisted upon visiting the site. Prior to the time the fraud was uncovered in 1987, the company's stock had a market value in excess of $211 million. Shortly thereafter, the stock was worthless. This case clearly illustrates the risks involved in accepting young companies with rapid growth, the need to investigate the background of key officers of a company, and the need to have a thorough understanding of the client's business.

Auditors should consider the financial strength and credit rating of a prospective client in order to help assess the overall risk of association with that business entity. This overall risk is often referred to as the auditors' **business risk.** The incentive for management to overstate operating results is increased when the client company is in a weak financial position or is greatly in need of additional capital. When an audit client goes bankrupt, the auditors often are named as defendants in lengthy and costly lawsuits. For that reason, some CPAs choose to avoid engagements entailing a relatively high risk of overstated operating results or of subsequent litigation; others may accept such engagements, recognizing the need to expand audit procedures to compensate for the unusually high levels of risk.

## Communication with Predecessor Auditors

The **predecessor auditors** are an excellent source of information about a prospective client. In fact, *SAS 7* (AU 315), "Communications between Predecessor and Successor Auditors," requires that the successor auditors attempt to communicate with the predecessor *before accepting the engagement.* Because auditors are ethically prohibited from disclosing confidential client information without the client's consent, the **successor auditors** should ask the prospective client to authorize the predecessor auditors to respond fully to the successors' inquiries. If a prospective client is reluctant to authorize communications with the predecessor auditors, the successor auditors should seriously consider the implications in deciding whether to accept the engagement.

When permission has been granted, the successor auditors' inquiries will include questions about disagreements with management over accounting principles, the predecessors' understanding of the reason for the change in auditors, and other matters that will assist the successor auditors in deciding whether to accept the engagement. This communication with the predecessor auditors is extremely important as it aids the successor auditors in evaluating the *integrity of management.* A review of cases involving management fraud reveals that a significant number of the companies involved had recently changed their auditors, often because of disagreements over accounting principles.

Regulations of the SEC require companies subject to its jurisdiction to file a Form 8-K reporting changes in independent auditors, and the reasons therefore. The companies must also report the details of any significant disagreements between management and the auditors occurring over the prior three years. The auditors that have resigned or been discharged must provide a response indicating whether they agree with the company's report and providing any necessary details. This requirement discourages management from the practice of **shopping for accounting principles,** in which a company changes auditors to a CPA firm that is more likely to sanction a disputed accounting principle. A company's management might, for example, search for auditors who would accept a questionable revenue recognition method as being in accordance with generally accepted accounting principles. Concern about this problem also led to the issuance of *SAS 50* (AU 625), "Reports on the Application of Accounting Principles," which provides guidance to public accountants when they get a request for a *written or oral* report on the accounting treatment of a prospective or completed transaction from a company that is audited by another CPA firm.

Before providing a report on accounting principles, *SAS 50* requires the accountants to take steps to make sure they have a complete understanding of the form and substance of the transaction, including consulting with the company's current accountants. They should also review existing accounting principles, and consult appropriate references and experts to provide an adequate basis for their conclusions. Although cases in which management actually shops for accounting principles are not common, it is clear that if management can change auditors casually, undue pressure is placed on auditors' independence.

## Other Communications

The auditors may also make inquiries of other third parties in obtaining background information about a prospective audit client. For example, the client's banker can provide information regarding the client's financial history and credit rating. The client's legal counsel can provide information about the client's legal environment, including such matters as pending litigation and regulatory proceedings.

## Other Considerations in Accepting an Audit Client

In addition to evaluating the integrity of management, the auditors will consider whether they can complete the audit in accordance with generally accepted auditing standards. As discussed in Chapter 4, the CPA firm must be independent of the client to perform an audit. Therefore, the auditors must determine whether there are any conditions that would prevent them from performing an *independent* audit of the client. Consideration will also be given to whether the partners and staff have appropriate training and experience to competently complete the engagement. If the auditors have no experience in a particularly complex industry, they may decide that a competent audit of a prospective client in that industry cannot be performed unless the CPA firm hires appropriately experienced personnel.

# OBTAINING THE ENGAGEMENT

After the auditors have collected the necessary information on the potential client, they will be in a position to assess the various risks involved with the audit and determine whether to attempt to obtain the engagement. To obtain the audit, the auditors may be asked to submit a competitive proposal that will include information on the nature of services that the firm offers, the qualifications of the firm's personnel, and other information to convince the prospective client to select the firm. The CPA firm may also be asked to make an oral presentation to the prospective client's audit committee and management to provide a basis for the selection.

## Audit Committees

Arrangements for the audit may be made through contact with the company's **audit committee.** Many companies organize such a committee within the board of directors to take an active role in overseeing the company's accounting and financial reporting policies and practices. Audit committees are required by the New York Stock Exchange, and have been endorsed by the SEC, the AICPA, and the American Stock Exchange.

An audit committee usually is composed of three to five *outside directors*—that is, directors who are neither officers nor employees of the company. The exclusion of officer-directors from the audit committee allows the CPAs to discuss more openly various factors concerning the company. During the course of the audit the discussions with the audit committee will focus on weaknesses in internal control, disagreements with management as to accounting principles, and indications of management fraud or other illegal acts by corporate officers. Since these communications assist the audit committee in its oversight of the financial reporting process of the company, they are required by generally accepted auditing standards. Chapters 8 and 18 present a detailed discussion of the required communications to audit committees.

Not all entities have audit committees. For example, the concept of an audit committee does not apply to businesses organized as sole proprietorships, partnerships, and small, closely held corporations. Arrangements for an audit of these businesses often are made with the owners, a partner, or an executive, such as the president, the treasurer, or the controller.

Fee Arrangements.    When the business engages the services of independent public accountants, it will usually ask for an estimate of the cost of the audit. Staff time is the basic unit of measurement for audit fees. Each public accounting firm develops a per hour or per diem fee schedule for each category of audit staff, based on direct salaries and such related costs as payroll taxes and insurance. The direct rate is then increased for overhead costs and a profit element. In addition to standard per diem or per hour fees, clients are charged for direct costs incurred by the public accounting firm for staff travel, report processing, and other out-of-pocket expenditures.

Estimating a fee for an audit involves the application of the CPA firm's daily or hourly rates to the estimated time required. Since the exact number of hours cannot be determined in advance, the auditors may merely give a rough estimate of the fee. Or they may multiply the rates by the estimated time and quote a range or bracket of amounts within which the total fee will fall. In today's competitive environment, a fixed fee is often quoted that is ''discounted'' from the standard to meet the competition.

Per diem rates for audit work vary considerably in different sections of the country, and even within a given community, in accordance with the reputation and experience of the accounting firm. Of course, the salaries paid to audit staff members are much less than the rates at which audit time is billed to clients. In many firms, salaries represent about 30 percent of billing rates; the remainder is required to cover the cost of nonbillable time when auditors are not assigned, overhead expenses of the office, and a profit to the partners.

Engagement Letters.   The preliminary understanding with the client should be summarized by the auditors in an **engagement letter,** making clear the nature of the engagement, any limitations on the scope of the audit, the work to be performed by the client's staff, scheduled dates for performance and completion of the examination, and the basis for computing the auditors' fee. When the engagement letter is accepted by the authorized client official, it represents an *executory contract* between the auditor and the client. Engagement letters do not follow any standard form; a typical engagement letter is presented in Figure 7–1.

The use of engagement letters is not limited to audit engagements. Professional standards for accounting and review services also require that the accountant have an understanding with the client as to the nature of the services to be performed. This "understanding" *preferably should be in writing* and signed by the client and the CPA.

*[handwritten margin note: explain type 86 opinion do expect to give if not unqualified]*

# AUDIT PLANNING

Once the client has been obtained, the planning process intensifies as the auditors concentrate their efforts on obtaining a detailed understanding of the client's business, and developing an overall audit strategy.

## Obtaining an Understanding of the Client's Business

When should a health club recognize its revenue from the sale of lifetime memberships? Is a company organized to produce a single motion picture a going concern? Is it appropriate for a real estate developer to use the percentage-of-completion method of revenue recognition? What is a reasonable depreciable life for today's most advanced computer systems? We will not attempt to answer these questions in this textbook; we raise them simply to demonstrate that the auditors must obtain a good working knowledge of an audit client's business and its industry if they are to design an effective strategy to allow them to issue an opinion on the fairness of its financial statements.

After the engagement is accepted, the auditors must obtain a detailed understanding of such factors as the client's organizational structure, accounting policies and procedures, capital structure, product lines, and methods of production and distribution. In addition, the CPA should be familiar with matters affecting the industry within which the client operates, including economic conditions and financial trends, inherent types of risk, governmental regulations, changes in technology, and widely used accounting methods. Without such a knowledge of the client's business environment, the auditor would not be in a position to evaluate the appropriateness of the accounting principles in use or the reasonableness of the many estimates and assumptions embodied in the client's financial statements.

Figure 7–1    Engagement Letter for Financial Statement Audit

---

ADAMS, BARNES & CO.

◆

*Certified Public Accountants*

Ms. Loren Steele, Controller
Keystone Computers & Networks, Inc.
14645 40th. Street
Phoenix, Arizona 85280                                                                    September 1 ,19X5

Dear Ms. Steele:

This letter is to confirm our arrangements for our audit of the financial statements of Keystone Computers & Networks, Inc. for the year ended December 31, 19X5.

We will audit the Corporation's balance sheet as of December 31, 19X5, and the related statements of income, retained earnings, and cash flows for the year then ended. The financial statements are the responsibility of the Company's management. Our responsibility is to express an opinion on the financial statements based on our audit. We will also issue a report on compliance with various debt covenants as required by your debt agreement with Western Financial Services.

We will conduct our audit in accordance with generally accepted auditing standards. Those standards require that we plan and perform the audit to obtain reasonable assurance about whether the financial statements are free of material misstatement. An audit includes examining, on a test basis, evidence supporting the amounts and disclosures in the financial statements. An audit also includes assessing the accounting principles used and significant estimates made by management, as well as evaluating the overall financial statement presentation. We believe that our audit will provide a reasonable basis for our opinion.

Our procedures will include tests (by statistical sampling, if feasible) of documentary evidence supporting the transactions recorded in the accounts, tests of the physical existence of inventories, and direct confirmation of receivables and certain other assets and liabilities by correspondence with selected customers, creditors, legal counsel, and banks. At the conclusion of our audit, we will request certain written representations from you about the financial statements and matters related thereto.

Your accounting department personnel will prepare the necessary detailed trial balance and supporting schedules.

Our engagement is subject to the inherent risk that material errors, irregularities, or illegal acts, including fraud or defalcations, if they exist, will not be detected. However, we will inform you of any such matters that come to our attention.

Our examination is scheduled for performance and completion as follows:

| | |
|---|---|
| Begin field work | November 10, 19X5 |
| Completion of field work | February 20, 19X6 |
| Delivery of audit report | March 5, 19X6 |

Our fees for this examination will be based on the time spent by various members of our staff at our regular rates, plus direct expenses. We will notify you immediately of any circumstances we encounter that could significantly affect our initial fee estimate of $12,000.

In order for us to work as efficiently as possible, it is understood that your accounting staff will provide us with a year-end trial balance by January 15, 19X6, and also with the schedules and account analyses described on the separate attachment.

If these arrangements are in accordance with your understanding, please sign this letter in the space provided and return a copy to us at your earliest convenience.

Very truly yours,

*Charles Adams*

Charles Adams, CPA

Accepted by: _____

Date: _____

> **♦ ILLUSTRATIVE CASE ♦**
>
> Volkswagen AG reported that "criminal manipulation" of its foreign-exchange positions has cost the firm as much as $259 million. The fraud prompted the resignation of the company's chief financial officer and the firing of its foreign-exchange manager. The auditors did not detect the irregularities until fraudulent contracts came due and were rejected by banks. An insider suggested that auditors often don't know enough about complicated currency instruments to detect such problems.

Numerous sources of information on prospective clients are available to the auditors. AICPA *Audit and Accounting Guides* and *Industry Risk Alerts,* trade publications, and governmental agency publications are useful in obtaining an orientation to the client's industry. Previous audit reports, annual reports to stockholders, SEC filings, and prior years' tax returns are excellent sources of financial background information. Informal discussions between the auditor-in-charge and key officers of the prospective client can provide information about the history, size, operations, accounting records, and internal controls of the enterprise.

Tour of Plant and Offices.   Another useful preliminary step for the auditors is to arrange an inspection tour of the plant and offices of a prospective client. This tour will give the auditors some understanding of the plant layout, manufacturing process, principal products, and physical safeguards surrounding inventories. During the tour, the auditors should be alert for signs of potential problems. Rust on equipment may indicate that plant assets have been idle; excessive dust on raw materials or finished goods may indicate a problem of obsolescence. A knowledge of the physical facilities will assist the auditors in planning how many audit staff members will be needed to participate in observing the physical inventory.

The tour affords the auditors an opportunity to observe firsthand what types of computer applications and internal documentation are used to record such activities as receiving raw materials, transferring materials into production, and shipping finished goods to customers. An understanding of these computer applications and documentation is essential to the auditors' consideration of internal control.

In visiting the offices, the auditors will learn the location of various computer terminals and accounting records. The auditors can ascertain the practical extent of segregation of duties within the client organization by observing the number of office employees. In addition, the tour will afford an opportunity to meet the key personnel whose names appear on the organization chart. The auditors will record the background information about the client in a *permanent file* available for reference in future engagements.

## Developing an Overall Audit Strategy

After obtaining a knowledge of the client's business, the auditors should formulate an overall audit strategy for the upcoming engagement. The best audit strategy is the approach that results in the most *efficient* audit—that is, an effective audit performed at the least possible cost. *SAS 47* (AU 312), "Audit Risk and Materiality in Conducting an

Audit'' states that in planning an audit, the auditors must consider carefully the appropriate levels of *materiality* and *audit risk*.

Materiality.   Materiality, for planning purposes, is the auditor's preliminary estimate of the smallest amount of misstatement that would probably influence the judgment of a reasonable person relying upon the financial statements. Auditors must modify their opinions whenever there are *material* deficiencies in the client's financial statements. However, they may issue an unqualified report if the deficiencies are *immaterial*.

The auditors' purpose in considering materiality at the planning stage of the audit is to determine the appropriate scope of their audit procedures. Audit procedures should be designed to detect material misstatements, but not so as to waste time searching for immaterial misstatements that cannot affect the auditors' report. As described in Chapter 6, the scope of the auditors' procedures for an account is directly related to the risk of material misstatement of that account. The auditors will perform extensive procedures on an account with a high degree of risk of material misstatement. Ordinarily, no audit procedures will be performed on an account that is immaterial.

While planning the audit, the auditors may also become aware of a number of accounting expediencies followed by the client which may result in immaterial misstatements. The concept of materiality often allows auditors to ''pass over'' such conceptual accounting errors as:

1. Charging all purchases of office supplies directly to expense accounts and making no effort to record as an asset the small quantities of office supplies remaining on hand at year-end.
2. Charging low-cost items such as small tools or desk-top calculators directly to expense accounts.
3. Not accruing liabilities for payroll taxes when the period ends between payroll dates. Many companies follow this policy in order to keep their accounting records consistent with the deductibility of payroll taxes for income tax purposes.

The auditors need to carefully consider the likelihood that the effect of these accounting expediencies may differ materially from results obtained following generally accepted accounting principles. Accounting expediencies are not acceptable simply because the client's management says the amounts involved are immaterial or because the amounts involved were considered immaterial in the past.

Quantifying Planning Materiality at the Overall Financial Statement Level.   Auditing standards require auditors to consider preliminary estimates of materiality for the audit, but they are not required to quantify the amount. Many CPA firms, however, have found it beneficial to quantify planning materiality to make sure that all of the professional staff on an audit view materiality for the audit in the same way.

Auditors use various approaches in determining a materiality measure for planning purposes. Some auditors rely upon judgment to estimate the amount that would materially distort the individual financial statements. The auditors may, for example, estimate that a $100,000 misstatement of net income on the income statement is material, while a $200,000 misstatement of total assets on the balance sheet is material. Since most misstatements affect both net income and total assets, the auditors would then design their audit to detect the smallest misstatement that would be material to any one of the financial statements, in this case $100,000. Auditors may also use *rules of thumb* related to a financial statement base, such as net income, total revenues, or total assets, to develop these estimates of overall materiality. Rules of thumb that are commonly used in practice include:

+ 5% to 10% of net income before taxes
+ 1/2% to 1% of total assets
+ 1/2% to 1% of total revenues
+ 1% of total equity

The appropriate financial statement base for computing materiality will vary based on the nature of the client's business. For example, total revenues for a financial institution is often too small to use as the base, in conjunction with the percentages presented above. In addition, if a company is in a near breakeven position, net income for the year will be much too small to be used as the financial statement base. In that situation, the auditors will often choose another financial statement base or use an average of net income over a number of prior years.

Auditors typically use a "sliding scale" for calculating overall materiality. For example, they might use 1 percent of total sales for materiality on the audit of a small business and 1/2 percent of total sales on the audit of a large corporation. This is because the absolute amount of materiality is also important. Consider a small business with $2,000,000 in revenue. If 1/2 percent of total revenue was used as a rule of thumb, $10,000 would be calculated as overall materiality. However, it is unlikely that $10,000 would affect a user's decision about the financial position and results of operations of any company. In addition, it would be impractical to audit the company to that level of precision.

Qualitative Considerations about Materiality.  Qualitative factors can also affect the determination of materiality for the audit. As indicated in Chapter 2, materiality depends not only on the amount of the item, but also on its nature. An illegal payment of a relatively small amount, for example, might be considered material to the company's financial statements. Other examples include the following:

+ A misstatement of the financial statements that would affect a company's compliance with a contractual agreement might be material regardless of its amount. As an example, assume that a company's long-term debt agreement requires the company to maintain working capital of at least $500,000; otherwise, the total debt becomes payable upon demand. If the company's working capital on the balance sheet was only slightly more than $500,000, a small misstatement might disguise a violation of the debt agreement. Since the violation would mean that the company's long-term debt should be reclassified as a current liability, the small misstatement becomes material to the financial statements.
+ A misstatement that reverses a trend of earnings for the company might be material regardless of its amount. For example, if a company has reported a 2 percent increase in net earnings for each of the last five years, an audit adjustment that would alter this trend by reporting no increase in net earnings might affect an investor's decision on whether to invest in the company.

◆ ILLUSTRATIVE CASE ◆

One of the Big 6 CPA firms has developed the following table to assist its audit staff in determining planning materiality based on the greater of total assets or total sales.

| If the Greater of Total Assets or Total Revenues Is: | | Materiality Is: | |
| --- | --- | --- | --- |
| **Over** | **But Not Over** | **Times** | **the Excess Over** |
| $              0 | $           30,000 | $              0 + .05900 | $                 0 |
| 30,000 | 100,000 | 1,780 + .03100 | 30,000 |
| 100,000 | 300,000 | 3,970 + .02140 | 100,000 |
| 300,000 | 1,000,000 | 8,300 + .01450 | 300,000 |
| 1,000,000 | 3,000,000 | 18,400 + .01000 | 1,000,000 |
| 3,000,000 | 10,000,000 | 38,300 + .00670 | 3,000,000 |
| 10,000,000 | 30,000,000 | 85,500 + .00460 | 10,000,000 |
| 30,000,000 | 100,000,000 | 178,000 + .00313 | 30,000,000 |
| 100,000,000 | 300,000,000 | 397,000 + .00214 | 100,000,000 |
| 300,000,000 | 1,000,000,000 | 826,000 + .00145 | 300,000,000 |
| 1,000,000,000 | 3,000,000,000 | 1,840,000 + .00100 | 1,000,000,000 |
| 3,000,000,000 | 10,000,000,000 | 3,830,000 + .00067 | 3,000,000,000 |
| 10,000,000,000 | 30,000,000,000 | 8,550,000 + .00046 | 10,000,000,000 |
| 30,000,000,000 | 100,000,000,000 | 17,800,000 + .00031 | 30,000,000,000 |
| 100,000,000,000 | 300,000,000,000 | 39,700,000 + .00021 | 100,000,000,000 |
| 300,000,000,000 | — | 82,600,000 + .00015 | 300,000,000,000 |

To illustrate application of the table, assume that a company has $12,670,000 of total assets and $20,520,000 of total revenue. Planning materiality would be calculated as described below:

$$\$85,500 + .00460 (\$20,520,000 - \$10,000,000) = \$133,892$$

While some qualitative factors can be considered when the audit is being planned, most cannot because the auditors do not know what types of misstatements will be found. Of course, the auditors will consider both the quantitative and qualitative aspects of the detected misstatements when they subsequently *evaluate the results* of their audit procedures. Evaluating the results of audit procedures is described in Chapter 18.

Allocating Overall Materiality to Individual Accounts.    Once the auditors have determined planning materiality for the overall financial statements, the auditors may decide to allocate materiality to individual financial statement accounts. The auditors generally allocate materiality only when they intend to use audit sampling for substantive testing of one or more of the accounts. When materiality is allocated to a particular account, it is referred to as the amount of *tolerable misstatement* of the account. Chapters 10 and 11 illustrate how tolerable misstatement is used in conjunction with substantive tests using audit sampling.

Allocating materiality to individual accounts is very complex and there are several techniques that are commonly used in practice. Before describing these techniques it is important to understand that simply allocating materiality to all accounts dollar for dollar, so that the total amount of all the tolerable misstatements is equal to overall planning materiality, is far too conservative. This is because misstatements of various accounts often counterbalance each other. That is, the overstatement of one asset may be offset by the understatement of another. Another reason that materiality should not be allocated dollar for dollar is the double-entry bookkeeping system, which allows detection of misstatements in an account by auditing a related account. For example, if at year-end a purchase of inventory on credit is recorded at an improper amount, the misstatement may be detected by the tests of inventories or by the tests of accounts payable.

As indicated above, several techniques are used to allocate materiality to individual accounts in practice—we will describe two. When using the first technique, the auditors multiply the amount of overall planning materiality by some factor, usually from 1.5 to 2. This amount is then allocated to the various balance sheet accounts.

The second technique involves allocating materiality only to those accounts that are to be tested with audit sampling. When using this approach, the auditors typically reduce overall materiality by an estimate of the aggregate amount of misstatement that will go undetected. Undetected misstatement is expected because the auditors design their tests to detect only material misstatement—smaller amounts often go undetected. The amount of overall materiality, reduced by this estimate of undetected misstatement, is then used as tolerable misstatement for every account that is being tested with audit sampling. Since estimating the amount of undetected misstatement is very difficult, many CPA firms have developed rules of thumb—25 to 50 percent of overall materiality is often used as an estimate of the amount of undetected misstatement.

---

♦ ILLUSTRATIVE CASE ♦

To illustrate the allocation of materiality to individual accounts, assume that the auditors have determined that overall materiality for the entire financial statements is $100,000. Using the first technique described above with a factor of 2, the auditors would allocate a total of $200,000 ($100,000 × 2) to the various balance sheet accounts. For audit efficiency, the auditors should allocate more of this amount to those accounts that are more time-consuming to audit, and little or no amount to those that are easy to audit. For example, cash can usually be audited to the penny at a low cost; therefore, no amount of materiality may be allocated to that account. The auditors will allocate the majority of the $200,000 to accounts that are difficult to audit, such as accounts receivable and inventories.

Assume that the auditors have decided to use the second technique to allocate materiality and are planning to use audit sampling in the substantive tests of two accounts, inventories and accounts receivable. If the auditors use 40 percent of overall materiality as an estimate of the amount undetected misstatement, they will use $60,000 ($100,000 − (40% × $100,000)) as tolerable misstatement for each of the two accounts.

Audit Risk.   As discussed in Chapter 6, the term **audit risk** refers to the possibility that the auditors may unknowingly fail to appropriately modify their opinion on financial statements that are materially misstated. At the overall financial statement level, audit risk is the chance that a material misstatement exists in the financial statements, and the auditors do not detect the misstatement with their audit procedures.

Auditors are aware that few audits involve material misstatements of financial statements, but when such misstatements do exist, they can result in millions of dollars of potential liability to the auditors. Experience has shown that many undetected misstatements of financial statements are intentional irregularities, rather than unintentional errors.

---

◆ ILLUSTRATIVE CASE ◆

An analysis of 456 court cases filed against CPAs indicates that management fraud was present approximately 44 percent of the time. Other employee defalcations were believed to be present 2 percent of the time. An assortment of accounting and auditing errors was alleged in the remaining cases.

---

In developing an audit plan, the auditors must consider factors that affect audit risk. An essential concept here is that the risk of misstatement is higher for some audits than for others. Figure 7–2 presents a list of risk factors, or "red flags" which may indicate a higher than normal risk of misstated financial statements. While none of these risk factors in and of itself would normally indicate the existence of material misstatement with certainty, each one should be considered by the auditors in planning the audit.

Analytical Procedures.   As described in Chapter 6, **analytical procedures** involve comparisons of financial statement balances and ratios for the period under audit with auditor expectations developed from sources such as the client's prior years' financial statements, published industry statistics, and budgets. When used for planning purposes, analytical procedures assist the auditors in planning the nature, timing, and extent of audit procedures that will be used for the specific accounts. The approach used is one of obtaining an understanding of the client's business and transactions, and identifying areas that may represent higher risks. The auditors will then plan a more thorough investigation of these potential problem areas, and perform a more effective audit. *SAS 56* (AU 329), "Analytical Procedures," requires the auditors to perform analytical procedures as a part of the planning process for *every* audit.

An example of the use of an analytical procedure for planning purposes is the comparison of the client's inventory turnover for the current year with comparable statistics from prior years. A significant decrease in inventory turnover might lead the auditors to consider the possibility that the client has excessive amounts of inventory. As a result, the auditors would plan a more extensive search for inventory items that may be obsolete.

First-Year Procedures.   A new client should be informed as to the extent of investigation of the beginning balances of such accounts as plant and equipment and inventories. To determine the propriety of depreciation expense for the current year and the proper

Figure 7–2    Financial Statement Risk of Misstatement Factors*

**Management Characteristics**

— Management operating and financing decisions are dominated by a single person.

— Management's attitude toward financial reporting is unduly aggressive.

— Management turnover (particularly senior accounting personnel) is high.

— Management places undue emphasis on meeting earnings projections.

— Management's reputation in the business community is poor.

**Operating Characteristics**

— Profitability of entity relative to its industry is inadequate or inconsistent.

— Sensitivity of operating results to economic factors (inflation, interest rates, unemployment, etc.) is high.

— Rate of change in entity's industry is rapid.

— Direction of change in entity's industry is declining with many business failures.

— Organization is decentralized without adequate monitoring.

— Internal or external matters are present that bring into question the entity's ability to continue as a going concern.

**Engagement Characteristics**

— Many contentious or difficult accounting issues are present.

— Significant difficult-to-audit transactions or balances.

— Significant and unusual related party transactions not in the ordinary course of business.

— Nature, cause (if known), or the amount of known and likely misstatements detected in the audit of prior period's financial statements is significant.

— New client with no prior audit history or sufficient information is not available from the predecessor auditor.

*AICPA, *Statement on Auditing Standards 53*, "The Auditor's Responsibility to Detect and Report Errors and Irregularities" (New York, 1988), AU 316.

balances in plant and equipment accounts at the balance sheet date, the auditors must investigate the validity of the property accounts at the beginning of the current period. Similarly, if the auditors are unable to obtain satisfactory evidence as to the balance of *beginning inventory,* they will not have sufficient evidence about cost of goods sold, and it will be necessary to disclaim an opinion on the income statement.

When satisfactory preceding-year audits of the business have been performed by reputable predecessor auditors, the auditors may be able to accept the opening balances of the current year with a minimum of verification work; in cases in which no satisfactory recent audit has been made, an extensive analysis of transactions of prior years will be necessary to establish account balances as of the beginning of the current year. In these latter situations, where appropriate, the client should be informed that the scope and cost of the initial audit may exceed that of repeat engagements, which will not require analysis of past years' transactions.

**Use of the Client's Staff.**   The auditors should obtain an understanding with the client as to the extent to which the client's staff, including the internal auditors, can help prepare for the audit. The client's staff should have the accounting records up-to-date when the auditors arrive. In addition, many audit working papers can be prepared for the auditors by the client's staff, thus reducing the cost of the audit and freeing the auditors from routine work. The auditors may set up the columnar headings for such working papers and give instructions to the client's staff as to the information to be gathered. As indicated in Chapter 6, these working papers should bear the label *Prepared by Client,* or *PBC,* and also the initials of the auditor who verifies the work performed by the client's staff. Working papers prepared by the client should never be accepted at face value; such papers must be reviewed and tested by the auditors.

Among the tasks that may be assigned to the client's employees are the preparation of a trial balance of the general ledger, preparation of an aged trial balance of accounts receivable, analyses of accounts receivable written off, lists of property additions and retirements during the year, and analyses of various revenue and expense accounts. Many of these "working papers" may be in the form of computer spreadsheets and other computerized data files.

**Other CPAs.**   When a portion of the client is audited by another CPA firm (e.g., a subsidiary in a distant city) efforts may be coordinated. For example, if the accounts of the subsidiary are to be consolidated with the overall enterprise, and if that subsidiary is audited by another CPA firm, the auditors must coordinate timing of necessary reports and procedures to be performed. Use of the work of other auditors was discussed in Chapter 3.

**Arranging Specialists.**   CPAs may lack the qualifications necessary to perform certain technical tasks relating to the audit. For example, judging the valuation of a diamond inventory may require employing a specialist in gem appraisal. Effective planning involves arranging for the appropriate use of specialists both inside and outside of the client organization. Using the work of specialists was discussed in detail in Chapter 6.

## Audit Plans

The planning process is documented in the audit working papers through the preparation of *audit plans, audit programs,* and *time budgets.* These "planning and supervision" working papers serve a dual purpose. First, they provide documentary evidence of the CPA firm's compliance with the "adequate planning" requirement of the first standard of field work. Second, these working papers provide the auditor-in-charge with a means of coordinating, scheduling, and supervising the activities of the audit staff members involved in the engagement.

An **audit plan** is an overview of the engagement, outlining the nature and characteristics of the client's business operations and the overall audit strategy. Although audit plans differ in form and content among public accounting firms, a typical plan includes details on the following:

1. Description of the client company—its structure, business, and organization.
2. Objectives of the audit (e.g., audit for stockholders, special-purpose audit, SEC filings).
3. Nature and extent of other services, such as preparation of tax returns, to be performed for the client.
4. Timing and scheduling of the audit work, including determining which procedures may be performed before the balance sheet date, what must be done on or after the balance sheet date and setting dates for such critical procedures as cash counts, accounts receivable confirmations, and inventory observation.
5. Work to be done by the client's staff.
6. Staffing requirements during the engagement.
7. Target dates for completing major segments of the engagement, such as the consideration of internal control, tax returns, the audit report, and SEC filings.
8. Any special audit risks for the engagement.
9. Preliminary judgments about materiality levels for the engagement.

The audit plan is normally drafted before starting work at the client's offices. However, the plan may be modified throughout the engagement as special problems are encountered and as the auditors' consideration of internal control lead to identification of areas requiring more or less audit work. An audit plan is included as a part of the illustrative audit case at the end of this chapter.

## Time Budgets for Audit Engagements

Public accounting firms usually charge clients on a time basis, and detailed time budgets can assist the auditors in estimating the audit fee. A **time budget** for an audit is constructed by estimating the time required for each step in the audit program for each of the various grades of auditors and totaling these estimated amounts. Time budgets serve other functions in addition to providing a basis for estimating fees. The time budget communicates to the audit staff those areas the manager or partner believe are critical and require more time. It also is an important tool of the audit senior—it is used to measure the efficiency of the staff and to determine at each stage of the engagement whether the work is progressing at a satisfactory rate.

There is always pressure to complete an audit within the estimated time. The staff assistant who takes more than the normal time for a task is not likely to be popular with supervisors or to win rapid advancement. Ability to do satisfactory work when given abundant time is not a sufficient qualification, *for time is never abundant in public accounting*.

The development of time budgets is facilitated in repeat engagements by reference to the preceding year's detailed time records. Sometimes time budgets prove quite unattainable because the client's records are not in satisfactory condition, or because of other special circumstances that arise. Even when time estimates are exceeded, there can be no compromise with qualitative standards in the performance of the field work. The CPA firm's professional reputation and its legal liability to clients and third parties do not permit any shortcutting or omission of audit procedures to meet a predetermined time estimate.

---

◆ ILLUSTRATIVE CASE ◆

A problem for some CPA firms is staff members understating the hours they have actually worked—a practice informally called "eating time." One study revealed that over 50 percent of respondents in the profession complete work on their own time without reporting the chargeable hours. This is generally accomplished by arriving early, staying late, or working through lunch or on weekends without recording the extra hours on the time sheet. Such a practice results in several problems for the CPA firm, including underbilling of clients, unrealistic future time budgets, and lower staff morale. This is a particularly difficult problem to eliminate since the in-charge auditors tend to benefit from the practice, because the audit engagement is completed in less time than was budgeted.

---

## Planning a Recurring Engagement

Planning a repeat engagement is far easier than planning for a first audit of a new client. The auditor-in-charge of a repeat engagement generally was involved in the previous year's audit and has a good working knowledge of the client's business. Also, the previous year's audit working papers contain a wealth of information useful in planning the recurring engagement. For example, the audit plan provides background information about the client and explains the overall strategy employed in the last audit. The prior year's audit program shows in detail the procedures performed and the length of time required to perform them. In addition, last year's working papers substantiate the beginning balances for the current year's audit.

While the prior year's working papers are extremely useful in planning the new engagement, the auditor-in-charge should not merely duplicate last year's audit program. Each audit should be a learning experience for the auditors, enabling them to design a more efficient audit in the following year. Also, the auditors may need to modify their approach to the audit for any changes in the client's operations, internal control structure, or business environment.

# DESIGNING AUDIT PROGRAMS

An **audit program** is a detailed list of the audit procedures to be performed in the course of the examination. A tentative audit program is developed as part of the advance planning of an audit. This tentative program, however, requires frequent modification as the audit progresses. For example, the nature, timing, and extent of substantive test procedures are influenced by the auditor's assessment of control risk. Thus, not until the consideration of internal control has been completed can a relatively final version of the audit program be drafted. Even this version may require modification if the auditors revise their preliminary estimates of materiality or risk for the engagement, or if the substantive tests disclose unexpected problems.

# The Audit Trail

In developing audit procedures, the auditors are assisted by the organized manner in which accounting systems record, classify, and summarize data. The flow of accounting data begins with the recording of thousands of individual transactions on such documents as invoices and checks. The information recorded on these original "source" documents is summarized in journals and the amounts in the journals are posted to ledger accounts. At the end of the year, the balances in the ledger accounts are arranged in the form of financial statements.

In thinking of the accounting records as a whole, we may say that a continuous trail of evidence exists—a trail of evidence that links the thousands of individual transactions comprising a year's business activity with the summary figures in the financial statements. In a manual accounting system, this *audit trail* consists of source documents, journal entries, and ledger entries. An audit trail also exists within a computer-based accounting system, although it may have a substantially different form; this will be discussed in Chapter 9.

Just as a hiker may walk in either direction along a mountain path, an auditor may follow the audit trail in either of two directions. For example, the auditor may follow specific transactions from their origin forward to their inclusion in the financial statement summary figures. This approach provides the auditor with assurance that all transactions have been properly interpreted and processed; it is a test of the completeness assertion.

On the other hand, the auditor may follow the stream of evidence back to its sources. This type of verification consists of tracing the various items in the statements (such as cash, receivables, sales, and expenses) back to the ledger accounts, and from the ledgers on back through the journals to original documents, evidencing transactions. This process of working backward from the financial statement figures to the detailed evidence of individual transactions ensures that financial statement figures are based upon valid transactions; it tests the existence assertion.

Although the technique of working along the audit trail is a useful one, bear in mind that the auditors must acquire other types of evidence obtained from sources other than the client's accounting records.

# Organization of the Audit Program

The audit program usually is divided into two major sections. The first section deals with the procedures to assess the effectiveness of the client's internal control structure (the "systems portion"), and the second section deals with the "substantive testing" of financial statement amounts, as well as the adequacy of financial statement disclosures.

### The Systems (Internal Control Structure) Portion of the Program.

The systems portion of the audit program is generally organized around the major **transaction cycles** of the client's internal control structure. For example, the systems portion of the audit program for a manufacturing company might be subdivided into separate programs for such areas as: (1) revenue (sales and collections) cycle, (2) acquisition (purchases and disbursements) cycle, (3) conversion (production) cycle, (4) payroll cycle, (5) investing cycle, and (6) financing cycle.

To illustrate one of these transaction cycles, let us consider sales and collections. The procedures used in processing sales transactions might include receiving a customer's purchase order, credit approval, shipment of merchandise, preparation of sales invoices, recording the sale, recording the account receivable, billing, and handling and recording the cash received from the customer.

Audit procedures in the systems portion of the program typically include obtaining an understanding of the internal controls for each transaction cycle, preparation of flowcharts for each cycle, tests of the significant internal controls, and the assessment of control risk for the related financial statement assertions.

In conjunction with their consideration of internal control, the auditors will make appropriate modification in the substantive test portion of the audit program. For example, as a result of weaknesses in internal control over the proper recording of sales, the auditors may assess control risk for the assertion of existence of accounts receivable to be high, and decide to send additional accounts receivable confirmations.

The Substantive Test Portion of the Program.   The portion of the audit program aimed at substantiating financial statement amounts usually is organized in terms of major balance sheet accounts, such as cash, accounts receivable, inventories, and plant and equipment. Considering the importance of the income statement, why do audit programs emphasize the substantiation of balance sheet items? In part, this method of organizing the work may be a carryover from the days when the auditors' objective was verification of the balance sheet alone. Even though present-day auditors are very much concerned with the reliability of the income statement, they still find the balance sheet approach to be an effective method of organizing their substantive audit procedures.

One advantage of the balance sheet approach is that highly competent evidence generally is available to substantiate assets and liabilities. Assets usually are subject to direct verification by such procedures as physical observation, inspection of externally created documentary evidence, and confirmation by outside parties. Liabilities usually can be verified by examination of externally created documents, confirmation, and inspection of canceled checks after the liability has been paid.

In contrast, consider the nature of revenues and expenses in double-entry accounting. The entry to record revenues or expenses has two parts: first, the recognition of the revenue or expense; and second, the corresponding change in an asset or liability account. Revenues and expenses have no tangible form; they exist only as entries in the client's accounting records, representing changes in owners' equity. Consequently, the best evidence supporting the existence of revenues or expenses usually is the verifiable change in the related asset or liability account.

Indirect Verification of Income Statement Accounts.   Figure 7–3 shows the relationship between income statement accounts and the related changes in cash or other balance sheet items. By substantiating the changes in the asset and liability accounts, the auditors indirectly verify revenue, cost of goods sold, and expenses. For example, most revenue transactions involve a debit to either Cash or Accounts Receivable. If the auditors are able to satisfy themselves that all cash receipts and all changes in accounts receivable during the year have been properly recorded, they have indirect evidence that revenue transactions have been accounted for properly.

Figure 7–3 The Auditors' Approach to Auditing Financial Statement Accounts

| | Income Statement Items | | Cash Transactions | | Balance Sheet Items | | |
|---|---|---|---|---|---|---|---|
| | | | | | Beginning balance | | Ending balance |
| | Revenue | = | Cash receipts from customers | − | Beginning balance of Accounts Receivable | + | Ending balance of Accounts Receivable |
| | Cost of goods sold | = | Cash payments for merchandise | − | Beginning balance of Accounts Payable | + | Ending balance of Accounts Payable |
| | | | | + | Beginning balance of Inventory | − | Ending balance of Inventory |
| | | | | − | Beginning balances of Accrued Expenses | + | Ending balances of Accrued Expenses |
| | Expenses | = | Cash payments for expenses | + | Beginning balances of Prepaid Expenses | − | Ending balances of Prepaid Expenses |
| Financial statement relationships | ↑ | | ↑ | | ↑ | | ↑ |
| Auditors' approach to substantiation | Verify indirectly by substantiating right-hand side of equation; also use analytical procedures and (if possible) direct computations. | | Substantiate by testing transactions; also perform reconciliations of cash accounts. | | Substantiate by reference to last year's audit working papers. | | Substantiate by substantive tests in current year. |

209

Direct Verification of Income Statement Accounts.    Not all of the audit evidence pertaining to income statement accounts is indirect. The verification of a major balance sheet item often involves several closely related income statement accounts that can be verified through computation or other direct evidence. For example, in substantiating the marketable securities owned by the client, it is a simple matter to compute the related interest revenue, dividends revenue, and gains or losses on sales of securities. In substantiating the balance sheet items of plant assets and accumulated depreciation, the auditors make computations that also substantiate depreciation expense. Uncollectible accounts expense is substantiated in conjunction with the balance sheet item Allowance for Doubtful Accounts. In addition to these computations, the auditors' *analytical procedures* provide direct evidence as to the reasonableness of various revenues and expenses.

Comparison of the Systems Approach and the Substantive Approach.    Auditing literature frequently refers to a CPA firm following a systems approach or a substantive approach to an audit. The **systems approach** involves extensive testing of the design and operating effectiveness of internal controls to justify low control risk assessments; the **substantive approach** relies more heavily upon substantive testing to restrict detection risk as the basis for the auditors' opinion. Actually, almost all audits involve a blend of procedures aimed at testing the effectiveness of internal controls and substantive testing. Thus, *systems approach* and *substantive approach* are relative terms, indicating the emphasis that a particular CPA firm places in the system and substantive portions of its audit program on a given engagement. Some CPA firms may lean toward one approach or the other as a matter of firm policy. However, in the audit of a client with weak internal control, the resulting high level of control risk allows the auditors no choice but to emphasize the substantive approach.

## Objectives of Audit Programs

An audit program is designed to accomplish audit objectives with respect to each major account in the financial statements. These objectives follow directly from the assertions that are contained in the clients' financial statements. Recall that those assertions are:

1. Existence or occurrence.
2. Completeness.
3. Rights and obligations.
4. Valuation or allocation.
5. Presentation and disclosure.

From these assertions, general objectives may be developed for each major type of balance sheet account, including assets, liabilities, and owners' equity.

## General Objectives of Audit Programs for Asset Accounts

The audit program for each financial statement account must be tailored to accomplish the specific audit objectives for that account. The specific objectives for auditing cash are not identical to the specific objectives for auditing accounts receivable. For example, questions about proper net realizable value causes valuation to be a bigger concern for accounts receivable. However, it is useful to realize that each audit program follows basically the same general approach to verifying the balance sheet items and related income statement amounts. To varying degrees, the substantive audit program for each asset category will need to include procedures to address the following general objectives:

---

**Substantive Audit Program for Asset Accounts Stated in Terms of General Objectives**

A.  Establish the *existence* of assets.
B.  Establish that the company has *rights* to the assets.
C.  Establish *completeness* of recorded assets.
D.  Determine the appropriate *valuation* of the assets.
E.  Establish the *clerical accuracy* of the underlying records.
F.  Determine the appropriate financial statement *presentation and disclosure* of the assets.

---

The above objectives for asset accounts include a "clerical accuracy" objective— Objective E. Clerical accuracy, a distinct part of several assertions, including completeness, existence, and valuation, may either be considered separately or as a part of the other objectives. Changes in these audit objectives, with respect to audit programs for liability and owners' equity accounts, will be discussed in later chapters.

## Substantiation of Account Balances

The central purpose of the auditors' consideration of internal control is to assess control risk for each major **assertion** concerning a financial statement account to determine the nature, timing, and extent of the audit work necessary to substantiate the account balance. In subsequent chapters, considerable attention will be given to the consideration of internal control; let us now discuss the objectives of the auditors' substantive procedures.

## Existence of Assets

The first step in substantiating the balance of an asset account is to verify the existence of the asset. For assets such as cash on hand, marketable securities, and inventories, existence of the asset usually may be verified by physical inspection, and by *vouching* from the recorded entry to the documents created when the assets were acquired.

When assets are in the custody of others, such as cash in banks and inventory on consignment, the appropriate audit procedure may be direct confirmation with the outside party. The existence of accounts receivable normally is verified by confirming with customers the amounts receivable. Verifying the existence of intangibles is more difficult; the auditors must gather evidence that costs have been incurred and that these costs represent probable future economic benefits.

## Rights to the Assets

Usually, the same procedures that verify existence also establish the company's rights to the asset. For example, confirming cash balances in bank accounts establishes existence of the cash and the company's ownership rights to that cash. Similarly, inspecting marketable securities verifies both existence and ownership because the registered owner's name usually appears on the face of the security certificate.

With other assets, such as plant and equipment, physical examination establishes existence *but not ownership*. Plant and equipment may be rented or leased rather than owned. To verify the client's rights to plant assets, the auditors must inspect documentary evidence such as property tax bills, purchase documents, and deeds.

The client may not hold legal title to all assets that are appropriately included in the financial statements. Instead, the client may own *rights* to use the assets conveyed by contracts, such as leases. The ownership of these rights may be established by reviewing the underlying contracts.

## Establishing Completeness

An effective internal control structure that provides assurance that acquisitions are recorded helps the auditors to establish the completeness of recorded assets. When such controls are found to be ineffective, the scope of substantive tests must be increased, but this is often a difficult task. When the auditors are testing the completeness of assets, they are looking for assets that have been acquired but not recorded in the accounting records. Therefore, analyzing recorded entries in the asset accounts will not be effective for this purpose; the auditors must take a different approach.

Many tests for unrecorded assets involve *tracing* from the "source documents" created when the assets were acquired to entries recording the assets in the accounting records. To test for unrecorded accounts receivable, for example, the auditors might select a sample of shipping documents issued during the year and trace the details to recorded sales transactions. Observation and physical examination are important to testing the completeness of recorded physical assets. To illustrate, during the observation of the client's physical inventory, the auditors are alert for inventory items that are not counted or included in the inventory summary. Physically examining equipment may reveal purchases that have not been properly capitalized.

Analytical procedures also may be used to bring conditions to light that indicate that all assets may not be recorded. For example, a low gross profit percentage for the current year in comparison to prior years may indicate that the client has a substantial amount of unrecorded inventory.

### Verifying the Cutoff of Transactions.

As a part of the auditors' procedures for establishing completeness as well as existence of recorded assets, the auditors will verify the client's cutoff of transactions included in the period. The financial statements should reflect all transactions occurring through the end of the period and none that occur subsequently. The term *cutoff* refers to the process of determining that transactions occurring near the balance sheet date are assigned to the proper accounting period.

The impact of cutoff errors upon the financial statements varies with the nature of the error. For example, a cutoff error in recording acquisitions of plant assets affects the balance sheet, but probably does not affect the income statement since depreciation usually is not recorded on assets acquired within a few days of year-end. On the other hand, a cutoff error in recording shipments of merchandise to customers affects both inventory and the cost of sales. In order to improve their financial picture, some clients may "hold their records open" to include in the current year cash receipts and revenue from the first part of the next period.

To verify the client's cutoff of transactions, the auditors should review transactions recorded shortly before and after the balance sheet date to ascertain that these transactions are assigned to the proper period. When such documents as checks, receiving reports, and shipping documents are serially numbered, noting the last serial number issued during the period will assist the auditors in determining that a proper cutoff has been made in recording transactions.

Direction of Testing.   In the above discussion of the existence and completeness assertions, two similar tests are described. In one test, *existence* of assets was verified by *vouching* from the recorded entry to the source documents. In the second test, the *completeness* of recording of assets was verified by *tracing* from the source documents to the recorded entry. Figure 7–4 illustrates these concepts.

In the first test, the auditors are looking for unsupported entries in the journals (or ledgers). Vouching from right to left on Figure 7–4 one might identify journal entries that are not supported and, possibly, are not valid. Note that transactions that are not supported

Figure 7–4   Direction of Tests

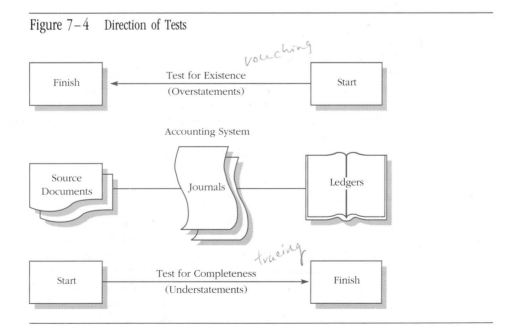

*can never* be found by tracing forward from source documents to the journal entries (left to right).

In the second test, the auditors are determining the *completeness* of posted transactions. If a transaction was never posted, the omission can be detected only by tracing in the direction from the source documents to the journals and ledgers. Transactions improperly omitted from ledger accounts cannot be brought to light by tracing existing ledger entries back to their source. Of course, some errors, such as transposition errors in entering transactions and postings to the wrong account, may be discovered by tracing or vouching.

## Valuation of Assets

Determining the proper valuation of assets requires a thorough knowledge of generally accepted accounting principles. The auditors must not only establish that the accounting method used to value a particular asset is generally accepted, they must also determine that the method of valuation is appropriate in the circumstances. Once the auditors are satisfied as to the appropriateness of the method, the auditors will perform procedures to test the accuracy of the client's application of the method of valuation to the asset.

Most assets are valued at cost. Therefore, a common audit procedure is to vouch the acquisition cost of assets to paid checks and other documentary evidence. If the acquisition cost is subject to depreciation or amortization, the auditors must evaluate the reasonableness of the cost allocation program and verify the computation of the remaining unallocated cost. Assets valued at the lower of cost or market necessitate an investigation of current market prices as well as acquisition costs.

## Clerical Accuracy of Records

The amount appearing as an asset on a financial statement is almost always the accumulation of many smaller items. For example, the amount of inventory on a financial statement might consist of the cost of thousands or, perhaps, hundreds of thousands of individual products. The auditors must test the clerical accuracy of the underlying records to determine that they accumulate to the total appearing in the general ledger and, therefore, the amount in the financial statements. The auditors often use their generalized audit programs to perform these tests of clerical accuracy of the records.

## Financial Statement Presentation and Disclosure

Even after all dollar amounts have been substantiated, the auditors must perform procedures to ensure that the financial statement presentation conforms to the requirements of authoritative accounting pronouncements and the general principle of adequate disclosure. Procedures falling into this category include the review of subsequent events; search for related party transactions; investigation of loss contingencies; review of disclosure of such items as accounting policies, leases, compensating balances, and pledged assets; and consideration of the categories and descriptions used on all of the financial statements.

## An Illustration of Audit Program Design

The above general objectives apply to all types of assets. Audit procedures for a particular asset account must be designed to accomplish the *specific audit objectives* regarding that asset. These specific objectives vary with the nature of the asset and the generally accepted accounting principles that govern its valuation and presentation.

In designing an audit program for a specific account, the auditors start by developing general objectives from the financial statement assertions. Then, specific objectives are developed for the account under audit and, finally, audit procedures are designed to accomplish each specific audit objective. Figure 7–5 provides a description of this process for accounts receivable and illustrates the relationship between management assertions, audit objectives, and audit procedures.

Figure 7–5 includes an example of only one substantive audit procedure for each specific objective. Usually, additional procedures must be performed to accomplish the audit objectives. For example, the audit objective of determining that receivables are properly presented in the balance sheet is not achieved solely by performing procedures focusing on the disclosure of related party transactions. The audit program must include procedures that focus on other aspects of presentation and disclosure, such as procedures designed to identify receivables pledged as collateral for debt. In addition, the complete

**Figure 7–5   Relationship of Assertions, Objectives, and Procedures**

| Management Assertions | General Audit Objectives for Assets | Specific Audit Objectives for Accounts Receivable | Example Audit Procedures |
|---|---|---|---|
| Existence or occurrence | Existence of assets | All receivables exist | Confirm a sample of receivables by direct communication with debtors |
| Rights and obligations | Rights to assets | The client has rights to the receivables | Vouch a sample of recorded receivables to sales agreements |
| Completeness | Completeness of assets | All receivables are recorded | Compare a sample of shipping documents to related sales invoices |
| | Clerical accuracy of records | Receivables records are accurate and agree with general ledger | Obtain an aged trial balance of receivables, test its clerical accuracy, and reconcile to the ledgers |
| Valuation or allocation | Valuation of assets | Receivables are presented at net realizable value | Investigate the credit ratings for delinquent and large receivables accounts |
| Presentation and disclosure | Financial statement presentation of assets | Receivables are properly presented in the balance sheet, with appropriate disclosures | Perform procedures to identify receivables from related parties |

audit program will include tests of the client's internal control structure that provide support for the auditors' assessments of control risk.

Chapters 12 through 18 consider the manner in which auditors design tests of controls and substantive procedures for various financial statement accounts. Specific audit objectives and sample audit procedures are presented for various accounts to provide a framework for our discussion. It is important to remember that the audit procedures presented in the textbook are merely illustrations of *typical* procedures. In actual practice, audit programs must be tailored to each client's business environment and internal control structure. The audit procedures comprising audit programs may vary substantially from one engagement to the next.

## Verification of Related Income Statement Accounts

Income statement amounts often can be verified conveniently in conjunction with the substantiation of the related asset account. For example, after notes receivable have been verified, the related interest revenue can be substantiated by mathematically computing the interest applicable to the notes. In other cases, income statement amounts are determined by the same audit procedures used in determining the valuation of the related asset. Determining the undepreciated cost of plant assets, for example, necessitates computing (or testing) the depreciation expense for the period. Similarly, determining the net valuation of accounts receivable involves estimating the amount of the uncollectible accounts expense.

Some income statement items, such as sales revenue, do not lend themselves to direct verification in conjunction with related asset accounts. However, when the auditors establish that recorded accounts receivable are legitimate assets, and have been properly valued, they have substantial *indirect* evidence that sales transactions also have been properly measured.

## THE AUDIT PROCESS

Although specific audit procedures vary from one engagement to the next, the fundamental steps which follow initial planning are essentially the same in almost every engagement:

1. Obtain an understanding of internal control sufficient to plan the audit.
2. Determine the planned assessed level of control risk.
3. Design and perform additional tests of controls.
4. Reassess control risk and modify planned substantive tests.
5. Perform substantive tests and complete the audit.
6. Form an opinion and issue the audit report.

1.  Obtain an Understanding of Internal Control Sufficient to Plan the Audit.    **The second standard** of field work states:

> A sufficient understanding of the internal control structure is to be obtained to plan the audit and to determine the nature, timing, and extent of tests to be performed.

The nature and extent of the audit work to be performed on a particular engagement depends largely upon the effectiveness of the client's internal control in preventing or detecting material misstatements in the financial statements. Before auditors can evaluate the effectiveness of the structure, they need a knowledge and understanding of how it works: what procedures are performed and who performs them, what controls are in effect, how various types of transactions are processed and recorded, and what accounting records and supporting documentation exist. Thus, obtaining an understanding of the client's internal control structure is a logical first step in every audit engagement.

Information about the client's internal control structure comes from interviews with client personnel, audit working papers from prior years' engagements, plant tours, and the client's manuals. In gathering information about the structure, it is often useful to study the sequence of procedures used in processing major categories of transaction cycles. As they obtain an understanding of the internal control structure, the auditors often perform tests of the operating effectiveness of certain controls.

A working knowledge of the client's internal control structure is needed throughout the audit; consequently, the auditors prepare working papers fully describing their understanding of the structure. Frequent reference to these working papers will be made to aid in designing audit procedures, ascertaining where documents are filed, familiarizing new audit staff with the structure, and as a refresher in beginning next year's engagement.

The description of internal control is usually prepared in the form of systems flowcharts. As an alternative to flowcharts, parts of the structure may be described by written narratives or by the completion of specially designed questionnaires. All of these working papers are illustrated and discussed in Chapter 8.

2.  Determine the Planned Assessed Level of Control Risk.    After analyzing the design of the internal control structure, the auditors must decide whether the structure, as designed, seems strong enough to prevent or to detect and correct material misstatements. In terms of the audit risk model, the auditors determine the planned assessed level of **control risk** for each significant assertion. If they assess internal control to be weak (control risk is high), they will rely primarily on substantive tests to reduce audit risk for the assertion to an acceptable level. On the other hand, if the structure seems capable of preventing or detecting and correcting misstatements, the auditor must decide which additional controls, if any, can efficiently be tested.

3.   Design and Perform Additional Tests of Controls.   Tests of controls are performed to determine whether key internal control procedures have been *properly designed and are operating effectively*. To illustrate a *test of a control,* consider the control procedure in which the accounting department accounts for the serial sequence of all shipping documents before preparing the related journal entries. The purpose of this control is to ensure that each shipment of merchandise is recorded in the accounting records; that is, to ensure the completeness of recorded sales and accounts receivable. To test the operating effectiveness of the control procedure, the auditors might review evidence of the client's accounting for the sequence of shipping documents, and select a sample of shipping documents prepared at various times throughout the year and inspect the related journal entries.

Notice that a test of an internal control measures the effectiveness of a particular *control procedure;* it *does not* substantiate the dollar amount of an account balance. Actually, a particular control procedure may affect several financial statement amounts. If, for example, the tests described above indicate that the accounting department does not effectively account for the serial sequence of shipping documents, the auditors should be alert to the possibility of material misstatements in sales revenue, accounts receivable, cost of goods sold, and inventories.

4.   Reassess Control Risk and Modify Planned Substantive Tests.   After completing their tests of controls, the auditors are in a position to reassess control risk based on the results of the tests, and determine whether it is necessary to modify their planned substantive tests. **Substantive tests** are procedures designed to substantiate the fairness of specific financial statement assertions. Examples of substantive tests include confirmation of accounts receivable and observation of the client's physical inventory. A major objective of internal control is to produce accurate and reliable accounting data. Thus, auditors should make an intensive investigation of account balances in areas for which internal control is weak; however, they are justified in performing less extensive testing of financial statement assertions for which they have determined that controls are operating effectively. This process of deciding upon the matters to be emphasized during the audit, based upon the assessment of internal control, means that the auditors will modify their audit program by expanding substantive tests in some areas and by reducing them in others.

Not all weaknesses in internal control require action by the auditors. For example, poor internal control over a small petty cash fund is not likely to have a material impact upon the fairness of the financial statements. On the other hand, if one employee is responsible for initiating cash disbursements and also for signing checks, this combination of duties might result in material error in the financial statements or substantial defalcations. In each instance, the auditors must exercise professional judgment in determining whether to modify the nature, timing, and extent of their audit procedures and whether to make recommendations to the client for improving internal control.

When significant deficiencies in internal control are discovered, the auditors should communicate the details to the client. In general, significant weaknesses (reportable conditions) must be communicated to top management and to the audit committee of the board of directors. In addition, a *management letter* is often issued in which the auditors discuss less significant matters and provide management with workable suggestions for improvements in the system. If the assessment of internal control is completed before the balance sheet date, the auditors' recommendations may be implemented quickly enough to contribute to the reliability of the financial statements for the year under audit.

### 5.   Perform Substantive Tests and Complete the Audit.   Some procedures for verifying account balances may be performed early in the audit. However, only after having completed the consideration of internal control are the auditors in a position to complete the procedures necessary to substantiate account balances.

### 6.   Form an Opinion and Issue the Audit Report.   The date upon which the last audit procedures are completed is termed the *last day of field work*. Although the audit report is dated as of the last day of field work, it is not actually issued on that date. Since the audit report represents an acceptance of considerable responsibility by the CPA firm, a partner will make a final review of the working papers from the engagement to determine that a thorough audit has been completed, and that the appropriate type of audit report is being issued. The process usually results in audit report issuance a week or more after the last day of field work.

## Relationship between Tests of Controls and Substantive Tests

Tests of controls provide auditors with evidence as to whether prescribed internal control procedures are in use and operating effectively. The results of these tests assist the auditors in evaluating the *likelihood* of material misstatements having occurred. Substantive tests, on the other hand, are designed to *detect* material misstatements if they exist in the financial statements. The amount of substantive testing done by the auditors is greatly influenced by their assessment of the likelihood that material misstatements exist.

To illustrate, assume that a client's procedures manual indicates that the finished goods warehouse is to be locked at all times and accessible only to authorized personnel. Through tests of controls consisting of inquiry and observation, the auditors learn that the warehouse often is unlocked and that several employees who are not authorized to be in the warehouse regularly eat lunch there. As the client's internal control procedure is not operating properly, the auditors should recognize that the *risk* of inventory shortages is increased. However, the tests of controls have *not* determined that an inventory shortage does, in fact, exist.

The principal substantive test to detect shortages of inventories is the auditors' observation of a physical inventory taken by the client. As part of this observation, the auditors make test counts of various items. In our case of the unlocked warehouse, the auditors' test has shown that internal control cannot be relied upon to prevent shortages. Therefore, the auditors should increase the number of test counts in an effort to verify the existence of inventory.

## Timing of Audit Work

The value of audited financial statements is enhanced if the statements are available on a timely basis after the year-end. To facilitate an early release of the audit report, auditors normally begin the audit well before the balance sheet date. The period before the balance sheet date is termed the **interim period.** Audit work that can always be performed during the interim period includes the consideration of internal control, issuance of the management letter, and substantive tests of transactions that have occurred to the interim date.

Interim tests of certain financial statement balances, such as accounts receivable, may also be performed, but this results in additional risk that must be controlled by the auditors. Significant errors or irregularities could arise in these accounts during the *remaining period* between the time that the interim test was performed and the balance sheet date. Thus, to rely on the interim test of a significant account balance, the auditors must perform additional tests of the account during the remaining period.

Performing audit work during the interim period has numerous advantages in addition to facilitating the timely release of the audited financial statements. The independent auditors may be able to assess internal control more effectively by observing and testing controls at various times throughout the year. Also, they can give early consideration to accounting problems. Another advantage is that interim auditing creates a more uniform work load for CPA firms. With a large client, such as General Motors, the auditors may have office space within the client's buildings and carry on auditing procedures throughout the entire year.

---

## ◆ ILLUSTRATIVE AUDIT CASE: KEYSTONE COMPUTERS & NETWORKS, INC.

### Part I: Audit Planning

The Keystone Computers & Networks, Inc. (KCN) case is used throughout the text to illustrate audit procedures and methodology. KCN is a company that sells and installs microcomputers and networking software to business customers. The CPA firm of Adams, Barnes & Co. has audited the financial statements of KCN for the past three years. This part of the case illustrates selective audit planning working papers prepared by the staff of Adams, Barnes & Co. for this year's audit. You should read through the information to obtain an understanding of the nature of the information that is important to planning an audit engagement. The working papers include:

- The balance sheet and income statement for the company for the prior year, 19X4.
- A trial balance for 12/31/X5, with comparative amounts for 12/31/X4.
- The analytical ratios working paper that is partially completed. (The ratios for 19X5 have been left off.)
- The audit plan for the audit of the financial statements for the year ended 12/31/X5.
- The engagement letter for the audit presented on page 196 of this chapter.

**KEYSTONE COMPUTERS & NETWORKS, INC.**
**Balance Sheet**
**December 31, 19X4**

**Assets**

Current Assets

| | |
|---|---:|
| Cash | $    27,089 |
| Trade receivables, less allowance for doubtful accounts of $9,600 | 843,852 |
| Accounts receivables—officers | 57,643 |
| Inventory | 694,744 |
| Prepaid expenses | 40,640 |
| Total current assets | $1,663,968 |

Equipment and Leasehold Improvements, at cost

| | |
|---|---:|
| Office equipment and furniture | $  280,881 |
| Leasehold improvements | 17,645 |
| | $  298,526 |
| Less accumulated depreciation | 125,976 |
| | $  172,550 |
| | $1,836,518 |

**Liabilities and Stockholders' Equity**

Current Liabilities

| | |
|---|---:|
| Line of credit | $  309,346 |
| Accounts payable | 504,641 |
| Current maturities of capital lease obligations | 20,183 |
| Accrued expenses | 115,332 |
| Total current liabilities | $  949,502 |
| Capital Lease Obligations, less Current maturities | $  135,465 |
| Total liabilities | $1,084,967 |

Stockholders' Equity

| | |
|---|---:|
| Common stock, $1 par value; 100,000 shares authorized; 20,000 shares issued and outstanding | $    20,000 |
| Additional paid-in capital | 41,647 |
| Retained earnings | 689,904 |
| | $  751,551 |
| | $1,836,518 |

**KEYSTONE COMPUTERS & NETWORKS, INC.**
**Statements of Income and Retained Earnings**
**Year Ended December 31, 19X4**

| | | | |
|---|---:|---:|---:|
| Net sales | | | $10,227,474 |
| Cost of goods sold | | | 6,867,473 |
| Gross profit | | | $ 3,360,001 |
| Selling expenses: | | | |
| Salaries | $513,040 | | |
| Payroll benefits and taxes | 97,478 | | |
| Advertising and promotion | 81,644 | | |
| Travel and entertainment | 37,628 | | |
| Miscellaneous | 16,322 | | |
| | | $ 746,112 | |
| Operating and administration expenses: | | | |
| Operating salaries | $852,988 | | |
| Administrative salaries | 437,889 | | |
| Payroll benefits and taxes | 223,433 | | |
| Rent | 124,344 | | |
| Utilities | 92,455 | | |
| Insurance | 109,723 | | |
| Legal and accounting | 23,544 | | |
| Bad debt | 34,545 | | |
| Supplies | 93,844 | | |
| Depreciation | 25,644 | | |
| Software development | 83,341 | | |
| Miscellaneous | 37,644 | | |
| | | $2,139,394 | |
| Total selling, operating, and administrative expenses | | | $ 2,885,506 |
| Operating income | | | $ 474,495 |
| Interest expense | | | 68,743 |
| Income before income taxes | | | $ 405,752 |
| Income taxes: | | | |
| Current | | $ 71,342 | |
| Deferred | | 3,245 | |
| | | | 74,587 |
| Net income | | | $ 331,165 |
| Retained earnings, January 1, 19X4 | | | $ 358,739 |
| Retained earnings, December 31, 19X4 | | | $ 689,904 |

# KEYSTONE COMPUTERS & NETWORKS, INC.
## Working Trial Balance
### For the Period Ended December 31, 19X5

| Account # | Account Name | Prior Period Balance 12/31/X4 | Unadjusted Trial Balance Dr (Cr) | Ref# | Adjustments Dr (Cr) | Balance Sheet Dr | Balance Sheet Cr |
|---|---|---|---|---|---|---|---|
| 1000.10 | Cash—First Natl. Bank | 26,489 | 46,753 | | | | |
| 1000.30 | Cash in register | 600 | 600 | | | | |
| 1050.10 | Accounts receivable—trade | 853,452 | 1,023,545 | | | | |
| 1050.40 | Accounts receivable—officers | 57,643 | 84,670 | | | | |
| 1050.90 | Allowance for bad debts | (9,600) | (10,400) | | | | |
| 1100.10 | Inventories | 694,744 | 903,766 | | | | |
| 1300.10 | Prepaid expenses | 40,640 | 42,555 | | | | |
| 2050.10 | Furniture & fixtures | 35,432 | 41,633 | | | | |
| 2050.30 | Office equipment | 245,449 | 305,450 | | | | |
| 2050.80 | Leasehold improvements | 17,645 | 17,645 | | | | |
| 2050.90 | Accumulated depreciation | (125,976) | (154,732) | | | | |
| 2100.00 | Software development cost | | 58,674 | | | | |
| 3050.10 | Accounts payable—trade | (504,641) | (586,699) | | | | |
| 3100.00 | Capital lease obligations—current | (20,183) | (21,050) | | | | |
| 3200.10 | Accrued liabilities | (115,332) | (130,040) | | | | |
| 3300.30 | Unearned service revenue | | (22,100) | | | | |
| 3400.50 | Line of credit | (309,346) | (365,867) | | | | |
| 4400.10 | Capital lease obligations—noncurrent | (135,465) | (114,415) | | | | |
| 5050.10 | Capital stock | (20,000) | (20,000) | | | | |
| 5100.10 | Paid-in-capital | (41,647) | (41,647) | | | | |
| 5700.10 | Retained earnings | (689,904) | (689,904) | | | | |
| 5900.00 | Dividends | | 90,000 | | | | |
| | | 0 | 458,437 | | | | |
| | | 0 | (458,437) | | | | |
| | | 0 | 0 | | | | |

223

# KEYSTONE COMPUTERS & NETWORKS, INC.
## Working Trial Balance
### For the Period Ended December 31, 19X5

Prepared by _WL_
Reviewed by _KW_

Page 2

| Account # | Account Name | Prior Period Balance 12/31/X4 | Unadjusted Trial Balance Dr (Cr) | Ref # | Adjustments Dr (Cr) | Income Statement Dr | Cr |
|---|---|---|---|---|---|---|---|
| 6000.10 | Sales of computers | (9,044,432) | (10,156,898) | | | | |
| 6010.10 | Service revenue | (187,423) | (210,845) | | | | |
| 6020.10 | Consulting revenue | (995,619) | (1,234,763) | | | | |
| 7020.10 | Cost of sales | 6,867,473 | 7,397,368 | | | | |
| 7070.10 | Salaries—sales | 513,040 | 583,438 | | | | |
| 7070.50 | Payroll benefits—sales | 97,478 | 125,354 | | | | |
| 7075.10 | Advertising & promotion | 81,644 | 92,645 | | | | |
| 7080.10 | Travel & entertainment | 37,628 | 44,655 | | | | |
| 7080.30 | Miscellaneous exp.—sales | 16,322 | 21,455 | | | | |
| 7090.10 | Salaries—operations | 852,988 | 1,003,455 | | | | |
| 7090.30 | Salaries—administrative | 437,889 | 596,060 | | | | |
| 7090.50 | Payroll benefits—admin. | 223,433 | 319,876 | | | | |
| 7100.10 | Rent | 124,344 | 166,988 | | | | |
| 7140.10 | Utilities | 92,455 | 110,876 | | | | |
| 7200.10 | Insurance | 109,723 | 123,454 | | | | |
| 7260.30 | Legal & accounting | 23,544 | 31,787 | | | | |
| 7320.10 | Bad debt expense | 34,545 | 56,477 | | | | |
| 7410.10 | Supplies | 93,844 | 129,967 | | | | |
| 7600.10 | Depreciation | 25,644 | 28,756 | | | | |
| 7650.10 | Software development | 83,341 | 63,222 | | | | |
| 7700.10 | Miscellaneous exp.—admin. | 37,644 | 45,333 | | | | |
| 7800.10 | Interest expense | 68,743 | 77,434 | | | | |
| 7900.10 | Current income taxes | 71,342 | 122,467 | | | | |
| 7900.70 | Deferred income taxes | 3,245 | 3,002 | | | | |
| 9000.00 | P & L Summary | 331,165 | | | | | |
| | | 0 | (458,437) | | | | |
| | | 0 | 458,437 | | | | |
| | | 0 | 0 | | | | |

**KEYSTONE COMPUTERS & NETWORKS, INC.**
**Analytical Review Ratios**
**For the Period Ended December 31, 19X5**

Prepared by _WL_

Reviewed by _KW_

| Ratio | Ending 12/31/X5 | Ending 12/31/X4 | Industry |
|---|---|---|---|
| Current ratio | | 1.752 | 1.300 |
| Days sales in accounts receivable, computed with average accounts receivable | | 33.224 | 37.000 |
| Allowance for doubtful accounts/accounts receivable | | .011 | — |
| Bad debt expense/net sales | | .003 | — |
| Inventory turnover computed with average inventory | | 10.397 | 10.000 |
| Days inventory on hand computed with average inventory | | 35.222 | 36.000 |
| Total liabilities to net worth | | 1.444 | 2.900 |
| Return on total assets | | .180 | .090 |
| Return on net worth | | .441 | .290 |
| Return on net sales | | .032 | .023 |
| Gross profit/net sales | | .329 | .240 |
| Selling, operating and administrative expense/net sales | | .282 | .239 |
| Times interest earned | | 6.902 | 5.500 |

**KEYSTONE COMPUTERS & NETWORKS, INC.**
Audit Plan
December 31, 19X5

| | | **Date** |
|---|---|---|
| **Prepared by:** | Warren Love (Senior) | August 14, 19X5 |
| **Reviewed by:** | Karen West (Manager) | August 28, 19X5 |
| **Reviewed by:** | Charles Adams (Partner) | September 5, 19X5 |

## Objectives of the Engagement

Audit of the financial statements of Keystone Computers & Networks, Inc. (KCN) for the year ended December 31, 19X5. Also, the company's debt agreement with Western Financial Services requires the company to furnish the lender a report by our firm on KCN's compliance with various restrictive debt covenants.

## Business and Industry Conditions

KCN sells and installs microcomputers and networking hardware and software to business customers. The company provides repair, maintenance, training, and software customization services. KCN has also begun developing its own computer networking software to be sold as a product to its customers. The company's primary competitive advantage is the technical expertise and broad range of services that it is able to provide to the customers that purchase its products.

The market for microcomputers and related products is extremely competitive. KCN competes with large retailers of microcomputers, such as Businessland, Computerland, and Microage. The company also competes with other value-added resellers who provide microcomputers and software products directly to customers. To effectively compete, the company must be able to obtain inventories of state-of-the-art equipment on a timely basis.

The market for microcomputer products is also very sensitive to economic conditions.

## Planning Meetings

On July 20, Karen West and I met with Loren Steele, controller, and Sam Best, president, of KCN to discuss the planning of the audit for the current year. On August 2, a planning meeting was held in our office with all members of the engagement team assigned to the audit.

## Audit Approach

The company has had no significant changes in its internal control structure from the prior year. Therefore, consistent with the approach used in last year's audit, we plan to perform tests of controls to assess control risk at less than the maximum for most financial statement assertions.

## Risk Factors

Several factors affect the risk of this engagement including:

- ◆ KCN is a closely-held company owned by five stockholders, Terry Keystone, Mark Keystone, John Keystone, Keith Young, and Rita Young. Terry and Mark Keystone are active members of the company's board of directors. None of the other owners take an active part in the business.

* Audited financial statements are required by Western Financial Services as a part of the company's line of credit agreement.

* The company has earned profits for the last few years, and it does not appear to be having financial difficulties.

These factors indicate that the engagement to audit KCN has only moderate risk.

## Significant Accounting and Auditing Matters

The company began offering for sale extended warranties on computers during the current year. We need to review the method of revenue recognition to determine whether it complies with the requirements of FASB Technical Bulletin 90-1.

In the prior year, the KCN began developing networking software products for sale. This year the company has started capitalizing certain costs of development. We need to review the method of accounting for the cost of software development to determine whether it complies with the requirements of FASB Statement No. 86.

## Planning Materiality

Because the firm has experienced steady growth in sales and earnings over the last 3 years, we believe that operating results are the most appropriate basis for estimating planning materiality as described below:

Comparison of Bases:

| Financial Statement Base | Annualized for 12/31/X5 |
|---|---|
| Sales | $11,000,000 |
| Total assets | 2,000,000 |
| Pretax net income | 525,000 |

Computation of planning materiality:

| Base | Amount | Percentage | Materiality Estimate |
|---|---|---|---|
| Sales | $11,000,000 | 1% | $110,000 |
| Total assets | 2,000,000 | 1% | 20,000 |
| Pretax net income | 525,000 | 10% | 52,500 |

The range for planning materiality is from $20,000 to $110,000. Based on the company's steady growth in sales and earnings and the fact that the company is not a public company, we have selected $70,000 as a reasonable materiality amount for planning purposes.

## Scheduling and Staffing Plan

Based on discussions with Ms. Steele, the following are tentative dates of importance for the audit:

| | |
|---|---|
| Begin interim audit work | November 10, 19X5 |
| Complete interim audit work | by November 15, 19X5 |
| Issue management letter on interim work | by November 30, 19X5 |
| Observe physical inventory | December 31, 19X5 |
| Begin year-end audit work | February 12, 19X6 |
| Complete field work | by February 20, 19X6 |
| Closing conference | February 25, 19X6 |
| Issue audit report | by March 5, 19X6 |
| Issue letter required by financing agreement | by March 5, 19X6 |
| Issue updated management letter | by March 10, 19X6 |

Staffing time requirements for the engagement are described below:

| | Assistant | Senior | Manager | Partner | Total |
|---|---|---|---|---|---|
| Interim | 16 | 20 | 6 | 4 | 46 |
| Final | 30 | 24 | 10 | 8 | 72 |
| | 46 | 44 | 16 | 12 | 118 |

## ◆ CHAPTER SUMMARY

This chapter explained the manner in which auditors plan an audit and design audit programs. To summarize:

1.  Investigating a potential audit client is essential because auditors want to avoid accepting clients that have unscrupulous management. As a part of their investigation the auditors are required to communicate with the predecessor auditors. Arrangements for the engagement are set forth in the engagement letter, which makes clear the nature of the engagement, any limitations on the work, and the responsibilities of the client.

2.  Once the client has been accepted, the auditors will perform procedures to obtain a more detailed understanding of the client's business and industry, and will develop an overall audit strategy which considers both materiality and audit risk.

3.  When planning an audit the auditors are required to perform preliminary analytical procedures, which help them to obtain a better understanding of the nature of the client's business and identify accounts that have a higher risk of material misstatement.

4.  The planning process is documented with audit plans, time budgets, and audit programs. Audit programs generally include both a systems portion that focuses on the client's internal control structure, and a substantive testing portion. The audit procedures that are contained in the audit program are designed around the assertions of management that are embodied in the financial statements.

5.  Subsequent to planning, the audit process consists of considering and testing the client's internal control structure, performing substantive tests, forming an opinion on the financial statements, and issuing the audit report.

# ◆ KEY TERMS INTRODUCED OR EMPHASIZED IN CHAPTER 7

**Analytical procedures**   Tests that involve comparisons of financial data for the current year to that of prior years, budgets, nonfinancial data, or industry averages. From a planning standpoint, analytical procedures help the auditors obtain an understanding of the client's business, and identify financial statement amounts that appear to be affected by errors or irregularities, or other potential problems.

**Audit committee**   A committee composed of outside directors (members of the board of directors who are neither officers nor employees) charged with responsibility for maintaining contact with the company's internal and independent auditors.

**Audit plan**   A broad overview of an audit engagement prepared in the planning stage of the engagement. Audit plans usually include such matters as the objectives of the engagement, nature of the work to be done, a time schedule for major audit work and completion of the engagement, and staffing requirements.

**Audit program**   A detailed listing of the specific audit procedures to be performed in the course of an audit engagement. Audit programs provide a basis for assigning and scheduling audit work and for determining what work remains to be done. Audit programs are specially tailored to each engagement.

**Audit risk**   The risk that the auditors may unknowingly fail to appropriately modify their opinion on financial statements that are materially misstated.

**Business risk of the auditors**   The overall risk to the CPA firm of association with a particular audit client. The primary elements involved are the risk of loss of reputation and litigation if the client has financial difficulties.

**Control risk**   The risk that a material misstatement that could occur in an account will not be prevented or detected on a timely basis by internal control.

**Detection risk**   The risk that the auditors' procedures will lead them to conclude that a financial statement assertion is not materially misstated, when in fact such misstatement does exist.

**Engagement letter**   A formal letter sent by the auditors to the client at the beginning of an engagement summarizing the nature of the engagement, any limitations on the scope of audit work, work to be done by the client's staff, and the basis for the audit fee. The purpose of engagement letters is to avoid misunderstandings, and they are essential on nonaudit engagements as well as audits.

**Interim period**   The time interval from the beginning of audit work to the balance sheet date. Many audit procedures can be performed during the interim period to facilitate early issuance of the audit report.

**Management assertions**   Representations of management that are communicated, explicitly or implicitly, by the financial statements.

**Predecessor auditor**   The CPA firm that formerly served as auditor but has resigned from the engagement or has been notified that its services have been terminated.

**Shopping for principles**   Conduct by some enterprises that discharge one independent auditing firm after seeking out another firm that will sanction a disputed financial statement principle or presentation.

**Substantive approach (to an audit)**    An approach to auditing in which the auditors' opinion is based primarily upon the evidence obtained by substantiating the individual financial statement assertions. This approach places less emphasis upon the consideration of internal control than does the systems approach and is particularly appropriate when internal control is weak.

**Substantive tests**    Tests of account balances and transactions designed to detect any material misstatements in the financial statements. The nature, timing, and extent of substantive testing are determined by the auditors' consideration of the client's internal control structure.

**Successor auditor**    An auditor who has accepted an engagement or who has been invited to make a proposal for an engagement to replace the CPA firm that formerly served as auditors.

**Systems approach (to an audit)**    An approach to auditing in which the auditors place a relatively high degree of reliance upon their consideration of the client's internal control and, therefore, perform a minimum of substantive testing. Whether an auditor follows a systems approach or a substantive approach is merely a matter of degree; every engagement involves both an assessment of control risk and substantive testing.

**Time budget**    An estimate of the time required to perform each step in the audit.

**Transaction cycle**    The sequence of procedures applied by the client in processing a particular type of recurring transaction. The term *cycle* reflects the idea that the same sequence of procedures is applied to each similar transaction. The auditors' consideration of internal control often is organized around the client's major transactions cycles.

# ◆ GROUP I: REVIEW QUESTIONS

7-1    What information should a CPA firm seek in its investigation of a prospective client?

7-2    In planning an audit the auditors must consider those factors that affect the risk of the particular engagement. List three risk factors relating to each of the following: management characteristics, operating characteristics, engagement characteristics.

7-3    What topics should be discussed in a preliminary meeting with a prospective audit client?

7-4    Are auditors justified in relying upon the accuracy of working papers prepared for them by employees of the client?

7-5    Describe the preferred composition and role of the audit committee of a board of directors.

7-6    State the purpose and nature of an engagement letter.

7-7    Criticize the following statement: "Throughout this audit, for all purposes, we will define a 'material amount' as $500,000."

7-8    Define and differentiate between an *audit plan* and an *audit program*.

7-9    Should a separate audit program be prepared for each audit engagement, or can a standard program be used for most engagements?

7-10    "An audit program is desirable when new staff members are assigned to an engagement, but an experienced auditor should be able to conduct an audit without reference to an audit program." Do you agree? Discuss.

7-11    Suggest some factors that might cause an audit engagement to exceed the original time estimate. Would the extra time be charged to the client?

7-12    What problems are created for a CPA firm when audit staff members underreport the amount of time spent in performing specific auditing procedures?

7-13   Why is audit work usually organized around balance sheet accounts rather than income statement items?

7-14   Identify the general objectives of the auditors' substantive procedures with respect to any major asset category.

7-15   What is meant by making a proper year-end *cutoff* ? Explain the effects of errors in the cutoff of sales transactions in both the income statement and the balance sheet.

7-16   What are the purposes of the audit procedures of *(a)* tracing a sample of journal entries forward into the ledgers and *(b)* vouching a sample of ledger entries back into the journals?

7-17   Charles Halstead, CPA, has a number of clients who desire audits at the end of the calendar year. In an effort to spread his work load more uniformly throughout the year, he is preparing a list of audit procedures that could be performed satisfactorily before the year-end balance sheet date. What audit work, if any, might be done in advance of the balance sheet date?

7-18   Define and differentiate between a test of a controls and a substantive test.

# ◆ GROUP II: QUESTIONS REQUIRING ANALYSIS

7-19   Morgan, CPA, is approached by a prospective audit client who wants to engage Morgan to perform an audit for the current year. In prior years, this prospective client was audited by another CPA. Identify the specific procedures that Morgan should follow in deciding whether or not to accept this client.

7-20   How does a knowledge of the client's business help the auditors in planning and performing an audit in accordance with generally accepted auditing standards?

7-21   Arthur Samuels, CPA, agreed to perform an audit of a new client engaged in the manufacture of power tools. After some preliminary discussion of the purposes of the audit and the basis for determination of the audit fee, Samuels asked to be taken on a comprehensive guided tour of the client's plant facilities. Explain specific ways that the knowledge gained by Samuels during the plant tour may help in planning and conducting the audit.

7-22   A CPA has been asked to audit the financial statements of a publicly held company for the first time. All preliminary discussions have been completed between the CPA, the company, the predecessor auditor, and all other necessary parties. The CPA is now preparing an engagement letter. List the items that should be included in the engagement letter.

7-23   The audit plan, the audit program, and the time budget are three important working papers prepared early in an audit. What functions do these working papers serve in the auditor's compliance with generally accepted auditing standards? Discuss.

7-24   The first standard of field work requires, in part, that "the work is to be adequately planned." An effective tool that aids the auditor in adequately planning the work is an audit program. What is an audit program and what purposes does it serve?

7-25   How can a CPA make use of the preceding year's audit working papers in a recurring audit?

7-26   When planning an audit, the auditors must assess the levels of risk and materiality for the engagement. Explain how the auditors' judgments about these two factors affect the auditors' planned audit procedures.

7-27    In planning every audit, the auditors are required to consider preliminary judgment about materiality levels for audit purposes. Described below are financial statement data from two separate companies:

| | Franklin Co. | Tyler Co. |
|---|---|---|
| Total assets | $34,900,000 | $2,700,000 |
| Total revenue | 29,600,000 | 4,500,000 |
| Equity | 13,800,000 | 1,000,000 |
| Net income before taxes | 1,600,000 | 90,000 |

*Required:*    a.    Develop an estimate of the appropriate amount of planning materiality for Franklin Co. and describe how you arrived at the estimate.
   b.    Develop an estimate of the appropriate amount of planning materiality for Tyler Co. and describe how you arrived at the estimate.

7-28    The auditors sometimes decide to allocate the amount of planning materiality to various financial statement accounts.

*Required:*    a.    Explain why auditors typically decide to allocate planning materiality to individual financial statement accounts.
   b.    Describe why the total amount of planning materiality allocated to individual accounts may exceed overall materiality.

7-29    Ann Knox, president of Knox Corporation, is a close friend of a client of yours. In response to a strong recommendation of your audit work by her friend, Ann Knox has retained you to make an audit of Knox Corporation's financial statements. Although you have had extensive auditing experience, you have not previously audited a company in the same line of business as Knox Corporation.

   Ann Knox informs you that she would like to have an estimate of the cost of the audit. List all the steps you would take in order to have an adequate basis for providing an estimate of the audit fee for the Knox Corporation engagement.

7-30    Select the best answer for each of the following. Explain the reasons for your selection.
   a.    The audit committee of a company should normally be made up of:
      (1)    Representatives from the client's management, investors, suppliers, and customers.
      (2)    The audit partner, the chief financial officer, the legal counsel, and at least one outsider.
      (3)    Representatives of the major equity interests, such as preferred and common stockholders.
      (4)    Members of the board of directors who are not officers or employees.
   b.    Which of the following should not normally be included in the engagement letter for an audit?
      (1)    A description of the responsibilities of client personnel to provide assistance.
      (2)    An indication of the amount of the audit fee.
      (3)    A description of the limitations of an audit.
      (4)    A listing of the client's branch offices selected for testing.
   c.    Appointing the independent auditors early will enable:
      (1)    A more thorough audit to be performed.
      (2)    A sufficient understanding of internal control to be obtained.
      (3)    Sufficient competent evidential matter to be obtained.
      (4)    A more efficient audit to be planned.
   d.    Which portion of an audit may *not* be completed before the balance sheet date?
      (1)    Tests of controls.
      (2)    Issuance of a management letter.

      (3)   Substantive testing.

      (4)   Assessment of control risk.

   *e.*  Which of the following should the auditors obtain from the predecessor auditor before accepting an audit engagement?

      (1)   Analysis of balance sheet accounts.

      (2)   Analysis of income statement accounts.

      (3)   All matters of continuing accounting significance.

      (4)   Facts that might bear on the integrity of management.

   *f.*  As one step in testing sales transactions, a CPA traces a random sample of sales journal entries to debits in the accounts receivable subsidiary ledger. This test provides evidence as to whether:

      (1)   Each recorded sale represents a bona fide transaction.

      (2)   All sales have been recorded in the sales journal.

      (3)   All debit entries in the accounts receivable subsidiary ledger are properly supported by sales journal entries.

      (4)   Recorded sales have been properly posted to customer accounts.

(AICPA, adapted)

7-31   Auditing literature frequently makes reference to the substantive approach and the systems approach to auditing.

*Required:*  *a.*  Distinguish between the substantive approach and the systems approach to an audit.

        *b.*  Explain the circumstances under which each approach would be most appropriate.

7-32   Listed below are several of the auditors' general objectives in performing substantive tests of an asset account:

    1.  Establish the existence of assets.

    2.  Establish that the company has rights to the assets.

    3.  Establish the completeness of recorded assets.

    4.  Determine the appropriate valuation of the assets.

    5.  Establish the clerical accuracy of the underlying records.

    6.  Determine the appropriate financial statement presentation and disclosure of the assets.

*Required:*  Indicate the general objective (or objectives) of each of the following audit procedures:

      *a.*  Count petty cash on hand.

      *b.*  Locate on the client's premises a sample of the equipment items listed in the subsidiary plant and equipment ledger.

      *c.*  Obtain a listing of inventory and reconcile the total to the general ledger.

      *d.*  Trace a sample of shipping documents to recorded sales transactions.

      *e.*  Obtain representation letter from management stating that no inventory or accounts receivable have been pledged to secure specific liabilities.

      *f.*  Vouch selected purchases of securities to brokers' advices.

7-33   Richard Foster, an assistant auditor, was assigned to the year-end audit work of Sipher Corporation. Sipher is a small manufacturer of language translation equipment. As his first assignment, Foster was instructed to test the cutoff of year-end sales transactions. Since Sipher uses a calendar year-end for its financial statements, Foster began by obtaining the computer-generated sales ledgers and journals for December and January. He then traced ledger postings for a few days before and after December 31 to the sales journals, noting the dates of the journal entries. Foster noted no journal entries that were posted to the ledger in the wrong accounting period. Thus, he concluded that the client's cutoff of sales transactions was effective.

*Required:*  Comment on the validity of Foster's conclusion. Explain fully.

# ◆ GROUP III: PROBLEMS

7-34   Valley Finance Company opened four personal loan offices in neighboring cities on January 2. Small cash loans are made to borrowers who repay the principal with interest in monthly installments over a period not exceeding two years. Ralph Norris president of the company, uses one of the offices as a central office and visits the other offices periodically for supervision and internal auditing purposes.

*Required:*   Assume that you agreed to audit Valley Finance Company's financial statements for the year ended December 31. No scope limitations were imposed.

   *a.*   How would you determine the scope necessary to complete your audit satisfactorily? Discuss.

   *b.*   Would you be responsible for the discovery of fraud in this audit? Discuss.

7-35   You are invited by John Bray, the president of Cheviot Corporation, to discuss with him the possibility of your conducting an audit of the company. The corporation is a small, closely held manufacturing organization that appears to be expanding. No previous audit has been made by independent certified public accountants. Your discussions with Bray include a review of the recent monthly financial statements, inspection of the accounting records, and review of policies with the chief accountant. You also are taken on a guided tour of the plant by the president. He then makes the following statement:

   "Before making definite arrangements for an audit, I would like to know about how long it will take and about how much it will cost. I want quality work and expect to pay a fair price, but since this is our first experience with independent auditors, I would like a full explanation as to how the cost of the audit is determined. Will you please send me a memorandum covering these points?"

   Write the memorandum requested by John Bray.

7-36   Precision Industries, Inc. is a manufacturer of electronic components. When a purchase order is received from a customer, a salesclerk prepares a serially numbered sales order and sends copies to the shipping and accounting departments. When the merchandise is shipped to the customer, the shipping department prepares a serially numbered shipping advice and sends a copy to the accounting department. Upon receipt of the appropriate documents, the accounting department records the sale in the accounting records. All shipments are *FOB shipping point.*

*Required:*   *a.*   How can the auditors determine whether Precision Industries, Inc. has made a proper year-end cutoff of sales transactions?

   *b.*   Assume all shipments for the first five days of the following year were recorded as occurring in the current year. If not corrected, what effect will this cutoff error have upon the financial statements for the current year?

7-37   You are a new staff assistant with the Houston office of a national public accounting firm. Yesterday you read an article in *The Wall Street Journal* in which the managing partner of your firm's New York office discussed the problems caused for the public accounting profession by auditors underreporting the number of hours worked on audits.

   You found this article interesting because of the experience you are having on the audit of Regal Industries, one of your office's largest clients. The field work at Regal is being run by Mark Thomas, a very hard-working senior who is highly regarded within your office. Thomas made senior in record time, and has established a reputation for bringing jobs in on schedule. Four staff assistants, including yourself, are working under Thomas. At the end of the engagement, Thomas will write a performance report on each assistant, which will be placed in the assistant's personnel file. The manager on the engagement also writes a performance evaluation on each assistant and on Thomas. You have heard, however, that managers usually agree with whatever the senior has said about an assistant's performance.

The budgeted time estimates for almost every audit procedure being performed at Regal seem too short. No one is able to finish anything on schedule. Last week, Thomas approached all of the staff assistants about working Saturday to "catch up." He said that he was going to work a short day on Saturday and would not report the hours on his time sheet. He said that if you would do the same, he would buy lunch after you finished up on Saturday. You and two other assistants agreed. The fourth assistant, Dave Scott, declined, saying that he was going to a baseball game on Saturday.

The work on Saturday ran smoothly, and it was nice to wear jeans instead of dress clothes. You did quit a little early, although it was about 3:30, not noon. Afterward, Thomas bought everyone lunch at a popular restaurant.

During the following workweek, you noticed that Thomas seemed quite friendly toward you and the other two assistants who had worked on Saturday. He also was complimentary of your work. He was not complimentary of Scott's work; in fact, you heard him comment to the engagement manager that he thought Scott would be a "short-timer," a phrase used to describe staff assistants who do not last long in public accounting. You were not too sympathetic to Scott's plight, however, as you and the other staff assistants also feel that Scott's work on the engagement has been substandard.

It is now Thursday afternoon, and Thomas has just asked the three of you who worked last Saturday if you will do the same thing again this week. He did not ask Scott. Again, Thomas offered to buy lunch if you would leave the hours off of your time sheets. You suspect that Thomas has read the article in *The Wall Street Journal,* because he seemed a little defensive about asking you to underreport your time. He pointed out that you are not paid by the hour anyway, so leaving the extra hours off of your time sheet "doesn't really cost you anything."

Required:  *a.*   Briefly explain why the managing partner of an office would probably oppose the practice of underreporting hours worked by the audit staff.

*b.*   Briefly explain why a senior might *not* oppose the practice.

*c.*   Explain how you think the other two staff assistants asked to work Saturday will probably respond. If you would respond differently, explain.

*d.*   Suggest quality control procedures that you think could be implemented by a CPA firm to discourage the underreporting of time by audit staff members.

---

## ◆ GROUP IV: RESEARCH AND DISCUSSION CASE

7-38   Tammy Potter, a new partner with the regional CPA firm of Tower & Tower, was recently appointed to the board of directors of a local civic organization. The chairman of the board of the civic organization is Lewis Edmond, who is also the owner of a real estate development firm, Tierra Corporation.

Potter was quite excited when Edmond indicated that his corporation needed an audit, and he wished to discuss the matter with her. During the discussion, Potter was told that Tierra Corporation needed the audit to obtain a substantial amount of additional financing to acquire another company. Presently, Tierra Corporation is successful, profitable, and committed to growth. The audit fee for the engagement should be substantial.

Since Tierra Corporation appeared to be a good client prospect, Potter tentatively indicated that Tower & Tower wanted to do the work. Potter then mentioned that Tower & Tower's quality control policies require an investigation of new clients and approval by the managing partner, Lee Tower.

Potter obtained the authorizations of Edmond to make the necessary inquiries for the new client investigation. Edmond was found to be a highly respected member of the community. Also, Tierra Corporation was highly regarded by its banker and its attorney, and the Dun & Bradstreet report on the corporation reflected nothing negative.

As a final part of the investigation process, Potter contacted Edmond's former tax accountant, Bill Turner. Potter was surprised to discover that Turner did not share the others' high opinion of Edmond. Turner related that on an IRS audit 10 years ago, Edmond was questioned about the details of a large capital loss reported on the sale of a tract of land to a trust. Edmond told the IRS agent that he had lost all of the supporting documentation for the transaction, and that he had no way of finding out the names of the principals of the trust. A search by an IRS auditor revealed that the land was recorded in the name of Edmond's married daughter and that Edmond himself was listed as the trustee. The IRS disallowed the loss and Edmond was assessed a civil fraud penalty. Potter was concerned about these findings, but eventually concluded that Edmond had probably matured to a point where he would not engage in such activities.

*Required:*   *a.*   Present arguments supporting a decision to accept Tierra Corporation as an audit client.

*b.*   Present arguments supporting a decision *not* to accept Tierra Corporation as an audit client.

*c.*   Assuming that you are Lee Tower, set forth your decision regarding acceptance of the client, identifying those arguments from parts *(a)* or *(b)* that you found most persuasive.

## ◆ SUGGESTED REFERENCES

AICPA, *Professional Standards, Volume 2,* Commerce Clearing House, *Statements on Quality Control Standards,* Section QC 10.07.

AICPA, *Statement on Auditing Standards 53,* ''The Auditor's Responsibility to Detect and Report Errors and Irregularities,'' (New York, 1988) AU 316.

## ◆ GROUP V: AUDIT CASE EXERCISES

7-39   The audit plan for the audit of Keystone Computers & Networks, Inc. appears on pages 226 through 228. Review each major section of the audit plan and briefly describe the purpose and content of the section. Organize your solution in the following manner:

| Section | Purpose | Content |
|---|---|---|
| OBJECTIVES OF THE ENGAGEMENT | To describe the services that are to be rendered to the client | The objectives are: (1) audit of KCN's financial statements for the year ended 12/31/X5, and (2) issuance of a letter on compliance with covenants of the client's letter of credit agreement |

7-40   In the audit plan for the audit of Keystone Computers & Networks, Inc. on page 227 there is a section on significant accounting and auditing matters. The first of the matters described in this section involves the appropriate accounting for the sale of extended warranty contracts. Research this accounting issue and write a brief memorandum for the working papers describing the issue and summarizing the appropriate method of accounting for the revenue received from these contracts.

7-41   In the audit plan for the audit of Keystone Computers & Networks on page 227 there is a section on significant accounting and auditing matters. The second matter described involves the capitalization the costs of developing a software program for sale.

*Required:*    *a.*    Research this issue and write a brief memorandum for the working papers describing the issue and summarizing the appropriate method of accounting for the development costs.

         *b.*    Based on your research, describe the major audit issue that you believe will be involved in auditing the software development costs.

7-42   A partially completed analytical ratios working paper for Keystone Computers & Networks, Inc. is presented on page 225.

*Required:*    *a.*    Complete the working paper by computing the financial ratios for 19X5.

         *b.*    After completing *(a)*, review the ratios and identify financial statement accounts that should be investigated because the related ratios are not comparable to prior-year ratios and industry averages.

         *c.*    For each account identified in *(b)*, list potential reasons for the unexpected account balances and related ratios.

# INTERNAL CONTROL

## CHAPTER OBJECTIVES

After studying this chapter, you should be able to:

- Define what is meant by an internal control structure.
- Describe management's responsibility for internal control.
- Distinguish among the major elements of a client's internal control structure: the control environment, the accounting system, and control procedures.
- Explain the characteristics of effective internal control.
- Describe the auditors' consideration of the internal control structure.
- Discuss the techniques used by auditors to obtain an understanding of internal control and describe the results in their working papers.
- Describe the auditors' responsibility for communication of internal control structure related matters.

The second standard of field work states:

> A sufficient understanding of the internal control structure is to be obtained to plan the audit and to determine the nature, timing, and extent of tests to be performed.

Our consideration of internal control in this chapter has three major objectives: first, to explain the meaning and significance of internal control; second, to discuss the major components of a client's internal control structure; and third, to show how auditors go about obtaining an understanding of internal control to meet the requirements of the second standard of field work. No attempt is made in this chapter to present in detail the internal control procedures applicable to particular kinds of assets or liabilities or to particular types of transactions, such as purchases or sales. Detailed information along those lines will be found in succeeding chapters as each phase of the audit is presented.

As discussed in Chapter 1, internal control has attained greatest significance in large-scale business organizations. Accordingly, the greater part of the discussion in this chapter is presented in terms of the large corporation. A separate section is presented at the end of the chapter, however, dealing with the problem of achieving internal control in a small business.

# THE MEANING OF INTERNAL CONTROL

Many people interpret the term *internal control* as the steps taken by a business to prevent employee fraud. Actually, such measures are only a part of internal control. In the broadest sense, an organization's **internal control structure** (also referred to as internal control system) consists of the policies and procedures established by management to provide reasonable assurance that the organization's objectives will be achieved. The concept of *reasonable assurance* recognizes that no structure is perfect and that the cost of an entity's internal control should not exceed the benefits expected to be derived. As one might expect, when considering internal control, an *organization's objectives* include safeguarding assets and providing reliable financial information. But internal control extends beyond the accounting and financial functions; its scope is companywide and touches all activities of the organization. It includes the methods by which top management delegates authority and assigns responsibility for such functions as selling, purchasing, accounting, and production. Internal control also includes the program for preparing, verifying, and distributing to various levels of management those current reports and analyses that enable executives to maintain control over the variety of activities and functions that constitute a large corporate enterprise. The use of budgetary techniques, production standards, inspection laboratories, time and motion studies, and employee training program involves engineers and many others far removed from accounting and financial activities; yet all of these devices are part of the mechanism referred to as an internal control structure. This broad concept of internal control is reflected in the integrated criteria that were recently developed to provide management with a basis for evaluating an organization's internal control.

## Internal Control Criteria for Management

As a result of a number of instances of fraudulent financial reporting in the 1970s and early 1980s, the major accounting organizations[1] sponsored the National Commission on Fraudulent Financial Reporting (the Treadway Commission) to study the causal factors that are associated with fraudulent reporting, and to make recommendations to reduce its incidence. The Commission made a number of recommendations that directly addressed internal control. For example, it emphasized the importance of a competent and involved audit committee and an active and objective internal audit function in preventing fraudulent practices. It also called on the sponsoring organizations to work together to develop an integrated framework to be used by management and others to evaluate internal control. As a result, the Committee of Sponsoring Organizations (COSO) commissioned a study for that purpose, and its report, titled *Internal Control—Integrated Framework,* was issued in 1992. The stated purposes of the study are to:

- Establish a common definition of internal control to serve the needs of different parties.
- Provide a standard against which business and other entities can assess their control systems and determine how to improve them.

The framework in this report provides management with a basis to evaluate internal controls not only over financial reporting, but also over the effectiveness and efficiency of operations and compliance with laws and regulations.

## The Foreign Corrupt Practices Act of 1977

The importance of establishing and maintaining effective internal control is also illustrated by the passage of the **Foreign Corrupt Practices Act.** In the mid-1970s, a number of American corporations acknowledged having made payments (bribes and kickbacks) to officials in foreign countries to obtain business. In most cases, the payments were legal under the laws of the countries in which they were made, but they were not in accordance with American standards of business ethics. In some instances, these questionable payments were made without the authorization or knowledge of top executives of the corporations involved. By passing the Foreign Corrupt Practices Act of 1977, Congress ordered an end to this practice. Payments to foreign officials for the purpose of securing business are specifically prohibited by the antibribery provisions of the act. To prevent top management from asserting that they were not aware of the payments, internal control provisions also were included in the act. These provisions require every corporation under the jurisdiction of the SEC (regardless of whether the corporation has international operations) to maintain a system of internal control that will provide reasonable assurance that:

---

[1]The sponsoring organizations included the American Institute of Certified Public Accountants, the American Accounting Association, the Financial Executives Institute, the Institute of Internal Auditors, and the Institute of Management Accountants.

1. Transactions are executed with the knowledge and authorization of management.
2. Transactions are recorded as necessary to permit the preparation of reliable financial statements and maintain accountability for assets.
3. Access to assets is limited to authorized individuals.
4. Accounting records of assets are compared to existing assets at reasonable intervals and appropriate action is taken with respect to any differences.

Violations of the Foreign Corrupt Practices Act can result in fines of up to $1 million and imprisonment of the members of management that are responsible. Thus, an effective system of internal control, long viewed as essential to the operation of a large organization, is required by federal law.

## Means of Achieving Internal Control

Internal control structures vary significantly from one organization to the next. The specific control features used depend upon such factors as the size, nature of operations, and objectives of the organization for which the structure was designed. Yet certain features are essential to satisfactory internal control in almost any large-scale organization. For purposes of financial statement audits, the relevant features are generally those that pertain to the entity's ability to record, process, summarize, and report financial data. These features may be divided into three elements: (1) the control environment; (2) the accounting system; and (3) control procedures.

# CONTROL ENVIRONMENT

The control environment is the collective effect of various overall factors that establish, enhance, or mitigate the effectiveness of specific control policies and procedures. The control environment reflects the overall attitude, awareness, and actions of the board of directors, management, owners, and others concerning the importance of control and the way it is used in the entity. This chapter emphasizes internal environmental factors, although you should recognize that external factors such as audits by regulatory agencies are also a part of the company's control environment. Internal environmental control factors include management's philosophy and operating style; the company's organizational structure; personnel policies and procedures; methods of assigning authority and responsibility; management control methods; the internal audit function; and the audit committee.

---

The COSO report, *Internal Control—Integrated Framework,* states that the control environment sets the tone of the organization, influencing the control consciousness of its people. It is the foundation for all other components of internal control, providing discipline and structure. Effectively controlled entities strive to have competent people, instill an enterprisewide attitude of integrity and control consciousness, and set a positive "tone at the top."

## Management Philosophy and Operating Style

Managements differ in both their philosophies toward financial reporting and their attitudes toward taking business risks. Some managements are extremely aggressive in financial reporting and place great emphasis on meeting or exceeding earnings projections. They may be willing to undertake activities with high risk on the prospects of high returns. Other managements are extremely conservative and risk averse. These differing philosophies and operating styles may have an impact on the overall reliability of the financial statements. Therefore, this factor is important to the auditor's assessment of the entity's control environment.

## Organizational Structure

Another control environment factor is the entity's **organizational structure.** A well-designed organizational structure provides a basis for planning, directing, and controlling operations. It divides authority, responsibilities and duties among members of an organization by dealing with such issues as centralized versus decentralized decision making and appropriate segregation of duties among the various departments. When management decision making is centralized and dominated by one individual, that individual's moral character is extremely important to the auditors. When a decentralized style is used, procedures to monitor the decision making of the many managers involved become more important.

The organizational structure of an entity should separate responsibilities for (1) *authorization* of transactions, (2) *recordkeeping* for transactions, and (3) *custody* of assets. In addition, to the extent possible, execution of the transaction should be segregated from these other responsibilities. The effectiveness of such structure is usually obtained by having designated department heads who are evaluated on the basis of the performance of their respective departments. The top executives of the major departments should be of equal rank and should report directly to the president or to an executive vice president. The partial organization chart in Figure 8–1 illustrates such an arrangement. If, for example, the controller were a line subordinate to the vice president of production, the organizational independence of the accounting department would be greatly impaired.

---

◆ ILLUSTRATIVE CASE ◆

During an examination of the Foster Company, the auditors' study of organizational lines of authority and their use of an internal control questionnaire disclosed that the receiving department personnel were under the direction of the purchasing agent. Accounts payable department employees had also been instructed to accept informal memoranda from the purchasing agent as evidence of receipt of merchandise and propriety of invoices.

Because of this deficiency in internal control, the auditors made a very thorough examination of purchase invoices and came across a number of large December invoices from one supplier bearing the notation: "Subject to adjustment at time of delivery of merchandise." Investigation of these transactions disclosed that the merchandise had not

*(continued)*

## Figure 8–1  Partial Organization Chart

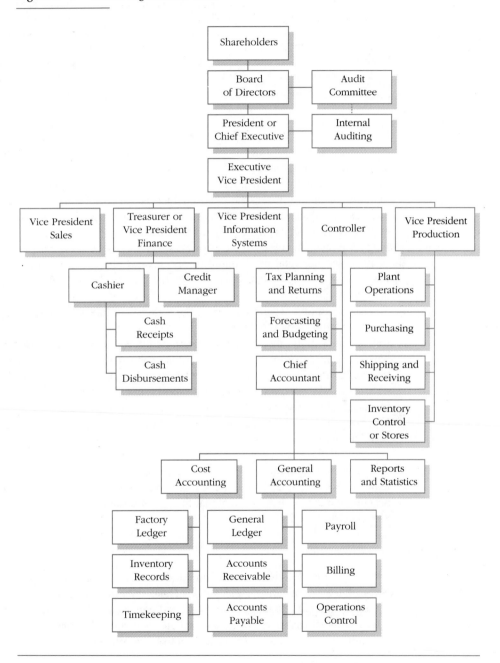

yet been delivered, but the invoices had been paid. The purchasing agent explained that he had requested the advance billing in an effort to reduce taxable income for the year under audit, during which profits had been higher than usual. Further investigation revealed that the purchasing agent held a substantial personal interest in the supplier making the advance billings, and that top management of the client company was not aware of this conflict of interest.

**Responsibilities of Finance and Accounting Departments.**   Finance and accounting are the two departments most directly involved in the financial affairs of a business enterprise. The division of responsibilities between these departments illustrates the separation of the accounting function from operations and also from the custody of assets. Under the direction of the *treasurer,* the finance department is responsible for financial operations and custody of liquid assets. Activities of this department include planning future cash requirements, establishing customer credit policies, and arranging to meet the short- and long-term financing needs of the business. In addition, the finance department has custody of bank accounts and other liquid assets, invests idle cash, handles cash receipts, and makes cash disbursements. In short, it is the finance department that conducts financial activities.

The accounting department, under the authority of the *controller,* is responsible for all accounting functions and the design and implementation of internal control. With respect to financial activity, the accounting department records financial transactions but does not handle financial assets. Accounting records establish accountability over assets, as well as providing the information necessary for financial reports, tax returns, and daily operating decisions. With respect to internal control, the accounting department maintains the independent records with which quantities of assets and operating results are compared. Often, this reconciliation function is performed by the *operations control group* or some other subdepartment within accounting.

Many of the subdepartments often found within accounting are illustrated in Figure 8–1. It is important for many of these subdepartments to be relatively independent of one another. For example, if the operations control group reconciles assets on hand to the accounting records, it is essential that the operations control personnel not maintain those records.

## Personnel Policies and Procedures

Ultimately, the effectiveness of an internal control structure is affected by the characteristics of the organization's personnel. Thus, management's policies and practices for hiring, training, evaluating, promoting, and compensating employees have a significant effect on the effectiveness of the control environment. Effective personnel policies often can mitigate other weaknesses in the control environment.

**Fidelity Bonds.**   Effective personnel management is not a guarantee against losses from dishonest employees. It is often the most trusted employees who engineer large embezzlements. The fact that they are so highly trusted explains why they have access to cash, securities, and company records and are in a position that makes embezzlement possible.

**Fidelity bonds** are a form of insurance in which a bonding company agrees to reimburse an employer, within limits, for losses attributable to theft or embezzlement by bonded employees. Most employers require employees handling cash or other negotiable assets to be bonded. Companies with only a few employees at risk may obtain individual fidelity bonds; larger concerns may prefer to obtain a blanket fidelity bond covering many employees. Before issuing fidelity bonds, underwriters investigate thoroughly the past records of the employees to be bonded. This service offers added protection by preventing the employment of persons with dubious records in positions of trust. Bonding companies are much more likely to prosecute fraud cases vigorously than are employers; general awareness of this fact is another deterrent against dishonesty on the part of bonded employees.

## Methods of Assigning Authority and Responsibility

Personnel within an organization need to have a clear understanding of their responsibilities and the rules and regulations that govern their actions. Therefore, to enhance the control environment, management develops employee job descriptions and computer systems documentation, and clearly defines authority and responsibility within the enterprise. Policies also may be established regarding such matters as acceptable business practices, conflicts of interest, and codes of conduct.

## Management Control Methods

Management control methods are used to exercise control over the authority delegated to others. Such methods involve developing plans and monitoring the progress toward accomplishment of those plans. A financial forecast and budgeting system is a prime example of a management control method. A financial forecast for an enterprise is an estimate of the expected financial position, results of operations, and cash flows for one or more future periods.[2] It establishes definite goals providing management with a yardstick for evaluating and controlling actual performance. During the year, monthly reports may be prepared comparing actual operating results with forecast figures. These reports should be accompanied by explanations of all significant variations between forecast and actual results, with a definite assignment of responsibility for such variances.

## Internal Auditing

Another basic component of the internal control environment is an internal auditing staff. **Internal auditors** investigate and appraise the internal control structure and the efficiency with which the various units of the business are performing their assigned functions, and report their findings and recommendations to top management. As representatives of top management, the internal auditors are interested in determining whether each branch or department has a clear understanding of its assignment, is adequately staffed, maintains good records, protects cash and inventories and other assets properly, cooperates harmoniously with other departments, and in general carries out effectively and efficiently its designated function. The manner in which the CPAs use the work of internal auditors is

---

[2]AICPA, *Guide for Prospective Financial Information* (New York, 1993), paragraph 3.04.

discussed later in this chapter; the internal auditing profession is discussed in detail in Chapter 20.

## Audit Committee

As discussed in Chapter 7, an audit committee should be composed of members of the board of directors who are neither officers nor employees of the client organization. Because of this independence from management of the firm, audit committees help maintain a direct line of communication between the board of directors and the entity's independent and internal auditors. They also monitor top management of the organization, serving as a deterrent to management override of other internal controls and management fraud.

# THE ACCOUNTING SYSTEM

The accounting system consists of the methods and records established to identify, assemble, analyze, classify, record, and report an entity's transactions and to maintain accountability for the related assets and liabilities. An accounting system should include methods and records to accomplish the following objectives:

1. Identify and record all valid transactions.
2. Describe on a timely basis the transactions in sufficient detail to permit proper classification of transactions for financial reporting.
3. Measure the value of transactions in a manner that permits recording their proper monetary value in the financial statements.
4. Determine the time period in which transactions occurred to permit recording of transactions in the proper accounting period.
5. Present properly the transactions and related disclosures in the financial statements.

In addition to the typical system of journals, ledgers, and other recordkeeping devices, an accounting system should include a chart of accounts and a manual of accounting policies and procedures. A *chart of accounts* is a classified listing of all accounts in use, accompanied by a detailed description of the purpose and content of each. A *manual of accounting policies and procedures* states clearly in writing the methods of treating transactions. In combination, the chart of accounts and manual of accounting policies and procedures should allow proper and uniform handling of transactions.

# CONTROL PROCEDURES

In addition to the control environment and the accounting system, management establishes other controls over the entity's transactions and assets. While there are many specific control procedures that may be implemented by a company, they may be categorized as procedures for: (1) proper authorization of transactions and activities; (2) appropriate segregation of duties; (3) adequate documentation and recording of transactions and events; (4) effective safeguards over access to and use of assets and records; and (5) independent checks on performance and proper valuation of recorded amounts.

## Authorization of Transactions

Authorization of transactions may be either general or specific. *General authorization* occurs when management establishes criteria for acceptance of a certain type of transaction. For example, top management may establish general price lists and credit policies for new customers. Transactions with customers that meet these criteria can be approved by the credit department. *Specific authorization* occurs when transactions are authorized on an individual basis. For example, top management may consider individually and specifically authorize any sales transaction in excess of a specified amount, say $100,000.

## Segregation of Duties

A fundamental concept of internal control is that no one department or person should handle all aspects of a transaction from beginning to end. We have already discussed the segregation of responsibilities among departments. In a similar manner, no one individual should perform more than one of the functions of authorizing transactions, recording transactions, and maintaining custody over assets. Also, to the extent possible, individuals executing the specific transaction should be segregated from these functions. The goal is to reduce the opportunities for any one person to be in a position to both perpetrate and conceal errors or irregularities in the normal course of his or her duties.

A credit sales transaction may be used to illustrate appropriate authorization and segregation procedures. Top management may have generally authorized the sale of merchandise at specified credit terms to customers who meet certain requirements. The credit department may approve the sales transactions by ascertaining that the extension of credit and terms of sale are in compliance with company policies. Once the sale is approved, the shipping department executes the transaction by obtaining custody of the merchandise from the inventory stores department and shipping it to the customer. The accounting department uses copies of the documentation created by the sales, credit, and shipping departments as a basis for recording the transaction and billing the customer. With this segregation of duties, no one department or individual can initiate and execute an unauthorized transaction.

## Adequate Documentation

A system of well-designed forms and documents is necessary to create a record of the activities of all departments. In the case of a credit sales transaction, the accounting department receives copies of internal documents prepared by the sales, credit, and shipping departments to properly record the transaction.

An internal control device of wide applicability is the use of serial numbers on documents. Serial numbers provide control over the number of documents issued. Checks, tickets, sales invoices, purchase orders, stock certificates, and many other business papers can be controlled in this manner. For some documents, such as checks, it may be desirable to account for the sequence used by a monthly or weekly inspection of the documents issued. For other documents, as in the case of serially numbered admission tickets, control may be achieved by noting the last serial number issued each day, and thereby computing the total value of tickets issued during the day. Adequate safeguarding and numerical control should be maintained at all times for unissued prenumbered documents.

## Safeguards over Assets and Records

Only individuals who are properly authorized should be allowed access to the company's assets. Direct physical access to assets may be controlled through the use of safes, locks, fences, and guards. Improper indirect access to assets, generally accomplished by creating unauthorized transactions or by falsifying financial records, must also be controlled. This may be accomplished by securing documents, accounting records, and computer data files and monitoring their use.

## Independent Checks on Performance and Proper Valuation

The accuracy of the work of various individuals in a company may be verified by independent checks on performance and valuation such as clerical checks, computer program controls, independent review reports, and reconciliations. When the accounting and custodial departments are relatively independent, the work of each department serves to verify the accuracy of the work of the other. Periodic comparisons should be made of accounting records and the physical assets on hand. Investigation as to the cause of any discrepancies will uncover weakness either in procedures for safeguarding assets or in maintaining the related accounting records. If the accounting records were not independent of the custodial department, the records could be manipulated to conceal waste, loss, or theft of the related assets.

---

◆ ILLUSTRATIVE CASE ◆

A manufacturer of golf clubs operated a large storeroom containing thousands of sets of golf clubs ready for shipment. Detailed perpetual inventory records were maintained by the employee in charge of the storeroom. A shortage of several sets of clubs developed as a result of theft by another employee who had acquired an unauthorized key to the storeroom. The employee responsible for the storeroom discovered the discrepancy between the clubs in stock and the quantities of clubs as shown by the records. Fearing criticism of his recordkeeping, he changed the inventory records to agree with the quantities on hand. The thefts continued, and large losses were sustained before the shortages were discovered. If the inventory records had been maintained by someone not responsible for physical custody of the merchandise, there would have been no incentive to conceal a shortage by falsifying the records.

---

Figure 8-2 illustrates the use of an independently maintained record to establish accountability for assets. It is *not* essential that all three parties in the diagram (A, B, and C) be employees of the company; one or more may be an outside party or a mechanical device. For example, if A is a bank with custody of cash on deposit, B would be the company employees maintaining records of cash receipts and disbursements, and C might be a computer program that performs periodic bank reconciliations. Or, if A is a salesclerk with custody of cash receipts from sales, B could be a cash register with a locked-in tape, and C could be the departmental supervisor. Regardless of the nature of the parties involved, the principle remains the same: Accounting records should be maintained in-

Figure 8–2   Establishing Accountability for Assets

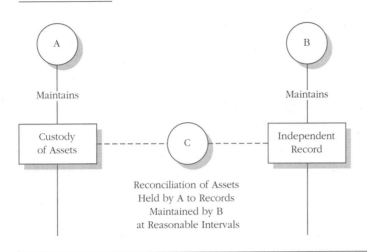

dependently of custody of the related assets and should be compared at reasonable intervals to asset quantities on hand.

## Limitations of Internal Control

Internal control can do much to protect against both errors and irregularities and ensure the reliability of accounting data. Still, it is important to recognize the existence of inherent limitations in any internal control structure. Errors may be made in the performance of control procedures as a result of carelessness, misunderstanding of instructions, or other human factors. In addition, without active participation by the board of directors and an effective internal audit department, top management can easily override the internal control structure. Finally, control procedures dependent upon separation of duties may be circumvented by collusion among employees.

The extent of the internal controls adopted by a business is limited by cost considerations. It is not feasible from a cost standpoint to establish a control structure that provides absolute protection from fraud and waste; reasonable assurance in this regard is the best that generally can be achieved.

# THE AUDITORS' CONSIDERATION OF INTERNAL CONTROL

The second standard of field work requires the auditors to obtain a sufficient understanding of the internal control structure to plan the audit and to determine the nature, timing, and extent of tests to be performed. As stated in SAS No. 55 (AU 319), "Consideration of the Internal Control Structure in a Financial Statement Audit," the auditors' understanding of their clients' internal control provides a basis both to (1) *plan the audit* and (2) *assess control risk*.

In planning an audit, it is essential that the auditors have a sufficient understanding of the client's control environment, accounting system, and control procedures. This encompasses both an understanding of the *design* of the policies, procedures, and records, and a knowledge of whether they have been *placed in operation* by the client. With this understanding the auditors are able to (1) identify the types of potential misstatements of the financial statements, (2) consider factors that affect the risk of material misstatements, and (3) design effective substantive tests of the financial statement balances. It is difficult to imagine designing tests of financial statement balances without an understanding of the control structure. For example, auditors who do not understand the client's policies and procedures for executing and recording credit sales would have a difficult time substantiating the balances of accounts receivable and sales.

The auditors' consideration of the internal control structure also provides a basis for their assessment of **control risk**—the risk that material misstatements will not be prevented or detected by the client's internal control structure. If the auditors determine that the client's internal control is effective, they will assess control risk to be low. The auditors can then accept a higher level of detection risk, and substantive testing can be decreased. Conversely, if internal controls are weak, control risk is high and the auditors must increase the extent of their substantive tests to limit the level of detection risk. Therefore, the auditors' understanding of internal control is a major factor in determining the nature, timing, and extent of substantive testing necessary to verify the financial statement assertions.

Since an effective internal control structure is a major factor in an audit, the question arises as to what action the auditors should take when internal control is found to be seriously deficient. Can the auditors complete a satisfactory audit and properly express an opinion on the fairness of financial statements of a company in which control risk is considered to be extremely high? The answer to this question depends on whether the auditors believe that inherent risk is at a satisfactory level so that substantive tests can be designed that will reduce audit risk to an acceptable level. For example, the auditors of a small business with a limited segregation of duties often apply an approach of restricting detection risk through extensive substantive tests of financial statement assertions, rather than performing tests of internal control.

## Obtain an Understanding of the Internal Control Structure

In every audit, the auditors must obtain an understanding of the internal control structure sufficient to plan the audit—this includes an understanding of the control environment, the accounting system, and control procedures.

Control Environment.   The auditors must obtain sufficient knowledge to understand management's and the board of directors' attitudes, awareness, and actions concerning the control environment. It is important that the auditors concentrate on the substance of controls, rather than their form. For example, a budgetary reporting system may provide reports, but the reports may not be analyzed and acted upon by management.

Accounting System.    To understand the accounting system the auditors must first understand the major types of transactions engaged in by the entity. Next, the auditors must become familiar with the treatment of those transactions, including how they are initiated, the related accounting records, and the manner in which the transactions are processed. Finally, the auditors must understand the financial reporting process used to prepare the financial statements, including the approaches used to develop accounting estimates.

Control Procedures.    While obtaining an understanding of the control environment and the accounting system, the auditors will generally obtain some knowledge about the client's control procedures. For example, while obtaining an understanding of documents relating to cash transactions, it is likely that the auditors will discover whether the bank accounts are reconciled. Whether it is necessary for the auditors to devote additional attention to obtaining an understanding of other control procedures depends on the circumstances of the engagement.

The auditors may find it necessary to understand and test certain control procedures to audit a particular assertion. For example, when auditing a charitable organization that receives significant cash donations, the auditors may be unable to effectively plan the audit for the completeness assertion for cash contributions without understanding and testing control procedures related to cash receipts. In other circumstances, the auditors may conclude that it would be too costly to audit a particular assertion using only substantive procedures; the most efficient course of action is to increase their understanding and testing of the client's internal control procedures.

Transaction Cycles.    In obtaining an understanding of the client's accounting system and the related control procedures, auditors generally find it useful to divide the overall system into its major transaction cycles. The term **transaction cycle** refers to the policies and the sequence of procedures for processing a particular type of transaction. For example, the accounting system in a manufacturing business might be subdivided into the following major transaction cycles:

1.   *Revenue (or sales and collections) cycle*—including procedures and policies for obtaining orders from customers, approving credit, shipping merchandise, preparing sales invoices (billing), recording revenue and accounts receivable, and handling and recording cash receipts.

2.   *Acquisition (or purchases and disbursements) cycle*—including procedures and policies for initiating purchases of inventory, other assets, and services; placing purchase orders, inspecting goods upon receipt and preparing receiving reports; recording liabilities to vendors; authorizing payment; and making and recording cash disbursements.

3.   *Conversion (production) cycle*—including procedures and policies for storing materials, placing materials into production, assigning production costs to inventories, and accounting for the cost of goods sold.

4.   *Payroll cycle*—including procedures and policies for hiring, terminating, and determining pay rates; timekeeping; computing gross payroll, payroll taxes, and amounts

withheld from gross pay; maintaining payroll records and preparing and distributing paychecks.

5.  *Financing cycle*—including procedures and policies for authorizing, executing, and recording transactions involving bank loans, leases, bonds payable, and capital stock.

6.  *Investing cycle*—including procedures and policies for authorizing, executing, and recording transactions involving investments in fixed assets and securities.

The transaction cycles within a particular company depend upon the nature of the company's business activities. A bank, for example, has no production cycle, but has both a lending cycle and a demand deposits cycle. Also, different auditors may elect to define a given company's transaction cycles in different ways. For example, the sales and collection cycle may alternatively be defined as two separate transaction cycles for (1) the processing and recording of credit sales, and (2) the handling and recording of cash receipts. The important point to recognize is that dividing internal control into transaction cycles enables the auditor to focus upon the internal control procedures that affect the reliability of specific assertions about accounts in the financial statements.

Sources of Information about Internal Control.   How do auditors gain an understanding of the client's internal control structure? Auditors obtain information about internal control by *inquiry* of appropriate client personnel, *inspecting* various entity documents and records, and *observing* control activities and operations as they are performed. In repeat engagements, their investigation for the current year will stress areas shown as having questionable controls in prior years. It is imperative, however, that auditors recognize that the pattern of operations is an ever-changing one—internal controls that were adequate last year may now be obsolete.

Auditors may ascertain the duties and responsibilities of client personnel by inspecting organization charts and job descriptions, and interviewing client personnel. Many clients have procedures manuals and flowcharts describing the approved practices to be followed in all phases of operations. Another excellent source of information is in the reports, working papers, and audit programs of the client's internal auditing staff.

The auditors' understanding of the internal control structure encompasses not only the design of the policies and procedures, but also whether they have been placed in operation. The term *placed in operation* means that the policy or procedure actually exists and is in use; that is, it does not just exist in theory or on paper.

While obtaining an understanding of internal control, the auditors may also obtain evidence about the operating effectiveness of various controls. *Operating effectiveness* deals with (1) how a control is applied, (2) the consistency with which it is applied, and (3) who applies the control. The distinction between knowing that a control has been placed in operation and obtaining evidence on its operating effectiveness is important. To properly plan the audit, auditors are required to determine that the major controls have been placed in operation; they are *not* required to evaluate their operating effectiveness. However, if the auditors wish to assess control risk at a level lower than the maximum, they must have evidence of the operating effectiveness of the controls. This evidence is obtained by performing tests of controls, which are discussed later in this chapter.

Document the Understanding of the Internal Control Structure.   As the independent auditors obtain a working knowledge of the internal control structure to plan the audit, they must document the information in their working papers. The form and extent of this documentation is affected by the size and complexity of the client, as well as the nature of the client's internal control structure. The documentation usually takes the form of internal control questionnaires, written narratives, or flowcharts.

Internal Control Questionnaire.   The traditional method of describing an internal control structure is to fill in a standardized **internal control questionnaire.** Many public accounting firms have developed their own questionnaires for this purpose. The questionnaire usually contains a separate section for each major transaction cycle, enabling the work of completing the questionnaire to be divided conveniently among several audit staff members.

Most internal control questionnaires are designed so that a ''no'' answer to a question indicates a weakness in internal control. In addition, questionnaires may provide for a distinction between major and minor control weaknesses, indication of the sources of information used in answering questions, and explanatory comments regarding control deficiencies. A disadvantage of standardized internal control questionnaires is their lack of flexibility. They often contain many questions that are ''not applicable'' to specific systems, particularly systems for small companies. Also, the situation in which an internal control strength compensates for a weakness in the structure may not be obvious from examining a completed questionnaire. An internal control questionnaire relating to cash receipts is illustrated in Figure 8–3.

Written Narrative of Internal Control.   An internal control questionnaire is intended as a means for the auditors to document their understanding of internal control. If completion of the questionnaire is regarded as an end in itself, there may be a tendency for the auditors to fill in the ''yes'' and ''no'' answers in a mechanical manner, without any real understanding or study of the transaction cycle. For this reason, some public accounting firms prefer to use written narratives or flowcharts in lieu of, or in conjunction with, questionnaires. **Written narratives** usually follow the flow of each major transaction cycle, identifying the employees performing various tasks, documents prepared, records maintained, and the division of duties. Figure 8–4 is a written narrative, describing internal control over cash receipts.

Flowcharts of Internal Control.   Many CPA firms consider systems flowcharts to be more effective than questionnaires or narrative descriptions in documenting their understanding of a client's accounting system and the related control procedures. A **systems flowchart** is a diagram—a symbolic representation of a system or a series of procedures with each procedure shown in sequence. To the experienced reader, a flowchart conveys a clear image of the system, showing the nature and sequence of procedures, division of responsibilities, sources and distribution of documents, and types and location of accounting records and files. The standard symbols used in systems flowcharting are illustrated in Figure 8–5; however, the symbols used and flowcharting technique vary somewhat among different public accounting firms.

## Figure 8–3    Internal Control Questionnaire

**Internal Control Questionnaire**
**Cash Receipts — Sales Cycle**

Client _Bennington Co., Inc._                    Audit Date _December 31, 199X_

Names and Positions of Client Personnel Interviewed:
_Lorraine Martin — Cashier; Helen Ellis — head bookkeeper; Wm. Dale — Manager_

| Question | Not Appl. | Yes | No | Weakness Major | Weakness Minor | Remarks |
|---|---|---|---|---|---|---|
| 1. Are all persons receiving or disbursing cash bonded? | | ✓ | | | | |
| 2. Is all incoming mail opened by a responsible employee who does not have access to accounting records? | | | ✓ | ✓ | | H. Ellis is head bookkeeper |
| 3. Does the employee assigned to the opening of incoming mail prepare a list of all checks and money received? | | | ✓ | | ✓ | See mitigating control in #13 |
| 4. a) Is a copy of the listing of mail receipts forwarded to the accounts receivable department for comparison with the credits to customers' accounts? | ✓ | | | | | |
| b) Is a copy of this list turned over to an employee other than the cashier for comparison with the cash receipts records? | ✓ | | | | | |
| 5. Are receipts from cash sales and other over-the-counter collections recorded by sales registers or point-of-sale terminals? | ✓ | | | | | |
| 6. Are the daily totals of cash registers or other mechanical devices verified by an employee not having access to cash? | ✓ | | | | | |
| 7. Are physical facilities and mechanical equipment for receiving and recording cash adequate and conducive to good control? | | ✓ | | | | |
| 8. Is revenue from investments, rent, concessions, and similar sources scheduled in advance so that nonreceipt on due date would be promptly investigated? | ✓ | | | | | |
| 9. Do procedures for sale of scrap materials provide for direct reporting to accounting department concurrently with transfer of receipts to cashier? | ✓ | | | | | |
| 10. Are securities and other negotiable assets in the custody of someone other than the cashier? | ✓ | | | | | |
| 11. Are collections by branch offices deposited daily in a bank account subject to withdrawal only by home office executives? | ✓ | | | | | |
| 12. Are each day's receipts deposited intact and without delay by an employee other than the accounts receivable bookkeeper? | | ✓ | | | | |
| 13. Are the duplicate deposit tickets returned by the bank and compared with the cash receipts record and mailroom list of receipts by an employee other than the cashier or accounts receivable bookkeeper? | | ✓ | | | | W. Dale Manager |
| 14. Are the duplicate deposit tickets properly filed and available for inspection by auditors? | | ✓ | | | | Chronological sequence |
| 15. Are NSF checks or other items returned by the bank delivered directly to an employee other than the cashier and promptly investigated? | | ✓ | | | | W. Dale Manager |
| 16. Is the physical arrangement of offices and accounting records designed to prevent employees who handle cash from having access to accounting records? | | | ✓ | | ✓ | Small Company doesn't permit this |

Prepared by _V.M. Harris_    Date _Sept. 6, 9X_    Manager Review _____    Date _____

Senior Review _____    Date _____    Partner Review _____    Date _____

Figure 8–4    Written Narrative on Internal Control

_____

**Bennington Co., Inc.**
**Cash Receipts Procedures**
**December 31, 199X**

All cash receipts are received by mail in the form of checks. Lorraine Martin, cashier, picks up the mail every morning at the post office and delivers it unopened to Helen Ellis, the head bookkeeper.

Ellis opens and distributes the mail. Customers' checks are given to Martin, who records the remittances in the cash receipts journal, prepares duplicate deposit slips, and mails the day's receipts intact to First National Bank. The bank returns the validated duplicate deposit slips by mail, and Ellis files them in chronological order. Ellis posts the accounts receivable subsidiary ledger from the cash receipts journal on a daily basis.

Any customers' checks charged back by the bank are given by Ellis to the manager, William Dale, who follows up and redeposits the checks. Ellis also forwards monthly bank statements unopened to Dale. Dale reconciles the monthly bank statement, compares the dates and amounts of deposits with the entries in the cash receipts journal, and reviews the propriety of sales discounts recorded in the cash receipts journal.

Martin, Ellis, and Dale are all bonded.

Val Martin Hawkins
September 6, 199X

_____

Separate systems flowcharts are prepared for each major transaction cycle. In addition, each flowchart is divided into vertical columns representing the various departments (or employees) involved in processing the transactions. Departmental responsibility for procedures, documents, and records is shown by reviewing the related flowcharting symbol beneath the appropriate departmental heading. Flowcharts usually begin in the upper left-hand corner; directional flowlines then indicate the sequence of activity. The normal flow of activity is from top to bottom and from left to right. These basic concepts of systems flowcharting are illustrated in Figure 8–6.

The special advantage of a flowchart over a questionnaire or a narrative is that a flowchart provides a clearer, more specific portrayal of the client's system. There is less opportunity for misunderstanding, blank spots, or ambiguous statements when one uses lines and symbols rather than words to describe internal control. Furthermore, in each successive annual audit, updating a flowchart is a simple process requiring only that the auditor add or change a few lines and symbols.

A possible disadvantage of flowcharts is that internal control weaknesses are not identified as prominently as in questionnaires. A "no" answer in an internal control questionnaire is a conspicuous red flag calling attention to a dangerous situation. A flowchart may not provide so clear a signal that a particular internal control is absent or is not being properly enforced. For that reason, some CPA firms use both flowcharts and questionnaires to describe internal control. The flowchart clearly depicts the system, while

## Figure 8–5  Widely Used Flowcharting Symbols

**Document**—any paper document, such as a check or sales invoice.

**Manual Process**—any manual operation, such as preparation of a sales invoice or reconciling a bank statement.

**Process**—any operation, whether performed manually, mechanically, or by EDP. Often used interchangeably with the manual process symbol.

**Offline Storage**—a file or other storage facility for documents or EDP records.

**Flowlines**—lines indicating the directional flow of documents. Normally downward or to the right unless otherwise indicated by arrowheads.

**Annotation**—used for explanatory comments, such as filing sequence (by date, alphabetical, etc.)

**Connector**—exit to or entry from another part of the flowchart. Used to avoid excessive crossing of flowlines. Exit and entry connectors are keyed by letters or numbers.

**Off-Page Connector**—indicates source or destination of items entering or exiting the flowchart.

**Input/Output**—used in place of an off-page connector to indicats information entering or exiting the flowchart.

**Decision**—indicates alternative courses of action resulting from a yes or no decision.

### Special Symbols for EDP Systems

| Magnetic Disk | Punched Card | Punched Tape | On-Line Storage | Magnetic Tape |

# Figure 8–6

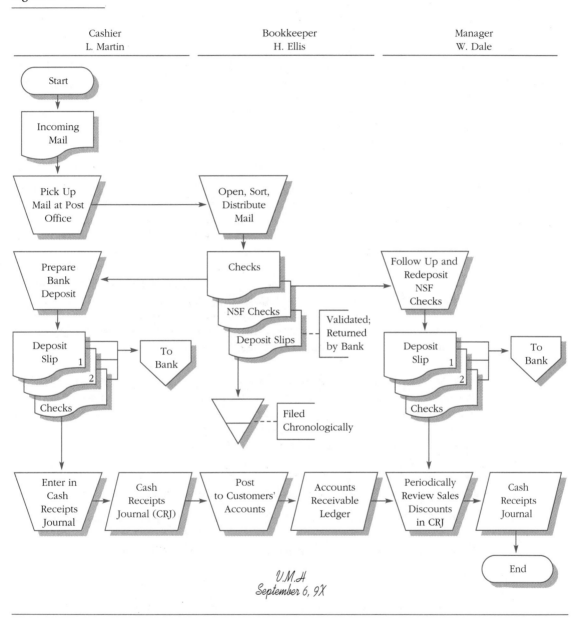

the questionnaire serves to remind the auditors of controls that should be present in the system.

Walk-Through Test.    After describing internal control in their working papers, the auditors will generally verify that the system has been placed in operation by performing a walk-through of each transaction cycle. The term **walk-through** refers to tracing several transactions (perhaps only one or two) through each step in the cycle. To perform a walk-through of the sales and collection cycle, for example, the auditors might begin by selecting several sales orders and following the related transactions through the client's sequence of procedures. The auditors would determine whether such procedures as credit approval, shipment of merchandise, preparation of sales invoices, recording of the accounts receivable, and processing of the customers' remittances were performed by appropriate client personnel and in the sequence indicated in the audit working papers. If the auditors find that the system functions differently from the working paper description, they will amend the working papers to describe the actual system.

## Assess Control Risk

Assessing control risk involves evaluating the effectiveness of a client's internal control policies and procedures in preventing or detecting material misstatements in the financial statements. Recall from Chapter 6 that most of the independent auditors' work involves gathering and evaluating evidence about the major financial statement assertions—existence or occurrence; completeness; rights and obligations; valuation or allocation; and presentation and disclosure. Therefore, the auditors assess control risk in terms of these five assertions. The process of arriving at the auditors' assessments of control risk is an iterative process that is refined as the auditors obtain more and more evidence about the effectiveness of various internal control policies and procedures. It may be summarized as the following steps: *(a)* determine the planned assessed level of control risk, *(b)* design and perform additional tests of controls, *(c)* reassess control risk and modify planned substantive tests, and *(d)* document the assessed level of control risk.

### Determine the Planned Assessed Level of Control Risk.

After documenting their understanding of internal controls, the auditors will determine a **planned assessed level of control risk** for the various financial statement assertions. For assertions with weaker internal controls, the auditors may simply plan to assess control risk at the maximum level, and no tests of the related controls need to be performed.

For financial statement assertions that appear to have more effective controls, the auditors may plan to assess control risk at a lower level. To assess control risk at less than the maximum level for a particular assertion, the auditors must:

1. Identify those internal control structure policies and procedures that are likely to prevent or detect material misstatements of the assertion.
2. Perform tests of controls to evaluate the effectiveness of such policies and procedures.

The auditors' planned assessed level of control risk is used to develop the initial audit program of substantive testing. For assertions with a high planned assessed level of control risk the auditors will plan substantial substantive procedures. Planned substantive procedures can be restricted or eliminated for assertions with a low planned assessed level of control risk.

Therefore, in making decisions about the planned assessed levels of control risk, the auditors must consider the trade-off between tests of controls and substantive testing.

**Tests of controls** allow the auditors to reduce their assessments of control risk, which, in turn, allows them to reduce the time spent performing substantive procedures. For each test of control, the auditors must ask themselves "Is the time required to perform the test justified in terms of its resulting decrease in the scope of substantive testing?"

Design and Perform Additional Tests of Controls.  The auditors may have gathered some evidence about the effectiveness of certain policies and procedures while they obtained an understanding of the client's internal control structure. In some audits, especially those involving small clients, these preliminary tests of controls may be adequate to support the auditors' planned assessed level of control risk. In these cases, the auditors need not perform additional tests of controls and may proceed directly to documenting their assessed level of control risk and completing the planned substantive tests. However, for many audits additional tests of controls are necessary to support the auditors' assessed level of control risk. The auditors will use their understanding of the internal control structure to design these additional tests of controls.

The audit procedures used to test the effectiveness of internal control policies and procedures include: (1) *inquiries* of appropriate client personnel, (2) *inspection* of documents and reports, (3) *observation* of the application of accounting policies or procedures, and (4) *reperformance* of the policy or procedure. Tests of controls focus on the performance of policies and procedures rather than on the accuracy of financial statement amounts.

To illustrate this distinction, assume that the client has implemented the control procedure of requiring a second person to review the quantities, prices, extensions, and footing of each sales invoice. The purpose of this control procedure is to prevent material errors in the billing of customers and the recording of sales transactions. A substantive test of financial statement amounts might involve selecting a sample of recorded sales transactions to determine that they have been properly recorded and included in the year's total sales. In this manner, the test only considers the internal control indirectly.

To test the effectiveness of this control procedure the auditors may make inquiries of client personnel and observe application of the procedure. They might also select a sample of, say, 30 sales invoices prepared throughout the year. They would inspect the invoice copy for the initials of the reviewer, and reperform the procedure by comparing the quantities to those listed on the related shipping documents, comparing unit prices to the client's price lists, and verifying the extensions and footings. The results of this test provide the auditors with evidence as to the existence and valuation of the recorded sales and accounts receivable. If numerous deviations from the control procedure are found, the auditors will expand their substantive procedures with respect to existence and valuation of accounts receivable and sales transactions.

The control procedure described above leaves documentary evidence of performance, allowing it to be tested by sampling. Other internal control procedures must be tested entirely through observation by the auditors and inquiry of client personnel. Segregation of duties, for example, is tested by observing the client's employees as they perform their duties, and inquiring as to who performed those duties throughout the period under audit. The auditors also should determine whether employees performed **incompatible functions** when other employees were absent from work on sick leave or vacation.

Reassess Control Risk and Modify Planned Substantive Tests.    After the auditors have completed the test of controls, they are in a position to reassess control risk based on the results of the tests. The results of the tests of controls may reveal that the level of control risk is actually higher than the planned level. If this is the case, modifications must be made in the nature, timing, and extent of the planned substantive tests in the audit program. For example, the auditors may decide to increase the extent of their substantive testing, or perform certain substantive tests at year-end rather than at an interim date.

Document the Assessed Level of Control Risk.    The auditors' **assessed level of control risk** will have identified the financial statement assertions with maximum control risk, and those assertions for which control risk is considered to be less than the maximum level. The auditors must document these conclusions in their working papers. They must also describe the basis for their assessments of control risk that are at less than the maximum level. A working paper, such as Figure 8–7, is often used to summarize the auditors' assessments of control risk and the resulting modifications in substantive tests. Notice that the extensions and limitations of audit procedures are described in detail to facilitate completion of the final version of the audit program.

The auditors' consideration of internal control is very complex. Figure 8–8 is a flowchart that highlights the major steps in the auditors' consideration of internal control.

## Decision Aids for Audit Program Modification

Modifying audit programs for various levels of control risk, while considering other factors such as levels of materiality and inherent risk, involves complex judgments. How many additional items should the auditors sample to compensate for high control risk? Is control risk for a particular account low enough to make it feasible to test the account at an interim date rather than at year-end? Without guidance from the CPA firm, different auditors within that firm might arrive at different answers to these questions. In fact, research on these types of audit judgments has revealed just that; there is a good deal of variance in auditors' program decisions.

CPA firms initially reacted to this problem by developing policies that put limits on individual auditors' decisions. The establishment of minimum audit sample sizes for particular types of tests is an example of such a policy. More recently, CPA firms have attempted to add even more structure to auditors' program decisions through the use of decision aids or guides. A **decision aid** is a checklist, standard form, or a computer program that helps the auditors make a particular decision by ensuring that they consider all relevant information or assisting them in combining the information to make the decision. By reducing the variance in auditors' program judgments, decision aids promote the performance of audits that meet firm and professional requirements.

## Consideration of the Work of Internal Auditors

Many of the audit procedures performed by internal auditors are similar in nature to those employed by independent auditors. This raises the question of how the work of the internal auditors affects the independent auditors' work. The Auditing Standards Board

Figure 8–7    Working Paper for Summarizing Assessment of Control Risk

---

**WP Index** *CR-1*

## Understanding of the Internal Control Structure, Control Risk Assessment, and Impact on Substantive Procedures

**Client**    *Arntco, Inc.*                                              **Balance Sheet Date** *12/31/X3*

**Completed by:**  *R.W.*    **Date:** *9/15/X3*            **Reviewed by:**  *K.J.*    **Date:** *10/28/X3*

We obtained sufficient knowledge of the design of the control environment, the accounting system, and control procedures to plan the audit, and determined that the policies and procedures have been placed in operation.

Workpapers related to our understanding of the control structure are included at *Perm. Files ICS 1 through ICS-7*. Except as noted below, and on the reference workpapers, we have assessed control risk to be at the maximum and have designed our substantive audit procedures accordingly.

For those significant assertions related to the account balances indicated below, we have assessed control risk at less than the maximum, and the effects of such assessment have been reflected in our audit program. For assertions for each account balance or class of transactions where control risk has been assessed at less than the maximum, tests of controls have been performed to provide evidential matter sufficient to evaluate the effectiveness of the policies and procedure relevant to the various assertions.

**CASH**                                                                **WORKPAPER REF** ___

---

---

---

**ACCOUNTS RECEIVABLE**                                                  **WORKPAPER REF** *C-2*

*Control risk is assessed as slightly below the maximum for the following assertions: existence and valuation (other than for net realizable value which risk is assessed at the maximum). Control risk for completeness is assessed as moderate. Accordingly, primary audit evidence for existence, ownership and valuation (other than net realizable value) will be obtained by year-end confirmation of all key items (over $3,500), a nonstatistical representative sample of the remaining population (see workpaper C-5) and cutoff tests at year-end. Evidence about the net realizable value objective will be obtained by procedures set forth in the audit program, which consider: subsequent cash collections, the aged trial balance, analytical procedures, and review of specific accounts with the owner-manager. Audit evidence for completeness will be obtained by application of (1) year-end cutoff tests and (2) analytical procedures applied to sales (see workpaper C-6).*

**INVENTORY**                                                           **WORKPAPER REF** *D-5*

*Prior experience and tests of controls indicate good controls over physical counts and pricing of material items in inventory. These tests of controls provide sufficient evidence to support a low control risk assessment for the existence and valuation assertions.*

:
:
:

**EXPENSE ACCOUNTS**                                                    **WORKPAPER REF** ___

---

Source: Adapted from AICPA, *Audit Guide: Consideration of the Internal Control Structure in a Financial Statement Audit* (New York, 1990).

## Figure 8–8   The Auditors' Consideration of Internal Control

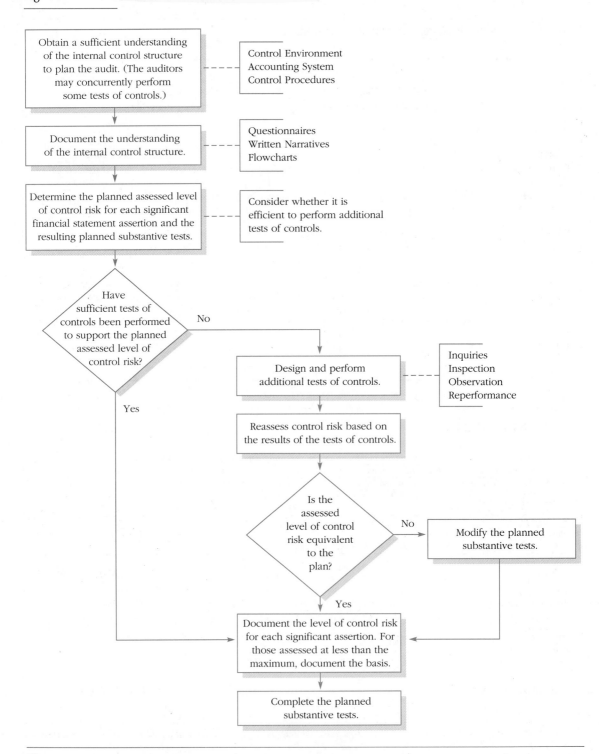

has addressed this issue in *SAS No. 65* (AU 322), "The Auditor's Consideration of the Internal Audit Function in an Audit of Financial Statements."

The internal audit function is an important aspect of the client's control environment. Therefore, the independent auditors consider the existence and quality of an internal audit function in their assessment of the client's internal control structure. Through its contribution to internal control, the work of the internal auditors may reduce the amount of audit testing performed by the independent auditors.

The independent auditors first obtain an understanding of the work of the internal auditors to determine its relevance to the audit. They make inquiries about such matters as the internal auditors' activities and audit plans. If the independent auditors conclude that the internal auditors' work is relevant and that it would be efficient to consider it, they assess the *competence* and *objectivity* of the internal audit staff, and evaluate the quality of their work.

In evaluating the competence of the internal auditors, the independent auditors consider the educational level, professional experience, and professional certifications of the internal audit staff. They also investigate the internal auditors' policies, programs, procedures, working papers, and reports; and the extent to which the internal auditors' activities are supervised and reviewed. Objectivity is evaluated by considering the organizational status of the director of internal audit, including whether the director reports to an officer of sufficient status to ensure broad audit coverage, and has direct access to the audit committee of the board of directors. The internal auditors' policies for assigning independent staff to audit areas are also reviewed.

After evaluating the competence and objectivity of the internal auditors, the independent auditors evaluate and test their work. This evaluation includes a review of the scope of the internal auditors' work, and the quality of their programs and reports. This investigation and evaluation provides the independent auditors with a sound basis for determining the extent to which the work of the internal auditors allows them to limit their audit procedures.

In addition to reducing the extent of the independent auditors' substantive procedures, the internal auditors' work may affect the independent auditors' procedures when obtaining an understanding of the client's internal control structure and assessing risk. The internal auditors also may provide direct assistance to the independent auditors in preparing working papers and performing certain audit procedures. However, the independent auditors should not overrely on the internal auditors' work; they must obtain sufficient, competent, evidential matter to support their opinion on the financial statements. Regardless of the extent of the internal auditors' work, the independent auditors must perform direct testing of those financial statement assertions with a high risk of material misstatement. Judgments about assessments of inherent and control risks, the materiality of misstatements, the sufficiency of tests performed, and other matters affecting the opinion must be those of the independent auditors. Also, the independent auditors should be directly involved in evaluating audit evidence that requires significant subjective judgment.

## Communication of Control Structure Related Matters

Deficiencies in the internal control structure identified by the auditors' procedures should be communicated to the client, along with the auditors' recommendations for corrective action. This is a service in addition to issuance of the audit report. *SAS 60* (AU 325),

"Communication of Internal Control Structure Related Matters Noted in an Audit" uses the term *reportable conditions* to refer to those matters that must be communicated by the auditors to the audit committee of the board of directors (or an individual or group with equivalent responsibility if no audit committee exists). A **reportable condition** is a significant deficiency in the design or operation of the internal control that could adversely affect the organization's ability to record, process, summarize, and report financial data. Reportable conditions may be communicated orally, but they are usually set forth in a letter, such as shown in Figure 8–9.

A reportable condition may be so significant as to be considered a **material weakness in internal control;** that is, a condition that results in more than a relatively low risk of material misstatement of the financial statements. Clients may request the auditors to identify in their communication on internal control those reportable conditions that are considered to be material weaknesses in internal control. While a written communication may indicate that the auditors found no material weaknesses, one should never be issued that states that the auditors identified no reportable conditions.

Auditors often communicate operational suggestions and less significant weaknesses in greater detail to management in a report called a **management letter.** This report serves as a valuable reference document for management and may also serve to minimize the auditors' legal liability in the event of a defalcation or other loss resulting from a weakness in internal control. Many auditing firms place great emphasis upon providing clients with a thorough and carefully considered management letter. These firms recognize that such a report can be a valuable and constructive contribution to the efficiency and effectiveness of the client's operations. The quality of the auditors' recommendations reflects their professional expertise and creative ability and the thoroughness of their investigation.

## Internal Control in the Small Company

The preceding discussion of internal control and its consideration by the independent auditors has been presented in terms of large corporations. In the large concern, excellent internal control may be achieved by extensive segregation of duties, so that no one person handles a transaction completely from beginning to end. In the very small concern, with only one or two office employees, there is little or no opportunity for division of duties and responsibilities. Consequently, internal control tends to be weak, if not completely absent, unless the owner/manager recognizes the importance of internal control and participates in key activities.

Because of the absence of strong internal control in small concerns, the independent auditors must rely much more on substantive tests of account balances and transactions than is required in larger organizations. Although it is well to recognize that internal control can seldom be strong in a small business, this limitation is no justification for ignoring available forms of control. Auditors can make a valuable contribution to small client companies by encouraging the installation of such control procedures as are practicable in the circumstances. The following specific practices are almost always capable of use in even the smallest business:

1. Record all cash receipts immediately.
   a. For over-the-counter collections, use cash registers easily visible to customers. Record register readings daily.

## Figure 8–9   Report to Audit Committee

*Wilson & Quinn*

Certified Public Accountants
1134 California St.
San Diego, California 92110

March 12, 19X2

Audit Committee of the Board of Directors
Fleet Feet Shoe Stores, Inc.
2567 University Blvd.
San Diego, California 92105

Gentlemen:

In planning and performing our audit of the financial statements of the Fleet Feet Shoe Stores, Inc. for the Year ended December 31, 19X1, we considered its internal control structure in order to determine our auditing procedures for the purpose of expressing our opinion on the financial statements and not to provide assurance on the internal control structure. However, we noted a matter involving the internal control structure and its operation that we consider to be a reportable condition under standards established by the American Institute of Certified Public Accountants. Reportable conditions involve matters coming to our attention relating to significant deficiencies in the design or operation of the internal control structure that, in our judgment, could adversely affect the organization's ability to record, process, summarize, and report financial data consistent with the assertions of management in the financial statements.

Our audit revealed that personnel at individual stores fail to prepare receiving reports for shipments of goods directly from wholesalers. This weakness increases the chance that the company will pay for merchandise that has not been received. We recommend that prenumbered receiving reports be prepared upon receipt of these shipments.

This report is intended solely for the information and use of the audit committee, management, and others in the organization.

Sincerely,

*James Wilson*

Wilson & Quinn, CPAs

*b.* Prepare a list of all mail remittances immediately upon opening the mail and retain this list for subsequent comparison with bank deposit tickets and entries in the cash receipts journal.

2. Deposit all cash receipts intact daily.

3. Make all payments by serially numbered checks, with the exception of small disbursements from petty cash.

4. Reconcile bank accounts monthly and retain copies of the reconciliations in the files.

5. Use serially numbered sales invoices, purchase orders, and receiving reports.

6. Issue checks to vendors only in payment of approved invoices that have been matched with purchase orders and receiving reports.

7. Balance subsidiary ledger with control accounts at regular intervals, and prepare and mail customers' statements monthly.

8. Prepare comparative financial statements monthly in sufficient detail to disclose significant variations in any category of revenue or expense.

Adherence to these basic control practices significantly reduces the risk of material error or major defalcation going undetected. If the size of the business permits a segregation of the duties of cash handling and recordkeeping, a fair degree of control can be achieved. If it is necessary that one employee serve as both accounting clerk and cashier, then active participation by the owner in certain key functions is necessary to guard against the concealment of fraud or errors. In a few minutes each day the owner, even though not trained in accounting, can create a significant amount of internal control by personally (1) reading daily cash register totals, (2) reconciling the bank account monthly, (3) signing all checks and canceling the supporting documents, (4) approving all general journal entries, and (5) critically reviewing comparative monthly statements of revenue and expense.

---

## ◆ CHAPTER SUMMARY

This chapter explained the meaning and significance of internal control, the major components of a client's internal control structure, and the manner in which auditors consider internal control. To summarize:

1. An organization's internal control structure consists of the policies and procedures established to provide reasonable assurance that the organization's objectives will be achieved. Internal control from management's perspective is a broad concept that encompasses all the policies and procedures that contribute to effective and efficient operations, reliable financial reporting, and compliance with laws and regulations. The portion of the internal control structure relevant to auditors is that which pertains to the entity's ability to record, process, summarize, and report financial data. The three elements of an internal control structure include the control environment, accounting system, and control procedures.

2. The control environment reflects the overall attitude, awareness, and actions of the board of directors, management, owners, and others concerning the importance of control and the way it is used in the entity.

3. The accounting system consists of the methods and records established to identify, assemble, analyze, classify, record, and report an entity's transactions, and to maintain accountability for the related assets and liabilities.

4. The control procedures represent other controls over the entity's transactions and assets, including proper authorization of transactions, segregation of duties, adequate documentation, safeguards over assets and records, and independent checks on performance and proper valuation of recorded amounts.

5. The auditors' consideration of internal control is performed to obtain information necessary to plan the audit and to assess control risk. An adequate understanding of the control environment, accounting system, and control procedures must be documented on all audits. This documentation may be accomplished by use of internal control questionnaires, written narratives, and flowcharts.

6. The auditors assess control risk for each major financial statement assertion to determine the nature, timing, and extent of the substantive tests of that assertion. If the auditors assess control risk at less than the maximum, they must perform tests of controls to determine that the related internal controls are operating effectively. Tests of controls consist of inquiries of appropriate client personnel, inspection of documents and reports, observation of the application of accounting policies and procedures, and reperformance of policies and procedures.

7. Auditors are required to report all reportable conditions that they discover during the audit to the audit committee. A reportable condition is a significant deficiency in the design or operation of an internal control that could adversely affect the organization's ability to record, process, summarize, and report financial data.

## ◆ KEY TERMS INTRODUCED OR EMPHASIZED IN CHAPTER 8

**Assessed level of control risk**   The level of control risk used by the auditors in determining the acceptable detection risk for a financial statement assertion and, accordingly, in deciding on the nature, timing, and extent of substantive testing.

**Audit decision aids**   Standard checklists, forms, or computer programs that assist auditors in making audit decisions by ensuring that they consider all relevant information, or that aid them in weighting and combining the information to make a decision.

**Control risk**   The possibility that a material error or irregularity in a financial statement assertion will not be prevented or detected by the client's internal control.

**Fidelity bonds**   A form of insurance in which a bonding company agrees to reimburse an employer for losses attributable to theft or embezzlement by bonded employees.

**Foreign Corrupt Practices Act**   Federal legislation prohibiting payments to foreign officials for the purpose of securing business. The act also requires all companies under SEC jurisdiction to maintain a system of internal control providing reasonable assurance that transactions are executed only with the knowledge and authorization of management.

**Incompatible duties**   Assigned duties that put an individual in a position to both perpetrate and conceal errors or irregularities in the normal course of job performance.

**Internal auditors**   Corporation employees who design and execute audit programs to test the effectiveness and efficiency of all aspects of internal control. The primary objective of internal auditors is to evaluate and improve the efficiency of the various operating units of an organization rather than to express an opinion as to the fairness of financial statements.

**Internal control questionnaire** One of several alternative methods of describing an internal control structure in audit working papers. Questionnaires are usually designed so that "no" answers prominently identify weaknesses in internal control.

**Internal control structure (system)** An organization's policies and procedures that have been established to provide reasonable assurance that its related objectives will be achieved. An internal control structure is composed of the control environment, the accounting system, and control procedures.

**Management letter** A report to management containing the auditors' recommendations for correcting any deficiencies disclosed by the auditors' consideration of internal control. In addition to providing management with useful information, a management letter may also help limit the auditors' liability in the event a control weakness subsequently results in a loss by the client.

**Material weakness in internal control** A reportable condition (see definition) in which the control system design or the degree of compliance do not reduce to a relatively low level the risk that material errors or irregularities might occur and not be detected.

**Operational audit** A review of a department or other unit of a business to evaluate the effectiveness and efficiency of operations.

**Organizational structure** The division of authority, responsibility, and duties among members of an organization.

**Planned assessed level of control risk** The level of control risk the auditor uses in developing a preliminary audit strategy which includes an appropriate combination of tests of controls and substantive tests.

**Reportable condition** A matter coming to the auditors' attention that represents a significant deficiency in the design or operation of the control structure, that could adversely affect the organization's ability to record, process, summarize, and properly report financial data.

**Systems flowcharts** A symbolic representation of a system or series of procedures with each procedure shown in sequence. Systems flowcharts are a widely used method of describing an internal control structure in audit working papers.

**Tests of controls** Tests directed toward the design or operation of an internal control structure policy or procedure to assess its effectiveness in preventing or detecting material misstatements of financial statement assertions.

**Transaction cycle** The sequence of procedures applied by the client in processing a particular type of recurring transaction. The auditors' working paper description of internal control often is organized around the client's major transaction cycles.

**Walk-through of the system** A test of the accuracy and completeness of the auditors' working paper description of internal control. A walk-through is performed by tracing several transactions through each step of the related transaction cycle, noting whether the sequence of procedures actually performed corresponds to that described in the audit working papers.

**Written narrative of internal control** A written summary of internal control for inclusion in audit working papers. Written narratives are more flexible than questionnaires, but by themselves are practical only for describing relatively small, simple systems.

# ◆ GROUP I: REVIEW QUESTIONS

**8-1** What is the basic purpose of the internal control structure? What measures comprise the structure?

**8-2** "All experienced auditors would design exactly the same audit program for a particular audit engagement." Do you agree? Explain.

**8-3** Identify the three elements of an organization's internal control structure.

8-4    List the factors that make up an organization's control environment.

8-5    How does separation of the recordkeeping function from custody of assets contribute to internal control?

8-6    Name three factors you consider of greatest importance in protecting a business against losses through embezzlement.

8-7    The owner of a medium-size corporation asks you to state two or three principles to be followed in dividing responsibilities among employees in a manner that will produce strong internal control. What would be your reply?

8-8    One basic concept of internal control is that no one employee should handle all aspects of a transaction. Assuming that a general category of transactions has been authorized by top management, how many employees (or departments) should participate in each transaction, as a minimum, to achieve strong internal control? Explain in general terms the function of each of these employees.

8-9    Compare the objectives of the internal auditors with those of the independent auditors.

8-10   What consideration, if any, may independent auditors give to the work of a client's internal audit staff?

8-11   What are the purposes of the consideration of internal control required by generally accepted auditing standards?

8-12   A prospective client informs you that all officers and employees of the company are bonded, and he requests that under these circumstances you forgo a consideration of internal control in order to reduce the cost of an audit. Construct a logical reply to this request.

8-13   Suggest a number of sources from which you might obtain the information needed to prepare a description of internal control in the audit working papers.

8-14   Under what circumstances are tests of controls *efficient* audit procedures?

8-15   How is the auditors' understanding of the client's internal control structure documented in the audit working papers?

8-16   What is a management letter? What is the letter's significance?

8-17   In view of the consideration afforded internal control by the auditors, how do you account for the fact that the auditors' standard report makes no reference to internal control in describing the scope of the audit?

8-18   You have discussed with the president of Vista Corporation several material weaknesses in internal control that have come to your attention during your audit. At the conclusion of this discussion, the president states that he will personally take steps to remedy these problems and that there is no reason for you to bring these matters to the attention of the board of directors. He explains that he believes the board should deal with major policy decisions and not be burdened with day-to-day management problems. How would you respond to this suggestion? Explain fully.

## ♦ GROUP II: QUESTIONS REQUIRING ANALYSIS

8-19   An auditor is required to obtain a sufficient understanding of each of the elements of an entity's internal control structure to plan the audit of the entity's financial statements and to assess control risk for the assertions embodied in the account balance, transaction type, and disclosure components of the financial statements.

*Required:*   *a.*   Identify the elements of an entity's internal control structure.

*b.*   For what purposes should an auditor's understanding of the internal control structure elements be used in planning an audit?

*c.*   Explain why an auditor might decide to assess control risk at the maximum level for one or more financial statement assertions.

*d.*   What must an auditor do to support assessing control risk at less than the maximum level when the auditor has determined that controls have been placed in operation?

8-20   Auditors may restrict substantive tests based on their assessment of control risk.

*Required:*   *a.*   Discuss and contrast the concepts of (1) the planned assessed level of control risk, (2) the (final) assessed level of control risk, and (3) control risk.

*b.*   Using internal control for the existence assertion for accounts receivable, provide an example which distinguishes among the three concepts discussed in part *a* above.

8-21   The auditors' consideration of internal control begins with obtaining an understanding of the internal control structure.

*Required:*   *a.*   Describe the remaining stages of the auditors' consideration.

*b.*   Provide examples of audit procedures that are performed at each stage (including the stage of obtaining an understanding).

8-22   Henry Bailey, CPA, is planning the audit of The Neighborhood Store, a local grocery cooperative. Because The Neighborhood Store is a small business operated entirely by part-time volunteer personnel, internal controls are weak. Bailey has decided that he will assess control risk at the maximum level for all assertions, and not restrict audit procedures in any area. Under these circumstances, may Bailey omit the consideration of the internal control structure in this engagement?

   8-23   Adherence to generally accepted auditing standards requires, among other things, a proper understanding of the existing internal control structure. The most common approaches to documenting the understanding of the system of internal control include the use of a questionnaire, preparation of a written narrative, preparation of a flowchart, and combinations of these methods.

*Required:*   *a.*   Discuss the advantages to CPAs of documenting internal control by using:

(1)   An internal control questionnaire.

(2)   A written narrative.

(3)   A flowchart.

*b.*   If they are satisfied that no material weaknesses exist in the structure after completing their description of internal control, is it necessary for the CPAs to conduct tests of controls? Explain.

(AICPA, adapted)

8-24   The process of gathering evidential matter to support an opinion on a client's financial statements involves several types of testing procedures. In the course of the examination, auditors perform detailed tests of samples of transactions from large-volume populations. Auditors may also audit various types of transactions by tracing a few transactions of each type through all stages of the accounting system.

*Required:*   What are the audit objectives associated with:

*a.*   A sample of transactions from a large-volume population?

*b.*   Tracing a few transactions of each type through all stages of the accounting system?

(AICPA, adapted)

8-25  During your first audit of a medium-size manufacturing company, the owner, John Bell, explains that in order to establish clear-cut lines of responsibility for various aspects of the business, he has made one employee responsible for the purchasing, receiving, and storing of merchandise. A second employee has full responsibility for maintenance of accounts receivable records and collections from customers. A third employee is responsible for personnel records, timekeeping, preparation of payrolls, and distribution of payroll checks. Bell asks your opinion concerning this plan of organization. Explain fully the reasons supporting your opinion.

8-26  Internal auditing is a staff function found in virtually every large corporation. The internal audit function is also performed in many smaller companies as a part-time activity of individuals who may or may not be called internal auditors. The differences between the audits by independent auditors and the work of internal auditors are more basic than is generally recognized.

*Required:*  *a.*  Briefly discuss the auditing work performed by the independent public accountant and the internal auditor with regard to:
    (1)  Auditing objectives.
    (2)  General nature of auditing work.

    *b.*  In conducting their audit, the independent auditors may consider the work of the internal auditors. Discuss briefly the reason for this consideration.

8-27  Select the best answer for each of the following questions. Explain the reason for your selection.
    *a.*  Which of the following would be least likely to be considered an objective of internal control?
        (1)  Checking the accuracy and reliability of accounting data.
        (2)  Detecting management fraud.
        (3)  Encouraging adherence to managerial policies.
        (4)  Safeguarding assets.
    *b.*  Which of the following symbols indicate that a file has been consulted?

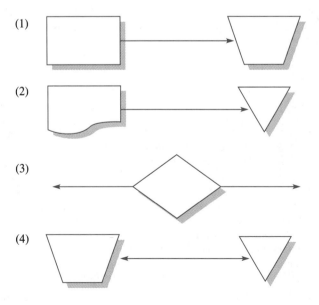

c. When a CPA decides that the work performed by internal auditors may have an effect on the nature, timing, and extent of the CPA's procedures, the CPA should consider the competence and objectivity of the internal auditors. Relative to objectivity, the CPA should:
  (1) Consider the organizational level to which the internal auditors report the results of their work.
  (2) Review the internal auditors' work.
  (3) Consider the qualifications of the internal audit staff.
  (4) Review the training program in effect for the internal audit staff.

d. Effective internal control in a small company that has an insufficient number of employees to permit proper separation of responsibilities can be improved by:
  (1) Employment of temporary personnel to aid in the separation of duties.
  (2) Direct participation by the owner in key recordkeeping and control activities of the business.
  (3) Engaging a CPA to perform monthly write-up work.
  (4) Delegation to each employee of full, clear-cut responsibility for a separate major transaction cycle.

e. Of the following statements about internal control, which one is *not* valid?
  (1) No one person should be responsible for the custody and the recording of an asset.
  (2) Transactions must be properly authorized before such transactions are processed.
  (3) Because of the cost/benefit relationship, a client may apply control procedures on a test basis.
  (4) Control procedures reasonably ensure that collusion among employees *cannot* occur.

f. Proper segregation of functional responsibilities calls for separation of the:
  (1) Authorization, recordkeeping, and custodial functions.
  (2) Authorization, execution, and payment functions.
  (3) Receiving, shipping, and custodial functions.
  (4) Authorization, approval, and execution functions.

8-28  During your first audit of a manufacturing company with approximately 100 production employees, you find that all aspects of factory payroll are handled by one employee and that none of the usual internal controls over payroll are observed. What action will you take?

# ◆ GROUP III: PROBLEMS

8-29  Orange Corp., a high-technology company, utilizes the following procedures for recording raw materials and transferring them to work in process.
  1. Upon receipt of raw materials by stores, the storeskeeper prepares a stock-in report with part number and quantities, files the original by date, and sends a copy to accounting.
  2. The inventory accounting clerk uses the stock-in report to post the perpetual inventory records using standard costs, and files the stock-in report by date.
  3. Raw materials requisitions, which show part number and quantity, are prepared by the manufacturing clerk and approved by the supervisor of manufacturing. A copy of the requisition is sent to accounting, and the original is filed by job order.
  4. The inventory accounting clerk reviews the requisitions for completeness, transfers the cost from raw materials to work in process, and files the requisitions by date.

*Required:*  Prepare a flowchart which describes the client's system of recording raw materials and transferring them to work in process.

(CIA, adapted)

8-30   At the Main Street Theatre the cashier, located in a box office at the entrance, receives cash from customers and operates a machine that ejects serially numbered tickets. To gain admission to the theater a customer hands the ticket to a door attendant stationed some 50 feet from the box office at the entrance to the theater lobby. The attendant tears the ticket in half, opens the door for the customer, and returns the stub to the customer. The other half of the ticket is dropped by the door attendant into a locked box.

*Required:*    *a.*    What internal controls are present in this phase of handling cash receipts?

       *b.*    What steps should be taken regularly by the manager or other supervisor to give maximum effectiveness to these controls?

       *c.*    Assume that the cashier and the door attendant decided to collaborate in an effort to abstract cash receipts. What action might they take?

       *d.*    Continuing the assumption made in *(c)* of collusion between the cashier and the door attendant, what features of the control procedures would be likely to disclose the embezzlement?

8-31   Island Trading Co., a client of your CPA firm, has requested your advice on the following problem. It has three clerical employees who must perform the following functions:

(1)    Maintain general ledger.

(2)    Maintain accounts payable ledger.

(3)    Maintain accounts receivable ledger.

(4)    Maintain cash disbursements journal and prepare checks for signature.

(5)    Issue credit memos on sales returns and allowances.

(6)    Reconcile the bank account.

(7)    Handle and deposit cash receipts.

*Required:*    Assuming that there is no problem as to the ability of any of the employees, the company requests your advice on assigning the above functions to the three employees in such a manner as to achieve the highest degree of internal control. It may be assumed that these employees will perform no other accounting functions than the ones listed and that any accounting functions not listed will be performed by persons other than these three employees.

       *a.*    List four possible unsatisfactory combinations of the above-listed functions.

       *b.*    State how you would recommend distributing the above functions among the three employees. Assume that, with the exception of the nominal jobs of the bank reconciliation and the issuance of credits on returns and allowances, all functions require an equal amount of time.

8-32   Prospect Corporation, your new audit client, processes its sales and cash receipts in the following manner:

    **1. Sales.**    Salesclerks prepare sales invoices in triplicate. The original and second copy are presented to the cashier, and the third copy is retained by the salesclerk in the sales book. When the sale is for cash, the customer pays the salesclerk, who presents the money to the cashier with the invoice copies.

    A credit sale is approved by the cashier from an approved credit list. After receiving the cash or approving the invoice, the cashier validates the original copy of the sales invoice and gives it to the customer. At the end of each day the cashier recaps the sales and cash received, files the recap by date, and forwards the cash and the second copy of all sales invoices to the accounts receivable clerk.

    The accounts receivable clerk balances the cash received with cash sales invoices and prepares a daily sales summary. Cash sales are posted by the accounts receivable clerk to the cash receipts journal, and the daily sales summary is filed by date. Cash from cash sales is included in the daily bank deposit (preparation of the bank deposit is described with cash receipts in the following section). The accounts receivable clerk posts credit sales invoices to the accounts receivable ledger and then sends all invoices to the inventory control clerk in the sales department.

The inventory clerk posts to the inventory control cards and files the sales invoices numerically.

**2. Cash receipts.**    The mail is opened each morning by a mail clerk in the sales department. The mail clerk prepares a remittance advice (showing customer and amount paid) for each check and forwards the checks and remittance advices to the sales department supervisor. The supervisor reviews the remittance advices and forwards the checks and advices to the accounting department supervisor.

The accounting department supervisor, who also functions as credit manager in approving new credit and all credit limits, reviews all checks for payments on past-due accounts and then gives the checks and remittance advices to the accounts receivable clerk, who arranges the advices in alphabetical order. The remittance advices are posted directly to the accounts receivable ledger cards. The checks are endorsed by stamp and totaled. The total is posted to the cash receipts journal. The remittance advices are filed chronologically.

After receiving the cash from the previous day's cash sales from the cashier, the accounts receivable clerk prepares the daily deposit slip in triplicate. The original and second copy of the deposit slip accompany the bank deposit, and the third copy is filed by date. The bank deposit is sent directly to National Bank.

*Required:*  *a.*  Prepare a systems flowchart of internal control over sales transactions as described in part 1 above.

*b.*  Prepare a systems flowchart of internal control over cash receipts as described in part 2 above.

8-33  You have been asked by the board of trustees of a local church to review its accounting procedures. As part of this review you have prepared the following comments relating to the collections made at weekly services and recordkeeping for members' pledges and contributions:

(1)  The church's board of trustees has delegated responsibility for financial management and internal audit of the financial records to the finance committee. This group prepares the annual forecast and approves major disbursements, but is not involved in collections or recordkeeping. No internal or independent audit has been considered necessary in recent years because the same trusted employee has kept church records and served as financial secretary for 15 years.

(2)  The offering at the weekly service is taken by a team of ushers. The head usher counts the offering in the church office following each service. He then places the offering and a notation of the amount counted in the church safe. The next morning the financial secretary opens the safe and recounts the offering. He withholds about $100 to meet cash expenditures during the coming week and deposits the remainder of the offering intact. In order to facilitate the deposit, members who contribute by check are asked to draw their checks to cash.

(3)  At their request a few members are furnished prenumbered, predated envelopes in which to insert their weekly contributions. The head usher removes the cash from the envelopes to be counted with the loose cash included in the offering and discards the envelopes. No record is maintained of issuance or return of the envelopes, and the envelope system is not encouraged.

(4)  Each member is asked to prepare a contribution pledge card annually. The pledge is regarded as a moral commitment by the member to contribute a stated weekly amount. Based upon the amounts shown on the pledge cards, the financial secretary furnishes a letter to requesting members to support the tax deductibility of their contributions.

*Required:*  Describe the weaknesses and recommend improvements in procedures for:

*a.*  Offerings given at weekly services.

*b.*  Recordkeeping for members' pledges and contributions.

Organize your answer sheets as follows:

| Weakness | Recommended Improvement |
|---|---|
|  |  |

(AICPA, adapted)

---

# ◆ GROUP IV: RESEARCH AND DISCUSSION CASE

**8-34** You are performing your first audit of Merit Drug Supply Company, a small company that is owned and managed by William Hicks. Merit employs only two other office workers, Tom Howe, the bookkeeper, and Glenda Monroe, the receptionist-secretary.

In obtaining an understanding of internal control over cash receipts, you ascertain that all cash receipts are received and deposited by Hicks. He prepares a list of the details of the receipts that is used by Howe to post the accounts receivable records. Neither Hicks nor Howe have any other incompatible duties in processing cash. You feel that this separation of responsibilities of custody of cash from recordkeeping is good, but you are uneasy about relying on controls applied by an owner/manager.

*Required:*   *a.*   Present arguments for relying on the owner/manager control.
  *b.*   Present arguments against relying on the owner/manager control.
  *c.*   Express your own opinion, referring back to points from *(a)* or *(b)* that support your opinion.

---

# ◆ SUGGESTED REFERENCES

AICPA, *Statement on Auditing Standards No. 55,* "Consideration of the Internal Control Structure in a Financial Statement Audit" (New York, 1988) AU 319.

AICPA, *Statement on Auditing Standards No. 53,* "The Auditor's Responsibility to Detect and Report Errors and Irregularities" (New York, 1988) AU 316.

Rayburn, D. D., *Auditing Research Monograph, No. 5,* "Audit Problems Encountered in Small Business Engagements" (New York: AICPA, 1982), pp. 77–81.

# TECHNOLOGY AND SAMPLING APPROACHES

# CONSIDERATION OF INTERNAL CONTROL IN A COMPUTER ENVIRONMENT

## CHAPTER OBJECTIVES

After studying this chapter, you should be able to:

- Contrast the characteristics of a computer accounting system with those of a manual system.

- Describe the nature of various types of computer systems.

- Distinguish among general controls, application controls, and user controls in a computer system.

- Explain the manner in which the auditors obtain an understanding of the internal control structure in a computer environment.

- Discuss the ways in which the auditors may test internal controls in a computer environment.

- Describe the nature of generalized audit software programs and the ways that they are used by the auditors.

The rapid increase in computerized data processing by business continues to have a dramatic effect on public accounting. No longer is the challenge of auditing computer activities limited to large clients only. With the advent of inexpensive microcomputer systems, even the smallest audit clients are likely to use a computer for most accounting functions.

In a traditional computer environment, information is processed on a large mainframe computer by a separate information systems department, using software developed by that department. The other departments of the company, referred to as *user departments,* send their data to the information systems department and receive computer-generated reports when processing is complete. However, with the advent of microcomputers, many data processing activities have been decentralized. Computer processing applications are performed more frequently by personnel within user departments throughout the company, utilizing **off-the-shelf software** packages. This eliminates the need for the client to employ computer programmers for those applications.

A typical small business uses a microcomputer to run an off-the-shelf general ledger package that provides the basis for its accounting system. Often, the computing power of a single microcomputer is sufficient to meet all of the computer needs of a small business. A large business might have a number of microcomputers at remote locations that are connected to the corporate mainframe system. Data are entered and reports are generated at the various locations by user department personnel; the nature of the application determines whether processing is actually performed on the mainframe computer or on a microcomputer. As these examples illustrate, auditors must be prepared to work in an ever-changing environment in which the client's accounting records are maintained on anything from a microcomputer to a multimillion-dollar mainframe system.

Although the computer has created some challenging problems for professional accountants, it has also broadened their horizons and expanded the range and value of the services they offer. The computer is more than a tool for performing routine accounting tasks with unprecedented speed and accuracy. It makes possible the development of information that could not have been gathered in the past because of time and cost limitations. When a client maintains accounting records with a complex and sophisticated computer system, auditors often find it helpful, and even necessary, to utilize the computer in performing many auditing procedures.

This chapter will consider some of the most significant ways in which auditing work is being affected by computers, but it cannot impart extensive knowledge of technical computer skills. Independent auditors will find additional familiarity with the computer, including technical skills such as programming, to be of ever-increasing value in the accounting profession.

# NATURE OF COMPUTER SYSTEMS

Before considering the impact of computer systems on the work of the certified public accountant, some understanding of the nature of a computer and its capabilities is needed. An electronic data processing (EDP) business system usually consists of a digital computer and peripheral equipment known as *hardware* and equally essential *software,* consisting of various programs and routines for operating a computer.

Hardware.    The principal hardware component of a digital computer is the *central processing unit* (CPU). The CPU consists of a *control unit,* which processes a program of instructions for manipulating data; a *storage unit* for storing the program of instructions and the data to be manipulated; and an *arithmetic unit* capable of addition, subtraction, multiplication, division, and comparison of data at speeds measured in *nanoseconds*.

Digital computer circuitry has two states in that any given circuit may be "on" or "off." By using an internal code, or machine language, capable of representing with two symbols any kind of data, all data may be expressed internally by the computer by a combination of on and off circuits. An example of a machine language is the *binary* number system.

Peripheral to the central processing unit are devices for recording input and devices for secondary storage, output, and communications. Peripheral devices in direct communication with the CPU are said to be **online,** in contrast to **offline** equipment not in direct communication with the CPU.

A first step in computer processing is to convert the data to machine-readable form. This is the role of recording and input devices, such as card readers, optical scanners, electronic cash registers, and intelligent terminals. Each of these devices either records data in some medium for later reading into the storage unit or communicates data directly to the CPU.

Secondary storage devices are utilized to augment the capacity of the storage unit of the CPU. Examples of secondary storage devices are magnetic tape and magnetic disk drives. Magnetic disk drives have the advantage of **direct access,** which allows for faster location and retrieval of data. Data on magnetic tapes must be stored sequentially and is retrieved by a systematic search.

Machines must also be used to translate the output of the computer back into a recognizable code or language. Output equipment includes printers and display terminals.

Software.    Computer systems use two major types of software: *system software* and *application software*. **System software** consists of programs that control and coordinate hardware components and provide other support to application software. Important components of system software are utility programs for recurring tasks of data processing, such as sorting, sequencing, and merging of data. The system software known as the **operating system** is important to the control of computer operations because it may be programmed to control access to programs and stored data and to maintain a log of all system activities.

Programs designed to perform a specific data processing task, such as payroll processing, are known as **application software.** Early application programs were laboriously written in machine language, but today programming languages such as COBOL (common business-oriented language) and C are much like English. Programming in C and other *source languages* is made possible by another element of software, the *compiler,* which is a computer program utilized in translating a *source-language program* into machine language. The machine-language version of a program is called an *object program*.

## Characteristics of Various Types of Computer Systems

In some ways, computer systems enhance the reliability of financial information. Computers process transactions uniformly and eliminate the human errors that may occur in a manual system. On the other hand, defects in programs can result in a computer processing all transactions incorrectly. Also, errors or irregularities that do occur in computer processing may not be detected by the client's personnel because few people are involved with data processing. Thus, computer hardware precision does not ensure that computer output will be reliable.

Computer systems differ as to their characteristics. A system, regardless of its size, may possess one or more of the following elements:

1. Batch processing.
2. Online capabilities.
3. Data base storage.
4. Computer networks.
5. End user computing.

Batch Processing.   When **batch processing** is used, input data are gathered and processed periodically in discrete groups. An example of batch processing is accumulating all of a day's sales transactions and processing them as a "batch" at the end of that day. While batch processing systems do not provide up-to-the-minute information, they are often more efficient than other types of systems.

Online Capabilities.   **Online systems** allow users to have direct (on-line) access to the data stored in the system. When an online system is in use, individual transactions may be entered directly from the originators at remote locations. The transactions may be held in a transaction file and later posted to the records as a batch, or real-time processing may be used. In *online, real-time* (OLRT) systems, transactions are processed immediately and all accounting records are updated instantaneously. These systems are frequently encountered in banks and savings institutions. Online, real-time systems allow a teller at any branch to update a customer's account immediately by recording deposits or withdrawals on a computer terminal. At most financial institutions, customers are able to transact business directly with the computer by inserting an identification card in an automatic teller terminal.

The use of an online, real-time system results in significant changes in the internal control structure. Original source documents may not be available to support input into the computer and the overall amount of the hard copy (printed) audit trail may be substantially reduced. Essential controls must be programmed into the computer. For example, the validity of data must be checked by the computer as they are entered into the system.

Data Base Storage.   In a traditional computer system, each computer application has its own application **files.** For example, the **master file** of accounts receivable is an application file, maintained by the accounts receivable department, that contains customer account activity for a period of time and information about each customer. Much of the information in this file is also included in the customer master file maintained by the sales department. This data redundancy is expensive in terms of computer storage cost. Also, data inconsistencies may arise because the information may not be up-to-date in all files.

In a **data base system,** separate application files are replaced with integrated data bases that are shared by many users and application programs. A data base system eliminates much data redundancy, and since the data base is normally stored on a direct access device, the system responds quickly to users' requests for information. Both batch and online, real-time systems can utilize data base storage.

From an internal control standpoint, it is essential that the data base be secured against improper access or alteration. Organizations that use data base systems often create a *data base administrator* function, with responsibility for administering the data base and controlling access to the data.

Computer Networks.   The advent of **telecommunications**—the electronic transmission of information by radio, wire, **fiber optics, microwave,** laser, and other electromagnetic systems—has made it possible to transfer information between computers. **Networks** of computers linked together through telecommunication links enable companies to communicate information back and forth between geographically dispersed business locations.

Networks that span a large geographical area are called **wide area networks** (WANs). In these networks, information generally is transmitted from one computer to another with modems or satellite dishes. In contrast, a **local area network** (LAN) is a communications network that allows resources, data, and program sharing within a limited geographical area. An example is a network that connects computers and printers within a single building.

Networking enables companies to implement **distributed data processing,** in which information and programs are shared by a large number of users. The network may provide company executives with on-line access to the vast amount of data stored in the company's main computer. They may selectively retrieve data and process it to their personal specifications with microcomputers located in their department.

Because data in a computer network may potentially be altered at any location that can access the system, weak internal controls at a single location can jeopardize the reliability of the entire system. Accordingly, computer security should be established at each location to ensure that data can be changed and accessed only by authorized personnel.

End User Computing.   When a company implements **end user computing,** the user groups are responsible for the development and execution of certain computer applications. The user department both generates and utilizes the necessary information. For these applications, the information systems department is eliminated, although certain files may be privately held for user departments in mainframe storage. End user computing is possible because of the processing power now available with microcomputers. The end user computer system is the exact opposite of the traditional data processing environment, in which all information needed by users was provided by programs that were purchased or written and tested by the information systems department.

Internal controls over end user computing are only as good as those instituted by the user departments. For example, if user departments do not adequately test new programs, the reliability of the entire system may be compromised. As is the case with computer networks, computer security must be established at each location to prevent unauthorized access to the company's data.

## Impact of Computers on the Audit Trail

In a manual or mechanical data processing system, an audit trail (transaction trail) of hard-copy documentation links individual transactions with the summary figures in the financial statements. Computers, on the other hand, are able to electronically create, update, and erase data in computer-based records without any visible evidence of a change being made. In addition, the development of telecommunications has created an environment in which data may be altered not only within a specific computer, but by various computers both within and outside the client's organization.

During the early development of computer systems, the electronic transfer of information led to some concern among accountants that computerized processing would obscure or even eliminate the audit trail. Although it is technically possible to design an information system that would leave no audit trail, such a system would be neither practical nor desirable. An adequate audit trail is necessary to enable management to direct and control the operations of the business, to permit file reconstruction in the event of transmission and processing errors or computer failure, and to accommodate the needs of independent auditors and governmental agencies.

An audit difficulty with advanced computer systems is that while an audit trail may exist, it may not exist in printed form; it may be available only in machine-readable form. Also, when it is no longer needed, the audit trail information may be transferred to a low-cost storage medium, such as microfiche. Another development that has significantly affected the audit trail is the **electronic data interchange system** (EDI) in which a company and its customers or suppliers use telecommunication links to exchange business data electronically. Source documents, such as invoices, purchase orders, checks, and bills of lading are replaced with electronic transactions. For example, in an EDI system a purchase transaction may be automatically initiated by the client's computer by sending an electronic message (purchase order) directly to a supplier's computer system. Invoicing and payment for the purchase may also be processed electronically. When EDI is being used the auditors should consider client data retention and processing policies in planning the nature and timing of their audit procedures. For example, the auditors might identify transactions to be tested at the time they are processed, so that information about the transactions can be obtained before it is removed from the computer system. Also, emphasis should be placed on coordinating the efforts of external and internal auditors to ensure adequate audit coverage.

Fears that computers would eliminate the audit trail have not materialized. During the design of a computer system, management will normally consult with both its internal and external auditors to ensure that an adequate audit trail is built into the system. In a computer system, of course, the audit trail may consist of computer printouts and documents stored in machine-readable form, rather than the more traditional handwritten source documents, journals, and ledgers.

## Internal Control in a Computer Environment

The discussion of internal control in Chapter 8 stressed the need for a proper division of duties. In a manual system, no one employee should have complete responsibility for a transaction, and the work of one person should be verified by the work of another handling other aspects of the same transaction. The division of duties in such a manner ensures accurate records and reports, and protects the company against losses from fraud or carelessness.

In a computerized system, work normally divided among many employees may be performed by the computer. Consolidation of activities and integration of functions are to be expected, since the computer can conveniently handle many related aspects of a transaction. For example, when payroll is processed by a computer, it is possible to carry out a variety of related tasks with only a single use of the computer files. These tasks could include maintaining personnel files with information on seniority, rate of pay, insurance and the like; performing certain aspects of the timekeeping function; distributing labor costs; and preparing payroll checks and payroll records.

Despite the integration of several functions in a computer system, the importance of internal control is not in the least diminished. The essential factors described in Chapter 8 for a satisfactory internal control structure remain relevant. Separation of duties and clearly defined responsibilities continue to be key factors. These traditional control concepts are augmented, however, by controls written into the computer programs and controls built into the computer hardware. Our discussion of computer controls will be organized around the three elements of the internal control structure—*control environment, accounting system,* and *control procedures.*

## CONTROL ENVIRONMENT IN A COMPUTER SYSTEM

The control environment reflects the overall attitude, awareness, and actions of the board of directors, management, and owners concerning the importance of internal control and the way it is used in the company. Use of a computerized system may affect any number of the control environment factors that were discussed in Chapter 8. For example, when a company has a sophisticated decentralized computer system, the dispersion of authority and decentralization of data entry points results in a need for more extensive methods of assigning authority and responsibility and additional management control methods for follow-up on performance. A computerized environment also may affect the organizational structure of the company and the manner in which the internal auditors perform their work.

## Organizational Structure in a Computerized Environment

Because of the ability of the computer to process data efficiently, there is a tendency to combine the performance of many data processing functions. In a manual or mechanical system, these combinations of functions may be considered incompatible from a standpoint of achieving strong internal control. For example, in a manual system the function of recording cash receipts is generally segregated from responsibility for posting entries to the subsidiary accounts receivable. Because one of these procedures serves as a check upon the other, assigning both functions to one employee would enable the employee to conceal his or her own errors. A properly programmed computer, however, has no tendency or motivation to conceal its errors and may record these transactions simultaneously. Therefore, what appears to be an incompatible combination of functions may be combined in an information systems department without weakening internal control.

When apparently incompatible functions are combined in the information systems department, compensating controls are necessary to prevent improper human intervention with computer processing. A person with the opportunity to make unauthorized changes in computer programs or data files is in a position to exploit the concentration of data processing functions in the information systems department. For example, a computer program used to process accounts payable may be designed to approve a vendor's invoice for payment only when that invoice is supported by a purchase order and receiving report. An employee able to make unauthorized changes in that program could cause unsubstantiated payments to be made to specific vendors.

Computer programs and data files cannot be changed without the use of data processing equipment. When changes are made, however, there may be no visible evidence of the alteration. Thus, the organization plan of the information systems department should prevent its personnel from having unauthorized access to equipment, programs, or data files. This is accomplished by providing definite lines of authority and responsibility, segregation of functions, and clear definition of duties for each employee in the department. The organization of the information systems department varies from one company to another in terms of reporting responsibility, relationships with other departments, and responsibilities within the department. As illustrated by Figure 9–1, the organizational structure of a well-staffed information systems department should include the following separation of responsibilities.

Information Systems Management.   The information systems manager (director) should supervise the operation of the department, and may report to the vice president of finance or administrative services, or to the controller. However, when the information systems

Figure 9–1   Organization of Information Systems Department

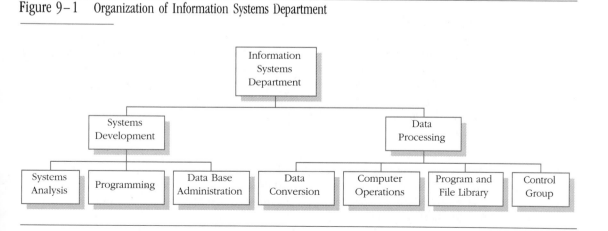

manager reports to the controller, the controller should not have direct involvement with computer operations. Alternatively, the position may be elevated to the vice president level, with reporting responsibility directly to the president.

Systems Analysis.    Systems analysts are responsible for designing the information system. After considering the objectives of the business and the data processing needs of the various user departments, they determine the goals of the system and the means of achieving them. Utilizing system flowcharts and detailed instructions, they outline the data processing system.

Programming.    Guided by the specifications provided by the systems analysts, the programmers design flowcharts of the computer programs required by the system. They then code the required programs in computer language, generally making use of specialized programming languages, such as C, and software elements, such as assemblers, compilers, and utility programs. They test the programs with **test data** composed of genuine or dummy records and transactions and perform the necessary debugging. Finally, the programmers prepare the necessary application documentation, such as the computer operator instructions.

Data Base Administration.    The data base administrator has the responsibility for planning and administering the company's data base. The primary objectives of this individual are to design the data base and to control its use.

Data Conversion.    Personnel involved with this function prepare and verify input data for processing. A keypunching operation is a traditional example of a data conversion department that has now been replaced with new technology. In today's systems, data may be input via terminals or scanned directly from source documents to magnetic tape, disk, or another computer-readable form. Data in an online, real-time system may be entered directly into the computer by user groups through telecommunication links from remote terminals with computer files being updated immediately.

Computer Operations.    The computer operators manipulate the computer in accordance with the instructions developed by the programmers. On occasion, the computer operators may need to intervene through the computer console during a run in order to correct an indicated error. The computer's operating system should be programmed to maintain a detailed log of all operator intervention. The separation of computer operations from programming is an important one from the standpoint of achieving effective internal control. An employee performing both functions may have an opportunity to make unauthorized changes in computer programs.

Program and File Library.    The purpose of the file library is to protect computer programs, master files, transaction (detail) tapes, and other records from loss, damage, and unauthorized use or alteration. To ensure adequate control, the librarian maintains a formal checkout system for making files and programs available to authorized users.

In many systems, a portion of the library function is performed by the computer. The computer operators or the users enter special code numbers or passwords to gain access to programs and files stored within the system. The computer automatically maintains a log showing when these programs and files are used and by whom.

Control Group.   The control group of an information processing department reviews and tests all input procedures, monitors computer processing, reviews exception reports, handles the reprocessing of exceptions detected by the computer, and reviews and distributes all computer output. This group also reviews the computer log of operator interventions and the library log of program usage. In smaller organizations, control group functions are performed by the user departments.

Other Organizational Controls.   Besides segregating functions, the information systems organization plan should provide for rotation of programmer assignments, rotation of operator assignments, mandatory vacations, and adequate fidelity bonds for information system employees. At least two of the qualified data processing personnel should be present whenever the computer facility is in use. Careful screening policies in hiring information systems personnel are also important in achieving effective internal control.

Computer-Centered Fraud.   The history of computer-centered fraud shows that the person responsible for frauds in many situations set up the system and controlled its use as programmer and operator.

---

### ◆ ILLUSTRATIVE CASE ◆

A programmer for a large bank wrote a program for identifying and listing all overdrawn accounts. Later, as operator of the bank's computer, he was able to insert a **patch** in the program to cause the computer to ignore overdrafts in his own account. The programmer-operator was then able to overdraw his bank account at will, without the overdraft coming to management's attention. The fraud was not discovered until the computer broke down and the listing of overdrawn accounts had to be prepared manually.

---

The number of personnel and the organizational structure will of course determine the extent to which segregation of duties is possible. At a minimum, the function of programming should be separated from the function controlling input to the computer programs, and the function of the computer operator should be segregated from the functions having detailed knowledge or custody of the computer programs. If one person is permitted to perform duties in several of these functions, internal control is weakened, and the opportunity exists for fraudulent data to be inserted in the system.

Whenever the responsibilities for recordkeeping and custody of the related assets are combined, the opportunities for an employee to conceal the abstraction of assets are increased. Since recordkeeping is an essential part of the information system's function, it is highly desirable to limit the access of information systems personnel to company assets. However, these employees have direct access to cash if data processing activity includes the preparation of signed checks. They also have indirect access to assets if, for example, the computer is used to generate shipping orders authorizing the release of inventory.

This combination of recordkeeping with access to assets seriously weakens internal control unless adequate *compensating controls* are present. One type of compensating control is the use of predetermined *batch totals,* such as document counts and totals of significant data fields, prepared in departments independent of information systems. For example, if the information systems department performs the function of printing checks, another department should be responsible for authorizing the preparation of the checks. The authorizing department should maintain a record of the total number and dollar amount of checks authorized. These independently prepared batch totals should then be compared with the computer output before the checks are released.

Organizational controls are reasonably effective in preventing an individual employee from perpetrating a fraud, but they do not prevent fraud involving collusion. If key employees or company officers conspire in an effort to commit fraud, internal controls that rely upon separation of duties can be rendered inoperative.

---

♦ ILLUSTRATIVE CASE ♦

Equity Funding Corporation of America went into bankruptcy after it was discovered that the company's financial statements had been grossly and fraudulently misleading for a period of years. A subsidiary of the company had been manufacturing bogus insurance policies on fictitious persons and then selling these policies to other insurance companies. When the fraud was discovered, Equity Funding's balance sheet included more than $120 million in fictitious assets, far exceeding the $75 million net income reported over the 13-year life of the company.

Perhaps the most startling revelation of the Equity Funding scandal was that numerous officers and employees of the company had worked together for years to perpetrate and conceal the fraud. The fictitious transactions had been carefully integrated into the company's computer-based accounting system. A wide variety of fraudulent supporting documents had been prepared for the sole purpose of deceiving auditors and governmental regulatory agencies. Upon disclosure of the activities, several members of top management were convicted of criminal charges.

The Equity Funding scandal is often described as a computer-based fraud. It was not the use of computers, however, that enabled the company to deceive auditors and government investigators. Rather, the fraudulent activities were successfully concealed for a number of years because of the unprecedented willingness of a large number of company officers and employees to participate in the scheme. Collusion of the magnitude existing at Equity Funding would render any internal control structure ineffective.

---

## Internal Auditing in a Computerized Environment

An internal audit function should exist separate and distinct from the control group of the information systems department. The control group is primarily concerned with day-to-day maintenance of the internal controls for data processing, whereas the internal auditors are interested in evaluating the overall efficiency and effectiveness of information systems operations and the related internal controls.

The internal auditors should participate in the design of the computer system to ensure that the system provides a proper audit trail and includes adequate internal controls. Once the system becomes operative, internal auditors review all aspects of the system on a test basis to determine whether prescribed internal controls are operating as planned. Among other things, the internal auditors perform tests to determine that no changes are made in the system without proper authorization, programming personnel are functionally separate from computer operating personnel, adequate documentation is maintained, input controls are functioning effectively, and the control group is performing its assigned functions.

# ACCOUNTING SYSTEM IN A COMPUTER SYSTEM

The nature of the accounting system may be profoundly affected by the use of computerized processing. Handwritten journals and ledgers are replaced by electronic transactions, computer files, and computer printouts. Transactions may be initiated by the computer itself, and source documents, such as receiving reports, may be generated only when needed.

The nature of computerized accounting systems varies significantly from one company to another. A small company might use commercial off-the-shelf accounting software to produce computer printed forms and records that closely resemble those of a manual accounting system. The accounting systems of larger companies are generally developed by information system personnel and include advanced features such as distributive data processing and electronic data interchange.

# CONTROL PROCEDURES IN A COMPUTER SYSTEM

Computer control procedures often are classified as general controls, application controls, and user controls. Whereas **general controls** apply to all computer applications, **application controls** and **user controls** relate to only a specific application, such as the preparation of payroll. Application control procedures include both *programmed control procedures* which are written into the computer programs, and *manual follow-up procedures* performed on the exception reports that are generated by the computer. *User control procedures* are those performed by users to test the accuracy and completeness of computer reports. Figure 9–2 illustrates the relationship among these three types of computer control procedures.

## General Control Procedures

General controls affect all computer applications and include procedures to control: *(a)* developing new programs and systems; *(b)* changing existing programs and systems; *(c)* access to programs and data; and *(d)* computer operations.

Figure 9-2    Computer Control Procedures

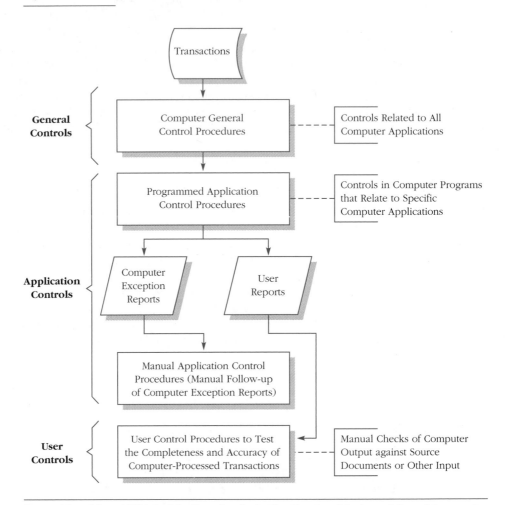

Source: Adapted from AICPA *Auditing Procedure Study: Consideration of the Internal Control Structure in a Computer Environment: A Case Study.*

Developing New Programs and Systems.   These controls ensure that the systems and programs that are developed by the information systems department meet users' needs, are free from errors, and include adequate controls and documentation. Examples include policies requiring user involvement in the development process, and appropriate testing of systems and programs before they are implemented. By requiring the information systems department to obtain technical assistance from personnel in other departments, such as the internal auditors, assurance is provided that the hardware and system software being purchased or developed will include appropriate controls. Among the more common hardware and system software controls are the following:

1. *Echo check*. The purpose of the echo check is to ensure that peripheral equipment, such as a printer, complies with computer instructions. A signal is returned to the computer verifying transmitted data or acknowledging the performance of an assigned task.

2. *Self-diagnosis*. Many computers are supplied with hardware or systems software routines that allow the computer to test its own circuitry. Self-diagnosis routines can identify a defective circuit or memory module before the system fails.

3. *Duplicate process check*. A duplicate process check consists of performing an operation twice and comparing the two results. In the duplicate process check known as *read after write,* the computer reads back data after they have been moved in the system and verifies their accuracy.

4. *Parity check*. Data are processed by the computer in arrays of *bits* (binary digits of 1 or 0). In addition to bits necessary to represent the numeric or alphabetic character, a *parity* bit is added when necessary to make the sum of the 1 bits always odd or even, depending upon the model of the computer. As data are transferred at rapid speeds between computer components, the parity check is applied by the computer to ensure that bits are not lost during the transfer process.

Another important consideration in developing new computer systems and applications is the preparation of adequate *system documentation*. The purpose of system documentation is to provide an overall description of the processing system in the form of system flowcharts and descriptions of the nature of input, operations, and output. It also establishes responsibilities for entering data, performing control tasks, and correcting and reprocessing erroneous data. Documentation describing each application program, as a minimum, should include:

1. A description of the purpose of the program.
2. A list and explanation of processing controls associated with the program.
3. A record of layouts showing the organization of data on magnetic tapes or disks.
4. Examples of computer output, including exception reports.
5. **Program flowcharts** showing the major steps and logic of the computer program.
6. Program listings in source language.
7. Program approval and change sheets showing proper authorization for all initial programs and subsequent changes.
8. An **operations manual** containing instructions for running the program.
9. A users' manual containing instructions for inputting data and applying user control procedures.
10. Test data utilized in testing and debugging the program.

Changing Existing Programs and Systems.    Frequently, changes in programs are suggested by users who have noted various difficulties associated with a processing system. These suggestions are generally documented in a **change request log,** which is used to initiate various program changes.

The process of changing programs and systems must be carefully controlled. The information systems manager should review all changes, and the modified program should be thoroughly tested before it is implemented. In addition, all changes should be appropriately documented.

### Access to Programs and Data.

Every computer system should have adequate security controls to safeguard equipment, files, and programs against loss, damage, and access by unauthorized personnel. When programs or files can be accessed from microcomputers or on-line terminals, users should be required to enter a secret password in order to gain access to the system. These passwords should be changed periodically and updated frequently to reflect changes in personnel. The computer's operating system also should be programmed to maintain a log of all terminal usage and should produce a warning if repeated attempts are made to gain access to data by use of incorrect passwords. The importance of these controls has been illustrated by several highly publicized incidents of youthful "hackers" using home computers to gain entry to both military and commercial computer systems.

Access to programs and data within the information systems department should also be carefully controlled. Systems programmers should not have access to input data or application programs that are currently in use; computer operators should have access to only the application programs currently being used. These programs should be compiled in machine language to make alteration difficult. Generally, only the information systems manager and the data base administrator should have access to all data files, especially the files of authorized users and passwords.

Physical controls are necessary to protect the equipment against sabotage, fire, and water damage. The best way to prevent deliberate damage is to limit access to the facility to authorized personnel. Visitors to the facility should be accompanied by authorized personnel. The information systems personnel should be carefully screened before employment, and management should always be alert to the possibility of damage by a disgruntled employee. Frequently, the location of the computer facility is kept relatively secret. The facility should have no windows and few doors; entrances should be controlled by guards or badge-activated locks. In addition, the computer room should be fire-resistant, air conditioned, and above likely flood levels.

### Computer Operations Controls.

To minimize the opportunity for unauthorized changes in programs, the computer operators should have access only to the *operations manual* that contains the instructions for processing programs, and not detailed program documentation. The operations manual should be sufficient to allow operators to solve routine operational problems and to train new operators.

Careful job scheduling and monitoring helps control the possibility of inappropriate program modification. The control group should monitor the computer operator's activities by reviewing the operations log, which records a description of each run, the elapsed time for the run, operator console interventions, machine halts, and files utilized.

Magnetic tapes or disks can be damaged by exposure to magnetic fields or excessive heat. Also, it is possible that a program or a file will accidentally be erased while it is being processed by the computer. As a precaution against such accidents, duplicate copies should be made of all files and programs, and integrated data bases should be transferred to backup disks or tapes at regular intervals. These backup copies should be stored at a separate location from the originals.

In a batch processing system, three generations of master files should be retained to enable reproduction of files lost or destroyed. Under this *grandfather-father-son* principle of file retention, the current updated master file is the *son,* the master file utilized in the updating run that produced the son is the *father,* and the previous father is the *grandfather.* Records of transactions for the current and the prior period also should be retained to facilitate updating the older master files in the event that the current master file is accidentally destroyed. The three generations should be stored in separate locations to minimize the risk of losing all three generations at once.

## Application Control Procedures

Application controls begin with requirements for proper authorization of the transactions to be processed. When transaction data are originally recorded on **hard-copy** source documents, such as sales orders, authorization may be indicated by the appropriate person initialing the document. In online systems, transaction data may be entered directly into the computer from remote terminal devices located in the departments initiating the transactions. Authorization of transactions may be accomplished by assigning to authorized terminal users an identification number that must be entered into the terminal before the computer will accept the input data. Also, the operating system should maintain a log of activity at each terminal to be reviewed by the system's control group for evidence of unauthorized use.

As indicated in Figure 9–2, application control procedures may be classified as programmed control procedures or manual follow-up procedures.

### Programmed Control Procedures. *Programmed control procedures* are those written into computer programs that help ensure the accuracy of computer input and processing. A major aspect of programmed control procedures are *input validation (edit) checks* that are performed on the data being entered. Examples of these controls include:

1. *Limit test.* A test of the reasonableness of a field of data, given a predetermined upper and/or lower limit.

2. *Validity test.* A comparison of data (for example, employee, vendor, and other codes) against a master file for authenticity.

3. *Self-checking number.* A self-checking number contains redundant information, such as the last two digits being a mathematical combination of the others, permitting a check for accuracy when the number is input, or after it has been transmitted from one device to another.

Input validation checks increase the accuracy of input data by rejecting any data that fail to meet a test requirement and by leading to a request for revised data from the user. The data can also be tested for completeness as they are entered at a terminal.

Input controls in batch processing systems are used to determine that no data are lost or added to the batch. The sequence of serial numbers or source documents comprising each batch should be accounted for. In addition, the following controls help ensure the accuracy and completeness of batch processing:

1. *Item (or record) count*. A count of the number of items or transactions being input in a given batch.
2. *Control total*. A control total is the total of one field of information for all items in a batch. An example would be total sales for a batch of sales orders.
3. *Hash total*. A hash total is a total of one field of information for all items in a batch, used in the same manner as a control total. The difference between a hash total and a control total is that a hash total has no intrinsic meaning. An example of a hash total would be the sum of the employee social security numbers being input for payroll processing.

Comparison of totals may be either performed by the computer or manually by the control group.

*Processing controls* are designed to ensure the reliability and accuracy of data processing activities. A number of the input controls described above are programmed as processing controls, including limit tests, validity tests, self-checking numbers, item counts, and control and hash totals. In addition, *file labels,* such as **header labels,** may be used to ensure that the proper transaction file or master file is being used on a specific run. *Internal labels* that are machine-readable are used in conjunction with gummed-paper external labels to prevent operators from accidentally processing the wrong file.

Manual Follow-Up Procedures.    Most manual follow-up procedures consist of review and analysis of outputs that have been generated in the form of *exception reports*. When exceptions or errors are disclosed by program controls, the computer processing may halt, or the exceptions may be printed out. Exception reports should be transmitted directly to the control group for follow-up. The control group's responsibility includes making certain that corrections of exceptions are properly entered and that duplicate corrections are avoided.

The effectiveness of manual follow-up procedures depends upon the effectiveness of the programmed control procedures that produce the exception reports. Thus, if a program does not generate an exception for an improper transaction, no manual follow-up is likely since the transaction is not included on the exception report.

## User Control Procedures

User control procedures are designed to test the completeness and accuracy of computer-processed transactions. These controls are generally designed to ensure the reliability of computer output and to determine that output is distributed to authorized personnel. Reconciliation of control totals generated by the computer to the totals developed at the input phase is an important aspect of user controls. In some systems, user departments may appraise the reliability of output from the information systems processing department by extensive review and testing. For example, sales invoices generated by the computer may be tested for clerical accuracy and pricing by an accounting clerk. Although these user controls can be very effective, it is generally more efficient to implement effective application controls and have users merely test the overall reasonableness of the output.

## Control in Microcomputer Systems

Although technology is reducing the extent of the differences between microcomputers and large mainframe computers, microcomputers generally are less flexible, smaller in memory capacity, and slower at processing data than mainframe computers. However, microcomputers have the advantage of giving office personnel and salespeople direct access to the computer without the turnaround time associated with a centralized system. For that reason, even audit clients with sophisticated centralized computer systems are likely to use microcomputers for a variety of on-site recordkeeping functions.

The advent of microcomputers has resulted in a decentralization of data processing activities. In a microcomputer environment, computers are located in user departments and operated by user personnel who have little or no computer training. Processing usually is performed with commercial off-the-shelf packages. For secondary storage when the computer is operating, microcomputers use hard disk drives where programs are stored. Floppy disks or magnetic tapes are used as backup for the hard disk.

Internal control over microcomputers is enhanced when data processing procedures are documented and operators are well trained. To ensure that the client can reconstruct financial records, duplicate (backup) diskettes or tapes of files should be made frequently and stored away from the originals in a secure location. Since microcomputers are located in user departments, there is a greater risk of use by unauthorized personnel. Therefore, the microcomputer's operating system should require the operator to enter authorization codes to gain access to menus that control specific programs and files. As a means of detecting improper activities, there should be an independent review of activity logs generated by the microcomputer. In addition, management should consider locking away critical software or installing a locking on/off switch on the microcomputer to prevent unauthorized use of the machine after business hours. The auditors are concerned with these and other internal controls over microcomputers when the information processed by them may affect the reliability of the information in the client's financial statements.

# THE AUDITORS' CONSIDERATION OF INTERNAL CONTROL IN A COMPUTER ENVIRONMENT

Regardless of whether the client's financial statements are produced by a manual or computerized data processing system, the auditors must adequately consider internal control. Their consideration provides the auditors with a basis for assessing control risk which affects the nature, timing, and extent of the work necessary to complete the audit. In discussing the auditors' consideration of internal control in a computer environment we will describe how the auditors obtain an understanding of internal control, document this understanding, and assess control risk.

## Obtaining an Understanding of the Computerized Internal Control System

Specialized skills may be needed to understand the internal control structure or to design effective audit tests for clients with computer systems. Therefore, training and education about computer systems and controls are an important part of the professional development programs of many CPA firms. Some CPA firms have trained *computer specialists* who act as consultants to the firm's other auditors on audits that involve particularly complex computer systems. Other CPA firms rely on outside consultants to provide this assistance on complex engagements. In either case, the auditor in charge of the engagement should have sufficient computer-related knowledge to review the adequacy of the procedures performed by the specialist. The results of the specialist's procedures must be considered when planning the nature, timing, and extent of other audit procedures.

## Documenting the Computerized Internal Control System

The auditor's documentation of the client's computer system varies depending on the complexity of the system. For a client with a simple internal control structure a *written narrative* might be adequate. However, computerized systems are usually documented by the use of systems flowcharts or specially designed internal control questionnaires.

Systems Flowcharts.   As explained in Chapter 8, *systems flowcharts* are a commonly used technique for documenting internal control in audit working papers. An advantage of using systems flowcharts is that the information systems department will normally have them available as part of the standard documentation.

An illustration of a systems flowchart for sales, accounts receivable, and cash receipts appears in Figure 9–3. The following description of the illustrated procedures and processing systems should be helpful in studying the illustrated flowchart.

1. Orders are received from sales representatives, and sales invoices are generated on an **intelligent terminal.** A computer file of sales transactions is generated by the terminal as a by-product of sales invoice preparation. Two copies of the invoices are mailed to the customer, one copy is sent to the shipping department, and one copy is filed offline.

2. Individual cash remittances from customers are received from the mail room and verified to a batch total, which is also received from the mail room. These remittances are entered via terminals to a computer file of cash receipts transactions, with the total input being compared to the batch total. After comparison of batch totals any necessary corrections are made to the transactions file.

3. The accounts receivable master file is updated by processing both the sales transactions file and the cash receipts transactions file. A by-product of the updating of the accounts receivable master file is an exception report for the run and a printout (on an online terminal) of any job messages.

The client's documentation of data processing activities usually includes program flowcharts as well as systems flowcharts. Program flowcharts illustrate the detailed logic of specific computer programs. In some circumstances auditors may use program flowcharts to obtain an understanding of the program controls contained in specific computer applications. This, however, involves careful consideration of the detailed logic of the program, is extremely time-consuming, and generally exceeds the level of knowledge required to plan the audit.

## Figure 9–3   Systems Flowchart

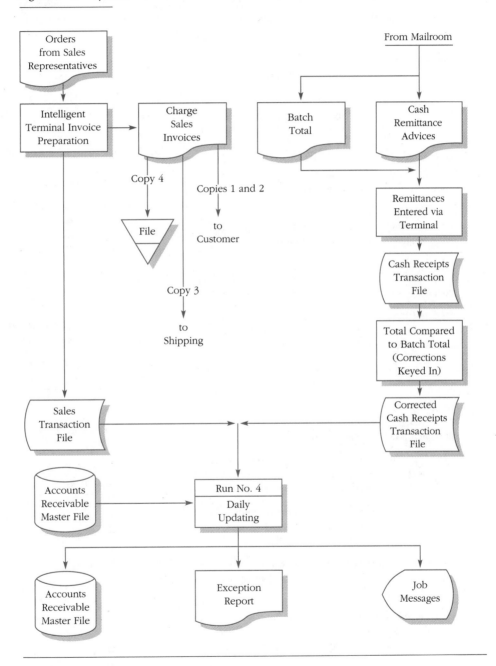

**Internal Control Questionnaires for Computer Systems.**    As an alternative or supplement to systems flowcharts, the auditor may decide to document a computer system with specialized questionnaires. A specialized computer internal control questionnaire for the general controls over access to the computer system is illustrated by Figure 9–4.

Figure 9–4    Control Procedures Questionnaire

| | Access to System Resources | Yes, No, N/A | KP 8/15/X1 Comments |
|---|---|---|---|
| 1. | Does the company have documented policies and procedures for computer security? | No | No written policies. |
| 2. | Are there adequate physical controls to restrict access to the computer room to authorized individuals? | Yes | Card key access. Visitors are accompanied by authorized personnel. |
| 3. | Are programmers restricted from access to application programs, job control language, and live data files? | Yes | The operating system security program restricts access to other programs and data. |
| 4. | Has a test library procedure been established so that programming is not performed using live data files and application programs? | Yes | Test data files are used for testing programs. |
| 5. | Are operators restricted from access to source programs? | Yes | Source programs cannot be accessed by operators. |
| 6. | Are utility programs that can alter data without any audit trail adequately controlled and their use logged for subsequent management reviews? | Yes | Access to utility programs are restricted by the security program. |
| 7. | Is there terminal access control software that restricts who can access the system, what programs can be used, and what files the user and/or program can access? | Yes | Access restricted by use of passwords. |
| 8. | Does terminal access control rely on passwords or other identification/validation processes to control access to the system? | Yes | Unattended terminals log off automatically after ten minutes of inactivity. |
| 9. | Are passwords controlled to ensure that they are confidential, unique, and updated to reflect needed changes on a timely basis? | Yes | Policies restrict access to passwords. |
| 10. | Are all significant events (security violations, use of critical software, or system commands, etc.) logged and promptly investigated by appropriate management personnel? | Yes | Reviewed by security manager. |

Source: Adapted from the AICPA Audit Guide, *Consideration of the Internal Control Structure in a Financial Statement Audit* (New York, 1990).

# Assessing Control Risk—Testing Computer System Controls

Assessing control risk involves evaluating the effectiveness of a client's internal control structure computer and manual policies and procedures in preventing or detecting material misstatements in the financial statements. As presented in Chapter 8, it may be summarized as having the following four steps: *(a)* determine the planned assessed level of control risk, *(b)* design and perform additional tests of controls, *(c)* reassess control risk and modify planned substantive tests, and *(d)* document the assessed level of control risk. In this section we emphasize testing of controls pertaining to computer systems.

### Determine the Planned Assessed Level of Control Risk.   
After obtaining an understanding of the client's control environment, the flow of transactions through the computer system, and basic control procedures, the auditors are in a position to determine the planned assessed level of control risk. If the auditors assess control risk at the maximum, they will omit additional tests of controls. On the other hand, if it appears that the controls will prove sufficiently reliable to justify the audit effort of testing the procedures, the auditors will plan lower assessments of control risk, and design additional tests of controls.

When the client's computer system is relatively simple and produces hard-copy documents and records, the auditors may decide that it is efficient to assess control risk at, or near, the maximum and bypass the computer. Using this approach, the auditors will process input data manually on a test basis. The auditors' results are then compared to those obtained by the client's data processing and any discrepancies are investigated. This technique is called *auditing around the computer* because the auditors bypass the computer rather than utilize it in conducting their tests. While auditing around the computer can be an effective approach in certain circumstances, it is unacceptable if the reason for its use is merely the auditors' lack of understanding of the client's computer processing activities.

### Design and Perform Additional Tests of Controls.   
The purpose of tests of controls is to provide reasonable assurance that the controls described in the audit working papers are actually operating as planned. Regardless of the nature of the client's data processing system, auditors must conduct tests of those controls they intend to consider in their assessment of control risk. The nature of the data processing system may, however, affect the specific procedures employed by the auditors in testing the controls.

Tests of controls for the control environment and the accounting system will consist of inquiries of appropriate personnel, inspection of documents and reports, observation of the application of accounting policies and procedures, and reperformance of certain procedures. The auditors will observe management's involvement in the accounting function, inspect management's operating plan and budgets, and hold discussions with the internal auditors. Similarly, they may make inquiries, observe and inspect evidence related to the accounting system, and trace several transactions through the system.

### Procedures to Test General Controls.   
The auditors will usually begin their consideration of computer control procedures by testing general controls. This is an efficient approach since the effectiveness of specific application controls is dependent on the existence of effective general controls over all computer activities. The auditors, for example, would

get little audit evidence from testing programmed controls in a payroll program in an environment where programmers can easily make unauthorized changes in any program. In the absence of controls over program modification, the auditors have no evidence that the program being tested is identical to the one used to process data during the year. Such weaknesses would limit the auditors' ability to rely on application controls to reduce their assessment of control risk.

Tests of the effectiveness of controls for development of new programs and systems may include making inquiries of personnel, reviewing the minutes of meetings of users and the computer staff, and inspecting the documentation of the tests performed on the systems before they were implemented. The auditors may have discussions with users to determine that they understand the systems and to obtain their assessments of the operation of the system.

To test controls over program changes, the auditors may review the documentation of any changes made and compare them to the log of manager approvals. Manuals being used by users and operators may be inspected to determine that they are the most recent versions.

Controls over access to programs and data may be tested through inquiry of client personnel and observation of the segregation of duties and physical controls over equipment. The computer-generated log of access violations may be inspected for evidence of review and follow-up by control group personnel.

Operations controls may be tested through inquiry of computer operators about adherence to policies and follow-up on exceptions and other problems. The auditor may also review reports summarizing appropriate corrective action taken on operations problems by computer operators, vendors, programmers, the data base administrator, and users.

**Procedures to Test Application Controls.**   Tests of application controls vary significantly, depending upon the nature of the system and application. For example, in a batch system, input controls may be tested by accounting for the serial sequence of source documents in selected batches, reviewing and verifying reconciliations of batch control totals, and comparing control totals to computer output. In an online, real-time system, on the other hand, batch data are not available, and the auditors will design tests that ensure that only authorized data are accepted as input, and that input validation checks are applied to ensure the accuracy of the data.

A primary approach to assessing application controls is to test the manual follow-up procedures by inspecting the exception reports generated by the computer, and reviewing the way in which the exceptions were handled by the control group. Analysis of exception reports may be especially effective when commercial off-the-shelf software is being used and when the auditor has a high degree of confidence that programs have not been modified. In such circumstances the auditor may be familiar with the nature, strengths, and limitations of these well-publicized software programs. Thus, testing the operation of the system itself may be of lesser importance than in circumstances in which the client has designed its own software or modified commercial off-the-shelf software.

When the auditor is unsure of the software's operation, techniques using computer-assisted audit techniques become especially helpful. These techniques include the use of **test data, integrated test facilities, controlled programs, program analysis, tagging and tracing,** and **generalized audit software programs.** Computer-assisted audit techniques are used by both external and internal auditors.

Test Data (Decks).   In the audit of a manual accounting system, the auditors trace sample transactions through the **records** from their inception to their final disposition. In the audit of a computer system, a comparable approach is the use of *test data*. The test data developed by the client's programmers may be utilized by the independent auditors once they have satisfied themselves by study of flowcharts and printouts that the tests are valid. As an alternative, the auditors may develop their own test data, but this approach is often too time-consuming to be practicable.

To test programmed controls, the test data should include significant exceptions that would affect the auditors' assessment of control risk. Among these would be transactions with missing data, erroneous transactions, illogical transactions, out-of-balance batches, and out-of-sequence records. The auditors will carefully appraise the programmed controls that relate to financial statement assertions for which they wish to assess control risk at a level below the maximum. Dummy transactions and records used in test data can be specially coded to avoid contamination of the client's genuine records and files. If the client's computer system includes an integrated test facility, the auditors may use this facility to prevent their test data from contaminating the client's files.

Integrated Test Facility.   One method used by internal and external auditors to test and monitor accounting controls in data processing applications is an **integrated test facility.** An integrated test facility is a subsystem of dummy records and files built into the regular data processing system. These dummy files permit test data to be processed simultaneously with regular (live) input without adversely affecting the live data files or output. The test data, which include transactions and exceptions pertaining to controls to be tested, affect only the dummy files and dummy output. For this reason, an integrated test facility is often called the *minicompany approach* to testing the system. Integrated test facilities may be used in either online, real-time, or batch processing systems.

The auditors monitor the processing of test data, studying the effects upon the dummy files, exception reports, and other output produced, and the follow-up on exceptions by the control group. An integrated test facility for payroll applications, for example, could be set up by including a fictitious department and records for fictitious employees in the payroll master file. Input data for the dummy department would be included with input data from actual departments. The auditors would monitor all output relating to the dummy department, including payroll records, exception reports, and payroll checks. (In this situation, strict control would be necessary to prevent misuse of the dummy payroll checks.)

A problem with integrated test facilities is the risk that someone may manipulate the real data files by transferring data to or from the dummy files. Controls should exist to prevent unauthorized access to the dummy files, and the auditors should monitor all activity in these files. Also, the test facility must be carefully designed to ensure that real files are not inadvertently contaminated with the fictitious test data.

Controlled Programs.   As an alternative or supplement to the test data approach, the auditors may monitor the processing of current data by using a duplicate program that is held under their control. They then compare their output to that developed by the client's copy of the program. They may also reprocess historical data with their controlled program for comparison with the original output. Reprocessing historical data may alert the auditors to undocumented changes in the client's programs.

Controlled programs are advantageous because the auditor may test the client's program with both genuine (live) and test data. Through controlled programs, auditors may test programmed controls without risk of contaminating the client's files. Also, the testing may be conducted at an independent computer facility without utilizing the client's computer or data processing personnel.

### Program Analysis Techniques.

Programs have been developed that can generate computer-made flowcharts of other programs. A trained auditor can examine the flowcharts to test the logic of applications programs and to ensure that the client's program documentation describes the program that is actually being used.

### Tagging and Tracing Transactions.

This technique involves *tagging* transactions with an indicator when they are entered into the system. The computer provides the auditors with a printout of the details of the steps in processing tagged transactions. This printout is examined for evidence of unauthorized program steps.

### Generalized Audit Software.

Many large CPA firms have developed **generalized audit software** (computer programs) that may be used to test the reliability of the client's programs as well as to perform many specific auditing functions. This audit software is suited for use on a wide variety of computer systems.

One application of computer audit software is to verify the reliability of the client's programs through a process termed *parallel simulation*. The generalized audit software may be directed to perform processing functions essentially equivalent to those of the client's programs. If the client's program is operating properly, the output of the client's processing of a group of transactions should be equivalent to the output from the generalized audit software package.

A significant value of generalized audit software lies in the fact that the auditors are able to conduct independent processing of live data. Often, the verification of the client's output would be too large a task to be undertaken manually, but can be done efficiently through a parallel computer program. Even when manual verification would be possible, the use of a parallel program allows the auditors to expand greatly the size of the sample of transactions to be tested. An extensive examination of the client's files may become a feasible and economic undertaking. It is not necessary, however, to duplicate all of the client's data processing. Testing should be performed only to the extent necessary to support the auditors' assessment of control risk.

### Procedures to Test User Controls.

Tests of user control procedures will vary significantly with the nature of the control. However, the primary objective is to obtain assurance that users are, at a minimum, testing computer output for reasonableness. Therefore, typical tests involve inquiries of users about test procedures performed and inspection of any documentation that exists.

### Reassess Control Risk and Modify Planned Substantive Tests.

Auditors test internal controls to determine the extent to which they may be relied upon to produce reliable accounting data and thereby reduce the assessed level of control risk. This assessment in

Figure 9–5   Relationship of General, Application, and User Controls to Assessed Level of Control Risk

| Assessment of Adequacy of: | Existence/ Occurrence | Completeness | Rights and Obligations | Valuation/ Allocation | Presentation and Disclosure |
|---|---|---|---|---|---|
| General Controls | Strong | Strong | N/A | Strong | N/A |
| Application Controls | Strong | Weak | N/A | Moderate | N/A |
| User Controls | Strong | Weak | N/A | Moderate | N/A |
| Assessed Level of Control Risk | Low | Slightly below the maximum | At the maximum | Moderate | At the maximum |
| Comments | Results of tests of controls support a low assessed level of control risk. | Weak application and user controls negate the strong general controls. | N/A | Combined assessment of results generally support a moderate assessed level of control risk. | N/A |

turn affects the nature, timing, and extent of the substantive testing necessary for the auditors to express an opinion as to the fairness of the financial statements.

Conceptually, considering internal controls over computer activities is no different from considering other aspects of the system. Substantive testing procedures must be expanded in those areas where control risk is high and may be restricted in areas where control risk is low. Figure 9–5 provides an example of a situation in which the auditors decided to assess control risk for the rights/obligations assertion and disclosure/presentation at the maximum level. The other risks were assessed by combining the assessments of the various major types of controls.

Document the Assessed Level of Control Risk.   As indicated in Chapter 8, the auditors must also document the assessed level of control risk, and the basis for assessing control risk at less than the maximum. When auditing a client with a computer system, the auditors' tests of general controls, application controls, and user controls will help provide the basis for the auditors' assessment of control risk at less than the maximum.

# SUBSTANTIVE TESTING WITH COMPUTERS

Substantive testing of computerized systems often requires auditors to directly access client computer files. Generalized audit software is widely used for retrieving data from the client's system for use by the auditors in substantiating account balances. In performing retrieval functions, the audit software interfaces with the client's computer files and locates specific data requested by the auditors. The audit software may then be used to rearrange the data in a format more useful to the auditors, compare the data to other files, make computations, and select random samples. Applications of this nature include:

1. *Examining the client's records for overall quality, completeness, and valid conditions.* In auditing a manual system, the auditors become aware of the general quality, accuracy, and validity of the client's records through visual observation. Since the auditors do not have the same physical contact with computer-based records, the audit software may be used to scan the client's files for various improprieties. For example, the accounts receivable file may be scanned for account balances in excess of credit limits, and the depreciation expense may be recomputed for each item in the plant assets file. The great speed of the computer often makes it possible to perform such calculations for each item in the population, rather than having to rely upon a sample-based test.

2. *Rearranging data and performing analyses.* The audit software may be used to rearrange the data in the client's files into a format more useful to the auditors. For example, the accounts receivable file may be reorganized into the format of an aged trial balance. Data from the client's files may be printed out in the format of the auditors' working papers. In addition, the audit software can make analytical computations, such as computing turnover ratios to identify slow-moving inventory.

3. *Selecting audit samples.* Audit samples may be selected from the client's files on a random basis or using any other criteria specified by the auditors. Examples include selection of the inventory items to be test counted and the accounts receivable to be confirmed. An additional time savings may result if the audit software is used to print out the actual confirmation requests.

4. *Comparing data on separate files.* When similar data are contained in two or more files, the audit software can compare the files and identify any discrepancies. For example, the changes in accounts receivable over a period of time may be compared to the details of the cash receipts and credit sales transactions files. Also, actual operating results may be compared to forecasts.

5. *Comparing the results of audit procedures with the client's records.* Data obtained by the auditors may be converted to machine-readable form and compared to the data in computer-based files. For example, the results of the auditors' inventory test counts can be compared to the perpetual inventory file.

Using Audit Software: An Illustration.   To illustrate some of the possible uses of generalized audit software, let us consider a specific example. Assume that an auditor is planning to observe a client's physical count of inventories at a specific date. All inventory is stored either in the client's distribution center or at a public warehouse. The client maintains computer-based perpetual inventory records, which are updated daily. This inventory file contains the following information:

| | |
|---|---|
| Part number. | Cost per unit. |
| Description of item. | Date of last purchase. |
| Location. | Date of last sale. |
| Quantity on hand. | Quantity sold during the year. |

The client has provided the auditor with a duplicate tape of the inventory file as of the date of the physical count.

Figure 9–6   Illustration of the Uses of Generalized Audit Software

| Basic Inventory Audit Procedure | How Generalized Audit Software Might Be Used |
|---|---|
| 1. Observe the physical count, making appropriate test counts. | 1. Determine which items are to be test counted by selecting from the inventory file a sample of items that provides the desired dollar coverage. |
| 2. Test the mathematical accuracy of the inventory extensions and footings. | 2. For each item in the inventory file, multiply the quantity on hand by the cost per unit and add the extended amounts. |
| 3. Compare the auditors' test counts to the inventory records. | 3. Arrange the test counts in a tape format identical to the inventory file and compare the two tapes. |
| 4. Compare the client's physical count data to the inventory records. | 4. Compare the quantity of each item counted to the quantity on hand in the inventory file. |
| 5. Perform a lower-of-cost-or-market test by obtaining a list of current costs per item from vendors. | 5. Compare the current costs per unit to the cost per unit in the inventory file; print out the extended value for each item, using the lower of two unit costs, and add extended amounts. |
| 6. Test purchases and sales cutoff. | 6. List a sample of items on the inventory file for which the date of last purchase or last sale is on, or immediately before, the date of the physical count. |
| 7. Confirm the existence of items located in public warehouses. | 7. List items located in public warehouses and print confirmations. |
| 8. Analyze inventory for evidence of obsolescence or slow-moving items. | 8. List items from the inventory file for which the turnover ratio (quantity sold divided by quantity on hand) is low or for which the date of last sale indicates a lack of recent transactions. |

Source: AICPA, adapted from Uniform CPA Examination.

The left-hand column in Figure 9–6 indicates typical inventory audit procedures the CPA might perform. The right-hand column indicates how the CPA's generalized audit software might be helpful in the performance of these procedures.

Auditors do not need extensive technical computer knowledge in order to make use of generalized audit software. They will find it necessary to perform only a modest amount of programming. In fact, many CPA firms have found that they can train audit staff members to complete specification sheets and operate a generalized audit program within a time span of a few days. Because of the simplified procedures that have been developed, auditors can, after limited training, program and operate the generalized audit software independently—that is, without assistance from the client's information systems personnel.

# COMPUTER SERVICE CENTERS

Computer service centers provide data processing services to customers who decide not to invest in their own computer facilities. Customers may transmit data in batches to the service center, and the service center processes the data and returns the output to the customers.

Some computer centers operate on a time-sharing basis. The subscribers to a commercial time-sharing system can, through their terminals, run programs, store these programs in the computer for subsequent use, use the programs developed by the time-sharing company, and store files of data in the computer for subsequent use. In brief, the user of a time-sharing system has available most of the services that would be available through ownership of a computer.

When a service center performs data processing for a client, the center's internal controls interact with the client's control structure. Accordingly, the auditors' understanding of the internal control structure must be based, in part, on an understanding of processing activities at the computer service center. A visit to the center may be necessary to obtain this understanding. In addition, if the auditors plan to reduce their assessed level of control risk based on certain controls, they must obtain evidence of their operational effectiveness regardless of whether those controls are applied by the client or by the service center.

The auditors may find that controls applied by the client are adequate to ensure that errors or irregularities in transactions are detected. For example, the client's personnel may develop input control totals and compare them to the service center's output. They may also reperform computer calculations on a test basis. When such controls are adequate, the auditors need test only client controls to reduce their assessment of control risk; there is no need to perform tests of controls at the service center.

In other situations, the controls performed at the computer service center are necessary to achieve the client's control objectives. This means that the auditors' assessment of control risk cannot be significantly reduced without evidence that controls at the center are operating effectively. To obtain this evidence, the auditors may have to perform tests at the service center.

Reports of Service Auditors.   Most service centers perform similar processing services for numerous clients. If the auditors of each client (called *user auditors*) were to visit the service center for the purpose of reviewing internal controls, they would ask similar questions and perform similar tests of controls. It may be advantageous for the service center to engage its own auditors (called *service auditors*) to study their internal control structure and issue a report on it. The user auditors may then elect to rely on this report as an alternative to visiting the service center themselves.

*SAS 70* (AU 324), ''Reports on the Processing of Transactions by Service Organizations,'' presents two types of reports that service auditors may provide: (1) reports on policies and procedures placed in operation, and (2) reports on policies and procedures placed in operation and tests of operating effectiveness. A report on policies and procedures placed in operation provides a detailed description of the service center's internal control structure; it provides the user auditors with an understanding of the system, but it does not provide a basis for reliance on the operating effectiveness of control procedures at the service center.

To consider the service center's controls in their assessments of control risk, the user auditors must have evidence that those controls are operating effectively. This evidence can be obtained only from tests performed directly by the user auditors, or a report on policies and procedures placed in operation and tests of operating effectiveness by the service auditors. If the service auditors' report provides an adequate basis for the user auditors' assessment of control risk, usually there is no need for the user auditors to perform their own tests at the center. They may decide to rely solely on the results of the service auditors' tests. However, the user auditors should take steps to satisfy themselves as to the professional reputation of the service auditors.

## ◆ CHAPTER SUMMARY

This chapter describes the auditors' consideration of internal control in a computer environment. To summarize:

1. Auditors are likely to encounter computerized recordkeeping in every audit engagement. Even the smallest of audit clients can be expected to at least use a microcomputer to process its accounting records.

2. The use of a computer system by a client does not change the need to establish effective internal controls; however, it does change the nature of those controls. More advanced computerized features, such as online capabilities, data base storage, computer networks, and end user computing, present special control risks. Therefore, specialized internal controls are needed, including computer passwords, validity tests, and computer logs.

3. The use of a computerized accounting system may significantly affect the control environment of the organization, especially its organizational structure and the work of the internal auditors. From an organizational standpoint, it is essential to segregate the function of programming from that of authorizing input to the system, and the function of operating the computer from those having details of the operations of the programs. Internal auditors often use computerized techniques to monitor the internal controls in a computerized system.

4. Computer control procedures are often classified as general controls, application controls, and user controls. General controls apply to all computer applications, and application controls and user controls relate only to a specific application. The auditors often consider general controls first, because applications and user controls cannot be operated effectively if the general controls are weak.

5. To test application controls, the auditors will often use computer-assisted audit techniques, such as test data, integrated test facilities, controlled programs, program analysis techniques, and tagging and tracing transactions.

6.  While generalized audit software also may be used to test applications controls, it is more often used by the auditors to perform substantive tests of computerized records. Generalized audit software may be used to perform such functions as testing the clerical accuracy of records, making comparisons of related data, and selecting random samples.

# ◆ KEY TERMS INTRODUCED OR EMPHASIZED IN CHAPTER 9

**Application controls**   Internal control procedures relating to a specific computer task, such as preparation of payroll.

**Batch processing**   A system in which like transactions are processed periodically as a group.

**C**   A programming language that is widely used because of its portability across various types of hardware.

**Change request log**   A log which consists of suggestions for changes in programs. These changes have often been initiated by users who have noted various difficulties associated with a program.

**Controlled programs**   Duplicate client application programs that are maintained under the auditors' control in order to test the programmed controls.

**Data base system**   A system that eliminates data redundancy by storing data for two or more computer applications in an integrated data base.

**Direct (random) access**   A storage technique in which each piece of data is assigned an address and may be retrieved without searching through other stored data. A magnetic disk drive is a direct access device.

**Distributed data processing network**   A network of computers that uses communication links to share data and programs among various users in remote locations throughout the organization. The users may process the data in their own departments.

**Electronic data interchange (EDI)**   A system in which data are exchanged electronically between the computers of different companies. In an EDI system source documents are replaced with electronic transactions created in a standard format.

**End user computing**   A system in which a user is responsible for developing and executing a computer application that generates information that is utilized by that same user.

**Fiber optic transmission**   Transmission using a glass or plastic filament cable used to communicate signals in the form of light waves

**File**   An organized collection of related records, such as a customer file.

**General controls**   Control procedures applicable to all or many computer systems in an organization. General controls include controls over the development of programs and systems, controls over changes to programs and systems, controls over computer operations, and controls over access to programs and data.

**Generalized audit software**   A group of computer programs used by auditors to locate and process data contained in a client's computer-based records. The programs perform such functions as rearranging the data in a format more useful to the auditors, comparing records, selecting samples, and making computations. This software is compatible with a wide variety of different computer systems.

**Hard copy**   Computer output in printed form, such as printed listings, reports, and summaries.

**Header label**   A machine-readable record at the beginning of a file that identifies the file.

**Integrated test facility**   A set of dummy records and files included in a computer system enabling test data to be processed simultaneously with live input.

**Intelligent terminals**   Visual display or keyboard/printer terminals that have a minimum amount of processing capabilities. They are often used to input transactions directly to magnetic tapes or disks for subsequent computer processing.

**Local area network (LAN)**   A communications facility that interconnects computers within a limited area, typically a building or a small cluster of buildings.

**Master file**   A file of relatively permanent data or information that is updated periodically.

**Microwave transmission**   Transmission using electromagnetic waves of certain radio frequencies.

**Network system**   A communications facility that interconnects computers.

**Offline**   Pertaining to peripheral devices or equipment not in direct communication with the central processing unit of the computer.

**Off-the-shelf software**   Commercially available software created for a variety of users in the same industry or with the same application.

**Online**   Pertaining to peripheral devices or equipment in direct communication with the central processing unit of the computer.

**Operating system**   Software that coordinates and controls hardware components. For example, authorization procedures may be programmed into the operating system to restrict access to files and programs to authorized personnel.

**Operations manual**   A manual that contains the instructions for processing a program. The manual should include sufficient information to allow operators to effectively operate programs, but should not include detailed program documentation.

**Patch**   A new section of coding added in a rough or expedient way to modify a program.

**Program analysis techniques**   Techniques for testing programmed controls that involve the examination of computer-generated flowcharts of application programs.

**Program flowchart**   A graphic representation of the major steps and logic of a computer program.

**Record**   A group of related items or fields of data handled as a unit.

**Report of service auditor**   A report issued by the auditor of a service center to attest to the internal controls at a computer service center. User auditors make use of these reports in considering the internal control over data processing performed for their clients by the service center.

**Sequential access**   A storage technique in which data are read and written in numerical (e.g., account number) sequence. A magnetic tape drive is a sequential storage device.

**System software**   Programs that control and coordinate hardware components and provide other support to application software.

**Tagging and tracing**   A technique for testing programmed controls in which selected transactions are tagged when they are entered for processing. A computer program provides a printout of the steps in processing the tagged transactions that may be reviewed by the auditors.

**Telecommunications**   The electronic transmission of information by radio, wire, fiber optics, microwave, laser, and other electromagnetic systems.

**Test data (decks)**   A set of dummy records and transactions developed to test the adequacy of a computer program or system.

**User controls**   Controls performed by users of computer information to test its accuracy and completeness.

**Wide area network (WAN)**   A communication facility that interconnects computers within a large geographical area.

# ◆ GROUP I: REVIEW QUESTIONS

9-1   Computer systems use two types of software: system software and application software. Explain the difference between these two types of software.

9-2   Distinguish between an end user computing and a distributed data processing network.

9-3   What is meant by a local area network?

9-4   Distinguish between user control procedures and manual application control procedures.

9-5   What are internal and external file labels? Why are they used?

9-6   Distinguish general controls from application controls and give examples of the types of controls included in each of these broad categories.

9-7   An information systems department usually performs numerous data processing functions that would be separated in a manual system. Does this imply that separation of duties is not a practical means of achieving internal control in a computerized system? Explain.

9-8   Explain briefly what is meant by an "online, real-time system."

9-9   Explain briefly the meaning of the term *documentation* as it pertains to computers and an information systems department. How might a client's documentation be used by the auditors?

9-10  The number of personnel in an information systems department may limit the extent to which segregation of duties is feasible. What is the minimum amount of segregation of duties that will permit satisfactory internal control?

9-11  Compare the responsibilities and objectives of the information systems control group to those of the internal auditors with respect to data processing activities

9-12  Define and give the purpose of each of the following controls:
   *a.*  Record counts.
   *b.*  Limit test.
   *c.*  Duplicate processing.
   *d.*  Hash totals

9-13  Differentiate between a system flowchart and a program flowchart.

9-14  Auditors should be familiar with the terminology employed in electronic data processing. The following statements contain some of the terminology so employed. Indicate whether each statement is true or false.
   *a.*  A recent improvement in computer hardware is the ability to automatically produce error listings. Previously, this was possible only when provisions for such a report were included in the program.
   *b.*  The control of input and output to and from the information systems department should be performed by an independent control group.
   *c.*  An internal-audit computer program that continuously monitors computer processing is a feasible approach for improving internal control in OLRT systems.
   *d.*  An internal label is one of the controls built into the hardware by the manufacturer of a magnetic tape system.
   *e.*  A limit test in a computer program is comparable to a decision that an individual makes in a manual system to judge a transaction's reasonableness.
   *f.*  A principal advantage of using magnetic tape files is that data need not be recorded sequentially.
   *g.*  A major advantage of disk files is the ability to gain random access to data on the disk.

    *h.* The term *grandfather-father-son* refers to a method of computer record security rather than to generations in the evolution of computer hardware.

    *i.* When they are not in use, tape and disk files should be stored apart from the computer room under the control of a librarian.

9-15    Describe briefly the internal controls that should be established over the operation of a micro-computer to prevent use by unauthorized personnel.

9-16    What is meant by the term *telecommunications?*

9-17    Explain briefly what is meant by a distributed data processing system.

9-18    Describe what is meant by electronic data interchange (EDI). How does EDI affect a company's audit trail?

9-19    Is it probable that the use of computers will eventually eliminate the audit trail, making it impossible to trace individual transactions from their origin to the summary totals in the financial statements? Explain the reasons for your answer.

9-20    Do auditors usually begin their consideration of internal control over computer activities with a review of general or application controls? Explain.

9-21    Describe the audit technique known as *tagging* and *tracing*. What is the purpose of the technique?

9-22    What is a service center? Are the auditors of a client that uses a service center concerned about the controls applied at the center? Explain.

# ◆ GROUP II: QUESTIONS REQUIRING ANALYSIS

9-23    The first requirement of an effective internal control structure is a satisfactory plan of organization. Explain the characteristics of a satisfactory plan of organization for an information systems department, including the relationship between the department and the rest of the organization.

9-24    Distinguish between batch processing and online, real-time (OLRT) processing. In which of these systems is strong internal control over input most easily attained? Explain.

9-25    Auditors encounter the use of microcomputers on almost every audit engagement.

    *a.* How do microcomputers differ from large computers?

    *b.* When are the auditors concerned with internal control over the use of microcomputers?

9-26    The use of test data is one method of performing tests of processing controls in a computer system. Identify and discuss several other methods by which auditors may test internal processing controls over computer activity.

9-27    Discuss how generalized audit software can be used to aid the auditors in examining accounts receivable in a fully computerized system.

9-28    An integrated test facility (ITF) is a method used by both internal and external auditors for testing computer system controls. Discuss the advantages and disadvantages of implementing an ITF.

        (CIA, adapted)

9-29    Many companies have part or all of their data processing done by computer service centers.

    *a.* What controls should the company maintain to ensure the accuracy of processing done by a service center?

    *b.* How do auditors assess internal control over applications processed for an audit client by a service center?

    *c.* What is a service auditors' report on the processing of transactions by a computer service center?

     *d.*  What two types of reports are provided by service auditors?

     *e.*  How do user auditors use each type of report?

9-30  Select the best answer for each of the following questions. Explain the reasons for your selection.

     *a.*  When erroneous data are detected by computer program controls, data may be excluded from processing and printed on an exception report. The exception report should probably be reviewed and followed-up on by the:

       (1)  Control group.

       (2)  System analyst.

       (3)  Supervisor of computer operations.

       (4)  Computer programmer.

     *b.*  An accounts payable program posted a payable to a vendor not included in the online vendor master file. A control which would prevent this error is a:

       (1)  Validity check.

       (2)  Range check.

       (3)  Limit test.

       (4)  Parity check.

     *c.*  When an online, real-time (OLRT) electronic data processing system is in use, internal control can be strengthened by:

       (1)  Providing for the separation of duties between data input and error listing operations.

       (2)  Attaching plastic file protection rings to reels of magnetic tape before new data can be entered on the file.

       (3)  Making a validity check of an identification number before a user can obtain access to the computer files.

       (4)  Preparing batch totals to provide assurance that file updates are made for the entire input.

     *d.*  Which of the following is an advantage of generalized audit software packages?

       (1)  They are all written in one identical computer language.

       (2)  They can be used for audits of clients that use differing computing equipment and file formats.

       (3)  They have reduced the need for the auditor to study input controls for computer-related procedures.

       (4)  Their use can be substituted for a relatively large part of the required tests of controls.

     *e.*  The increased presence of the microcomputer in the workplace has resulted in an increasing number of persons having access to the computer. A control that is often used to prevent unauthorized access to sensitive programs is:

       (1)  Backup copies of the diskettes.

       (2)  Passwords for each of the users.

       (3)  Input validation checks.

       (4)  Record counts of the number of input transactions in a batch being processed.

     *f.*  An auditor will use the computer test data method in order to gain assurances with respect to the:

       (1)  Input data.

       (2)  Machine capacity.

       (3)  Controls contained within the program.

       (4)  Degree of keypunching accuracy.

(CIA, adapted)

# ◆ GROUP III: PROBLEMS

9-31    The Ultimate Life Insurance Company recently established a data base management system. The company is now planning to provide its branch offices with terminals that have online access to the central computer facility.

*Required:*   *a.*   Define a "data base."
       *b.*   Give one fundamental advantage of a data base.
       *c.*   Describe three security steps to safeguard the data base from improper access through the terminals.

(CIA, adapted)

9-32    CPAs may audit around or through computers in the audit of the financial statements of clients who utilize computers to process accounting data.

*Required:*   *a.*   Describe the auditing approach referred to as "auditing around the computer."
       *b.*   Under what conditions do CPAs decide to audit through the computer instead of around the computer?
       *c.*   In auditing through the computer, CPAs may use test data.
          (1)   What is test data?
          (2)   Why do CPAs use test data?
       *d.*   How can the CPAs be satisfied that the computer programs presented to them for testing are actually those used by the client for processing accounting data?

(AICPA, adapted)

9-33    Johnson, CPA, was engaged to audit the financial statements of Horizon Incorporated, which has its own computer installation. While obtaining an understanding of the internal control structure, Johnson found that Horizon lacked proper segregation of the programming and operating functions. As a result, Johnson intensified the consideration of internal control surrounding the computer and concluded that the existing compensating general controls provided reasonable assurance that the objectives of internal control were being met.

*Required:*   *a.*   In a properly functioning computer environment, how is the separation of the programming and operating functions achieved?
       *b.*   What are the compensating general controls that Johnson most likely found?

(AICPA, adapted)

9-34    As you are planning the annual audit of Norton Corporation, you are informed that the company has purchased a number of microcomputers for use in various locations. One of the machines has been installed in the stores department which has the responsibility for disbursing stock items and for maintaining stores records. In your audit, you find that an employee receives the requisitions for stores, disburses the stock, maintains the records, operates the computer, and authorizes adjustments to the total amounts of stock accumulated by the computer.

    When you discuss the applicable controls with the department manager, you are told that the microcomputer is assigned exclusively to that department. Therefore, the manager contends that it does not require the same types of controls applicable to large computer systems.

*Required:*   *a.*   Comment on the manager's contention.
       *b.*   Discuss five types of control that would apply to this microcomputer application.

(CIA, adapted)

9-35    A CPA's client, The Outsider, Inc., is a medium-sized manufacturer of products for the leisure time activities market (camping equipment, scuba gear, bows and arrows, and so on). During the past year, a computer system was installed, and inventory records of finished goods and parts were converted to computer processing. The inventory master file is maintained on a disk. Each record of the file contains the following information:

Item or part number.

Description.

Size.

Unit of measure code.

Quantity on hand.

Cost per unit.

Total value of inventory on hand at cost.

Date of last sale or usage.

Quantity sold or used this year.

Economic order quantity.

Code number of major vendor.

Code number of secondary vendor.

In preparation for year-end inventory, the client has two identical sets of preprinted inventory count cards. One set is for the client's inventory counts and the other is for the CPA's use to make audit test counts. The following information has been keypunched into the cards and interpreted on their face:

Item or part number.

Description.

Size.

Unit of measure code.

In taking the year-end inventory, the client's personnel will write the actual counted quantity on the face of each card. When all counts are complete, the counted quantity will be keypunched into the cards. The cards will be processed against the disk file, and quantity-on-hand figures will be adjusted to reflect the actual count. A computer listing will be prepared to show any missing inventory count cards and all quantity adjustments of more than $100 in value. These items will be investigated by client personnel, and all required adjustments will be made. When adjustments have been completed, the final year-end balances will be computed and posted to the general ledger.

The CPA has available generalized audit software that can process both cards and disk files.

*Required:*  a.  In general and without regard to the facts above, discuss the nature of generalized audit software and list the various types of uses of such software.

b.  List and describe at least five ways generalized audit software can be used to assist in the audit of inventory of The Outsider, Inc. (For example, the software can be used to read the disk inventory master file and list items of high unit cost or total value. Such items can be included in the CPA's test counts to increase the dollar coverage of the audit verification.)

(AICPA, adapted)

9-36  You will be auditing for the first time the financial statements of Central Savings and Loan Association for the year ending December 31. The CPA firm that audited the association's financial statements for the prior year issued an unqualified audit report.

At the beginning of the current year, the association installed an online, real-time computer system. Each teller in the association's main office and seven branch offices has an online, input-output terminal. Customers' mortgage payments and savings account deposits and withdrawals are recorded in the accounts by the computer from data input by the teller at the time of the transaction. The teller keys the proper account by account number and enters the information in the terminal keyboard to record the transaction. The computer is housed at the main office.

*Required:*   You would expect the association to have certain internal controls in effect because an online, real-time computer system is employed. List the internal controls that should be in effect solely because this system is employed, classifying them as:

    *a.*   Those controls pertaining to input of information.

    *b.*   All other types of computer controls.

9-37   Lee Wong, CPA, is auditing the financial statements of the Alexandria Corporation, which recently installed a batch processing computer system. The following comments have been extracted from Wong's notes on computer operations and the processing and control of shipping notices and customer invoices:

    To minimize inconvenience Alexandria converted without change its existing data processing system, which utilized tabulating equipment. The computer company supervised the conversion and has provided training to all computer department employees in systems design, operations, and programming.

    Each computer run is assigned to a specific employee, who is responsible for making program changes, running the program, and answering questions. This procedure has the advantage of eliminating the need for records of computer operations because each employee is responsible for his or her own computer runs.

    At least one computer department employee remains in the computer room during office hours, and only computer department employees have keys to the computer room.

    System documentation consists of those materials furnished by the computer company—a set of record formats and program listings. These and the disk and tape library are kept in a corner of the computer department.

    The corporation considered the desirability of program controls, but decided to retain the manual controls from its existing system.

    Company products are shipped directly from public warehouses, which forward shipping notices to general accounting. There a billing clerk enters the price of the item and accounts for the numerical sequence of shipping notices from each warehouse. The billing clerk also prepares daily adding machine tapes (control tapes) of the units shipped and the unit prices.

    Shipping notices and control tapes are forwarded to the computer department for inputting and processing. Extensions are made on the computer. Output consists of invoices (in six copies) and a daily sales register. The daily sales register shows the aggregate totals of units shipped and unit prices, which the computer operator compares to the control tapes.

    All copies of the invoice are returned to the billing clerk. The clerk mails three copies to the customer, forwards one copy to the warehouse, maintains one copy in a numerical file, and retains one copy in an open invoice file that serves as a detailed accounts receivable record.

*Required:*   Describe weaknesses in internal control over information and data flows and the procedures for processing shipping notices and customer invoices, and recommend improvements in these controls and processing procedures. Organize your answer sheets as follows:

| Weakness | Recommended Improvement |
| --- | --- |
|  |  |

(AICPA, adapted)

# AUDIT SAMPLING— CONCEPTS AND TECHNIQUES

## CHAPTER OBJECTIVES

After studying this chapter, you should be able to:

- Define audit sampling.
- Explain the difference between sampling and nonsampling risk.
- Distinguish between statistical and nonstatistical sampling.
- Describe how basic sampling concepts apply to audit sampling.
- Distinguish among attributes, discovery, classical variables, and probability-proportional-to-size sampling plans.
- Discuss the effects of changes in various population characteristics and changes in sampling risk on required sample size.
- Describe how auditors plan, perform, and evaluate samples for tests of controls.
- Explain how the auditors use attributes sampling to perform tests of controls.
- Describe in general how auditors plan, perform, and evaluate samples for substantive tests.

I n Chapter 6 we discussed the need for sufficient, competent evidential matter as the basis for audit reports. As business entities have evolved in size, auditors increasingly have had to rely upon sampling procedures as the only practical means of obtaining this evidence. This reliance upon sampling procedures is one of the basic reasons that audit reports are regarded as expressions of opinion, rather than absolute certifications of the fairness of financial statements.

Audit sampling, whether statistical or nonstatistical, is the process of selecting a group of items (called the *sample*) from a large group of items (called the **population** or *field*) and using the characteristics of the sample to draw inferences about the characteristics of the entire population of items. The underlying assumption is that the sample is **representative** of the population, meaning that, for the characteristics being considered, the sample is essentially the same as the population. Basic to audit sampling is **sampling risk**—the risk that the auditors' conclusion based on a sample might be different from the conclusion they would reach if they examined every item in the entire population.

Sampling risk is reduced by increasing the size of the sample. At the extreme, when an entire population is examined there is no sampling risk. But, auditing large samples or the entire population is costly. A key element in efficient sampling is to balance the sampling risk against the cost of using larger samples.

Auditors may also draw erroneous conclusions because of *nonsampling errors*—those due to factors not directly caused by sampling. For example, the auditors may fail to apply appropriate audit procedures, or they may fail to recognize errors in the documents or transactions that are examined. The risk pertaining to nonsampling errors is referred to as **nonsampling risk.** Nonsampling risk can generally be reduced to low levels through effective planning and supervision of audit engagements and implementation of appropriately designed quality control procedures by the CPA firm. The procedures discussed throughout this text help control nonsampling risk. In the remainder of this and the following chapter we will emphasize sampling risk.

## COMPARISON OF STATISTICAL AND NONSTATISTICAL SAMPLING

A sample is said to be nonstatistical (or judgmental) when the auditors estimate sampling risk by using professional judgment rather than by using statistical techniques. This is not to say that nonstatistical samples are carelessly selected samples. Indeed, both nonstatistical and statistical audit samples should be selected in a way that they may be expected to allow the auditor to draw valid inferences about the population. In addition, the misstatements found in either a nonstatistical or a statistical sample should be used to estimate the total amount of misstatement in the population (called the *projected misstatement*). However, nonstatistical sampling provides no means of quantifying sampling risk. Thus, the auditors may find themselves taking larger and more costly samples than are necessary, or unknowingly accepting a higher than acceptable degree of sampling risk.

The use of statistical sampling does not eliminate professional judgment from the sampling process. It does, however, allow the auditors to measure and control sampling risk. Through statistical sampling techniques, the auditors may specify in advance the sampling risk that they want in their sample results and then compute a sample size that controls sampling risk at the desired level. Since statistical sampling techniques are based upon the laws of probability, the auditors are able to control the extent of the sampling risk in relying upon sample results. Thus, statistical sampling may assist auditors in (1) designing efficient samples, (2) measuring the sufficiency of the evidence obtained, and (3) objectively evaluating sample results. However, these advantages are not obtained without additional costs of training the audit staff, designing sampling plans, and selecting items for examination. For these reasons, nonstatistical samples are widely used by auditors, especially for tests of relatively small populations. Both statistical and nonstatistical sampling can provide auditors with sufficient competent evidential matter.[1]

## Selecting a Random Sample

A common misinterpretation of statistical sampling is to equate this process with random sampling. Random sampling is simply a method of *selecting* items for inclusion in a sample; it can be used in conjunction with either statistical or nonstatistical sampling. To emphasize this distinction, we will use the term **random selection** rather than random ''sampling'' to refer to the procedure of selecting the items for inclusion in a sample.

The principle involved in unrestricted random selection is that every item in the population has an equal chance of being selected for inclusion in the sample. Although random selection results in an *unbiased sample,* the sample is not necessarily representative. Sampling risk still exists that purely by chance a sample will be selected that does not possess essentially the same characteristics as the population. However, since the risk of a nonrepresentative random sample stems from the laws of probability, this risk may be measured by statistical formulas.

The sample also may not be representative of the actual population because the population being sampled differs from the actual population. The auditors select an audit sample from a **physical representation** of the population. For example, a sample of accounts payable may be selected from a computer listing (the physical representation) of recorded accounts payable. Any conclusions based on this sample relate only to the population on the computer listing. The auditors' conclusions do not consider the possibility that certain creditors (with balances due) are completely omitted from the listing. Stated in terms of the financial statement assertions, existence is addressed to a greater extent than is completeness. Therefore, it is essential that the auditors consider whether the physical representation reflects the proper population.

The concept of a random sample requires that the person selecting the sample will not influence or bias the selection either consciously or unconsciously. Thus, some type of impartial selection process is necessary to obtain a truly random sample. Techniques often used for selecting random samples include *random number tables, random number generators,* and *systematic selection.*

Random Number Tables.    One of the easiest methods of selecting items at random is the use of a random number table. A portion of a random number table is illustrated in Figure 10–1. The random numbers appearing in Figure 10–1 are arranged into columns

---

[1]*SAS 39* (AU 350), ''Audit Sampling,'' and the AICPA Audit and Accounting Guide, *Audit Sampling,* provide auditors with guidelines for planning, performing, and evaluating both statistical and nonstatistical samples.

Figure 10–1   Table of Random Numbers

| Row | Columns | | | | |
|-----|-----|-----|-----|-----|-----|
| | **(1)** | **(2)** | **(3)** | **(4)** | **(5)** |
| 1 . . . . . . . . . . . . . . | 04734 | 39426 | 91035 | 54839 | 76873 |
| 2 . . . . . . . . . . . . . . | 10417 | 19688 | 83404 | 42038 | 48226 |
| 3 . . . . . . . . . . . . . . | 07514 | 48374 | 35658 | 38971 | 53779 |
| 4 . . . . . . . . . . . . . . | 52305 | 86925 | 16223 | 25946 | 90222 |
| 5 . . . . . . . . . . . . . . | 96357 | 11486 | 30102 | 82679 | 57983 |
| 6 . . . . . . . . . . . . . . | 92870 | 05921 | 65698 | 27993 | 86406 |
| 7 . . . . . . . . . . . . . . | 00500 | 75924 | 38803 | 05386 | 10072 |
| 8 . . . . . . . . . . . . . . | 34862 | 93784 | 52709 | 15370 | 96727 |
| 9 . . . . . . . . . . . . . . | 25809 | 21860 | 36790 | 76883 | 20435 |
| 10 . . . . . . . . . . . . . . | 77487 | 38419 | 20631 | 48694 | 12638 |

of five digits. Except that the columnar arrangement permits the reader of the table to select numbers easily, the columns are purely arbitrary and otherwise meaningless. Each digit on the table is a random digit; the table does *not* merely represent a listing of random five-digit numbers. The columnar arrangement is for convenience only.

In using a random number table, the first step is to establish correspondence between the digits in the table and the items in the population. This is most easily done when the items in the population are consecutively numbered. On occasion, however, auditors may find it necessary to renumber the population to obtain correspondence. For example, if transactions are numbered A–001, B–001, and so on, the auditors may assign numbers to replace the alphabetic characters. Next, the auditors must select a starting point and a systematic route to be used in reading the random number table. Any route is permissible, as long as it is followed consistently.

To illustrate the use of a random number table, assume that a client's accounts receivable are numbered from 0001 to 5,000 and that the auditors want to select a random sample of 110 accounts for confirmation. Using the table in Figure 10–1, the auditors decide to start at the top of Column 2 and to proceed from top to bottom. Reading only the first four digits of the numbers in Column 2, the auditors would select 3942, 1968, and 4837 as three of the account numbers to be included in their sample. The next number, 8692, would be ignored, since there is no account with that number. The next numbers to be included in the sample would be 1148, 592, 2186, and so on.

In using a random number table, it is possible that the auditors will draw the same number more than once. If they ignore the number the second time it is selected and go on to the next number, they are *sampling without replacement*. This term means that an item once selected is not replaced in the population of eligible items, and consequently it cannot be drawn for inclusion in the sample a second time.

The alternative to sampling without replacement is *sampling with replacement*. Sampling with replacement means that once an item has been selected, it is immediately replaced into the population of eligible items and may be selected a second time. When applied to a random number table, the procedure is to include the number in the analysis as frequently as it occurs in the sample.

Statistical formulas can be used to compute sample size either with or without replacement. Most frequently auditors discard duplicate numbers and use sampling without replacement. This results in a slightly smaller required sample size, and eliminates questions about the propriety of including items more than once in evaluating the sample results.

Random Number Generators.   Even when items are assigned consecutive numbers, the selection of a large sample from a random number table may be a very time-consuming process. Computer programs called *random number generators* may be used to provide any length list of random number applicable to a given population. Random number generators may be programmed to select random numbers with specific characteristics, so that the list of random numbers provided to the auditors includes only numbers present in the population. A random number generator is a standard program in all generalized audit software packages.

Systematic Selection.   An approach that is less time-consuming than selecting a random number for each item to be included in the sample is **systematic selection.** This technique involves selecting every *n*th item in the population following one or more *random starting points*.

To illustrate systematic selection, assume that auditors wish to examine 200 paid checks from a population of 10,000 checks. If only one random starting point is used, the auditors would select every 50th check (10,000 ÷ 200) in the population. As a starting point, the auditors would select at random one of the first 50 checks. If the random starting point is check No. 37, check Nos. 37, 87 (37 + 50), and 137 (87 + 50) would be included in the sample, as well as every 50th check number after 137. If the auditors had elected to use five random starting points, 40 checks (200 ÷ 5) would have to be selected from each random start. Thus, the auditors would select every 250th check number (10,000 ÷ 40) after each of the five random starting points between one and 250.

Selecting every *n*th item in the population results in a random sample only when positions in the population were assigned in random order. For example, if expensive inventory parts are always assigned an identification number ending in 9, systematic selection could result in a highly biased sample that would include too many expensive items or too many inexpensive items.

To prevent drawing a nonrandom or biased sample when systematic selection is used, the auditors should first determine that the population is arranged in random order. If the population is not in random order, the auditors should use several random starting points for their systematic selection process.

The systematic selection technique has the advantage of enabling the auditors to obtain a sample from a population of unnumbered documents or transactions. If the documents to be examined are unnumbered, there is no necessity under this method to number them either physically or mentally, as required under the random number table selection technique. Rather, the auditors merely count off the sampling interval to select the documents or use a ruler to measure the interval. Generalized audit software packages include routines for systematic selection of audit samples from computer-based files.

## Other Methods of Sample Selection

Two other selection techniques that are used by auditors include haphazard selection and block selection. Neither of these two methods applies probabilistic methods to selecting the items for the sample. For that reason, they should not generally be used in conjunction with statistical sampling plans.

Haphazard Selection.   When haphazard sample selection is used, the auditors select the items from the population on an arbitrary basis, but without any conscious bias. For example, a haphazard sample of vouchers contained in a file drawer might be selected by pulling vouchers from the drawer without regard for the voucher's size, shape, or location in the drawer. If used, haphazard samples should not consist of items selected in a careless manner; the sample should be expected to be representative of the population.

Block Selection.   A block sample consists of all items in a selected time period, numerical sequence, or alphabetical sequence. For example, in testing internal control over cash disbursements, the auditors might decide to vouch all disbursements made during the months of April and December. In this case, the sampling unit is months rather than individual transactions. Thus, the sample consists of two blocks selected from a population of 12. Due to the relatively large number of blocks needed to form a reasonable audit conclusion, block sampling cannot generally be relied upon to efficiently produce a representative sample.

## Stratification

Auditors often *stratify* a population before computing the required sample size and selecting the sample. **Stratification** is the technique of dividing a population into relatively homogeneous subgroups called *strata*. These strata then may be sampled separately; the sample results may be evaluated separately, or combined, to provide an estimate of the characteristics of the total population. Whenever items of extremely high or low values or other unusual characteristics are segregated in this manner, each stratum becomes more homogeneous. The effect is to require a smaller number of sample items to evaluate the several strata separately than to evaluate the total population without the use of stratification.

Besides increasing the efficiency of sampling procedures, stratification enables auditors to relate sample selection to the materiality or other characteristics of items and, possibly, to apply different audit procedure to each stratum. For example, in selecting accounts receivable for confirmation, auditors might stratify and test the population as follows:

| Stratum | Composition of Stratum | Method of Selection Used | Type of Confirmation Request* |
|---------|------------------------|--------------------------|-------------------------------|
| 1 | All accounts of $10,000 and over | 100 percent confirmation | Positive |
| 2 | All accounts of $5,000 to $9,999.99 | Random number generator | Positive |
| 3 | All accounts of less than $5,000 | Random number generator | Negative |

*A positive confirmation request asks the respondent to reply, indicating the amount owed; a negative request asks for a response only if the respondent does not agree with the amount indicated on the request. Confirmation of accounts receivable is discussed in more detail in Chapter 13.

When the auditors are using audit sampling for substantive testing, stratification is almost always applied. For example, the auditors generally will not accept sampling risk for any item that by itself could materially misstate the population. For that reason, the auditors will test every item with a book balance of more than the tolerable misstatement. They will then select samples from each of the other strata.

## Types of Statistical Sampling Plans

The sampling procedures used to accomplish specific audit objectives are called sampling plans. Statistical sampling plans may be used to estimate many different characteristics of a population, but every estimate is either of (1) an occurrence rate or (2) a numerical quantity. The sampling terms corresponding to occurrence rates and numerical quantities are **attributes** and **variables,** respectively. Specifically, the major types of statistical sampling plans used for audit sampling include the following:

1. *Attributes sampling.* This sampling plan enables the auditors to estimate the rate of occurrence of certain characteristics in the population (e.g., deviations from performance of a prescribed control procedure). **Attributes sampling** frequently is used in performing tests of controls. For example, the auditor might use attributes sampling to estimate the percentage of the cash disbursements processed during the year that were not approved.

2. *Discovery sampling.* This form of attributes sampling is designed to locate at least one deviation (exception) in the population. **Discovery sampling** often is used in situations in which the auditors expect a very low rate of occurrence of some critical deviation. As an example, the auditors might use discovery sampling to attempt to locate a fraudulent cash disbursement.

3. *Classical variables sampling.* These sampling applications provide the auditors with an estimate of a numerical quantity, such as the dollar balance of an account. As would be expected, this technique is primarily used by auditors to perform substantive tests. For example, variables sampling might be used to plan, perform, and evaluate a sample of accounts receivable selected for confirmation. Frequently used variables sampling plans include **mean-per-unit estimation, ratio estimation,** and **difference estimation.**

4. *Probability-proportional-to-size sampling (PPS).* This technique, which is also referred to as *dollar-unit sampling,* applies attributes sampling theory to develop an estimate of the total dollar amount of misstatement in a population. **Probability-proportional-to-size sampling** is used as an alternative to classical variables sampling methods for performing substantive tests of transactions or balances. Unlike classical variables sampling techniques that define the sampling unit as each transaction or account balance in the population, PPS sampling defines the sampling unit as each *individual dollar* making up the book value of the population. A transaction or account is selected for audit if a dollar from that transaction or account is selected from the population. Therefore, each transaction or account has a probability proportional to its size of being selected for inclusion in the sample.

Sometimes one sampling plan may be used for the **dual purposes** of (1) testing an internal control procedure and (2) substantiating the dollar amount of an account balance. For example, a single sampling plan might be used to evaluate the effectiveness of the client's internal controls over recording sales transactions and to estimate the total overstatement or understatement of the sales account.[2]

## Allowance for Sampling Risk (Precision)

Whether the auditors' objective is estimating attributes or variables, the sample results may not be *exactly* representative of the population. Some degree of **sampling error**— the difference between the actual rate or amount in the population and that indicated by the sample—is usually present. In utilizing statistical sampling techniques, auditors are able to measure and control the risk of material sampling error by deciding on the appropriate levels of sampling risk and the allowance for sampling risk.

The allowance for sampling risk is the amount used to create a range, set by + or − limits from the sample results, within which the true value of the population characteristic being measured is likely to lie. For example, assume a sample is taken to determine the occurrence rate of a certain type of deviation from the performance of an internal control procedure. The sample indicates a deviation rate of 2.1 percent. We have little assurance that the deviation rate in the population is exactly 2.1 percent, but we know that the sample result probably approximates the population deviation rate. Therefore, using statistical sampling techniques, we may set an interval around the sample result within which we expect the population deviation rate to be. An allowance for sampling risk of ±1 percent would indicate that we expect the true population deviation rate to lie between 1.1 and 3.1 percent.

The wider the interval we allow, the more confident we may be that the true population characteristic is within it. In the preceding example, an allowance for sampling risk of ±2 percent would mean that we assume the population deviation rate to be between 0.1 percent and 4.1 percent.

---

[2]The size of a sample used for a dual purpose test should be the larger of the two samples that would have been required for the two separate purposes.

The allowance for sampling risk may also be used to construct a dollar interval. For example, we may attempt to establish the total dollar value of receivables within an interval of ±$10,000. As is discussed later in this chapter, the allowance for sampling risk required by auditors usually is determined in light of the amount of a tolerable misstatement. **Tolerable misstatement** is an estimate of the maximum monetary misstatement that may exist in an account that, when combined with the misstatement in other accounts, will not cause the financial statements to be materially misstated.

## Sample Size

The size of the sample has a direct effect upon both the allowance for sampling risk and sampling risk. With a very small sample, we cannot have low sampling risk unless we allow a very large **allowance for sampling risk (precision)**. As the sample size increases, both sampling risk and the allowance for sampling risk decrease. In other words, the smaller the allowance for sampling risk or the sampling risk desired by the auditors, the larger the required sample.

Sample size is also affected by certain characteristics of the population being tested. As the population increases in size, the sample size necessary to estimate the population with specified sampling risk and allowance for sampling risk will increase; however, if the population size is above approximately 500 an increase in its size has only a very small effect on the required sample size. In attributes sampling, sample size also increases as the **expected population deviation rate** increases. Finally, in classical variables sampling, greater variability among the item values in the population (a larger standard deviation) increases the required sample size.

# AUDIT SAMPLING FOR TESTS OF CONTROLS

Tests of controls are used to determine whether the client's internal control structure policies and procedures are operating in a way that would prevent or detect material misstatements in the financial statements. As discussed in Chapter 8, audit sampling cannot be used to test the operating effectiveness of all internal control procedures. In general, sampling can be used only when performance of the internal control procedure leaves some *evidence of performance,* such as a completed document or the initials of the person performing the procedure. This evidence of performance allows the auditors to determine whether or not the control procedure was applied to each item included in the sample. The results of tests of controls are most frequently presented in terms of the **rate of deviation** from performance of the prescribed internal control procedure.

A deviation from performance of a control procedure does not necessarily indicate a misstatement of the financial statements. To illustrate the distinction between deviations and financial statement misstatements, assume that the auditors have selected a sample of 50 cash disbursement vouchers to test for approval by the assistant controller. If the auditors find that 5 of the 50 vouchers were not properly approved, the deviation rate in the sample is 10 percent (5 deviations ÷ 50 vouchers), but the financial statements may not be misstated. All five vouchers may represent valid cash disbursements that were properly recorded. However, the auditors may conclude from the results of this test that there is a relatively high risk of invalid cash disbursements, because the sample results indicate that the assistant controller fails to approve about 10 percent of the vouchers processed. The auditors will use this evidence to increase the assessed level of control risk for the financial statement accounts that are affected by the cash disbursements cycle.

## Sampling Risk for Tests of Controls

When performing tests of internal control procedures, the auditors are concerned with two aspects of sampling risk:

1. *The risk of assessing control risk too high.* This risk is the possibility that the sample results will cause the auditors to assess control risk at a higher level than is warranted based on the actual operating effectiveness of the internal control procedure.
2. *The risk of assessing control risk too low.* This more important risk is the possibility that the sample results will cause the auditors to assess control risk at a lower level than is warranted based on the actual operating effectiveness of the internal control procedure.

Figure 10–2 illustrates these two aspects of sampling risk for tests of controls.

The **risk of assessing control risk too high** relates to the **efficiency** of the audit process. When the sample results cause the auditors to assess control risk at a higher level than it actually is, the auditors will perform more substantive testing than is necessary in the circumstance. This unnecessary testing reduces the *efficiency* of the audit, but it does not lessen the **effectiveness** of the audit as a means of detecting material misstatements in the client's financial statements. For that reason, the auditors usually do not attempt to directly control the risk of assessing control risk too high.

The **risk of assessing control risk too low** is of utmost concern. If the auditors assess control risk to be lower than it actually is, they will inappropriately reduce the extent of their substantive tests. This unwarranted reduction is substantive testing lessens the over-

---

Figure 10–2  Sampling Risk for Tests of Controls

| The Tests of Controls Sample Indicates: | Actual Extent of Operating Effectiveness of the Control Procedure Is: | |
|---|---|---|
| | Adequate for Planned Assessed Level of Control Risk | Inadequate for Planned Assessed Level of Control Risk |
| Extent of operating effectiveness is adequate | Correct decision | Incorrect decision (risk of assessing control risk too low) |
| Extent of operating effectiveness is inadequate | Incorrect decision (risk of assessing control risk too high) | Correct decision |

all *effectiveness* of the audit as a means of detecting material misstatements in the client's financial statements. Therefore, the auditors carefully control the risk of assessing control risk too low when performing tests of controls.

# ATTRIBUTES SAMPLING

As indicated previously, attributes sampling is widely used for tests of controls when auditors are estimating the rate of deviations from prescribed internal control procedures. For example, if an attributes sample indicates a deviation rate of 5 percent with an allowance for sampling risk of ±3 percent, the auditors could infer that between 2 and 8 percent of the items in the population contain deviations. In this example, 2 percent is the *lower deviation rate (lower precision limit)* and 8 percent is the *upper deviation rate (upper precision limit)* for the sample estimate. Tests of controls are designed to provide the auditors with assurance that deviation rates do not exceed acceptable levels. Therefore, the auditors are concerned only with the upper deviation rate for the sample estimate. The relevant question from the above example is whether the auditors can accept a deviation rate as high as 8 percent, not whether they can accept a deviation rate as low as 2 percent. The lower deviation rate is not pertinent to the objective of the test. For this reason, auditors generally use one-sided tests in attributes sampling; they consider only the upper deviation rate that will permit them to assess control risk at the planned level. In tests of controls the upper deviation rate is called the **tolerable deviation rate**.

Attributes sampling for tests of controls generally involves the following ten steps:

1. Determine the objective of the test.
2. Define the attributes and deviation conditions.
3. Define the population to be sampled.
4. Specify the risk of assessing control risk too low and the tolerable deviation rate.
5. Estimate the expected population deviation rate.
6. Determine the sample size.
7. Select the sample.
8. Test the sample items.
9. Evaluate the sample results.
10. Document the sampling procedure.

## Determine the Objective of the Test

The objective of tests of controls is to provide evidence about the design or operating effectiveness of internal control structure policies and procedures. The auditors perform tests of controls to support their planned assessed level of control risk. Accordingly, an attributes sample will be selected and tested to provide evidence that a particular internal control structure procedure is operating adequately to support the auditors' planned assessed level of control risk.

## Define the Attributes and "Deviation" Conditions

The auditors use professional judgment to define the attributes and deviation conditions for a particular test of controls. *Attributes* are characteristics that provide evidence that an internal control procedure was actually performed. An example is the existence of the initials of the individual performing the internal control procedure on the appropriate document. When a sample item does not have one or more of the attributes it is classified as a *deviation*. Usually several different conditions indicate that an internal control policy or procedure was not properly performed. As an example, assume that the auditors are performing a test of controls for the valuation of sales transactions. One of the control procedures that the auditors decide to test is the review of sales invoices that is performed by an accounting clerk. The clerk's review includes: (1) comparing quantities on each invoice to shipping documents, (2) comparing prices on each invoice to authorized price lists, (3) testing the clerical accuracy of each invoice, and (4) initialing a copy of the invoice to indicate that the procedure was performed. In performing the test of this control procedure, the auditors would classify a transaction as a deviation if any one or more of the following deviation conditions exist:

1.   The invoice copy is not initialed by the accounting clerk.
2.   The quantities on the invoice do not agree with the shipping documents.
3.   The prices on the invoice do not agree with authorized price lists.
4.   The invoice has a clerical inaccuracy.

It is important that the attributes and deviation conditions be precisely defined before the test of control is performed; otherwise, a staff accountant may not make the appropriate decision about which sample items represent deviations.

If a document selected for testing cannot be located, the auditors generally will not be able to apply alternate procedures to determine whether the control was applied. Simply selecting another item is *not* appropriate. In such circumstances, at a minimum, the misplaced document should be treated as a deviation for evaluation purposes. Also, because the disappearance of documents is consistent with many possible explanations, ranging from unintentional misfiling to material irregularities, the auditors should carefully consider the overall implications of the situation.

## Define the Population

The auditors should determine that the population from which the sample is to be selected is appropriate for the specific audit objective. For example, if the auditors wish to test the operating effectiveness of an internal control procedure designed to ensure that all shipments have been recorded as sales, they will *not* select a sample from the sales journal—that population is created by recorded sales and could not be expected to contain shipments that were not recorded. The appropriate population for detecting such deviations would be a population that contains all of the items shipped (e.g., the file of shipping documents).

## Specify the Risk of Assessing Control Risk Too Low and the Tolerable Deviation Rate

How do auditors determine the appropriate risk of assessing control risk too low and the tolerable deviation rate for a test of a control? The answer, in short, is *professional judgment*. The risk of assessing control risk too low—that is, the risk that the actual deviation rate *exceeds* the tolerable deviation rate—is a critical risk in tests of controls. As discussed previously, this risk impacts the effectiveness of the audit. Since the results of tests of controls play a major role in determining the nature, timing, and extent of other audit procedures, auditors usually specify a low level of risk—5 or 10 percent is often used.[3]

Auditors specify the tolerable deviation rate based on (1) their planned assessed level of control risk, and (2) the degree of assurance desired from the evidential matter in the sample. The lower the planned assessed level of control risk (or more assurance desired from the sample), the lower the tolerable deviation rate.

---

The AICPA's *Audit Sampling Guide* includes the following overlapping ranges to illustrate the relationship between the planned assessed level of control risk and the tolerable deviation rate:

| Planned Assessed Level of Control Risk | Tolerable Deviation Rate |
|---|---|
| Low | 2%–7% |
| Moderate | 6%–12% |
| Slightly below the maximum | 11%–20% |
| Maximum | omit test |

---

## Estimate the Expected Population Deviation Rate

In addition to the tolerable deviation rate and the risk of assessing control risk too low, the expected population deviation rate also affects the sample size in attributes sampling. This expected deviation rate is significant because it represents the rate that the auditors expect to discover in their sample from the population.

In estimating the expected population deviation rate, the auditors often use the sample results from prior years, as documented in their working papers. The auditors may also estimate the rate based on their experience with similar tests for other clients or by examining a small pilot sample.

## Determine the Sample Size

As indicated above, the three major factors that determine the sample size for a test of control are the risk of assessing control risk too low, the tolerable deviation rate, and the expected population deviation rate. The population size also has an effect on sample size,

---

[3]Some sources use the term *confidence level* to represent the complement of the risk of assessing control risk too low. Thus, a 95 percent confidence level is identical to a 5 percent risk of assessing control risk too low (100 percent − 5 percent).

Figure 10–3   Factors Affecting Sample Size for Tests of Controls

| Factor | Change in Factor | Effect upon Required Sample Size |
|---|---|---|
| **Auditors' requirements:** | | |
| Risk of assessing control risk too low | Increase | Decrease |
| Tolerable deviation rate | Increase | Decrease |
| **Population characteristics:** | | |
| Population deviation rate (expected) | Increase | Increase |
| Population size | Increase | Increase (if population is small) |

but only when the population is very small. Figure 10–3 summarizes the effects of these factors on the required sample size for a test of controls.

Tables to Determine Sample Size.   To enable auditors to use attributes sampling without resorting to complex mathematical formulas, tables such as the ones in Figures 10–4 and 10–5 have been developed.

Figures 10–4 and 10–5 may be used to determine required sample sizes at a 5 or 10 percent risk of assessing control risk too low, respectively. The horizontal axis of each figure is the tolerable deviation rate specified by the auditors. The vertical axis is the deviation rate estimated by the auditors to exist within the population. The numbers in the body of the table indicate the required sample sizes. The number in parentheses shown after the required sample size is the allowable number of deviations that may be observed in the sample for the results to support the auditors' planned assessed level of control risk.[4]

To use Figures 10–4 and 10–5, the auditors stipulate the expected deviation rate in the population and the tolerable deviation rate.[5] The appropriate table is selected based on the desired risk of assessing control risk too low. Then, the auditors read the sample size from the table at the intersection of the stipulated tolerable deviation rate and the expected population deviation rate. For example, assume that the auditors specify a 5 percent risk of assessing control risk too low, allowing them to use Figure 10–4 to determine the required sample size. They estimate the deviation rate in the population to be 1 percent and specify a 9 percent tolerable deviation rate to justify their planned assessed level of control risk related to this control procedure. Figure 10–4 shows that these specifications result in a sample size of 51 items, which must contain no more than 1 control procedure deviation if the auditors' planned control risk assessment is to be supported by the test.

---

[4]The number of deviations allowable in a sample sometimes exceeds the estimated deviation rate multiplied by the sample size. This is because the allowable number of deviations is always rounded to the nearest whole number as it is not possible to observe a partial deviation in a sample item. The sample sizes have been adjusted to reflect this rounding.

[5]Some tables require the auditors to specify population size. Figures 10–4 through 10–7 assume an infinite population. When populations are finite required sample sizes are only slightly smaller.

Figure 10–4     Statistical Sample Sizes for Tests of Controls 5 Percent Risk of Assessing Control Risk Too Low
                (with allowable number of deviations in parentheses)

| Expected Population Deviation Rate (in percentage) | Tolerable Deviation Rate | | | | | | | | | | |
|---|---|---|---|---|---|---|---|---|---|---|---|
| | 2% | 3% | 4% | 5% | 6% | 7% | 8% | 9% | 10% | 15% | 20% |
| 0.00% | 149(0) | 99(0) | 74(0) | 59(0) | 49(0) | 42(0) | 36(0) | 32(0) | 29(0) | 19(0) | 14(0) |
| 0.25 | 236(1) | 157(1) | 117(1) | 93(1) | 78(1) | 66(1) | 58(1) | 51(1) | 46(1) | 30(1) | 22(1) |
| 0.50 | * | 157(1) | 117(1) | 93(1) | 78(1) | 66(1) | 58(1) | 51(1) | 46(1) | 30(1) | 22(1) |
| 0.75 | * | 208(2) | 117(1) | 93(1) | 78(1) | 66(1) | 58(1) | 51(1) | 46(1) | 30(1) | 22(1) |
| 1.00 | * | * | 156(2) | 93(1) | 78(1) | 66(1) | 58(1) | 51(1) | 46(1) | 30(1) | 22(1) |
| 1.25 | * | * | 156(2) | 124(2) | 78(1) | 66(1) | 58(1) | 51(1) | 46(1) | 30(1) | 22(1) |
| 1.50 | * | * | 192(3) | 124(2) | 103(2) | 66(1) | 58(1) | 51(1) | 46(1) | 30(1) | 22(1) |
| 1.75 | * | * | 227(4) | 153(3) | 103(2) | 88(2) | 77(2) | 51(1) | 46(1) | 30(1) | 22(1) |
| 2.00 | * | * | * | 181(4) | 127(3) | 88(2) | 77(2) | 68(2) | 46(1) | 30(1) | 22(1) |
| 2.25 | * | * | * | 208(5) | 127(3) | 88(2) | 77(2) | 68(2) | 61(2) | 30(1) | 22(1) |
| 2.50 | * | * | * | * | 150(4) | 109(3) | 77(2) | 68(2) | 61(2) | 30(1) | 22(1) |
| 2.75 | * | * | * | * | 173(5) | 109(3) | 95(3) | 68(2) | 61(2) | 30(1) | 22(1) |
| 3.00 | * | * | * | * | 195(6) | 129(4) | 95(3) | 84(3) | 61(2) | 30(1) | 22(1) |
| 3.25 | * | * | * | * | * | 148(5) | 112(4) | 84(3) | 61(2) | 30(1) | 22(1) |
| 3.50 | * | * | * | * | * | 167(6) | 112(4) | 84(3) | 76(3) | 40(2) | 22(1) |
| 3.75 | * | * | * | * | * | 185(7) | 129(5) | 100(4) | 76(3) | 40(2) | 22(1) |
| 4.00 | * | * | * | * | * | * | 146(6) | 100(4) | 89(4) | 40(2) | 22(1) |
| 5.00 | * | * | * | * | * | * | * | 158(8) | 116(6) | 40(2) | 30(2) |
| 6.00 | * | * | * | * | * | * | * | * | 179(11) | 50(3) | 30(2) |
| 7.00 | * | * | * | * | * | * | * | * | * | 68(5) | 37(3) |

Note: This table assumes a large population.
*Sample size is too large to be cost effective for most audit applications.
Source: AICPA, Audit and Accounting Guide, *Audit Sampling* (New York, 1983).

## Select the Sample

When the auditors are using attributes sampling, it is essential that the sample items are selected in a random manner. Random samples may be selected using random number tables, random number generators, or systematic sampling. When selecting the sample items, the auditors often select extra items to be substituted for any voided, unused, or inapplicable items. An inapplicable item is one that would not be expected to have a particular attribute. For example, assume the auditors are testing a sample of cash disbursement transactions to determine that they are all supported with receiving reports. If a rent payment is selected, the item would be inapplicable, because it would not be expected to be supported with a receiving report.

## Test the Sample Items

When testing the sample items, an auditor examines each sample item for the attributes of interest. Each item will be classified as to whether or not it contains a deviation from the prescribed internal control procedure. The auditor performing the test should also be

Figure 10–5   Statistical Sample Sizes for Tests of Controls 10 Percent Risk of Assessing Control Risk Too Low (with allowable number of deviations in parentheses)

| Expected Population Deviation Rate | Tolerable Deviation Rate | | | | | | | | | | |
|---|---|---|---|---|---|---|---|---|---|---|---|
| | **2%** | **3%** | **4%** | **5%** | **6%** | **7%** | **8%** | **9%** | **10%** | **15%** | **20%** |
| 0.00% | 114(0) | 76(0) | 57(0) | 45(0) | 38(0) | 32(0) | 28(0) | 25(0) | 22(0) | 15(0) | 11(0) |
| 0.25 | 194(1) | 129(1) | 96(1) | 77(1) | 64(1) | 55(1) | 48(1) | 42(1) | 38(1) | 25(1) | 18(1) |
| 0.50 | 194(1) | 129(1) | 96(1) | 77(1) | 64(1) | 55(1) | 48(1) | 42(1) | 38(1) | 25(1) | 18(1) |
| 0.75 | 265(2) | 129(1) | 96(1) | 77(1) | 64(1) | 55(1) | 48(1) | 42(1) | 38(1) | 25(1) | 18(1) |
| 1.00 | * | 176(2) | 96(1) | 77(1) | 64(1) | 55(1) | 48(1) | 42(1) | 38(1) | 25(1) | 18(1) |
| 1.25 | * | 221(3) | 132(2) | 77(1) | 64(1) | 55(1) | 48(1) | 42(1) | 38(1) | 25(1) | 18(1) |
| 1.50 | * | * | 132(2) | 105(2) | 64(1) | 55(1) | 48(1) | 42(1) | 38(1) | 25(1) | 18(1) |
| 1.75 | * | * | 166(3) | 105(2) | 88(2) | 55(1) | 48(1) | 42(1) | 38(1) | 25(1) | 18(1) |
| 2.00 | * | * | 198(4) | 132(3) | 88(2) | 75(2) | 48(1) | 42(1) | 38(1) | 25(1) | 18(1) |
| 2.25 | * | * | * | 132(3) | 88(2) | 75(2) | 65(2) | 42(1) | 38(1) | 25(1) | 18(1) |
| 2.50 | * | * | * | 158(4) | 110(3) | 75(2) | 65(2) | 58(2) | 38(1) | 25(1) | 18(1) |
| 2.75 | * | * | * | 209(6) | 132(4) | 94(3) | 65(2) | 58(2) | 52(2) | 25(1) | 18(1) |
| 3.00 | * | * | * | * | 132(4) | 94(3) | 65(2) | 58(2) | 52(2) | 25(1) | 18(1) |
| 3.25 | * | * | * | * | 153(5) | 113(4) | 82(3) | 58(2) | 52(2) | 25(1) | 18(1) |
| 3.50 | * | * | * | * | 194(7) | 113(4) | 82(3) | 73(3) | 52(2) | 25(1) | 18(1) |
| 3.75 | * | * | * | * | * | 131(5) | 98(4) | 73(3) | 52(2) | 25(1) | 18(1) |
| 4.00 | * | * | * | * | * | 149(6) | 98(4) | 73(3) | 65(3) | 25(1) | 18(1) |
| 5.00 | * | * | * | * | * | * | 160(8) | 115(6) | 78(4) | 34(2) | 18(1) |
| 6.00 | * | * | * | * | * | * | * | 182(11) | 116(7) | 43(3) | 25(2) |
| 7.00 | * | * | * | * | * | * | * | * | 199(14) | 52(4) | 25(2) |

Note: This table assumes a large population.
*Sample size is too large to be cost effective for most audit applications.
Source: AICPA, Audit and Accounting Guide, *Audit Sampling* (New York, 1983).

alert for evidence of any unusual matters, such as evidence of fraud or related party transactions.

## Evaluate the Sample Results

After testing the sample items and summarizing the deviations from a prescribed internal control procedure, the auditors evaluate the sample results. In evaluating the results the auditors must consider not only the actual number of deviations observed, but also the nature of the deviations. The auditors' evaluation will include the following four steps:

1.  *Determine the deviation rate.* Calculating the deviation rate in the sample involves dividing the number of observed deviations by the sample size.

2.  *Determine the achieved upper deviation rate.* The auditors will use a computer program or table to determine the achieved upper deviation rate (also referred to as the *achieved upper precision limit*). This deviation rate represents the maximum population deviation rate that the auditors can expect based on the results of the sample.

3.  *Consider the qualitative aspects of the deviations.* In addition to considering the deviation rate in the sample, the auditors will consider the nature of the deviations and any implications for other phases of the audit. Deviations that result from intentional acts (irregularities) are of much more concern than those that are due to misunderstanding of instructions or carelessness.

4.  *Reach an overall conclusion.* The auditors will combine the sample evidence with the results of other relevant tests of controls to determine if the combined results support the auditors' planned assessed level of control risk. If not, the auditors will increase the assessed level of control risk which will result in an increase in the extent of the planned substantive tests.

Tables to Evaluate Sample Results.   Figures 10−6 and 10−7 allow auditors to obtain the *achieved upper deviation rate* from a sample result. The achieved upper deviation rate is the actual maximum deviation rate that is supported by the sample results. When the achieved upper deviation rate is more than the tolerable deviation rate, the planned assessed level of control risk relating to the control procedure is not supported.

To illustrate evaluation of a sample, assume that 2 deviations are found in the sample of 51. As indicated previously, the auditors selected this sample with a specified risk of

---

**Figure 10−6**   Statistical Sampling Results Evaluation Table for Tests of Controls: Achieved Upper Deviation Rate at 5 Percent Risk of Assessing Control Risk Too Low

| Sample Size | **Actual Number of Deviations Found** | | | | | | | | | | |
| --- | --- | --- | --- | --- | --- | --- | --- | --- | --- | --- | --- |
| | **0** | **1** | **2** | **3** | **4** | **5** | **6** | **7** | **8** | **9** | **10** |
| 25 | 11.3 | 17.6 | * | * | * | * | * | * | * | * | * |
| 30 | 9.5 | 14.9 | 19.6 | * | * | * | * | * | * | * | * |
| 35 | 8.3 | 12.9 | 17.0 | * | * | * | * | * | * | * | * |
| 40 | 7.3 | 11.4 | 15.0 | 18.3 | * | * | * | * | * | * | * |
| 45 | 6.5 | 10.2 | 13.4 | 16.4 | 19.2 | * | * | * | * | * | * |
| 50 | 5.9 | 9.2 | 12.1 | 14.8 | 17.4 | 19.9 | * | * | * | * | * |
| 55 | 5.4 | 8.4 | 11.1 | 13.5 | 15.9 | 18.2 | * | * | * | * | * |
| 60 | 4.9 | 7.7 | 10.2 | 12.5 | 14.7 | 16.8 | 18.8 | * | * | * | * |
| 65 | 4.6 | 7.1 | 9.4 | 11.5 | 13.6 | 15.5 | 17.4 | 19.3 | * | * | * |
| 70 | 4.2 | 6.6 | 8.8 | 10.8 | 12.6 | 14.5 | 16.3 | 18.0 | 19.7 | * | * |
| 75 | 4.0 | 6.2 | 8.2 | 10.1 | 11.8 | 13.6 | 15.2 | 16.9 | 18.5 | 20.0 | * |
| 80 | 3.7 | 5.8 | 7.7 | 9.5 | 11.1 | 12.7 | 14.3 | 15.9 | 17.4 | 18.9 | * |
| 90 | 3.3 | 5.2 | 6.9 | 8.4 | 9.9 | 11.4 | 12.8 | 14.2 | 15.5 | 16.8 | 18.2 |
| 100 | 3.0 | 4.7 | 6.2 | 7.6 | 9.0 | 10.3 | 11.5 | 12.8 | 14.0 | 15.2 | 16.4 |
| 125 | 2.4 | 3.8 | 5.0 | 6.1 | 7.2 | 8.3 | 9.3 | 10.3 | 11.3 | 12.3 | 13.2 |
| 150 | 2.0 | 3.2 | 4.2 | 5.1 | 6.0 | 6.9 | 7.8 | 8.6 | 9.5 | 10.3 | 11.1 |
| 200 | 1.5 | 2.4 | 3.2 | 3.9 | 4.6 | 5.2 | 5.9 | 6.5 | 7.2 | 7.8 | 8.4 |

Note: This table presents upper limits as percentages. This table assumes a large population.
*Over 20 percent.
Source: AICPA, Audit and Accounting Guide, *Audit Sampling* (New York, 1983).

Figure 10–7   Statistical Sampling Results Evaluation Table for Tests of Controls: Achieved Upper Deviation Rate at 10 Percent Risk of Assessing Control Risk Too Low

| Sample Size | Actual Number of Deviations Found | | | | | | | | | | |
|---|---|---|---|---|---|---|---|---|---|---|---|
| | **0** | **1** | **2** | **3** | **4** | **5** | **6** | **7** | **8** | **9** | **10** |
| 20 | 10.9 | 18.1 | * | * | * | * | * | * | * | * | * |
| 25 | 8.8 | 14.7 | 19.9 | * | * | * | * | * | * | * | * |
| 30 | 7.4 | 12.4 | 16.8 | * | * | * | * | * | * | * | * |
| 35 | 6.4 | 10.7 | 14.5 | 18.1 | * | * | * | * | * | * | * |
| 40 | 5.6 | 9.4 | 12.8 | 16.0 | 19.0 | * | * | * | * | * | * |
| 45 | 5.0 | 8.4 | 11.4 | 14.3 | 17.0 | 19.7 | * | * | * | * | * |
| 50 | 4.6 | 7.6 | 10.3 | 12.9 | 15.4 | 17.8 | * | * | * | * | * |
| 55 | 4.1 | 6.9 | 9.4 | 11.8 | 14.1 | 16.3 | 18.4 | * | * | * | * |
| 60 | 3.8 | 6.4 | 8.7 | 10.8 | 12.9 | 15.0 | 16.9 | 18.9 | * | * | * |
| 70 | 3.3 | 5.5 | 7.5 | 9.3 | 11.1 | 12.9 | 14.6 | 16.3 | 17.9 | 19.6 | * |
| 80 | 2.9 | 4.8 | 6.6 | 8.2 | 9.8 | 11.3 | 12.8 | 14.3 | 15.8 | 17.2 | 18.6 |
| 90 | 2.6 | 4.3 | 5.9 | 7.3 | 8.7 | 10.1 | 11.5 | 12.8 | 14.1 | 15.4 | 16.6 |
| 100 | 2.3 | 3.9 | 5.3 | 6.6 | 7.9 | 9.1 | 10.3 | 11.5 | 12.7 | 13.9 | 15.0 |
| 120 | 2.0 | 3.3 | 4.4 | 5.5 | 6.6 | 7.6 | 8.7 | 9.7 | 10.7 | 11.6 | 12.6 |
| 160 | 1.5 | 2.5 | 3.3 | 4.2 | 5.0 | 5.8 | 6.5 | 7.3 | 8.0 | 8.8 | 9.5 |
| 200 | 1.2 | 2.0 | 2.7 | 3.4 | 4.0 | 4.6 | 5.3 | 5.9 | 6.5 | 7.1 | 7.6 |

Note: This table presents upper limits as percentages. This table assumes a large population.
*Over 20 percent.
Source: AICPA, Audit and Accounting Guide, *Audit Sampling* (New York, 1983).

assessing control risk too low of 5 percent and a tolerable deviation rate of 9 percent. Referring to Figure 10–6, we find that the exact sample size of 51 does not appear. When this happens the auditors may interpolate; use more detailed tables, sometimes generated by a computer program; or use the largest sample size listed on the table that does not exceed the sample size actually selected. Using the latter approach, we evaluate the results using a slightly smaller size of 50. Figure 10–6 indicates that when 2 deviations are found in a sample size of 50, the achieved upper deviation rate is 12.1 percent. This tells the auditors that, statistically, there is a 5 percent chance that the actual deviation rate is higher than 12.1 percent; but this exceeds the 9 percent tolerable deviation rate. The most likely effect of this sample result will be an increase in the assessed level of control risk, with a corresponding increase in the scope of substantive testing for the related financial statement assertions. Only when the upper deviation rate found in Figure 10–6 (or Figure 10–7 if testing at a 10 percent risk level) is less than or equal to the tolerable deviation rate would the sample results support the auditors' planned assessed level of control risk.

## Document the Sampling Procedure

Finally, the auditors will document the significant aspects of the prior nine steps in the working papers.

## Detailed Illustration of Attributes Sampling

The following procedures for applying attributes sampling are based upon the use of the tables in Figure 10–4 and 10–6; however, only slight modifications of the approach are necessary if other tables are used.

1. *Determine the objective of the test.*    Assume that the auditors wish to test the effectiveness of the client's internal control procedure of matching receiving reports with purchase invoices as a step in authorizing payments for purchases of materials. They are interested in the clerical accuracy of the matching process and in determining whether the control procedure that requires the matching of purchase invoices and receiving reports is operating effectively.

2. *Define the attributes and deviation conditions.*    The auditors define the deviation conditions as any one or more of the following with respect to each invoice and the related receiving report:

*a.*   Any invoice not supported by a receiving document.

*b.*   Any invoice supported by a receiving document that is applicable to another invoice.

*c.*   Any difference between the invoice and the receiving document as to quantities shipped.

For this test, the only procedure required is inspection of the documents and matching of the receiving reports with invoices.

3. *Define the population to be sampled.*    The client prepares a serially numbered **voucher** for every purchase of materials. The receiving report and purchase invoice are attached to each voucher. Therefore, the sampling unit for the test is an individual voucher. Since the test of controls is being performed during the interim period, the population to be tested consists of 3,653 vouchers for purchases of material during the first 10 months of the year under audit. If at any point the auditor determines that the physical representation of the population (the 3,653 vouchers) has omitted vouchers that should be included in the first 10 months, the auditors should also test those vouchers.

4. *Specify the risk of assessing control risk too low and the tolerable deviation rate.*    The auditors realize that errors in matching receiving reports with purchase orders can affect the financial statements through overpayments to vendors and misstatements of purchases and accounts payable. They also plan to assess control risk at a low level for the assertions of existence, occurrence, and valuation of purchases, inventories, and accounts payable. Based on these considerations, the auditors decide upon a tolerable deviation rate of 7 percent, with a 5 percent risk of assessing control risk too low.

5. *Estimate the expected population deviation rate.*    In the audits of the previous three years, the auditors observed that exceptions for the type described above produced deviation rates of 1.2 percent, 1.3 percent, and 1.1 percent. Therefore, the auditors conservatively select an *expected deviation rate* of 1.5 percent.

6. *Determine the sample size.*    Since the stipulated risk of assessing control risk too low is 5 percent, Figure 10–4 is applicable. At the intersection of the column for a tolerable deviation rate of 7 percent and the row for a 1.5 percent expected deviation rate, the sample size is found to be 66 items. The allowable number of deviations in the sample is one.

7. *Select the sample.*    Since the vouchers are serially numbered, the auditors decide to use a generalized audit software program to generate a list of random numbers to select the sample for testing.

8. *Test the sample items.*   The auditors proceed to examine the vouchers and supporting documents for each of the types of deviations previously defined. As they perform the test, the auditors will be alert for any unusual matters, such as evidence of fraud.

9. *Evaluate the sample results.*   In evaluating the sample results, the auditors consider not only the actual number of deviations observed, but also the nature of the deviations. We will discuss three possible sets of circumstances: (1) the actual number of deviations is equal to or less than, the allowable number; (2) the actual number of deviations is more than the allowable number; and (3) one or more deviations observed contain evidence of a deliberate manipulation or circumvention of internal control.

First, assume that one deviation has been identified and there is no evidence of a deliberate manipulation or circumvention of the internal control structure. Recall that the allowable number of deviations from Figure 10–4 was one. Because the number of deviations (here, one) did not exceed the allowable number, the auditors may conclude that there is less than a 5 percent risk that the population deviation rate is greater than 7 percent. In this case, the sample results support the auditors' planned assessed level of control risk.

Next, assume that the number of deviations observed in the sample is three, and none of the observed deviations indicate deliberate manipulation or circumvention of internal control. Because this exceeds the allowable one deviation, the achieved upper deviation rate is greater than 7 percent. Referring to Figure 10–6, for a sample size of 65 (the highest number still less than the actual sample size), the auditors find that when three deviations are observed the achieved upper deviation rate is 11.5 percent. In light of these results, the auditors should increase the assessed level of control risk in this area and increase the extent of their substantive testing procedures (i.e., decrease detection risk). As a preliminary step to any modification of their audit program, the auditors should investigate the cause of the unexpectedly high deviation rate.

Finally, assume that one or more of the deviations discovered by the auditors indicates an irregularity such as circumvention of the internal control structure. In such a circumstance other auditing procedures become necessary. The auditors must evaluate the effect of the deviation on the financial statements and adopt auditing procedures that are specifically designed to detect the type of deviation observed. Indeed, the nature of the deviation may be more important than its rate of occurrence.

10. *Document the sampling procedures.*   Finally, each of the nine prior steps, as well as the basis for overall conclusions, should be documented in the auditors' working papers. Figure 10–8 is an illustrative working paper that documents the results of this test of controls, as well as tests of other controls for the purchasing cycle.

## Other Statistical Attributes Sampling Approaches

### Discovery Sampling.
Discovery sampling is actually a modified case of attributes sampling. The purpose of a discovery sample is to detect at least *one deviation,* with a predetermined risk of assessing control risk too low, if the deviation rate in the population is greater than the specified tolerable deviation rate. One important use of discovery sampling is to locate examples of a suspected fraud.

Although discovery sampling is designed to locate relatively rare items, it cannot locate a needle in a haystack. If an extremely small number of deviations exist within a population (e.g., 0.1 percent or less), no sample of reasonable size can provide adequate

Figure 10-8   Documentation of the Results of Tests of Controls

Scantech Inc.                                                            R-22
Attributes Sampling Summary—Purchase Transactions                        WEB
December 31, 19X2                                                         11/23/X1

**Objectives of test:**   (1) To test the operating effectiveness of the procedures for matching receiving reports with purchase invoices; (2) To test the operating effectiveness of the procedures for matching purchase orders with purchase invoices; (3) To test the operating effectiveness of the procedures for testing the clerical accuracy of purchase invoices.

**Population:**   Voucher register entries for the first ten months of the year    **Size:**  3,653

**Sampling unit:**   Individual vouchers

**Random selection procedure:**   Random number generator

**Risk of assessing control risk too low:**   5 percent

| | Planning Parameters: | | | Sample Results: | |
|---|---|---|---|---|---|
| Attributes Tested: | Tolerable Deviation Rate | Expected Deviation Rate | Sample Size | Number of Deviations | Achieved Maximum Rate |
| 1.  Quantity and other data on receiving report agree with purchase invoice. | 7% | 1.5% | 66 | 1 | 7% |
| 2.  Prices and other data on purchase order agree with purchase invoice. | 10% | 1% | 46 | 0 | 6.5% |
| 3.  Clerical accuracy of purchase invoice has been verified. | 7% | 0% | 42 | 0 | 7% |

**Conclusion:**   The results support the assessment of a low level of control risk for existence and valuation of purchases, inventory and accounts payable.

assurance that an example of the deviation will be encountered. Still, discovery sampling can (with a very high degree of confidence) ensure detection of deviations occurring at a rate as low as 0.3 to 1 percent.

Discovery sampling is used primarily to search for *critical deviations*. When a deviation is critical, such as evidence of fraud, any deviation rate may be intolerable. Consequently, if such deviation is discovered, the auditors may abandon their sampling procedures and undertake a thorough examination of the population. If no deviations are found in discovery sampling, the auditors may conclude (with the specified risk of assessing control risk too low) that the critical deviation does not occur to the extent of the tolerable deviation rate.

To use discovery sampling, the auditors must specify their desired risk of assessing control risk too low and the tolerable deviation rate for the test. The required sample size then may be determined by referring to an appropriate attribute sampling table, *with the assumption that the expected deviation rate in the population is 0 percent.*

To illustrate discovery sampling, assume that auditors have reason to suspect that someone has been preparing fraudulent purchase orders, receiving reports, and purchase invoices in order to generate cash disbursements for fictitious purchase transactions. In order to determine whether this has occurred, it is necessary to locate only one set of the fraudulent documents in the client's file of paid vouchers.

Assume the auditors desire a 5 percent risk that their sample will not bring to light a fraudulent voucher if the population contains 2 percent or more fraudulent items. Referring to Figure 10–4, the auditors find that a sample size of 149 is required for an expected population deviation rate of zero percent and a tolerable deviation rate of 2 percent. Assuming that the auditors select and examine the 149 vouchers and no fraudulent vouchers are found, they may conclude that there is only a 5 percent risk that there are more than 2 percent fraudulent vouchers in the population.

Sequential (Stop-or-Go) Sampling.   Another approach used in practice is **sequential (stop-or-go) sampling.** Under a sequential sampling plan, the audit sample is taken in several stages. The auditors start by examining a small sample. Then, based on the results of this initial sample, they decide whether to (1) assess control risk at the planned level, (2) assess control risk at a higher level than planned, or (3) examine additional sample items to get more information. If the sample results do not provide enough information to make a clear-cut decision about internal control, the auditors examine additional items and repeat the decision process until the tables being used indicate that a decision as to the assessed level of control risk can be made.

The primary advantage of a sequential approach is that for very low population deviation rates lower sample sizes may be required as compared to the fixed-sized sample plans. Disadvantages of sequential approaches include the fact that sample sizes may be larger for populations with moderate deviation rates and the process of drawing samples at several stages may not be as efficient.

## Nonstatistical Attributes Sampling

The major differences between statistical and nonstatistical sampling in attributes sampling are the steps for determining sample size and for evaluating sample results. As is the case with statistical sampling, auditors who use nonstatistical sampling need to consider the risk of assessing control risk too low and the tolerable deviation rate when determining the required sample size. But these factors need not be quantified. When evaluating results, the auditors should compare the deviation rate of the sample to the tolerable deviation rate. If the sample size was appropriate and the sample deviation rate is somewhat lower than the tolerable deviation rate, the auditors can generally conclude that the risk of assessing control risk too low is at an acceptable level. As the sample deviation rate gets closer to the tolerable deviation rate, it becomes less and less likely that the population's deviation rate is lower than the tolerable level. The auditors must use their professional judgment to determine the point at which the assessed level of control risk should be increased above the planned level.

# AUDIT SAMPLING FOR SUBSTANTIVE TESTS

Substantive tests are designed to detect misstatements, both errors and irregularities, that exist in the financial statements. The sampling plans that are used for substantive tests are designed to estimate the dollar amount of misstatements in a particular account balance or class of transactions. Based on the sample result, the auditors then conclude whether there is an unacceptably high risk of material misstatement in the balance.

## Sampling Risk for Substantive Tests

Similar to sampling risk for tests of controls, there are two aspects of sampling risk for substantive tests, including:

1.  The risk of **incorrect rejection** (alpha risk) of an account. This is the possibility that sample results will indicate that an account balance is materially misstated when, in fact, it is not misstated.

2.  The risk of **incorrect acceptance** (beta risk) of an account. This is the possibility that sample results will indicate that an account balance is *not* materially misstated when, in fact, it is materially misstated.

Figure 10-9   Sampling Risk for Substantive Tests

| The Substantive Test Sample Indicates: | The Population Actually Is: | |
|---|---|---|
| | Not Materially Misstated | Materially Misstated |
| The population is not materially misstated | Correct decision | Incorrect decision (risk of incorrect acceptance) |
| The population is materially misstated | Incorrect decision (risk of incorrect rejection) | Correct decision |

The nature of these risks parallels the sampling risks of tests of controls. If the auditors make the first type of error and incorrectly reject an account balance, their audit will lack *efficiency* since they will perform additional audit procedures that will eventually reveal that the account is not materially misstated. Thus, the risk of incorrect rejection does not relate to the effectiveness of the audit.

If the auditors make the second type of error, incorrect acceptance, the *effectiveness* of the audit is compromised. Therefore, the risk of incorrect acceptance is of primary concern to auditors; failure to detect a material misstatement may lead to accusations of negligence and to extensive legal liability. Figure 10–9 illustrates both aspects of sampling risk for substantive tests.

# STATISTICAL SAMPLING FOR SUBSTANTIVE TESTS

As indicated previously, there are several statistical techniques that enable the auditors to estimate the dollar amount of an account balance. These techniques include classical variables sampling plans and probability-proportional-to-size sampling. Regardless of the technique used, audit sampling for substantive tests involves the following eight steps:

1.  Determine the objective of the test.
2.  Define the population and sampling unit.
3.  Choose an audit sampling technique.
4.  Determine the sample size.
5.  Select the sample.
6.  Test the sample items.
7.  Evaluate the sample results.
8.  Document the sampling procedure.

## Determine the Objective of the Test

When using audit sampling for substantive tests, the auditors' objective is to test the reasonableness of one or more assertions about a financial statement balance, for example, the existence of accounts receivable. In achieving this objective the auditors use the sample results to estimate the total amount of misstatement in the balance.

## Define the Population and Sampling Unit

The population consists of all the items that constitute the financial statement balance. The auditors must determine that the population selected is appropriate for the objective of the test. For example, when performing a substantive test of completeness of accounts payable, the auditors would not define the population as the recorded accounts, because an unrecorded account could not be selected from that population. The appropriate population would be one that may include unrecorded items, such as the population of cash disbursements made after the financial statement date.

The auditors must also define the sampling unit. The *sampling unit* is any of the individual elements that constitute the population. A particular population may have several potential sampling units. For example, when confirming accounts receivable the auditors may decide to use either individual account balances or invoice amounts as the sampling unit. In this case the sampling unit that is easiest for the customers to confirm would probably be selected.

## Choose an Audit Sampling Technique

Assuming that the auditors have decided to use statistical techniques for the substantive test, the auditors generally must decide whether to use classical variables or probability-proportional-to-size sampling. In making this decision, the auditors will consider the relative advantages and disadvantages of these statistical techniques, as described in Figure 10–10.

---

Figure 10–10    Relative Advantages and Disadvantages of Classical Variables Sampling and Probability-Proportional-to-Size Sampling

### Classical Variables Sampling

| Advantages | Disadvantages |
|---|---|
| 1. When there are many misstatements in the population, variables sampling techniques will result in a smaller sample size. | 1. To determine the sample size, the standard deviation of the population must be estimated. |
| 2. Items with zero and negative balances do not require any special treatment. | 2. To evaluate results, the sample's standard deviation must be calculated. |
| 3. Sample size may be somewhat easier to expand if that becomes necessary. | 3. Variables sampling (especially mean-per-unit) usually must be stratified, requiring the use of a computer to perform the computations. |

### Probability-Proportional-to-Size (PPS) Sampling

| Advantages | Disadvantages |
|---|---|
| 1. The technique is generally easier to use. | 1. Special considerations are required to handle understated amounts and negative balances. |
| 2. No estimate of the standard deviation of the population is needed. | 2. Each item in the population must have a book value. |
| 3. Automatically stratifies the population because items are selected based on their dollar amount. | 3. When misstatements are found, the technique might overstate the allowance for sampling risk. |
| 4. When there are few misstatements, the technique will generally result in a smaller sample size. | 4. For accounts with many misstatements, the sample size may exceed that of the classical techniques. |
| 5. Sample selection can begin before the entire population is available. | |

---

# Determine the Sample Size

Several factors determine the appropriate sample size for a substantive test, including:

1. Risk of incorrect rejection.
2. Risk of incorrect acceptance.
3. Tolerable misstatement.
4. Characteristics of the population.

Risk of Incorrect Rejection.   As indicated above, the risk of incorrect rejection relates directly to the efficiency of the audit. The effectiveness of the audit is not affected by this type of risk. However, rejecting a materially correct account balance may be quite costly in terms of the additional audit work that must be performed to determine that the original conclusion from the sample was not correct. Therefore, the auditors will often specify the risk of incorrect rejection based on a consideration of these potential costs.

Risk of Incorrect Acceptance.   The risk of incorrect acceptance relates directly to the effectiveness of the substantive test of details. It measures the extent of the evidence obtained from the test—the lower the risk of incorrect acceptance, the greater the amount of evidence obtained from the test. From the discussion in Chapter 6, we know that the extent of the substantive tests is determined by the levels of inherent and control risk for the assertions being tested. This relationship was illustrated by the formula for audit risk that is presented below:

$$AR = IR \times CR \times DR$$

where:

$AR$ = The allowable audit risk that a material misstatement might remain undetected for the account balance and related assertions.

$IR$ = Inherent risk, the risk of a material misstatement in an assertion, assuming there were no related internal controls.

$CR$ = Control risk, the risk that a material misstatement that could occur in an assertion will not be prevented or detected on a timely basis by the internal control structure.

$DR$ = Detection risk, the risk that the auditors' procedures will fail to detect a material misstatement if it exists.

Since substantive procedures may consist of both tests of details using sampling and other types of substantive tests, such as analytical procedures, one modification of this formula is necessary to calculate the risk of incorrect acceptance for a substantive test. Detection risk must be separated into two components:

$AP$ = the risk that analytical procedures and any other substantive procedures not using audit sampling will fail to detect a material misstatement.

$TD$ = the allowable risk of incorrect acceptance for the substantive test of details.

With this modification, the revised formula is presented below:

$$AR = IR \times CR \times AP \times TD$$

Mathematically we may rearrange the terms in the formula as follows to solve for the appropriate risk of incorrect acceptance for the substantive test of details:

$$TD = \frac{AR}{IR \times CR \times AP}$$

To illustrate, assume that the auditors are willing to accept a 5 percent audit risk of material misstatement in the assertion of existence of the client's accounts receivable. They believe that the inherent risk of that assertion is 100 percent. After considering internal control over the revenue cycle, they assess control risk at a level of 50 percent, and they believe that the analytical procedures performed to test the assertion have a 40 percent risk of failing to detect a material misstatement. The appropriate level of risk of incorrect acceptance may be calculated as follows:

$$TD = \frac{AR}{IR \times CR \times AP} = \frac{0.05}{(1.00) \times (0.50) \times (0.40)} = 0.25$$

Thus, the auditors must plan an audit sample for the substantive test of details with a risk of incorrect acceptance of 25 percent.

Implementing this formula in practice is quite difficult—it is not easy to precisely quantify the various levels of risks. For this reason, most CPA firms have implemented approaches that are less mathematical. However, the formula is useful in illustrating the relationships between the various types of risk. We know from the formula that in circumstances in which the auditors assess inherent risk and control risk as high and do not perform other effective tests of the assertion, the risk of incorrect acceptance must be set at a very low level. Decreases in inherent risk, control risk, or the risk that other procedures will fail to detect a material misstatement allow the auditors to accept a higher risk of incorrect acceptance for the substantive test of details.

Tolerable Misstatement.   The sample size also is affected by the amount of tolerable misstatement—that is, the maximum monetary misstatement that may exist in the account without causing the financial statements to be materially misstated. Tolerable misstatement for a particular account is directly related to the auditors' preliminary estimate of materiality for the audit, as described in Chapter 7. Tolerable misstatement amounts are determined by allocating overall materiality for the entire financial statements to the individual accounts.

Characteristics of the Population.   Certain characteristics of the population being audited affect the required sample size. As indicated previously, the population size affects the required sample size, but only when the population is small. If the auditors are using classical variables sampling, the size of the sample also is affected by the variability of the

Figure 10–11   Factors Affecting Sample Size for Substantive Tests

| Factor | Change in Factor | Effect upon Required Sample Size |
|---|---|---|
| **Auditors' requirements:** | | |
| Risk of incorrect rejection | Increase | Decrease |
| Risk of incorrect acceptance | Increase | Decrease |
| Tolerable misstatement | Increase | Decrease |
| **Population characteristics:** | | |
| Population size | Increase | Increase (if population is small) |
| Standard deviation (if classical variables sampling is used) | Increase | Increase |
| Expected misstatement | Increase | Increase |

items in the population. The larger the variability as measured by the **standard deviation,** the larger the required sample size. Of course, stratification of the population can be used to minimize the effects of variability in the population.

When the auditors use probability-proportional-to-size (PPS) sampling, the expected amount of misstatement in the population affects the required sample size. The larger the amount of expected misstatement, the larger the required sample size.[6]

Summary of the Factors Affecting Sample Size.   Figure 10–11 summarizes the effects of the various factors on the required sample size for a substantive test.

## Select the Sample

The method of selecting the sample will generally be determined by the sampling technique used. If a classical variables technique is being used, the population will normally be stratified and a computer program will be used to select the items within each stratum. If PPS sampling is used, a random sample of dollars from the population is selected using a random number generator, random number tables, or systematic selection. When a dollar is selected from a particular sampling unit, that unit is included in the sample.

## Test the Sample Items

After the sample is selected, the auditors will perform audit procedures to test each sample item. The audit procedures performed to test the items will allow the auditors to determine the *audited value* of each item. The difference between the book value of each item and its audited value is the amount of the item's misstatement.

---

[6]Although not modified in this text, classical sample size formulas may be adjusted to reflect expected misstatement by subtracting the expected misstatement from the tolerable misstatement. This will result in a larger required sample size.

In some circumstances, the auditors may not be able to apply audit procedures to particular sample items. This might occur, for example, because the necessary supporting documents are missing. If considering these unexamined items to be completely misstated (i.e., with an audited value of $0) will not cause the auditors to reject the account balance, the auditors may decide not to audit them. Otherwise, the auditors should attempt to devise alternative procedures that will provide sufficient evidence about the audited values of the items. In all cases, the auditors must consider the overall implications of the situation.

## Evaluate the Sample Results

In evaluating the results of a statistical sample for a substantive test, the auditors will perform the following three steps:

1. Project the sample misstatement to the population.
2. Consider sampling risk.
3. Consider the qualitative aspects of the misstatements.

Project the Sample Misstatement to the Population.   The auditors will use the sample results to estimate the total audited value of the population and the total amount of misstatement, the *projected misstatement* in the population. To illustrate one way this may be done, assume that a population of 2,000 accounts with a total book value of $8,000,000 is being audited. The population thus has an average book value of $4,000 ($8,000,000 / 2,000 accounts). Also, assume that the CPAs audited a random sample of 160 accounts from this population and that the tolerable misstatement amount was established as $300,000. When evaluating the sample the auditors found that the average audited value of the 160 accounts in the sample is $3,900.

Various methods are discussed in Chapter 11 for calculating the projected misstatement in the account. The *mean-per-unit* estimation method uses the average (mean) audited value of the sample to estimate the account's total audited value. In this example, the estimated total audited value is calculated to be $7,800,000 as shown below:

$$\text{Estimated total audited value} = \text{Mean audited value} \times \text{Number of accounts}$$
$$= \$3,900 \times 2,000 \text{ accounts}$$
$$= \$7,800,000$$

The projected misstatement is calculated as the difference between the estimated total audited value and the book value:

$$\text{Projected Misstatement} = \text{Estimated total audited value} - \text{Book value of the population}$$
$$= \$7,800,000 - \$8,000,000$$
$$= \$200,000 \text{ overstatement}$$

Consider Sampling Risk.   When statistical sampling is used for a substantive test, the auditors utilize statistical formulas to determine whether the account balance should be accepted. Continuing our example from the preceding section, assume that the auditors are applying a classical mean-per-unit variables sampling plan to the population. Application of this statistical technique will result in computation of an acceptance interval around the estimated total audited value. If the book value of the client's accounts receivable, here $8,000,000, falls within this interval, the auditors will accept the balance as being materially correct. Otherwise, the auditors will conclude that there is an unacceptably high risk that the inventory account is materially misstated.

In cases in which the client's book value falls *outside* the interval, the auditor must decide whether: (1) the client's book value is actually materially misstated or (2) the sample is not representative of the population. To decide which is the case, the auditors should carefully examine the misstatements found in the sample. For example, if few misstatements were found, this may indicate that the sample is not representative. Based on the results of this misstatement analysis, the auditors may decide to (1) increase the sample size of the test, (2) perform other audit tests of the account, or (3) work with the client's personnel to locate other misstated items in the account.

Consider the Qualitative Aspects of the Misstatements.   In addition to evaluating the frequency and amounts of the misstatements, the auditors will also consider their qualitative aspects. The discovery of an irregularity usually has much broader implications than the discovery of an error. In addition, the discovery of an unexpectedly large number of misstatements may cause the auditors to reassess control risk for the assertions about the account balance.

## Document the Sampling Procedure

Finally, the auditors will document all of the significant aspects of the prior seven steps in their working papers.

---

# ◆ CHAPTER SUMMARY

This chapter presented the concepts and techniques used by auditors to perform audit sampling. To summarize:

1.  Audit sampling is defined as applying an audit procedure to less than 100 percent of the items in a population to make some conclusion about that population.

2.  Auditors may use statistical or nonstatistical sampling to perform tests of controls or substantive tests. Statistical sampling allows the auditors to measure and control sampling risk. Sampling risk is the risk that the auditors will make an incorrect conclusion from the sample results, because the sample is not representative of the population.

3.  The major type of statistical sampling plan for tests of controls is attributes sampling, which can provide the auditors with an estimate of the extent of the deviations from a prescribed internal control policy or procedure.

4.  The two aspects of sampling risk for tests of controls include the risk of assessing control risk too high, which relates to the efficiency of the audit, and the risk of assessing control risk too low, which is critical because it relates to the effectiveness of the audit.

5.  The major factors that affect the required sample size for an attributes sample are the risk of assessing control risk too low, the tolerable deviation rate, and the expected deviation rate in the population.

6.  The two aspects of sampling risk for substantive tests include the risk of incorrect rejection and the risk of incorrect acceptance. The risk of incorrect acceptance is the critical risk, because if the auditors accept a materially misstated account balance, they may issue an inappropriate audit opinion.

7.  In performing sampling for substantive tests the auditors typically use classical variables sampling or probability-proportional-to-size sampling.

8.  The primary factors that affect the sample size for a substantive sample include the risk of incorrect acceptance, the amount of tolerable misstatement for the account, and the variance of items included in the account.

## ◆ KEY TERMS INTRODUCED OR EMPHASIZED IN CHAPTER 10

**Allowance for sampling risk (ASR, precision)**   An interval around the sample results in which the true population characteristic is expected to lie.

**Attributes sampling**   A sampling plan enabling the auditors to estimate the rate of deviation (occurrence) in a population.

**Deviation rate (occurrence rate, exception rate)**   A defined rate of departure from prescribed control procedures.

**Difference estimation**   A sampling plan that uses the difference between the audited (correct) values and book values of items in a sample to calculate the estimated total audited value of the population. Difference estimation is used in lieu of ratio estimation when the differences are not nearly proportional to book values.

**Discovery sampling**   A sampling plan for locating at least one deviation, providing that the deviation occurs in the population with a specified frequency.

**Dual-purpose test**   A test designed to test an internal control procedure and to substantiate the dollar amount of an account using the same sample.

**Effective audit**   An audit that achieves the planned degree of effectiveness in detecting any material misstatement in the client's financial statements.

**Efficient audit**   An effective audit that is performed at the lowest possible cost.

**Expected deviation rate**   An advance estimate of a deviation rate. This estimate is necessary for determining the required sample size in an attributes sampling plan.

**Mean-per-unit estimation**   A sampling plan enabling the auditors to estimate the average dollar value (or other variable) of items in a population by determining the average value of items in a sample.

**Nonsampling risk**   The aspects of audit risk not due to sampling. This risk normally relates to "human" rather than "statistical" errors.

**Physical representation of the population**   The population from which the auditors sample. The physical representation of the population differs from the actual population when it does not include items that exist in the actual population. For example, the auditors sample from a trial balance of receivables which may or may not include all actual receivables.

**Population**   The entire field of items from which a sample might be drawn.

**Precision**   See allowance for sampling risk.

**Probability-proportional-to-size sampling**   A variables sampling procedure that uses attributes theory to express a conclusion in monetary (dollar) amounts.

**Random selection**   Selecting items from a population in a manner in which every item has an equal chance of being included in the sample.

**Ratio estimation**   A sampling plan that uses the ratio of audited (correct) values to book values of items in the sample to calculate the estimated total audited value of the population. Ratio estimation is used in lieu of difference estimation when the differences are nearly proportional to book values.

**Representative sample**   A sample possessing essentially the same characteristics as the population from which it was drawn.

**Risk of assessing control risk too high**   This risk is the possibility that assessed level of control risk based on the sample is greater than the true operating effectiveness of the internal control procedure.

**Risk of assessing control risk too low**   This most important risk is the possibility that the assessed level of control risk based on the sample is less than the true operating effectiveness of the internal control procedures.

**Risk of incorrect acceptance**   The risk that sample results will indicate that a population is *not* materially misstated when, in fact, it is materially misstated.

**Risk of incorrect rejection**   The risk that sample results will indicate that a population is materially misstated when, in fact, it is not.

**Sampling error**   The difference between the actual rate or amount in the population and that of the sample. For example, if an actual (but unknown) deviation rate of 3 percent exists in the population, and the sample's deviation rate is 2 percent, the sampling error is 1 percent.

**Sampling risk**   The risk that the auditors' conclusion based on a sample might be different from the conclusion they would reach if the test were applied to the entire population. For tests of controls, sampling risks include the risks of assessing control risk too high and too low; for substantive testing, sampling risks include the risks of incorrect acceptance and rejection.

**Sequential sampling**   A sampling plan in which the sample is selected in stages, with the need for each subsequent stage being conditional on the results of the previous stage.

**Standard deviation**   A measure of the variability or dispersion of item values within a population; in a normal distribution, 68.3 percent of all item values fall within $\pm$ 1 standard deviation of the mean, 95.4 percent fall within $\pm$ 2 standard deviations, and 99.7 percent fall within $\pm$ 3 standard deviations.

**Stratification**   Dividing a population into two or more relatively homogeneous subgroups (strata). Stratification increases the efficiency of most sampling plans by reducing the variability of items in each stratum. The sample size necessary to evaluate the strata separately is often smaller than would be needed to evaluate the total population.

**Systematic selection**   The technique of selecting a sample by drawing every $n$th item in the population, following one or more random starting points.

**Tolerable deviation rate**   The maximum population rate of deviations from a prescribed control procedure that the auditor will tolerate without modifying the planned assessment of control risk.

**Tolerable misstatement**   An estimate of the maximum monetary misstatement that may exist in an account balance without causing the financial statements to be materially misstated.

**Variables sampling**   Sampling plans designed to estimate a numerical measurement of a population, such as a dollar value.

**Voucher**   A document authorizing a cash disbursement. A voucher usually provides space for employees performing various approval functions to initial. The term *voucher* may also be applied to the group of supporting documents used as a basis for recording liabilities or for making cash disbursements.

# ◆ GROUP I: REVIEW QUESTIONS

10-1   Define, and differentiate between, nonstatistical (judgmental) sampling and statistical sampling.

10-2   What statistical sampling plan appears to be most useful in accomplishing the basic objectives of tests of controls? Explain.

10-3   In selecting items for examination, an auditor considered three alternatives: *(a)* random number table selection, *(b)* systematic selection, and *(c)* random number generator selection. Which, if any, of these methods would lead to a random sample if properly applied?

10-4   Explain briefly the term *systematic selection* as used in auditing and indicate the precautions to be taken if a random sample is to be obtained. Is systematic selection applicable to unnumbered documents? Explain.

10-5   Explain briefly how the auditors using statistical sampling techniques may measure the possibility that the sample drawn has characteristics not representative of the population.

10-6   What would be the difference in an attributes sampling plan and a variables sampling plan in a test of inventory extensions?

10-7   Distinguish between attributes sampling and variables sampling.

10-8   Explain the meaning of *sampling without replacement* and *sampling with replacement*.

10-9   If a sample of 100 items indicates a deviation rate of 3 percent, should the auditors conclude that the entire population also has approximately a 3 percent deviation rate?

10-10   What relationship exists between the expected population deviation rate and sample size?

10-11   Describe the difference between sampling risk and nonsampling risk.

10-12   The 10 following statements apply to unrestricted random sampling with replacement. Indicate whether each statement is true or false. Briefly discuss each false statement.
   *a.*   When sampling from the population of accounts receivable for certain objectives, the auditor might sample only active accounts with balances.
   *b.*   To be random, every item in the population must have an equal chance of being selected for inclusion in the sample.
   *c.*   In general, all items in excess of a material misstatement need to be examined and sampling of them is inappropriate.
   *d.*   It is likely that five different random samples from the same population could produce five different estimates of the true population mean.
   *e.*   A 100 percent sample would have to be taken to attain an allowance for sampling risk range of ±$0 with no sampling risk.
   *f.*   The effect of the inclusion by chance of a very large or very small item in a random sample can be lessened by increasing the size of the sample.
   *g.*   The standard deviation is a measure of the variability of items in a population.
   *h.*   The larger the standard deviation of a population, the smaller the required sample size.
   *i.*   Unrestricted random sampling with replacement may result in a larger sample size than unrestricted random sampling without replacement.
   *j.*   Unrestricted random sampling normally results in a smaller sample size than does stratified sampling.

10-13   In performing a substantive test of the book value of a population, auditors must be concerned with two aspects of sampling risk. What are these two aspects of sampling risk, and which aspect is of greater importance to auditors? Explain.

10-14 Do the risk of incorrect acceptance and the risk of assessing control risk too low relate most directly to the efficiency or the effectiveness of an audit? Explain.

10-15 While performing a substantive test, the auditors determined that the sample results supported the conclusion that the recorded account balance was materially misstated. It was, in fact, not materially misstated. What type of sampling risk does this illustrate?

10-16 If certain forms are not consecutively numbered, which type of sample selection is likely to be most efficient—a random number generator, systematic, or block? Why?

10-17 Explain what is meant by the following statement: "When sampling, the auditors must determine that the *physical representation* of the actual population is complete."

10-18 Does stratification eliminate the variability in a nonhomogeneous population? Explain.

10-19 When performing attributes sampling, may auditors combine several types of exceptions in their definition of a deviation? Explain.

10-20 What effects will an auditor's belief that the population's actual deviation rate exceeds the tolerable deviation rate have on the test of controls sample size?

10-21 What is a dual purpose test?

10-22 When performing a dual purpose test, how does the auditor arrive at the required sample size?

10-23 An auditor is *sampling with replacement* and, by chance, a particular account has been selected twice. Should it be included two times in the sample?

10-24 Which technique results in a smaller sample size, sampling with or without replacement?

10-25 What are the three major factors that determine the sample size for an attributes sampling plan?

10-26 When using attributes sampling the auditors must estimate the expected population deviation rate. What sources are used to make this estimate?

10-27 Does required sample size increase or decrease as one changes from a 5 percent risk of assessing control risk too low to a 10 percent risk of assessing control risk too low? (Do not use a table.)

10-28 Explain what is meant by an allowance for sampling risk of ±1 percent with a risk of 10 percent of assessing control risk too low.

10-29 Describe what is meant by a *sequential sampling plan*.

10-30 What options are available to an auditor when the client's book value falls *outside* the acceptance interval calculated using the estimate of the total value of the population ± the adjusted allowance for sampling risk?

# ◆ GROUP II: QUESTIONS REQUIRING ANALYSIS

10-31 CPAs may decide to apply nonstatistical or statistical techniques to audit testing.

*Required:*   *a.* List and explain the advantages of applying statistical sampling techniques to audit testing.
  *b.* List and discuss the decisions involving professional judgment that must be made by the CPAs in applying statistical sampling techniques to tests of controls.
  *c.* You have applied attributes sampling to the client's pricing of the inventory and discovered from your sampling that the sample deviation rate exceeds your tolerable rate. Discuss the courses of action you can take.

10-32 One of the generally accepted auditing standards states that sufficient competent evidential matter is to be obtained through inspection, observation, inquiries, and confirmation to afford a reasonable basis for an opinion regarding the financial statements under audit. Some degree of uncertainty is implicit in the concept of "a reasonable basis for an opinion," because the concept of sampling is well established in auditing practice.

*Required:*   *a.*   Explain the auditor's justification for accepting the uncertainties that are inherent in the sampling process.

*b.*   Discuss the nature of sampling risk and nonsampling risk. Include the effect of sampling risk on substantive tests of details and on tests of internal control.

(AICPA, adapted)

10-33   In performing a test of controls for sales order approvals, the CPAs stipulate a tolerable deviation rate of 8 percent with a risk of assessing control risk too low of 5 percent. They anticipate a deviation rate of 2 percent.

*Required:*   *a.*   What type of sampling plan should the auditors use for this test?

*b.*   Using the appropriate table or formula from this chapter, compute the required sample size for the test.

*c.*   Assume that the sample indicates four deviations. May the CPAs conclude with a 5 percent risk of assessing control risk too low that the population deviation rate does not exceed the tolerable rate of 8 percent?

10-34   An auditor has reason to suspect that fraud has occurred through forgery of the treasurer's signature on company checks. The population under consideration consists of 3,000 checks. Can discovery sampling rule out the possibility that any forged checks exist?

10-35   Select the best answer for each of the following questions. Explain the reasons for your selection.

*a.*   Which of the following is an element of sampling risk?

(1)   Choosing an audit procedure that is inconsistent with the audit objective.

(2)   Concluding that no material misstatement exists in a materially misstated population based on taking a sample that includes no misstatement.

(3)   Failing to detect an error on a document that has been inspected by an auditor.

(4)   Failing to perform audit procedures that are required by the sampling plan.

*b.*   The primary purpose of using stratification as a sampling method in auditing:

(1)   To decrease the nonsampling risk of a given sample.

(2)   To determine the exact occurrence rate of a given characteristic in the population being studied.

(3)   To decrease the effect of variance in the total population.

(4)   To determine the allowance for sampling risk of the sample selected.

*c.*   In assessing sampling risk, the risk of incorrect rejection and the risk of assessing control risk too high relate to the:

(1)   Efficiency of the audit.

(2)   Effectiveness of the audit.

(3)   Selection of the sample.

(4)   Audit quality controls.

*d.*   When forms are not consecutively numbered:

(1)   Selection of a random sample probably is not possible.

(2)   Systematic sampling may be appropriate.

(3)   Stratified sampling should be used.

(4)   Random number tables cannot be used.

*e.*   In which of the following circumstances is it *least* likely that tests of controls will be performed?

(1)   The expected deviation rate exceeds the tolerable deviation rate.

(2)   The planned assessed level of control risk is at a level slightly below the maximum.

(3)   The risk of assessing control risk too low is less than the expected deviation rate.

(4)   The tolerable deviation rate exceeds the risk of assessing control risk too low.

  *f.* When using audit sampling for substantive tests, the auditors' estimate of the total misstatement in an account is referred to as the:
    (1) Tolerable misstatement.
    (2) Materiality level.
    (3) Projected misstatement.
    (4) Allowance for sampling risk.

10-36  The professional development department of a large CPA firm has prepared the following illustration to familiarize the audit staff with the relationships of sample size to population size and variability and the auditors' specifications as to the tolerable misstatement and the risk of incorrect acceptance.

| | Characteristics of Population 1 Relative to Population 2 | | Audit Specifications as to a Sample from Population 1 Relative to a Sample from Population 2 | |
| --- | --- | --- | --- | --- |
| | Size | Variability | Tolerable Misstatement | Planned Risk of Incorrect Acceptance |
| Case 1 . . . . . . . | Larger | Equal | Equal | Equal |
| Case 2 . . . . . . . | Equal | Larger | Larger | Equal |
| Case 3 . . . . . . . | Larger | Equal | Smaller | Equal |
| Case 4 . . . . . . . | Smaller | Smaller | Equal | Lower |
| Case 5 . . . . . . . | Smaller | Equal | Larger | Higher |

*Required:*  For each of the five cases in the above illustration, indicate the relationship of the sample size to be selected from population 1 relative to the sample from population 2. Select your answer from the following numbered responses and state the reasoning behind your choice. The required sample size from population 1 is:
    (1) Larger than the required sample size from population 2.
    (2) Equal to the required sample size from population 2.
    (3) Smaller than the required sample size from population 2.
    (4) Indeterminate relative to the required sample size from population 2.

# ◆ GROUP III: PROBLEMS

10-37  The use of statistical sampling techniques in an audit of financial statements does not eliminate judgmental decisions.

*Required:*  *a.* Identify and explain four areas in which judgment may be exercised by CPAs in planning a statistical test of controls.
    *b.* Assume that the auditors' sample shows an unacceptable deviation rate. Discuss the various actions that they may take based upon this finding.

c.  A nonstratified sample of 80 accounts payable vouchers is to be selected from a population of 3,200. The vouchers are numbered consecutively from 1 to 3,200 and are listed, 40 to a page, in the voucher register. Describe four different techniques for selecting a random sample of vouchers for inspection.

(AICPA, adapted)

10-38   Sampling for attributes is often used to allow an auditor to reach a conclusion concerning a rate of occurrence in a population. A common use in auditing is to test the rate of deviation from a prescribed internal control procedure to determine whether the planned assessed level of control risk is appropriate.

*Required:*   *a.*  When an auditor samples for attributes, identify the factors that should influence the auditors' judgment concerning the determination of:
(1)   Acceptable level of risk of assessing control risk too low.
(2)   Tolerable deviation rate.
(3)   Expected population deviation rate.

*b.*  State the effect on sample size of an increase in each of the following factors, assuming all other factors are held constant:
(1)   Acceptable level of the risk of assessing control risk too low.
(2)   Tolerable deviation rate.
(3)   Expected population deviation rate.

*c.*  Evaluate the sample results of a test for attributes if authorizations are found to be missing on 7 check requests out of a sample of 100 tested. The population consists of 2,500 check requests, the tolerable deviation rate is 8 percent, and the acceptable level of risk of assessing control risk too low is 5 percent.

*d.*  How may the use of statistical sampling assist the auditors in evaluating the sample results described in *c,* above?

(AICPA, adapted)

10-39   Scott Duffney, CPA, has randomly selected and audited a sample of 100 of Will-Mart's accounts receivable. Will-Mart has 3,000 accounts receivable accounts with a total book value of $3,000,000. Duffney has determined that the account's tolerable misstatement is $250,000.
His sample results are as follow:

Average audited value        $990
Average book value           $998

*Required:*   Calculate the accounts receivable estimated audited value and projected misstatement using the mean-per-unit method.

10-40   As part of your audit of the Abba Company accounts payable function, your audit program includes a test of controls addressing the company policy requiring that all vouchers be properly approved. You estimate the population deviation rate to be 3 percent.

*Required:*   *a.*  In addition to an estimate of population deviation rate, what factors affect the size of the sample needed?

*b.*  What bases could be used to provide an estimate of the population deviation rate?

*c.*  Assume that a sample of 100 has been drawn, audit tests performed, and a sample deviation rate of 4 percent computed. Furthermore, you have selected a 5 percent risk of assessing control risk too low as appropriate. Use the appropriate table to determine the achieved upper deviation rate.

*d.*  What actions can be taken to deal with a situation in which the achieved upper deviation rate exceeds the tolerable rate?

10-41   The auditors of Dunbar Electronics want to limit the risk of material misstatement in the valuation of inventories to 2 percent. They believe that there exists a 50 percent risk that a material misstatement could have bypassed the client's internal control and that the inherent risk of the account is 80 percent. They also believe that the analytical procedures performed to test the assertion have a 40 percent risk of failing to detect a material misstatement.

*Required:*   *a.*   Briefly discuss what is meant by audit risk, inherent risk, control risk, and the risk that analytical procedures might fail to detect a material misstatement.

   *b.*   Calculate the maximum allowable risk of incorrect acceptance for the substantive test of details.

   *c.*   What level of detection risk is implicit in this problem?

# AUDIT SAMPLING—APPLICATIONS FOR SUBSTANTIVE TESTING

## CHAPTER OBJECTIVES

After studying this chapter, you should be able to:

- Identify the various statistical techniques used for substantive testing.

- Describe how to plan, perform, and evaluate an audit sample using mean-per-unit estimation.

- Distinguish between ratio and difference estimation techniques.

- Describe how to plan, perform, and evaluate an audit sample using probability-proportional-to-size sampling.

- Explain how nonstatistical sampling may be used in performing substantive tests.

- Describe how to plan, perform, and evaluate an audit sample using a structured nonstatistical sampling approach.

C hapter 10 introduced the concepts of audit sampling as they relate to substantive testing. This chapter describes in detail the sampling plans that are used most frequently for substantive tests of account balances, including those using classical variables methods, probability-proportional-to-size sampling, and nonstatistical sampling techniques.

## CLASSICAL VARIABLES SAMPLING

As indicated in Chapter 10, classical variables sampling plans enable auditors to estimate a numerical quantity, such as the dollar amount of an account balance. This makes these techniques particularly useful for performing substantive tests. Classical variables sampling methods include **mean-per-unit estimation, ratio estimation,** and **difference estimation.**

### Mean-per-Unit Estimation

Mean-per-unit estimation enables auditors to estimate the *mean audited* value of the items in a population, with specified sampling risk and allowance for sampling risk (precision), by determining the *mean audited* value of items in a sample. An estimate of the total audited value of the population is obtained by multiplying the mean audited value of the sample (the **sample mean**) times the number of items in the population. The **projected misstatement** may then be calculated as the difference between this estimated total audited value and the client's book value. The assumption underlying mean-per-unit estimation is that a sample's mean audited value will, for a certain sampling risk and allowance for sampling risk, represent the true audited mean of the population.

For variables sampling, even if computer software is used to determine the required sample size, some familiarity with statistical theory and terminology is useful. Of particular importance are the concepts of **normal distribution** and **standard deviation.**

Normal Distribution.   Many populations, such as the heights of all men, may be described as normal distributions. A normal distribution is illustrated by the familiar bell-shaped curve, shown in Figure 11–1, in which the values of the individual items tend to congregate around the **population** mean. Notice that the distribution of individual item values is symmetrical on both sides of the mean. There is no tendency for deviations to be to one side rather than the other.

Even when the items within the population are not normally distributed, the concept of a normal distribution is relevant to sampling theory. If auditors were to draw from any population hundreds of samples of a given size, *the means of these samples would form a normal distribution* around the true population mean. This characteristic allows auditors to apply mean-per-unit estimation to populations that are not normally distributed, even though only one sample is usually taken.

Figure 11 – 1    Normal Distribution

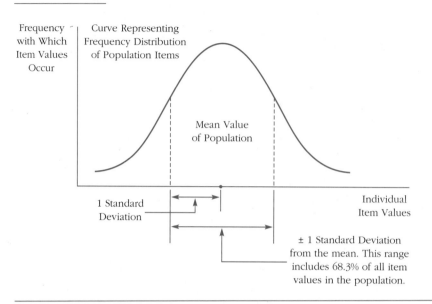

Standard Deviation.    The **standard deviation** of a population is a measure of the *variability* or *dispersion* of individual item values about its mean.[1] The less variation among item values, the smaller the standard deviation; the greater the variation among item values, the larger the standard deviation. It is inherent in the definitions of normal distribution and standard deviation that 68.3 percent of the item values in a normal distribution fall within ± 1 standard deviation of the population mean, that 95.4 percent fall within ± 2 standard deviations, and that 99.7 percent fall within ± 3 standard deviations. These percentage relationships hold true by definition; however, the dollar amount of the standard deviation will vary from one population to another.

In calculating the sample size, the auditors need an estimate of the population's standard deviation of *audited* values. They may obtain this estimate by calculating the standard deviation of the book values of the population or by using the standard deviation of the audited values obtained in the previous year's audit. Alternatively, auditors may obtain an estimate of the standard deviation of the audited values by taking a *pilot sample*

---

[1]The standard deviation is the square root of the following quotient: the sum of the squares of the deviation of each item value from the population mean, divided by the number of items in the population. Symbolically, the formula for calculating the standard deviation is:

$$\sqrt{\frac{\Sigma(x-\overline{X})^2}{N}}$$

where:

$x$ = each population item.

$\overline{X}$ = the mean of the population.

$N$ = the number of items in the population.

of approximately 50 items.[2] Generalized audit software packages include routines designed to estimate the standard deviation of the book values of a population either from a pilot sample or from the population book values.

## Controlling Sampling Risk

In Chapter 10 we described the two aspects of sampling risk for substantive tests, including:

1. *The risk of incorrect rejection of an account.* The possibility that the sample results will indicate that an account balance is materially misstated when, in fact, it is not misstated.
2. *The risk of incorrect acceptance of an account.* The possibility that the sample results will indicate that an account balance is not materially misstated when, in fact, it is materially misstated.

When planning a variables sampling plan, these two types of risks may be controlled independently of one another. For example, auditors may design a sample that limits both risks to 10 percent, or they may hold the **risk of incorrect acceptance** to 5 percent while allowing the **risk of incorrect rejection** to rise to 40 percent or more. In establishing the planned level of the risk of incorrect acceptance, auditors must consider the extent of the evidence that must be obtained from the substantive test. As indicated in Chapter 10, this is determined by the auditors' assessments of inherent risk and control risk for the assertions being tested, and the extent of the evidence obtained from any other substantive tests of those assertions. In stipulating the planned risk of incorrect rejection, on the other hand, the auditors should consider the time and other costs involved in performing additional audit procedures when the sample results *erroneously* indicate that a correct book balance is materially misstated.

In mean-per-unit estimation, as was the case with attributes sampling, the allowance for sampling risk is used to control sampling risk. The appropriate planned allowance for sampling risk may be determined from the following formula.

$$\text{Planned allowance for sampling risk} = \frac{\text{Tolerable misstatement}}{1 + \dfrac{\text{Incorrect acceptance coefficient}}{\text{Incorrect rejection coefficient}}}$$

The **tolerable misstatement** is the maximum monetary misstatement that may exist in the account without causing the financial statements to be materially misstated. The *risk coefficients* are taken from a table, such as the one in Figure 11–2.

---

[2]An *estimate* of the standard deviation may be made from a sample by taking the square root of the following quotient: the sum of the squares of the deviation of each sample item value from the sample mean, divided by one less than the number of items in the sample. Symbolically, the formula for estimating the standard deviation is:

$$\sqrt{\frac{\Sigma(x-\overline{X})^2}{n-1}}$$

Figure 11–2   Risk Coefficients

| Acceptable Level of Risk | Incorrect Acceptance Coefficient | Incorrect Rejection Coefficient |
|:---:|:---:|:---:|
| 1.0% | 2.33 | 2.58 |
| 4.6 | 1.68 | 2.00 |
| 5.0 | 1.64 | 1.96 |
| 10.0 | 1.28 | 1.64 |
| 15.0 | 1.04 | 1.44 |
| 20.0 | 0.84 | 1.28 |
| 25.0 | 0.67 | 1.15 |
| 30.0 | 0.52 | 1.04 |
| 40.0 | 0.25 | 0.84 |
| 50.0 | 0.00 | 0.67 |

## Determination of Sample Size

The factors directly included in the sample size formula for mean-per-unit estimation are (1) the population size, (2) the planned risk of incorrect rejection, (3) the estimated variability (standard deviation) among item values in the population, and (4) the planned allowance for sampling risk. The relationship of these factors to the required sample size is expressed by the following formula:[3]

$$\text{Sample size} = \left( \frac{\text{Population size} \times \text{Incorrect rejection coefficient} \times \text{Estimated standard deviation}}{\text{Planned allowance for sampling risk}} \right)^2$$

## Evaluation of Sample Results

Recall that the auditors determined sample size based on the planned sampling risks and on an estimate of the standard deviation of the population. When the auditors' estimate of the population's standard deviation is exactly the same as that found in the sample, the planned allowance for sampling risk may be used for evaluation purposes. However, this is seldom the case. The auditors' estimate of the population standard deviation usually differs from that of the subsequent sample. When this occurs, the sample taken does not

---

[3]This formula is based upon an infinite population. The effect on sample size when the population is finite but of significant size is small. Symbolically, this formula may be stated:

$$n = \left( \frac{N \times U_r \times SD}{A} \right)^2$$

where $n$ = sample size, $N$ = population size, $U_r$ = incorrect rejection coefficient, $SD$ = estimated standard deviation, and $A$ = planned allowance for sampling risk.

control both risks at their planned levels because the auditors have under- or overestimated the variability of the population in computing the required sample size. Although there are various ways of adjusting the allowance for sampling risk, one that maintains the risk of incorrect acceptance at its planned level is described below:

$$\begin{matrix} \text{Adjusted} \\ \text{allowance for} \\ \text{sampling risk} \end{matrix} = \begin{matrix} \text{Tolerable} \\ \text{misstatement} \end{matrix} - \frac{(\text{Population size} \times \text{Incorrect acceptance coefficient} \times \text{Sample standard deviation})}{\sqrt{\text{Sample size}}}$$

Once the auditors calculate the adjusted allowance for sampling risk, the client's book value is accepted or rejected based on whether it falls within the interval constructed by the audited sample mean ± the adjusted allowance for sampling risk. If the book value falls within the interval, the sample results support the conclusion that the account balance is materially correct. On the other hand, if the client's book value does *not* fall within the interval the sample results indicate that there is too great a risk that the account balance is materially misstated.

## Illustration of Mean-per-Unit Estimation

1. *Determine the objective of the test.*   Assume that the auditors wish to test the existence and gross valuation of recorded accounts receivable of a small public utility client. They wish to test the book value of accounts receivable by confirming a sample of the accounts through direct correspondence with the customers.

2. *Define the population and sampling unit.*   The client's records have 100,000 accounts recorded at a total book value of $6,250,000. The auditors believe that the customers will be able to confirm the total outstanding account balance. Therefore, the account balance is used as the sampling unit instead of the individual transactions making up the balance. Figure 11–3 summarizes the accounts.

3. *Choose an audit sampling technique.*   The auditors have decided to use the mean-per-unit technique.

4. *Determine the sample size.*   To calculate the required sample size the auditors must determine (1) the tolerable misstatement for accounts receivable, (2) the planned levels of sampling risk (the risks of incorrect acceptance and rejection), (3) the estimate of the population standard deviation, and (4) the population size.

Based on their consideration of internal control, the auditors believe that all accounts are included in the 100,000 accounts in the clients' subsidiary ledger (the physical representation of the population). In view of the materiality of the dollar amounts involved, the auditors assess the tolerable misstatement to be $364,000. Since internal control over existence and valuation of accounts receivable is very weak, the auditors assess control risk at the maximum level, that is, 100 percent. In addition, they assess inherent risk at 100 percent and plan to perform only very limited other substantive tests of these assertions. Therefore, the auditors decide on a 5 percent risk of incorrect acceptance. Based on a consideration of the costs of performing additional procedures when an account is improperly rejected, a 4.6 percent risk of incorrect rejection is planned by the auditors.

From this information and by using risk coefficients obtained from Figure 11–2, the planned allowance for sampling risk may be calculated as follows:

$$\text{Planned allowance for sampling risk} = \frac{\text{Tolerable misstatement}}{1 + \dfrac{\text{Incorrect acceptance coefficient}}{\text{Incorrect rejection coefficient}}}$$

$$= \frac{\$364{,}000}{1 + \dfrac{1.64}{2.00}}$$

$$= \$200{,}000$$

To estimate the standard deviation of the population, the auditors use a generalized audit software program to calculate the standard deviation of the recorded book values of the individual customers' accounts. The result is $15.

---

Figure 11–3    Population of Accounts Receivable

**ABC COMPANY**
**Accounts Receivable**
**December 31, 19X3**

| Account Number | Account Name | Book Value |
|---|---|---|
| 000,001 | Aaron, William | $      65.55 |
| 000,002 | Adams, James | 66.44 |
| 000,003 | Adams, Susan | 82.42 |
| 000,004 | Ahohn, Jennifer | 55.14 |
| 000,005 | Ahrons, Kenneth | 44.96 |
| ⋮ | ⋮ | ⋮ |
| 003,000 | Carhon, Sandra | 65.00 |
| ⋮ | ⋮ | ⋮ |
| 099,999 | Zenit, Darlene | 82.50 |
| 100,000 | Zyen, Chem | 99.20 |
| TOTAL BOOK VALUE | | $6,250,000.00 |
| | | |
| MEAN ACCOUNT VALUE* | | $      62.50 |

---

*$6,250,000/100,000.

Using the sample size formula, the required sample size may now be computed as follows:

$$\text{Sample size} = \left(\frac{\text{Population size} \times \text{Incorrect rejection coefficient} \times \text{Estimated standard deviation}}{\text{Planned allowance for sampling risk}}\right)^2$$

$$= \left(\frac{100,000 \times 2.00 \times \$15}{\$200,000}\right)^2 = \left(\frac{\$3,000,000}{\$200,000}\right)^2$$

$$= 225 \text{ accounts}$$

5.  *Select the sample.*  The client's accounts receivable are from residential customers and do not vary greatly in size. For this reason, the auditors decide to use a random number table to select an unstratified random sample.

6.  *Test the sample items.*  The auditors send the confirmations and perform additional procedures as appropriate.

7.  *Evaluate the sample results.*  Confirmation of the 225 accounts, as summarized on Figure 11-4, results in a sample with a mean audited value of $61 per account. Figure 11-4 also indicates that the mean *book value* of the 225 accounts in the sample was $63. Notice that this $63 mean sample book value differs somewhat from the mean book value of the entire population, $62.50, in Figure 11-3. *This difference of $0.50 per account is due to chance and is not directly used in the mean-per-unit analysis.*

As a first case, assume that the confirmation results also indicate a standard deviation of the sample's audited values of $15. Since the sample's standard deviation equals that

Figure 11-4   Auditors' Sample of Accounts Receivable

**ABC COMPANY**
**Sample of Accounts Receivable**
**December 31, 19X3**

| Sample Item Number | Account Number | Account Name | Book Value | Audited Value | Difference |
|---|---|---|---|---|---|
| 001 | 000,002 | Adams, James | $ 66.44 | $ 66.44 | $ 0.00 |
| 002 | 000,005 | Ahrons, Kenneth | 44.9 | 43.00 | 1.96 |
| 003 | 001,100 | Banner, Jane | 92.16 | 92.16 | 0.00 |
| 004 | 002,200 | Boynton, Willis | 72.12 | 68.50 | 3.62 |
| 005 | 003,000 | Carhon, Sandra | 65.00 | 65.00 | 0.00 |
| ⋮ | ⋮ | ⋮ | ⋮ | ⋮ | ⋮ |
| 224 | 093,212 | Yelbow, Sharlene | 82.50 | 82.50 | 0.00 |
| 225 | 100,000 | Zyen, Chem | 99.20 | 92.00 | 7.20 |
| TOTAL VALUE (Sample) | | | $14,175.00 | $13,725.00 | $450.00 |
| MEAN VALUES (Total Value/225) | | | $ 63.00 | 61.00 | 2.00 |

used in planning, the adjusted allowance for sampling risk equals the planned allowance of $200,000. In this case, the auditors' estimate of the total audited value of the population is $6,100,000, and the acceptance interval for the sample result is that amount plus or minus the allowance for sampling risk of $200,000, calculated as follows:

$$\text{Estimated total audited value} = \text{Mean audited value} \times \text{Number of accounts}$$

$$\text{Estimated total audited value} = \$61 \times 100,000 \text{ accounts} = \$6,100,000$$

$$\text{Acceptance interval} = \text{Estimated total audited value} \pm \text{Allowance for sampling risk}$$

$$= \$6,100,000 \pm \$200,000$$

$$= [\$5,900,000 \text{ to } \$6,300,000]$$

Because the client's book value of $6,250,000 falls within this acceptance interval, the sample results indicate that the client's valuation of accounts receivable is not materially misstated. However, the sample results indicate a **projected misstatement** of $150,000, calculated as follows:

$$\text{Projected misstatement} = \text{Estimated total audited value} - \text{Book value of population}$$

$$= \$6,100,000 - \$6,250,000$$

$$= \$150,000 \text{ overstatement}$$

This projected misstatement will be considered when the auditors are analyzing the total amount of potential misstatement in the financial statements. Also, the auditors may suggest that the client correct any accounts that their test revealed to be misstated, even though the misstatements are less than the tolerable misstatement amount.

How do the auditors evaluate the results if the sample's standard deviation differs from the estimate? They may use the formula discussed above to calculate an adjusted allowance for sampling risk. For example, if the standard deviation of the sample's audited values had instead been equal to $16, the adjusted allowance for sampling risk may be calculated as follows:

$$\begin{aligned}\text{Adjusted allowance for sampling risk} &= \frac{\text{Tolerable}}{\text{misstatement}} - \frac{(\text{Population size} \times \text{Incorrect acceptance coefficient} \times \text{Sample standard deviation})}{\sqrt{\text{Sample size}}} \\ &= \$364,000 - \frac{(100,000 \times 1.64 \times \$16)}{\sqrt{225}} \\ &= \$189,067\end{aligned}$$

Thus, the acceptance interval would be constructed as $6,100,000 ± $189,067 ($5,910,933 to $6,289,067). As illustrated by Figure 11–5, the client's book value ($6,250,000) also falls within this interval. Therefore, the sample results still indicate that the account does not contain a material misstatement.

As in other types of sampling, the auditors should consider the qualitative aspects of any misstatements found in their sample. "What caused the misstatements?" "Do any of the misstatements indicate fraud?" and "What are the implications of the misstatements for other audit areas?" are questions the auditors would attempt to answer in their qualitative evaluation of the results.

8. *Document the sampling procedures.*   Each of the prior seven steps, as well as the basis for overall conclusions, should be documented in the auditors' working papers.

Figure 11–5    Acceptance Interval for Substantive Test

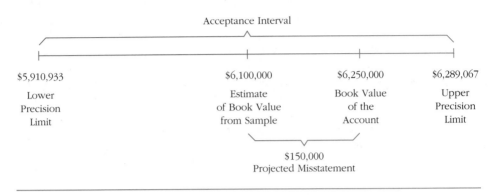

Acceptance Interval

| $5,910,933 | $6,100,000 | $6,250,000 | $6,289,067 |
| Lower Precision Limit | Estimate of Book Value from Sample | Book Value of the Account | Upper Precision Limit |

$150,000
Projected Misstatement

## Ratio and Difference Estimation

Mean-per-unit estimation uses the mean audited value of the sample as the basis for estimating the total value of the population. Two alternatives to this approach are ratio and difference estimation. Although closely related, ratio estimation and difference estimation are two distinct sampling plans; each is appropriate under slightly different circumstances.

In ratio estimation, the auditors use a sample to estimate the *ratio* of the audited (correct) value of a population to its book value. This ratio is estimated by dividing the total audited value of a sample by the total book value of the sample items.[4] An estimate of the correct population value is obtained by multiplying this estimated ratio by the total book value of the population.

In applying difference estimation, the auditors use a sample to estimate the *average difference* between the audited value and book value of items in a population. The average difference is estimated by dividing the net difference between the audited value and book value of a sample by the number of items in the sample.[5] The total difference between the book value of the population and its estimated correct value is determined by multiplying the estimated average difference by the number of items in the population.

---

[4]Symbolically, this process is expressed:

$$\hat{R} = \frac{\Sigma a_j}{\Sigma b_j}$$

where $\hat{R}$ (pronounced R caret) represents the estimated ratio of audited value to book value, $a_j$ represents the audited value of each sample item, and $b_j$ represents the book value of each sample item. Alternatively, the same ratio may be calculated using the ratios of the sample's mean audited and book values.

[5]Symbolically, the estimated difference is computed:

$$\hat{d} = \frac{1}{n} \sum_{j=1}^{n} (a_j - b_j)$$

where $\hat{d}$ represents the estimated average difference between audited value and book value; $n$ represents the number of items in the sample; and $a_j$ and $b_j$ represent the audited and book values, respectively.

Use of Ratio and Difference Estimation. The use of ratio or difference estimation techniques requires that (1) each population item has a book value, (2) an audited value may be determined for each sample item, and (3) differences between audited and book values (misstatements) are relatively frequent. If the occurrence rate of misstatements is very low, a prohibitively large sample is required to disclose a representative number of misstatements. However, when these requirements are met, ratio estimation or difference estimation is often more efficient than mean-per-unit estimation.

Ratio estimation is most appropriate when the size of misstatements is nearly proportional to the book values of the items. That is, it is appropriate when larger accounts have large misstatements and smaller accounts have small misstatements. When the size of misstatements is not approximately proportional to book value, difference estimation is the more appropriate technique.

## Illustration of Ratio and Difference Estimation

The information presented in Figures 11–3 and 11–4 may be used to illustrate the use of ratio and difference estimation techniques. Recall that the population consists of 100,000 accounts with an aggregate book value of $6,250,000. The auditors calculate the required sample size, randomly select the accounts to be sampled, and apply auditing procedures to determine the correct account balances. In actuality, differences in the sample size formulas[6] would cause the sample size to differ from that obtained using the mean-per-unit method, but in this illustration we will continue to assume a sample size of 225, as summarized on Figure 11–4.

Ratio Estimation. Using ratio estimation, the auditors would estimate the audited value of the population as

$$\text{Estimated total audited value} = \left[\frac{\text{Audited value of sample}}{\text{Book value of sample}}\right] \times \text{Book value of population}$$

$$\text{Estimated total audited value} = \left[\frac{\$13,725}{\$14,175}\right] \times \$6,250,000 = \$6,051,587$$

The ratio approach thus indicates a projected misstatement of a $198,413 overstatement ($6,051,587 − $6,250,000) for accounts receivable. Alternatively, the projected misstatement may be calculated directly as:

$$\text{Projected misstatement} = \left[\frac{\text{Sample net misstatement}}{\text{Book value of sample}}\right] \times \text{Book value of population}$$

$$\text{Projected misstatement} = \left[\frac{\$450}{\$14,175}\right] \times \$6,250,000 = \$198,413$$

---

[6]The major differences in the formulas is that the standard deviations used would be those for the ratios and differences.

Difference Estimation. If difference estimation is used, the auditors would estimate the average difference per item to be a $2 overstatement ($63 − $61). Multiplying the $2 by the 100,000 accounts in the population indicates that the projected misstatement for accounts receivable is a $200,000 overstatement. The estimated total audited value would be $6,050,000 ($6,250,000 − $200,000). Formulas are available for both ratio and difference estimation to calculate an adjusted allowance for sampling risk to control sampling risk in a manner similar to the mean-per-unit method.

# PROBABILITY-PROPORTIONAL-TO-SIZE (PPS) SAMPLING

Probability-proportional-to-size (PPS) sampling[7] is a technique that applies the theory of attributes sampling to estimate the total dollar amount of misstatement in a population. It has gained popularity because of its ease of use and because it often results in smaller size samples than classical variables approaches. Figure 10–10 in Chapter 10 provides a description of advantages and disadvantages of PPS sampling.

Whereas classical variables sampling plans define the population as a group of accounts or transactions, PPS sampling defines the population as the *individual dollars* comprising the population's book value. Thus, a population of 5,000 accounts receivable with a total dollar value of $2,875,000 is viewed as a population of 2,875,000 items (dollars), rather than 5,000 items (accounts).

## Determination of Sample Size

The factors affecting sample size in PPS sampling are (1) the population book value, (2) the reliability factor, (3) the tolerable misstatement, (4) the expected misstatement in the account, and (5) the expansion factor. Specifically, the sample size for PPS may be computed as follows:

$$\text{Sample size} = \frac{\text{Population book value} \times \text{Reliability factor}}{\text{Tolerable misstatement} - (\text{Expected misstatement} \times \text{Expansion factor})}$$

Several of the factors in the PPS formula need very little additional explanation. The book value of the population is the recorded amount of the population being audited. The tolerable misstatement is the maximum monetary misstatement that may exist in the population without causing the financial statements to be materially misstated. The expected misstatement is the auditors' estimate of the dollar amount of misstatement in the population. The auditors estimate the expected misstatement using professional judgment based on prior experience and knowledge of the client. The other factors used to calculate sample size are based on the auditors' desired risk of incorrect acceptance and are obtained from tables, such as the one in Figure 11–6. The "zero misstatements" row of Figure 11–6 is always used for obtaining the reliability factor for determining sample

---

[7]Variations of this sampling technique are called *dollar-unit sampling* and *monetary-unit sampling*.

Figure 11–6    Reliability Factors for Misstatements of Overstatement

| Number of Overstatement Misstatements | Risk of Incorrect Acceptance | | | | | | | | |
|---|---|---|---|---|---|---|---|---|---|
| | 1% | 5% | 10% | 15% | 20% | 25% | 30% | 37% | 50% |
| 0* | 4.61 | 3.00 | 2.31 | 1.90 | 1.61 | 1.39 | 1.21 | 1.00 | 0.70 |
| 1 | 6.64 | 4.75 | 3.89 | 3.38 | 3.00 | 2.70 | 2.44 | 2.14 | 1.68 |
| 2 | 8.41 | 6.30 | 5.33 | 4.72 | 4.28 | 3.93 | 3.62 | 3.25 | 2.68 |
| 3 | 10.05 | 7.76 | 6.69 | 6.02 | 5.52 | 5.11 | 4.77 | 4.34 | 3.68 |
| 4 | 11.61 | 9.16 | 8.00 | 7.27 | 6.73 | 6.28 | 5.90 | 5.43 | 4.68 |
| 5 | 13.11 | 10.52 | 9.28 | 8.50 | 7.91 | 7.43 | 7.01 | 6.49 | 5.68 |
| 6 | 14.57 | 11.85 | 10.54 | 9.71 | 9.08 | 8.56 | 8.12 | 7.56 | 6.67 |
| 7 | 16.00 | 13.15 | 11.78 | 10.90 | 10.24 | 9.69 | 9.21 | 8.63 | 7.67 |
| 8 | 17.41 | 14.44 | 13.00 | 12.08 | 11.38 | 10.81 | 10.31 | 9.68 | 8.67 |
| 9 | 18.79 | 15.71 | 14.21 | 13.25 | 12.52 | 11.92 | 11.39 | 10.74 | 9.67 |
| 10 | 20.15 | 16.97 | 15.41 | 14.42 | 13.66 | 13.02 | 12.47 | 11.79 | 10.67 |

*Always used for reliability factor in sample size formula and for basic precision.
Source: AICPA, Audit and Accounting Guide, *Audit Sampling* (New York, 1983).

Figure 11–7    Expansion Factors for Expected Misstatement

| | Risk of Incorrect Acceptance | | | | | | | | |
|---|---|---|---|---|---|---|---|---|---|
| | 1% | 5% | 10% | 15% | 20% | 25% | 30% | 37% | 50% |
| Factor | 1.9 | 1.6 | 1.5 | 1.4 | 1.3 | 1.25 | 1.2 | 1.15 | 1.0 |

Source: AICPA, Audit and Accounting Guide, *Audit Sampling* (New York, 1983).

size. Thus, if a 10 percent risk of incorrect acceptance is desired, the auditors use a reliability factor of 2.31. The expansion factor comes directly from Figure 11–7. For a 10 percent risk of incorrect acceptance, the factor is 1.5.

## Controlling Sampling Risk

As is the case with classical variables approaches, the auditors decide on an appropriate level of risk of incorrect acceptance, based on the extent of the evidence required from the sample. This level of risk is then used to obtain the appropriate factors to calculate sample size. The risk of incorrect rejection is indirectly controlled by the auditors' estimate of expected misstatement that is used to calculate the PPS sample size. To reduce the risk of incorrect rejection, the auditors will increase their estimate of expected misstatement. If the auditors underestimate the expected misstatement, the sample size will not be large enough and additional testing may be necessary in order to accept the account balance as being materially correct.

## Method of Sample Selection

Auditors generally use a **systematic selection** approach when using PPS. However, since the sampling unit is based on dollars, not individual accounts, the sampling interval is also based on dollars. The sampling interval is calculated as follows:

$$\text{Sampling interval} = \frac{\text{Population book value}}{\text{Sample size}}$$

To illustrate this method of selection, assume that the auditors are sampling from a population of accounts receivable totaling $300,000, and the sampling interval is calculated to be $1,500. A random starting point is selected between $1 and $1,500, say, $412. The account with the 412th dollar will then be the first sample item. Then, the sample will include the accounts receivable that contain every $1,500 from the starting point, as illustrated in Figure 11–8. The accounts included in Figure 11–8 are considered "logical units" because when applying PPS the auditors generally *cannot* audit only the dollar selected but must audit the entire account, invoice, or voucher. Consider the confirmation of accounts receivable. Sending a confirmation of a specific dollar in a selected balance is not generally feasible; the auditors must confirm the entire account balance or transaction from the account balance. Also note that when using a systematic sampling plan every account with a book value as large or larger than the sampling interval will be included in the sample. Thus, for example, since every 1500th dollar is being selected in Figure 11–8, account 0003 for $1,700 will always be included.

## Evaluation of Sample Results

After the sample has been selected and procedures applied to arrive at audited values for the individual accounts, the PPS sample is evaluated. The PPS evaluation procedure involves calculating an **upper limit on misstatement,** which is an estimate of the max-

---

Figure 11–8   PPS Selection Process

| Account Number | Book Value | Cumulative Total | Dollar Selected | Sample Item Book Value |
|---|---|---|---|---|
| 0001 | $1,000 | $  1,000 | $  412 | $1,000 |
| 0002 | 42 | 1,042 | | |
| 0003 | 1,700 | 2,742 | 1,912 | 1,700 |
| 0004 | 666 | 3,408 | | |
| 0005 | 50 | 3,458 | 3,412 | 50 |
| . | . | . | . | . |
| . | . | . | . | . |
| . | . | . | . | . |
| | | $300,000 | | |

imum amount of misstatement in the account. The upper limit on misstatement has two already familiar components—the **projected misstatement** and the **allowance for sampling risk.** However, in PPS sampling, the allowance for sampling risk is made up of two other components, the **basic precision** and the **incremental allowance.** Mathematically, these relationships may be described as follows:

$$
\underset{\text{on misstatement}}{\text{Upper limit}} = \underset{\text{misstatement}}{\text{Projected}} + \overbrace{\underset{\text{precision}}{\text{Basic}} + \underset{\text{allowance}}{\text{Incremental}}}^{\substack{\text{Allowance for} \\ \text{sampling risk}}}
$$

As is the case with the classical approaches, the projected misstatement may be viewed as the auditors' "best estimate" of the misstatement in the population. The *projected misstatement* in the population is determined by summing the projected misstatement for each account, or other logical unit, in the sample. Thus, when the sample includes no misstatements, the projected misstatement is zero. If misstatements do exist in the sample, the method used to project the misstatements in a particular account depends on whether or not the book value of the account found to be in error is less than the sampling interval. For accounts with book values that are less than the amount of the sampling interval, the projected misstatement is calculated by multiplying the percent of misstatement in the account, known as the **tainting,** times the sampling interval. Thus, if an account with a book value of $100 is found to have an audited value of $60, the misstatement in the account is $40 ($100 − $60) and the tainting is 40 percent ($40/$100). The tainting of 40 percent would then be multiplied by the sampling interval to get the projected misstatement for that account. Accounts with balances less than the sampling interval represent other unselected items in that interval. Thus, for accounts with book values that are less than the sampling interval, the account's tainting percentage is projected to the entire interval from which it was selected.

For accounts with book values equal to or greater than the sampling interval, the actual misstatement in the account is equal to the projected misstatement. The reason for the difference in the methods of calculation of the projected misstatement is that every account with a book value equal to or greater than the sampling interval will be included in the sample. These items do not represent other unselected items in the population; therefore, the actual misstatement in the account is equal to the projected misstatement.

The next step in determining the upper limit on misstatements involves calculating the two components of the allowance for sampling risk—the basic precision and the incremental allowance. The basic precision is always found by multiplying the reliability factor for zero misstatements from Figure 11–6 by the sampling interval.

When misstatements are discovered in the sample, the incremental allowance is found by (1) ranking the projected misstatements for the accounts with book values less than the sampling interval from largest projected misstatement to smallest projected misstatement, (2) multiplying each projected misstatement by an incremental factor calculated from the reliability factors in Figure 11–6, and (3) summing the resulting amounts. When no misstatements of accounts with book values less than the sampling interval are found in the sample, the incremental allowance is zero.

To complete the quantitative evaluation of the sample results, the auditors compute the upper limit on misstatements. When misstatements are found, the upper limit is computed by adding together the projected misstatement, the basic precision, and the incremental allowance. Of course, if no misstatements are found in the sample, the upper limit on misstatements consists only of the basic precision.

After the upper limit on misstatements is calculated, the auditors compare it to the tolerable misstatement for the account. If the upper limit on misstatements is less than or equal to tolerable misstatement, the sample results support the conclusion that the population is not misstated by more than tolerable misstatement at the specified level of sampling risk. On the other hand, if the upper limit on misstatements exceeds the amount of tolerable misstatement, the sample results do not provide the auditor with enough assurance that the misstatement in the population is less than tolerable misstatement.

## Illustration of PPS Sampling

The case used to illustrate mean-per-unit sampling on pages 359 through 363 will be used to illustrate PPS sampling. The population, in that case, had a book value of $6,250,000 and the auditors decided on a tolerable misstatement for the account of $364,000, and a 5 percent risk of incorrect acceptance. Additionally, assume that based on prior audits, the auditors expect $50,000 of misstatement in the population.

Since the auditors are using a risk of incorrect acceptance of 5 percent, the reliability factor from Figure 11–6 is 3.00, and the expansion factor from Figure 11–7 is 1.6. Remember for calculating sample size that the zero misstatement row of Figure 11–6 is always used. Using this information, the sample size and sampling interval may be calculated as follows:

$$\text{Sample size} = \frac{\text{Population book value} \times \text{Reliability factor}}{\text{Tolerable misstatement} - (\text{Expected misstatement} \times \text{Expansion factor})}$$

$$= \frac{\$6,250,000 \times 3.00}{\$364,000 - (\$50,000 \times 1.6)} = 66$$

$$\frac{\text{Sampling}}{\text{interval}} = \frac{\text{Population book value}}{\text{Sample size}}$$

$$= \frac{\$6,250,000}{66} = \$95,000 \text{ (approximately)}$$

Using the PPS selection method, the auditors select the accounts for confirmation, perform confirmation procedures, and find the following three misstatements:

| Book Value | Audited Value |
|---|---|
| $      100 | $    90 |
| 2,000 | 1,900 |
| 102,000 | 102 |

Based on the above results, the projected misstatement, basic precision, and the incremental allowance are calculated in Figure 11–9.

Figure 11–9    PPS Illustration of Calculation of Upper Limit on Misstatement

**Projected Misstatement:**

| Book Value | Audited Value | Misstatement | Tainting Percentage | Sampling Interval | Projected Misstatement | |
|---|---|---|---|---|---|---|
| $    100 | $   90 | $      10 | 10% | $95,000 | $   9,500 | |
| 2,000 | 1,900 | 100 | 5 | 95,000 | 4,750 | |
| 102,000 | 102 | 101,898 | NA | NA | 101,898 | |
| $104,100 | $2,092 | $102,008 | | | | $116,148 |

**Basic Precision =** Reliability factor × Sampling interval

=          3.0          ×        $95,000          =                                          285,000

**Incremental Allowance:**

| Reliability Factor | Increment | (Increment − 1) | Projected Misstatement | Incremental Allowance | |
|---|---|---|---|---|---|
| 3.00 | — | — | — | — | |
| 4.75 | 1.75 | 0.75 | $9,500 | $7,125 | |
| 6.30 | 1.55 | 0.55 | 4,750 | 2,613 | 9,738 |

**Upper Limit on Misstatement**                               $ 410,886

The calculation of projected misstatement is straightforward, and no table values are required. Note that the tainting percentages for the first two misstatements are computed by dividing the misstatement amount by the book value of the account. Then, the tainting percentages are multiplied by the sampling interval to calculate the projected misstatement. Because the book value of the account containing the third misstatement is greater than the sampling interval of $95,000, the projected misstatement for that account is equal to the amount of the misstatement.

The second element of the upper limit on misstatement, basic precision, is simply the reliability factor for zero misstatements, and a risk of incorrect acceptance of 5 percent from Figure 11–6 multiplied by the sampling interval.

The calculation of the incremental allowance uses the projected misstatements of the accounts with book values less than the sampling interval. These projected misstatements are ranked by size from largest projected misstatement to smallest and multiplied by the incremental reliability factors, minus one. These incremental reliability factors are derived from the factors in Figure 11–6. Because a 5 percent risk of incorrect acceptance was selected and two misstatements were found in accounts with balances less than the sampling interval, the factors of 3.00, 4.75, and 6.30 are taken from Figure 11–6. An incremental factor is calculated as the difference between successive factors. For example, the incremental factor for the first error is 4.75 − 3.00, or 1.75. Then one is subtracted from each incremental factor to arrive at the factor that is multiplied by the first projected misstatement, in this case 0.75. This process is repeated for each additional projected misstatement.

Because the upper limit ($410,886) is in excess of the tolerable misstatement ($364,000), the auditors would not accept the population as being materially correct. Thus, adjustment of the account, expansion of the test, or audit report modification would be appropriate.[8] In this situation, the most logical approach would be to persuade the client to adjust for the $102,008 in actual misstatements found in the sample. This would reduce the upper limit on misstatements to $308,878 ($410,886 − $102,008) and enable the auditors to accept the account as being materially correct.

## Considerations in Using PPS Sampling

Although the formulas for PPS sampling at first seem difficult, once a user becomes familiar with them, they are easier to apply in practice than the classical variables sampling methods. As indicated in Chapter 10, an estimate of the standard deviation of the population does not have to be made, and the PPS selection method automatically results in an efficient stratification of the sample. The method also provide smaller sample sizes when few misstatements are expected in the sample.

The advantages of PPS sampling do not come without cost. If there are many differences between recorded and audited amounts, classical variables sampling methods will result in a smaller sample size. Also, when using PPS sampling special consideration must be given to (1) accounts with zero balances, (2) accounts with negative balances, and (3) accounts that are understated. CPA firms use various methods to overcome these limitations.

# NONSTATISTICAL SAMPLING FOR SUBSTANTIVE TESTS

The major differences between statistical and nonstatistical sampling in substantive testing are in the procedures used to determine the sample size and evaluate the sample results. When using nonstatistical sampling the auditors may decide not to quantify the factors used to arrive at the sample size, although they will consider the relationships that are summarized in Figure 10–11 of the previous chapter. In evaluating the sample results, the auditors also will project the misstatements found in the sample to the population and consider sampling risk, but the level of risk is not quantified. While the auditors may use unassisted judgment for determining the sample size and for evaluating the sample results, many CPA firms have adopted structured approaches to nonstatistical sampling that are based on statistical methods. This increases the consistency of sampling judgments that are made by various auditors throughout the firm.

---

[8]In many circumstances such as this, the client requests that the auditors expand the test to either identify the specific misstatements or to determine that the account is not materially misstated.

## Illustration of Nonstatistical Sampling

The following example illustrates the use of a structured nonstatistical sampling plan that is based on PPS sampling theory.

1.  *Determine the objective of the test.*   Assume that the auditors are performing a test of the valuation of inventory by testing the pricing of a sample of inventory items by reference to vendors' invoices. The inventory consists of 2,000 items with a book value of $3,000,000.

2.  *Define the population and sampling unit.*   The physical representation of the population consists of a listing of the inventory items on hand at year-end, and the auditors have determined that the sampling unit will be each individual product.

3.  *Choose the audit sampling technique.*   The auditors have decided to use a structured approach to nonstatistical sampling.

4.  *Determine the sample size.*   To determine the required sample size the auditors will use the following formula:

$$\text{Sample size} = \left[ \frac{\text{Population book value} \times \text{Reliability factor}}{\text{Tolerable misstatement}} \right]$$

The reliability factor for the formula is selected from a table such as the one that is illustrated by Figure 11–10. It is based on the auditors' combined assessment of inherent and control risk and the auditors' assessment of the risk that other substantive procedures will fail to detect a material misstatement of the assertions. Both risks are assessed on qualitative scales from maximum risk (100 percent) to low risk.

In our example, assume that the auditors have assessed the combination of inherent and control risk at slightly below the maximum. They have also performed analytical procedures on the inventory account that the auditors believe have a moderate risk of not detecting a material misstatement in the valuation of the inventory account. Using these assessments of risk, the auditors obtain a reliability factor of 2.0 from the table in Figure 11–10. If the auditors have decided that $100,000 is the amount of tolerable misstatement for the inventory account, the sample size would be calculated as follows:

---

Figure 11–10   Reliability Factors for Nonstatistical Sampling Plan

| Assessment of Inherent and Control Risk | Risk That Other Substantive Procedures (e.g., analytical procedures) Will Fail to Detect a Material Misstatement | | |
|---|---|---|---|
| | **Maximum** | **Moderate** | **Low** |
| Maximum | 3.0 | 2.3 | 1.9 |
| Slightly below maximum | 2.7 | 2.0 | 1.6 |
| Moderate | 2.3 | 1.6 | 1.2 |
| Low | 1.9 | 1.2 | 1.0 |

Note: This table is applicable when the auditors expect few misstatements in the population.

$$\text{Sample size} = \left[\frac{\text{Population book value} \times \text{Reliability factor}}{\text{Tolerable misstatement}}\right]$$

$$= \left[\frac{\$3,000,000 \times 2.0}{\$100,000}\right]$$

$$= 60 \text{ items}$$

5. *Select the sample.* Even though nonstatistical sampling is being used, the auditors should generally select the sample on a **stratified** basis. In this case, the auditors decide to use the PPS selection method so that each item has a probability proportional to its size of being selected.

6. *Test the sample items.* The auditors examine vendors' invoices supporting the price of each product selected for testing. Assume that the auditors find two products that were priced at improper prices, resulting in a total overstatements of the account of $6,600. In addition, the total dollar value of the sample is calculated to be $1,100,000.

7. *Evaluate the sample results.* In evaluating the sample results, the auditors will begin by projecting the misstatements found in the sample to the population. A number of methods may be used. However, the auditors typically use the ratio or difference method illustrated on pages 363 through 365. In this example, the auditors decide to use the ratio method of projecting the misstatement, as illustrated below:

$$\text{Projected misstatement} = \left[\frac{\text{Sample net misstatement}}{\text{Book value of sample}}\right] \times \text{Book value of population}$$

$$= \left[\frac{\$6,600}{\$1,100,000}\right] \times \$3,000,000$$

$$= \$18,000$$

After calculating the projected amount of misstatement in the population, the auditors will then compare that amount with the amount of tolerable misstatement. In this situation, the auditors compare $18,000 with $100,000, and use professional judgment to evaluate whether there is a sufficiently low risk of material misstatement of the account. Since the projected misstatement is only 18 percent ($18,000/$100,000) of tolerable misstatement, the auditors would likely conclude that the account balance is acceptable. As the amount of projected misstatement gets closer to the amount of tolerable misstatement for the account, the auditors are more likely to conclude that the risk of material misstatement is too high. When the auditors conclude that the risk of misstatement is high they will not accept the client's book balance as being materially correct.

The auditors will also perform a qualitative evaluation of the misstatements found in the population to determine if there are implications for other aspects of the audit. Intentional misstatements would generally have greater implications for the audit than clerical errors.

Document the Sampling Procedure. The nonstatistical sampling procedures described above would be documented in a manner similar to that used for statistical sampling plans.

## ◆ CHAPTER SUMMARY

This second chapter on audit sampling describes in detail applications of audit sampling for substantive testing, using classical variables sampling, probability-proportional-to-size (PPS) sampling, and nonstatistical sampling. To summarize:

1. When a classical variables sampling plan is used, the required sample size is determined by the risk of incorrect acceptance, the risk of incorrect rejection, the amount of tolerable misstatement for the account, and the standard deviation of the items in the account.

2. Classical variables sampling methods include mean-per-unit estimation, ratio estimation, and difference estimation.

3. When evaluating the results of a classical variables sampling plan, the auditors compute an acceptance interval; if the client's book value falls within the interval, it is accepted as being materially correct. Otherwise, the auditors generally must perform additional testing to determine whether the client's balance is actually misstated or the sample was not representative.

4. PPS sampling is a technique that uses attributes sampling theory to estimate the total dollar misstatement of the population. PPS sampling defines the population as the individual dollars making up the account balance; it obtains its efficiency from the fact that every item in the population has a probability proportional to its size of being selected.

5. In PPS sampling the required sample size is determined by the population book value, the risk of incorrect acceptance, the tolerable misstatement for the account balance, and the expected misstatement in the account.

6. To evaluate a PPS sample the auditors compute the upper limit on misstatement. The account balance is accepted as being materially correct if the upper limit on misstatement is not more than tolerable misstatement for the account.

7. Many CPA firms use structured approaches to nonstatistical sampling for substantive tests. Such approaches increase the consistency of sampling decisions by various staff members within the firms.

## ◆ KEY TERMS INTRODUCED OR EMPHASIZED IN CHAPTER 11

**Allowance for sampling risk (ASR, precision)**   An interval around the sample results in which the true population characteristic is expected to lie.

**Basic precision**   In probability-proportional-to-size sampling, the reliability factor (for zero misstatements at the planned risk of incorrect acceptance) times the sampling interval.

**Confidence level**   The complement of the risk of incorrect acceptance.

**Difference estimation**   A classical variables sampling plan for estimating the average difference between the audited (correct) values of items in a population and their book values. Difference estimation is used in lieu of ratio estimation when the differences are not nearly proportional to book values.

**Dollar-unit sampling**   See probability-proportional-to-size sampling.

**Incremental allowance**   In probability-proportional-to-size sampling, an amount determined by ranking the misstatements for logical units that are less than the sampling interval and considering incremental changes in reliability factors.

**Mean**   The average item value, computed by dividing total value by the number of items comprising total value.

**Mean-per-unit estimation**   A classical variables sampling plan enabling the auditors to estimate the average dollar value (or other variable) of items in a population by determining the average value of items in a sample.

**Normal distribution**   A frequency distribution in which item values tend to congregate around the mean with no tendency for deviation toward one side rather than the other. A normal distribution is represented graphically by a bell-shaped curve.

**Population**   The entire field of items from which a sample might be drawn.

**Probability-proportional-to-size sampling**   A variables sampling procedure that uses attributes theory to express a conclusion in monetary (dollar) amounts.

**Projected misstatement**   An estimate of the most likely amount of monetary misstatement in a population.

**Ratio estimation**   A classical variables sampling plan for estimating the ratio of the audited (correct) values of items to their book values. Extending the book value of the population by this ratio provides an estimate of audited total population value. Ratio estimation is a highly efficient technique when errors are nearly proportional to item book values.

**Reliability**   See confidence level.

**Risk of incorrect acceptance**   The risk that sample results will indicate that a population is *not* materially misstated when, in fact, it is materially misstated.

**Risk of incorrect rejection**   The risk that sample results will indicate that a population is materially misstated when, in fact, it is not.

**Standard deviation**   A measure of the variability or dispersion of item values within a population; in a normal distribution, 68.3 percent of all item values fall within $\pm$ 1 standard deviation of the mean, 95.4 percent fall within $\pm$ 2 standard deviations, and 99.7 percent fall within $\pm$ 3 standard deviations.

**Stratification**   Dividing a population into two or more relatively homogeneous subgroups (strata). Stratification increases the efficiency of most sampling plans by reducing the variability of items in each stratum. The sample size necessary to evaluate the strata separately is often smaller than would be needed to evaluate the total population.

**Systematic selection**   The technique of selecting a sample by drawing every $n$th item in the population, following one or more random starting points.

**Tainting**   In probability-proportional-to-size sampling, the percentage of misstatement of an item (misstatement amount divided by book value).

**Tolerable misstatement**   An estimate of the maximum monetary misstatement that may exist in an account balance without causing the financial statements to be materially misstated.

**Upper limit on misstatement**   In probability-proportional-to-size sampling, the sum of projected misstatement, basic precision, and the incremental allowance. This total is used to evaluate sample results.

# ◆ GROUP I: REVIEW QUESTIONS

11-1   "One of the difficulties involved with the classical variables methods is that they require computation of a standard deviation and therefore that the population follows a normal distribution." Evaluate this statement.

11-2   Explain how the auditors may obtain an estimate of a population's standard deviation to determine an appropriate sample size.

11-3   When using the mean-per-unit method to evaluate results, explain how the auditors use the differences between the audited values and the book values of the individual items in their sample.

11-4   For what purposes is the planned allowance for sampling risk used in mean-per-unit sampling?

11-5   Using the approach presented in this chapter for mean-per-unit sampling, when is it necessary to calculate an *adjusted allowance for sampling risk?*

11-6   What conditions are necessary for the auditors to use either the ratio or difference estimation techniques?

11-7   The mean of the audited values in a sample is $20. The accounts in that sample have a mean book value of $21. The entire population of 10,000 accounts has an average book value of $19. Using mean-per-unit sampling, calculate the estimated total audited value of the account.

11-8   List the factors affecting sample size in a PPS sample.

11-9   "When using a systematic sample selection technique with PPS sampling, every account larger than the sampling interval will automatically be included in the sample." Do you agree? Explain.

11-10  When using PPS sampling, do auditors select sample items based on individual dollars, audit individual dollars, or both?

11-11  "When no misstatements are found in a PPS sample, the upper limit on misstatement is equal to zero." Is this statement correct? Explain.

11-12  A PPS sample with a sampling interval of $2,000 includes an item with an audited value of $90. This value was $30 lower than the account's book value. Calculate the tainting percentage for this account.

11-13  The *reliability factor* table provides factors for as many as three computations when planning and evaluating the results of a PPS sample. Describe in general terms each of these computations.

11-14  A company has an inventory with a book value of $4,583,231, which includes 116 product lines and a total of 326,432 units. How many items comprise this population for purposes of applying a probability-proportional-to-size sampling plan? Explain.

11-15  In a probability-proportional-to-size sample with a sampling interval of $20,000, an auditor discovered that a selected account receivable with a recorded amount of $10,000 had an audit amount of $2,000. Calculate the projected misstatement for this one item.

11-16  Is it correct to say that when using nonstatistical variables sampling one is unable to project the misstatements identified to the entire population? Explain why this is or is not the case.

11-17  When using nonstatistical sampling, what relationship must exist between the projected misstatement and tolerable misstatement in order for the auditors to conclude that an account balance is acceptable?

---

# ◆ GROUP II: QUESTIONS REQUIRING ANALYSIS

11-18   An auditor used a nonstatistical sampling plan to audit the inventory of an auto supply company. The auditor tested the recorded cost of a sample of inventory items by reference to vendors' invoices. In performing the test, the auditor verified all the items on two pages selected at random from the client's 257-page inventory listing. The sampling plan resulted in a test of $50,000 of the total book value of $5,000,000, and the auditor found a total of $5,000 in overstatements in the sample. Since the senior indicated that a material misstatement in the Inventory account was $100,000, the auditor concluded that the recorded inventory value was materially correct.

*Required:*   Evaluate the auditor's sampling plan and the manner in which the results were evaluated.

11-19   Cathy Williams is auditing the financial statements of Westerman Industries. In the performance of a mean-per-unit estimation of credit sales, Williams has decided to limit the risk of incorrect rejection to 25 percent and the risk of incorrect acceptance to 10 percent. Williams considers the tolerable misstatement in this revenue account to be ± $500,000. Calculate the planned allowance for sampling risk.

11-20   Chris York, CPA, is considering the use of probability-proportional-to-size sampling in examining the sales transactions and accounts receivable of Carter Wholesale Company.

*Required:*   *a.*   How does the definition of the items in an accounts receivable population vary between probability-proportional-to-size sampling and mean-per-unit sampling?

*b.*   Should a population of accounts receivable be stratified by dollar value before applying probability-proportional-to-size sampling procedures? Discuss.

11-21   Select the best answer for each of the following questions. Explain the reasons for your selection.

*a.*   An auditor needs to estimate the average highway weight of tractor-trailer trucks using a state's highway system. Which estimation method is most appropriate?
   (1)   Mean-per-unit.
   (2)   Difference.
   (3)   Ratio.
   (4)   Probability-proportional-to-size (IIA).

*b.*   When using classical variables sampling techniques, the measure of variability that is most useful is the:
   (1)   Median.
   (2)   Range.
   (3)   Mean.
   (4)   Standard deviation.

*c.*   All other relevant factors remaining constant in a probability-proportional-to-size sampling plan, an increase in the expected misstatement has what effect on required sample size?
   (1)   Increase.
   (2)   Decrease.
   (3)   Effect depends upon the level of sampling risk being accepted.
   (4)   No effect.

*d.*   The auditors have sampled 50 accounts from a population of 1,000 accounts receivable. The sample items have a mean book value of $200, and a mean audited value of $203. The book value in the population is $198,000. What is the estimated audited value of the population using the *mean-per-unit* method?
   (1)   $198,000
   (2)   $200,000

    (3) $201,000

    (4) $203,000

e.  Using the same facts as in *d* above, what is the estimated total audited value of the population using the *difference* method?

    (1) $198,000

    (2) $200,000

    (3) $201,000

    (4) $203,000

f.  In a *probability-proportional-to-size* sample with a sampling interval of $15,000, an auditor discovered that a sampled account receivable with a recorded amount of $2,000 was overstated by $400. The projected misstatement of this sample was:

    (1) $400

    (2) $3,000

    (3) $3,750

    (4) $12,000

**11-22**  Ratio estimation and difference estimation are two widely used variables sampling plans.

*Required:*  a.  Under what conditions are ratio estimation or difference estimation appropriate sampling plans for estimating the total dollar value of a population?

        b.  What relationship determines which of these two plans will be most efficient in a particular situation?

**11-23**  Bill Jones wishes to use nonstatistical sampling to select a sample of his client's 3,000 accounts receivable, which total $330,000. He believes that $30,000 represents a reasonable tolerable misstatement. He also has assessed both the combination of inherent and control risk at the maximum level, and the risk that other substantive procedures will fail to detect a material misstatement at the maximum. He wishes to use a structured approach. Use the formula presented in the text to calculate the required sample size.

**11-24**  During an audit of Potter Company, an auditor needs to estimate the total value of the 5,000 invoices processed during June. The auditor estimates the standard deviation of the population to be $30. Determine the size sample the auditor would select to achieve an allowance for sampling risk (precision) of± $25,000 with 4.6 percent risk of incorrect rejection.

                                                        (AICPA, adapted)

**11-25**  Robert Rotter, CPA, is considering the use of a mean-per-unit estimation sampling plan. Explain the factors that Rotter would consider in determining—

    a.  The acceptable risk of incorrect rejection.

    b.  The tolerable misstatement in the population.

    c.  The acceptable risk of incorrect acceptance.

---

## ◆ GROUP III: PROBLEMS

**11-26**  The auditors wish to use mean-per-unit sampling to evaluate the reasonableness of the book value of the accounts receivable of Smith, Inc. Smith has 10,000 receivable accounts with a total book value of $1,500,000. The auditors estimate the population's standard deviation to be equal to $25. After examining the overall audit plan, the auditors believe that the account's tolerable misstatement is $60,000, and that a risk of incorrect rejection of 5 percent and a risk of incorrect acceptance of 10 percent are appropriate.

*Required:*   *a.*   Calculate the required sample size.
           *b.*   Assuming the following results:

Average audited value          = $146
Standard deviation of sample = $ 28

Use the mean-per-unit method to:
(1)   Calculate the point estimate of the account's audited value.
(2)   Calculate the projected misstatement for the population.
(3)   Calculate the adjusted allowance for sampling risk.
(4)   State the auditors' conclusion in this situation.

11-27   In the audit of Potomac Mills, the auditors wish to test the costs assigned to manufactured goods. During the year, the company has produced 2,000 production lots with a total recorded cost of $5.9 million. The auditors select a sample of 200 production lots with an aggregate book value of $600,000 and vouch the assigned costs to the supporting documentation. Their examination discloses misstatements in the cost of 52 of the 200 production lots; after adjustment for these misstatements, the audited value of the sample is $582,000.

*Required:*   *a.*   Show how the auditors would compute an estimate of the total cost of production lots manufactured during the year using each of the following sampling plans. (Do not compute the allowance for sampling risk or the risk of incorrect acceptance of the estimates.)
               (1)   Mean-per-unit estimation.
               (2)   Ratio estimation.
               (3)   Difference estimation.
           *b.*   Explain why mean-per-unit estimation results in a higher estimate of the population value than does ratio estimation in this particular instance.

11-28   To test the pricing and mathematical accuracy of sales invoices, the auditors selected a sample of 200 sales invoices form a total of 41,600 invoices that were issued during the year under audit. The 200 invoices represented total recorded sales of $22,800. Total sales for the year amounted to $5 million. The examination disclosed that of the 200 invoices audited, 5 were not properly priced or contained errors in extensions and footings. The five incorrect invoices represented $720 of the total recorded sales, and the errors found resulted in a net understatement of these invoices by $300.

*Required:*   Explain what conclusions the auditors may draw from the above information, assuming the sample was selected:
          *a.*   Using nonstatistical sampling.
          *b.*   As part of a difference estimation plan for estimating the total population value.
          *c.*   As part of an attributes sampling plan using a stipulated tolerable deviation rate of 5 percent, and a risk of assessing control risk too low of 5 percent. (Use the concepts presented in Chapter 10 for this portion of the problem.)

11-29   The auditors wish to test the valuation of accounts receivable in the audit of Desert Enterprises of Bullhead City. The client has $500,000 of total recorded receivables, composed of 850 accounts. The auditors have determined the following:

Tolerable misstatement          $25,000
Risk of incorrect acceptance        5%
Expected misstatement           $ 2,000

The auditors have decided to use probability-proportional-to-size sampling.

*Required:* a. For planning the sample, calculate:
   (1)  Required sample size.
   (2)  Sampling interval.
   b. Assume that the auditors have tested the sample and discovered three misstatements:

| Book Value | Audited Value |
|---|---|
| $   50 | $   47 |
| 800 | 760 |
| 8,500 | 8,100 |

Calculate:
   (1)  Projected misstatement.
   (2)  Basic precision.
   (3)  Incremental allowance.
   (4)  Upper limit on misstatement.
   c. Explain how the auditors would consider the results calculated in *b*.

11-30  Edwards has decided to use probability-proportional-to-size (PPS) sampling, sometimes called dollar-unit sampling, in the audit of a client's accounts receivable balance. Few, if any, misstatements of the account balance are expected.
   Edwards plans to use the following PPS sampling table:

### Reliability Factors for Misstatements of Overstatement

| Number of Overstatement Misstatements | Risk of Incorrect Acceptance | | | | |
|---|---|---|---|---|---|
| | 1% | 5% | 10% | 15% | 20% |
| 0 | 4.61 | 3.00 | 2.31 | 1.90 | 1.61 |
| 1 | 6.64 | 4.75 | 3.89 | 3.38 | 3.00 |
| 2 | 8.41 | 6.30 | 5.33 | 4.72 | 4.28 |
| 3 | 10.05 | 7.76 | 6.69 | 6.02 | 5.52 |
| 4 | 11.61 | 9.16 | 8.00 | 7.27 | 6.73 |

*Required:* a. Identify the advantages of using PPS sampling over classical variables sampling.
   b. Calculate the sampling interval and the sample size Edwards should use given the following information:

Tolerable misstatement . . . . . . . . . . . . . . . . . . . . . . . . .  $15,000
Risk of incorrect acceptance . . . . . . . . . . . . . . . . . . . . . .   5%
Estimated misstatement . . . . . . . . . . . . . . . . . . . . . . . .   0
Recorded amount of accounts receivable . . . . . . . . . . . . . . .  $300,000

Note: Requirements *b* and *c* are *not* related.
   c. Calculate the total projected misstatement if the following three errors were discovered in a PPS sample:

| | Recorded Amount | Audited Amount | Sampling Interval |
|---|---|---|---|
| 1st misstatement | $   400 | $   320 | $1,000 |
| 2nd misstatement | 500 | 0 | 1,000 |
| 3rd misstatement | 3,000 | 2,500 | 1,000 |

(AICPA, adapted)

11-31   The auditors of Landi Corporation wish to use a structured approach to nonstatistical sampling to evaluate the reasonableness of the accounts receivable. Landi has 15,000 receivable accounts with a total book value of $2,500,000. The auditors have a combined assessed level of inherent and control risk at a moderate level, and believes that their other substantive procedures are so limited as to require a "maximum" risk assessment. After considering the overall audit plan, the auditors believe that the account's tolerable misstatement is $57,500.

*Required:*   a.   Calculate the required sample size.
b.   Assuming the following results:

Number of items in sample                 100
Total audited value of sample items   $16,200
Total book value of sample items         17,000

(1)  Use the ratio estimation method to calculate the projected misstatement of the population.
(2)  Use the difference estimation method to calculate the projected misstatement of the population.

c.   Use the results obtained *b* to come to a conclusion as to whether to "accept" or "reject" the population.

# ◆ INTEGRATING PROBLEM

11-32   Bill Pei, CPA, is about to begin his audit of the accuracy of his client's accounts receivable. Based on experience, he expects that approximately 1 percent of the client's 40,000 accounts have errors. The total book value of receivables is $5 million. Pei has established $390,000 as the amount for tolerable misstatement, 5 percent for the risk of incorrect acceptance, and 10 percent for the risk of incorrect rejection. The auditors estimate the standard deviation of the accounts to be $45.

*Required:*   a.   Using mean-per-unit sampling, calculate the required sample size.
b.   Now ignore part *a*. Assume that as part of an attribute sampling plan using a stipulated tolerable rate of 5 percent, and a risk of assessing control risk too low of 5 percent, the auditors wish to test the receivables valuation—that is, each account will either be considered as correct, or a deviation. What sample size would be required for this test?

*Additional information for parts c through g.*
Now ignore your *a* and *b* answers and assume that the auditor selected a random sample of 208 accounts (square root = 14.4), representing a total book value of receivables of $40,800. He found five errors, representing a $20,300 overstatement as follows:

| Misstatement | Book Value | Audited Value |
|---|---|---|
| 1 | $26,000 | $5,950 |
| 2 | 1,000 | 900 |
| 3 | 220 | 200 |
| 4 | 180 | 120 |
| 5 | 100 | 30 |
| | $27,500 | $7,200 |

The standard deviation of the book value of the sample was $50, while the standard deviation of the audited values of the sample was $55. For part *g* assume a sampling interval of $24,038 ($5,000,000/208).

*Required:*  c.  Using mean-per-unit estimation, what is the projected misstatement for the population?

d.  Using mean-per-unit sampling, calculate the adjusted allowance for sampling risk and use it to calculate the appropriate interval for use in deciding whether to ''accept'' or ''reject'' the population.

e.  Using difference estimation, calculate the projected misstatement for the population.

f.  Given the five misstatements presented above, what statistical conclusion may be made using attribute sampling (recall part *b* above)?

g.   Using PPS sampling, calculate:

(1)  Projected misstatement.

(2)  Basic precision.

(3)  Incremental allowance for sampling risk.

# TESTING CYCLE CONTROLS AND PERFORMING SUBSTANTIVE TESTS

# 12

# REVENUE CYCLE—OBTAINING AN UNDERSTANDING AND TESTING CONTROLS

## CHAPTER OBJECTIVES

After studying this chapter, you should be able to:

- Explain the nature of sales and cash receipts transactions in the revenue cycle.

- Describe the documents, records, and accounts that comprise the revenue cycle.

- Identify and explain the fundamental internal control policies and procedures for sales transactions.

- Identify and explain the fundamental internal control policies and procedures for cash receipts transactions.

- Relate specific internal control structure policies and procedures to financial statement assertions.

- Design typical tests of controls used by auditors to assess control risk for the financial statement assertions as they relate to the revenue cycle.

T his chapter presents information about the nature of the revenue cycle. In broad terms, this cycle includes the receiving of orders from customers, the delivery and billing of goods and services, and the recording and collection of accounts receivable. The chapter begins by explaining the nature of the sales and cash receipts transactions in the revenue cycle and the fundamental internal controls. Then, it describes the nature of the understanding auditors need to plan the audit and the manner in which auditors design tests of controls for this cycle.

# INTERNAL CONTROL OVER THE REVENUE CYCLE

## Internal Control over Sales

Internal control, from the point of receiving an order from a customer through the point of billing the customer for the sale, is essential. When internal controls over sales on account are inadequate, large credit losses are almost inevitable. For example, merchandise may be shipped to a customer whose credit standing has not been approved. Shipments may be made to a customer without notice being given to the billing department; consequently, no sales invoice will be prepared and no account receivable will be recorded. Sales invoices may contain errors in prices and quantities; and if sales invoices are not controlled by serial numbers, some may be lost and never recorded as accounts receivable. To avoid such difficulties, effective internal control procedures over credit sales are necessary.

Internal control over credit sales is strengthened by a division of duties so that different departments or individuals are responsible for (1) preparation of the sales order, (2) credit approval, (3) issuance of merchandise from stock, (4) shipment, (5) billing, (6) invoice verification, (7) maintenance of control accounts, (8) maintenance of customers' ledgers, (9) approval of sales returns and allowances, and (10) authorization of write-offs of uncollectible accounts. When this degree of segregation of duties is feasible, accidental errors are likely to be detected quickly through the comparison of documents and amounts emerging from independent units of the company, and the opportunity for fraud is reduced. While our discussion of internal control will be developed primarily in terms of these sales activities of manufacturing companies, most of the principles also apply to nonmanufacturing companies. The sales transactions portion of the revenue cycle for a typical manufacturing company is illustrated by Figure 12–1.

### Controlling Customers' Orders.
The controlling and processing of orders received from customers require carefully designed operating policies and control procedures if costly errors are to be avoided. Important initial steps include the listing of the **customer's purchase order** (see page 388), a review of items and quantities to determine whether the order can be filled within a reasonable time, and the preparation of a sales order. The **sales order** (see page 388) is a translation of the terms of the customer's order into a set of specific instructions for the guidance of various divisions, including the credit, finished goods stores, shipping, billing, and accounts receivable units. If the sales order is generated by the computer, input validation (edit) checks should be established to ensure that customer numbers are valid, that part numbers and descriptions are accurate, and that the terms of sale are in accordance with established company policies. The actions to be taken

DIXIELINE INDUSTRIES LTD.
CREDIT SALES SYSTEMS FLOWCHART
DECEMBER 31, 19XX

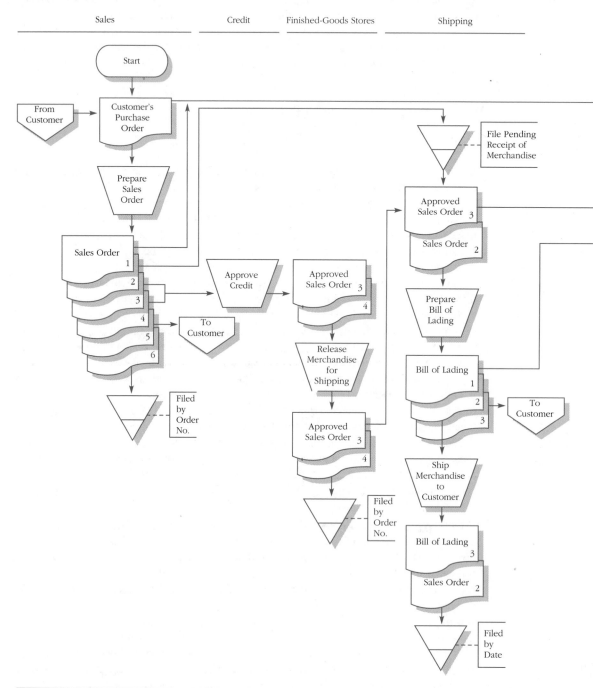

Figure 12–1    (*continued*)

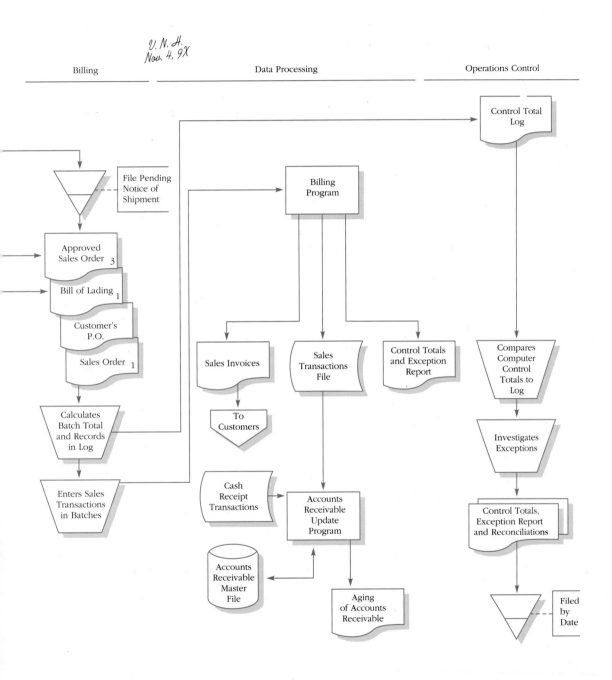

*V. N. H.*
*Nov. 4, 9X*

Billing                          Data Processing                          Operations Control

```
                                        78644
              PURCHASE ORDER
                 Pilot Stores
                  1425 G St.
               Irvine, CA 92345


To:  Wood Supply Co.        Date:  Nov. 10, 19XX
     21 Main St.
     Suisun, CA 95483       Ship via:  Jon Trucking

                            Terms:  2/10, n/40

Enter our order for
```

| Qty | Description | Price | Total |
|---|---|---|---|
| 20 doz. | Q Clamps #26537489 | $235.00 | $4700.00 |
| 10 | 120 hp Generators #45983748 | 355.00 | 3550.00 |

```
                            Wood Supply Co.
                            By:  Bill Jones
```

```
                                        476538

              SALES ORDER

             Wood Supply Co.
                 21 Main St.
              Suisun, CA 95483


To:  Pilot Stores          Date:  Nov. 23, 19XX
     1425 G St.
     Irvine, CA 92345      Credit Approval:  MS

Cust. No.:  987604
```

| Description | Part No. | Quantity |
|---|---|---|
| Q Clamps | 26537489 | 20 doz. |
| 120 hp Generators | 45983748 | 10 |

by the factory upon receipt of a sales order will depend upon whether the goods are standard products carried in stock or are to be produced to specifications set by the customer.

Credit Approval. Before sales orders are processed, the credit department must determine whether goods may be shipped to the customer on open account. This department is supervised by a credit manager who reports to the treasurer or the vice president of finance. The credit department implements management's credit policies and uses them to evaluate prospective and continuing customers by studying the customers' financial statements and by referring to reports of credit agencies, such as those provided by Dun & Bradstreet. Once a new customer has been granted a line of credit, approval of a particular sales transaction involves a simple determination of whether the customer has sufficient unused credit. This process is often performed by the computer. If the sales transaction will cause the customer's credit limit to be exceeded, the computer will print out the details for the credit department, which will initiate the process of determining whether to increase the customer's line of credit. When credit is not approved, the customer is notified and an effort is made to negotiate some other terms, such as cash on delivery.

Issuing Merchandise. Companies that carry standard products in stock maintain a finished goods storeroom supervised by a storeskeeper. The storeskeeper issues the goods upon receipt of an approved sales order or shipping instructions printed out on the computer terminal in the stores department. The computer then updates the perpetual inventory records for the items that were transferred and shipped. To segregate the recording and custody functions, perpetual inventory records of finished goods should be maintained by the accounting department, not by the storeskeeper.

```
                                                    10026574
                        BILL OF LADING

Wood Supply Co.
21 Main St.
Suisun, CA 95483            Date:  Nov. 25, 19XX

Cosigned to:               Order No.:  476538
      Pilot Stores
      1425 G St.           Shipper:  Jon Trucking
      Irvine, CA 92345
```

| Quantity | Description | Weight |
|----------|-------------|--------|
| 5 Boxes | 20 doz. Q Clamps #26537489 | 142 |
| 10 Crates | 10-Generators #45983748 | 2560 |
| | | 2702 |

Shipper's Acceptance: _Bill Warren_

```
                                                     7462537
                           INVOICE
                       Wood Supply Co.
                         21 Main St.
                       Suisun, CA 95483

Sold to:  Pilot Stores      Date:  Nov. 27, 19XX
          1425 G St.
          Irvine, CA 92345  Your order no.:  78644

                            Shipped:  Nov. 25, 19XX

                            Shipped via  Jon Trucking
```

| Qty | Description | Price | Total |
|-----|-------------|-------|-------|
| 20 doz. | Q Clamps | $ 235.00 | $ 4700.00 |
| 10 | 120 hp Generators | 355.00 | 3550.00 |
| | | | $ 8250.00 |

Shipping. When the goods are transmitted by the finished goods storeroom to the shipping department, this group must arrange for space in railroad cars, aircraft, or motor freight carriers. **Shipping documents,** such as **bills of lading,** are created when the goods are loaded into cars or trucks. The shipping documents, regardless of whether they are generated manually or by the computer, should be numerically controlled. Shipping documents are critical source documents because they provide evidence of the transfer of title to the goods to the customer; this is typically the point of occurrence of the sales transaction. When shipments are made by truck, some type of gate control is also needed to ensure that all goods leaving the plant have been recorded as shipments. This may require the surrender to the gatekeeper of copies of shipping documents.

Billing. The term *billing* means notifying the customer of the amount due for goods or services delivered. This notification is accomplished by preparing and mailing a **sales invoice.** Billing should be performed by a department not under the control of sales executives. The function is generally assigned to a separate section within the accounting, data processing, or finance department. The billing section has the responsibility of (1) accounting for the serially numbered shipping documents, (2) comparing shipping documents with sales orders and customers' purchase orders and change notices, (3) entering pertinent data from these documents on the sales invoice, (4) applying prices and discounts from price lists to the invoice, (5) making the necessary extensions and footings, and (6) accumulating the total amounts billed. When a formal contract exists, as is often the case when dealing with governmental entities, that contract usually specifies prices, delivery procedures, inspection and acceptance routines, method of liquidating advances, and numerous other details. Accordingly, the contract is an extremely important source of information for preparation of the sales invoice. Sales invoices are often generated by the computer based upon information that has already been entered into the system. The shipping data provide the computer with information about the quantities of goods sold, and prices to be charged have either been entered by the sales department when the sales order was generated, or are contained in a computer master file of sales prices. As the sales invoices are printed, the computer also creates a computerized sales transactions file that is used in conjunction with the cash receipts transactions file to update the master file of accounts receivable. Periodically, the computer updates the general ledger and prints the sales journal and the subsidiary ledger of accounts receivable. The computer also generates monthly statements for mailing to customers.

Internal control procedures should be established to ensure the accuracy of the invoices before they are mailed to customers. When a manual accounting system is in use, these procedures might consist of a second-person review of the accuracy of prices, credit terms, transportation charges, extensions, and footings. When a computerized billing system is in use this objective is generally achieved by implementing input validation (edit) checks and various batch processing controls.

Adjustments to Sales and Receivables.   All adjustments to sales for allowances, returns, and write-offs of accounts receivable should be supported by serially numbered credit memoranda signed by an officer or responsible employee having no duties relating to cash handling or to the maintenance of customers' ledgers. Good internal control over credits for returned merchandise usually includes a requirement that the goods be received and examined before credit is given. The credit memoranda should then bear the serial number of the receiving report on the returned shipment.

The process of uncollectible receivable write-off should be initiated by the credit manager, with subsequent authorization by the treasurer. Receivables that are written off should then either be turned over to a collection agency or retained and transferred to a separate ledger and control account. The records may be of a memorandum nature rather than part of the regular accounting system. Also, when possible— generally when the debtor is still in existence—statements requesting payment should continue to be mailed. Otherwise, any subsequent collections may be embezzled by employees without the necessity of falsifying records to conceal the theft.

---

CREDIT MEMORANDUM

Wood Supply Co.
21 Main St.
Suisun, CA 95483

Customer: Howe Carpet Co.       Date: Dec. 15, 19XX
894 Reed St.
Orange, CA 92786

Customer No.: 687960       Invoice No. 7598597
Receiving Report No.: N/A

| Description | Amount |
| --- | --- |
| Allowance for substandard goods | $550.00 |

Authorized by: *Janis Morris*

## Internal Control over Cash Receipts

Most of the functions relating to cash handling—both receipts and disbursements—are the responsibility of the finance department, under the direction of the treasurer. These functions include handling and depositing cash receipts; signing checks; investing idle cash; and maintaining custody of cash, marketable securities, and other negotiable assets. In addition, the finance department should forecast cash requirements and make both short-term and long-term financing arrangements.

Ideally, the functions of the finance department and the accounting department should be integrated in a manner that provides assurance that:

1. All cash that should have been received *was* in fact received, recorded accurately, and deposited promptly.
2. Cash disbursements have been made only for authorized purposes and have been properly recorded.
3. Cash balances are maintained at adequate, but not excessive, levels by forecasting expected cash receipts and payments related to normal operations. The need to obtain loans or invest excess cash is thus made known on a timely basis.

A detailed study of the operating routines of the individual business is necessary in developing the most efficient control procedures, but some general guidelines for achieving internal control over cash receipts may be summarized as follows:

1. Do not permit any one employee to handle a transaction from beginning to end.
2. Separate cash handling from recordkeeping.
3. Centralize receiving of cash to extent possible.
4. Record cash receipts on a timely basis.
5. Encourage customers to obtain receipts and observe cash register totals.
6. Deposit cash receipts daily.
7. Have monthly bank reconciliations prepared by employees not responsible for the custody of cash or issuance of checks. The completed reconciliation should be reviewed promptly by an appropriate official.
8. Forecast expected cash receipts (and disbursements) and investigate variances from forecasted amounts.

Typical internal controls over the cash receipts portion of the revenue cycle are illustrated by Figure 12–2.

Cash Sales.   Control over cash sales is stronger when two or more employees (usually a salesclerk and a cashier) participate in each transaction with a customer. Restaurants and cafeterias often use a centrally located cashier who receives cash from the customer along with a sales check prepared by another employee. Theaters generally have a cashier selling prenumbered tickets, which are collected by a door attendant when the customer is admitted. If tickets or sales checks are serially numbered and all numbers accounted for, this separation of responsibility for the transaction is an effective means of preventing fraud.

# Figure 12–2    Cash Receipts Cycle

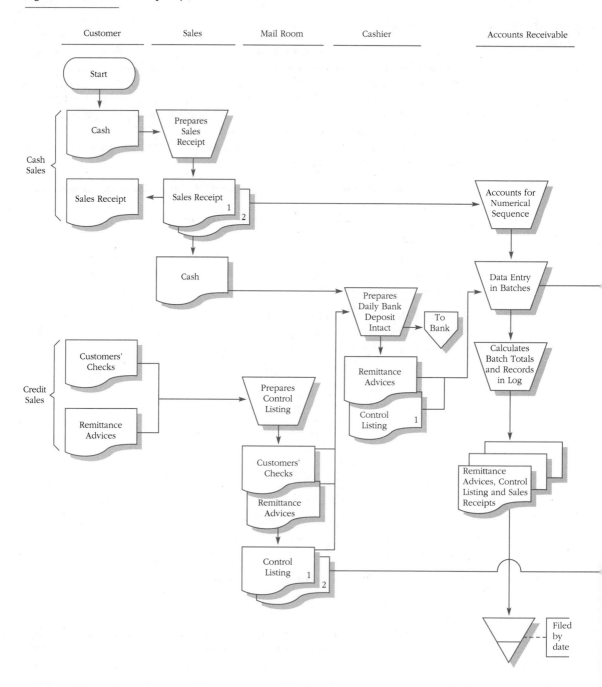

Figure 12-2    (*continued*)

Data Processing                    Operations Control                Bank

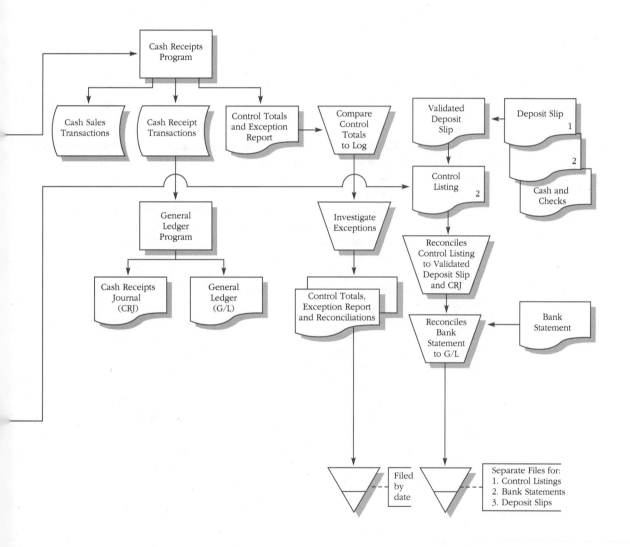

In many retail establishments, the nature of the business is such that one employee must make over-the-counter sales, deliver the merchandise, receive cash, and record the transaction. In this situation, dishonesty may be discouraged by proper use of cash registers or electronic point-of-sale systems. The protective features of cash registers include (1) visual display of the amount of the sale in full view of the customer; (2) a printed receipt, which the customer is urged to take with the merchandise; and (3) accumulation of a locked-in total of the day's sales. Finally, cash sales (as well as collections on receivables) should be deposited daily.

Electronic Point-of-Sale (POS) Systems.   Many retail stores use various types of electronic cash registers, including online computer terminals. With some of these devices, an electronic scanner is used to read the sales price and other data from specially prepared product tags. The salesperson need only pass the tag over the scanner for the register to record the sale at the product's price. Thus, the risk of a salesperson recording sales at erroneous prices is substantially reduced.

Besides providing strong control over cash sales, electronic registers often may be programmed to perform numerous other control functions. For example, online registers may verify the credit status of charge account customers, update accounts receivable and perpetual inventory records, and provide special printouts accumulating sales data by product line, salesperson, department, and type of sale.

Collections from Credit Customers.   In most manufacturing and wholesale companies, cash receipts consist principally of checks received through the mail. This situation poses little threat of defalcation unless one employee is permitted to receive and deposit these checks and also to record the credits to the customers' accounts. Strong internal control requires that the accounts receivable clerk have no access to the cash receipts, and that the master file of accounts receivables be periodically reconciled with the general ledger. When the nature of operations permits, different employees should be assigned responsibility for (1) initial listing of cash receipts, (2) custody and depositing of cash receipts, (3) maintenance of customers' accounts, (4) reconciliation of customers' ledgers with controlling accounts, (5) mailing monthly statements to customers, and (6) collection activity and past-due accounts. A typical internal control structure for cash receipts through the mail is described below.

Incoming mail is opened in the mail room, where an employee endorses the checks "for deposit only" to the company's account and prepares a *control listing* of the incoming cash receipts. This listing shows the amount received from each customer and identifies the customer by name or account number. A copy of the control listing is forwarded to operations control. Another copy of the control listing and the cash receipts are forwarded to the cashier. The remittance advices and a copy of the control listing are forwarded to the employee responsible for maintaining the customers' accounts. An employee who does not handle cash receipts or customers' accounts mails monthly statements to customers detailing their billings and payments.

Which controls tend to prevent the mail room employee from abstracting the receipts from several customers, destroying the remittance advices, and omitting these receipts from the control listing? First, incoming cash receipts consist primarily of checks made payable to the company. Second, if customers' accounts are not credited for payments made, they will complain to the company's accounting personnel after reviewing their monthly statements. If these customers can produce paid checks supporting their claims of payment and these checks do not appear on the mail room control listings, responsibility for the embezzlement is quickly focused upon the mail room employee.

The cash is transferred to the cashier (with a copy of the control listing) who deposits the day's receipts intact in the bank. Control is exercised over the cashier by periodic reconciliation of the operations control copies of the mail room control listings with the cash receipts journal and the details of the validated deposit slips received from the bank.

Businesses receiving a large volume of cash receipts through the mail often use a lockbox system to strengthen internal control and hasten the depositing of the remittances. The **lockbox** is actually a post office box controlled by the company's bank. The bank picks up mail at the post office box several times a day, credits the company's checking account for cash received, and sends the remittance advices to the company. Internal control is strengthened by the fact that the company's personnel have no access to cash and bank personnel have no access to the company's accounting records.

The employee responsible for the customers' accounts ledger enters the details of cash receipts into the computer in batches. The cash receipts program creates a file of cash receipt transactions that is used to update the general ledger and the master file of accounts receivable. This computer program creates control and cash totals exception reports that detail any invalid customer account numbers or unusual payment amounts. Manual follow-up procedures on exception reports and the necessary reconciliations are performed by the operations control group.

## Internal Audit Activities

As a part of their audit activities, the internal auditors may periodically take over the mailing of monthly statements to customers or send confirmations and investigate any discrepancies reported; they also may perform extensive reviews of shipping reports, invoices, cash receipts, credit memoranda, and aged trial balances of receivables to determine whether authorized procedures are being carried out consistently.

# OBTAINING AND DOCUMENTING AN UNDERSTANDING OF THE INTERNAL CONTROL STRUCTURE

When obtaining an understanding of the internal control structure, the auditors consider the control environment, the accounting system, and control procedures, as discussed in Chapter 8.

**Control Environment.**  The control environment reflects the overall attitude, awareness, and actions of management and the board of directors concerning the importance of internal control and the way it is used in the entity. The elements of the control environment affect the overall internal control structure and all transaction cycles of the company. Of particular importance to the auditors' consideration of the revenue cycle is the company's organizational structure as it relates to the processing of sales transactions. The auditors will determine whether the major functions are appropriately segregated. The

**Figure 12-3** Overview of the Revenue Cycle—Documents and Accounts

**Sales**

```
                                              78644
              PURCHASE ORDER
                  Pilot Stores
                   1425 G St.
                 Irvine, CA 92345


  To:  Wood Supply Co.        Date:  Nov. 10, 19XX
       21 Main St.
       Suisun, CA 95483       Ship via:  Jon Trucking

                              Terms:  2/10, n/40

  Enter our order for
```

| Qty | Description | Price | Total |
|-----|-------------|-------|-------|
| 20 doz. | Q Clamps #26537489 | $235.00 | $4700.00 |
| 10 | 120 hp Generators #45983748 | 355.00 | 3550.00 |

```
                       Wood Supply Co.
                    By:  Bill Jones
```

```
                                            10026574
                  BILL OF LADING

  Wood Supply Co.
  21 Main St.
  Suisun, CA 95483        Date:  Nov. 25, 19XX

  Cosigned to:            Order No.:  476538
       Pilot Stores
       1425 G St.
       Irvine, CA 92345   Shipper:  Jon Trucking
```

| Quantity | Description | Weight |
|----------|-------------|--------|
| 5 Boxes | 20 doz. Q Clamps #26537489 | 142 |
| 10 Crates | 10-Generators #45983748 | 2560 |
|  |  | 2702 |

```
               Shipper's Acceptance:  Bill Warren
```

```
                                             476538
               SALES ORDER

              Wood Supply Co.
                21 Main St.
              Suisun, CA 954583

  To:  Pilot Stores          Date:  Nov. 23, 19XX
       1425 G St.
       Irvine, CA 92345      Credit Approval:  MS

  Cust. No.:  987604
```

| Description | Part No. | Quantity |
|-------------|----------|----------|
| Q Clamps | 26537489 | 20 doz. |
| 120 hp Generators | 45983748 | 10 |

**Cash Receipts**

Check

```
  Pilot Stores
  1425 G St.
  Irvine, CA 92345               Date: Dec. 5, 19XX
  Pay to the
  order of    Wood Supply Co.           $8085.00
       Eight thousand eighty-five and no/100

  First National Bank          Pilot Stores
  California                   Jackie Cohen
```

```
                    Remittance Advice
  Wood Supply Co.

  Inv. #7462537                      $8085.00
```

Figure 12-3 (*continued*)

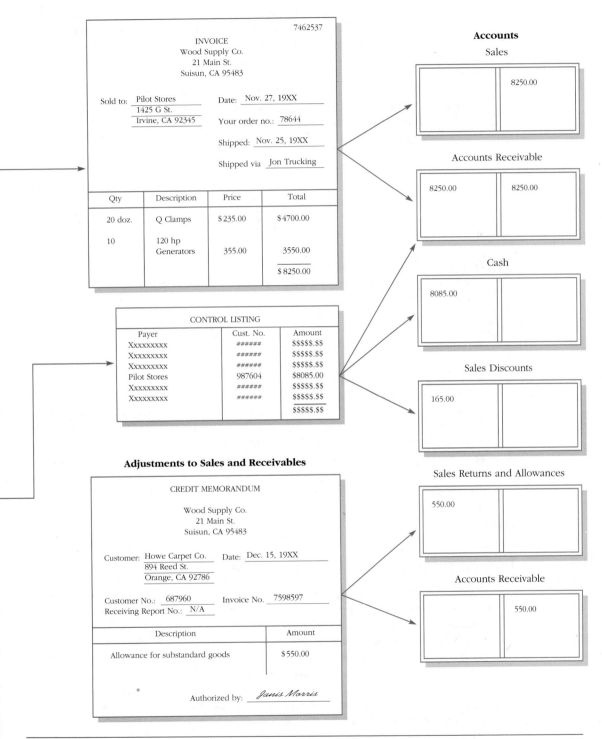

auditors also will obtain an understanding of management's control methods for these transactions. Questions that are relevant include the following: Are sales forecasts and budgets prepared? Are cash budgets used? Are variances from sales budgets investigated and is appropriate action taken? and Are sales budgets used to evaluate employee performance?

With regard to the company's personnel policies and procedures, the auditors will determine whether employees who handle cash are bonded. In addition, internal control is improved when these individuals are required to take vacations, and when assigned duties are rotated periodically.

Accounting System and Control Procedures.    The auditors' consideration of the accounting system and control procedures relating to the revenue cycle may begin with the preparation of a written description or flowchart and the completion of an internal control questionnaire. Typical of the questions comprising an internal control questionnaire for the cycle are questions such as the following: Are orders from customers initiated and reviewed by the sales department? Are sales invoices prenumbered and all numbers accounted for? Are all sales approved by the credit department before shipment? An internal control questionnaire for cash receipts was illustrated in Chapter 8.

After the auditors have prepared a flowchart (or other description) of the internal control policies and procedures, they should determine whether the client is actually using the policies and procedures—that is, they must determine whether the controls have been *placed in operation*. As the auditors verify their understanding of the revenue cycle, they will observe whether there is an appropriate segregation of duties and inquire as to who performed various functions throughout the year. They may also perform a walk-through of the cycle. The term *walk-through* means to trace a few transactions through each step of the system to determine that transactions actually are being processed in the manner indicated by the flowchart. In addition the auditors will inspect various documents, such as bills of lading, sales invoices, and remittance advices, and review document files to determine that the client is appropriately accounting for the sequence of prenumbered documents. Figure 12–3 illustrates these documents and the primary accounts involved in the revenue cycle.

# TESTING CONTROLS AND ASSESSING CONTROL RISK

To assess control risk, the auditors evaluate the effectiveness of a client's internal control policies and procedures in preventing or detecting material misstatements in the financial statements. Control risk is assessed in terms of the five financial statement assertions—existence or occurrence; completeness; rights and obligations; valuation or allocation; and presentation and disclosure. An understanding of the internal control structure relating to the revenue cycle enables the auditors to determine a planned assessed level of control risk for the various assertions about sales and accounts receivable. When control risk is to be assessed at a level lower than the maximum, appropriate tests of controls are performed to justify such an assessment. In the following section, typical tests of controls are presented as they relate to the primary financial statement assertions.

## Existence or Occurrence

Tests of controls for the existence or occurrence assertion address whether the recorded sales transactions occurred during the period and whether the resulting recorded accounts receivable exist. When performing these tests of controls, the auditors carefully review the terms of the "sale" to determine whether revenue should be recognized. For example, extremely liberal "return" privileges may raise a question as to whether a sale may properly be reported. Also, various accounting standards address when revenue may be recognized for sales of items such as real estate, receivables with recourse, and assets that are leased back.

An appropriate segregation of duties for the revenue cycle provides assurance in support of the assertion of existence or occurrence, as well as most others. Since the segregation of duties leaves no documentary evidence of performance, the auditors' tests of controls include observation of employees performing various functions and inquiry as to who performed the functions throughout the year.

Tests of controls over existence of receivables and occurrence of sales may also involve examination of the significant aspects of a sample of sales transactions. Because these tests involve inspection and reperformance procedures, the auditors may use either statistical or nonstatistical sampling techniques, as discussed in Chapter 10. Generalized audit software may be used to select the transactions to be tested.

In manufacturing companies, the audit procedures for verifying the occurrence of a sales transaction may begin with selection of a sample of sales invoices and comparison with the customer's purchase order and the client's sales order. The date of each invoice is then compared with the date of the shipping document and the date of entry in the accounts receivable subsidiary ledger. The auditors also examine evidence that credit approval was obtained for the sale prior to the time that the goods were shipped.

If the client has established effective computer application controls for sales transactions, the auditors might decide to test these controls directly instead of testing a sample of sales transactions. Tests of application controls might involve inspecting evidence of the operations control group's reconciliation of batch control totals for sales transactions, and the follow-up on any transactions that are listed on exception reports. The auditors might also observe the application of input validity tests as sales transactions are entered. They may even enter test data to obtain additional evidence about performance of application controls.

The auditors should also investigate the internal controls for sales to related parties. Effective control over intercompany or interbranch transfers of merchandise often requires the same kind of formal procedures for billing, shipping, and collections as for outsiders; hence, these movements of merchandise are often invoiced and recorded as sales. When the operations of the several organizational units are combined or consolidated into one income statement, however, it is apparent that any transactions not representing sales to outsiders should be eliminated from consolidated sales. In the audit of a client that operates subsidiaries or branches, the auditors should also investigate the procedures for recording movements of merchandise among the various units of the company.

Tests of controls over existence of accounts receivable may also involve evaluation of the client's procedures for mailing monthly statements to customers. The auditors may inquire about these procedures and inspect any evidence of follow-up on errors reported by customers.

Controls over cash receipts are important to the existence assertion of accounts receivable. If cash receipts are received but not recorded, accounts receivable may remain in the client's records when they no longer exist. The client's segregation of duties and policies for reconciling of bank accounts are likely to provide relatively strong assurance about accurate recording of cash receipts. To test the client's reconciliation procedures, the auditors may select a sample of the bank (financial institution) reconciliations performed during the year, noting who performed them. The auditors will review the reconciliations and in some cases may decide to *reperform* the reconciliation process by reference to accounting records, bank statements, and canceled checks.

Satisfactory internal control over cash receipts demands that each day's collections be deposited intact that day, or no later than the next banking day. To provide assurance that cash receipts have been deposited intact, the auditors should compare the detail of selected original cash receipts listings (mail room listings and register tapes) to the detail of the daily deposit slips.

Comparison of the daily entries in the cash receipts journal with bank deposits may disclose a type of fraud known as lapping. *Lapping* means the concealment of a cash shortage by delaying the recording of cash receipts. If cash collected from customer A is withheld by the cashier, a subsequent collection from customer B may be entered as a credit to A's account. B's account will not be shown as paid until a collection from customer C is recorded as a credit to B. Unless the money abstracted by the cashier is replaced, the accounts receivable as a group remain overstated; but judicious shifting of the overstatement from one account receivable to another may avert protests from customers receiving monthly statements. The following schedule makes clear how a lapping activity may be carried on. In companies in which the cashier has access to the general accounting records, shortages created in this manner have sometimes been transferred to inventory accounts or elsewhere in the records for temporary concealment.

| Date | Actually Received From | Actual Cash Receipts | Recorded as Received From | Receipts Recorded and Deposited | Receipts Withheld |
|------|------|------|------|------|------|
| Dec. 1 | Abbott | $ 750 |  |  | $ 750 |
|  | Crane | 1,035 | Crane | $1,035 |  |
| 2 | Barstow | 750 | Abbott | 750 |  |
|  | White | 130 | White | 130 |  |
| 3 | Crawford | 1,575 | Barstow | 750 | 825 |
|  | Miller | 400 | Miller | 400 |  |
|  |  | $4,640 |  | $3,065 | $1,575 |

Lapping is most easily carried on when an employee who receives collections from customers is responsible for the posting of customers' accounts. Familiarity with customers' accounts makes it relatively easy to lodge a shortage in an account that will not be questioned.

## Completeness

Tests of controls for completeness for the revenue cycle provide assurance that all sales and receivables have been recorded. As is the case with the existence or occurrence assertion, an appropriate segregation of duties generally provides the best assurance for completeness. Therefore, the auditors will observe and inquire about how functions critical to the recording of sales transactions and collection of receivables are performed. In addition, to determine that all transactions have been properly recorded the auditors will assess controls over the process of budgeting sales and cash receipts to determine whether the client's personnel are likely to detect unrecorded transactions.

When describing tests of controls for existence or occurrence, tests that involved examining the significant aspects of a sample of sales transactions were discussed. Those procedures would not disclose orders that had been shipped but not recorded or billed, because the direction of the tests was from the recorded entry to the supporting documents. To test controls for the completeness assertion, the auditors perform tests to determine that shipping documents have been prepared and maintained for all shipments. For example, the auditors may determine whether a shipping document is required before any goods leave the warehouse.

After establishing that the shipping documents represent the actual shipments, the auditors may select a sample of shipping documents issued during the year and compare them to sales invoices. In making this test, particular emphasis should be placed upon accounting for all shipping documents by serial number. Any voided shipping documents should have been canceled and retained in the files. The purposeful or accidental destruction of shipping documents before the creation of a sales invoice might go undetected if this type of test were not performed.

When shipping data are entered into the computer system by personnel in the shipping department, the auditors' test of completeness controls might involve tests of the application controls. As an example, the auditors might inspect evidence that the operations control group performed reconciliations of the item counts and control totals of the batches of shipping documents.

When auditing adjustments to sales and receivables, the auditors should review the use and authorization of the credit memoranda. Selected credits to customers' accounts may be compared to credit memoranda and other supporting documents. In this way the auditors may determine that the client's procedures for controlling sales returns and allowances and write-offs of uncollectible accounts are operating effectively.

When auditing clients with substantial amounts of cash sales, the auditors may compare selected cash register readings or tapes with daily totals in the sales journal. The serial number of all sales tickets used during selected periods should be accounted for and individual tickets should be tested for accuracy of calculations.

## Rights and Obligations

Evidence about rights and obligations for the revenue cycle relates most directly to whether a legally valid sale has occurred, and whether the client retains rights to the receivables involved. When inventory has been consigned, no sale or receivable should be recorded until the appropriate conditions have been met relating to the consignee's sale of the goods. Also, the factoring of receivables may result in a situation in which the receivables are no longer owned by the client. The auditors should inquire about the client's procedures for identifying consigned goods and factored accounts receivable, and examine any supporting documentation.

## Valuation or Allocation

Effective pricing and sales discount policies for customer invoices are a necessary element of good internal control over valuation of sales and accounts receivable. After discussing the policies with management, the policies may be tested by inspecting selected invoices for evidence of the "second person" review of the invoices. The invoices selected for testing may be verified by comparison with authorized price lists, catalogs, or contracts with customers. After inspecting and recalculating the accuracy of selected individual invoices, the auditors may decide to trace the invoices to the sales journal and to postings in the accounts receivable subsidiary ledger. The extensions and footings of sampled invoices also may be tested for arithmetical accuracy.

When a computerized billing system is in use, the auditors will test the control procedures for developing the billing information. For example, the client's program that updates prices may produce an edit report that details the price changes made. Sales personnel may be required to review the report to determine that only authorized changes are made and indicate approval by initialing the report. The auditors may test this control by examining a sample of the edit reports generated during the year. The auditors may also test the input validation checks that test the validity and completeness of information as it is entered into the system. Tests of these controls might involve observation of the application of these controls as real data are being entered by client personnel. To obtain additional evidence, the auditors may decide to enter test data into the system.

Appropriate valuation of accounts receivable requires that the client's allowance for uncollectible accounts be adequate in amount. Therefore, the auditors will review the client's policies for evaluating the creditworthiness of customers and establishing customer credit limits. The policies may be tested by reviewing selected customer credit files. As indicated previously, the auditor will also test selected sales transactions to determine that credit was approved prior to shipment of goods.

The auditors are also concerned with the client's procedures for following up on past due accounts. To test these procedures the auditors may examine selected aged trial balances that were reviewed by credit personnel, and inspect available evidence of the procedures used to follow up on past due accounts.

## Presentation and Disclosure

The presentation and disclosure assertion relating to the revenue cycle deals with whether the related components of the financial statements are properly classified, described, and disclosed. Here, the auditors will assess the client's controls for identifying required disclosures such as those for related-party transactions, consignments, and various restrictions on accounts. For example, these controls might include the use of a chart of accounts, and an independent review of the classification of sales transactions by accounting personnel. Because this assertion deals largely with disclosures required in the financial statements, auditors often choose to assess control risk at a high level and rely upon substantive testing procedures to determine that the disclosures are presented properly.

# Reassess Control Risk

When the auditors have completed the procedures described in the preceding sections, they should reassess the extent of control risk for each financial statement assertion for accounts involved in the revenue cycle, including receivables, sales, and cash. Figure 12–4 summarizes the relationships among the assertions, the internal control policies and procedures, and typical tests of controls. This figure illustrates which internal control policies and procedures affect the auditors' assessments of control risk for the various assertions. Substantive tests will be designed based on the reassessed levels of control risk.

# Figure 12-4 Assessing Control Risk for Receivables and Sales

| Internal Control Policy or Procedure | Typical Tests of the Control Policy or Procedure | Existence or occurrence | Completeness | Rights and obligations | Valuation or allocation | Presentation & disclosure |
|---|---|---|---|---|---|---|
| Segregate duties over sales and collections of receivables | Observe and make inquiries about the performance of various functions | X | X | X | X | |
| Match sales invoices with shipping documents, purchase orders, and sales orders | Select a sample of sales invoices and compare details to shipping documents, purchase orders, and sales orders | X | | X | X | |
| Review of the clerical accuracy of sales invoices by a second person | Select a sample of sales invoices and examine them for evidence of second-person review | | | | X | |
| Obtain credit approval of sales prior to shipment | Make inquiries about credit policies; select a sample of sales transactions and examine evidence of credit approval | X | | | X | |
| Mail monthly statements to customers and follow up on errors reported | Observe and make inquiries about the mailing of statements and review evidence of follow-up | X | X | X | X | |
| Reconcile bank (financial institution) accounts monthly | Review a sample of bank reconciliations performed during the year | X | | X | X | |
| Use control listing to control cash collections | Observe, make inquiries about the process, and reconcile selected listings to the bank and accounting records | X | X | X | X | |
| Use budgets and analyze variances from actual amounts | Examine budgets and evidence of follow-up on variances | X | X | X | X | |
| Use prenumbered shipping and billing documents and account for the sequence | Observe and make inquiries about the use of prenumbered documents and inspect evidence of accounting for the sequence | | X | | | |
| Use credit memoranda for authorization of adjustments to sales and receivables | Select a sample of credits to customers' accounts and inspect credit memoranda and other supporting documents | | X | | X | |
| Use a chart of accounts and an independent review of account classifications | Inspect the chart of accounts and evidence of the review of account classifications | | | | | X |

# ◆ ILLUSTRATIVE AUDIT CASE: KEYSTONE COMPUTERS & NETWORKS, INC.

# PART II: CONSIDERATION OF INTERNAL CONTROL

This second part of the audit case of Keystone Computers & Networks, Inc. (KCN) illustrates the manner in which auditors obtain an understanding of the internal control structure, perform tests of controls, and assess control risk. The process is illustrated with the revenue cycle, and includes the following working papers:

◆ A questionnaire to evaluate the control environment of the company. Since this questionnaire is designed for nonpublic companies, it does not address control environment factors that are generally found only in public companies, such as an audit committee of the board of directors and an internal audit function.

◆ An organizational chart for the company. This working paper helps the auditors evaluate the overall segregation of functions within the company.

◆ A flowchart description of the revenue cycle of the company and the related internal control policies and procedures prepared by the staff of Adams, Barnes & Co. (ABC), CPAs.

◆ ABC's working paper for assessment of control risk for accounts receivable and sales as it would appear before any tests of controls are performed. This working paper identifies the internal controls and weaknesses for the revenue cycle. It also relates the internal controls and weaknesses to the various financial statement assertions about sales and accounts receivable.

◆ The audit program for tests of controls for the revenue cycle. This working paper describes the various tests of controls that were performed by the staff of ABC to obtain evidence about the operating effectiveness of the internal control policies and procedures. These tests provide the support for the auditors' assessed level of control risk.

◆ ABC's working paper documenting the results of tests of controls that were performed using audit sampling.

◆ ABC's working paper for assessment of control risk for accounts receivable and sales as it would appear after all tests of controls are performed. Notice that the auditors have checked the boxes indicating that the controls are operating effectively. This allows ABC's staff to arrive at the final assessed level of control risk as indicated at the bottom of the working paper.

You should read through the information to obtain an understanding of the way in which auditors document their understanding of internal control and the assessment of control risk for a transaction cycle. You may also wish to review the planning documentation presented on pages 220 through 228 of Chapter 7 to refresh your knowledge about the nature of the company's business.

## Obtaining and Documenting an Understanding of the Revenue Cycle

ABC's consideration of the internal controls relating to the revenue cycle began by updating various working papers, including the following:

◆ Control Environment Questionnaire—IC-3 and IC-4.
◆ Organizational Chart of KCN—IC-5.
◆ Revenue Cycle Flowchart—IC-8.
◆ Assessment of Control Risk Worksheet (before tests of controls are performed)—IC-20.

The Control Environment Questionnaire (IC-3 and IC-4), the Organizational Chart (IC-5), and the Revenue Cycle Flowchart (IC-8) required only limited updating as there were few changes in internal control during the year, and key personnel are the same as in the preceding year. After completing the description of internal control the audit staff of ABC observed operation of the system and found that the internal controls had been placed in operation.

The staff of ABC then used the documentation of internal control to identify controls and weaknesses on Schedule IC-20. This schedule includes a check box in the appropriate column to designate the financial statement assertions that are addressed by the internal control policy or procedure. For the weaknesses, an "X" is included in the appropriate columns. Before tests of controls are performed the check boxes are blank because the auditors do not know whether the controls are operating effectively.

## Testing Controls and Assessing Control Risk

When obtaining an understanding of the overall internal control structure, ABC's audit staff first considered the elements of the control environment as documented with the Control Environment Questionnaire, IC-3 and IC-4. As indicated on the questionnaire, they found that the control environment is strong and reflects an atmosphere conducive to the effective operation of the accounting system and control procedures.

Based on their understanding of internal control, ABC's staff planned assessed levels of control risk at a low level for completeness, and at a moderate level for existence or occurrence, rights, and valuation. As with most small businesses, the auditors found that KCN had no effective internal controls to address the presentation and disclosure assertion. Based on the planned assessed levels, the audit staff of ABC designed a program (IC-12 and IC-13) to test the controls. Schedule IC-15 illustrates how they determined sample size and evaluated the results of tests of controls that involved audit sampling.

The completed Schedule IC-20[1] on pages 417–18 includes check marks to indicate that the tests of controls demonstrated that the related internal controls were operating effectively. Based on these results, the auditors' assessed levels of control risk—indicated in the last row of Schedule IC-20—were supported at their planned levels. These assessments will be used to determine the nature, timing, and extent of substantive tests of sales and accounts receivable. These tests will be illustrated in Part III of the case in Chapter 13.

---

[1]This schedule is included twice (incomplete and complete) for illustrative purposes. In an actual audit, only the completed schedule would be included.

| **Control Environment Questionnaire—Nonpublic Companies** | | | IC-3 |
| --- | --- | --- | --- |

*WL*
*11/10/X5*

**Client:** *Keystone Computers & Networks, Inc.*

**Financial Statement Date:** *12/31/X5*

|  | Yes | No | N/A | Comments |
| --- | --- | --- | --- | --- |

**Management Philosophy and Operating Style**

1. Does management have clear objectives in terms of budget, profit, and other financial and operating goals? — √

2. Are such objectives clearly written, actively communicated, and monitored? — √

3. Does management adequately consider the potential effects of taking large or unusual business risks prior to doing so? — √

4. Are business risks adequately monitored? — √

**Organizational Structure**

5. Is the organization of the entity clearly defined in terms of lines of authority and responsibility? — √

6. Does the entity have a current organizational chart and related materials such as job descriptions? — √

7. Are policies and procedures for authorization of transactions established at an adequately high level? — √

8. Are such policies and procedures adequately adhered to? — √

**Methods of Assigning Authority and Responsibility**

9. Are authority and responsibility to deal with organizational goals and objectives, operating functions, and regulatory requirements adequately delegated? — √

10. Has management established and communicated policies about appropriate business practices and conduct and conflicts of interest? — √

11. Has the entity developed computer systems documentation which indicates the procedures for authorizing transactions and approving systems changes? — √

| **Control Environment Questionnaire—Nonpublic Companies,** continued | IC-4 |

*WL*
*11/10/X5*

**Client:** *Keystone Computers & Networks, Inc.*

**Financial Statement Date:** *12/31/X5*

|  | Yes | No | N/A | Comments |
|---|---|---|---|---|
| **Management Control Methods** | | | | |
| 12. Are there regular meetings of the board of directors to set policies and objectives, review the entity's performance, and take appropriate action, and are minutes of such meetings prepared and signed on a timely basis? | ✓ | | | |
| 13. Has the entity established planning and reporting systems that set forth management's plans and the results of actual performance? | ✓ | | | |
| 14. Do the planning and reporting systems adequately identify variances from planned performance? | ✓ | | | *Monthly* |
| 15. Does the entity have established policies for developing and modifying accounting systems and control procedures? | ✓ | | | |
| **Personnel Policies and Procedures** | | | | |
| 16. Does the entity employ sound hiring practices, including background investigations, where appropriate? | ✓ | | | |
| 17. Are employees adequately trained to meet their job responsibilities? | ✓ | | | |
| 18. Is employee performance evaluated at regular intervals? | ✓ | | | |
| 19. Are employees in positions of trust bonded? | ✓ | | | |
| 20. Are employees in positions of trust required to take vacations and are their duties rotated while they are on vacation? | ✓ | | | |

Conclusion:   *The control environment of the company appears to be strong and reflects an atmosphere conducive to the effective operation of the accounting system and control procedures.*

**KEYSTONE COMPUTERS & NETWORKS, INC.**
Organizational Chart
12/31/X5

IC-5

*WL*
*11/11/X5*

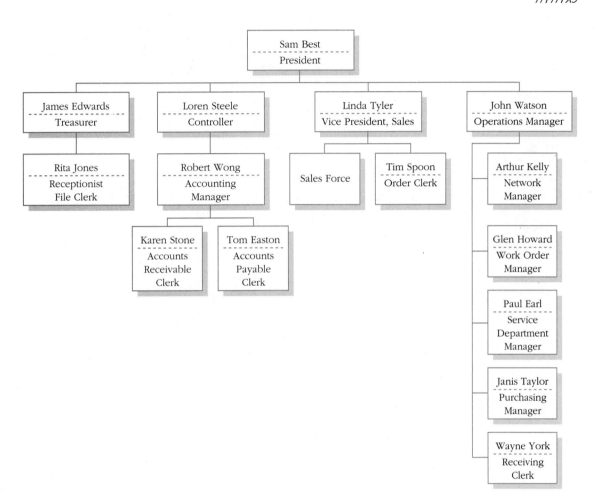

**KEYSTONE COMPUTERS & NETWORKS, INC.**

Internal Control Structure—Revenue Cycle

12/31/X5

IC-8

*WL*

*11/11/X5*

| Order Clerk Tim Spoon | Work Order Manager Glen Howard | Accounts Receivable Clerk Karen Stone |
|---|---|---|

Receives Customer Order from Salesman

Credit for New Customers Approved by President

Order Keyed into Computer

Computer Generates Sales Invoice → Sales Transactions File

Sales Invoice

To Customer

Computer Generates Sales Invoice

Shipping Order

Prepares Equipment for Delivery

Inputs Shipping Information into Computer

Computer Generates Delivery Receipt

Delivery Receipt

Goods Delivered by Salesman or Truck Driver (Customer Signs Copy of Receipt)

Signed Delivery Receipt from Salesman and Truck Driver

Signed Delivery Receipt

Sales Invoice Copy

Matches Invoice and Delivery Receipt and Accounts for Numerical Sequences

Filed by #

Prelisting 2

Copies of Checks

Inputs Cash Receipts from Copies of Checks and Prelisting

Cash Receipts Journal

Sales Transactions File

Computer Updates Accounts Receivable Master File

Cash Receipt Transactions

Accounts Receivable Master File

Exception Reports

Computer Prints Reports

Sales Journal

Accounts Receivable Ledger

Aged Accounts Receivable Schedule

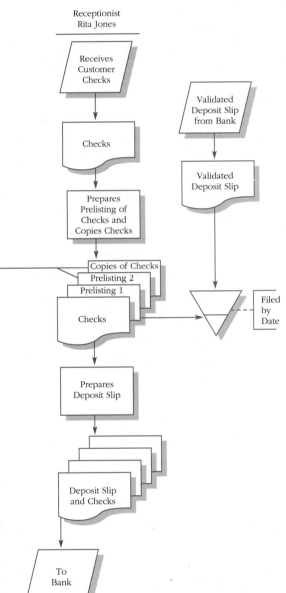

Notes:

1. The company uses MAS 90, a commercial accounting software package that has not been modified.

2. The company has a local area network, with computer terminals in the purchasing, work order, and accounting departments.

3. Sales orders are entered on an online terminal that applies the following application controls:

   • The order clerk's password is verified before transactions are accepted.

   • Customer numbers are agreed to customer master file information.

   • Computer determines whether the customer has sufficient credit limit remaining to make the purchase. If rejected, the customer's credit limit must be increased by the president or the terms must be changed to cash on delivery.

   • Computer will require override of the transaction by the order clerk any time the sales price of an item is less than its cost.

   • Computer assigns number to sales invoice.

4. Shipping information is entered to an on-line terminal that applies the following controls:

   • The work order manager's password is verified before shipping data are accepted.

   • The shipping data are agreed to details of the sales transactions that were entered by the sales order clerk. If the name of the customer or the quantities shipped do not agree the system will reject the data. Override will only be accepted by the system from the vice president of sales by password.

   • Computer assigns number to delivery receipt.

5. Cash receipts are entered to an on-line terminal that applies the following controls:

   • The accounts receivable clerk's password is verified before transactions are accepted.

   • When the customer number is entered the company name is presented on screen for comparison by clerk.

6. As the computer updates the accounts receivable master file, it produces an exception report that contains any items with invalid customer numbers and any unusually large cash payments in relation to the customer's account balance. The accounting manager reviews and follows up on exceptions and any corrections are made the same day.

7. The accounting manager reconciles the master file of accounts receivable to the general ledger on a monthly basis.

8. Monthly statements are mailed to customers.

9. The receptionist endorses incoming checks "for deposit only" to the company's account.

10. Cash sales are minor in amount and the cash is accepted by the receptionist who maintains the company's cash fund.

11. Cash deposits are made daily.

12. Computer summaries of cash collections of accounts receivable and cash sales are reconciled to validated bank deposits slips and the prelisting of cash receipts by the accounting manager.

13. Sales returns and allowances are approved by the vice president—sales.

14. Write-offs of accounts receivable are approved by the president after initiation by the controller, but not on a regular basis.

15. Accounting manager reconciles bank account on a monthly basis.

**KEYSTONE COMPUTERS & NETWORKS, INC.**                    IC-20
Assessment of Control Risk—Revenue Cycle
12/31/X5                                          *WL*
                                                  *11/13/X5*

| Internal Controls | Existence or Occurrence | Complete-ness | Rights | Valuation | Presenta-tion and Disclosure |
|---|:---:|:---:|:---:|:---:|:---:|
| **Sales** | | | | | |
| 1. Separation of duties for authorization, credit approval, shipping, and accounting for sales transactions. | ☐ | ☐ | ☐ | ☐ | |
| 2. Company uses an unmodified commercial software package. | ☐ | ☐ | ☐ | ☐ | |
| 3. Credit lines are approved by the president. | | | | ☐ | |
| 4. Computer verifies the order clerk's password before sales data can be entered. | ☐ | | ☐ | ☐ | |
| 5. Application controls (input validation checks) are applied to ensure the accuracy of the billing process. | | | | ☐ | |
| 6. Computer assigns numbers to sales invoices. | | ☐ | | | |
| 7. Computer verifies the work order manager's password before shipping data can be entered. | ☐ | | ☐ | ☐ | |
| 8. Input validation checks are applied to shipping data as they are entered. | | | | ☐ | |
| 9. Computer assigns numbers to delivery receipts. | | ☐ | | | |
| 10. Accounts receivable clerk matches invoices with delivery receipts and accounts for numerical sequences. | | ☐ | | | |
| 11. Accounting manager reconciles the accounts receivable master file to the general ledger monthly. | ☐ | ☐ | ☐ | ☐ | |
| 12. Monthly statements are mailed to customers. | ☐ | ☐ | ☐ | ☐ | |
| 13. Sales returns and allowances are approved by the vice president of sales. | | | | ☐ | |

| Cash Receipts | Existence or Occurrence | Complete-ness | Rights | Valuation | Presenta-tion and Disclosure |
|---|---|---|---|---|---|
| 14. Separation of duties of custody of cash from records of cash receipts and accounts receivable. | ☐ | | ☐ | ☐ | |
| 15. Checks are prelisted and stamped with restrictive endorsement when received. | ☐ | | ☐ | ☐ | |
| 16. Application controls (input validation checks) are applied to ensure the accuracy of the recording of cash receipts. | | | | ☐ | |
| 17. Control totals are reconciled by the accounting manager. | ☐ | ☐ | ☐ | ☐ | |
| 18. Exception reports are reviewed and followed up on by the accounting manager. | | | | ☐ | |
| 19. Computer summaries of cash collections and cash sales are reconciled to bank deposits and prelisting of cash receipts by accounting manager. | ☐ | ☐ | ☐ | ☐ | |
| 20. Accounting manager reconciles bank account on a monthly basis. | ☐ | ☐ | ☐ | ☐ | |
| **Internal Control Weaknesses** | | | | | |
| 1. Sales invoices are prepared and mailed prior to delivery of goods. | X | | X | X | |
| 2. Accounts receivable are not written-off on a regular basis. | | | | X | |
| **Assessed Level of Control Risk** | *Moderate* | *Low* | *Moderate* | *Moderate* | *Maximum* |

| | | IC-12 |
|---|---|---|
| **Audit Program—Tests of Controls—Revenue Cycle** | | *WL* |
| | | *11/12/X5* |

**Client:** *Keystone Computers & Networks, Inc.*

**Financial Statement Date:** *12/31/X5*

| Procedure | Performed by | |
|---|---|---|
| | **Initials** | **Date** |

**Sales Transactions**

| Procedure | Initials | Date |
|---|---|---|
| 1. Observe and inquire about the segregation of duties for sales transactions. | *WL* | *11/15/X5* |
| 2. Inspect documentation of the MAS 90 software package. | *WL* | *11/15/X5* |
| 3. Inquire about the president's procedures for approving credit limits. | *WL* | *11/15/X5* |
| 4. Observe the order clerk when entering customer orders and enter several test transactions to determine that: | | |
|    *a.* Password must be entered to enter customer orders. | *MP* | *11/14/X5* |
|    *b.* The system performs a validity check for the customer's number. | *MP* | *11/14/X5* |
|    *c.* The system determines that the customer's credit limit is not exceeded. | *MP* | *11/14/X5* |
|    *d.* The system compares sales price to cost of product and requires override when cost exceeds sales price. | *MP* | *11/14/X5* |
| 5. Observe that the computer assigns numbers to sales invoices. | *MP* | *11/14/X5* |
| 6. Review the sales invoice file with delivery reports attached to obtain evidence that all numbers are accounted for and all invoices have an attached delivery report. | *MP* | *11/14/X5* |
| 6. Inquire about the accounting manager's procedures for reconciling the accounts receivable master file to the general ledger. | *WL* | *11/15/X5* |
| 7. Observe the mailing of monthly statements. | *MP* | *1/6/X6* |
| 8. Inquire about the procedures for approval of sales returns and allowances by the vice president–sales. | *WL* | *11/15/X5* |

| | | IC-13 |
|---|---|---|
| **Audit Program—Tests of Controls—Revenue Cycle,** continued | | *WL*<br>*11/12/X5* |

**Client:** *Keystone Computers & Networks, Inc.*

**Financial Statement Date:** *12/31/X5*

| | Performed by | |
|---|---|---|
| **Procedure** | **Initials** | **Date** |

**Cash Receipts**

9. Observe and inquire about the segregation of duties for cash receipts. — *WL* — *11/15/X5*

10. Observe the prelisting and endorsement of checks by the receptionist. — *MP* — *11/13/X5*

11. Observe the accounts receivable clerk entering cash receipts to determine that:

    *a.* Password must be entered to enter cash receipts. — *MP* — *11/14/X5*

    *b.* Customer's name is shown on screen when customer number is entered. — *MP* — *11/14/X5*

12. Test the procedures for reconciling control totals from the accounts receivable program as follows:

    *a.* Inquire about the procedures. — *WL* — *11/14/X5*

    *b.* Select a sample of printouts of the control totals and inspect them for evidence of reconciliation. Use the following parameters:
    (1) Risk of assessing control risk too low—10%.
    (2) Tolerable deviation rate—7%.
    (3) Expected deviation rate—1%. — *WL* — *11/14/X5*

13. Test the procedures for review and follow-up on the exception reports from the accounts receivable program as follows:

    *a.* Inquire about the procedures. — *WL* — *11/14/X5*

    *b.* Select a sample of exception reports and inspect them for evidence of follow-up on the exceptions. Use the following parameters:
    (1) Risk of assessing control risk too low—10%.
    (2) Tolerable deviation rate—10%.
    (3) Expected deviation rate—0%. — *WL* — *11/14/X5*

14. Test the procedures for reconciling the computer summary of cash collections and cash sales to the deposit slips and prelisting of cash receipts as follow:

    *a.* Inquire about the procedures. — *WL* — *11/14/X5*

    *b.* Select a sample of the computer summaries and inspect them for evidence of the reconciliation. Use the following parameters:
    (1) Risk of assessing control risk too low—10%.
    (2) Tolerable deviation rate—10%.
    (3) Expected deviation rate—1%. — *WL* — *11/14/X5*

15. Inquire about the procedures for reconciliation of bank accounts. — *WL* — *11/14/X5*

16. Inspect _4_ bank reconciliations performed during the year. — *WL* — *11/14/X5*

### KEYSTONE COMPUTERS & NETWORKS, INC.
### Attributes Sampling Summary—Revenue Cycle
### December 31, 19X5

IC-15

*WL*
*11/14/X5*

**Objectives of test:** *(1) To test the operating effectiveness of the procedures for reconciling control totals of computer run for updating accounts receivable; (2) To test the operating effectiveness of the procedures for review and follow-up on the exception reports from the computer run for updating accounts receivable; (3) To test the operating effectiveness of the procedures for reconciling the computer summary of cash collections and cash sales to the deposit slips and prelisting of cash receipts.*

| Test | Population | Size |
|------|-----------|------|
| 1 | Control total reports | 234 |
| 2 | Exception reports | 234 |
| 3 | Computer summaries of collections and cash sales | 234 |

**Sampling unit:** *Individual reports*

**Random selection procedure:** *Random number table*

**Risk of assessing control risk too low:** *10 percent*

| | Planning Parameters | | | Sample Results | |
|---|---|---|---|---|---|
| **Attributes Tested:** | **Tolerable Deviation Rate** | **Expected Deviation Rate** | **Sample Size** | **Number of Deviations** | **Achieved Maximum Rate** |
| 1. Existence of a reconciliation of control totals initialed by the accounting manager. | 7% | 1% | 55 | 1 | 7% |
| 2. Indication of disposition of exceptions initialed by the accounting manager. | 10% | 0% | 22 | 0 | 10% |
| 3. Existence of a reconciliation of cash collections and cash sales to prelisting and deposit slips initialed by the accounting clerk. | 10% | 1% | 38 | 0 | 6.4% |

**Conclusion:** *The results support the assessment of control risk for completeness at a low level, and for existence, occurrence, rights and valuation at a moderate level.*

**KEYSTONE COMPUTERS & NETWORKS, INC.**
**Assessment of Control Risk—Revenue Cycle**
**12/31/X5**

IC-20

*WL*
*11/13/X5*

| Internal Controls | Existence or Occurrence | Complete-ness | Rights | Valuation | Presenta-tion and Disclosure |
|---|:---:|:---:|:---:|:---:|:---:|
| **Sales** | | | | | |
| 1.  Separation of duties for authorization, credit approval, shipping, and accounting for sales transactions. | ☑ | ☑ | ☑ | ☑ | |
| 2.  Company uses an unmodified commercial software package. | ☑ | ☑ | ☑ | ☑ | |
| 3.  Credit lines are approved by the president. | | | | ☑ | |
| 4.  Computer verifies the order clerk's password before sales data can be entered. | ☑ | | ☑ | ☑ | |
| 5.  Application controls (input validation checks) are applied to ensure the accuracy of the billing process. | | | | ☑ | |
| 6.  Computer assigns numbers to sales invoices. | | ☑ | | | |
| 7.  Computer verifies the work order manager's password before shipping data can be entered. | ☑ | | ☑ | ☑ | |
| 8.  Input validation checks are applied to shipping data as they are entered. | | | | ☑ | |
| 9.  Computer assigns numbers to delivery receipts. | | ☑ | | | |
| 10. Accounts receivable clerk matches invoices with delivery receipts and accounts for numerical sequences. | | ☑ | | | |
| 11. Accounting manager reconciles the accounts receivable master file to the general ledger monthly. | ☑ | ☑ | ☑ | ☑ | |
| 12. Monthly statements are mailed to customers. | ☑ | ☑ | ☑ | ☑ | |
| 13. Sales returns and allowances are approved by the vice president of sales. | | | | ☑ | |

| Cash Receipts | Existence or Occurrence | Complete-ness | Rights | Valuation | Presenta-tion and Disclosure |
|---|:---:|:---:|:---:|:---:|:---:|
| 14. Separation of duties of custody of cash from records of cash receipts and accounts receivable. | ☑ | | ☑ | ☑ | |
| 15. Checks are prelisted and stamped with restrictive endorsement when received. | ☑ | | ☑ | ☑ | |
| 16. Application controls (input validation checks) are applied to ensure the accuracy of the recording of cash receipts. | | | | ☑ | |
| 17. Control totals are reconciled by the accounting manager. | ☑ | ☑ | ☑ | ☑ | |
| 18. Exception reports are reviewed and followed up on by the accounting manager. | | | | ☑ | |
| 19. Computer summaries of cash collections and cash sales are reconciled to bank deposits and prelisting of cash receipts by accounting manager. | ☑ | ☑ | ☑ | ☑ | |
| 20. Accounting manager reconciles bank account on a monthly basis. | ☑ | ☑ | ☑ | ☑ | |
| **Internal Control Weaknesses** | | | | | |
| 1. Sales invoices are prepared and mailed prior to delivery of goods. | X | | X | X | |
| 2. Accounts receivable are not written-off on a regular basis. | | | | X | |
| **Assessed Level of Control Risk** | *Moderate* | *Low* | *Moderate* | *Moderate* | *Maximum* |

---

## ◆ CHAPTER SUMMARY

This chapter explained the details of the revenue cycle (sales and cash receipts) and the auditors' consideration of the internal control structure for this transaction cycle. To summarize:

1. The revenue cycle includes the receiving of orders from customers, the delivery and billing of goods and services, and the recording and collection of accounts receivable. Effective internal control over sales transactions is best achieved by having separate departments responsible for preparing sales orders, approving credit, shipping mer-

chandise, billing customers, maintaining the accounts receivable subsidiary ledger, and authorizing adjustments to sales and accounts receivable.

2.  Internal control over cash receipts should provide assurance that all cash received is recorded promptly and accurately. Control over cash sales is strongest when two or more employees participate in each transaction, or when collections are controlled by a cash register or an electronic point-of-sale system. When cash receipts consist of checks received through the mail, the receipts should be listed and controlled by personnel who do not maintain cash or accounts receivable records. The control listing should be reconciled to the entries in the cash receipts journal and deposit records from the financial institution.

3.  The auditors' consideration of internal control over the revenue cycle provides them with a basis for assessing control risk for the financial statement assertions about sales and receivable accounts. To assess control risk at less than the maximum for a particular assertion, the auditors must perform tests of the operating effectiveness of the revenue cycle controls. The auditors' assessment of control risk then is used to determine the nature, timing, and extent of the substantive tests of the sales and receivables. These tests are described in Chapter 13.

## ◆ KEY TERMS INTRODUCED OR EMPHASIZED IN CHAPTER 12

**Bill of lading**   A shipping document acknowledging items shipped (e.g., number of cartons), freight amount, weight, and so on. A bill of lading is required for common carriers and is essentially a shipping contract. A bill of lading may be prepared by either the company shipping goods or by a common carrier.

**Customer purchase order**   The document prepared by the customer indicating the goods the customer wishes to purchase and the related terms.

**Lockbox**   A post office box controlled by the company's bank at which cash remittances from customers are received. The bank picks up the remittances, immediately credits the cash to the company's bank account, and forwards the remittance advices to the company.

**Sales invoice**   A document prepared by the seller and sent to a customer containing information about the goods sold, including formal notice to the purchaser about the terms of payment.

**Sales order**   A document prepared by the company which translates the terms of the customer's purchase order into a set of specific instructions for guidance of various divisions within the organization, including the credit, finished goods, shipping, billing, and accounts receivable departments.

**Shipping document**   A document that may either be a formal bill of lading when a common carrier is involved, or a less formal document describing the items being shipped to a customer.

## ◆ GROUP I: REVIEW QUESTIONS

12-1   ''Strong internal control in a large company dictates that a separate credit department be established to authorize credit and the write-off of doubtful accounts.'' Do you agree with the quoted statement? Explain.

12-2    The auditors' work on cash may include preparing a description of internal controls and performing tests of controls. Which of these two steps should be performed first? What is the purpose of tests of controls?

12-3    Describe the types of control procedures that help ensure the accuracy of posting of cash receipts to customer accounts in a batch computer processing system.

12-4    What prevents the person who opens incoming mail from being able to abstract cash collections from customers?

12-5    Prepare an example of lapping of cash receipts, showing actual transactions and the cash receipts journal entries.

12-6    State briefly the objective of the billing function. What important document is created by the billing department?

12-7    Criticize the following quotation: ''A credit memorandum should be issued only when an account receivable is determined to be uncollectible.''

12-8    Explain the difference between a *customer's order* and a *sales order,* as these terms might be used by a manufacturing company making sales on credit.

12-9    Describe the role of the credit department in a manufacturing company.

12-10   The controller of a new client operating a medium-size manufacturing business complains to you that he believes the company has sustained significant losses on several occasions because certain sales invoices were misplaced and never recorded as accounts receivable. What internal control procedure can you suggest to guard against such problems?

12-11   In the examination of credit memoranda covering allowances to customers for goods returned, how can the auditors ascertain whether the customer actually did return merchandise in each case in which accounts receivable were reduced?

12-12   Among specific procedures that contribute to good internal control over accounts receivable are *(a)* the approval of uncollectible account write-offs and credit memoranda by an executive and *(b)* the sending of monthly statements to all customers. State three other procedures conducive to strong internal control.

12-13   An inexperienced clerk assigned to the preparation of sales invoices in a manufacturing company became confused as to the nature of certain articles being shipped, with the result that the prices used on the invoices were far less than called for in the company's price lists. What internal control procedures could be established to guard against such errors?

12-14   The accounts receivable section of the accounting department in Wind Power, Inc. maintains subsidiary ledgers that are posted from copies of the sales invoices transmitted daily from the billing department. How may the accounts receivable section be sure that it receives promptly a copy of each sales invoice prepared?

12-15   A company that ships goods to its customers must establish procedures to ensure that a sales invoice is prepared for every shipment. Describe procedures to meet this requirement.

12-16   What is meant by a ''lockbox system'' for cash receipts?

12-17   Auditors test controls through (1) inquiry of appropriate client personnel, (2) inspection of documents, (3) observation, and (4) reperformance of procedures. Which of these approaches are likely to be effective in testing the segregation of duties for sales transactions?

12-18   Comment on the following: ''Any voided prenumbered shipping documents should be properly mutilated and disposed of to eliminate any possibility of improper shipment of goods.''

12-19   Which other responsibilities are incompatible with the granting of credit memoranda to customers for returns of merchandise?

12-20   When testing for the completeness of recorded sales, would the auditors test from source documents to the recorded entries, or vice versa? Explain.

# ◆ GROUP II: QUESTIONS REQUIRING ANALYSIS

12-21   Fluid Controls, Inc., a manufacturing company, has retained you to perform an audit for the year ended December 31. Prior to the year-end, you begin to obtain an understanding of the new client's internal controls over cash.

You find that nearly all of the company's cash receipts are in the form of checks received through the mail, but there is no prelisting of cash receipts before they are recorded in the accounts. You find that the incoming mail is opened either by the cashier or by the employee maintaining the accounts receivable subsidiary ledger, depending on which employee has time available. The controller stresses the necessity of flexibility in assignment of duties to the 20 employees comprising the office staff, in order to keep all employees busy and achieve maximum economy of operation.

*Required:*   *a.*   Explain how prelisting of cash receipts strengthens internal control.
           *b.*   List specific duties that should not be performed by an employee assigned to prelist the cash receipts in order to avoid any opportunity for that employee to conceal embezzlement of cash receipts.

(AICPA, adapted)

12-22   Although the primary objective of an independent audit is not the discovery of fraud, the auditors in their work on cash take into consideration the high inherent risk associated with this asset. Evidence of this attitude is illustrated by the CPA's alertness for signs of lapping.

*Required:*   *a.*   Define lapping.
           *b.*   Explain the audit procedures that CPAs might utilize to uncover lapping.

12-23   If you were preparing a credit sales system flowchart, what document would you show as:
    *a.*   The source for posting debits to a customer's account in the accounts receivable ledger?
    *b.*   Authorization to the finished goods stores to release merchandise to the shipping department?
    *c.*   The source for preparing a sales order?
    *d.*   The source for preparing a bill of lading?
    *e.*   The source for an entry in the sales journal?

12-24   Select the best answer for each of the following and explain fully the reason for your selection.
    *a.*   To determine that all sales have been recorded, the auditors would select a sample of transactions *from* the:
        (1)   Shipping documents file.
        (2)   Sales journal.
        (3)   Accounts receivable subsidiary ledger.
        (4)   Remittance advices.
    *b.*   Identify the control that is most likely to prevent the concealment of a cash shortage resulting from the improper write-off of a trade account receivable:
        (1)   Write-offs must be approved by a responsible official after review of credit department recommendations and supporting evidence.
        (2)   Write-offs must be approved by the accounts receivable department.
        (3)   Write-offs must be authorized by the shipping department.

(4)   Write-offs must be supported by an aging schedule showing that only receivables overdue by several months have been written off.

*c.*   To ensure effective internal control over cash receipts, a client may:
(1)   Use a lockbox system.
(2)   Allow sales only to customers who have passed a rigid credit check.
(3)   Decentralize receiving of cash to the extent possible.
(4)   Separate cash handling from cash custody responsibilities.

*d.*   Which of the following segregation of duties would make "lapping" of accounts receivable least likely?
(1)   Segregate the cash receipts from cash disbursements functions.
(2)   Segregate cash receipts from reconciliation of bank accounts.
(3)   Segregate cash receipts from posting of customer accounts.
(4)   Segregate cash receipts from cash sales.

*e.*   For effective internal control, employees who maintain the accounts receivable subsidiary ledger should not also approve:
(1)   Employee overtime.
(2)   Write-off customer accounts.
(3)   Cash disbursements.
(4)   Purchases.

*f.*   Which of the following is *not* likely to be an effective control over cash sales?
(1)   Encourage customers to obtain receipts and observe cash register totals.
(2)   Deposit cash sales daily.
(3)   Install electronic point-of-sale systems.
(4)   Separate credit authorization from analysis of past-due accounts.

# ◆ GROUP III: PROBLEMS

**12-25**   The Art Appreciation Society operates a museum for the benefit and enjoyment of the community. During hours when the museum is open to the public, two clerks who are positioned at the entrance collect a five-dollar admission fee from each nonmember patron. Members of the Art Appreciation Society are permitted to enter free of charge upon presentation of their membership cards.

At the end of each day one of the clerks delivers the proceeds to the treasurer. The treasurer counts the cash in the presence of the clerk and places it in a safe. Each Friday afternoon the treasurer and one of the clerks deliver all cash held in the safe to the bank and receive an authenticated deposit slip that provides the basis for the weekly entry in the cash receipts journal.

The board of directors of the Art Appreciation Society has identified a need to improve its internal control over cash admission fees. The board has determined that the cost of installing turnstiles, sales booths, or otherwise altering the physical layout of the museum will greatly exceed any benefits which may be derived. However, the board has agreed that the sale of admission tickets must be an integral part of its improvement efforts.

Smith has been asked by the board of directors of the Art Appreciation Society to review the internal control over cash admission fees and provide suggestions for improvement.

*Required:*   Indicate weaknesses in the existing internal control over cash admission fees, which Smith should identify, and recommend one improvement for each of the weaknesses identified.

Organize the answer as indicated in the following illustrative example:

| Weakness | Recommendation |
|---|---|
| 1. There is no documentation to establish the number of paying patrons. | 1. Prenumbered admission tickets should be issued upon payment of the admission fee. |

(AICPA, adapted)

12-26  John Harris, CPA, has been engaged to audit the financial statements of the Spartan Drug Store, Inc. Spartan is a medium-sized retail outlet that sells a wide variety of consumer goods. All sales are for cash or check. Cashiers utilize cash registers to process these transactions. There are no receipts by mail and there are no credit card or charge sales.

*Required:*  Construct the "Processing Cash Collections" segment of the internal control questionnaire on "Cash Receipts" to be used in the evaluation of the internal control structure for the Spartan Drug Store, Inc. Each question should elicit either a yes or no response. Do *not* discuss the internal controls over cash sales.

(AICPA, adapted)

12-27  The cashier of Mission Corporation intercepted customer A's check, payable to the company in the amount of $500, and deposited it in a bank account that was part of the company petty cash fund, of which he was custodian. He then drew a $500 check on the petty cash fund bank account payable to himself, signed it, and cashed it. At the end of the month, while processing the monthly statements to customers, he was able to change the statement to customer A to show that A had received credit for the $500 check that had been intercepted. Ten days later he made an entry in the cash receipts journal that purported to record receipt of a remittance of $500 from customer A, thus restoring A's account to its proper balance but overstating cash in the bank. He covered the overstatement by omitting from the list of outstanding checks in the bank reconciliation two checks, the aggregate amount of which was $500.

*Required:*  Discuss briefly what you regard as the more important deficiencies in internal control in the above situation and, in addition, include what you consider a proper remedy for each deficiency.

12-28  The following are typical questions that might appear on an internal control questionnaire for accounts receivable:
   1. Are sales invoices checked for proper pricing, terms, and clerical accuracy?
   2. Are shipping documents prenumbered and all numbers accounted for?
   3. Is customer credit approval obtained from the credit department prior to shipment of goods?

*Required:*  a. Describe the purpose of each of the above internal control procedures.
   b. Describe the manner in which the operating effectiveness of each of the above procedures might be tested.
   c. Assuming that the operating effectiveness of each of the above procedures is found to be inadequate, describe how the auditors might alter their substantive tests to compensate for the increased level of control risk.

12-29  The flowchart on page 424 depicts the activities relating to the sales, shipping, billing, and collecting processes used by Newton Hardware, Inc.

*Required:*  Identify the weaknesses in internal control relating to the activities of
   a. The warehouse clerk.
   b. Bookkeeper A.
   c. The collection clerk.

(AICPA, adapted)

12-30  A CPA's audit working papers include the narrative description below of the cash receipts and billing portions of the internal control structure of Parktown Medical Center, Inc. Parktown is a small health care provider that is owned by a publicly held corporation. It employs 7 salaried

| Sales Clerk | Warehouse Clerk | Bookkeeper A |
|---|---|---|

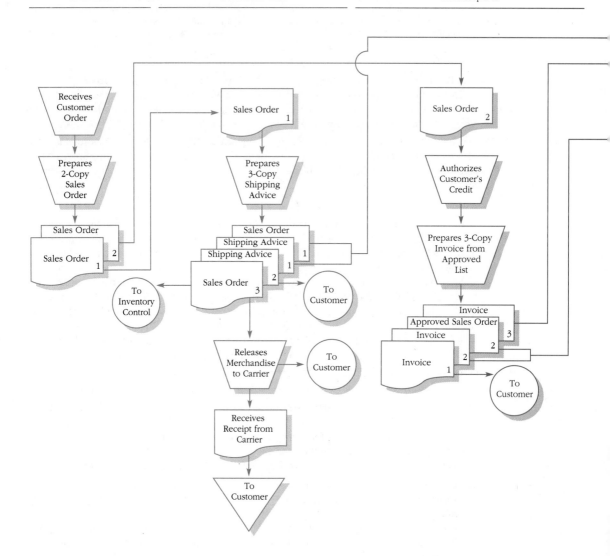

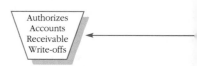

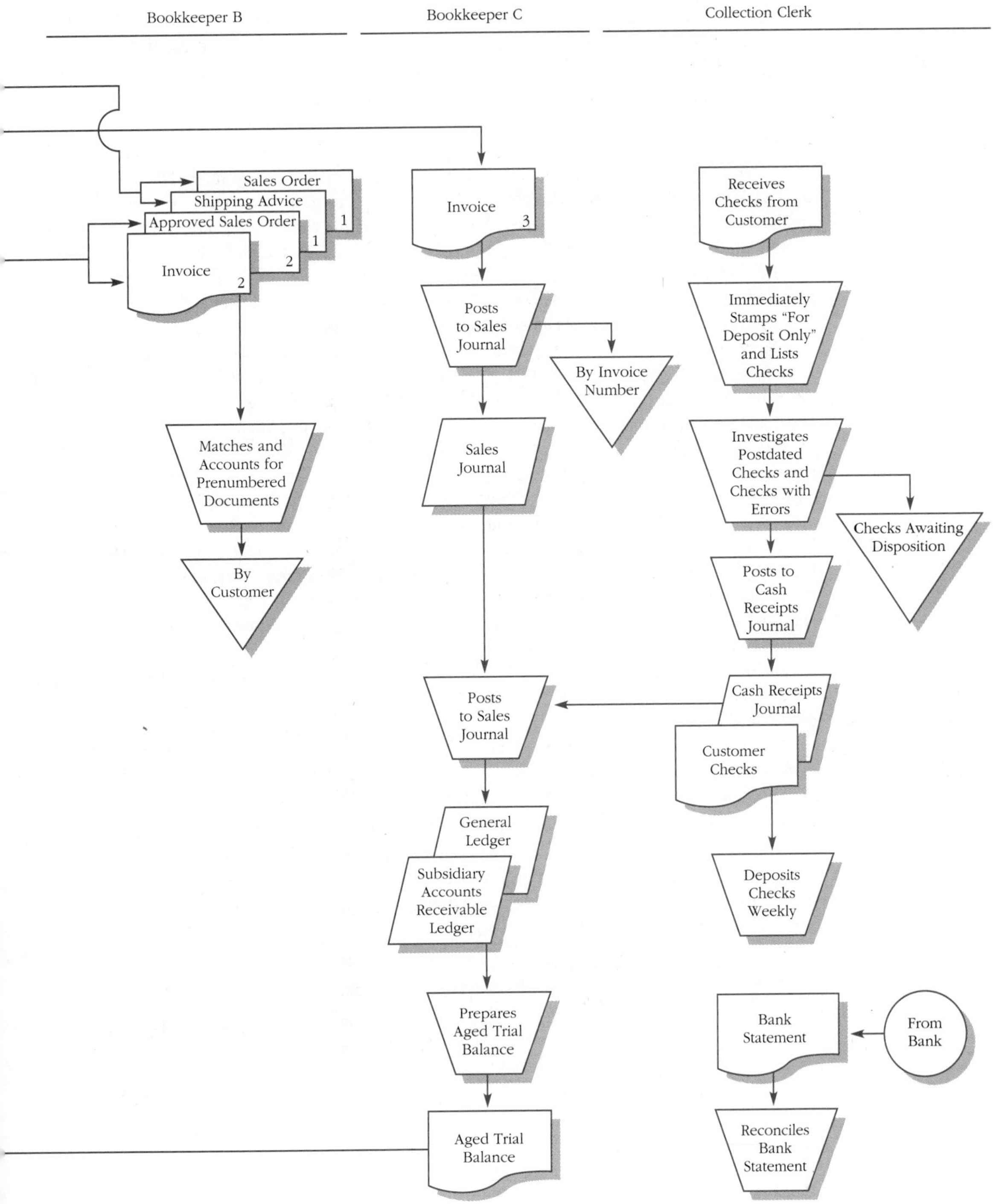

| Bookkeeper B | Bookkeeper C | Collection Clerk |
|---|---|---|

Sales Order

Shipping Advice

Approved Sales Order 1

1

Invoice 2

2

Invoice 3

Receives Checks from Customer

Posts to Sales Journal

By Invoice Number

Immediately Stamps "For Deposit Only" and Lists Checks

Matches and Accounts for Prenumbered Documents

Sales Journal

Investigates Postdated Checks and Checks with Errors

Checks Awaiting Disposition

By Customer

Posts to Cash Receipts Journal

Posts to Sales Journal

Cash Receipts Journal

Customer Checks

General Ledger

Subsidiary Accounts Receivable Ledger

Deposits Checks Weekly

Prepares Aged Trial Balance

Bank Statement

From Bank

Aged Trial Balance

Reconciles Bank Statement

physicians, 10 nurses, 3 support staff in a common laboratory, and 3 clerical workers. The clerical workers perform such tasks as reception, correspondence, cash receipts, billing, and appointment scheduling and are adequately bonded. They are referred to in the narrative as "office manager," "clerk 1," and "clerk 2."

### Narrative

Most patients pay for services by cash or check at the time services are rendered. Credit is not approved by the clerical staff. The physician who is to perform the respective services approves credit based on an interview. When credit is approved, the physician files a memo with the billing clerk (clerk #2) to set up the receivable from data generated by the physician.

The servicing physician prepares a charge slip that is given to clerk #1 for pricing and preparation of the patient's bill. Clerk #1 transmits a copy of the bill to clerk #2 for preparation of the revenue summary and for posting in the accounts receivable subsidiary ledger.

The cash receipts functions are performed by clerk #1, who receives cash and checks directly from patients and gives each patient a prenumbered cash receipt. Clerk #1 opens the mail and immediately stamps all checks "for deposit only" and lists cash and checks for deposit. The cash and checks are deposited daily by the office manager. The list of cash and checks together with the related remittance advices are forwarded by clerk #1 to clerk #2. Clerk #1 also serves as receptionist and performs general correspondence duties.

Clerk #2 prepares and sends monthly statements to patients with unpaid balances. Clerk #2 also prepares the cash receipts journal and is responsible for the accounts receivable subsidiary ledger. No other clerical employee is permitted access to the accounts receivable subsidiary ledger. Uncollectible accounts are written off by clerk #2 only after the physician who performed the respective services believes the account to be uncollectible and communicates the write-off approval to the office manager. The office manager then issues a write-off memo that clerk #2 processes.

The office manager supervises the clerks, issues write-off memos, schedules appointments for the doctors, makes bank deposits, reconciles bank statements, and performs general correspondence duties.

Additional services are performed monthly by a local accountant who posts summaries prepared by the clerks to the general ledger, prepares income statements, and files the appropriate payroll forms and tax returns. The accountant reports directly to the parent corporation.

*Required:*  Based only on the information in the narrative, describe the internal control weaknesses and one resulting misstatement that could occur and not be prevented or detected by Parktown's internal control structure concerning the cash receipts and billing function. Do *not* describe how to correct the weaknesses and potential misstatements. Use the format illustrated below.

| *Internal Control Weakness* | *Potential Misstatement* |
|---|---|
| There is no control to verify that fees are recorded and billed at authorized rates and terms. | Accounts receivable could be overstated and uncollectible accounts understated because of the lack of controls. |

(AICPA, adapted)

---

# ◆ GROUP IV: AUDIT CASE EXERCISES

12-31   A summary of the internal controls for the revenue cycle of Keystone Computers & Networks, Inc. appears on pages 405 through 418.

*Required:* *a.* For the following three internal controls over sales indicate one type of error or irregularity that the control serves to prevent or detect. Organize your solution as follows:

| *Internal Control Procedure* | *Error or Irregularity Controlled* |
| --- | --- |
| 1. Application controls are applied when customer orders are entered by the sales order clerk. | |
| 2. The computer assigns numbers to sales invoices when they are prepared. | |
| 3. Monthly statements are mailed to customers. | |

*b.* For the following three internal controls over cash receipts indicate one type of error or irregularity that the control serves to prevent or detect. Organize your solution as follows:

| *Internal Control Procedure* | *Error or Irregularity Controlled* |
| --- | --- |
| 1. Cash receipts are prelisted by the receptionist. | |
| 2. The accounting manager reconciles control totals generated by the accounts receivable computer program. | |
| 3. The computer summaries of cash collections and cash sales are reconciled to prelistings of cash receipts and cash deposits by the accounting manager. | |

12-32 As indicated on the risk assessment working paper on page 418, the auditors identified two weaknesses in internal control over the revenue cycle of KCN. Describe the implications of each of the two weaknesses in terms of the type of errors or irregularities that could result.

12-33 As indicated on the working paper on page 416, the auditors decided to apply audit sampling to three internal control procedures for the revenue cycle.

*Required:* *a.* Describe the characteristic that a control procedure must possess in order for it to be tested with audit sampling.

*b.* Assume that the auditors decided to use audit sampling to test the operating effectiveness of the procedures for matching sales invoices with delivery receipts. Determine the required sample size, using the following parameters:

- Risk of assessing control risk too low—10 percent
- Tolerable deviation rate—15 percent
- Expected deviation rate—1 percent

*c.* Prepare a working paper similar to the one on page 416 documenting the planned audit procedure described in part *b.*

# REVENUE CYCLE—SUBSTANTIVE TESTS

After studying this chapter, you should be able to:

- Describe the sources and nature of receivables and sales transactions.

- Identify the auditors' objectives for the examination of the receivables and sales accounts.

- Explain the nature of the typical substantive procedures for the examination of receivables and sales.

- Describe the sources and nature of cash transactions and balances.

- Identify the auditors' objectives for the examination of cash accounts.

- Relate the auditors' objectives for the examination of receivables, sales, and cash accounts to the typical substantive procedures for these accounts.

Accounts receivable, notes receivable, sales, and cash are the fundamental financial statement accounts that are associated with the revenue cycle. This chapter describes the manner in which auditors design substantive tests for these accounts. Recall that the nature, timing, and extent of substantive tests are determined by the auditors' assessed levels of inherent and control risk. The manner in which auditors assess inherent risk for various accounts was described in Chapter 6. Chapter 12 described the auditors' consideration of internal control structure policies and procedures for the revenue cycle, including the auditors' assessment of control risk. This chapter is divided into two sections. The first section presents the way in which auditors design substantive tests for sales and receivables. Substantive tests for the cash account are described in the later section of the chapter.

# DESIGNING SUBSTANTIVE TESTS OF RECEIVABLES AND SALES

Receivables include not only claims against customers arising from the sale of goods or services, but also a variety of miscellaneous claims such as loans to officers or employees, loans to subsidiaries, claims against various other companies, claims for tax refunds, and advances to suppliers.

Trade notes and accounts receivable usually are relatively large in amount and should appear as separate items in the current assets section of the balance sheet at their net realizable value. Auditors are especially concerned with the presentation and disclosure of loans to officers, directors, and affiliated companies. These related-party transactions are commonly made for the convenience of the borrower rather than to benefit the lending company. Consequently, such loans are often collected only at the convenience of the borrower. It is a basic tenet of financial statement presentation that transactions not characterized by arm's-length bargaining should be fully disclosed.

Typically, notes receivable are used for handling transactions of substantial amounts; these negotiable documents are widely used by both industrial and commercial concerns. In banks and other financial institutions, notes receivable usually constitute the single most important asset.

An installment note or contract is a negotiable instrument that grants possession of the goods to the purchaser but permits the seller to retain a lien on the goods until the final installment under the note has been received. Installment notes are widely used in the sale of industrial machinery, farm equipment, and automobiles. Other transactions that may lead to the acquisition of notes receivable include the disposal of items of plant and equipment, the sale of divisions of a company, the issuance of capital stock, and the making of loans to officers, employees, and affiliated companies.

## Objectives for Substantive Tests of Receivables and Sales

The audit *objectives* for substantive tests of receivables and sales are to:

1. Substantiate the *existence* of receivables and the *occurrence* of sales transactions.
2. Establish the *completeness* of receivables and sales transactions.
3. Determine that the client has *rights* to the recorded receivables.

4. Establish the *clerical accuracy* of records and supporting schedules of receivables and sales.

5. Determine that the *valuation* of receivables and sales is at appropriate net realizable values.

6. Determine that the *presentation* and *disclosure* of receivables and sales is adequate, including the separation of receivables into appropriate categories, adequate reporting of any receivables pledged as collateral, and disclosure of related-party sales and receivables.

## SUBSTANTIVE TESTS FOR RECEIVABLES AND SALES

Figure 13–1 presents typical substantive tests used to meet the primary audit objectives for accounts receivable, notes receivable, and sales. In the following sections we describe these procedures in detail.

### Obtain Aged Schedule of Accounts Receivable

| Primary Audit Objective: |
| --- |
| Clerical accuracy ☑ |

An **aged trial balance** of trade accounts receivable at the audit date is commonly prepared by employees of the client for the auditors, often in the form of a computer printout. The audit software-prepared schedule illustrated in Figure 13–2 is a multipurpose format

Figure 13–1   Objectives of Major Substantive Tests of Receivables and Sales Transactions

| Substantive Tests | Primary Audit Objectives |
| --- | --- |
| Obtain aged listing of receivables and reconcile to ledgers<br>Obtain analyses of notes receivable and related interest | Clerical accuracy |
| Inspect notes on hand and confirm those not on hand<br>Confirm receivables with debtors | Existence and occurrence; Rights; and Valuation |
| Review the year-end cutoff of sales transactions<br>Perform analytical procedures<br>Verify interest earned on notes receivable | Existence and occurrence; Rights; and Completeness |
| Evaluate the propriety of client's accounting for transactions<br>Evaluate adequacy of allowance for uncollectible accounts | Valuation |
| Investigate the existence of pledged receivables<br>Investigate receivables from related parties<br>Evaluate financial statement presentation and disclosure | Presentation and disclosure |

designed to display the aging of customers' accounts, the estimate of probable credit losses, and the confirmation control information. The summary of so many phases of the examination of receivables in a single working paper is practicable only for small concerns with a limited number of customers. If the client has any accounts receivable other than trade accounts, the auditors also should obtain similar analyses of those accounts.

When trial balances or analyses of accounts receivable are furnished to the auditors by the client's employees, some independent verification of the listing is essential. Determination of the proper extent of testing should be made in relation to the adequacy of the internal controls over receivables. The auditors should test footings, crossfootings, and

## Figure 13–2   Aging of Accounts Receivable

The Fairview Corporation
Account No. 121
Accounts Receivable--Trade
December 31, 199X

B-1
*V.M.H.*
*1/12/9X*

*Prepared by Client*

| Confir-mation Number | Customer | Balance 12/31/9X | Billed for December | Billed for November | Billed for October | Billed prior to October | Credit Balances | Collections Subsequent to 12/31/9X | Estimated Uncollectible |
|---|---|---|---|---|---|---|---|---|---|
| 1 *cx* | Adams & Sons | $ 8,055.60 *uy* | $ 7,921.60 *i* | | $  334.00 *i* | | | $ 7,912.60 | |
| 2 *c* | Baker Company, Inc. | 205.00 *uy* | | $  205.00 *i* | | | | 205.00 | |
| 3 *c* | Cross Mfg. Corp | 7,310.20 *uy* | 1,500.20 *uy* | 1,210.00 *i* | 500.00 *i* | | | 4,100.00 | |
| | Douglas Supply Co. | 22.00 *uy* | | | | $4,100.00 *i* | | | 22.00 |
| 4 *c* | Electric Mfg. Co., Inc. | 1,250.00 *uy* | 1,250.00 *i* | | | 22.00 *i* | | 1,250.00 | |
| | J.R. Farmer | 3,000 *uy* | 3,000.00 *i* | | | | | | |
| 64 *cx* | Young Industries | 1,825.00 *uy* | 1,575.00 *i* | | 250.00 *i* | | | | |
| | Zappa M'fg. | 47.19 *uy* | 47.19 *i* | | | | | 47.19 | |
| | | $78,624.62 ✓ | $48,801.67 | $21,245.60 | $2,278.20 | $6,302.15 | $(600.00) | $62,406.44 | $ 4,100.00 |
| | | (3,000.00) | (3,000.00) | | | | | | |
| | | 75,624.62 | 45,801.67 | | | | | | |

*u* = Footed and cross-footed.
✓ = Agreed to general ledger.
*y* = Traced to accounts receivable subsidiary ledger.
*i* = Verified aging.
*c* = Confirmed; no exception.
*cx* = Confirmed with exception. See G-1-1.

*See audit program (B-2) for extent of confirmation and other auditing procedures.*

Conclusion:
   *The results of the confirmation and other tests described in the audit program (B-2) provide sufficient appropriate evidence of existence of, and rights to, trade accounts receivable in the aggregate amount of $75,624.62.*

*A.J.E. 12*
*Accounts Receivable — Officers      3,000.00*
   *Accounts Receivable — Trade                     3,000.00*
*Correct classification of account*
*receivable from J.R. Farmer,*
*President*

*V.M.H.*
*Jan. 20, 9X*

agings. In testing the aging, it is important to test some accounts classified as current, as well as those shown as past due. These selected accounts should be traced to the subsidiary ledgers. The totals of schedules prepared by client personnel should also be compared with related controlling accounts. In addition, the balances of the subsidiary ledger records should be verified by footing the debit and credit columns on a test basis. Generalized computer audit programs may be used to perform these tests when the client's accounts receivable are processed by a computer system.

## Obtain Analyses of Notes Receivable

| Primary Audit Objective: |  |
| --- | --- |
| Clerical accuracy | ☑ |

An analysis of notes receivable supporting the general ledger controlling account may be prepared for the auditors by the client's staff. The information to be included in the analysis normally will include the name of the maker, date, maturity, amount, interest rate, and amounts of interest earned and accrued. In addition to verifying the accuracy of the analysis prepared by the client, the auditors should trace selected items to the accounting records and to the notes themselves.

## Inspect Notes Receivable

| Primary Audit Objectives: |  |
| --- | --- |
| Existence | ☑ |
| Rights | ☑ |

The inspection of notes receivable on hand should be performed concurrently with the count of cash and securities to prevent the concealment of a shortage by substitution of cash for misappropriated negotiable instruments, or vice versa. Any securities held by the client as collateral for notes receivable should be inspected and listed at the same time. Complete control over all negotiable instruments should be maintained by the auditors until the count and inspection are completed.

Notes receivable owned by the client may be held by others at the time of the audit. Confirmation in writing from the *holder* of the note is considered as an acceptable alternative to inspection; it does not, however, eliminate the need for securing confirmation from the *maker* of the note. The confirmation letter sent to a bank, collection agency, secured creditor, or other holder should contain a request for verification of the name of the maker, the balance of the note, the interest rate, and the due date.

Printed note forms are readily available at any bank; an unscrupulous officer or employee of the client company desiring to create a fictitious note could do so by obtaining a bank note form and filling in the amount, date, maturity, and signature. The relative ease of creating a forged or fictitious note suggests that physical inspection by the auditors represents a less significant and conclusive audit procedure in verification of notes receivable than for cash or securities.

## Confirm Receivables

| Primary Audit Objectives: |  |
| --- | --- |
| Existence | ☑ |
| Rights | ☑ |
| Valuation | ☑ |

The term **confirmation** was defined in Chapter 7 as a type of documentary evidence secured from outside the client organization and transmitted directly to the auditors. Direct communication with debtors is the most essential and conclusive step in the verification of the existence of accounts and notes receivable. By confirming an account receivable, the auditors prove that the receivable and customer *exist*. Written acknowledgment of the debt by the debtor serves the purposes of *(a)* establishing the existence and gross valuation of the asset, and *(b)* providing some assurance that no lapping or other manipulation affecting receivables is being carried on at the balance sheet date. However, the confirmation of a receivable provides only limited evidence about the completeness and net valuation assertions, because only recorded amounts are confirmed, and debtors may acknowledge debts even though they are not able to pay them.

A better understanding of the emphasis placed on confirmation of receivables can be gained by a brief review of auditing history. Audit objectives and procedures were drastically revised in the late 1940s. Before that time the usual audit did not include procedures to ensure that the receivables were genuine claims against existing companies or that inventories actually existed and had been accurately counted. For the auditors to confirm receivables (or to observe the taking of physical inventory) was considered too expensive and not particularly important. Auditors generally relied in that early era upon a written statement by management concerning the validity of receivables and the existence of inventories. This approach was drastically revised after several spectacular fraud cases involving millions of dollars in fictitious receivables and inventories showed the need for stronger audit evidence.

*SAS 67* (AU 330), ''The Confirmation Process,'' summarizes the current status of the confirmation procedure. It indicates that there is a presumption that the auditor will confirm accounts receivable, unless: *(a)* accounts receivable are immaterial, *(b)* the use of confirmations would be ineffective, or *(c)* the auditor's combined assessment of inherent risk and control risk is low, and that assessment, in conjunction with other substantive tests, is sufficient to reduce audit risk for the applicable assertions to an acceptably low level. When receivables are not confirmed the auditors must document the basis for the decision.

All requests for confirmation of notes and accounts receivable should be mailed in envelopes bearing the CPA firm's return address. A stamped or business reply envelope addressed to the office of the auditors should be enclosed with the request. Confirmation requests should be deposited personally by the auditors at the post office or in a government mailbox. These procedures are designed to prevent the client's employees from having any opportunity to alter or intercept a confirmation request or the customer's reply thereto. The entire process of confirming receivables will obviously contribute nothing toward the detection of overstated or fictitious accounts if the confirmation requests or replies from customers pass through the hands of the client. Requests returned as undeliverable by the post office may be of prime significance to the auditors and hence should be returned directly to their office.

An important part of confirming notes and accounts receivable is considering the validity of the debtors' addresses. The auditors should investigate thoroughly any suspicious circumstances, such as an excessive number of individual debtors with addresses that are post office boxes; the boxes may have been rented under fictitious debtors' names by employees of the client company who are engaged in accounts receivable fraud.

---

### ◆ ILLUSTRATIVE CASE ◆

In the Equity Funding Corporation of America fraud, fictitious receivables selected for confirmation by the auditors bore addresses of relatives of employees who were conspirators in the fraud. The fictitious confirmation requests were thus signed and returned to the auditors by the recipients.

To improve the rate of response to confirmation requests, the auditors should carefully design the form to make sure that the person receiving the confirmation has easy access to the information requested. For example, customers that use a voucher system for cash disbursements may be better able to confirm unpaid transactions, rather than total receivable balances. The auditors should also try to include on the form the details of the transactions, such as customers' purchase order numbers.

Positive and Negative Confirmation Requests.   There are two methods of confirming receivables by direct communication with the debtor. In each type of communication, the client makes the formal request for confirmation, although the auditors control the entire confirmation process.

The **positive method** consists of a request addressed to the debtor asking for a reply. Most positive forms ask the debtor to confirm directly to the auditors the accuracy of the dollar amount shown on the confirmation request—see Figure 13–3. Other positive forms, referred to as *blank forms,* do not state the amount on the request, but ask the debtor company to fill in the balance.

The **negative method** consists of a communication addressed to the debtor asking it to advise the auditors *only* if the balance shown is incorrect. A negative confirmation request may be in the form of a letter or it may be made merely by applying a rubber stamp to the customer's regular monthly statement, or by attaching a gummed label worded such as that shown in Figure 13–4.

The positive form generally provides more assurance because the auditors are alerted to the need for further investigation if a reply is not received. However, when recipients are asked to confirm the accuracy of information provided on the confirmation request, there is a risk that the recipient may simply sign and return the request without verifying the information. Blank forms control for this possibility by requiring the recipient to provide the information. But, blank confirmations may result in lower response rates and, therefore, require more follow-up procedures.

When the negative form of confirmation request is used, the lack of a reply from a given customer is interpreted as satisfactory evidence, when in fact the customer may simply have ignored the confirmation request. Since the auditors need not follow up on nonreplies, the expense of using negative confirmation requests is less than for the positive form; thus, more customers can be contacted for the same cost.

Although positive confirmation requests may be used in any circumstance, the use of only negative requests should be reserved for situations in which *(a)* the combined assessed level of inherent and control risk is low, *(b)* a large number of small balances is involved, and *(c)* the auditors have no reason to believe that the recipients of the requests are not likely to give them consideration. When the auditors use negative requests, they should consider supplementing the confirmation process with other substantive procedures. In many situations a combination of positive and negative forms is used, with the positive form used for large balances and the negative form for small balances.

Size of Sample.   In the audit of most companies, the confirmation process for accounts receivable is limited to a sample. The sample should always be large enough to warrant the drawing of valid inferences about the entire population of receivables. Generally, auditors are able to stratify the population in a manner so as to allow confirmation of a majority of the dollar amount of receivables.

Figure 13–3    Positive Form of Accounts Receivable Confirmation Request

---

## SMITH & CO. ——————————————————————

*1416 Eighteenth Street  •  Los Angeles  •  California  •  90035*

December 31, 199X

Martin, Inc.
6700 Holmes Street
Kansas City, Missouri 64735

Dear Sirs:

Please confirm directly to our auditors

Adams, Barnes & Co.
Certified Public Accountants
1800 Avenue of the Stars
Los Angeles, California 90067

the correctness of the balance of your account payable to us as shown below
and on the enclosed statement at December 31, 199X. If the amount is not in
agreement with your records at that date, please provide any information which
will aid our auditors in reconciling the difference.

Your prompt return of this form in the enclosed stamped envelope is
essential to the completion of the auditors' examination of our financial
statements and will be appreciated.

Smith & Co.

By _M.J. Crowley_
(Controller)

THIS IS NOT A REQUEST FOR PAYMENT, BUT MERELY FOR
CONFIRMATION OF YOUR ACCOUNT.
- - - - - - - - - - - - - - - - - - - - - - - - - - - - - - - - - - - - - - - - - - - - -

The statement of our account showing a balance of $24,689.00 due Smith &
Co. at December 31, 199X is correct except as noted below.

Martin, Inc.

Date: _January 16, 199X_            By _Howard Martin_

Exceptions: _None_

---

Figure 13-4   Negative Form of Accounts Receivable Confirmation Request

Please examine this statement carefully. If it does not agree with your records, please report any differences to our auditors

    Adams, Barnes & Co.
    Certified Public Accountants
    1800 Avenue of the Stars
    Los Angeles, California 90067

A business reply envelope requiring no postage is enclosed for your convenience.

THIS IS NOT A REQUEST FOR PAYMENT

---

As discussed in Chapters 10 and 11, the size of the sample will vary with the levels of sampling risk accepted (the risk of incorrect rejection and acceptance), the tolerable misstatement, and certain characteristics of the population. The results of confirmation tests in prior years serve as another guide to the auditors in setting sample size; significant exceptions in prior years' confirmation results signal the need for extensive confirmation of the current year's receivables. Finally, the choice between the positive and negative forms of confirmation requests influences the size of the sample. The number of confirmations mailed is usually increased when the negative form is used.

In selecting the individual accounts to be confirmed, it is customary to include all customers with balances above a selected dollar amount and to select a sample of accounts from the remaining receivables. Generalized computer audit programs are useful in stratifying computer-processed accounts receivable to facilitate the selection of a representative sample.

Discrepancies in Customers' Replies.   The auditors should resolve unusual or significant differences reported by customers. The majority of such reported discrepancies arise because of normal lags in the recording of cash receipts or sales transactions, or because of misunderstanding on the part of the customer as to the date of the balance it is asked to confirm. Some replies may state that the balance listed is incorrect because it does not reflect recent cash payments; in such instances, the auditors normally trace the reported payments to the cash records.

Alternative Audit Procedures for Nonrespondents.   The percentage of replies to positive confirmation requests that can be expected will vary greatly according to the type of debtor. When using positive confirmation requests, the auditors should generally follow up with a second and sometimes a third request to produce replies. When replies are still not received, the auditors should apply alternative procedures to the accounts, unless (a) the amount of the nonresponses is not significant when projected as a 100 percent misstatement to the total balance of receivables, and (b) there are no unusual characteristics related to the nonresponses. The best *alternative auditing procedure* is examination of subsequent cash receipts in payment of the receivable. However, in order to make certain that the payment is for a receivable that existed at year-end, the auditors also may need to examine shipping documents, customer purchase orders, or sales invoices for the sales transactions making up the receivable. Examination of these sales documents is also the alternative procedure used for receivables that are not paid during the subsequent period.

The Confirmation Process in Perspective.   When all expected replies to confirmation requests have been received, a summary should be prepared outlining the extent and nature of the confirmation program and the overall results obtained. Such a summary is a highly important part of the audit working papers.

The auditors face more than one type of risk in relying upon the confirmation process to form an opinion about the fairness of the accounts receivable as a whole. We have already recognized the risk that some accounts with erroneous balances may not be included in the sample confirmed, and also the risk that replies may not be received from some customers having erroneous balances. Finally, there is the risk that customers may routinely return confirmation requests without actually comparing the balance with their records. Such responses would give the auditors a false sense of security. Despite these risks, however, the confirming of accounts receivable provides valuable evidence and represents an important part of the auditors' work.

It has sometimes been said that the best proof available to the auditors as to the existence of an account receivable is its collection during the course of their examination. But this statement requires qualification, as indicated by the following situation:

---

◆ ILLUSTRATIVE CASE ◆

During the first audit of a small manufacturing company, the auditors sent confirmation requests to all customers whose accounts showed balances in excess of $1,000. Satisfactory replies were received from all but one account, which had a balance of approximately $30,000. A second confirmation request sent to this customer produced no response; but before the auditors could investigate further, they were informed by the cashier-accountant that the account had been paid in full. The auditors asked to examine the customer's check and the accompanying remittance advice, but were told that the check had been deposited and the remittance advice destroyed. Further questioning concerning transactions with this customer evoked such vague responses that the auditors decided to discuss the account with the officers of the company. At this point the cashier-accountant confessed that the account in question was a fictitious one created to conceal a shortage and that to satisfy the auditors he had "collected" the account receivable by diverting current collections from other customers whose accounts had already been confirmed.

---

Reviewing and Confirming Accounts and Notes Written Off as Uncollectible.   If any accounts or notes receivable of significant amount were written off as uncollectible during the year, the auditors should determine that these write-offs were properly authorized. In the absence of proper authorization procedures, a dishonest employee could conceal permanently a theft of cash merely by a charge to accounts or notes receivable followed by a write-off of that asset.

A systematic review of the notes and accounts written off can conveniently be made by obtaining or preparing an analysis of the allowance for doubtful accounts and notes. Debits to the allowance may be traced to the authorizing documents and to the control record of accounts and notes written off; confirmation requests may be mailed to some of the debtors to determine that the account or note was genuine when it was first recorded in the accounts. Credit entries should be compared with the charges to uncollectible accounts and notes expense. Any write-off that appears unreasonable should be fully investigated. Charge-off of a note or account receivable from an officer, stockholder, or director is unreasonable on its face and warrants the most searching investigation by the auditors. The computation of percentages relating the year's write-offs to net credit sales, to uncollectible accounts expense, and to the allowance for doubtful accounts and notes may be useful in identifying any abnormal write-offs.

## Review Sales Cutoff

| Primary Audit Objectives: |
| --- |
| Existence ☑ |
| Rights ☑ |
| Completeness ☑ |

One of the more common methods of falsifying accounting records is to inflate the sales for the year by holding open the sales journal beyond the balance sheet date. Shipments occurring in the first part of January may be covered by sales invoices bearing a December date and included in December sales. The purpose of such misleading entries is to present a more favorable financial picture than actually exists. Since sales are frequently used as the base for computation of bonuses and commissions, an additional incentive for padding the Sales account is often present.

The auditors will compare the sales recorded for several days before and after the balance sheet date with the duplicate sales invoices and shipping documents. They will use results obtained from their consideration of internal control to determine the scope of tests of the cutoff of sales records. If warehousing, shipping, billing, and receiving have been found to be independently controlled through a proper segregation of duties, only a limited comparison of sales at year-end may be necessary. On the other hand, when one individual controls both shipping records and billing documents an attempt to manipulate both sets of records to overstate the year's sales is more likely. In situations such as this the auditors may not only compare sales invoices with shipping documents, but may also personally observe the shipping function at year-end to determine that a proper cutoff has occurred.

The term **window dressing** refers to actions taken around the balance sheet date to improve the financial picture presented in the financial statements. Fictitious sales, as well as predated shipments, are occasionally recorded at year-end as a means of window dressing the financial statements. The merchandise in question may even be shipped to customers without their prior knowledge, and subsequently returned. To guard against such manipulation, the auditors should review carefully all substantial sales returns following the balance sheet date that may apply to receivables originating in the year under audit. Consideration should be given to reflecting these returns in the current year's business by means of adjusting entries. Confirmation of accounts receivable, if made at the balance sheet date, should also serve to bring any large unauthorized shipments to the attention of the auditors.

## Perform Analytical Procedures

| Primary Audit Objectives: |
|---|
| Existence ☑ |
| Rights ☑ |
| Completeness ☑ |

Several ratios and relationships can be computed to indicate the overall reasonableness of the amounts shown for accounts receivable, sales, notes receivable, and interest revenue. Examples include: *(a)* the gross profit rate, *(b)* accounts receivable turnover, *(c)* the ratio of accounts receivable to the year's net credit sales, *(d)* the ratio of accounts written off during the year to the ending balance of accounts receivable, *(e)* the ratio of the valuation allowance to accounts receivable, *(f)* the ratio of interest revenue to notes receivable, and *(g)* the ratio of uncollectible account expense to credit sales.

These ratios and relationships should be compared with corresponding data for the preceding years and with comparable industry averages.

## Verify Interest on Notes Receivable

| Primary Audit Objectives: |
|---|
| Existence ☑ |
| Rights ☑ |
| Completeness ☑ |

The most effective verification of the Interest Earned account consists of an independent computation by the auditors of the interest earned during the year on notes receivable. The working paper used to analyze notes receivable should show the interest rate and date of issuance of each note. The interest section of this working paper consists of four columns, which show (for each note receivable owned during the year) the following information:

1. Accrued interest receivable at the beginning of the year (taken from the preceding year's audit working papers).
2. Interest earned during the year (computed from the terms of the notes).
3. Interest collected during the year (traced to cash receipts records).
4. Accrued interest receivable at the end of the year (computed by the auditors).

These four columns comprise a self-balancing set. The beginning balance of accrued interest receivable (first column) plus the interest earned during the year (second column) and minus the interest collected (third column) should equal the accrued interest receivable at the end of the year (fourth column). The totals of the four columns should be cross-footed to ensure that they are in balance; in addition, the individual column totals should be traced to the balances in the general ledger.

If the interest earned for the year as computed by the auditors does not agree with interest earned as shown in the accounting records, the next step is an analysis of the ledger account. When there is a significant difference found in this analysis, it may indicate that nonexistent notes are recorded or that not all the notes owned by the client are reflected in the accounts.

For financial institutions or other clients having numerous notes receivable, the auditors may verify interest computations on only a sample of the notes. In addition, they should test the reasonableness of total interest earned for the year by applying a weighted average rate of interest to the average balance of the Notes Receivable ledger account during the year.

## Evaluate Accounting for Transactions

| Primary Audit Objective: |
| --- |
| Valuation ☑ |

Many instances of misstatements in financial statements have involved inappropriate recognition of sales revenue and related receivables. The auditors must carefully evaluate the propriety of the client's valuation and treatment of certain transactions. Problems that the auditors might discover include:

1.  An allowance for sales returns may not be set up for goods shipped to customers who are given the right to return the goods under certain circumstances.
2.  Cash receipts from franchise fees may be included in revenue and receivables when services have not been rendered to the franchisees.
3.  Leases properly accounted for using the operating method of accounting may be improperly accounted for as sale-type capital leases overstating revenues and receivables.
4.  Management might use the percentage-of-completion method of revenue recognition in inappropriate circumstances or might overestimate the amount of revenue earned.
5.  Notes receivable may not bear reasonable interest rates at the time they are accepted, resulting in a need to discount the notes to present values.

The above examples make it clear that auditors must have a thorough understanding of generally accepted accounting principles and the *substance*, as well as the form, of the client's sales transactions. The auditors carefully examine the various documents pertaining to the transactions to determine that proper accounting principles have been followed.

## Evaluate Allowance for Uncollectible Accounts

| Primary Audit Objective: |
| --- |
| Valuation ☑ |

If the balance sheet is to reflect fairly the financial position of the business, the receivables must be stated at net realizable value, that is, at face value less an adequate allowance for uncollectible notes and accounts receivable. The measurement of income requires an impartial matching of revenue and related expenses. Since one of the expenses involved is the expense caused by uncollectible notes and accounts, the auditors' review of uncollectible receivables should be looked upon as the verification of both income statement and balance sheet accounts.

As the audit approaches completion, considerable time will have elapsed since the balance sheet date. Consequently, many of the accounts receivable that were past due at the balance sheet date will have been collected; the others will be further past due. Thus, the auditors have the advantage of hindsight in judging the collectibility of the receivables owned at the balance sheet date.

The auditors' best evidence of the proper valuation of accounts and notes receivable is payment in full by the debtors subsequent to the balance sheet date. The auditors should note in the working papers any such amounts received; in the illustrated trial balance of trade accounts receivable (Figure 13–2), a special column has been provided for this purpose.

A note receivable, especially one obtained in settlement of a past-due account receivable, may involve as much credit risk as an account receivable. Provision for loss may reasonably be made for notes that have been repeatedly renewed, for installment notes on which payments have been late and irregular, for notes received in consequence of past-due accounts receivable, for defaulted notes, and for notes of companies known to be in financial difficulties. To appraise the collectibility of notes receivable, the auditors may investigate the credit standing of the makers of any large or doubtful notes. Reports from credit-rating agencies and financial statements from the makers of notes should be available for this purpose in the client's credit department.

Evaluation of any collateral supplied by the makers of notes is another step in determining the collectibility of notes receivable. The auditors should determine current market value of securities held as collateral by the client by reference to market quotations or by inquiry of brokers. Attention of the client should be called to any cases in which the market value of the collateral is less than the note; the deficiency might have to be considered uncollectible.

To conclude as to the adequacy of management's accounting estimate for the allowance for uncollectible accounts, the auditors may take the following steps:

1. Compare the details of the aging of accounts receivable to prior years' agings. Evaluate the past-due accounts receivable listed in the aging schedule that have not been paid subsequent to the balance sheet date, noting such factors as the size and recency of payments, settlement of old balances, and whether recent sales are on a cash or a credit basis. The client's correspondence file may furnish much of this information.

2. Investigate the credit ratings for delinquent and unusually large accounts. An account with a single customer may represent a major portion of the total receivables.

3. Review confirmation exceptions for an indication of amounts in dispute or other clues as to possible uncollectible accounts.

4. Summarize in a working paper those accounts whose collectibility is doubtful based on the preceding procedures. List customer names, doubtful amounts, and reasons considered doubtful.

5. Review with the credit manager the current status of significant doubtful accounts, ascertaining the collection action taken and the opinion of the credit manager as to ultimate collectibility. Indicate on the uncollectible accounts working paper the credit manager's opinion as to the collectible portion of each account listed, and use this information to assist in evaluating the collectibility of specific accounts.

6. Compute analytical relationships, such as the number-of-days-sales in accounts receivable and the relationship of the valuation allowance to (1) accounts receivable and (2) net credit sales, and compare to comparable ratios for prior years and industry averages. Investigate any unexpected results.

## Investigate Pledged Receivables

| Audit Objective: |
| --- |
| Presentation  ☑ |

The auditors should inquire directly as to whether any notes or accounts receivable have been pledged or assigned as such arrangements must be disclosed. The **pledging of receivables** may also be revealed through the medium of financial institution confirmation requests, which specifically call for a description of the collateral securing bank loans.

Analysis of the interest expense accounts may reflect charges from the pledging of receivables to finance companies.

Accounts receivable that have been pledged should be plainly labeled by stamping on the copy of the sales invoice a notice such as "Pledged to First National Bank under loan agreement of December 199X," and by inserting an identifying code in the accounts receivable records. Accounts labeled in this manner would be identified by the auditors in their initial review of receivables and confirmed by direct correspondence with the bank to which they were pledged. The auditors cannot, however, proceed on the assumption that all pledged receivables have been labeled to that effect, and they must be alert to detect any suggestions of an unrecorded pledging of accounts receivable.

## Investigate Related-Party Transactions

| Primary Audit Objective: |
| --- |
| Presentation ☑ |

Loans by a corporation to its officers, directors, stockholders, or affiliates require particular attention from the auditors because these related-party transactions are not the result of arm's-length bargaining by parties of opposing interests. Furthermore, such loans are often prohibited by the corporation's bylaws. It is somewhat difficult to reconcile substantial loans to insiders by a nonfinancial corporation with the avowed operating objectives of such an organization. The independent auditors have an obligation to stockholders, creditors, and others who rely upon audited statements to require disclosure of any self-dealing on the part of the management. It seems apparent that most loans to officers, directors, and stockholders are made for the convenience of the borrower rather than for the profit of the corporation. Because of the somewhat questionable character of such loans, they are sometimes paid off just before the balance sheet date and renewed shortly thereafter in an effort to avoid disclosure in financial statements. Under these circumstances, the renewed borrowing may be detected by the auditors through a scanning of notes and accounts receivable transactions subsequent to the balance sheet date. Financial statement disclosure of such transactions may be necessary.

## Evaluate Disclosures

| Primary Audit Objective: |
| --- |
| Presentation ☑ |

The auditors must ascertain that the financial presentation of accounts and notes receivable and the related disclosures are in accordance with generally accepted accounting principles. Related-party receivables should be shown separately with disclosure of the nature of the relationships and the amounts of the transactions. Any unusual terms of notes receivable should be disclosed in the footnotes. Also, the amounts of allowances for uncollectible receivables should be shown as deductions from the related receivables. Finally, significant concentrations of credit risk arising from trade accounts receivable should be disclosed in accordance with *FASB Statement No. 105*, "Disclosure of Information about Financial Instruments with Off-Balance-Sheet Risk and Financial Instruments with Concentrations of Credit Risk."

## Interim Audit Work on Receivables and Sales

Much of the audit work on receivables and sales can be performed one or two months before the balance sheet date. The **interim audit work** may consist of the consideration of internal controls and, in some cases, the confirmation of accounts receivable as well.

A decision to carry out the confirmation of receivables at an interim date rather than at year-end is justified only if control risk for existence of accounts receivable is not high.

If interim audit work has been performed on receivables and sales, the year-end audit work may be modified considerably. For example, if the confirmation of accounts receivable was performed at October 31, the year-end audit program would include preparation of a summary analysis of postings to the Accounts Receivable controlling account for the period from November 1 through December 31. This analysis would list the postings by month, showing the journal source of each. These postings would be traced to the respective journals, such as the sales journal and cash receipts journal. The amounts of the postings would be compared with the amounts in preceding months and with the corresponding months in prior years. The purpose of this work is to bring to light any significant variations in receivables during the months between the interim audit work and the balance sheet date.

In addition to this analysis of the entries to the receivables accounts for the intervening period, the audit work at year-end would include obtaining the aging of the accounts receivable at December 31, confirmation of any large accounts in the year-end trial balance that are new or delinquent, and the usual investigation of the year-end cutoff of sales and cash receipts.

### Audit Working Papers for Receivables and Sales

Besides preparing lead schedules for receivables and sales, the auditors obtain or prepare the following working papers:

1.  Aged trial balance of trade accounts receivable (often a computer printout).
2.  Analyses of other accounts receivable.
3.  Analysis of notes receivable and related interest.
4.  Analysis of allowance for uncollectible accounts and notes.
5.  Comparative analysis of sales transactions by month, by product, or by territory, or by relating forecasted sales to actual sales.
6.  Summary of the results of analytical procedures and related investigations of unexpected amounts.
7.  Confirmations and a summary of the results of confirmation of receivables.
8.  Memoranda describing evidence about the collectibility of selected accounts.
9.  Summary of the results of tests of sales transactions.

## DESIGNING SUBSTANTIVE TESTS OF CASH

Cash normally includes general, payroll, petty cash, and, less frequently, savings accounts. General accounts are checking accounts similar in nature to those maintained by individuals. Cash sales, collections of receivables, and investment of additional capital typically increase the account; business expenditures decrease it. Under the terms of a bank loan agreement, the cash in a company's general account sometimes must be maintained at a specified minimum balance referred to as a *compensating balance*.

Cash equivalents are often combined with cash items to create the current asset classification called "cash and cash equivalents." *Cash equivalents* include money market funds, certificates of deposit, savings certificates, and other similar types of deposits. Any item that cannot be converted to cash on short notice should be classified as an investment, receivable, or prepaid expense, rather than as a cash equivalent.

Payroll and petty cash accounts are "imprest" at a low balance. When payroll is paid, a check from the general account is drawn to deposit funds into the payroll account. Petty cash, used for very small expenditures, is replenished as necessary.

Normal internal control policies and procedures (e.g., reconciliation of bank accounts) detect most errors that occur in these accounts. On the other hand, the liquid nature of cash increases the risk of undetected irregularities.

## Objectives for Substantive Tests of Cash

The audit objectives for substantive tests of cash are to:

1. Substantiate the *existence* of recorded cash.
2. Establish the *completeness* of recorded cash.
3. Determine that the client has *rights* to recorded cash.
4. Establish the *clerical accuracy* of cash schedules.
5. Determine that the *presentation* and *disclosure* of cash, including restricted funds (such as compensating balances and bond sinking funds), are appropriate.

In connection with the audit of cash, the auditors will also verify the amounts of any interest revenue from cash deposits. As is the case with other assets, auditors are especially concerned with the likelihood of overstatements of the account; therefore, objective 1, the existence of recorded cash, is of utmost importance.

---

◆ ILLUSTRATIVE NOTE ◆

A recent research study reports the results of a study of lawsuits against public accountants. A total of 129 cases were examined and none of the suits concerned misstatements involving undervalued assets.

---

In addition to concerns about the overstatement of cash, auditors are aware that cash may have been improperly abstracted during the period, even though the year-end cash may be properly stated. To distinguish between the situations, assume that the client's balance sheet shows "Cash . . . . . $250,000." For most clients, the primary risks are that errors or irregularities either (1) create a situation in which $250,000 overstates actual cash, or (2) have improperly reduced the balance to $250,000.

Concerning the first risk (overstated cash), a shortage may have been concealed merely by the insertion of a fictitious check in the cash on hand at year-end or by the omission of an outstanding check from the year-end bank reconciliation. Note that the omission of an outstanding check may be indicative of either an error or an irregularity. For example, poor internal control may result in a situation in which human error resulted in the check not being recorded in disbursements. On the other hand, although recorded in cash disbursements, the check may have been omitted from the outstanding check list to allow the individual who has embezzled that amount of cash to hide an irregularity.

Concerning the second risk—when the year-end cash is correct, but should be higher—the auditors' problem is not misstated cash, but the irregularity itself and its effect on other accounts. Consequently, the auditors have in mind such basic questions as (1) Do the client's records reflect all cash transactions that took place during the year? and (2) Were all cash payments properly authorized and for a legitimate business purpose? Examples of irregularities that may be disclosed in searching for answers to these questions are:

1. Interception of cash receipts before any record is made.
2. Payment for materials not received.
3. Duplicate payments.
4. Overpayments to employees or payments to fictitious employees.
5. Payments for personal expenditures of officers or related parties.

Exceptions exist to the general rule that auditors are primarily concerned with overstatements of cash (and other assets). For example, the management of a privately held company may be motivated to understate assets (including cash) to minimize income taxes. Also, a client may maintain bank accounts not recorded on the books for such purposes as making illegal bribes. Thus, the auditors must consider whether all amounts of cash accounts are recorded (the completeness objective).

We have not included a "valuation" objective for cash. Valuation of cash is less a concern than for other assets because no allowance need be considered to arrive at a realizable value. However, when foreign subsidiaries are involved, the auditors must determine that translated currency is properly valued.

## How Much Audit Time for Cash?

The factor of materiality applies to audit work on cash as well as to other sections of the audit. The counting of a small petty cash fund, which is inconsequential in relation to the company's overall financial position, accomplishes little in achieving the auditors' objective of expressing an opinion on the financial statements. Nevertheless, auditors do devote a larger proportion of the total audit hours to cash than might be suggested by the relatively small amount of cash shown on the balance sheet. Although the year-end balance of cash may appear relatively small, the amount flowing into and out of the Cash account during the year is often greater than for any other account. Consequently, work on cash is important in virtually every audit.

Several reasons exist to explain the auditors' traditional emphasis on cash transactions. Liabilities, revenue, expenses, and most other assets flow through the Cash account; that is, these items either arise from or result in cash transactions. Thus, the examination of cash transactions assists the auditors in the substantiation of many other items in the financial statements.

Another reason contributing to extensive auditing of cash is that cash is the most liquid of assets and offers the greatest temptation for theft, embezzlement, and misappropriation. Inherent risk is high for liquid assets, and auditors tend to respond to high-risk situations with more intensive investigation. However, the detection of fraud is relevant to overall fairness of the client's financial statements only if such fraud is material in amount.

On occasion, auditors may encounter evidence of small-scale employee fraud. After determining that such fraud could *not* have a material effect upon the financial statements, the auditors should review the situation with the management and the audit committee of the board of directors before investigating the matter further. This discussion will alert the client to the situation, protect the auditors from charges of negligence, and avoid wasting audit time on matters that are not material with respect to the financial statements and that may better be pursued by client personnel.

# SUBSTANTIVE TESTS FOR CASH

Figure 13–5 presents typical substantive tests used to meet the primary audit objectives for cash. In the following sections we describe these procedures in detail.

## Obtain Analyses of Cash Accounts

| Primary Audit Objectives: |
|---|
| Clerical Accuracy   ☑ |

A schedule that lists all of the client's cash accounts at the audit date is commonly obtained from client personnel. For cash in bank accounts, this schedule will typically list the bank, the account number, account type, and the year-end balance per books. Selected accounts are traced by the auditors from the schedule to the accounting records.

Figure 13–5    Objectives of Major Substantive Tests of Cash Transactions and Balances

| Substantive Tests | Primary Audit Objectives |
|---|---|
| Obtain analyses of cash balances and reconcile to general ledger | Clerical accuracy |
| Send standard confirmation forms to financial institutions | Existence; Rights |
| Obtain reconciliations of bank balances and consider reconciling bank activity | |
| Obtain bank cutoff statement | |
| Count cash on hand | |
| Verify the client's cutoff of cash transactions | Existence; Rights; and Completeness |
| Analyze bank transfers occurring around year-end | |
| Investigate payments to related parties | Presentation and disclosure |
| Evaluate financial statement presentation and disclosure | |

## Confirm Cash Accounts

| Primary Audit Objectives: |
| --- |
| Existence ☑ |
| Rights ☑ |

One of the objectives of the auditors' work on cash is to substantiate the existence of the amount of cash shown on the balance sheet. A direct approach to this objective is to confirm amounts on deposit and obtain or prepare reconciliations between bank statements and the accounting records.

Confirmation of amounts on deposit by direct communication with financial institution officials is obtained in most audits. Account balances are confirmed with a standard form as illustrated by Figure 13–6. This standard confirmation form, agreed to by the AICPA, the American Bankers Association, and the Bank Administration Institute, addresses *only* the client's deposit and loan balances. Information identifying accounts and loans and their balances are typed on the form to assist the financial institution in completing it. Thus, the form is primarily used to *corroborate* the existence of recorded information. However, the confirmation may also lead to the *discovery* of additional accounts or loans and, therefore, it provides limited evidence about the *completeness* of recorded amounts. Although the personnel at the financial institution will not conduct a detailed search of the records, they will include information about additional deposits and loans that they note while completing the confirmation.

The details of other financial arrangements are also confirmed with financial institutions, using separate confirmation letters sent to the individual at the financial institution that is responsible for the client's financial arrangements or knowledgeable about those arrangements. For example, the auditors may send a separate confirmation letter to corroborate compensating balance arrangements, or authorized check signers. These confirmation letters are described in detail in Chapter 17.

## Analyze Reconciliations

| Primary Audit Objectives: |
| --- |
| Existence ☑ |
| Rights ☑ |

Determining a company's cash position at the close of the period requires a reconciliation of the balance per the bank statement at that date with the balance per the company's accounting records. Even though the auditors may not be able to begin their field work for some time after the close of the year, they will prepare a bank reconciliation as of the balance sheet date or test the one prepared by the client.

If the year-end reconciliation has been made by the client before the arrival of the auditors, there is no need for duplicating the work. However, the auditors should examine the reconciliation in detail to satisfy themselves that it has been properly prepared. Inspection of a reconciliation prepared by the client will include verifying the arithmetical accuracy, comparing balances to the bank statement and ledger account, and investigating the reconciling items. The importance of a careful review of the client's reconciliation is indicated by the fact that a cash shortage may be concealed merely by omitting a check from the outstanding check list or by purposely making an error in addition on the reconciliation.

There are many satisfactory forms of bank reconciliations. The form most frequently used by auditors begins with balance per bank and ends with unadjusted balance per the accounting records. The format permits the auditors to post adjusting entries affecting cash directly to the bank reconciliation working paper, so that the final adjusted balance can be cross-referenced to the cash lead schedule or to the working trial balance.

Figure 13-6   Confirmation Letter

## STANDARD FORM TO CONFIRM ACCOUNT
## BALANCE INFORMATION WITH FINANCIAL INSTITUTIONS

The Fairview Corporation
CUSTOMER NAME

| ORIGINAL |
|---|
| To be mailed to accountant |

We have provided to our accountants the following information as of

Financial Institution's Name and Address

Security National Bank
1000 Wilshire Boulevard
Los Angeles, California 90017-3562

the close of business on ___December 31___, 19 X3, regarding our deposit and loan balances. Please confirm the accuracy of the information, noting any exceptions to the information provided. If the balances have been left blank, please complete this form by furnishing the balance in the appropriate space below.* Although we do not request nor expect you to conduct a comprehensive, detailed search of your records, if during the process of completing this confirmation additional information about other deposit and loan accounts we may have with you comes to your attention, please include such information below. Please use the enclosed envelope to return the form directly to our accountants.

1. At the close of business on the date listed above, our records indicated the following deposit balance(s):

| ACCOUNT NAME | ACCOUNT NO. | INTEREST RATE | BALANCE* |
|---|---|---|---|
| General Account | 133-7825 | None | $89,548.92 |
| Payroll Account | 133-8765 | None | 8,212.05 |

2. We were directly liable to the financial institution for loans at the close of business on the date listed above as follows:

| ACCOUNT NO./ DESCRIPTION | BALANCE* | DATE DUE | INTEREST RATE | DATE THROUGH WHICH INTEREST IS PAID | DESCRIPTION OF COLLATERAL |
|---|---|---|---|---|---|
| 55-8965T Credit | $324,877 | 6/15/X7 | $12^{1}/_{2}\%$ | 12/15/X3 | Furniture & Fixtures |
| Line | $200,000 | 3/31/X4 | $13^{1}/_{4}\%$ | 12/31/X3 | Unsecured |

_Judith Fareri_
(Customer's Authorized Signature)

January 16, 19X4
(Date)

The information presented above by the customer is in agreement with our records. Although we have not conducted a comprehensive, detailed search of our records, no other deposit or loan accounts have come to our attention except as noted below.

_Jeanne M. Mebus_
(Financial Institution Authorized Signature)

January 31, 19X4
(Date)

_Audit Inquiry Clerk_
(Title)

| EXCEPTIONS AND/OR COMMENTS |
|---|
|  |

Please return this form directly to our accountants:

Douglas & Troon, CPAs
800 Hill Street
Los Angeles, CA 90014-7865

*Ordinarily, balances are intentionally left blank if they are not available at the time the form is prepared.

Approved 1990 by American Bankers Association, American Institute of Certified Public Accountants, and Bank Administration Institute. Additional forms availabe from: AICPA – Order Department, P.O. Box 1003, NY, NY 10108 – 1003

0451 5951

448

The mechanics of balancing the ledger account with the bank statement by no means completes the auditors' verification of cash on deposit. The authenticity of the individual items making up the reconciliation must be established by reference to their respective sources. The balance per the bank statement, for example, is not accepted at face value but is verified by direct confirmation with the bank, as described in the preceding pages. Other verification procedures associated with the reconciliation of the bank statement will now be discussed.

The auditors should investigate any checks outstanding for a year or more. If checks remain outstanding for long periods, internal control over cash disbursements is weakened. Employees who become aware that certain checks have long been outstanding and may never be presented have an opportunity to conceal a cash shortage merely by omitting the old outstanding check from the bank reconciliation. Such omissions will serve to increase the apparent balance of cash on deposit and may thus induce an employee to abstract a corresponding amount of cash on hand. It is good practice for the client to eliminate long-outstanding checks of this nature by an entry debiting the Cash account and crediting Unclaimed Wages or another special liability account. This will reduce the work required in bank reconciliations, as well as lessen the opportunity for irregularities.

When internal control over the recording of cash receipts and disbursements is considered weak, the auditors may use additional reconciliation procedures. For example, a **proof of cash** may be prepared, which in addition to reconciling the account balance, reconciles cash transactions occurring during a specified period. Specifically, the technique is used to identify

1. Cash receipts and disbursements recorded in the accounting records but not on the bank statement.
2. Cash deposits and disbursements recorded on the bank statement, but not on the accounting records.
3. Cash receipts and disbursements recorded at different amounts by the bank than in the accounting records.

A proof of cash is essentially a fraud detection procedure that may be used for any months during the year.

A proof of cash for the test period of September is illustrated in Figure 13–7. Notice that this working paper is so organized that the first and last columns reconcile the cash balance per bank and the balance per accounting records at the beginning of the test period (Column 1) and at the end of this period (Column 4). These outside columns are equivalent to typical monthly bank reconciliations. The two middle columns reconcile the bank's record of deposits with the client's record of cash receipts (Column 2) and the bank's record of paid checks with the client's record of cash disbursements (Column 3).

Next, consider the source of the figures used in this reconciliation. The amounts "per bank statement" are taken from the September 30 bank statement. The subsequent rows of deposits, checks, and other items are taken from the August and September bank reconciliations, and the amounts "per books" are taken from the client's Cash general ledger account and cash receipts and disbursements journals.

**Figure 13–7**    Proof of Cash

**THE FAIRVIEW CORPORATION**
**Account No. 101**
**Proof of Cash for September 199X**
**December 31, 199X**

A-6

SM
11/15/9X

| | Balance 8/31/9X | Deposits | Checks | Balance 9/30/9X |
|---|---|---|---|---|
| Per Bank Statement | $39,236.40 ✗ | $46,001.00 | $40,362.90 | $44,874.50 ✗ |
| Deposits in Transit | | | | |
| at 8/31/9X | 600.00 | (600.00) | | |
| at 9/30/9X | | 837.50 | | 837.50 |
| Outstanding Checks | | | | |
| at 8/31/9X | (1241.00) Ч | | (1241.00) | |
| at 9/30/9X | | | 3402.00 | (3,402.00) Ӵ |
| Bank Service Charge | | | | |
| August | (4.60) ✓ | | 4.60 | |
| September | | | 2.80 | 2.80 ✗ |
| Check of customer A.D. | | | | |
| Speeler charged back by Bank | | | | |
| 8/12/9X, redeposited 9/15/9X | | (900.00) | (900.00) | |
| Per Books | $38,600.00 M | $45,338.50 M | $41,625.70 M | $42,312.80 M |

✓   Traced to client's 8/31/9X bank statement.
✗   Traced to client's 9/30/9X bank statement.
⊘   Per adding machine tape at A-4-1.
Ч   Per adding machine tape at A-4-2.
Ӵ   Per adding machine tape at A-4-3.
M   Traced to general ledger.

Footed cash receipts journal and check register for 9/91. Accounted for numerical sequence of all checks issued September 199X (26610-6792). No exceptions noted.

K.W. 9/16/9X

## Obtain Cutoff Statement

| Primary Audit Objectives: | |
|---|---|
| Existence | ☑ |
| Rights | ☑ |

**A cutoff bank statement** is a statement covering a specified number of business days (usually 7 to 10) following the end of the client's fiscal year. The client will request the bank to prepare such a statement and mail it directly to the auditors. This statement is used to test the accuracy of the year-end reconciliation of the company's bank accounts. It allows the auditors to examine firsthand the checks listed as outstanding and the details of deposits in transit on the company's reconciliation.

With respect to checks that were shown as outstanding at year-end, the auditors should determine the dates on which these checks were paid by the bank. By noting the dates of payment of these checks, the auditors can determine whether the time intervals between the dates of the check and the time of payment by the bank were unreasonably long. Unreasonable delay in the presentation of these checks for payment constitutes a strong implication that the checks were not mailed by the client until some time after the close of the year. The appropriate adjusting entry in such cases consists of a debit to Cash and a credit to a liability account.

In examining the cutoff bank statement, the auditors will also watch for any paid checks issued on or before the balance sheet date but not listed as outstanding on the client's year-end bank reconciliation. Thus, the cutoff bank statement provides assurance that the amount of cash shown on the balance sheet was not overstated by omission of one or more checks from the list of checks outstanding.

## Count Cash on Hand

| Primary Audit Objectives: |   |
|---|---|
| Existence | ☑ |
| Rights | ☑ |

Cash on hand ordinarily consists of undeposited cash receipts, petty cash funds, and change funds. The petty cash funds and change funds may be counted at any time before or after the balance sheet date; many auditors prefer to make a surprise count of these funds.

The count of cash on hand is of special importance in the audit of banks and other financial institutions. Whenever auditors make a cash count, they should insist that the *custodian of the funds be present throughout the count*. At the completion of the count, the auditors should obtain from the custodian a signed and dated acknowledgment that the funds were counted in the custodian's presence and were returned intact by the auditors. Such procedures avoid the possibility of an employee trying to explain a cash shortage by claiming that the funds were intact when turned over to the auditors.

A first step in the verification of cash on hand is to establish control over all negotiable assets, such as cash funds, securities and other investments, notes receivable, and warehouse receipts. Unless all negotiable assets are verified at one time, an opportunity exists for a dishonest officer or employee to conceal a shortage by transferring it from one asset category to another.

It is not uncommon to find included in cash on hand some personal checks cashed for the convenience of officers, employees, and customers. Such checks, of course, should not be entered in the cash receipts journal because they are merely substitutes for currency previously on hand. The auditors should determine that these checks are valid and collectible, thus qualifying for inclusion in the balance sheet figure for cash. This may be accomplished by the auditors' examination of the last bank deposit for the period and determining that it includes all checks received through year-end. The auditors will retain a validated deposit slip from this deposit for comparison to any checks subsequently charged back by the bank.

## Verify Cash Cutoff

| Primary Audit Objectives: |   |
|---|---|
| Existence | ☑ |
| Rights | ☑ |
| Completeness | ☑ |

An accurate cutoff of cash receipts (and of cash disbursements) at year-end is essential to a proper statement of cash on the balance sheet. The balance sheet figure for cash should include all cash received on the final day of the year and none received subsequently. If the auditors can arrange to be present at the client's office at the close of business on the last day of the fiscal year, they will be able to verify the cutoff by counting the undeposited cash receipts. It will then be impossible for the client to include in the records any cash received after this cutoff point without the auditor being aware of such actions.

Of course, the auditors cannot visit every client's place of business on the last day of the fiscal year, nor is their presence at this time normally essential to a satisfactory verification of cash. As an alternative to a count on the balance sheet date, auditors can verify the cutoff of cash receipts by determining that deposits in transit as shown on the year-end bank reconciliation appear as credits on the bank statement on the first business day of the new year. Results of the auditors' consideration of internal control will dictate the necessary scope of audit procedures.

The auditors should be aware of possible **window dressing** related to cash transactions. For example, if the cash receipts are not deposited daily, cash received for a few days after the close of the year may be included in a deposit dated as of year-end, thus overstating the cash balance at the balance sheet date.

Other approaches to window dressing improve but do not outrightly misrepresent the cash position. For example, a corporate officer who has borrowed money from the corporation may repay the loan just before the end of the year and then promptly obtain the loan again after year-end; in such a situation disclosure in the notes to the financial statements may be appropriate.

Other forms of window dressing do not require action by the auditors. Many companies make strenuous efforts at year-end to achieve an improved financial picture by rushing shipments to customers, by pressing for collection of receivables, and sometimes by paying liabilities down to an unusually low level. Such efforts to improve the financial picture to be reported are not improper. Before giving approval to the balance sheet presentation of cash, the auditors must exercise their professional judgment to determine whether the client has engaged in window dressing of a nature that causes the financial statements to be misleading.

## Analyze Bank Transfers

| Primary Audit Objectives: | |
|---|---|
| Existence | ☑ |
| Rights | ☑ |
| Completeness | ☑ |

The purpose of tracing bank transfers is to disclose overstatements of cash balances resulting from **kiting.** Many businesses maintain checking accounts with a number of banks and often find it necessary to transfer funds from one bank to another. When a check drawn on one bank is deposited in another, several days (called the float period) usually pass before the check clears the bank on which it is drawn. During this period, the amount of the check is included in the balance on deposit at both banks. Kiting refers to manipulations that utilize such temporarily overstated bank balances to conceal a cash shortage or meet short-term cash needs.

Auditors can detect manipulations of this type by preparing a schedule of bank transfers for a few days before and after the balance sheet date. This working paper lists all bank transfers and shows the dates that the receipt and disbursement of cash were recorded in the cash journals and on the bank statements. An illustration of a schedule of bank transfers is shown on the following page.

Disclosure of Kiting.    By comparing the dates in this working paper, auditors can determine whether any manipulation of the cash balance has taken place. The increase in one bank account and decrease in the other bank account should be recorded in the cash

| Check No. | Bank Accounts | | Amount | Date of Disbursement | | Date of Receipt | |
|---|---|---|---|---|---|---|---|
| | From | To | | Books | Bank | Books | Bank |
| 5897 | General | Payroll | $30,620 | 12/28 | 1/3 | 12/28 | 12/28 |
| 6006 | General | Branch 4 | 24,018 | 1/2 | 1/4 | 12/30 | 12/30 |
| 6029 | Branch 2 | General | 10,000 | 1/3 | 1/5 | 1/3 | 12/31 |

journals in the same accounting period. Notice that Check No. 6006 in the transfer schedule was recorded in the cash journals as a receipt on December 30 and a disbursement of January 2. As a result of recording the debit and credit parts of the transaction in different accounting periods, cash is overstated on December 31. For the cash receipts journal to remain in balance, some account must have been credited on December 30 to offset the debit to Cash. If a revenue account was credited, the results of operations were overstated along with cash.

Kiting may also be used to conceal a cash shortage. Assume, for example, that a financial executive misappropriates $10,000 from a company's general checking account. To conceal the shortage on December 31, the executive draws a check transferring $10,000 from the company's branch bank account to the general account. The executive deposits the transfer check in the general account on December 31, but records the transfer in the accounting records as occurring early in January. As of December 31, the shortage in the general account has been replaced, no reduction has yet been recorded in the branch account, and no shortage is apparent. Of course, the shortage will reappear in a few days when the transfer check is paid from the branch account.

A bank transfer schedule should disclose this type of kiting because the transfer deposit appears on the general account bank statement in December, while the transaction was not recorded in the cash journals until January. Check No. 6029 in the transfer schedule illustrates this discrepancy. These illustrations suggest the following rules for determining when it is likely that a cash transfer has misstated the cash balance: (1) the dates of recording the transfer *per the books* (from the cash disbursements and cash receipts journals, respectively) are from different financial statement periods, or (2) the date the check was recorded *by the bank* (either the disbursement or the receipt, but not both) is from the financial statement period prior to when it is recorded on the books.

A third type of kiting uses the float period to meet short-term cash needs. For example, assume that a business does not have sufficient cash to meet the month-end payroll. The company might draw a check on its general account in one bank, deposit it in a payroll account in another bank, and rely upon subsequent deposits being made to the general account before the transfer check is presented for payment. If the transfer is properly recorded in the accounting records, this form of kiting will not cause a misstatement of the cash balance for financial reporting purposes. However, banks attempt to detect this practice and may not allow the customer to draw against the deposit until the check has cleared the other account. In some deliberate schemes to defraud banks, this type of kiting has been used to create and conceal overdrafts of millions of dollars.

## Investigate Related-Party Transactions

| Primary Audit Objectives: |
|---|
| Presentation ☑ |

Any large or unusual checks payable to directors, officers, employees, affiliated companies, or cash should be carefully reviewed by the auditors to determine whether the transactions *(a)* were properly authorized and recorded and *(b)* are adequately disclosed in the financial statements.

To provide assurance that cash disbursements to related parties were authorized transactions and were properly recorded, the auditors should determine that each such transaction has been charged to the proper account, is supported by adequate vouchers or other documents, and was specifically approved in advance by an officer other than the one receiving the funds.

To determine that such transactions are adequately disclosed, the auditors must obtain evidence concerning the relationship between the parties, the substance of each transaction (which may differ from its form), and the effect of each transaction upon the financial statements. Disclosure of related-party transactions should include the nature of the relationships, a description of the transactions, and the dollar amounts involved.

## Evaluate Disclosures

| Primary Audit Objectives: |
|---|
| Presentation ☑ |

The balance sheet figure for cash should include only those amounts that are available for use in current operations. A bank deposit that is restricted in use (for example, cash deposited with a trustee for payments on long-term debt) should not be included in cash. Agreements to maintain *compensating balances* should be disclosed. The auditors must also make sure that the caption, cash or cash and equivalents, on the client's balance sheet corresponds to that used in the statement of cash flows.

## Interim Audit Work on Cash

To avoid a concentration of audit work shortly after the year-end, CPA firms try to complete as many auditing procedures as possible on an interim basis during the year. The consideration of internal control over cash, for example, can be performed in advance of the client's year-end. The audit work on cash at year-end can then be limited to such substantive tests as a review of the client's bank reconciliations, confirmation of year-end bank balances, investigation of the year-end cutoff, and a general review of cash transactions during the interval between the interim work on cash and the end of the period.

## Audit Working Papers for Cash

In addition to preparing a lead schedule for cash, the auditors obtain or prepare the following working papers:

1. Reconciliations of cash accounts at financial institutions.
2. Confirmations from financial institutions.
3. Copies of cutoff bank statements.
4. Bank transfer schedule.
5. Summary of results of tests of cash transactions.

# ◆ ILLUSTRATIVE AUDIT CASE: KEYSTONE COMPUTERS & NETWORKS, INC.

# PART III: SUBSTANTIVE TESTS

This part of the audit case illustrates the manner in which the auditors design substantive tests of balances. The substantive tests are illustrated for two revenue cycle accounts—accounts receivable and sales. This aspect of the audit is illustrated with the following working papers:

- ◆ The substantive audit program of accounts receivable and sales.
- ◆ The audit sampling plan for the confirmation of accounts receivable.

The nature, timing, and extent of the substantive procedures for accounts receivable and sales were determined by the Adams, Barnes & Co. (ABC), CPAs, assessment of control risk as described in Part II of the audit case on pages 405 through 418 of Chapter 12. To refresh your knowledge of the case, review that part as well as Part I on pages 220 through 228 of Chapter 7.

| Audit Program—Substantive Tests—Accounts Receivable and Sales | B-6 |
|---|---|
| | *WL* |
| **Client:** *Keystone Computers & Networks, Inc.* | *11/13/X5* |

**Financial Statement Date:** *12/31/X5*

| | | Performed by | |
|---|---|---|---|
| | **Procedure** | **Initials** | **Date** |
| 1. | Obtain an aged trial balance of accounts receivable as of 12/31/X5. | *MP* | *1/6/X6* |
| 2. | Select a sample of customer's accounts at 12/31/X5 for positive confirmation using probability-proportional-to-size sampling based on the following parameters: | | |
| | *a.* Risk of incorrect acceptance of 25%. | | |
| | *b.* Tolerable misstatement of $35,000. | | |
| | *c.* Expected misstatement of $10,000. | *MP* | *1/7/X6* |
| 3. | Use generalized audit software to: | | |
| | *a.* Foot the master file of accounts receivable at 12/31/X5. | *MP* | *1/7/X6* |
| | *b.* Test the client-prepared aging of accounts receivable. | *MP* | *1/7/X6* |
| | *c.* Select the specific accounts for confirmation. | *MP* | *1/7/X6* |
| 4. | Mail accounts receivable confirmation requests. | *MP* | *1/8/X6* |
| 5. | Send second requests for all unanswered confirmation requests. | *MP* | *1/25/X6* |
| 6. | For confirmation requests to which no reply is received perform the following alternative procedures: | | |
| | *a.* Test items subsequently paid to remittance advices which identify the specific invoices paid. If necessary, reconcile the amounts paid to sales invoices and delivery receipts. | *MP* | *2/15/X6* |
| | *b.* For items not paid, inspect the invoices and delivery receipts for the sales transactions making up the account balance. | *MP* | *2/16/X6* |
| 7. | Resolve exceptions noted on confirmation requests. | *MP* | *2/16/X6* |
| 8. | Summarize the results of the confirmation procedures. | *MP* | *2/16/X6* |
| 9. | Review the adequacy of the allowance for uncollectible accounts by performing the following procedures: | | |
| | *a.* Review the aged trial balance of accounts receivable with the president. | *WL* | *2/13/X6* |
| | *b.* Review confirmation exceptions for indications of disputed amounts. | *WL* | *2/13/X6* |
| | *c.* Analyze and review trends in the following relationships: | | |
| | (1) Accounts receivable to net sales. | *WL* | *2/15/X6* |
| | (2) Allowance for bad debts to accounts receivable. | *WL* | *2/15/X6* |
| | (3) Bad debt expense to net sales. | *WL* | *2/15/X6* |

| Audit Program—Substantive Tests—Accounts Receivable and Sales, continued | | B-6 |
| --- | --- | --- |

*WL*

*11/13/X5*

**Client:** *Keystone Computers & Networks, Inc.*

**Financial Statement Date:** *12/31/X5*

|  | | Performed by | |
| --- | --- | --- | --- |
| **Procedure** | | **Initials** | **Date** |
| 10. | At year-end, review the file of sales invoices that are waiting to be matched with delivery receipts for any sales transactions that were not executed and, therefore, should be recorded in the subsequent period. | *MP* | *12/31/X5* |
| 11. | For all sales recorded in the last week of the year inspect the related delivery receipt to determine that the sale occurred before 12/31/X5. | *MP* | *2/12/X6* |
| 12. | Review credit memoranda for sales returns and allowances through the last day of field work to determine if an adjustment is needed to record the items as of year-end. | *MP* | *2/16/X6* |
| 13. | Perform analytical procedures for sales and accounts receivable including comparison of the following to prior years and/or industry data: | | |
| | *a.* Gross profit percentage. | *WL* | *2/12/X6* |
| | *b.* Accounts receivable turnover. | *WL* | *2/16/X6* |
| | *c.* Advertising expense as a percentage of sales. | *WL* | *2/16/X6* |
| | *d.* Net receivables as a percentage of total current assets. | *WL* | *2/16/X6* |
| 14. | Ascertain whether any accounts have been assigned, pledged, or discounted by review of agreements and confirmation with banks. | *WL* | *2/13/X6* |
| 15. | Ascertain by inquiry whether any accounts are owed by employees or related parties such as officers, directors, or shareholders, and: | | |
| | *a.* Obtain an understanding of the business purpose for the transactions that resulted in the balances. | *WL* | *2/16/X6* |
| | *b.* Ascertain the amounts involved. | *WL* | *2/16/X6* |
| | *c.* Confirm the balances. | *WL* | *1/25/X6* |

---

### KEYSTONE COMPUTERS & NETWORKS, INC.
### Audit Sample Plan for Confirmation of Accounts Receivable
### 12/31/X5

B9

*WL*
*1/7/X6*

**Objective:** *Establish the existence, occurrence, and gross valuation of accounts receivable and sales by confirmation.*

**Population:** *The trial balance of 433 accounts receivable at 12/31/X5, with a total book value of $1,023,545.*

**Definition of Misstatement:** *Any amount that is determined not to be a valid account receivable.*

**Sampling Technique:** *Probability-proportional-to-size*

**Sampling Parameters:**

1.  **Tolerable misstatement:**

    | | |
    |---|---:|
    | *Total materiality as indicated in the audit plan* | *$70,000* |
    | *Less: Estimate of undetected misstatement (50% of overall materiality)* | *35,000* |
    | *Tolerable misstatement for this test* | *$35,000* |

2.  **Risk of incorrect acceptance:**

    *Because we have assessed control risk at a moderate level and have performed analytical procedures that are moderately effective at detecting material misstatements, the risk of incorrect acceptance will be set at 25 percent.*

3.  **Expected misstatement:**

    *Based on prior-year audits, the expected misstatement for the account is $10,000.*

**Calculation of Sample Size and Sampling Interval:**

$$\text{Sample size} = \frac{\text{Book value of population} \times \text{Reliability factor}}{\text{Tolerable misstatement} - (\text{Expected misstatement} \times \text{Expansion factor})}$$

$$= \frac{\$1,023,545 \times 1.39}{\$35,000 - (\$10,000 \times 1.25)}$$

$$= 63$$

$$\text{Sampling interval} = \frac{\text{Book value of population}}{\text{Sample size}} = \frac{\$1,023,545}{63} = \$16,000 \text{ (rounded)}$$

*Actual sample size was only 50 because several accounts were more than twice the sampling interval.*

---

## ◆ CHAPTER SUMMARY

In this chapter we described the auditors' substantive tests of the revenue cycle accounts—sales, receivables, and cash. To summarize:

1.  The primary objectives for the auditors' substantive tests of sales and receivables are to *(a)* substantiate the existence of receivables, *(b)* establish the completeness of receivables and sales transactions, *(c)* determine that the client has rights to the recorded receivables, *(d)* establish the clerical accuracy of records and supporting schedules of receivables and sales, *(e)* determine that the valuation of receivables and sales is at appropriate net realizable values, and *(f)* establish that the presentation and disclosure of receivables and sales are appropriate.

2.  The most time-consuming and critical audit procedures for receivables and sales are those designed to test the assertions of existence, occurrence, and valuation. Among

the procedures designed to achieve these objectives is confirmation of accounts receivable, which is generally required in all audits. Acknowledgment of the debt provides evidence of existence of receivables and occurrence of sales, as well as the gross valuation of the amounts. An important part of obtaining evidence about the proper valuation of accounts receivable is the auditors' evaluation of the adequacy of the allowance for uncollectible accounts. Since this account is a management estimate, it is typically audited by a combination of inquiry of management, analytical procedures, and inspection of various documentation.

3. The principal objectives for the substantive tests of cash are to *(a)* substantiate the existence of the recorded cash, *(b)* establish the completeness of recorded cash, *(c)* determine that the client has rights to recorded cash, *(d)* determine that cash schedules are clerically accurate, and *(e)* evaluate the adequacy of the presentation and disclosure of the cash accounts. A primary substantive test of cash is confirmation of the balances of the company's accounts with financial institutions.

4. Since cash generally has a high degree of inherent risk, more audit time is devoted to the audit of the account than is indicated by its dollar amount.

# ◆ KEY TERMS INTRODUCED OR EMPHASIZED IN CHAPTER 13

**Aged trial balance** A listing of individual customers' accounts classified by age. Serves as a preliminary step in estimating the collectibility of accounts receivable.

**Confirmation** The process of obtaining evidence by written communication with the debtor or other party to a transaction.

**Cutoff bank statement** A bank statement covering a specified number of business days (usually 7 to 10) after the client's balance sheet date. Auditors use this statement to determine that checks issued on or before the balance sheet date and paid during the cutoff period were listed as outstanding on the year-end bank reconciliation. Another use is to determine that reconciling items shown on the year-end bank reconciliation have cleared the bank within a reasonable time.

**Interim audit work** Those audit procedures that can be performed before the balance sheet date. The purpose is to facilitate earlier issuance of the audit report and to spread the auditors' work more uniformly over the year.

**Kiting** Manipulations causing an amount of cash to be included simultaneously in the balance of two or more bank accounts. Kiting schemes are based on the float period—the time necessary for a check deposited in one bank to clear the bank on which it was drawn.

**Negative confirmation** A confirmation request addressed to the debtor requesting a reply only if the balance shown on the request is incorrect.

**Pledging of receivables** To assign to a bank, factor, finance company, or other lender an exclusive claim against accounts receivable as security for a debt.

**Positive confirmation** A confirmation request sent to the debtor asking it to confirm directly to the auditors the accuracy of the dollar amount shown on the request. Calls for a reply regardless of whether the amount is correct or incorrect.

**Proof of cash** An audit procedure that reconciles the bank's record of cash activity with the client's accounting records for a test period. The working paper used for the proof of cash is a four-column bank reconciliation.

**Standard Form to Confirm Account Balance Information with Financial Institutions** A standard confirmation form, agreed to by the AICPA, the American Bankers Association, and the Bank

Administration Institute, that is designed to provide corroborating evidence about the client's account balances and outstanding loans.

**Window dressing**   Action taken by the client shortly before the balance sheet date to improve the financial picture presented in the financial statements.

---

## ◆ GROUP I: REVIEW QUESTIONS

13-1   It is sometimes said that audit work on cash is facilitated by the existence of two independent records of the client's cash transactions, which are available for comparison by the auditors. Identify these two independent records.

13-2   Give two reasons why audit work on cash is likely to be more extensive than might appear to be justified by the relative amount of the balance sheet figure for cash.

13-3   Describe circumstances that might cause a client to understate assets such as cash and accounts receivable.

13-4   What information do CPAs request from a financial institution on the Standard Form to Confirm Account Balance Information with Financial Institutions?

13-5   How can the auditors corroborate compensating balance arrangements?

13-6   What action should be taken by the auditors when the count of cash on hand discloses a shortage?

13-7   During your reconciliation of bank accounts in an audit, you find that a number of checks for small amounts have been outstanding for more than a year. Does this situation call for any action by the auditor? Explain.

13-8   Explain the objectives of each of the following audit procedures for cash:
  *a.*   Obtain a cutoff bank statement subsequent to the balance sheet date.
  *b.*   Compare paid checks returned with bank statement to list of outstanding checks in previous reconciliation.
  *c.*   Trace all bank transfers during the last week of the audit year and the first week of the following year.
  *d.*   Investigate any checks representing large or unusual payments to related parties.

13-9   Explain two procedures by which auditors may verify the client's cutoff of cash receipts.

13-10   What is the meaning of the term *window dressing* when used in connection with year-end financial statements? How might the term be related to the making of loans by a corporation to one or more of its executives?

13-11   Give an example of a type of receivable originating without arm's-length bargaining. Comment on the presentation of such receivables in the balance sheet.

13-12   In selecting accounts receivable for confirmation, the auditors discover that the client company's records show the addresses of many individual customers to be post office boxes. What should be the auditors' reaction to this situation?

13-13   Cite various procedures auditors employ that might lead to the detection of an inadequate allowance for doubtful accounts receivable.

13-14   A CPA firm wishes to test the client's sales cutoff at June 30, 199X. Describe the steps that the auditors should include in this test.

13-15   Several accounts receivable confirmations have been returned with the notation ''verifications of vendors' statements are no longer possible because of our data processing system.'' What alternative auditing procedures could be used to verify these accounts receivable?

13-16   The confirmation of accounts receivable is an important auditing procedure. Should the formal request for confirmation be made by the client or by the auditors? Should the return envelope be addressed to the client, to the auditors in care of the client, or to the auditors' office? Explain.

13-17   In the audit of an automobile agency, you find that installment notes received from the purchasers of automobiles are promptly discounted with a bank. Would you consider it necessary to confirm these notes by a communication with the bank? With the makers? Explain.

13-18   Your review of notes receivable from officers, directors, stockholders, and affiliated companies discloses that several notes of small amounts were written off to the allowance for uncollectible notes during the year. Have these transactions any special significance? Explain.

13-19   What auditing procedures, if any, are necessary for notes receivable but are not required for accounts receivable?

13-20   What alternative auditing procedures may be undertaken in connection with the confirmation of accounts receivable where customers having substantial balances fail to reply after second request forms have been mailed directly to them?

13-21   In your first audit of Hydro Manufacturing Company, a manufacturer of outboard motors, you discover that an unusually large number of sales transactions were recorded just before the end of the fiscal year. What significance would you attach to this unusual volume?

13-22   In connection with an audit, what are the purposes of a review of sales returns and allowances subsequent to the balance sheet date?

13-23   State briefly the audit objectives that are addressed by the audit procedure of "Confirm accounts receivable and notes receivable by direct communication with debtors."

# ◆ GROUP II: QUESTIONS REQUIRING ANALYSIS

13-24   "When auditors are verifying a client's bank reconciliation, they are particularly concerned with the possibility that the list of outstanding checks may include a nonexistent or fictitious check, and also are concerned with the possibility of omission from the reconciliation of a deposit in transit." Criticize the above quotation and revise it into an accurate statement.

13-25   During the first few months of the year, John Smith, the cashier in a small company, was engaged in lapping operations. However, he was able to restore the amount of cash "borrowed" by March 31, and he refrained from any fraudulent acts after that date. Is it likely that the year-end audit will lead to the discovery of his lapping activities? Explain.

13-26   An assistant auditor received the following instructions from her supervisor: "Here is a cutoff bank statement covering the first seven business days of January. Compare the paid checks returned with the statement and dated December 31 or earlier with the list of checks outstanding at December 31." What type of irregularity might this audit procedure bring to light? Explain.

13-27   During the examination of cash, the CPAs are alert for any indications of kiting.

*Required:*   *a.* Define *kiting*.
*b.* Explain the audit procedures that should enable the CPAs to uncover kiting.

13-28   Explain how each of the following items would appear in a four-column proof of cash for the month of November. Assume the format of the proof of cash begins with bank balances and ends with the unadjusted balances per the accounting records.
*a.* Outstanding checks at November 30.
*b.* Deposits-in-transit at October 31.

    c.   Check issued and paid in November, drawn payable to Cash.

    d.   The bank returned $1,800 in NSF checks deposited by the client in November; the client redeposited $1,450 of these checks in November and $350 in December, making no additional entries in the accounting records.

13-29  During your audit of Miles Company, you prepared the following bank transfer schedule:

### MILES COMPANY
### Bank Transfer Schedule
### December 31, 199X

| Check | Bank Accounts | | | Date Disbursed Per | | Date Deposited Per | |
| Number | From | To | Amount | Books | Bank | Books | Bank |
|---|---|---|---|---|---|---|---|
| 2020 | 1st Natl. | Suburban | $32,000 | 1/4 | 1/5 | 12/31 | 1/3 |
| 2021 | 1st Natl. | Capital | 21,000 | 12/31 | 1/4 | 12/31 | 1/3 |
| 3217 | 2nd State | Suburban | 6,700 | 1/3 | 1/5 | 1/3 | 12/30 |
| 0659 | Midtown | Suburban | 5,500 | 12/30 | 1/5 | 12/30 | 1/3 |

*Required:*   a.  Describe the purpose of a bank transfer schedule.

             b.  Identify those transfers that should be investigated and explain the reason.

                                                  (AICPA, adapted)

13-30  In the audit of a client with a fiscal year ending June 30, the CPAs obtain a July 10 bank statement directly from the bank. Explain how this cutoff bank statement will be used:

*Required:*   a.  In the review of the June 30 bank reconciliation.

             b.  To obtain other audit information.

                                                  (AICPA, adapted)

13-31  In the audit of Wheat, Inc. for the year ended December 31, you discover that the client had been drawing checks as creditors' invoices became due but had not been mailing the checks immediately. Because of a working capital shortage, some checks have been held for two or three weeks.

       The client's controller informs you that unmailed checks totaling $48,500 were on hand at December 31 of the current year. He states that these December-dated checks had been entered in the cash disbursements journal and charged to the respective creditors' accounts in December because the checks were prenumbered. However, these checks were not actually mailed until early January. The controller wants to adjust the cash balance and accounts payable at December 31 by $48,500 because the Cash account had a credit balance. He objects to submitting audited financial statements to his bank showing an overdraft of cash.

*Required:*  Discuss the propriety of adjusting the cash balance and accounts payable by the indicated amount of outstanding checks.

13-32  Select the best answer for each of the following situations and give reasons for your choice.

    a.  You have been assigned to the year-end audit of a financial institution and are planning the timing of audit procedures relating to cash. You decide that it would be preferable for the auditors to:

       (1)  Count the cash in advance of the balance sheet date in order to disclose any kiting operations at year-end.

    (2)  Coordinate the count of cash with the cutoff of accounts payable.

    (3)  Coordinate the count of cash with the count of marketable securities and other negotiable assets.

    (4)  Count the cash immediately upon the return of the confirmation letters for the financial institution.

*b.*  To gather evidence on the balance per bank in a bank reconciliation, the auditors would examine all of the following *except:*

    (1)  Cutoff bank statement.

    (2)  Year-end bank statement.

    (3)  Bank confirmation.

    (4)  General ledger.

*c.*  Which of the following might be detected by the auditors' review of the client's sales cutoff?

    (1)  Excessive goods returned for credit.

    (2)  Unrecorded sales discounts.

    (3)  Lapping of year-end accounts receivable.

    (4)  Inflated sales for the year.

*d.*  To test the existence assertion for recorded receivables, the auditors would select a sample *from* the:

    (1)  Sales orders file.

    (2)  Customer purchase orders.

    (3)  Accounts receivable subsidiary ledger.

    (4)  Shipping documents (bills of lading) file.

*e.*  Which assertion relating to sales is most directly addressed when the auditors compare a sample of shipping documents to related sales invoices?

    (1)  Existence or occurrence.

    (2)  Completeness.

    (3)  Rights and obligations.

    (4)  Presentation and disclosure.

*f.*  Cooper, CPA, is auditing the financial statements of a small rural municipality. The receivable balances represent residents' delinquent real estate taxes. The internal control structure at the municipality is weak. To determine the existence of the accounts receivable balances at the balance sheet date, Cooper would most likely:

    (1)  Send positive confirmation requests.

    (2)  Send negative confirmation requests.

    (3)  Examine evidence of subsequent cash receipts.

    (4)  Inspect the internal records such as copies of the tax invoices that were mailed to the residents.

13-33  During the audit of Solar Technologies, Inc., the auditors sent confirmation requests to customers whose accounts had been written off as uncollectible during the year under audit. An executive of Solar protested, saying: "You people should be verifying that the receivables on the books are collectible. We know the ones we wrote off are no good."

*Required:*  *a.*  What purpose, if any, is served by this audit procedure?

    *b.*  Does the Solar executive's statement suggest some misunderstanding of audit objectives? Explain.

13-34  During preliminary conversations with a new staff assistant you instruct her to send out confirmation requests for both accounts receivable and notes receivable. She asks whether the confirmation requests should go to the makers of the notes or to the holders of the notes in the case of notes that have been discounted. Provide an answer to her question and give reasons for your answer.

13-35  Lakeside Company has retained you to conduct an audit so that it will be able to support its application for a bank loan with audited financial statements. The president of Lakeside states that you will have unlimited access to all records of the company and may carry out any audit procedures you consider necessary, except that you are not to communicate with customers. The president feels that contacts with customers might lead them to believe that Lakeside is in financial difficulty. Under these circumstances, will it be possible for you to issue the auditors' standard unqualified audit report? Explain.

13-36  In their work on accounts receivable and elsewhere in an audit, the independent auditors often make use of confirmation requests.

*Required:*   *a.* What is an audit confirmation request?

*b.* What characteristics should an audit confirmation request possess if a CPA firm is to consider it to be valid evidence?

*c.* Distinguish between a positive confirmation request and a negative confirmation request in the auditors' examination of accounts receivable.

*d.* In confirming a client's accounts receivable, what characteristics should be present in the accounts if the CPA firm is to use negative confirmation requests?

13-37  What are the implications to the auditors if, during their examination of accounts receivable, some of a client's customers do not respond to the auditors' request for positive confirmation of their accounts receivable?

What procedures should the auditors perform if there is no response to a second request for a positive confirmation?

(AICPA, adapted)

13-38  Walt Conn, CPA, is engaged to audit the financial statements of Matthews Wholesaling for the year ended December 31, 199X. Conn obtained and documented an understanding of the internal control structure relating to the accounts receivable and assessed control risk relating to accounts receivable at the maximum level. Conn requested and obtained from Matthews an aged accounts receivable schedule listing the total amount owed by each customer as of December 31, 199X, and sent positive confirmation requests to a sample of the customers.

*Required:*   What additional substantive audit procedures should Conn consider applying in auditing the accounts receivable?

(AICPA, adapted)

13-39  An assistant auditor was instructed to "test the aging of accounts receivable as shown on the trial balance prepared by the client." In making this test, the assistant traced all past-due accounts shown on the trial balance to the ledger cards in the accounts receivable subsidiary ledger and computed the aging of these accounts. The assistant found no discrepancies and reported to the senior auditor that the aging work performed by the client was satisfactory.

*Required:*   Comment on the logic and adequacy of this test of the aging of accounts receivable.

# ◆ GROUP III: PROBLEMS

13-40   The following client-prepared bank reconciliation is being examined by Kautz, CPA, during an audit of the financial statements of Cynthia Company:

**CYNTHIA COMPANY**
**Bank Reconciliation**
**Village Bank Account 2**
**December 31, 199X**

| | | |
|---|---:|---:|
| Balance per bank *(a)* . . . . . . . . . . . . . . . . . . . . . . . | | $18,375.91 |
| Deposits in transit *(b)* | | |
| 12/30 . . . . . . . . . . . . . . . . . . . . . . . . . . | $1,471.10 | |
| 12/31 . . . . . . . . . . . . . . . . . . . . . . . . . . | 2,840.69 | 4,311.79 |
| Subtotal . . . . . . . . . . . . . . . . . . . . . | | 22,687.70 |
| Outstanding checks *(c)* | | |
| 837 . . . . . . . . . . . . . . . . . . . . . . . . . . | 6,000.00 | |
| 1941 . . . . . . . . . . . . . . . . . . . . . . . . . . | 671.80 | |
| 1966 . . . . . . . . . . . . . . . . . . . . . . . . . . | 320.00 | |
| 1984 . . . . . . . . . . . . . . . . . . . . . . . . . . | 1,855.42 | |
| 1985 . . . . . . . . . . . . . . . . . . . . . . . . . . | 3,621.22 | |
| 1987 . . . . . . . . . . . . . . . . . . . . . . . . . . | 2,576.89 | |
| 1991 . . . . . . . . . . . . . . . . . . . . . . . . . . | 4,420.88 | (19,466.21) |
| Subtotal . . . . . . . . . . . . . . . . . . . . . | | 3,221.49 |
| NSF check returned | | |
| 12/29 *(d)* . . . . . . . . . . . . . . . . . . . . . . . | | 200.00 |
| Bank charges . . . . . . . . . . . . . . . . . . . . . | | 5.50 |
| Error Check No. 1932 . . . . . . . . . . . . . . . . . | | 148.10 |
| Customer note collected by the bank | | |
| ($2,750 plus $275 interest) *(e)* . . . . . . . . . . . . . . | | (3,025.00) |
| Balance per books *(f)* . . . . . . . . . . . . . . . . . . . . | | $550.09 |

*Required:*   Indicate one or more audit procedures that should be performed by Kautz in gathering evidence in support of each of the items *(a)* through *(f)* above.

(AICPA, adapted)

13-41   You are the senior auditor-in-charge of the July 31, 199X, audit of Reliable Auto Parts, Inc. Your newly hired staff assistant reports to you that she is unable to complete the four-column proof of cash for the month of April 199X, which you instructed her to do as part of the consideration of internal control for cash.

Your assistant shows you the working paper (on the next page) that she has prepared. Your review of your assistant's work reveals that the dollar amounts of all of the items in her working paper are correct. You learn that the accountant for Reliable Auto Parts, Inc. makes no journal entries for bank services charges or note collections until the month following the bank's recording of the item and that Reliable's accountant makes no journal entries whatsoever for NSF checks that are redeposited and cleared.

*Required:*   Prepare a corrected four-column proof of cash in good form for Reliable Auto Parts, Inc., for the month of April 199X.

## RELIABLE AUTO PARTS, INC.
### Proof of Cash for April 199X
### July 31, 199X

| | Balance 3/31/9X | Deposits | Checks | Balance 4/30/9X |
|---|---|---|---|---|
| Per bank statement | 71,682.84 | 61,488.19 | 68,119.40 | 65,051.63 |
| Deposits in transit: | | | | |
| At 3/31/9X | 2,118.18 | | | (2,118.18) |
| At 4/30/9X | | 4,918.16 | | 4,918.16 |
| Outstanding checks: | | | | |
| At 3/31/9X | (14,888.16) | | 14,888.16 | |
| At 4/30/9X | | | (22,914.70) | 22,914.70 |
| Bank service charges: | | | | |
| March 199X | (22.18) | | 22.18 | |
| April 199X | | | (19.14) | 19.14 |
| Note receivable collected by bank 4/30/9X | | 18,180.00 | | 18,180.00 |
| NSF check of customer L. G. Waite, charged back by bank 3/31/9X, redeposited and cleared 4/3/9X | (418.19) | 418.19 | | |
| Balances as computed | 58,472.49 | 85,004.54 | 60,095.90 | 108,965.45 |
| Balances per books | 59,353.23 | 45,689.98 | 76,148.98 | 28,894.23 |
| Unlocated difference | (880.74) | 39,314.56 | (16,053.08) | 80,071.22 |

13-42 During the audit of Sunset Building Supply, you are given the following year-end bank reconciliation prepared by the client:

## SUNSET BUILDING SUPPLY
### Bank Reconciliation
### December 31

| | |
|---|---|
| Balance per 12/31 bank statement. . . . . . . . . . . . . . . . . . . . . . | $48,734 |
| Add: Deposits in transit . . . . . . . . . . . . . . . . . . . . . . . . . . | 4,467 |
| | $53,201 |
| Less: Checks outstanding . . . . . . . . . . . . . . . . . . . . . . . . . | 20,758 |
| Balance per ledger, 12/31 . . . . . . . . . . . . . . . . . . . . . . . . . | $32,443 |

According to the client's accounting records, checks totaling $31,482 were issued between January 1 and January 14 of the following year. You have obtained a cutoff bank statement dated January 14 containing paid checks amounting to $50,440. Of the checks outstanding at December 31, $3,600 were not returned in the cutoff statement, and of those issued per the accounting records in January, $8,200 were not returned.

*Required:* a. Prepare a working paper comparing (1) the total of all checks returned by the bank or still outstanding with (2) the total per the client's records of checks outstanding at December 31 plus checks issued from January 1–14.

b. Suggest four possible explanations for the situation disclosed in your working paper. State what action you would take in each case, including any adjusting entry you would propose.

13-43   MLG Company's auditor received confirmations and cutoff statements with related checks and deposit tickets for MLG's three general-purpose bank accounts directly from the banks. The auditor has assessed control risk for the assertions about cash as low. The proper cutoff of external cash receipts and disbursements was established. No bank accounts were opened or closed during the year.

*Required:*   Prepare the audit program of substantive procedures to verify MLG's bank balances. Ignore any other cash accounts.

(AICPA, adapted)

13-44   Milton Chambers, CPA, was retained by Hall Corporation to perform an audit of its financial statements for the year ending December 31. In a preliminary meeting with company officials, Chambers learned that the corporation customarily accepted numerous notes receivable from its customers. At December 31, the client company's controller provided Chambers with a list of the individual notes receivable owned at that date. The list showed for each note the date of the note, amount, interest rate, maturity date, and name and address of the maker. After a careful consideration of the internal control relating to notes receivable, Chambers turned his attention to the list of notes receivable provided to him by the controller.

Chambers proved the footing of the list and determined that the total agreed with the general ledger control account for notes receivable and also with the amount shown in the balance sheet. Next he selected 20 of the larger amounts on the list of notes receivable for detailed investigation. This investigation consisted of confirming the amount, date, maturity, interest rate, and collateral, if any, by direct communication with the makers of the notes. By selection of the larger amounts, Chambers was able to verify 75 percent of the dollar amount of notes receivable by confirming only 20 percent of the notes. However, he also selected a random sample of another 20 percent of the smaller notes on the list for confirmation with the makers. Satisfactory replies were received to all confirmation requests.

The president of Hall Corporation informed Chambers that the company never required any collateral in support of the notes receivable; the replies to confirmation requests indicated no collateral had been pledged.

No notes were past due at the balance sheet date, and the credit manager stated that no losses were anticipated. Chambers verified the credit status of the makers of all the notes he had confirmed by reference to audited financial statements of the makers and Dun & Bradstreet credit ratings.

By independent computation of the interest accrued on the notes receivable at the balance sheet date, Chambers determined that the accrued interest receivable as shown on the balance sheet was correct.

Since Chambers found no deficiencies in any part of his audit, he issued an unqualified audit report. Some months later, Hall Corporation became insolvent and the president fled the country. Chambers was sued by creditors of the company, who charged that his audit was inadequate and failed to meet minimum professional standards. You are to comment on the audit program followed by Chambers with respect to notes receivable *only.*

13-45   As part of his audit of the financial statements of Marlborough Corporation for the year ended March 31, 199X, Mark Wayne, CPA, is reviewing the balance sheet presentation of a $1,200,000 advance to Franklin Olds, Marlborough's president. The advance, which represents 50 percent of current assets and 10 percent of total assets, was made during the year ended March 31, 199X. It has been described in the balance sheet as "miscellaneous accounts receivable" and classified as a current asset.

Olds informs the CPA that he has used the proceeds of the advance to purchase 35,000 shares of Marlborough's common stock, in order to forestall a takeover raid on the company. He is reluctant to have his association with the advance described in the financial statements because he does not have voting control and fears that this will "just give the raiders ammunition."

Olds offers the following four-point program as an alternative to further disclosure:

1. Have the advance approved by the board of directors. (This can be done expeditiously because a majority of the board members are officers of the company.)
2. Prepare a demand note payable to the company with interest of 12 percent (the average bank rate paid by the company).
3. Furnish an endorsement of the stock to the company as collateral for the loan. (During the year under audit, despite the fact that earnings did not increase, the market price of Marlborough common rose from $20 to $40 per share. The stock has maintained its $40 per share market price subsequent to year-end.)
4. Obtain a written opinion from the company attorney supporting the legality of the company's advance and the use of the proceeds.

*Required:*   *a.* Discuss the proper balance sheet classification of the advance to Olds and other appropriate disclosures in the financial statements and notes. (Ignore SEC regulations and requirements, tax effects, creditors' restrictions on stock repurchase, and the presentation of common stock dividends and interest revenue.)

*b.* Discuss each point of Olds's four-point program as to whether it is desirable and as to whether it is an alternative to further disclosure.

*c.* If Olds refuses to permit further disclosure, what action should the CPA take? Discuss.

*d.* In his discussion with the CPA, Olds warns that the raiders, if successful, probably will appoint new auditors. What consideration should the CPA give to this factor? Explain.

(AICPA, adapted)

13-46   Lawrence Company maintains its accounts on the basis of a fiscal year ending October 31. Assume that you were retained by the company in August to perform an audit for the fiscal year ending October 31, 199X. You decide to perform certain auditing procedures in advance of the balance sheet date. Among these interim procedures is the confirmation of accounts receivable, which you perform at September 30.

The accounts receivable at September 30 consisted of approximately 200 accounts with balances totaling $956,750. Seventy-five of these accounts with balances totaling $650,725 were selected for confirmation. All but 20 of the confirmation requests have been returned; 30 were signed without comments, 14 had minor differences that have been cleared satisfactorily, and 11 confirmations had the following comments:

1. We are sorry, but we cannot answer your request for confirmation of our account because Moss Company uses a computerized accounts payable voucher system.
2. The balance of $1,050 was paid on September 23, 199X.
3. The above balance of $7,750 was paid on October 5, 199X.
4. The above balance has been paid.
5. We do not owe you anything at September 30, 199X, since the goods represented by your invoice dated September 30, 199X, Number 25,050, in the amount of $11,550, were received on October 5, 199X, on FOB destination terms.
6. An advance payment of $2,500 made by us in August 199X should cover the two invoices totaling $1,350 shown on the statement attached.
7. We never received these goods.
8. We are contesting the propriety of the $12,525 charge. We think the charge is excessive.
9. Amount okay. As the goods have been shipped to us on consignment, we will remit payment upon selling the goods.

10. The $10,000, representing a deposit under a lease, will be applied against the rent due to us during 199X, the last year of the lease.

11. Your credit in the amount of $440, dated September 5, 199X, cancels the above balance.

*Required:*   What steps would you take to clear satisfactorily each of the above 11 comments?

(AICPA, adapted)

13-47   During your audit of the financial statements of Martin Mfg. Co., a new client, for the year ended March 31, 199X, you note the following entry in the general journal dated March 31, 199X:

| | | |
|---|---:|---:|
| Notes Receivable. . . . . . . . . . . . . . . . . . . . . . . . | 550,000 | |
| Land . . . . . . . . . . . . . . . . . . . . . . . . . | | 500,000 |
| Gain on Sale of Land . . . . . . . . . . . . . . . . . . . . | | 50,000 |

To record sale of excess plant-site land to Ardmore Corp. for 8 percent note due five years from date. No interest payment required until maturity of note.

Your review of the contract for sale between Martin and Ardmore, your inquiries of Martin executives, and your study of minutes of Martin's directors' meetings develop the following facts:

1. The land has been carried in your client's accounting records at its cost of $500,000.

2. Ardmore Corp. is a land developer and plans to subdivide and resell the land acquired from Martin Mfg. Co.

3. Martin had originally negotiated with Ardmore on the basis of a 12 percent interest rate on the note. This interest rate was established by Martin after a careful analysis of Ardmore's credit standing and current money market conditions.

4. Ardmore had rejected the 12 percent interest rate because the total outlay on a 12 percent note for $550,000 would amount to $880,000 at the end of five years, and Ardmore thought a total outlay of this amount would leave it with an inadequate return on the subdivision. Ardmore held out for a total cash outlay of $770,000, and Martin Mfg. Co. finally agreed to this position. During the discussions, it was pointed out that the present value of $1 due five years hence at an annual interest rate of 12 percent is approximately $0.567.

*Required:*   Ignoring income tax considerations, is the journal entry recording Martin's sale of the land to Ardmore acceptable? Explain fully and draft an adjusting entry if you consider one to be necessary.

---

## ◆ GROUP IV: RESEARCH AND DISCUSSION CASE

13-48   On October 21, Rand & Brink, a CPA firm, was retained by Suncraft Appliance Corporation to perform an audit for the year ended December 31. A month later, James Minor, president of the corporation, invited the CPA firm's partners, George Rand and Alice Brink, to attend a meeting of all officers of the corporation. Mr. Minor opened the meeting with the following statement:

"All of you know that we are not in a very liquid position, and our October 31 balance sheet shows it. We need to raise some outside capital in January, and our December 31 financial statements (both balance sheet and income statement) must look reasonably good if we're going to make a favorable impression upon lenders or investors. I want every officer of this company to do everything possible during the next month to ensure that, at December 31, our financial statements look as strong as possible, especially our current position and our earnings.

"I have invited our auditors to attend this meeting so they will understand the reason for some year-end transactions that might be a little unusual. It is essential that our financial statements carry the auditors' approval, or we'll never be able to get the financing we need. Now what suggestions can you offer?''

The vice president for sales was first to offer suggestions: ''I can talk some of our large customers into placing some orders in December that they wouldn't ordinarily place until the first part of next year. If we get those extra orders shipped, it will increase this year's earnings and also increase our current assets.''

The vice president in charge of production commented: ''We can ship every order we have now and every order we get during December before the close of business on December 31. We'll have to pay some overtime in our shipping department, but we'll try not to have a single unshipped order on hand at year-end. Also, we could overship some orders, and the customers wouldn't make returns until January.''

The controller spoke next: ''If there are late December orders from customers that we can't actually ship, we can just label the merchandise as sold and bill the customers with December 31 sales invoices. Also, there are always some checks from customers dated December 31 that don't reach us until January—some as late as January 10. We can record all those customers' checks bearing dates of late December as part of our December 31 cash balance.''

The treasurer offered the following suggestions: ''I owe the company $50,000 on a call note I issued to buy some of our stock. I can borrow $50,000 from my mother-in-law about Christmas time and repay my note to the company. However, I'll have to borrow the money from the company again early in January, because my mother-in-law is buying an apartment building and will need the $50,000 back by January 15.

''Another thing we can do to improve our current ratio is to write checks on December 31 to pay most of our current liabilities. We might even wait to mail the checks for a few days or mail them to the wrong addresses. That will give time for the January cash receipts to cover the December 31 checks.''

The vice president of production made two final suggestions: ''Some of our inventory, which we had tentatively identified as obsolete, does not represent an open-and-shut case of being unsalable. We could defer any write-down until next year. Another item is some machinery we have ordered for delivery in December. We could instruct the manufacturer not to ship the machines and not to bill us before January.''

The president, James Minor, spoke directly to Rand and Brink, the auditors. ''You can see I'm doing my best to give you full information and cooperation. If any of these suggested actions would prevent you from giving a clean bill of health to our year-end statements, I want to know about it now so we can avoid doing anything that would keep you from issuing an unqualified audit report. I know you'll be doing a lot of preliminary work here before December 31, but I'd like for you not to bill us before January. Will you please give us your reactions to what has been said in this meeting?''

*Required:*     Put yourself in the role of Rand & Brink, CPAs, and evaluate *separately* each suggestion made in the meeting. What general term is applicable to most of the suggested actions?

*b.*    Could you assure the client that an unqualified audit report would be issued if your recommendations were followed on all the matters discussed? Explain.

*c.*    Would the discussion in this meeting cause you to withdraw from the engagement?

---

## ◆ SUGGESTED REFERENCES

Appropriate chapters from any intermediate accounting textbook. This textbook, pages 438–39 and 452.

# ◆ GROUP V: AUDIT CASE EXERCISES

13-49   In Part II of the audit case, the audit staff of Adams, Barnes & Co. identified the following two internal control weaknesses:

    *a.*   Sales invoices are prepared and mailed prior to delivery of goods.

    *b.*   Accounts receivable are not written-off on a regular basis.

*Required:*   Review the audit program on pages 456 through 457 and identify the audit procedures that were designed specifically to address these two weaknesses.

13-50   Keystone Computers & Networks, Inc. (KCN) has 433 accounts receivable, with a total book value of $1,023,545. From that population Adams, Barnes & Co. (ABC), CPAs, selected a sample of 50 accounts for confirmation for the year ended December 31, 19X5 as illustrated by the working paper on page 458. First and second confirmation requests resulted in replies for all but seven of those accounts. ABC performed alternate procedures on those seven accounts and noted no exceptions. Of the 43 replies, 5 had exceptions as described below (with ABC follow-up):

    1.   "The balance of $1,200 is incorrect because we paid that amount in full on December 31, 19X5." *Follow-up: An analysis of the cash receipts journal revealed that the check had been received in the mail on January 9, 19X6.*

    2.   "Of the balance of $30,000, $330 is incorrect because on December 19 we returned a printer to Keystone when we found that we didn't need it. We ordered it in the middle of November when we had anticipated a need for it. When we received the printer we realized it was unnecessary and returned it unopened." *Follow-up: An analysis of the transaction revealed that it was received by Keystone on December 31, 19X5 and that the adjustment to the account had been processed on January 2, 19X6.*

    3.   "The balance of $300 is correct, and we paid it on January 5, 19X6." *Follow-up: An analysis of the cash receipts journal revealed that the check had been received on January 10, 19X6.*

    4.   "Of the balance of $13,000, $1,000 is incorrect because it represents goods that we didn't receive until January 5, 19X6." *Follow-up: Inspection of shipping records reveals that the item was delivered on January 3, 19X6.*

    5.   "Of the account's $1,800 balance, we paid $1,746 and the $54 (3 percent of the total) remains unpaid because the Keystone salesperson told us that she would be able to obtain a 'special' discount beyond the normal." *Follow-up: While inspection of the sales agreement indicated no such discount arrangement, discussions with Loren Steele (controller) and Sam Best (president) indicated that the salesperson had inappropriately granted such a discount to the client. On January 15 of 19X6 they processed the discount and credited the account for $54.*

*Required:*   *a.*   For each of the five exceptions, determine the account's proper "audited value."

    *b.*   Use the probability-proportional-to-size method with your analysis from part *a* to evaluate your sample's results. The risk of incorrect acceptance is 25 percent.

# AUDITING THE ACQUISITION CYCLE

## CHAPTER OBJECTIVES

After studying this chapter, you should be able to:

- Explain the nature of purchases and cash disbursements transactions in the acquisition cycle.

- Describe the documents, records, and accounts that comprise the acquisition cycle.

- Identify and explain the fundamental internal control policies and procedures for the acquisition cycle.

- Relate specific internal control structure policies and procedures to financial statement assertions.

- Design typical tests of controls used by auditors to evaluate the effectiveness of the controls over the acquisition cycle.

- Describe the nature of purchases, accounts payable, and other liabilities.

- Identify the auditors' objectives for the audit of purchases, accounts payable, and other liabilities.

- Describe the nature of appropriate substantive audit procedures to accomplish the objectives for the audit of purchases, accounts payable, and other liabilities.

T his chapter presents information on the nature of the acquisition cycle. This transaction cycle includes initiating and authorizing purchases, ordering goods and services, and recording and payment of accounts payable. The chapter begins by explaining the nature of the purchases and cash disbursements transactions in the acquisition cycle and the fundamental internal controls. Then it describes the nature of the understanding the auditors need to plan the audit, and the manner in which auditors design tests of controls for this cycle. Finally, the chapter describes the way in which auditors design and perform substantive tests for purchases, accounts payable, and other liabilities.

# INTERNAL CONTROL OVER THE ACQUISITION CYCLE

## Internal Control over Purchases

Adequate internal control over purchases requires, first of all, an organizational structure that delegates to a separate department of the company the exclusive authority to make all purchases of materials and services. The purchasing, receiving, and accounting functions should be clearly separated and lodged in separate departments. Although this type of departmentalized operation may not be possible in small companies, it is usually feasible to make one person responsible for all purchase transactions. This segregation of functions is apparent in the flowchart of the acquisition cycle in Figure 14–1.

|  |  |
|---|---|
| 1000985 | |
| **Morris Construction Co.** | |
| **Purchase Requisition** | |

| Department:<br><br>General Stores | Date: ___May 10, 19XX___<br><br>Date Required:<br>June 15, 19XX |
|---|---|

| Quantity | Description |
|---|---|
| 250 | Acme chrome faucets<br>#278473 |
| | Approved By:<br>*Don Warren* |

**Purchasing.** A purchase transaction begins with the issuance of a properly approved purchase requisition by the stores department or another department needing the goods or services. A copy of the requisition is sent to the purchasing department to provide a basis for preparing the serially numbered purchase order. The requisition should include a precise description of the type and quantity of the goods or services desired. In a sophisticated computerized system, purchase requisitions and purchase orders are generated by the computer based upon projected needs as indicated by production forecasts and perpetual inventory records. If the company uses

Figure 14–1  Flowchart of an Acquisition Cycle

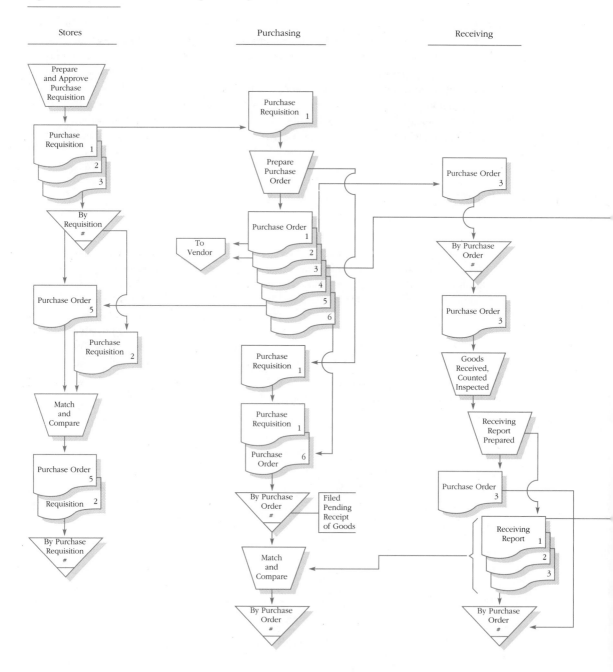

Figure 14-1 (*continued*)

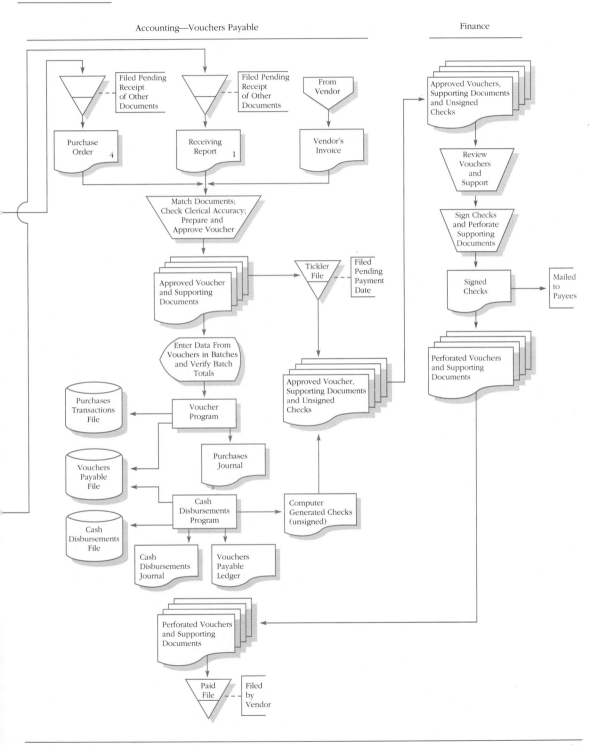

AA09847

PURCHASE ORDER
Morris Construction Co.
1212 Belaire Blvd.
Houston, TX 77062

To: Carson Supply Co.                    Date: May 12, 19XX
1671 21st St.
Houston, TX 77021         Ship via: SOS Delivery

Terms: 2/10. n/30

Enter our order for:

| Qty | Description | Price | Total |
|-----|-------------|-------|-------|
| 250 | Acme chrome faucets #278473 | $21.00 | $5,250.00 |

Morris Construction Co.

By: _Mary Goyer_

---

5874983

Morris Construction Co.
Receiving Report

| Received From: | Date: | May 30, 19XX |
|----------------|-------|--------------|
| Carson Supply Co. 1671 21st St. Houston, TX 77021 | Order No: AA09847 | Carrier: SOS Delivery |

| Quantity | Description |
|----------|-------------|
| 250 | Acme chrome faucets #278473 |

Received By:

_Bill Jones_

---

a system of **electronic data interchange (EDI),** the computer may communicate the purchase information directly to a supplier's computer system.

In most large organizations, purchase orders are issued only after compliance with extensive procedures for (1) determining the need for the items, (2) obtaining competitive bids, and (3) obtaining approval of the financial aspect of the commitment. The original purchase order is sent to the vendor and copies are sent to the accounting and receiving departments. The copy of the purchase order sent to the receiving department may have the quantities blacked out to increase the likelihood that receiving personnel will make independent counts of the merchandise received.

Receiving.   All goods received by the company—without exception—should be cleared through a receiving department that is independent of the purchasing and shipping departments. The receiving department is responsible for (1) determining quantities of goods received, (2) detecting damaged or defective merchandise, (3) preparing a receiving report, and (4) promptly transmitting goods received to the stores department. The receiving report should be serially numbered and prepared in a sufficient number of copies to permit prompt notification of the receipt to the purchasing and accounting departments, as well as to the department requesting the goods. In addition, to maintain control over receipts of goods, many companies use a receiving register to list all shipments received from suppliers.

If the company utilizes a computerized purchasing system, receiving information may be entered to the computer directly by receiving department personnel, and the computer will print the receiving report. In these systems, input validation (edit) checks should be established to help ensure the accuracy of the information as it is entered. For example, the details of quantities of products received from suppliers may be compared by the computer to the information in the file of open purchase orders. If the vendor's name or the quantities received do not agree with the purchase order data, the computer will request that the receiving clerk reconcile the differences and provide revised information.

Accounts Payable.   A **voucher** system is one method of achieving strong internal control over cash disbursements by providing assurance that all disbursements are properly authorized and reviewed before a check is issued. In a typical voucher system, the vouchers (accounts) payable department is responsible for assembling the appropriate documentation to support every cash disbursement. For example, before authorizing payment for merchandise purchased, the vouchers payable department assembles copies of the purchase order, receiving report, and **vendor's invoice,** and determines that these documents are in agreement. After determining that the transaction is properly supported, an accounting employee prepares a voucher, which is filed in a tickler file according to the date upon which payment will be made.

A *voucher,* in this usage, is an authorization sheet that provides space for the initials of the employees performing various authorization functions. Authorization functions include such procedures as extending and footing the vendor's invoice; determining the agreement of the invoice, purchase order, and receiving report; and recording the

3276485

INVOICE
Carson Supply Co.
1671 21st St.
Houston, TX 77021

Sold to: Morris Construction Co.    Date: June 5, 19XX
1212 Belaire Blvd.
Houston, TX 77062    PO No. AA09847

Ship to:   Same    Date shipped: May 15, 19XX

Terms:   2/10, n/30    Shipped via:
SOS Delivery

| Qty | Description | Price | Total |
|-----|-------------|-------|-------|
| 250 | Acme chrome faucets #278473 | $21.00 | $5,250.00 |
|  |  |  | $5,250.00 |

transaction in the accounts. Each step in the verification of an invoice should be evidenced by entering a date and signature on the voucher. Comparing the quantities listed on the invoice with those shown on the receiving report and purchase order will prevent the payment of charges for goods in excess of those ordered and received. A safeguard against the payment of excessive prices is provided by comparing the prices, discounts, and terms of shipment as shown on the purchase order to the vendor's invoice. Transactions are recorded in a **voucher register** (which normally replaces the purchases journal) by an entry debiting the appropriate asset, liability, or expense account, and crediting Vouchers Payable. The separation of the function of invoice verification and approval from the function of cash disbursement is another step that tends to prevent errors and irregularities. On the payment date, the voucher and supporting documents are removed from the tickler file and the check is prepared *but not signed*. The voucher, supporting papers, and the check (complete except for signature) are forwarded to the finance department for signature.

In a computerized purchasing system, vendor invoice information will be entered by the accounting department and it may be matched by the computer with purchase order and receiving information that was entered by the other departments. If the information matches, the computer will approve the payment and automatically record the voucher as a payable. Transactions with inconsistencies will not be processed, but will be listed on an exception report for review and follow-up by the operations control group. Just prior to its due date, the computer will generate a check in payment of the invoice. If the checks are signed by the computer, they should not be sent to the vouchers payable department for mailing.

Another control procedure the auditors may expect to find in a well-managed accounts payable department is the monthly balancing of the detailed records of accounts payable (or vouchers) to the general ledger control account. These reconciliations are saved as evidence of the performance of this procedure and as an aid in locating any subsequent errors.

**Vendors' statements,** received monthly, should be reconciled promptly with the accounts payable ledger or list of open vouchers, and any discrepancies fully investigated. In some industries, it is common practice to make advances to vendors, which are recovered by making percentage deductions from invoices. When advances are made, the auditors should ascertain that procedures are followed to ensure that deductions from the invoices are made in accordance with the terms of the agreement.

## Internal Control over Cash Disbursements

All disbursements should be made by check, except for payment of minor items from petty cash funds. A principal advantage of this method is obtaining evidence of a receipt from the payee in the form of an endorsement on the check. Other advantages include (1) the centralization of disbursement authority in the hands of a few designated officials — only persons authorized to sign checks; (2) a permanent record of disbursements; and (3) a reduction in the amount of cash kept on hand.

To secure in full the internal control benefits implicit in the use of checks, it is essential that all checks be prenumbered and all numbers of the series be accounted for. Unissued prenumbered checks should be adequately safeguarded against theft or misuse. Voided checks should be defaced to eliminate any possibility of further use and filed in the regular sequence of paid checks. Dollar amounts should be printed on all checks by the computer or a check-protecting machine. This practice makes it difficult for anyone to alter a check by increasing its amount.

Officials authorized to sign checks should review the documents supporting the payment and perforate (deface) these documents at the time the check is signed to prevent them from being submitted a second time. In a voucher system, this involves perforating the voucher and the supporting purchase order, receiving report, and vendor's invoice. The canceled vouchers are returned to the accounts payable department, where an entry is made to record the cash disbursement (usually a debit to Accounts or Vouchers Payable, and a credit to Cash). Paid vouchers usually are filed by voucher number in a paid voucher file.

Most companies issuing a large volume of checks use computers or check-signing machines. The authorized signature (usually that of the treasurer) may be printed automatically on each check as it is processed. If the computer generates signed checks, item counts, control totals, and hash totals (reconciled by finance department personnel) may be used to make certain that checks are issued only for authorized cash disbursements. When a check-signing machine is used, a key is required to retrieve the signed checks, and the facsimile signature plate should be removed from the machine and safeguarded when the machine is not in use. A second, manual signature may also be required on checks signed by a computer or a check-signing machine for large disbursements, say over $10,000.

Reconciliation of monthly bank statements is essential to adequate internal control over cash disbursements. Bank statements should be reconciled by the computer or an employee having no part in authorizing or accounting for cash transactions or in handling cash. Statements from the bank should come unopened to this employee. Each month the completed bank reconciliation should be reviewed by a responsible company official and approved in writing.

Strong internal control is inherent in this system because every disbursement is authorized and reviewed before a check is issued. Also, neither the accounts payable nor the finance department is in a position to disburse cash without a review of the transaction by the other department.

---

◆ ILLUSTRATIVE CASE ◆

One contracting company ignored basic controls over cash disbursements. The accounts payable clerk prepared and signed checks (using a facsimile signature plate) and reconciled the bank account. The clerk periodically recorded disbursements in the check register for a greater amount than was actually paid, and wrote herself a check for the difference. For example, if the company had been billed $7,500, she would write the check for $7,500, but record it for $10,000 in the register. She would then write a check to herself for the difference, here $2,500, and record that check as having been voided. Upon arrival of the bank statement, she would reconcile the account, and dispose of the ''voided'' check written to herself.

When detected, the clerk had abstracted over $400,000. The internal control policy of reconciliation of the bank account by another individual would have either prevented or detected this irregularity.

# OBTAINING AND DOCUMENTING AN UNDERSTANDING OF THE INTERNAL CONTROL STRUCTURE

As with other transaction cycles, the auditors are required to obtain an understanding of the control environment, the accounting system, and control procedures for the acquisition cycle.

Control Environment.   When obtaining an understanding of the internal control structure, the auditors consider the control environment, the accounting system, and control procedures, as discussed in Chapter 8. The control environment reflects the overall attitude, awareness, and actions of management and the board of directors concerning the importance of control and the way it is used in the entity. The elements of the control environment discussed in Chapter 8 affect the overall internal control structure and all transaction cycles. Accordingly, the auditors' analysis of them will be considered in conjunction with the detailed analysis of the accounting system and control procedures.

Certain aspects of the control environment, particularly relevant to the auditors' consideration of internal control for the acquisition cycle, include the following:

- The organizational structure of the company as it relates to the processing of purchase transactions.
- The use of budgets to control expenditures, including appropriate follow-up on variances from budgeted amounts.
- Personnel policies and procedures for the selection and training of purchasing and receiving employees and those involved in making cash disbursements.

Personnel policies and procedures are very important for employees involved in the acquisition cycle. If these employees are not competent or lack integrity, the company can sustain large losses. The importance of competence and integrity may be illustrated by considering the company's purchasing agents who negotiate the terms of purchases with the company's various suppliers. If these individuals are incompetent, they may commit the company to large purchases at unfavorable terms. Also, if purchasing agents accept "kickbacks," the company will not only lose the amounts accepted but may also make purchases at unfavorable terms.

Accounting System and Control Procedures.   The auditors must obtain an understanding of the transactions that make up the client's acquisition cycle. One approach is to flowchart the system, or to use flowcharts prepared by the client. The auditors may also prepare narrative descriptions of the system or complete an internal control questionnaire. Typical of the questions are the following: Is an accounts payable trial balance prepared monthly and reconciled to the general ledger controlling account? Are monthly statements from vendors reconciled with accounts payable ledgers or unpaid vouchers? Are advance payments to vendors recorded as receivables and controlled in a manner that ensures that they will be recovered by offset against vendors' invoices? Are debit memos issued to vendors for discrepancies in invoice prices, quantities, or computations? Are debit balances in vendors' accounts brought to the attention of the credit and purchasing departments?

After the auditors have prepared a flowchart (or other description) of internal control, they determine whether the client is actually using the internal controls described to them; that is, they determine whether the controls have been *placed in operation*. They will typically perform a walk-through of several purchase transactions, and observe the performance of various internal control policies and procedures.

As the auditors verify their understanding of the internal control structure, they will observe and inquire about the segregation of duties for purchases and cash disbursements. They will also inspect the various documents and reconciliations that are important to the client's internal control over the acquisitions cycle. For example, the reconciliations of monthly statements from vendors to the payables ledger will be inspected. Budgets for cash disbursements will be inspected and the auditors will review the evidence of the follow-up on variances from budgeted amounts of cash disbursements. Figure 14-2 illustrates these documents and the primary accounts involved in the acquisition cycle.

# TESTING CONTROLS AND ASSESSING CONTROL RISK

The auditors evaluate the effectiveness of a client's internal control policies and procedures in preventing or detecting material misstatements in the financial statements. As we have discussed throughout the text, auditors assess control risk in terms of the five financial statement assertions—existence or occurrence; completeness; rights and obligations; valuation or allocation; and presentation and disclosure.

The auditors' approach for assessing control risk in the acquisition cycle, as it is with other cycles, is one of using their understanding of the internal control structure to determine a planned assessed level of control risk for the various assertions. Appropriate tests of controls are performed to justify assessments at levels lower than the maximum.

## Existence or Occurrence

Internal control structure policies and procedures for the existence or occurrence assertion provide assurance that recorded purchases and disbursements actually occurred during the period and that the related accounts payable exist. An appropriate segregation of duties provides assurance in support of most financial statement assertions, including existence or occurrence. Since segregation of duties often leaves no evidence of performance, the auditors' tests of controls will include observation of employees performing various functions and inquiry as to who performed the functions throughout the period.

The auditors' tests of controls over existence or occurrence may also involve tests of purchase and disbursement transactions. The appropriate direction of these tests is from the recorded entry in the accounting records to the source documents, including the voucher, purchase order, receiving document, vendor's invoice, and canceled check. By examining these supporting documents for a sample of recorded cash disbursements and unpaid accounts payable, the auditors obtain evidence that the purchase was authorized and the goods were received, counted, and inspected. The auditors will also examine the voucher for the initials of the individuals who matched the vendor's invoice to the purchase order and the receiving report. The auditors may reperform these control procedures by comparing the details of the vendor's invoice to the purchase order and the receiving report. If the vendor's invoice has been paid, the auditors will inspect the

# Figure 14-2 Overview of the Acquisition Cycle—Documents and Accounts

## Purchases

| | 1000985 |
|---|---|
| | Morris Construction Co.<br>Purchase Requisition |

| Department:<br><br>General Stores | Date: May 10, 19XX<br><br>Date Required:<br>June 15, 19XX |
|---|---|

| Quantity | Description |
|---|---|
| 250 | Acme chrome faucets<br>#278473 |

Approved By:

*Don Warren*

| | 5874983 |
|---|---|
| | Morris Construction Co.<br>Receiving Report |

| Received From:<br><br>Carson Supply Co.<br>1671 21st St.<br>Houston, TX 77021 | Date: May 30, 19XX<br><br>Order No: AA09847<br><br>Carrier: SOS Delivery |
|---|---|

| Quantity | Description |
|---|---|
| 250 | Acme chrome faucets<br>#278473 |

Received By:

*Bill Jones*

AA09847

PURCHASE ORDER
Morris Construction Co.
1212 Belaire Blvd.
Houston, TX 77062

To: Carson Supply Co.
1671 21st St.
Houston, TX 77021

Date: May 12, 19XX

Ship via: SOS Delivery

Terms: 2/10. n/30

Enter our order for

| Qty | Description | Price | Total |
|---|---|---|---|
| 250 | Acme crome<br>faucets<br>#278473 | $21.00 | $5,250.00 |

Morris Construction Co.

By: *Mary Goyer*

## Figure 14–2   (*continued*)

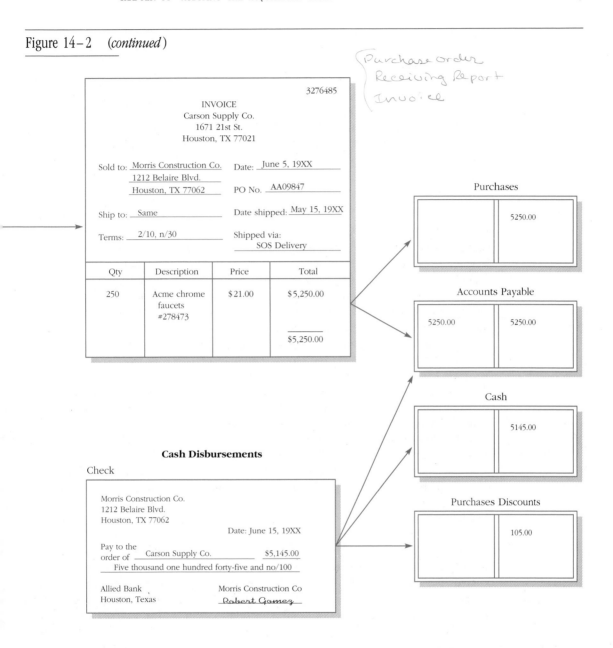

Purchase order
Receiving Report
Invoice

**INVOICE**
Carson Supply Co.
1671 21st St.
Houston, TX 77021

3276485

Sold to: Morris Construction Co.    Date: June 5, 19XX
1212 Belaire Blvd.
Houston, TX 77062    PO No. AA09847

Ship to: Same    Date shipped: May 15, 19XX

Terms: 2/10, n/30    Shipped via:
SOS Delivery

| Qty | Description | Price | Total |
|-----|-------------|-------|-------|
| 250 | Acme chrome faucets #278473 | $21.00 | $5,250.00 |
| | | | $5,250.00 |

Purchases

| | 5250.00 |
|--|--|

Accounts Payable

| 5250.00 | 5250.00 |
|--|--|

Cash

| | 5145.00 |
|--|--|

Purchases Discounts

| | 105.00 |
|--|--|

**Cash Disbursements**

Check

Morris Construction Co.
1212 Belaire Blvd.
Houston, TX 77062

Date: June 15, 19XX

Pay to the
order of   Carson Supply Co.           $5,145.00
Five thousand one hundred forty-five and no/100

Allied Bank                Morris Construction Co
Houston, Texas             Robert Gomez

supporting documents to determine that they have been perforated or canceled. The canceled check will also be inspected for an authorized signature and appropriate endorsement by the vendor.

When the client has established effective computer application controls for purchase transactions, the auditors may find it more efficient to test these controls rather than to test a sample of purchase transactions. Batch processing controls might be tested by inspecting evidence of the reconciliations of batch control totals by the control group. In addition, a sample of the exception reports printed by the computer when the vendors' invoices do not match purchasing and receiving information might be inspected, as well as evidence of follow-up on these exceptions.

## Completeness

Of critical concern to the auditors are the client's control policies and procedures to ensure completeness of recorded purchases and accounts payable. Unrecorded purchases of inventory will lead to overstated profits if the inventory items that were purchased are included in the count of inventory and thus included in the client's financial statement inventory amount. As is the case with the existence or occurrence assertion, a proper segregation of functions will help ensure that all transactions are recorded. Therefore, the auditors' observation and inquiry procedures described above will also provide evidence about internal controls over the completeness of purchases and accounts payable.

Prenumbered purchase orders and receiving reports that are accounted for by the accounts payable department facilitate the auditors' tests of controls over completeness. The auditors will review document logs to determine that client personnel have accounted for the numerical sequence of all of these documents. An equivalent test when the computer system controls the documents is inspection of a sample of the reconciliations of item counts generated by the computer with the batch totals accumulated when the items were entered.

Another significant internal control structure procedure over the completeness of recorded purchases and accounts payable is reconciliation of accounts payable to vendors' statements. The auditors can test this control by selecting a sample of vendors' statements and inspecting evidence that they were reconciled to the related accounts payable. The auditors also may reperform selected reconciliations.

The client's internal control policies and procedures for reconciling bank accounts and budgeting cash disbursements also provide evidence that all cash disbursements are recorded. Therefore, inspecting selected bank reconciliations is an important test of control for the completeness assertion. When an individual who is otherwise independent of cash receipts and disbursements performs that function the auditors will generally observe and make inquiries about the bank reconciliation process. The auditors' tests may also involve reperforming selected reconciliations. Tests of the company's budgeting process will include inspection of selected budgets and examination of evidence that management has followed up on all significant budget variances.

## Rights and Obligations

Evidence about rights and obligations for the acquisition cycle relates most directly to whether a legally valid purchase transaction occurred and, therefore, whether the client is obligated to pay the related account payable. Tests of controls for the existence or occurrence assertion provide evidence on rights and obligations and often involve examining related details on documents such as vendors' invoices. In addition, the auditors may review the client's control procedures for recording goods received on consignment. When goods are received on consignment, the client does not have legal title (right) to the inventory, nor an obligation to pay for them until the goods are sold.

## Valuation or Allocation

The objective of the client's control procedures for proper valuation of purchases and accounts payable is to determine that these transactions are recorded at the appropriate amount. To achieve this objective, client personnel will test all vendors' invoices for proper pricing and clerical accuracy before they are paid. When appropriate client personnel perform these functions, the auditors will inspect a sample of vouchers for the initials of those individuals. The auditors may also reperform these procedures by tracing the prices on the invoices to approved purchase orders and by extending and footing the invoice amounts.

If the computer approves the vendors' invoices by matching them with purchasing and receiving information and by verifying the clerical accuracy of the invoices, the auditors may decide to test these controls. Inspection of the exception reports generated by the system provides evidence that the computer is effectively testing the invoices before they are approved. The auditors also will examine evidence that the operations control group follows up on the exceptions. The test data approach might be used to test the input validation checks performed by the computer when purchasing and receiving data are entered.

## Presentation and Disclosure

The presentation and disclosure assertion for the acquisition cycle deals with whether purchase transactions and accounts payable are properly classified and described, and the notes to the financial statements include appropriate disclosure about these items. Accordingly, the auditors will test the client's controls for identifying unusual transactions, such as purchases from related parties. They may also test the client's controls that are designed to prevent the misclassification of expenses, such as use of a chart of accounts and investigation of budget variances. Often, the auditors will choose to assess control risk at a relatively high level for this assertion, and rely primarily on substantive procedures to determine that presentation and disclosure are appropriate.

## Reassess Control Risk

When the auditors have completed the procedures described in the preceding section, they should assess the level of control risk for each financial statement assertion about accounts payable and purchases. These assessments will determine whether the auditors should modify their planned substantive tests. Figure 14–3 summarizes the relationship between the financial statement assertions, the internal control structure policies and procedures, and typical tests of controls.

Figure 14–3    Assessing Control Risk for Acquisition Cycle

| Internal Control Policy or Procedure | Typical Tests of the Control Policy or Procedure | Existence or occurrence | Completeness | Obligations | Valuation | Presentation and disclosure |
|---|---|:---:|:---:|:---:|:---:|:---:|
| Segregate duties over purchases and disbursements | Observe and make inquiries about the performance of various functions | X | X | X | X | |
| Obtain approval of all purchase orders prior to issuance | Select a sample of purchase orders and inspect whether they have been properly approved | X | X | X | | |
| Use prenumbered purchase orders and receiving reports | Observe and make inquiries about the use of prenumbered documents and inspect evidence of accounting for the sequence | | X | | | |
| Match quantities on vendors' invoices to those on purchase orders and receiving reports | Select a sample of vendors' invoices and compare the quantities to those on purchase orders and receiving reports | X | | X | | |
| Approve vendors' invoices prior to payment | Select a sample of vendors' invoices and observe whether they have been approved | X | | X | X | |
| Prenumber checks and account for numbers | Select a sample of checks and account for sequence | | X | | | |
| Balance details of individual disbursements with totals to be posted to appropriate general ledger account distributions and total cash disbursement | Select a sample of daily individual disbursements, recompute totals, and compare to ledger postings | X | X | X | X | |
| Reconcile vendors' statements to the details of accounts payable records | Select a sample of vendors' statements and inspect evidence of reconciliation to the accounts payable records | | X | | | |
| Reconciliation of bank accounts monthly by an employee who is independent of invoice processing, cash disbursements, cash receipts, petty cash, and general ledger functions | Observe and make inquiries about the reconciliation process and inspect reconciliations | X | X | X | X | |
| Use budgets and analyze variance from actual amounts | Examine budgets and evidence of follow-up on variances | X | X | X | X | |
| Use a chart of accounts and an independent review of account classifications | Inspect the chart of accounts and evidence of the review of account classifications | | | | | X |

# DESIGNING SUBSTANTIVE TESTS OF ACCOUNTS PAYABLE AND PURCHASES

Typical transactions creating accounts payable, as described earlier in this chapter, include purchases of merchandise, raw materials, and supplies. In addition, other sources of accounts payable include purchases of plant assets, receipts of services, such as legal and accounting services, advertising, repairs, and utilities. Accounts payable arising from the purchase of goods or services are usually evidenced by invoices and statements received from the suppliers. However, **accrued liabilities** (sometimes called **accrued expenses**) generally accumulate over time, and management must make accounting estimates of the year-end liability. Such estimates are often necessary for salaries, pensions, interest, rent, taxes, and similar items.

## Objectives of Substantive Tests for Accounts Payable and Purchases

The audit *objectives* for substantive tests of accounts payable and purchases are to:

1. Substantiate the *existence* of recorded accounts payable and the *occurrence* of purchase transactions.
2. Establish the *completeness* of accounts payable and purchase transactions.
3. Determine that the client has *obligations* to pay the recorded accounts payable.
4. Establish the *clerical accuracy* of records and supporting schedules of accounts payable and purchases.
5. Determine that the *valuation* of accounts payable is in accordance with generally accepted accounting principles.
6. Determine that the *presentation* and *disclosure* of accounts payable and purchases are appropriate

Virtually all lawsuits against CPA firms allege that the auditors failed to detect an overstatement of earnings. Management, especially of publicly held companies, is often under some pressure to report increased earnings. In previous chapters, we discussed the auditors' concern about exaggeration of earnings that results from the overstatement of assets. In the audit of liabilities, the auditors are primarily concerned with the possibility of understatement, or omission, of liabilities. An *understatement of liabilities* will exaggerate the financial strength of a company and conceal fraud just as effectively as an *overstatement of assets*. Furthermore, the understatement of liabilities is usually accompanied by the understatement of expenses and an overstatement of net income. For example, delaying the recording of bills for December operating expenses until January overstates income while understating accounts payable. Therefore, audit procedures for liabilities should have as a primary objective the determination of the *completeness* of recorded payables.

Audit procedures for detecting understated liabilities differ from those used to detect overstated assets. Overstating an asset account usually requires an improper entry in the accounting records, as by the recording of a fictitious transaction. Such improper entries can be detected by the auditors through verification of the individual entries making up the balance of an asset account. By way of contrast, understating a liability account is generally possible merely by *failing to make an entry* for a transaction creating a liability.

Figure 14-4    Objectives of Major Substantive Tests of Accounts Payable and Purchases

| Substantive Tests | Primary Audit Objectives |
|---|---|
| Obtain trial balance of payables and reconcile with the ledgers | Clerical accuracy |
| Vouch balances payable to selected creditors by inspecting supporting documents | Existence or occurrence; Obligations; and Valuation |
| Reconcile liabilities with vendors' monthly statements <br><br> Confirm accounts payable <br><br> Perform analytical procedures | Completeness; Existence or occurrence; Obligations; and Valuation |
| Search for unrecorded accounts payable | Completeness |
| Perform procedures to identify accounts payable to related parties <br><br> Evaluate financial statement presentation and disclosure | Presentation and disclosure |

The omission of an entry is less susceptible to detection than is a fictitious entry. If the omission is detected, it is much easier to pass it off as an accidental error. Auditors have long recognized that the most difficult type of irregularity to detect is fraud based on the *nonrecording* of transactions.

When accounts payable entries have been recorded, the existence of a definite financial commitment makes accomplishment of the valuation audit objective less difficult than for assets (other than cash). The situation with accrued liabilities is different since in many circumstances exact measurement will be difficult; the CPAs must audit management's accounting estimates.

## Substantive Tests for Accounts Payable and Purchases

Figure 14-4 presents typical substantive tests used to meet the primary audit objectives for accounts payable. In the following sections we describe these procedures in detail.

## Obtain Trial Balance of Accounts Payable Accounts

| Primary Audit Objective: |
|---|
| Clerical accuracy   ☑ |

One purpose of this procedure is to prove that the liability figure appearing in the balance sheet is in agreement with the individual items comprising the detail records. A second purpose is to provide a starting point for substantive testing. The auditors will use the list of vouchers or accounts payable to select a representative group of items for careful examination.

The client company usually furnishes the auditors with a year-end trial balance. The auditors should verify the footing and the accuracy of individual amounts in the trial balance. If the schedule of individual items does not agree in total with the control account, the cause of the discrepancy must be investigated. In most situations, the auditors will arrange for the client's staff to locate such errors and make the necessary adjustments. Agreement of the control account and the list of individual account balances is not absolute proof of the completeness of recorded indebtedness; invoices received near the close of the period may not be reflected in either the control account or the subsidiary records, and other similar errors may exist without causing the accounts to be out of balance.

## Vouch Balances Payable

| Primary Audit Objectives: |
| --- |
| Existence         ☑ |
| Obligations       ☑ |
| Valuation         ☑ |

The vouching of selected creditors' balances to supporting vouchers, invoices, purchase orders, and receiving reports is a substantive test of the existence, obligations, and valuation of accounts payable as well as occurrence of purchases. For companies that use a voucher system, the verification of the individual vouchers is made most conveniently at the balance sheet date, when the vouchers will be together in the unpaid voucher file. The content of the unpaid voucher file changes daily; as vouchers are paid, they are removed from the file and filed alphabetically by vendor. Consequently, it is important that the client maintain a list of year-end unpaid vouchers. This listing should show the names of vendors, voucher numbers, dates, and amounts.

## Reconcile Vendors' Statements

| Primary Audit Objectives: |
| --- |
| Completeness      ☑ |
| Existence         ☑ |
| Obligations       ☑ |
| Valuation         ☑ |

In some companies, it is a regular practice each month to reconcile vendors' statements with the detailed records of payables. If the auditors find that this reconciliation is regularly performed by the client's staff, they may limit their review of vendors' statements to determining that the reconciliation work has been satisfactory.

If the client's staff has not reconciled vendors' statements and accounts payable, the auditors may do so. When control risk for accounts payable is high, the auditors may control incoming mail to ensure that all vendors' statements received by the client are made available to the auditors. Among the discrepancies often revealed by reconciliation of vendors' statements are charges by the vendor for shipments not yet received or recorded by the client. Although conceptually all purchases on which title has passed should be included in inventory (thus items shipped FOB (free on board) shipping point as of year-end and not yet received should be included), normal accounting procedures do not provide for recording invoices as liabilities until the merchandise has been received. In-transit shipments on which title has passed should be listed and a decision should be reached as to whether they are sufficiently material to warrant year-end adjustment.

## Confirm Accounts Payable

| Primary Audit Objectives: |
| --- |
| Completeness      ☑ |
| Existence         ☑ |
| Obligations       ☑ |
| Valuation         ☑ |

Although **confirmation** of accounts payable is a widely used procedure, it is generally considered less necessary than is the confirmation of accounts receivable. One reason for this difference is that for accounts payable the auditors will find in the client's possession externally created evidence such as vendors' invoices and statements that substantiate the accounts payable. No such external evidence is on hand to support accounts receivable.

Another reason for the difference in significance attached to confirmation of accounts payable is that the greatest risk in the audit of liabilities is the possibility of unrecorded

## Figure 14–5

---

**PACKAGE SYSTEMS, INC.**

9200 CHANNEL STREET
NEW ORLEANS, LOUSIANA 70128

January 2, 19X2

Grayline Container, Inc.
4800 Madison Street
Dallas, Texas 75221

Dear Sirs:

　　Our independent auditors, Nelson & Gray, CPAs, are performing an audit of our financial statements. For this reason, please inform them in the space provided below the amount, if any, owed to you by this company at December 31, 19X1.

　　Please attach an itemized statement supporting any balance owed, showing all unpaid items. Your reply should be sent directly to Nelson & Gray, CPAs, 6500 Lane Avenue, New Orleans, Louisiana 70128. A stamped addressed envelope is enclosed for your reply. Thank you.

Sincerely,

*Robert W. James*

Robert W. James
Controller

---------------------------------------------------------------

Nelson & Gray, CAs

　　Our records show that the amount of $_____26,800_____ was owed to us by Packaging Systems, Inc., at December 31, 19X1, as shown by the itemized statement attached.

Date:___Jan. 6, X2___

Signature ___*Sharon Steele*___

Title ___*Controller*___

amounts. While confirmation can provide evidence about completeness, it is a more effective procedure for establishing existence and valuation of an item. To make the confirmation procedure more effective at addressing the completeness of accounts payable, the auditors will often use a *blank form,* as illustrated by Figure 14–5. This form asks the vendor to fill in the amount of the liability rather than to confirm a recorded amount. Also, accounts payable confirmation requests will be mailed to vendors from whom substantial purchases have been made during the year, regardless of the size of their accounts at the confirmation date (even to suppliers whose accounts show zero balances). These substantial suppliers may be identified by reference to cash disbursement records or computer printouts of purchase volume by individual supplier; inquiry of purchasing department personnel; or examination of the accounts payable subsidiary ledger. Other accounts payable that often are confirmed by the auditors include those for which monthly statements are not available, accounts reflecting unusual transactions, accounts with parent or subsidiary corporations, and accounts secured by pledged assets.

## Perform Analytical Procedures

| Primary Audit Objectives: |
|---|
| Completeness ☑ |
| Existence ☑ |
| Obligations ☑ |
| Valuation ☑ |

To gain assurance as to the overall reasonableness of accounts payable and purchases, the auditor may compute ratios such as accounts payable divided by purchases and accounts payable divided by total current liabilities. These ratios are compared with ratios for prior years to disclose trends that warrant investigation.

The list of amounts payable to individual vendors should be reviewed to identify any companies from which the client does not ordinarily acquire goods or services. The amounts owed to individual creditors should also be compared with balances in prior years. By studying yearly variations in purchases and other accounts closely related to accounts payable, the auditors may become aware of errors in accounts payable and purchases. Finally, the portion of accounts payable that is past due at the year-end should be compared with corresponding data for previous years.

The auditors may test purchase discounts by computing the ratio of cash discounts earned to total purchases during the period and comparing this ratio from period to period. Any significant decrease in the ratio might indicate a change in terms of purchases, failure to take discounts, or fraudulent manipulation.

## Search for Unrecorded Accounts Payable

| Primary Audit Objective: |
|---|
| Completeness ☑ |

Throughout the audit the auditors must be alert for any unrecorded payables. For example, the preceding three steps of this program—reconciliation, confirmation, and analytical procedures—may disclose unrecorded liabilities. In addition to normal trade payables that may be unrecorded, other examples include unrecorded liabilities related to customers' deposits recorded as credits to accounts receivable, obligations for securities purchased but not settled at the balance sheet date, unbilled contractor or architect fees for a building under construction at the audit date, and unpaid attorney or insurance broker fees.

In addition to the prior audit steps, when searching for unrecorded accounts payable the auditors will examine transactions that were recorded following year-end. A comparison of cash payments occurring after the balance sheet date with the accounts payable trial balance is generally the most effective means of disclosing unrecorded accounts payable.

All liabilities must eventually be paid and will, therefore, be reflected in the accounts at least by the time they are paid. Regular monthly expenses, such as rent and utilities, are often posted to the ledger accounts directly from the cash disbursements journal without any account payable or other liability having been set up. Therefore, the auditors will often examine all cash disbursements, over a specified dollar amount, that are made by the client during the subsequent period.

The auditors should also consider sources of potential unrecorded payables such as the following:

1. Unmatched invoices and unbilled receiving reports. These documents are called work in process in a voucher system. The auditors should review such unprocessed documents at the balance sheet date to ascertain that the client has recorded an account payable where appropriate.

2. Vouchers payable entered in the voucher register subsequent to the balance sheet date. Inspection of these records may uncover an item that should have been recorded as of the balance sheet date.

3. Invoices received by the client after the balance sheet date. Not all vendors send invoices promptly when goods are shipped or services are rendered. Accordingly, the auditors' review of invoices received by the client in the subsequent period may disclose unrecorded accounts payable as of the balance sheet date.

4. **Consignments** in which the client acts as a consignee. The consignee assumes liability for consigned merchandise when those goods have been sold to third parties. Those sales, especially shortly before the year-end, may not have been set up as a liability to the consignor. While the auditors' overall knowledge about the accounting for such consigned items will dictate the appropriate procedures, those related to the revenue cycle such as tests of sales transactions around year-end may reveal such sales.

A form of audit working paper used to summarize unrecorded accounts payable discovered by the auditors is illustrated in Figure 14–6.

When unrecorded liabilities are discovered by the auditors, the next question is whether the omissions are sufficiently material to warrant proposing an adjusting entry. Will the adjustment cause a sufficient change in the financial statements to give a different impression of the company's current position or of its earning power?

To illustrate the factors to be considered in deciding upon the materiality of an unrecorded transaction, let us use as an example the December 31 annual audit of a small manufacturing company in good financial condition with total assets of $1 million and preadjustment net income of $100,000. The auditors' procedures bring to light the following unrecorded liabilities:

1. An invoice of $1,400, dated December 30 and bearing terms of FOB shipping point. The goods were shipped on December 30 but were not received until January 4. The invoice was also received and recorded on January 4.

In considering the materiality of this omission, the first point is that net income is not affected. The adjusting entry, if made, would add equal amounts to current assets (inventories) and to current liabilities; hence it would not change the amount of working capital. The omission does affect the current ratio very slightly. The auditor

## Figure 14-6

```
                          THE PALERNO COMPANY                          M-1-1
                        Unrecorded Accounts Payable
                           December 31, 19X3                            LK
                                                                       2/19/X4

           Invoice                                    Account
   Date    Number        Vendor and Description       Charged         Amount

12/31/X3    2851   Hayes Mfg. Co.-invoice and shipment in transit   Inventories    $10,650.00

12/28/X3    2428   Tax & Williams-unpaid legal fees-see M-4         Legal           1,000.00
                                                                    Expenses

12/31/X3      _    Allen Enterprises-12/19 account sales for        Sales          25,680.00
                   consigned goods

12/31/X3      _    Hart & Co.-machinery repairs (paid 1/1/X4)       Repair         12,600.00
                                                                    Expense

    _         _    Grant Co.-shipment received 12/31/X3 per         Inventories    15,820.00
                   receiving report no. 2907; invoice not yet
                   received

    _         _    Arthur & Baker-earned but unpaid architects'fee  Construction
                   for building under construction-see K-5          in Progress    23,370.00

                                                                                  $89,120.00
```

----------------------------------------------------------------------------

```
A.J.E. #8     131 Inventories              10,650.00
              501 Cost of Sales            15,820.00
              156 Construction in Progress 23,370.00
              401 Sales                    25,680.00
              518 Legal Expense             1,000.00
              527 Repairs Expense          12,600.00
              203 Accounts Payable                        89,120.00

              To record unrecorded accounts payable at 12/31/X3
```

The above payables were identified principally in the audit of accounts payable.
See audit program B-4 for procedures employed. In my opinion the $89,120
adjustment includes all material unrecorded accounts payable.

LK
2/23/X4

would probably consider this transaction as not sufficiently material to warrant adjustment.

2.   Another invoice for $4,000, dated December 30 and bearing terms of FOB shipping point. The goods arrived on December 31 and were included in the physical inventory taken that day. The invoice was not received until January 8 and was entered as a January transaction.

This error should be corrected because the inclusion of the goods in the physical inventory without recognition of the liability has caused an error of $4,000 in pretax income for the year. Since the current liabilities are understated, both the amount of working capital and the current ratio are exaggerated. The owners' equity is also overstated. These facts point to the materiality of the omission and constitute strong arguments for an adjusting entry.

3. An invoice for $9,500, dated December 31, for a new office safe. The safe was installed on December 31, but the invoice was not recorded until paid on January 15.

   Since the transaction involved only asset and liability accounts, the omission of an entry did not affect net income. However, working capital and the current ratio are affected by the error since the debit affects a noncurrent asset and the credit affects a current liability. Most auditors would probably not propose an adjusting entry for this item.

4. An invoice for $6,000, dated December 31, for advertising services rendered during October, November, and December. The invoice was not recorded until paid on January 15.

   The argument for treating this item as sufficiently material to warrant adjustment is based on the fact that net income is affected, as well as the amount of working capital and the current ratio. The adjusting entry should probably be recommended in these circumstances.

The preceding examples suggest that a decision as to the materiality of an unrecorded transaction hinges to an important extent on whether the transaction affects net income. Assuming that an omitted transaction does affect net income and there is doubt as to whether the dollar amount is large enough to warrant adjustment, the auditors should bear in mind that almost half of the effect of the error on net income may be eliminated by corporate income taxes. In other words, an adjusting entry to record an omitted expense item of $10,000 may reduce after-tax income by only $5,000. If the adjusting entry is not made, the only ultimate effect is a shift of $5,000 between the net incomes of two successive years. Unless the client requests all adjusting entries, the auditors should avoid proposing adjusting entries for errors in the year-end cutoff of transactions unless the effect on the statements is significant. However, it should be borne in mind that a number of insignificant individual misstatements may be material in their *cumulative* effect on the financial statements. Therefore, the auditors will accumulate the effects of the adjusting entries not proposed (passed) to consider them with misstatements detected in other accounts, as discussed in Chapter 18.

## Investigate Related-Party Transactions

| Primary Audit Objective: |
| :--- |
| Presentation ☑ |

Payables to a corporation's directors, principal stockholders, officers, employees, or affiliates require particular attention by the auditors since they are not the result of arm's-length bargaining by parties of opposing interests. Here the auditors should consider the possibility that these payables relate to purchases of inventory or other asset items for which there may be valuation questions.

The independent auditors must perform procedures directed toward identifying such payables. All material payables to related parties and the details of the related transactions must be disclosed in the financial statements.

## Evaluate Disclosures

| Primary Audit Objective: |
|---|
| Presentation ☑ |

Proper balance sheet presentation of accounts payable requires that any material amounts payable to related parties be listed separately from amounts payable to trade creditors. The notes to the financial statements should disclose the nature of the related party transactions, as well as the amounts involved.

Debit balances of substantial amounts sometimes occur in accounts payable because of such events as duplicate payments made in error, return of merchandise to vendors after payment has been made, and advances to suppliers. If these debit balances are material, a reclassification entry should be made in the audit working papers so that the debit balances will appear as assets in the balance sheet rather than being offset against other accounts payable with credit balances.

Accounts payable secured by pledged assets should be disclosed in the balance sheet or a note thereto, and cross-referenced to the pledged assets.

# SUBSTANTIVE TESTS OF OTHER LIABILITIES

In addition to the accounts payable previously considered, other items classified as current liabilities include:

1. Amounts withheld from employees' pay.
2. Sales taxes payable.
3. Unclaimed wages.
4. Customers' deposits.
5. Accrued liabilities.

## Amounts Withheld from Employees' Pay

Payroll deductions are notoriously numerous; among the more important are social security taxes and individual income taxes. Although the federal and state governments do not specify the exact form of records to be maintained, they do require that records of amounts earned and withheld be adequate to permit a determination of compliance with tax laws.

Income taxes withheld from employees' pay and not remitted as of the balance sheet date constitute a liability to be verified by the auditors. Accrued employer payroll taxes may be audited at the same time. This verification usually consists of tracing the amounts withheld to the payroll summary sheets, testing computations of taxes withheld and accrued, determining that taxes have been deposited or paid in accordance with federal and state laws and regulations, and reviewing quarterly tax returns.

Payroll deductions also are often made for union dues, charitable contributions, retirement plans, insurance, savings bonds, and other purposes. Besides verifying the liability for any such amounts withheld from employees and not remitted as of the balance sheet date, the auditors should review the adequacy of the withholding procedures and determine that payroll deductions have been properly authorized and accurately computed.

## Sales Taxes Payable

In most sections of the country, business concerns are required to collect sales taxes imposed by state and local governments on retail sales. These taxes do not represent an expense to the business; the retailer merely acts as a collecting agent. Until the amounts collected from customers are remitted to the taxing authority, they constitute current liabilities of the business. The auditors' verification of this liability includes a review of the client's periodic tax returns. The reasonableness of the liability also is tested by a computation applying the tax rate to total taxable sales. In addition, the auditors should examine a number of sales invoices to ascertain that customers are being charged the correct amount of tax. Debits to the liability account for remittances to the taxing authority should be traced to copies of the tax returns and should be vouched to the paid checks.

## Unclaimed Wages

Unclaimed wages are, by their very nature, subject to misappropriation. The auditors, therefore, are particularly concerned with the adequacy of internal control over this item. A list of unpaid wages should be prepared after each payroll distribution. The payroll checks should not be left for more than a few days in the payroll department. Prompt deposit in a special bank account provides much improved control. The auditors will analyze the Unclaimed Wages account for the purpose of determining that (1) the credits represent all unclaimed wages after each payroll distribution and (2) the debits represent only authorized payments to employees, remittances to the state under unclaimed property laws, or transfers back to general cash funds through approved procedures.

## Customers' Deposits

Many companies require that customers make deposits on returnable containers. Public utilities and common carriers also may require deposits to guarantee payment of bills or to cover equipment on loan to the customer. A review of the procedures followed in accepting and returning deposits should be made by the auditors with a view to disclosing any shortcomings in internal control. In some instances, deposits shown by the records as refunded to customers may in fact have been abstracted by employees.

The verification should include obtaining a list of the individual deposits and a comparison of the total with the general ledger controlling account. If deposits are interest-bearing, the amount of accrued interest should also be tested for reasonableness. As a general rule, the auditors do not attempt to confirm deposits by direct communication with customers; however, this procedure is desirable if the amounts involved are substantial or the internal control structure procedures are considered to be deficient.

## Accrued Liabilities

Most accrued liabilities (expenses) represent obligations payable sometime during the succeeding period (**subsequent period**) for services or privileges received before the balance sheet date. Examples include interest payable, accrued property taxes, accrued payrolls and payroll taxes, income taxes payable, and amounts accrued under service guarantees.

Because accrued items are based on client estimates of amounts which will subsequently become payable, subjective factors may make it difficult to establish control over them. As a result, these estimates may be particularly susceptible to misstatement, especially in circumstances in which management is under pressure to show increased earnings.

The basic auditing steps for accrued liabilities are:

1. Examine any contracts or other documents on hand that provide the basis for the accrual.

2. Appraise the accuracy of the detailed accounting records maintained for this category of liability.

3. Identify and evaluate the reasonableness of the assumptions made that underlie the computation of the liability.

4. Test the computations made by the client in setting up the accrual.

5. Determine that accrued liabilities have been treated consistently at the beginning and end of the period.

6. Consider the need for accrual of other accrued liabilities not presently considered (that is, test completeness).

The following sections describe the nature of the audit of various specific accrued liabilities.

Accrued Property Taxes.    Property tax payments are usually few in number and substantial in amount. It is, therefore, feasible for the audit working papers to include an analysis showing all of the year's property tax transactions. Tax payments should be verified by inspection of the property tax bills issued by local government units and by reference to the related paid checks. If the tax accruals at the balance sheet date differ significantly from those of prior years, an explanation of the variation should be obtained. The auditors should verify that property tax bills have been received on all taxable property or that an estimated tax has been accrued.

Accrued Payrolls.    The examination of payrolls from the standpoint of appraising the adequacy of internal controls and substantiating the expenditures for the period under audit is considered in Chapter 15. The present consideration of payrolls is limited to the procedures required for testing accrued payrolls at the balance sheet date.

Accrued gross salaries and wages appear on the balance sheets of virtually all concerns. The accuracy of the amount accrued may be significant in the determination of total liabilities and also in the proper matching of costs and revenue. The verification procedure consists principally of comparing the amounts accrued to the actual payroll of the subsequent period and reviewing the method of allocation at the balance sheet date. Payments made at the first payroll dates of the subsequent period are reviewed to determine that no significant *unrecorded* payroll liability existed as of the balance sheet date.

Pension Plan Accruals.    Auditing procedures for the accrued liability for pension costs may begin with a review of the copy of the pension plan in the auditors' permanent file. Then consideration should be given to the provisions of the Employee Retirement Income

Security Act (ERISA). The auditors must determine that the client's accrued pension liability is presented in accordance with *FASB No. 87*, "Employers' Accounting for Pensions," including consideration of service cost, interest cost, amortization of transition and service costs, and gains and losses on pension plan assets. In auditing these amounts the auditors will obtain representations from an actuary and confirm the activity in the plan with the trustee. In evaluating the evidence from the actuary, the auditors should comply with the requirements of *SAS 11* (AU 336), "Using the Work of a Specialist" (discussed in Chapter 6).

### Postemployment Benefits Other than Pensions.

Companies must also accrue liabilities for health and similar benefits that will be provided to their employees after retirement. Under *FASB No. 106*, "Employers' Accounting for Postretirement Benefits Other than Pensions," companies must accrue, during the years that employees perform services, the expected cost of providing the benefits to the employees, their beneficiaries, and their dependents. Determining the amount of these liabilities is a very complex procedure, because assumptions must be made about matters such as employee work lives and increases in medical costs. Since these assumptions are developed by actuaries and other specialists, the auditors should evaluate the assumptions and related computations in accordance with *SAS 11* (AU 336), "Using the Work of a Specialist."

### Accrued Vacation Pay.

Closely related to accrued salaries and wages is the liability that may exist for accrued vacation pay. This type of liability arises from two situations: (1) an employee entitled by contract to a vacation during the past year may have been prevented from taking it by an emergency work schedule, and (2) an employee may be entitled to a future vacation of which part of the cost must be accrued to achieve a proper matching of costs and revenue.

The auditors' verification of accrued vacation pay may begin with a review of the permanent file copy of the employment contract or agreement stipulating vacation terms. The computation of the accrual should then be verified both as to arithmetical accuracy and for agreement with the terms of the company's vacation policy.

### Product Warranty Liabilities.

The products of many companies are sold with a guarantee of free service or replacement during a rather extended warranty period. The costs of rendering such services should be recognized as expenses in the year the product is sold rather than in a later year in which the replacement is made or the repair service is performed. If this policy is followed, the company will make an annual charge to expense and credit to a liability account based on the amount of the year's sales and the estimated future service or replacement cost. As repairs and replacements take place, the costs will be charged to the liability account.

The auditors should review the client's annual provision for estimated future expenditures and compute the percentage relationship between the amount in the liability account and the amount of the year's sales. If this relationship varies sharply from year to year, the client should be asked for an explanation. The auditors should also review the charges to the liability account month by month and be alert for the improper recording of other expenses in this account. Sudden variations in the monthly charges to the liability account require investigation. In general, the auditors should determine that the balance in the liability account for service guarantees moves in reasonable relationship with the trend of sales. The auditors also should be alert for changes in the client's products or repair costs that might affect the amount of the warranty liability.

Current income tax laws prohibit the deduction of provisions for warranty liabilities; deductions are permitted only when actual expenditures are incurred. Accordingly, the auditors should ascertain that the client is properly allocating income taxes attributable to the nondeductible provisions.

Accrued Commissions and Bonuses.    Accrued commissions to sales representatives and bonuses payable to managerial personnel also require verification. The essential step in this case is reference to the authority for the commission or bonus. The basic contracts should be examined and traced to minutes of directors' meetings. If the bonus or commission is based on the total volume of sales or some other objective measure, the auditors should verify the computation of the accrual by applying the prescribed rate to the amount used as a base.

Income Taxes Payable.    Federal, state, and foreign income taxes on corporations represent a material factor in determining both net income and financial position. The auditors cannot express an opinion on either the balance sheet or income statement of a corporation without first obtaining evidence that the provision for income taxes has been properly computed. In the audit of small and medium-sized companies, it is customary for the audit engagement to include the preparation of the client's tax returns. If the income tax returns have been prepared by the client's staff or other persons, the auditors must nevertheless verify the reasonableness of the tax liability if they are to express an opinion on the fairness of the financial statements. In performing such a review of a tax return prepared by the client's staff or by others, the auditors may sometimes discover an opportunity for a tax saving that has been overlooked; obviously such a discovery tends to enhance the client's appreciation of the services rendered by the auditors.

The auditors should analyze the Income Taxes Payable account and vouch all amounts to income tax returns, paid checks, or other supporting documents. The final balance in the Income Taxes Payable account will ordinarily equal the computed federal, state, and foreign taxes on the current year's income tax returns, less any payments thereon.

The tax expected to be paid by a corporation often differs from the actual tax paid due to temporary differences between taxable income and pretax accounting income. These differences result in the need to establish deferred tax liabilities or assets. The auditors determine the amount of deferred tax liabilities using schedules referred to as ''tax accrual'' working papers, which usually are reviewed by one of the CPA firm's tax specialists.

Besides reviewing the computation of the income tax liability for the current year, the auditors should determine the date to which income tax returns for prior years have been examined by IRS agents and the particulars of any disputes or additional assessments. Review of the reports of revenue agents is also an essential step. In the first audit of a new client, the auditors should review any prior years' income tax returns not yet examined by revenue agents to make sure that there has been no substantial underpayment of taxes that would warrant presentation as a liability.

Accrued Professional Fees.   Fees of professional firms include charges for the services of attorneys, public accountants, consulting engineers, and other specialists who often render services of a continuing nature but present bills only at infrequent intervals. By inquiry of officers and by review of corporate minutes, the auditors may learn of professional services received for which no liability has yet been reflected in the accounts. Review of the expense account for legal fees is always essential because it may reveal damage suits, tax disputes, or other litigation warranting disclosure in the financial statements.

## Balance Sheet Presentation

Accrued expenses—interest, taxes, rent, and wages—are included in the current liability section of the balance sheet and sometimes combined into one figure. Income taxes payable, however, may be sufficiently material to be listed as a separate item. Deferred federal income taxes resulting from tax allocations should be classified as current liabilities (or assets) if they relate to the next year. Otherwise, deferred federal income taxes are classified as noncurrent.

Deferred credits to revenue for such items as rent or interest collected in advance that will be included in earnings in the succeeding period are customarily included in current liabilities. Deposits on contracts and similar advances from customers also are accorded the status of current liabilities because the receipt of an advance increases the current assets total and because the goods to be used in liquidating the advance are generally included in current assets.

## Time of Examination

The nature and amount of **accounts payable** may change greatly within a few weeks' time; consequently, the auditors' verification of these rapidly changing liabilities is most effective when performed immediately after the balance sheet date. As stressed at the beginning of this chapter, failure to record a liability will cause an overstatement of financial position. Audit work on accounts payable performed before the balance sheet date is of little value if the client fails to record important liabilities coming into existence during the remaining weeks of the year under audit. For this reason, many auditors believe that most of the audit work on accounts payable should be performed *after the balance sheet date*. Certainly, the auditors' search for unrecorded liabilities must be made after the balance sheet date because this search is concentrated on the transactions occurring during the first few weeks of the new year.

Some current liability accounts other than accounts payable are more suitable for preliminary audit work. The documents relating to accrued property taxes, for example, may be available in advance of the balance sheet date. Amounts withheld from employees' pay can be reviewed before the end of the year. The propriety of amounts withheld and of amounts remitted to the tax authorities during the year can be verified before the pressure of year-end work begins. The working papers relating to such liability accounts then may be completed very quickly after the end of the accounting period.

## ◆ CHAPTER SUMMARY

This chapter described the details of the acquisition cycle (purchases and cash disbursements), the auditors' consideration of the internal control for this transaction cycle, and the auditors' substantive tests of the acquisition cycle accounts—purchases, accounts payable, and other liabilities. To summarize:

1. The acquisition cycle includes initiating and authorizing purchases, ordering goods and services, and recording and paying accounts payable. Effective internal control over purchase transactions is best achieved by having separate departments responsible for purchasing, receiving, and accounting for the transactions. In this manner, payments are made only for those purchases that are properly authorized and received.

2. Internal control over cash disbursements is best achieved when all payments are made by check, except for payment of minor items from petty cash funds. Separation of the functions of preparation of the payments from that of signing checks tends to prevent errors and irregularities in cash disbursements.

3. The auditors' principal objectives in the examination of accounts payable and purchases are to: *(a)* substantiate the existence of recorded accounts payable and the occurrence of purchase transactions, *(b)* establish the completeness of accounts payable and purchase transactions, *(c)* determine that the client has obligations to pay the recorded accounts payable, *(d)* establish the clerical accuracy of records and schedules, *(e)* determine the appropriate valuation of accounts payable, and *(f)* determine that the presentation and disclosure of accounts payable and purchases are appropriate.

4. In auditing accounts payable and other liabilities, it is important for the auditors to remember that an understatement of liabilities will exaggerate the financial strength of a company in the same way as an overstatement of assets. Therefore, the auditors' substantive procedures primarily focus on the objective of determining the completeness of recorded amounts. A number of these procedures involve inspecting documents related to transactions occurring during the subsequent period to determine whether these items should have been recorded as liabilities at year-end.

5. Accrued liabilities represent obligations payable for services received before the balance sheet date that will be paid in the subsequent period. Examples include accrued warranty liabilities, accrued payroll, and accrued pension liabilities. The substantive procedures to audit these liabilities generally include inspection of documents, recomputation, and analytical procedures.

## ◆ KEY TERMS INTRODUCED OR EMPHASIZED IN CHAPTER 14

**Accounts payable**   Current liabilities arising from the purchase of goods and services from creditors, generally evidenced by invoices or statements received from the creditors.

**Accrued liabilities (accrued expenses)**   Short-term obligations for services of a continuing nature that accumulate on a time basis. Examples include interest, taxes, rent, salaries, and pensions. Accrued liabilities are not generally evidenced by invoices or statements.

**Confirmation**   Direct communication with vendors or suppliers to determine the amount of an account payable.

**Consignment**   A transfer of goods from the owner to another person who acts as the sales agent of the owner.

**Electronic data interchange (EDI)**   A computer network between companies that allows the interchange of data from one company's computer to the other's (e.g., allows purchases and sales between two firms to be processed electronically).

**Subsequent period**   The time extending from the balance sheet date to the date of the auditors' report.

**Vendor's invoice**   A document received from the supplier containing information about the goods purchased, including formal notice to the purchaser about the terms of payment. Also sometimes referred to as a *purchase invoice* or a *supplier's invoice*. This document is the "sales invoice" from the revenue cycle.

**Vendor's statement**   A monthly statement prepared by a vendor (supplier) showing the beginning balance, charges during the month for goods or services, amounts collected, and ending balance. This externally created document should correspond (except for timing differences) with an account in the client's accounts payable subsidiary ledger.

**Voucher**   A document authorizing a cash disbursement. A voucher usually provides space for employees performing various approval functions to initial. The term *voucher* may also be applied to the group of supporting documents used as a basis for recording liabilities or for making cash disbursements.

**Voucher register**   A journal used in a voucher system—generally replacing the purchases journal—to record liabilities requiring cash payment in the near future. Every liability recorded in a voucher register corresponds to a voucher authorizing future payment.

# ◆ GROUP I: REVIEW QUESTIONS

If a corporation overstates its earnings, are its liabilities more likely to be overstated or understated? Explain.

14-2   Lawsuits against CPA firms are most likely to allege that the auditors were negligent in not detecting which of the following? *(a)* overstatement of liabilities and earnings, *(b)* understatement of assets and earnings, *(c)* overstatement of owners' equity. Explain the reasoning underlying your choice.

14-3   Assume that a highly placed employee has stolen company assets and is now planning to conceal the fraud by failing to make an accounting entry for a large transaction. Would the omission probably be for a transaction creating an asset or a liability? Explain.

14-4   Suggest two reasons why the adjustments proposed by independent auditors more often than not call for reducing recorded earnings.

14-5   Explain how the auditors coordinate the year-end cutoff of accounts payable with their observation of the year-end physical inventory.

14-6   Identify three audit procedures (other than "search for unrecorded accounts payable") that are concerned directly or indirectly with disclosing unrecorded accounts payable.

14-7   What is the purpose of the auditors' review of cash payments subsequent to the balance sheet date?

14-8    The auditors usually find in the client's possession documentary evidence, such as invoices, supporting both accounts receivable and accounts payable. Is there any difference in the quality of such evidence for accounts receivable and for accounts payable? Explain.

14-9    Describe briefly an internal control procedure that would prevent a paid disbursement voucher from being presented for payment a second time.

14-10   Is the confirmation of accounts payable by direct communication with vendors as useful and important an audit procedure as is the confirmation of accounts receivable? Explain.

14-11   During the verification of the individual invoices comprising the total of accounts payable at the balance sheet date, the auditors discovered some receiving reports indicating that the merchandise covered by several of these invoices was not received until after the balance sheet date. What action should the auditors take?

14-12   What do you consider to be the most important single procedure in the auditors' search for unrecorded accounts payable? Explain.

14-13   Whitehall Company records its liabilities in an accounts payable subsidiary ledger. The auditors have decided to select some of the accounts for confirmation by direct communication with vendors. The largest volume of purchases during the year had been made from Ranchero Company, but at the balance sheet date this account has a zero balance. Under these circumstances should the auditors send a confirmation request to Ranchero Company, or would they accomplish more by limiting their confirmation program to accounts with larger year-end balances?

14-14   Compare the auditors' approach to the verification of liabilities with their approach to the verification of assets.

14-15   Most auditors are interested in performing as many phases of an audit as possible in advance of the balance sheet date. The verification of accounts payable, however, generally is regarded as something to be done after the balance sheet date. What specific factors can you suggest that make the verification of accounts payable less suitable than many other accounts for interim work?

14-16   The operating procedures of a well-managed accounts payable department will provide for the verification of several specific points before a vendor's invoice is recorded as an approved liability. What are the points requiring verification?

14-17   List the major responsibilities of an accounts payable department.

14-18   In achieving adequate internal control over operations of the accounts payable department, a company should establish procedures that will ensure that extensions and footings are proved on all invoices and that the propriety of prices is reviewed. What is the most effective means of ensuring consistent performance of these duties?

14-19   Which do you consider the more significant step in establishing strong internal control over accounts payable transactions: the approval of an invoice for payment, or the issuance of a check in payment of an invoice? Explain.

14-20   Outline a method by which the auditors may test the propriety of cash discounts taken on accounts payable.

14-21   For which documents relating to the accounts payable operation would you recommend the use of serial numbers as an internal control procedure?

14-22   What internal control procedure would you recommend to call attention to failure to pay invoices within the discount period?

14-23   As part of the investigation of accounts payable, auditors sometimes vouch entries in selected creditors' accounts back through the journals to original documents, such as purchase orders, receiving reports, invoices, and paid checks. What is the principal purpose of this procedure?

14-24   Vendors' statements and accounts payable confirmations are both forms of documentary evidence created outside the client organization and useful in audit work on accounts payable. Which of these two represents higher quality evidence? Why?

14-25   What documentary evidence created outside the client's organization is particularly important to the auditors in verifying accrued property taxes?

14-26   What differences should auditors expect to find in supporting evidence for accrued liabilities as contrasted with accounts payable?

14-27   Among the departments of J-R Company are a purchasing department, receiving department, accounting department, and finance department. If you were preparing a flowchart of a voucher system to be installed by the company, in which department would you show—
    *a.*   The assembling of the purchase order, receiving report, and vendor's invoice to determine that these documents are in agreement?
    *b.*   The preparation of a check?
    *c.*   The signing of a check?
    *d.*   The mailing of a check to the payee?
    *e.*   The perforation of the voucher and supporting documents?

14-28   During your audit of a small manufacturing firm, you find numerous checks of large amounts drawn payable to the treasurer and charged to the Miscellaneous Expense account. Does this require any action by the auditor? Explain.

## ◆ GROUP II: QUESTIONS REQUIRING ANALYSIS

14-29   Early in your first audit of Star Corporation, you notice that sales and year-end inventory are almost unchanged from the prior year. However, cost of goods sold is less than in the preceding year, and accounts payable also are down substantially. Gross profit has increased, but this increase has not carried through to net income because of increased executive salaries. Management informs you that sales prices and purchase prices have not changed significantly during the past year, and there have been no changes in the product line. Star Corporation relies on the periodic inventory system. Your initial impression of internal control is that several weaknesses may exist.

*Required:*   Suggest a possible explanation for the trends described, especially the decrease in accounts payable while sales and inventory were constant and gross profit increased. Explain fully the relationships involved.

14-30   Henry Mills is responsible for preparing checks, recording cash disbursements, and preparing bank reconciliations for Signet Corporation. While reconciling the October bank statement, Mills noticed that several checks totaling $937 had been outstanding for more than one year. Concluding that these checks would never be presented for payments, Mills prepared a check for $937 payable to himself, forged the treasurer's signature, and cashed the check. Mills made no entry in the accounts for this disbursement and attempted to conceal the theft by destroying the forged check and omitting the long-outstanding checks from subsequent bank reconciliations.

*Required:*     *a.*   Identify the weaknesses in Signet Corporation's internal control.
    *b.*   Explain several audit procedures that might disclose the fraudulent disbursement.

14-31  Compare the confirmation of accounts receivable with the confirmation of accounts payable under the following headings:

    *a.*  Generally accepted auditing procedures. (Justify the differences revealed by your comparison.)

    *b.*  Selection of accounts to be confirmed.

(AICPA, adapted)

14-32  In connection with their audit of the financial statements of Davis Company, the auditors reviewed the Federal Income Taxes Payable account.

*Required:*  *a.*  Discuss reasons why the auditors should review the federal income tax returns for prior years and the reports of internal revenue agents.

    *b.*  What information will these reviews provide? (Do not discuss specific tax return items.)

(AICPA, adapted)

14-33  The *subsequent period* in an audit is the time extending from the balance sheet date to the date of the auditors' report.

*Required:*  Discuss the importance of the subsequent period in the audit of trade accounts payable.

14-34  During the course of any audit, the auditors are always alert for unrecorded accounts payable or other unrecorded liabilities.

*Required:*  For each of the following audit areas (1) describe an unrecorded liability that might be discovered and (2) state what auditing procedure(s) might bring it to light.

    *a.*  Construction in progress (property, plant, and equipment).

    *b.*  Prepaid insurance.

    *c.*  License authorizing the client to produce a product patented by another company.

    *d.*  Minutes of directors' meetings.

14-35  Describe the audit steps that generally would be followed in establishing the propriety of the recorded liability for federal income taxes of a corporation you are auditing for the first time. Consideration should be given the status of *(a)* the liability for prior years and *(b)* the liability arising from the current year's taxable income.

14-36  In the course of your initial audit of the financial statements of Sylvan Company, you ascertain that of the substantial amount of accounts payable outstanding at the close of the period, approximately 75 percent is owed to six creditors. You have requested that you be permitted to confirm the balances owing to these six creditors by communicating with the creditors, but the president of the company is unwilling to approve your request on the grounds that correspondence in regard to the balances—all of which contain some overdue items—might give rise to demands on the part of the creditors for immediate payment of the overdue items and thereby embarass Sylvan Company.

    In the circumstances, what alternative procedure would you adopt in an effort to satisfy yourself that the accounting records show the correct amounts payable to these creditors?

(AICPA, adapted)

14-37  Select the best answer for each of the following and explain the reason for your selection.

    *a.*  Which of the following procedures is *least* likely to be completed before the balance sheet date?

      (1)  Confirmation of receivables.

      (2)  Search for unrecorded liabilities.

      (3)  Observation of inventory.

      (4)  Review of internal accounting control over cash disbursements.

b.  An examination of the balance in the accounts payable account is ordinarily *not* designed to:
   (1)   Detect accounts payable that are substantially past due.
   (2)   Verify that accounts payable were properly authorized.
   (3)   Ascertain the reasonableness of recorded liabilities.
   (4)   Determine that all existing liabilities at the balance sheet date have been recorded.

c.  Which of the following is the *best* audit procedure for determining the existence of unrecorded liabilities?
   (1)   Examine confirmation requests returned by creditors whose accounts appear on a subsidiary trial balance of accounts payable.
   (2)   Examine unusual relationships between monthly accounts payable balances and recorded purchases.
   (3)   Examine a sample of invoices a few days prior to and subsequent to year-end to ascertain whether they have been properly recorded.
   (4)   Examine selected cash disbursements in the period subsequent to year-end.

d.  Auditor confirmation of accounts payable balances at the balance sheet date may be *unnecessary* because:
   (1)   This is a duplication of cutoff tests.
   (2)   Accounts payable balances at the balance sheet date may *not* be paid before the audit is completed.
   (3)   Correspondence with the audit client's attorney will reveal all legal action by vendors for nonpayment.
   (4)   There is likely to be other reliable external evidence available to support the balances.

e.  A client erroneously recorded a large purchase twice. Which of the following internal control measures would be most likely to detect this error in a timely and efficient manner?
   (1)   Footing the purchases journal.
   (2)   Reconciling vendors' monthly statements with subsidiary payable ledger accounts.
   (3)   Tracing totals from the purchases journal to the ledger accounts.
   (4)   Sending written quarterly confirmation requests to all vendors.

f.  For effective internal control, the accounts payable department should compare the information on each vendor's invoice with the:
   (1)   Receiving report and the purchase order.
   (2)   Receiving report and the voucher.
   (3)   Vendor's packing slip and the purchase order.
   (4)   Vendor's packing slip and the voucher.

## ◆ GROUP III: PROBLEMS

14-38   The following are typical questions that might appear on an internal control questionnaire for accounts payable.
   1.   Are monthly statements from vendors reconciled with the accounts payable listing?
   2.   Are vendors' invoices matched with receiving reports before they are approved for payment?

*Required:*   a.   Describe the purpose of each of the above internal control procedures.
   b.   Describe the manner in which each of the above procedures might be tested.
   c.   Assuming that the operating effectiveness of each of the above procedures is found to be inadequate, describe how the auditors might alter their substantive tests to compensate for the increased level of control risk.

14-39   Taylor, CPA, is engaged in the audit of Rex Wholesaling for the year ended December 31. Taylor obtained an understanding of internal control relating to the purchasing, receiving, trade accounts payable, and cash disbursement cycles, and has decided not to proceed with tests of controls. Based upon analytical procedures, Taylor believes that the trade accounts payable on the balance sheet as of December 31 may be understated.

Taylor requested and obtained a client-prepared trade accounts payable schedule listing the total amount owed to each vendor.

*Required:*   What additional substantive audit procedures should Taylor apply in examining the trade accounts payable?

14-40   As part of your first audit of the financial statements of Marina del Rey, Inc., you have decided to confirm some of the accounts payable. You are now in the process of selecting the individual companies to whom you will send accounts payable confirmation requests. Among the accounts payable you are considering are the following:

| Company | Amount Payable at Year-End | Total Purchases from Vendor during Year |
|---|---|---|
| Dayco, Inc. . . . . . . . . . | $ — | $1,980,000 |
| Gearbox, Inc. . . . . . . . . | 22,650 | 46,100 |
| Landon Co. . . . . . . . . . | 65,000 | 75,000 |
| Western Supply . . . . . . . | 190,000 | 2,123,000 |

*Required:*   a.   Which two of the above four accounts payable would you select as the most important to confirm? Explain your choice in terms of the audit objectives in sending accounts payable confirmation requests.

b.   Assume that you are selecting accounts receivable to be confirmed. Assume also that the four companies listed above are customers of your client rather than suppliers and that the dollar amounts are accounts receivable balances and total sales for the year. Which two companies would you select as the most important to confirm? Explain your choice.

14-41   James Rowe, CPA, is the independent auditor of Raleigh Corporation. Rowe is considering the audit work to be performed in the accounts payable area for the current year's engagement.

The prior year's working papers show that confirmation requests were mailed to 100 of Raleigh's 1,000 suppliers. The selected suppliers were based on Rowe's sample that was designed to select accounts with large dollar balances. A substantial number of hours was spent by Raleigh employees and by Rowe resolving relatively minor differences between the confirmation replies and Raleigh's accounting records. Alternative audit procedures were used for those suppliers that did not respond to the confirmation requests.

*Required:*   a.   Identify the accounts payable audit objectives that Rowe must consider in determining the audit procedures to be followed.

b.   Identify situations in which Rowe should use accounts payable confirmations and discuss whether Rowe is required to use them.

c.   Discuss why the use of large dollar balances as the basis for selecting accounts payable for confirmation might not be the most efficient approach, and indicate what more efficient procedures could be followed when selecting accounts payable for confirmation.

(AICPA, adapted)

14-42   During the current year, your audit client, Video Corporation, was licensed to manufacture a patented type of television tube. The licensing agreement called for royalty payments of 50 cents for each tube manufactured by Video Corporation. What procedures would you follow in connection with your regular annual audit at December 31 to obtain evidence that the liability for royalties is correctly stated?

(AICPA, adapted)

14-43   Nancy Howe, your staff assistant on the April 30, 19X2, audit of Wilcox Company, was transferred to another audit engagement before she could complete the audit of unrecorded accounts payable. Her working paper, which you have reviewed and are satisfied is complete, appears below.

*Required:*   Prepare a proposed adjusting journal entry for the unrecorded accounts payable of Wilcox Company at April 30, 19X2. The amounts are material. (Do not deal with income taxes.)

|  |  |  |
|---|---|---|
|  | Wilcox Company | |
|  | Unrecorded Accounts Payable | M-1-1 |
|  | April 30, 19X2 | |
| **Invoice Date** | **Vendor and Description** | **Amount** |
|  | Hill & Harper—unpaid legal fees at Apr. 30, X2 (see lawyer's lstter at M-4) | 1000 𝑦 |
| Apr.1,X2 | Drew Insurance Agency—unpaid premium on fire insurance for period Apr. 1, X2— Mar. 31, X5 (see insurance broker letter at J-1-1) | 1800 𝑦 |
| Apr.30,X2 | Mays and Sage, Stockbrokers—advice for 100 shares of Madison Ltd. Common stock (settlement date May 7, X2) | 2125 −𝑦 |
|  | Lane Company—shipment received Apr. 30, X2 per receiver no. 3361 and included in Apr. 30, X2 physical inventory; invoice not yet received (amount is per purchase order) | 5863 −𝑦 |
|  |  | 10788 — |

𝑦-*Examined document described.*

*In my opinion, the $10,788 adjustment includes all material unrecorded accounts payable.*

*N.A.H*
*May 29, X2*

14-44   You were in the final stages of your audit of the financial statements of Scott Corporation for the year ended December 31, 19X0, when you were consulted by the corporation's president, who believes there is no point to your examining the 19X1 voucher register and testing data in support of 19X0 entries. He stated that (1) bills pertaining to 19X0 that were received too late to be included in the December voucher register were recorded as of the year-end by the corporation by journal entry, (2) the internal auditors made tests after the year-end, and (3) he would furnish you with a letter representing that there were no unrecorded liabilities.

*Required:*   *a.*   Should the independent auditors' test for unrecorded liabilities be affected by the fact that the client made a journal entry to record 19X0 bills that were received late? Explain.

*b.*   Should the independent auditors' test for unrecorded liabilities be affected by the fact that a letter is obtained in which a responsible management official represents that to the best of his knowledge all liabilities have been recorded? Explain.

*c.*   Should the independent auditors' test for unrecorded liabilities be eliminated or reduced because of the internal audit tests? Explain.

*d.*   Assume that the client company, which handled some government contracts, had no internal auditors but that auditors for a federal agency spent three weeks auditing the records and were just completing their work at this time. How would the independent auditors' unrecorded liability test be affected by the work of the auditors for a federal agency?

*e.*   What sources in addition to the 19X1 voucher register should the independent auditors consider to locate possible unrecorded liabilities?

(AICPA, adapted)

# AUDITING THE CONVERSION AND PAYROLL CYCLES

## CHAPTER OBJECTIVES

After studying this chapter, you should be able to:

- Explain the nature of the transactions in the conversion and payroll cycles.

- Identify and explain the fundamental internal control policies and procedures for conversion and payroll transactions.

- Relate specific internal control structure policies and procedures to financial statement assertions.

- Design typical procedures used by auditors to test the effectiveness of the controls over the conversion and payroll cycles.

- Describe the nature of inventory, payroll, and cost of goods sold accounts.

- Identify the audit objectives for substantive tests of the inventory and cost of goods sold accounts.

- Identify the audit objectives for substantive tests of payroll-related accounts.

- Describe the nature of appropriate substantive audit procedures to accomplish the objectives for the audit of inventory, cost of goods sold, and payroll.

This chapter presents information about the nature of the conversion and payroll cycles. Because labor costs are an important part of conversion costs, these two cycles are considered together.

For a manufacturing company, the conversion cycle involves combining raw materials, labor, and overhead to produce finished goods. For a retailing operation, this cycle involves the purchase of goods for resale to customers, and for a service company it involves providing labor services and limited materials to customers. This chapter emphasizes the conversion and payroll cycles for a manufacturing company, but it also describes differences involved for nonmanufacturing organizations.

The discussion of the conversion cycle may be integrated with information presented in the preceding three chapters on the acquisition and revenue cycles. The acquisition cycle includes the purchase of raw materials, labor, and overhead items to produce finished products, and the revenue cycle involves sales of those products. Figure 15–1 illustrates the relationships among the three cycles. This interrelationship between the cycles means that many of the controls that have been described in the preceding chapters also affect the conversion cycle. For example, Chapter 14 on the acquisition cycle pre-

**Figure 15 – 1    Relationships among Transaction Cycles**

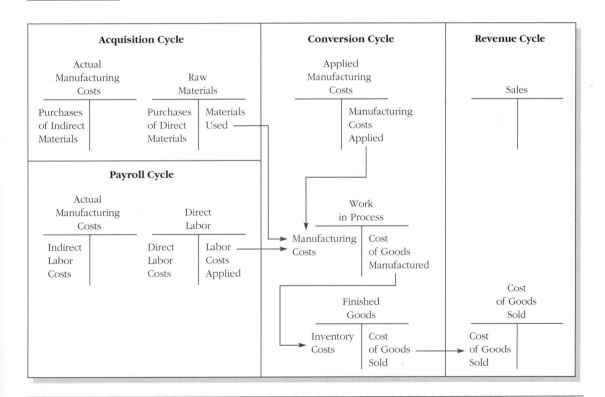

sented a variety of controls for selecting vendors, ordering merchandise and materials, inspecting goods received, recording the liability to the vendor, and authorizing and making cash disbursements for acquisitions. Chapter 12 considered controls over credit approval, issuing merchandise, shipping goods, billing customers, and collecting cash receipts for the revenue cycle. The emphasis in this chapter is on the process that occurs between the point at which raw materials and services are purchased to the point of sale of the finished product.

## Auditing the Conversion Cycle

### Internal Control over the Conversion Cycle

The importance of adequate internal control over inventories and cost of goods sold from the viewpoint of both management and the auditors can scarcely be overemphasized. In some companies, management stresses internal controls over cash and securities but pays little attention to control over inventories. Since many types of inventories are composed of items not particularly susceptible to theft, management may consider internal controls to be unnecessary in this area. Such thinking ignores the fact that internal control performs other functions that are just as important as fraud prevention.

Good internal control includes providing accurate cost data for inventories and goods sold, as well as ensuring accuracy in reporting physical quantities. Inadequate internal control may cause losses by permitting erroneous cost data to be used by management in setting prices and in making other decisions based on reported profit margins. If the accounts do not furnish a realistic picture of the cost of inventories on hand, the cost of goods manufactured, and the cost of goods sold, the financial statements may be misleading as to both earnings and financial position.

Internal control procedures for the conversion cycle affect nearly all of the functions involved in producing and disposing of the company's products. Purchasing, receiving, storing, issuing, processing, and shipping are the physical functions directly connected with inventories; the cost accounting system and the perpetual inventory records comprise the recording functions. Since the auditors are interested in financial statement amounts that are the final products of the recording function, it is necessary for them to understand and appraise the cost accounting system and the perpetual inventory records, as well as the various procedures and original documents underlying the preparation of financial data.

Purchasing.   Adequate internal control over purchases requires an organizational structure that delegates to a separate department of the company exclusive authority to make all purchases of materials and services. The purchasing, receiving, and recording functions should be clearly separated and lodged in separate departments. In small companies, this type of departmentalized operation may not be possible; but even in very small enterprises, it is usually feasible to make one person responsible for all purchase transactions and to review this individual's work. Chapter 14 discusses details of the necessary controls over purchasing.

Receiving.   All goods received by the company should be cleared through a receiving department that is independent of the purchasing, storing, and shipping departments. The receiving department is responsible for (1) the determination of quantities of goods received, (2) the detection of damaged or defective merchandise, (3) the preparation of a **receiving report,** and (4) the prompt transmittal of goods received to the stores department.

Storing Purchased Goods.   As goods are delivered to stores, they should be counted, inspected, and receipted for. The stores department should notify the accounting department of the amount received and placed in stock. In performing these functions, the stores department makes an important contribution to overall control of inventories. By signing for the goods, it fixes its own responsibility, and by notifying the accounting department of actual goods stored, it provides verification of the receiving department's work.

Issuing.   The stores department, being responsible for all goods under its control, has reason to insist that a prenumbered requisition be issued to serve as a receipt for all items issued to a department requesting the goods. Requisitions are usually prepared in triplicate. One copy is retained by the department making the request, another serves as the stores department's receipt, and the third is a notice to the accounting department for cost distribution. To prevent the indiscriminate writing of requisitions for questionable purposes, some organizations establish policies requiring that requisitions be drawn only upon the authority of a bill of materials, an engineering order, or a sales order. In wholesale and retail concerns, shipping orders, rather than factory requisitions, serve to authorize withdrawals from stores.

Conversion (Production).   Responsibility for the goods in production must be fixed, usually on factory supervisors or superintendents. **Routing sheets** document the flow of the goods and related responsibility as they progress through the conversion process. Thus, from the time materials are delivered to the factory until they are completed and routed to a finished goods storeroom, a designated supervisor should be in control and be prepared to answer for their location and disposition. These manual forms are unnecessary in a computerized system; entries into computer terminals throughout the plant maintain records of the movement of materials through the manufacturing process.

The internal control procedures for goods in process may include regular inspection procedures to reveal defective work. This aids in disclosing inefficiencies in the productive system and also tends to prevent inflation of the work in process inventory by the accumulation of cost of goods that will eventually be scrapped.

Control procedures should also ensure that goods scrapped during production are promptly reported to the accounting department so that the decrease in value of work in process inventories may be recorded. Scrapped materials may have substantial salvage value, and this calls for segregation and control of scrap inventories.

Storing Finished Goods.   When goods are completed they are transferred to finished goods stores to await sale and shipment. Transfers of goods to the shipping department should be made only after proper authorization has been received. This authorization will normally be a sales order approved by the credit department, although the shipping function also includes returning defective goods to suppliers. In this latter case, the authorization may take the form of a shipping authorization from a purchasing department executive.

Shipping.    The shipping department will prepare, or the computer system will generate, a prenumbered **shipping document** indicating the goods shipped. One copy of the shipping document should be retained by the shipping department as evidence of shipment; a second copy should be sent to the billing department where it will be used—with the customer's purchase order and the sales order—as the basis for invoicing the customer; and a third copy should be enclosed as a packing slip with the goods when they are shipped. The control aspect of this procedure is strengthened by the fact that an outsider, the customer, will generally inspect the packing slip and notify the company of any discrepancy between this list, the goods ordered, and the goods actually received.

When the goods are shipped using a common carrier, a fourth copy of the shipping document, required in this case to be a **bill of lading,** is provided to the carrier. In addition, the copy forwarded to billing will then include additional evidence of shipment: trucking bills, carriers' receipts, and freight bills. This facilitates subsequent audit by grouping together the documents showing that shipments were properly authorized and carried out.

Established shipping routines should be followed for all types of shipments, including the sale of scrap, return of defective goods to suppliers, and forwarding of materials and parts to subcontractors.

Cost Accounting.    An adequate cost accounting system is necessary to account for the usage of raw materials and supplies, to determine the content and value of work in process inventories, and to compute the finished goods inventory. This system comprises all the records, orders, and requisitions needed for proper accounting for the disposition of materials as they enter the flow of production and as they continue through the factory in the process of becoming finished goods. The cost accounting system also serves to accumulate labor costs and indirect costs that contribute to the work in process and the finished goods inventories. The cost accounting system thus forms an integral part of the internal control for the conversion cycle.

The figures produced by the cost accounting system should be controlled by general ledger accounts. The cost of direct materials and labor are recorded in individual work in process accounts for each job order or process. Periodically, manufacturing overhead is applied to the jobs or processes and recorded in the accounts. A single work in process inventory account controls individual work in process accounts.

Underlying this general ledger control of factory records is a system of production orders, material requisitions, job tickets or other labor distributions, and factory overhead distributions. Control is achieved by implementing various procedures that verify the accuracy of production records. Allocations of direct materials and labor costs are recomputed and reconciled to material and payroll records. Manufacturing overhead costs that are applied using predetermined rates are adjusted to actual costs at the end of the period.

Many companies have established standard cost systems that help identify the causes of ineffectiveness and waste. These systems provide for the prompt pricing of inventories and for control over operations through a study of variances between actual and standard costs. All the various types of cost accounting systems are alike in that they are designed to contribute to effective internal control by monitoring the execution of managerial directives in the factory, providing reliable inventory figures, and safeguarding company assets.

The Perpetual Inventory System.   Perpetual inventory records constitute an important part of internal control. These records, by showing the current quantity of goods on hand, provide information essential to intelligent purchasing, sales, and production-planning policies. With such a record it is possible to guide procurement by establishing points of minimum and maximum quantities for each standard item stocked.

The use of a **perpetual inventory system** allows companies to control the high costs of holding excessive inventory, while minimizing the risk of running out of stock. The company can control inventories through reorder points and economic order quantities, including *just-in-time* ordering systems in which inventory levels are kept to a minimum.

If perpetual inventory records are to produce the control implicit in their nature, it is desirable that the subsidiary records be maintained both in quantities and dollars for all stock, that the subsidiary records be controlled by the general ledger, that trial balances be prepared at reasonable intervals, and that both the detailed records and the general ledger control accounts be adjusted to agree with physical counts whenever taken.

Perpetual inventory records discourage inventory theft and waste, since storekeepers and other employees are aware of the accountability over goods established by this continuous record of goods received, issued, and on hand. The records, however, must be periodically verified through the physical counting of goods.

## Obtaining and Documenting an Understanding of the Internal Control Structure for the Conversion Cycle

A sufficient understanding of the internal control structure for the conversion cycle will involve consideration of the control environment, accounting system, and control procedures.

Control Environment.   The organizational structure of a manufacturing company will typically include a high-level official who is responsible for all aspects of the production function. The auditors will obtain an understanding of this officer's responsibilities as well as how the production function fits into the company's overall organizational structure.

Of particular importance to the auditor's consideration of the conversion cycle are management control methods. Production costs are often controlled with the use of budgets and standard costs. However, for these techniques to be effective, it is essential for management to analyze variances from budgets and standards and take timely corrective action for problems that are indicated.

Accounting System and Control Procedures.   The auditors must obtain an understanding of the entity's conversion cycle transactions. The consideration of internal controls may involve filling out a questionnaire, writing descriptive memoranda, or preparing flowcharts depicting the internal control structure for the cycle. The auditors should become familiar with the procedures for purchasing, receiving, storing, and issuing goods and for controlling production. They should also obtain an understanding of the cost accounting system and the perpetual inventory records.

The auditors should give consideration to the physical protection of inventories. Any deficiencies in storage facilities, in guard service, or in physical handling that may lead to losses from weather, fire, flood, or theft should be called to the attention of management.

The matters to be investigated in the auditors' consideration of internal controls over the conversion cycle are fairly well indicated by the following questions: Are perpetual inventory records maintained for each class of inventory? Are perpetual inventory records verified by physical inventories at least once each year? Do the procedures for physical inventories include the use of prenumbered tags, with all tag numbers accounted for? Are differences between physical inventory counts and perpetual inventory records investigated before the perpetual records are adjusted? Is a separate purchasing department responsible for purchasing all materials, supplies, and equipment? Are all incoming shipments, including returns by customers, processed by a separate receiving department? Are materials and supplies held in the custody of a stores department and issued only upon receipt of properly approved requisitions?

After the auditors have prepared flowcharts (or other descriptions) of internal control, they should determine that the client is using those procedures, that is, determine whether the controls have been placed in operation. This information may be obtained through inquiries of entity personnel, inspection of documents, and observation of activities. As the auditors obtain their understanding of the internal control policies and procedures, they will observe whether there is an appropriate segregation of duties, and inquire as to who performed various functions throughout the year. They will also inspect various documents, such as purchase requisitions, purchase orders, material requisitions, time tickets, and shipping advices, and review document files to determine that the client is appropriately accounting for the sequence of prenumbered documents. Inventory, production, and responsibility accounting reports will be examined and the auditors will review the evidence of follow-up on variances from standard costs. These procedures may provide the auditors with sufficient evidence on operating effectiveness to assess control risk for certain financial statement assertions about inventories and cost of goods sold as being at less than the maximum.

## Testing Controls and Assessing Control Risk for Conversion Cycle Accounts

The auditors evaluate the effectiveness of a client's internal control policies and procedures in preventing or detecting material misstatements to assess control risk. As we have discussed throughout the text, auditors assess control risk in terms of the five financial statement assertions—existence or occurrence; completeness; rights and obligations; valuation or allocation; and presentation and disclosure.

The auditors use their understanding of the internal control structure to determine a planned assessed level for control risk for the various assertions. Appropriate tests of controls are then performed to justify assessments at levels lower than the maximum.

### Existence or Occurrence.
Tests of the existence or occurrence assertion address whether conversion transactions occurred during the period and whether the related assets exist. The primary asset involved is inventories. As is the case with the other cycles, an

appropriate segregation of duties helps provide assurance about most assertions, including existence or occurrence. The auditors' tests of segregation of duties will include the observation of employees performing various functions and inquiry as to who performed the functions throughout the year.

The direction of tests of the existence or occurrence assertion is primarily from the recorded entry to source documents. Accordingly, the auditors' tests of controls may involve vouching recorded raw material purchases to purchase orders, receiving reports, and **vendors' invoices.** This step will normally be performed in conjunction with the tests of the acquisition cycle. Subsequently, tests will be performed to determine that transfers of product costs to work in process, finished goods, and cost of goods sold are handled properly. This process is discussed in detail under the valuation assertion.

Completeness.   The completeness assertion for the conversion cycle requires that all materials, labor, and overhead be recorded as product costs. Chapter 14 presents a number of tests of completeness for purchases transactions. The combination of a proper segregation of functions and control over the numerical sequence of source documents will be tested to obtain evidence that all materials, labor, and overhead costs are recorded. After original costs have been recorded, an effective cost accounting system will help ensure that costs are properly apportioned between work in process, finished goods, and cost of goods sold.

Valuation or Allocation.   Controls over the valuation or allocation assertion are inherent in the client's cost accounting system. A wide variety of practices will be encountered for the costing of finished products. The cost accounting records may be controlled by general ledger accounts or operated independently of the general accounting system. In the latter case, the cost of completed units may be difficult or impossible to verify and may represent nothing more than a well-reasoned guess. Because cost accounting methods vary so widely, even among manufacturing concerns in the same industry, audit procedures for a cost accounting system must be designed to fit the specific circumstances encountered in each case.

The function of any cost accounting system is to account for the three elements of manufacturing cost—direct materials, direct labor, and manufacturing overhead. Cost accounting systems may accumulate either actual costs or standard costs according to *process* or *jobs*. The auditors' tests of the client's cost accounting system are designed to determine that costs allocated to specific jobs or processes are appropriately accumulated.

To determine whether costs are appropriately computed, the auditors test the propriety of direct materials quantities and unit costs, direct labor hours and hourly rates, and overhead rates and allocation bases. Quantities of direct materials charged to jobs or processes are vouched to material requisitions, and unit materials costs are compared to the raw materials perpetual inventory records or vendor invoices. The auditors examine job tickets or time summaries supporting direct labor-hours accumulations and trace direct labor hourly rates to union contracts or individual employee personnel files. When the client utilizes a computerized system, the auditors' tests of the cost accounting system may focus on the application controls that ensure the accuracy of the data entered into the system. In computerized systems, terminals located throughout the plant maintain records of the movement and accumulated costs of goods. If passwords and input validation checks are included in the system, the auditors may test these controls by observation and, possibly, by entering test transactions.

If standard costs are in use, the auditors will compare them with actual costs for representative items to ascertain whether the standards reflect current materials and labor usage and unit costs. The composition of factory overhead, the basis for its distribution by department and product, and the effect of any change in basis during the year should be reviewed. The reasonableness of the standard costs for the selected products should be verified by testing computations, extensions, and footings and by tracing charges for labor, materials, and overhead to original sources.

The auditors' study of a manufacturing company's cost accounting system should give special attention to any changes in cost methods made during the year and the effect of such changes on the cost of goods sold. Close attention should also be given to the methods of summarizing costs of completed products and to the procedures for recording the cost of partial shipments.

If the client company has supply contracts with U.S. government agencies, the auditors should determine whether standards issued by the **Cost Accounting Standards Board** were complied with. Cost accounting standards issued to date have dealt with such matters as consistency in estimating, accumulating, allocating and reporting costs, and depreciation of plant assets.

Rights and Obligations.   Evidence on rights and obligations in the conversion cycle relate primarily to whether legally valid purchase transactions have occurred. For example, consignments of inventory represent a circumstance in which inventory items may be on hand, yet the client does not own the goods. Therefore, the auditors will test the client's procedures for identifying and segregating goods that are not owned.

Presentation and Disclosure.   The presentation and disclosure assertion for the conversion cycle deals with whether the related components of the financial statements are properly classified, described, and disclosed. For example, inventory must be classified as to raw materials, work in process, and finished goods. Therefore, the auditors will perform tests of the client's perpetual inventory system, including the procedures for reconciling the inventory records to production data and physical quantities on hand.

The auditors will also assess the client's controls relating to identifying required disclosures such as for purchase commitments. However, in the area of required disclosures, the auditors may choose to assess control risk at a relatively high level and rely upon substantive testing procedures to determine that required disclosures are presented properly.

Figure 15–2 summarizes the relationships among the assertions, the internal control policies and procedures, and typical tests of controls for the conversion cycle.

## Designing Substantive Tests of Inventories and Cost of Goods Sold

As we have discussed, the term *inventories* as used in this chapter includes (1) goods on hand ready for sale, either the merchandise of a trading concern or the finished goods of a manufacturer; (2) goods in the process of production; and (3) goods to be consumed directly or indirectly in production, consisting of raw materials, purchased parts, and

Figure 15–2    Assessing Control Risk for the Conversion Cycle

| Internal Control Policy or Procedure | Typical Tests of the Control Policy or Procedure | Existence or occurrence | Completeness | Rights and obligations | Valuation or allocation | Presentation and disclosure |
|---|---|---|---|---|---|---|
| Segregate duties over purchases and custody of inventories | Observe and make inquiries about the performance of various functions | X | X | X | X | |
| Use prenumbered requisitions, purchase orders, and receiving reports and account for the sequence of documents | Observe and make inquiries about the use of prenumbered documents and inspect evidence of accounting for the sequence | | X | | | |
| Establish procedures for authorizing purchase transactions, reconciling purchase invoices to purchase orders and receiving reports, and verifying the clerical accuracy of purchase invoices | Observe and make inquiries about purchase procedures, and test a sample of purchase transactions by inspecting evidence of authorizations and reconciliations, comparing the details to authorized purchase orders and receiving reports, and recomputing the invoice amounts | X | | X | X | |
| Establish general ledger control of inventories of raw materials, goods in process, and finished goods and periodically reconcile to production records | Inspect accounting and production records and selected reconciliations | X | | X | X | X |
| Establish controls for the cost accounting system that accumulates appropriate inventory costs on a job order or process cost basis, such as independent reviews of cost accumulations | Inspect evidence of independent reviews of cost accumulations, recompute material costs by reference to requisitions and purchase invoices, direct labor costs by reference to time and payroll records, and overhead application rates | | | | X | |
| Analyze variances from standard costs | Inspect inventory reports and examine evidence of follow-up on variances | X | X | | X | |
| Use perpetual records to control inventories | Inquire about the perpetual inventory procedures, and test the records by reference to purchase invoices, receiving reports, and production records | X | X | | X | X |
| Use appropriate procedures for taking the physical inventory | Review the inventory instructions and observe the inventory | X | X | X | X | |
| Establish appropriate physical controls over inventories | Observe and inquire about the physical control policies and procedures | X | | X | | |

supplies. The valuation of goods on hand and in process often presents complex issues. For example, items such as precious gems, sophisticated electronic parts, and construction in progress present significant problems of identification and valuation.

## The Objectives of Substantive Tests for Inventories and Cost of Goods Sold

The audit *objectives* for substantive tests of inventories and cost of goods sold are to:

1.  Determine the *existence* of inventories.
2.  Establish the *completeness* of inventories.
3.  Establish that the client has *rights* to the recorded inventories.
4.  Establish the *clerical accuracy* of records and supporting schedules for inventories and cost of goods sold.
5.  Determine that the *valuation* of inventories and cost of goods sold is arrived at by appropriate methods.
6.  Determine that the *presentation and disclosure* of inventories and cost of goods sold is adequate, including disclosure of classifications of inventories, accounting methods, and any inventories pledged as collateral for loans.

In conjunction with the audit of inventories and cost of goods sold, the auditors will also obtain evidence about the related purchases, sales, purchase returns, and sales returns accounts.

Importance of Inventory Observation.    The responsibilities of independent auditors with respect to inventories can best be understood by considering the *McKesson & Robbins* fraud case. The hearings conducted by the SEC in 1939 disclosed that the audited financial statements of McKesson & Robbins, Inc., a drug company listed on the New York Stock Exchange, contained $19 million of fictitious assets, about one fourth of the total assets shown on the balance sheet. The fictitious assets included $10 million of nonexistent inventories. How was it possible for the independent auditors to have conducted an audit and to have issued an unqualified opinion without discovering this gigantic fraud?

The audit program followed for inventories in this case was in accordance with customary auditing practice of the 1930s. But, in that period it was customary to limit the audit work on inventories to an examination of records only; the standards of that era did not require any observation, physical count, or other actual contact with inventories. Up to the time of the *McKesson & Robbins* case, auditors had avoided taking responsibility for verifying the accuracy of inventory quantities and the physical existence of the goods. With questionable logic, many auditors had argued that they were experts in handling figures and analyzing accounting records but were not qualified to identify and measure the great variety of raw materials and manufactured goods found in the factories, warehouses, and storage buildings of their clients.

The *McKesson & Robbins* case brought a quick end to such limited views of the auditors' responsibilities. In 1939, *Statements on Auditing Procedures 1* and *2,* the first formal auditing standards issued by the AICPA, affirmed the importance of the auditors' observation of physical inventories, but authorized the substitution of other auditing procedures under certain circumstances. *SAS 1* (AU 331.09-.11), which recodified the previous series of *Statements on Auditing Procedures,* continues to distinguish between companies that determine inventory quantities solely by an annual physical count (**periodic inventory system**) and companies with well-kept perpetual inventory records. The latter companies often have strong internal control over inventories and may employ sampling techniques to verify the records by occasional test counts throughout the year rather than by a complete annual count of the entire inventory. For those clients the auditors' observation of physical inventory may be limited to such counts as they consider appropriate, and these counts may occur during or after the end of the period being audited.

## Substantive Tests for Inventories and Cost of Goods Sold

Figure 15-3 presents typical substantive tests used to meet the primary audit objectives for inventories and cost of goods sold. These procedures are described in detail in the following sections.

**Figure 15-3**   Objectives of Major Substantive Tests of Inventories and Cost of Goods Sold

| Substantive Tests | Primary Audit Objectives |
|---|---|
| Obtain listings of inventory and reconcile to ledgers | Clerical accuracy |
| Evaluate the client's planning of physical inventory and plan observation<br><br>Observe the taking of the physical inventory<br><br>Confirm inventories in public warehouses and on consignment | Existence or occurrence; Completeness; Rights; and Valuation or allocation |
| Review the year-end cutoff of purchases and sales transactions | Existence or occurrence; Rights; and Completeness |
| Obtain a copy of the completed physical inventory and test its accuracy | Existence or occurrence; Completeness; Clerical accuracy; and Valuation or allocation |
| Test inventory pricing | Valuation or allocation |
| Perform analytical procedures | Existence or occurrence; Completeness; Rights; and Valuation or allocation |
| Determine whether any inventories have been pledged and review commitments | Valuation or allocation; Presentation and disclosure |
| Evaluate financial statement presentation and disclosure | Presentation and disclosure |

## Obtain Listings of Inventory

| Primary Audit Objective: |
| :--- |
| Clerical accuracy ☑ |

The auditors will obtain a schedule of listings of inventory that will be reconciled to both the general ledger and appropriate subsidiary ledgers. The nature of the listings will vary depending upon whether the client engages in manufacturing or simply sells products at retail. The auditors' goal in performing this step is to make certain that the inventory records agree with what is recorded in the financial statements.

## Evaluate Client's Planning of Physical Inventory and Plan Observation

| Primary Audit Objectives: |
| :--- |
| Existence ☑ |
| Completeness ☑ |
| Rights ☑ |
| Valuation ☑ |

Efficient and effective inventory taking requires careful advance planning. Cooperation between the auditors and client personnel in formulating the procedures to be followed will prevent unnecessary confusion and will aid in securing a complete and well-controlled count. A first step is the designation by the client management of an individual employee, often a representative of the controller, to assume responsibility for the physical inventory. This responsibility will begin with the drafting of procedures and will carry through to the final determination of the dollar value of all inventories.

In planning the physical inventory, the client should consider many factors, such as *(a)* selecting the best date or dates, *(b)* suspending production in certain departments of the plant, *(c)* segregating obsolete and defective goods, *(d)* establishing control over the counting process through the use of inventory tags or sheets, *(e)* achieving proper cutoff of sales and purchase transactions, and *(f)* arranging for services of engineers or other specialists to determine the quantity or quality of certain goods or materials.

Once the plan has been developed, it must be documented and communicated in the form of written instructions to the personnel taking the physical inventory. These instructions normally will be drafted by the client and reviewed by the auditors, who will judge their adequacy. In evaluating the adequacy of the instructions, the auditors should consider the nature and materiality of the inventories, as well as the existing internal control. Normally, the auditors will insist that the inventory be taken at or near the balance sheet date. However, if the client has an effective internal control structure, including perpetual records, the auditors may be satisfied to observe inventory counts performed during the year. If the client plans to use a statistical sampling technique to estimate the quantities of inventories, the auditors will evaluate the statistical validity of the sampling method and the propriety of the sampling risk and the allowance for sampling risk.

Advance planning by the senior auditor-in-charge is also necessary to ensure efficient use of audit staff members during the inventory taking. The auditor-in-charge should ascertain the dates of the counts, the extent of the test counts, the need for client assistance, the number of auditors needed at each location, and the estimated time required. When multiple locations are involved, the auditors must determine whether the assessed levels of inherent and control risk may justify omission of observation at certain locations. When only certain locations are to be observed, the auditors should consider not informing the client of the specific locations in advance. In addition, the observation should be planned in a manner so as to ensure that client employees are not aware of the exact nature of all items that are test-counted by the auditors.

---

**♦ ILLUSTRATIVE CASE ♦**

In 1992 it was reported that audits of Phar-Mor Inc., a discount drugstore chain, did not detect a $50 million overstatement of inventory. The allegedly fraudulent overstatements occurred at stores at which the client knew in advance the CPAs did not intend to observe inventory counts. The client refrained from making fraudulent adjustments at the stores where it knew that the inventories would be observed by the CPAs. In another case, auditors are reported to have permitted company officials to follow them and record where test counts of inventory were taken; the managers subsequently falsified counts for inventory items that weren't test counted by the auditors.

---

Advance planning may also reveal to the auditors a need to rely upon the advice of a **specialist** for discharging their responsibility for testing inventory. For example, the auditors of a retail jeweler might engage an independent expert in gems to assist in identifying the precious stones and metals included in the client's inventory. Similarly, the auditors of a chemical producer might rely upon the expert opinion of an independent chemist as to the identity of components of the client's inventories. Guidelines for using the work of a specialist are presented in Chapter 6.

When written instructions are prepared by the auditing firm for the use of its staff in a particular engagement, these instructions are not made available to the client. Their purpose is to help ensure that all auditors understand their assignments and can therefore work efficiently during the physical inventory—Figure 15–4 provides an example of such instructions.

## Observe the Physical Inventory Count

| Primary Audit Objectives: |
| --- |
| Existence ☑ |
| Completeness ☑ |
| Rights ☑ |
| Valuation ☑ |

It is not the auditors' function to *take* the inventory or to control or supervise the taking; this is the responsibility of management. The auditors' responsibility is to *observe* the inventory taking. However, to observe the inventory taking implies a much more active role than that of a mere spectator. **Observation** by the auditors includes determining that all usable inventory owned by the client is included in the count and that the client's employees comply with the written inventory instructions. As part of the process of observing the physical inventory, the auditors will be alert to inclusion of any obsolete or damaged merchandise in inventory. Excessive dust or rust on raw materials inventory items may be indicative of obsolescence or infrequent sale. Such merchandise should be segregated by the client and written down to its net realizable value.

---

**♦ ILLUSTRATIVE CASE ♦**

During their observation of the repair parts inventory on the first audit of an automotive agency client, the auditors noticed a large number of new fenders of a design and shape not used on the current model cars. Examination of perpetual inventory records revealed that only one of this type of fender had been sold during the past two years. The automobile dealer agreed that few, if any, of this model of fender would ever be sold and readily agreed with the auditors' suggestions that the fenders be valued at their scrap value.

---

**Figure 15–4**

### MCDONALD AND COMPANY
*Certified Public Accountants*

Glen Haven Department Stores, Inc.
Inventory Observation–Instructions for Audit Staff
August 1, 199X

We will observe physical inventory taking at the following stores of Glen Haven Department Stores, Inc., on August 5, 199X.

| Store | Store Manager | Our Staff |
|-------|---------------|-----------|
| Wilshire | J. M. Baker | John Rodgers, Faye Arnold |
| Crenshaw | Roberta Bryan | Weldon Simpkins |
| Valley | Hugh Remington | Roger Dawson |

Report to assigned stores promptly at 8:00 a.m. Attached are copies of the company's detailed instructions to employees who are to take the physical inventories and to supervisors who are to be in charge. These instructions appear to be complete and adequate; we should satisfy ourselves by observation that the instructions are being followed.

All merchandise counted will be listed on prenumbered inventory sheets. We should make test counts of approximately 5 percent of the stock items to ascertain the accuracy of the physical counts. A majority of the counts should be performed on the high-value stock, as described on the enclosed listing. Test counts are to be recorded in working papers, with the following information included:

> Department number
> Inventory sheet number
> Stock number
> Description of item
> Quantity
> Selling price per price tag

We should ascertain that adequate control is maintained over the prenumbered inventory sheets issued. Also, we should prepare a listing of the last numbers used for transfers, markdowns, and markups in the various departments and stores. Inventory sheets are not to be removed from the departments until we have "cleared" them; we should not delay this operation.

Each staff member's working papers should include an opinion on the adequacy of the inventory taking. The papers should also include a summary of time incurred in the observation.

No cash or other cutoff procedures are to be performed as an adjunct to the inventory observation.

During the inventory observation, the auditors are alert for, and follow up on, any unusual problems not anticipated in the client's written inventory instructions or improperly dealt with by the client's inventory teams.

The auditors will also *record the serial number of the final receiving and shipping documents issued before the taking of inventory* so that the accuracy of the cutoff can be determined at a later date. Shipments or receipts of goods taking place during the counting process should be closely observed and any necessary reconciliations made. Observation of the physical inventory by the auditors also stresses determining that the client is controlling the inventory tags or sheets properly. These should be prenumbered so that all tags or sheets can be accounted for.

During the inventory observation, the auditors will make test counts of selected inventory items. The extent of the test counts will vary widely, depending upon levels of inherent risk and control risk, and the materiality of the client's inventory. A representative number of test counts should be recorded in the audit working papers for subsequent comparison with the completed inventory listing.

Serially numbered inventory count tags are usually attached to each lot of goods during the taking of a physical inventory. The design of the tag and the procedures for using it are intended to guard against two common pitfalls: *(a)* accidental omission of goods from the count and *(b)* double counting of goods.

Many companies use two-employee teams to count the inventories. Each team is charged with a sequence of the serially numbered tags and is required to turn in to the physical inventory supervisor any voided or unused tags.

The actual counting, the filling in of inventory tags, and the pulling of these tags are done by the client's employees. While the inventory tags are still attached to the goods, the auditors may make such test counts as they deem appropriate in the circumstances. The auditors will list in their working papers the tag numbers for which test counts were made. The client employees will ordinarily not collect (pull) the inventory tags until the auditors indicate that they are satisfied with the accuracy of the count.

In comparing their test counts to the inventory tags, the auditors are alert for errors not only in quantities but also in part numbers, descriptions, units of measure, and all other aspects of the inventory item. For test counts of goods in process inventory, the auditors must ascertain that the percentage or stage of completion indicated on the inventory tag is appropriate.

If the test counts made by the auditors indicate discrepancies, the goods are recounted at once by the client's employees and the error corrected. If an excessive number of errors is found, the inventory for the entire department or even for the entire company should be recounted.

The information listed on the inventory tags often is transferred by the client to serially numbered inventory sheets. These sheets are used in pricing the inventory and in summarizing the dollar amounts involved. After the inventory tags have been collected, the client employee supervising the inventory will determine that all tags are accounted for by serial number. The auditors should ascertain that numerical control is maintained over both inventory tags and inventory sheets.

Clients using computer equipment may facilitate inventory counting and summarizing through machine-readable inventory tags. Prior to the physical inventory, the tags may be encoded with tag numbers, part numbers, descriptions, and unit prices. After the physical inventory, the information from the tags is entered into the computer, which extends quantity times unit price for each inventory item and prints out a complete inventory summary.

The test counts and tag numbers listed by the auditors in their working papers will be traced later to the client's inventory summary sheets. A discrepancy will be regarded not as an error in counting but as a mistake in copying data from the tags, a purposeful alteration of a tag, or creation of a fictitious tag.

---

**♦ ILLUSTRATIVE CASE ♦**

The auditors of Cenco Incorporated did not adequately review the control of physical inventory tags, even though their CPA firm's procedures required such a review. According to the SEC (Accounting and Auditing Enforcement Release No. 1, par. 4552), Cenco personnel altered quantities on the final inventory computer listings and created bogus inventory tags; the result was a $39 million overstatement of inventory with a reported value of $119 million. The auditors ignored several indications of the inventory overstatement, including numerous differences between the client's inventory computer listings and the auditors' test counts, lack of vendor invoices to support the purchase of quantities of certain inventory items reported to be on hand, and unusual adjustments of perpetual records to physical counts.

---

During the observation of physical inventories, the auditors should make inquiries to ascertain whether any of the materials or goods on hand are the property of others, such as goods held on **consignment** or customer-owned materials sent in for machine work or other processing.

Audit procedures applicable to goods held by the client on consignment may include a comparison of the physical inventory with the client's records of consigned goods on hand, review of contracts and correspondence with consignors, and direct written communication with the consignors to confirm the quantity and value of goods held at the balance sheet date and to disclose any client liability for unremitted sales proceeds or from inability to collect consignment accounts receivable.

Working papers will be prepared by each auditor participating in the observation of the inventory. These papers should indicate the extent of test counts, describe any deficiencies noted, and express a conclusion as to whether the physical inventory appeared to have been properly taken in accordance with the client's instructions. The auditor-in-charge should prepare a concise summary memorandum indicating the overall extent of observation and the percentage of inventory value covered by quantity tests. The memorandum may also include comments on the consideration given to the factors of quality and condition of stock, the treatment of consigned goods on hand, and the control of shipments and receipts during the counting process. Figure 15–5 illustrates this type of memorandum.

# Figure 15–5

THE WILSHIRE CORPORATION
Comments on Observation of Physical Inventory                D9

December 31, 199X

1. Advance Planning of Physical Inventory.

   A physical inventory was taken by the client on December 31, 199X. Two weeks in advance of this date we reviewed the written inventory instructions prepared by L. D. Frome, Controller. These instructions appeared entirely adequate and reflected the experience gained during the counts of previous years. The plan called for a complete closing down of the factory on December 31, since the preceding year's count had been handicapped by movements of productive material during the counting process. Training meetings were conducted by Frome for all employees assigned to participate in the inventory; at these meetings the written instructions were explained and discussed.

2. Observation of Physical Inventory.

   We were present throughout the taking of physical inventory on December 31, 199X. Prior to the count, all materials had been neatly arranged, labeled, and separated by type. Two-employee inventory teams were used: one employee counting and calling quantities and descriptions; the other employee filling in data on the serially numbered inventory tags. As the goods were counted, the counting team tore off the "first count" portion of the inventory tag. A second count was made later by another team working independently of the first; this second team recorded the quantity of its count on the "second count" portion of the tag.
   We made test counts of the numerous items, covering approximately 60 percent of the total inventory value. These counts were recorded on our working papers and used as noted below. Our observation throughout the plant indicated that both the first and second counts required by the inventory instructions were being performed in a systematic and conscientious manner. The careful and alert attitude of employees indicated that the training meetings preceding the count had been quite effective in creating an understanding of the importance of an accurate count. Before the "second count" portions of the tags were removed, we visited all departments in the company with Frome and satisfied ourselves that all goods had been tagged and counted.
   No goods were shipped on December 31. We ascertained that receiving reports were prepared on all goods taken into the receiving department on this day. We recorded the serial numbers of the last receiving report and the last shipping advice for the year 199X. (See D-9-1.) We compared the quantities per the count with perpetual inventory records and found no significant discrepancies.

3. Quality and Condition of Materials.

   Certain obsolete parts had been removed from stock prior to the count and reduced to a scrap carrying value. On the basis of our personal observation and questions addressed to supervisors, we have no reason to believe that any obsolete or defective materials remained in inventory. During the course of inventory observation, we tested the reasonableness of quantities of 10 items, representing the 40 percent of the value of the inventory, by comparing the quantity on hand with the quantity used in recent months; in no case did we find that the quantity in inventory exceeded three months' normal usage.

*U.M.H.*
*Jan. 3, 9X*

## Confirm Inventories in Public Warehouses and on Consignment

| Primary Audit Objectives: | |
|---|---|
| Existence | ☑ |
| Completeness | ☑ |
| Rights | ☑ |
| Valuation | ☑ |

The examination of warehouse receipts is not sufficient verification of goods stored in public warehouses. The AICPA has recommended direct confirmation in writing from outside custodians of inventories, and supplementary procedures when the amounts involved represent a significant proportion of the current assets or of the total assets of a concern. These supplementary procedures include review of the client's procedures for investigating prospective warehouses and evaluating the performance of warehouses having custody of the client's goods. The auditors should also consider obtaining accountants' reports on the warehouses' internal controls relevant to custody of stored goods. If the amounts are quite material, or if any reason for doubt exists, the auditors may decide to visit the warehouses and observe a physical inventory of the client's merchandise stored at the warehouses.

The verification of goods in the hands of consignees may conveniently be begun by obtaining from the client a list of all consignees and copies of the consignment contracts. Contract provisions concerning the payment of freight and other handling charges, the extension of credit, computation of commissions, and frequency of reports and remittances require close attention. After review of the contracts and the client's records of consignment shipments and collections, the auditors should communicate directly with the consignees and obtain full written information on consigned inventory, receivables, unremitted proceeds, and accrued expenses and commissions as of the balance sheet date.

Often, the client may own raw materials that are processed by a subcontractor before being used in the client's production process. The auditors should request the subcontractor to confirm quantities and descriptions of client-owned materials in the subcontractor's possession.

## Review Purchases and Sales Cutoffs

| Primary Audit Objectives: | |
|---|---|
| Existence | ☑ |
| Completeness | ☑ |
| Rights | ☑ |

An accurate cutoff of purchases is one of the most important factors in verifying the existence and completeness of the year-end inventory. Assume that a shipment of goods costing $10,000 is received from a supplier on December 31, but the vendor's invoice does not arrive until January 2 and is entered as a January transaction. If the goods are included in the December 31 physical inventory but there is no December entry to record the purchase and the liability, the result will be an overstatement of both net income for the year and retained earnings and an understatement of accounts payable, each error being in the full amount of $10,000 (ignoring income taxes).

Regardless of whether goods are on hand as of year-end, if title has passed to the client at the balance sheet date, that merchandise should be included in the client's year-end inventory. Title to the merchandise generally passes based on the terms of shipment. If merchandise is shipped "FOB Shipping Point," title to the goods passes when the merchandise is shipped by the vendor; this merchandise is often referred to as "Merchandise in Transit." If merchandise is shipped "FOB Destination," title to the goods passes when the merchandise is received.

As an illustration, assume that a vendor's invoice is received on December 31, indicating that merchandise was shipped to the client as of December 30. Furthermore, the merchandise covered by the invoice is not received until January 3. Whether the invoice and inventory should be recorded at year-end depends upon the shipping terms. If the merchandise was shipped "FOB Shipping Point," title has passed as of year-end and the liability to the supplier and the increase in inventory should be recorded in December; if the merchandise was shipped "FOB Destination," title has not passed as of year-end and the entry should be recorded in January.

How can the auditors determine that year-end purchases and their related liabilities to suppliers has been properly recorded? Their approach is to *examine on a test basis the vendors' invoices and receiving reports for several days before and after the inventory date*. Each vendor's invoice in the files should have a receiving report attached; if an invoice recorded in late December is accompanied by a receiving report dated December 31 or earlier, the goods must have been on hand and included in the year-end physical inventory and represent proper year-end purchases. However, if the receiving report carried a January date, the potential for error is high in that the goods were not included in the physical count made on December 31. When inventory accounts are adjusted to a physical count total, the potential for understating income and inventory exists in that the liability may be established as of year-end, but the inventory account does not reflect the purchase since it is established at the physical count total. The auditors then must consider the shipping terms to determine the period in which the transaction should properly be reported and that both inventory and accounts payable are properly stated.

A supplementary approach to the matching of vendors' invoices and receiving reports is to examine the records of the receiving department. For each shipment received near the year-end, the auditors should determine that the related vendor's invoice was recorded in the proper period.

Chapter 12 includes a discussion of the audit procedures for determining the accuracy of the sales cutoff. The sales cutoff is mentioned again at this point to emphasize its importance in determining the fairness of the client's inventory and cost of goods sold as well as accounts receivable and sales.

## Test Accuracy of Physical Inventory

| Primary Audit Objectives: |
| --- |
| Existence ☑ |
| Completeness ☑ |
| Clerical accuracy ☑ |
| Valuation ☑ |

The testing of extensions and footings on the final inventory listing may disclose misstatements of physical inventories. Often this test consists of "sight-footing" to the nearest hundred dollars or thousand dollars of the inventory listings. Generalized audit software may also be used to test extensions and footings.

In testing extensions, the auditors should be alert for two sources of substantial errors—misplaced decimal points and incorrect extension of *count* units by *price* units. For example, an inventory listing that extends 1,000 units times $1C (per hundred) as $1,000 will be overstated by $990. An inventory extension of 500 sheets of steel times $1 per pound will be substantially understated because each sheet of steel weighs much more than one pound.

The auditors also should trace to the completed physical inventory their test counts made during the observation of physical inventory. During this tracing, the auditors should be alert for any indications that inventory tags have been altered or that fictitious inventory tags have been created. The auditors also reconcile inventory tag number sequences in the physical inventory listing to tag numbers noted in their audit working papers for the inventory observation. This procedure is designed to determine that the client has not omitted inventory items from the listing, or included additional items that were not present during the physical inventory.

Another test of the clerical accuracy of the completed physical inventory is the reconciliation of the physical counts to inventory records. Both the quantities and the values of the items should be compared to the company's perpetual records. The totals of various types of inventory should also be compared with the corresponding control accounts. All substantial discrepancies should be investigated fully.

## Test Inventory Pricing

| Primary Audit Objective: |
| --- |
| Valuation    ☑ |

The auditors are responsible for determining that the bases and methods of pricing inventory result in a valuation in accordance with generally accepted accounting principles. As indicated earlier, a variety of pricing methods are generally acceptable.

The testing of costs applied to inventories of raw materials, purchased parts, and supplies by a manufacturing company is similar to the testing of costs of merchandise in a trading business. The costs are verified by reference to vendor invoices. Figure 15–6 illustrates a working paper prepared by an auditor in making price tests.

When auditing the pricing of goods in process and finished goods, the auditors make reference to the client's cost accounting records of accumulated direct materials, direct labor, and manufacturing overhead costs. When a standard cost system is used, the auditors test whether variances have been properly allocated between inventory accounts and costs of goods sold.

The auditors must recognize that a variety of methods are generally accepted for the application of manufacturing overhead to inventories. A predetermined rate of factory overhead applied on the basis of machine-hours, direct labor dollars, direct labor-hours, or some similar basis is used by many manufacturing companies. The auditors will ordinarily insist that any significant amount of under- or overabsorbed overhead be applied proportionately to the amounts of inventory and cost of goods sold.

A distinction between factory overhead, on the one hand, and selling and general administration costs, on the other, must be made under generally accepted accounting principles because the latter costs are expensed in the period incurred. The difference in the accounting treatment accorded to factory overhead and to nonmanufacturing costs implies a fundamental difference between these two types of cost. Nevertheless, as a practical matter it is often impossible to say with finality the exact proportions of a particular expenditure, such as the salary of a vice president in charge of production, that should be classified as factory overhead as contrasted to general and administrative expense. Despite this difficulty, a vital procedure in the audit of cost of goods sold for a manufacturing concern is determining that factory overhead costs are reasonably allocated in the accounts.

Failure to distribute factory costs to the correct accounts can cause significant distortions in the client's predetermined overhead rate and in under- or overapplied factory overhead. The auditors may find it necessary to obtain or prepare analyses of a number of the factory overhead subsidiary ledger accounts and to verify the propriety of the charges to them. Then, the auditors must determine that the propriety of the total machine-hours,

## Figure 15–6   Test of Inventory Pricing

```
                              The Wilshire Corporation
                   Test of Pricing - Raw Materials and Purchased Parts
                              December 31, 199X                              D-5
```

| Part No. | Description | Per Inventory Quantity/Price | Per Vendor's Invoice | | | | |
|---|---|---|---|---|---|---|---|
| | | | Vendor | Date | No. | Quantity @ Price | |
| 8Z 182 | Aluminum 48 x 144 x .025 | 910 sheets @ 10.10 | Hardy & Co. | Dec. 18, 9X | 5415 | 1000 @ 10.10 | ✓ |
| 8Z 195 | Aluminum 45/72 x .032 | 804 sheets @ 9.01 | Watson Mfg. Co. | Nov. 28, 9X | 3201 | 500 @ 9.01 | ✓ |
| | | | | Dec. 22, 9X | 3456 | 400 @ 9.01 | ✓ |
| K1125 | Stainless steel .025 x 23 | 80,625 lbs @ .80 | Ajax Steel Co. | Dec. 3, 9X | K182 | 100,000 @ .80 | ✓ |
| K1382 | Stainless steel .031 x 17 | 65,212 lbs @ .82 | Ajax Steel Co. | Dec. 3, 9X | K182 | 75,000 @ .82 | ✓ |
| XL3925 | 10 H.P. Electronic Motor | 50 units @ 400.00. | Cronyn Mfg. Co. | Nov. 18, 9X | D2532 | 100 @ 400.00 | ✓ |
| XJ3824 | 3/4 H.P. Electronic Motor | 645 units @ 30.50 | Long & Co. | Dec. 29, 9X | E9215 | 650/30.50 | ✓ |

Inventory value of raw materials and purchased parts selected for price testing—$301,825.56

Percent of total raw materials and purchased parts selected for price testing $301,825.56/$503,615.10 = 60%

See audit program B-4 for method of selecting raw materials and purchased parts for price testing.

✓ = agreed to prices on the vendor's invoice.

*Conclusion:*

*Based on our tests, the pricing of raw materials and purchased parts is materially correct.*

*CMB*
*1/4/9X*

direct labor-hours, or other aggregate allocation base used by the client company to determine the factory overhead rate.

## Perform Analytical Procedures

Primary Audit Objectives:

| | |
|---|---|
| Existence | ☑ |
| Completeness | ☑ |
| Rights | ☑ |
| Valuation | ☑ |

Material misstatements of inventory may be disclosed by analytical procedures designed to establish the general reasonableness of inventory figures. For example, major increases or decreases in the various types of inventory as compared to prior-year amounts may be identified and investigated. Also, scanning perpetual inventory records may reveal slow-moving items.

In certain lines of business, particularly retail and wholesale companies, gross profit margins may be quite uniform from year to year. Any major difference between the ending inventory estimated by the gross profit percentage method and the count of inventory at year-end should be investigated fully.

Another useful test is the computation of rates of inventory turnover (preferably by individual product) based on the relationship between the cost of goods sold for the year and the average inventory as shown on the monthly financial statements. These turnover rates may be compared with rates prevailing in prior years. A decreasing rate of turnover suggests the possibility of obsolescence or of unnecessarily large amounts of inventories. Alternatively, they may simply reflect deliberate stockpiling in anticipation of higher prices or shortages of certain strategic materials.

The auditors' analytical procedures for inventory transactions will often include a comparison of the volume of transactions from period to period. Comparisons of transactions, classified by vendor and type of product, may reveal unusual variations of quantities purchased, or unusual concentrations of purchases with particular vendors, indicating that a possible conflict of interest may be identified.

The auditors also should scan all general ledger accounts relating to costs of goods sold to make certain that they contain no apparent misstatements, for example, an error such as closing miscellaneous revenue and expense into the costs of goods sold.

The auditors of a manufacturer client should obtain from the client or prepare an analysis of costs of goods sold by month, broken down into raw materials, direct labor, and factory overhead elements. The analysis should also include a description of all unusual and nonrecurring charges or credits to costs of goods sold. These cost analyses may be compared to various production statistics, such as direct labor-hours and machine-hours.

## Identify Pledged Inventory and Review Commitments

| Primary Audit Objectives: |
|---|
| Valuation ☑ |
| Presentation ☑ |

The verification of inventories includes a determination by the auditors as to whether any goods have been *pledged* or subjected to a lien of any kind. Pledging of inventories to secure bank loans may be discovered when cash and indebtedness are confirmed.

A record of outstanding **purchase commitments** is usually readily available, since this information is essential to management in maintaining day-to-day control of the company's inventory position and cash flow. If either the price or the quantity of commitments seems excessive, the auditors should seek full information. Commitments at excessive prices may result in losses that should be reflected in the financial statements. Financial statement disclosure of all material purchase commitments is required.

**Sales commitments** are indicated by the client's backlog of unfilled sales orders. If estimated total costs to produce the goods ordered exceed fixed selling prices, the indicated loss and a related liability should be recorded in the client's financial statements for the current period.

## Evaluate Disclosures

| Primary Audit Objective: |
|---|
| Presentation ☑ |

One of the most important factors in proper presentation of inventories in the financial statements is disclosure of the inventory pricing method or methods in use. Other important disclosures include the following:

1. Changes in methods of valuing inventory, with the dollar effect and justification for the change reported, in accordance with APB *Opinion No. 20*.
2. The various classifications of inventory, such as finished goods, work in process, and raw materials.

3. The details of any arrangements relating to any pledged inventory.
4. Deduction of valuation allowance for inventory losses.
5. Existence and terms of inventory purchase commitments.

The auditors will review the client's disclosures of such matters to determine whether they comply with generally accepted accounting principles.

## Problems Associated with Inventory of First-Year Audit Clients

The need for the auditors to be present to observe the taking of the ending inventory has been strongly emphasized in auditing literature. However, the figure for beginning inventory is equally significant in determining the cost of goods sold and the net income for the year. In an initial audit of a client, the auditors may not have been present to observe the taking of inventory at the beginning of the year. What procedures can they follow to obtain evidence that the beginning inventories are fairly stated?

The first factor to consider is whether the client was audited by another CPA firm for the preceding year. If a review of the predecessor firm's working paper indicates compliance with generally accepted auditing standards, the new auditors can accept the beginning inventories with a minimum of investigation. That minimum might include the following steps: *(a)* study of the inventory valuation methods used; *(b)* inspection of the inventory records; *(c)* inspection of the inventory sheets used in taking the preceding year's physical inventory; and *(d)* comparison of the beginning and ending inventories, broken down by product classification.

If there has been no satisfactory audit for the preceding year, the investigation of the beginning inventories will include not only the procedures mentioned above but steps such as the following: *(a)* discussion with the person in the client's organization who supervised the physical inventory at the preceding balance sheet date; *(b)* study of the written instructions used in planning the inventory; *(c)* tracing of numerous items from the inventory tags or count sheets to the final summary sheets; *(d)* tests of the perpetual inventory records for the preceding period by reference to supporting documents for receipts and withdrawals; and *(e)* tests of the overall reasonableness of the beginning inventories in relation to sales, gross profit, and rate of inventory turnover. An investigation along these lines will sometimes give the auditors assurance that the beginning inventory was carefully compiled and reasonable in amount; however, in most cases, these procedures will not provide sufficient evidence about the validity of the beginning inventory figure. In these latter cases, the auditors will not be able to issue an unqualified opinion *as to the statements of income and cash flows.* They may be able, however, to give an unqualified opinion on the *balance sheet,* since this financial statement does not reflect the beginning inventories.

# AUDITING THE PAYROLL CYCLE

## Internal Control over the Payroll Cycle

The payroll in many companies is the largest operating cost, and therefore deserves the close attention of management as well as the auditors. In the past, payroll frauds were common and often substantial. Today, however, such frauds may be more difficult to conceal for several reasons: (1) extensive segregation of duties relating to payroll; (2) the use of computers, with proper controls, for preparation of payrolls, and (3) the necessity of filing frequent reports to the government, listing employees' earnings and tax with-holdings.

The establishment of strong internal control over payroll remains important for several reasons. Although payroll frauds are less frequent today, the possibility of large-scale payroll fraud still exists. Such frauds may involve listing fictitious persons on the payroll, overpaying employees, and continuing employees on the payroll after their separation from the company. A second reason for emphasizing internal control over payrolls is that a great mass of detailed information concerning hours worked and rates of pay must be processed quickly and accurately if workers are to be paid promptly and without error. Good employee relations demand that paychecks be ready on time and be free from error. As pointed out in previous chapters, internal control is a means of securing accuracy and dependability in accounting data as well as a means of preventing fraud.

Still another reason for emphasizing the importance of internal control over payrolls is the existence of various payroll tax and income tax laws which require that certain payroll records be maintained and that payroll data be reported to the employee and to govern-mental agencies. Complete and accurate records of time worked are also necessary if a company is to protect itself against lawsuits under the Fair Labor Standards Act.

To control payroll costs means to avoid waste and to obtain efficient production from the dollars expended for services of employees. As a means of establishing control over payroll costs, many companies delegate to department heads and other supervisors re-sponsibility for the control of costs in their respective units of the business. Budgets are prepared using estimates of departmental labor costs for the coming period. As the year progresses and actual labor costs are compiled, the controller submits monthly reports to top management comparing the budgeted labor costs and the actual labor costs for each department. The effectiveness of this control procedure will depend largely upon the extent to which top management utilizes these reports and takes action upon variances from the budget.

Most important of all internal controls over payroll is the division of payroll work among several departments of the company. Payroll activities include the functions of (1) employment (personnel), (2) timekeeping, (3) payroll preparation and recordkeeping, and (4) distribution of pay to employees. For effective internal control, each of these functions should be handled by a separate department of the company. These several phases of payroll activities will now be considered individually.

Employment (Personnel).   The first significant step in building strong internal control over payrolls should be taken by the personnel department when a new employee is hired. At this point, the authorized rate of pay should be entered on a pay-rate record. The employee also should sign a payroll deduction authorization specifying any amounts to be withheld and a withholding tax exemption certificate. These records should be kept in the personnel department, but a notice of the hiring of the new employee, the rate of pay, and the payroll deductions should be sent to the payroll department. When a computer is used, this information will be keyed into an employee payroll master file. The personnel de-partment, the payroll department, or data processing will enter the data into the computer system.

Under no circumstances should a name be added to the payroll without having received the formal authorization notice from the personnel department. When an employee's rate of pay is changed, the new rate should be entered on the pay-rate record (often computerized) that is maintained in the personnel department. An authorization for the new rate should be sent to the payroll department before the change can be made effective on the payroll. Upon termination of an employee, notice of termination should be sent from the personnel department to the payroll department. The work of the payroll department and the propriety of names and pay raises used in preparing the payroll, therefore, rest upon formal documents or computer input originating outside the payroll department.

Adequate internal control demands that the addition and removal of names from the company payroll, as well as rate changes and reclassification of employees, be evidenced by written approval of an executive in the personnel department and by the head of the operating department concerned. To permit the payroll department to initiate changes in pay rates, or to add names to the payroll without formal authorization from the personnel department, increases the likelihood of fraud.

Timekeeping.    The function of timekeeping consists of determining the number of hours (or units of production) for which each employee is to be paid. The use of electronic time-recording equipment is of considerable aid in establishing adequate internal control over the timekeeping function. In addition, supervisors should maintain contact with subordinates and prepare time reports summarizing the use of labor.

Internal control can be improved by the practice of regular comparison of the time reports prepared by timekeepers or supervisors with time clock records showing arrival and departure times of employees. If pay is based on piecework, a comparison may be made between the reports of units produced and the quantities that are added to the perpetual inventory records.

Salaried employees receiving a fixed monthly or weekly salary may not be required to use time clocks. Some companies require salaried employees to fill out a weekly or semimonthly report indicating the time devoted to various activities. If a salaried employee is absent, the department head usually has authority to decide whether a pay reduction should be made.

Payroll Preparation and Recordkeeping.    In a manual system, the payroll department has the responsibility for computing the amounts to be paid to employees and for preparing all payroll records. It is imperative that the payroll department *not* perform the related functions of timekeeping, employment, or distribution of pay to employees. The output of the payroll department may be thought of as: (1) the payroll checks (or pay envelopes, if wages are paid in cash); (2) individual employee statements of earnings and deductions; (3) a payroll journal; (4) an employees' ledger, summarizing earnings and deductions for each employee; (5) a payroll distribution schedule, showing the allocation of payroll costs to direct labor, overhead, and various departmental expense accounts; and (6) quarterly and annual reports to the government showing employees' earnings and taxes withheld. If the client utilizes a centralized computer, many of these functions may be delegated to data processing as illustrated by Figure 15–7, a partial computerized payroll processing system.

Figure 15-7   Summarized Computer Batch Processing System

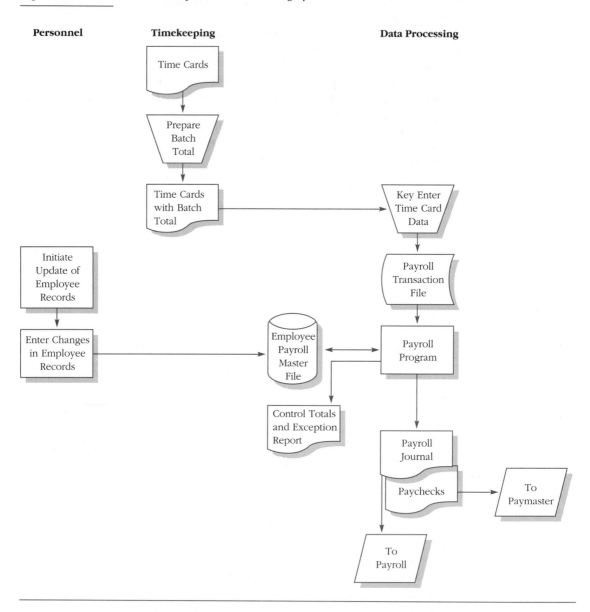

In a computerized system the payroll is calculated by the computer using the work hours reported by the timekeeping department and the authorized pay rates and payroll deductions reported by the personnel department. In addition to preparing the payroll journal, the payroll department prepares the payroll checks or the pay envelopes, if wages are paid in cash. Checks are then forwarded to the treasurer for signature.

Regardless of the system used, the auditors should expect the client's system to include such basic records as time cards, payroll journals, labor distributions, and employee earnings records. In a computerized system some or all of these documents may exist only in computer-readable form.

Distributing Paychecks or Cash.   The distribution of paychecks or pay envelopes to employees should be the task of the paymaster, an individual who performs no other payroll activity. If pay is deposited directly into employee bank accounts, controls over that process are necessary, such as authorization of deposits by personnel in the treasurer's department.

If employees are paid in cash, the paymaster will use a copy of the payroll journal and the information on the payroll envelopes (both prepared by the payroll department) to fill the payroll envelopes with cash. The paymaster will require proof of identity when distributing checks or cash to employees and require them to sign a receipt for any cash received. All checks or pay envelopes for an absent employee should be retained and neither returned to the payroll department nor turned over to another employee for delivery.

Most companies that pay employees by check use a special payroll bank account. A voucher for the entire amount of the weekly payroll may be prepared in the general accounting department based on the payroll summary prepared in the payroll department. This voucher is sent to the treasurer, who issues a check on the general bank account for the amount of the payroll. The check is deposited in the special payroll bank account and checks to individual employees are drawn on this account. It also is the practice of some companies to require dual signatures on large checks and to have printed on the check a statement that this type of check is not valid if issued for an amount in excess of a specified dollar amount.

If wages are paid in cash, any unclaimed wages should be deposited in the bank and credited to a special liability account. Subsequent disbursement of these funds to employees then will be controlled by the necessity of drawing a check and preparing supporting documents. The dangers inherent in permitting unclaimed pay envelopes to be retained by the paymaster, returned to the payroll clerk, or intermingled with petty cash are apparent.

# Obtaining and Documenting an Understanding of the Internal Control Structure for the Payroll Cycle

An understanding of the three elements of the internal control structure as they relate to payroll transactions will allow the auditors to plan an effective examination of payroll transactions and accounts.

Control Environment.   Several aspects of the client's control environment are particularly significant to the control of payroll transactions. For example, the auditors will consider whether the organizational structure of the company supports an independent personnel function.

A system of budgeting is also important for controlling payroll transactions, as are the personnel policies and procedures of the company. Effective personnel policies and procedures help ensure that the employees involved in the various payroll functions are competent to handle their job responsibilities. In addition, the internal auditors often devote a significant amount of time to auditing payroll activities, because of the concern with compliance with the many laws and regulations that apply to this area.

### Accounting System and Control Procedures.

The auditors' understanding of the payroll cycle encompasses a consideration of the employment, timekeeping, payroll preparation and recording, and payroll distribution functions. The auditors typically document the payroll cycle with a flowchart or internal control questionnaire. Matters that are generally considered include the following: Are employees paid by check? Is a payroll bank account maintained on an imprest basis? Are the activities of timekeeping, payroll compilation, payroll check signing, and paycheck distribution performed by separate departments or employees? Are all operations involved in the preparation of payrolls subjected to independent verification before the paychecks are distributed? Are employee time reports approved by supervisors? Is the payroll bank account reconciled monthly by an employee having no other payroll duties?

## Testing Controls and Assessing Control Risk for Payroll Cycle Accounts

As in the audit of other transaction cycles, the auditors' tests of controls for the payroll cycle will be organized around the financial statement assertions about the payroll accounts.

### Existence or Occurrence.

Since the direction of tests of the existence or occurrence assertion is primarily from recorded entries to source documents, the auditors often will vouch payroll transactions to appropriate time cards, time sheets, and other source documents. When pay is deposited directly into employee bank accounts, the auditors may compare records of the transfer to source documents in which the employee authorizes such direct deposit. In these circumstances, the employee will usually have provided the client with written authorization, including a sample deposit slip for the account involved. The auditors will also test the effectiveness of the client's segregation of functions by observing performance of the functions and by making appropriate inquiries of client personnel.

### Completeness.

Tests of controls for the assertion of completeness of payroll transactions involve inspection of the accounting for the numerical sequence of time cards, payroll checks, and other payroll source documents. In a computerized system, the auditors may examine reconciliations of various item counts, control totals, and hash totals.

### Rights and Obligations.

As they relate to rights and obligations, the auditors' tests will focus on the validity of payroll transactions. The auditors often will trace the amounts of various transactions to authorizations, including those required by the board of directors.

Valuation or Allocation.   Controls over the valuation of payroll transactions included as product costs will be tested in conjunction with the auditors' tests of controls over the conversion cycle. Valuation of payroll transactions not directly associated with the conversion cycle represents a lesser audit concern in that these labor costs are reflected in the income statement at their actual cost. Still, auditors may test the controls that ensure the accuracy of payroll rates, hours worked, and the clerical accuracy of payroll records.

Presentation and Disclosure.   Controls over presentation and disclosure of payroll transactions include those over the allocation of payroll costs to various functions. Accordingly, the auditors will test the client's procedures for controlling payroll cost distribution. For example, if payroll distribution reports are reviewed by an accounting executive, the auditors might test the control by inspecting evidence of the executive's review. The auditors' tests may also focus on the client's procedure for developing financial statement disclosures about pension, stock option, and executive bonus plans.

Figure 15–8 summarizes the relationships among the assertions, the internal control policies and procedures, and typical tests of controls for the payroll cycle.

## Substantive Tests for Payroll Accounts

The auditors may perform substantive tests of payroll such as the following:

1. Perform analytical procedures to test the reasonableness of payroll expense; for example, develop an expectation about the amount of payroll expense by multiplying the amount of one pay period by the number of pay periods in the year.
2. Investigate any extraordinary fluctuations in salaries, wages, and commissions.
3. Obtain or prepare a summary of compensation of officers for the year and trace to contracts, minutes of directors' meetings, or other authorization.
4. Test computations of compensation earned under profit-sharing or bonus plans.
5. Test commission earnings by examination of contracts and detailed supporting records.
6. Test pension obligations by reference to authorized pension plans and to supporting records.

Figure 15–9 relates the procedures to their primary audit objectives.

In addition to the above procedures, the auditors may plan a surprise observation of a regular distribution of paychecks to employees. The auditors' objective in observing the distribution of checks or cash to employees on a regular payday is to determine that every name on the company payroll is that of a bona fide employee presently on the job. This audit procedure is especially desirable if the various phases of payroll work are not sufficiently segregated by departments to afford good internal control. The history of payroll frauds shows that permitting one person to have custody of employment records, time cards, paychecks, and employees' earnings records has often led to the entering of fictitious names on the payroll, and to other irregularities, such as use of excessive pay rates and continuance of pay after the termination of an employee. When performing this procedure the auditors first will determine that they have possession of all the checks or envelopes comprising the payroll. They will then accompany representatives of the client

Figure 15–8   Assessing Control Risk for the Payroll Cycle

| Internal Control Policy or Procedure | Typical Tests of the Control Policy or Procedure | Existence or occurrence | Completeness | Rights and obligations | Valuation or allocation | Presentation and disclosure |
|---|---|---|---|---|---|---|
| Segregate payroll duties of employment, timekeeping, recordkeeping, and distributing checks | Observe and make inquiries about the performance of various functions. | X | X | X | X | |
| Require appropriate support for payroll check preparation | Vouch from payroll journal to time cards and other source documents | X | | | X | |
| Time cards are approved by appropriate personnel | Trace time shown on payroll register to time cards and time reports approved by supervisors | X | | | | |
| Use prenumbered payroll checks and account for sequence | Examine payroll checks and account for sequence | | X | | | |
| Reconciliation of payroll accounts monthly by an employee who is otherwise independent of the payroll process | Observe and make inquiries about the reconciliation process and inspect reconciliations | X | X | X | X | |
| Review and verify individual employee payroll calculations | Determine basis of deductions from payroll and compare with records of deductions authorized by employees | X | X | | X | |
| Review overall payroll calculations and distributions | Test extensions and footings of payroll, and inspect evidence of review | X | X | | X | X |
| Balance details of individual disbursements with totals posted to appropriate general ledger account distributions and total payroll disbursement | Select one or more payrolls, recompute totals, and compare to ledger postings | X | X | X | X | |
| Use budgets and analyze variance from actual amounts | Examine budgets and evidence of follow-up on variances | X | X | X | X | X |

Figure 15–9   Objectives of Major Substantive Tests of Payrolls

| Substantive Tests | Primary Audit Objectives |
| --- | --- |
| Perform analytical procedures<br><br>Investigate fluctuations in salaries, wages, and commissions<br><br>Obtain a summary of amounts of officers' compensation and trace to authorization | Existence or occurrence; Completeness; and Valuation |
| Test computations of compensation under profit-sharing or bonus plans<br><br>Test commission earnings<br><br>Test pension obligations | Valuation |

around the plant as all the checks or envelopes are distributed to employees. It is essential that the auditors establish the identity of each employee receiving payment.

# ◆ CHAPTER SUMMARY

This chapter described details of the conversion and payroll cycles, the auditors' consideration of the internal control for these cycles, and the auditors' substantive procedures for inventory and payroll accounts. To summarize:

1.  Effective internal control over the conversion cycle requires appropriate policies and procedures for purchasing, receiving and issuing supplies and materials, producing and shipping products, and cost accounting. A perpetual inventory system is also important.

2.  The primary internal control over the payroll cycle includes separation of the functions of employment, timekeeping, payroll preparation and recordkeeping, and the distribution of pay to employees.

3.  The auditors' understanding of the internal controls over the conversion and payroll cycles will allow them to design appropriate substantive tests of inventory, cost of goods sold accounts, and various payroll costs.

4.  In the audit of inventories, auditors are primarily concerned about the existence assertion, that is, the possibility of overstatement of year-end balances. Therefore, a primary substantive test for inventory accounts is observation of the client's physical inventory. Other substantive procedures include price tests of the valuation of inventory items, cutoff tests, analytical procedures, and tests of the financial statement presentation and disclosure.

5.  Substantive tests of payroll cycle accounts address the overall reasonableness of payroll costs and the proper allocation of these costs to the functional areas of manufacturing, selling, and administration. In addition, tests must be performed on the allocation of manufacturing costs to work in process, finished goods, and cost of goods sold.

## ◆ KEY TERMS INTRODUCED OR EMPHASIZED IN CHAPTER 15

**Bill of lading**   A shipping document acknowledging items shipped (e.g., number of cartons), freight amount, weight, and so on. A bill of lading is required for common carriers and is essentially a shipping contract. A bill of lading may be prepared by either the company shipping goods or by a common carrier.

**Consignment**   A transfer of goods from the owner to another person who acts as the sales agent of the owner.

**Cost Accounting Standards Board**   A five-member board established by Congress to narrow the available options in cost accounting under generally accepted accounting principles. Companies having significant supply contracts with certain U.S. government agencies are subject to the cost accounting standards established by the board.

**Observation**   The auditors' evidence-gathering technique of viewing a client activity to obtain physical evidence of performance.

**Periodic inventory system**   A method of accounting in which inventories are determined solely by means of a physical inventory at the end of the accounting period.

**Perpetual inventory system**   A method of accounting for inventories in which control accounts and subsidiary ledgers are maintained to record receipts and issuances of goods in quantities, and often also in dollar amounts. The accuracy of perpetual inventory records is tested periodically by physical inventories.

**Purchase commitment**   A contractual obligation to purchase goods at fixed prices, entered into well in advance of scheduled delivery dates.

**Receiving report**   A report normally filled out by the receiving department which specifies the quantity and quality of materials and parts received.

**Routing sheet**   A schedule that accompanies a specific job through the production process, and specifies the processes required for the job.

**Sales commitment**   A contractual obligation to sell goods at fixed prices, entered into well in advance of scheduled delivery dates.

**Shipping document**   A document that may either be a formal bill of lading when a carrier is involved, or a less formal internal document indicating the items being shipped to a customer.

**Specialist**   A person possessing special skill or knowledge in a field other than accounting or auditing, such as an appraiser.

**Vendor's invoice**   A document received from the supplier containing information about the goods purchased, including formal notice to the purchaser about the terms of payment. Also, sometimes referred to as a ''purchase invoice'' or a ''supplier's invoice.'' When considering the revenue cycle, this document is referred to as the ''sales invoice.''

## ◆ GROUP I: REVIEW QUESTIONS

15-1   Many auditors consider the substantiation of the figure for inventory to be a more difficult and challenging task than the verification of most other items on the balance sheet. List several specific factors that support this view.

15-2   The client's cost accounting system is often an important part of an audit of the financial statements of a manufacturing company. For what purposes do the auditors consider the cost accounting system?

15-3 What part, if any, do the independent auditors play in the planning for a client's physical inventory?

15-4 What are the purposes of the auditors' observation of the taking of the physical inventory? (Do not discuss the procedures or techniques involved in making the observation.)

15-5 For what purposes do the auditors make and record test counts of inventory quantities during their observation of the taking of the physical inventory? Discuss.

15-6 Once the auditors have completed their test counts of the physical inventory, will they have any reason to make later reference to the inventory tags used by the client's employees in the counting process? Explain.

15-7 When perpetual inventory records are maintained, is it necessary for a physical inventory to be taken at the balance sheet date? Explain.

15-8 What charges and credits may be disclosed in the auditors' analysis of the Cost of Goods Sold account of a manufacturing concern?

15-9 A client company wishes to conduct its physical inventory on a sampling basis. Many items will not be counted. Under what general conditions will this method of taking inventory be acceptable to the auditors?

15-10 ''A well-prepared balance sheet usually includes a statement that the inventories are valued at cost.'' Evaluate this quotation.

15-11 Darnell Equipment Company uses the LIFO method of valuation for part of its inventories and weighted-average cost for another portion. Would you be willing to issue an unqualified opinion under these circumstances? Explain.

15-12 ''If the auditors can determine that all goods in the physical inventory have been accurately counted and properly priced, they will have discharged fully their responsibility with respect to inventory.'' Evaluate this statement.

15-13 How do the independent auditors consider the client's backlog of unfilled sales orders in the examination of inventories?

15-14 The controller of a new client company informs you that most of the inventories are stored in bonded public warehouses. He presents warehouse receipts to account for the inventories. Will careful examination of these warehouse receipts constitute adequate verification of these inventories? Explain.

15-15 On October 1, Hana Ranch Company, which has never been audited, is asked by its bank to arrange for a year-end audit. The company retains you to make this audit and asks what measures, if any, it should take to ensure a satisfactory year-end physical inventory. Perpetual inventories are not maintained. How would you answer this inquiry?

15-16 Enumerate specific steps to be taken by the auditors to ascertain that a client's inventories have not been pledged or subjected to a lien of any kind.

15-17 What division of duties among independent departments is desirable to achieve maximum internal control over payrolls?

15-18 What specific procedures are suggested by the phrase ''test of controls over payroll transactions''?

15-19 What safeguards should be employed when the inaccessibility of banking facilities makes it desirable to pay employees in cash?

15-20 You are asked by a client to outline the procedures you would recommend for handling of unclaimed wages. What procedures do you recommend?

# ◆ GROUP II: QUESTIONS REQUIRING ANALYSIS

15-21    You are engaged in the audit of Reed Company, a new client, at the end of its first fiscal year, June 30, 19X1. During your work on inventories, you discover that all of the merchandise remaining in stock on June 30, 19X1, had been acquired July 1, 19X0, from Andrew Reed, the sole shareholder and president of Reed Company, for an original selling price of $10,000 cash and a note payable due July 1, 19X3, with interest at 15 percent, in the amount of $90,000. The merchandise had been used by the president when he operated a similar business as a sole proprietor. How can you verify the pricing of the June 30, 19X1, inventory of Reed Company? Explain.

15-22    The observation of a client's physical inventory is a mandatory auditing procedure when possible for the auditors to carry out and when inventories are material.

*Required:*    a.    Why is the observation of physical inventory a mandatory auditing procedure? Explain.
              b.    Under what circumstances is observation of physical inventory impossible?
              c.    Why is the auditors' review of the client's control of inventory tags important during the observation of physical inventory? Explain.

15-23    You have been asked to audit the financial statements of Wilson Corporation, a roadbuilding contractor that has not previously been audited. During your interim work, you learn that Wilson excludes a significant inventory item from its annual balance sheet. This inventory item, which Wilson management claims is approximately the same amount each year, is gravel that has been processed for use in road building and is placed at different road construction sites wherever it might be used. Wilson's controller states that any unused gravel at the completion of a construction contract is never moved to another job site; in fact, the gravel often disappears because of thefts during winter months when road construction is suspended.

         Would you be able to issue an unqualified opinion on the financial statements of Wilson Corporation? Explain.

15-24    Grandview Manufacturing Company employs standard costs in its cost accounting system. List the audit procedures that you would apply to ascertain that Grandview's standard costs and related variance amounts are acceptable and have not distorted the financial statements. (Confine your audit procedures to those applicable to raw materials.)

15-25    At the beginning of your annual audit of Crestview Manufacturing Company's financial statements for the year ended December 31, 199X, the company president confides in you that Henry Ward, an employee, is living on a scale in excess of that which his salary would support.

         The employee has been a buyer in the purchasing department for six years and has charge of purchasing all general materials and supplies. He is authorized to sign purchase orders for amounts up to $500. Purchase orders in excess of $500 require the countersignature of the general purchasing agent.

         The president understands that the usual audit of financial statements is not designed, and cannot be relied upon, to disclose fraud or conflicts of interest, although their discovery may result. The president authorizes you, however, to expand your regular audit procedures and to apply additional audit procedures to determine whether there is any evidence that the buyer has been misappropriating company funds or has been engaged in activities that were conflicts of interest.

*Required:*    List the audit procedures you would apply to the company records and documents in an attempt to discover evidence within the purchasing department of defalcations being committed by the buyer. Give the purpose of each audit procedure.

(AICPA, adapted)

15-26    A number of companies employ outside service companies that specialize in counting, pricing, extending, and footing inventories. These service companies usually furnish a certificate attesting to the value of the physical inventory.

Assuming that the service company took the client company's inventory on the balance sheet date:

    *a.* How much reliance, if any, can the auditors place on the inventory certificate of outside specialists? Discuss.

    *b.* What effect, if any, would the inventory certificate of outside specialists have upon the type of report the auditors would render? Discuss.

    *c.* What reference, if any, would the auditors make to the certificate of outside specialists in their audit report?

(AICPA, adapted)

15-27    Santa Rosa Corporation is a closely held furniture manufacturing company employing approximately 1,000 employees. On December 15, the corporation retained the firm of Warren and Wood, Certified Public Accountants, to perform a December 31 year-end audit. The president of the corporation explained that perpetual inventory records were maintained and that every attention was given to maintaining strong internal control. A complete count of inventories had been made at November 30 by the company's own employees; in addition, extensive test counts had been made in most departments at various intervals during the year. Although the company was not large, it employed an internal auditor and an assistant who had devoted their full time to analysis of internal control and appraisal of operations in the various organizational units of the company.

The certified public accountant who had audited Santa Rosa Corporation for several years had died during the current year, and the company had decided to forgo an annual audit. The physical inventory had therefore been taken at November 30 without being observed by an independent public accountant. Shortly thereafter, a major stockholder in the company had demanded that new auditors be retained. The president explained to Warren and Wood that the company was too far behind on its delivery schedules to take time out for another physical inventory, but that all the documentation used in the recent count were available for their review. The auditors reviewed the documentation, made a thorough analysis of the internal controls over inventory, and made test counts at December 31 of large items representing 10 percent of the total value of inventory. The items tested were traced to the perpetual inventory records, and no significant discrepancies were found. Inventories at December 31 amounted to $4 million out of total assets of $9 million.

*Required:*    Assume that the auditors find no shortcomings in any aspect of the audit apart from the area of inventories. You are to prepare:

    *a.* An argument setting forth the factors that indicate the issuance of an unqualified audit opinion.

    *b.* An opposing argument setting forth the factors that indicate the auditors should not issue an unqualified opinion.

15-28    One of the problems faced by the auditors in their verification of inventory is the possibility that slow-moving and obsolete items may be included in the goods on hand at the balance sheet date. In the event that such items are identified in the physical inventory, their carrying value should be written down to an estimated scrap value or other recoverable amount.

Prepare a list of the auditing procedures that the auditors should employ to determine whether slow-moving or obsolete items are included in the physical inventory.

15-29    During your observation of the November 30, 199X, physical inventory of Jay Company, you note the following unusual items:

    *a.* Electric motors in the finished goods storeroom not tagged. Upon inquiry, you are informed that the motors are on consignment to Jay Company.

b.  A cutting machine (one of Jay's principal products) in the receiving department, with a large REWORK tag attached.

c.  A crated cutting machine in the shipping department, addressed to a nearby U.S. naval base, with a Department of Defense "Material Inspection and Receiving Report" attached, dated November 30, 199X, and signed by the Navy Source Inspector.

d.  A small, isolated storeroom with five types of dusty raw materials stored therein. Inventory tags are attached to all of the materials, and your test counts agree with the tags.

*Required:*  What additional procedures, if any, would you carry out for each of the above? Explain.

15-30  Ace Corporation does not conduct a complete annual physical count of purchased parts and supplies in its principal warehouse, but uses statistical sampling instead to estimate the year-end inventory. Ace maintains a perpetual inventory record of parts and supplies and believes that statistical sampling is highly effective in determining inventory values and is sufficiently reliable to make a physical count of each item of inventory unnecessary.

*Required:*  a.  Identify the audit procedures that should be used by the independent auditor that change or are in addition to normal required audit procedures when a client utilizes statistical sampling to determine inventory value and does not conduct a 100 percent annual physical count of inventory items.

b.  List at least 10 normal audit procedures that should be performed *to verify physical quantities* whenever a client conducts a periodic physical count of all or part of its inventory.

(AICPA, adapted)

15-31  Nolan Manufacturing Company retains you on April 1 to perform an audit for the fiscal year ending June 30. During the month of May, you make extensive studies of internal control over inventories.

All goods purchased pass through a receiving department under the direction of the chief purchasing agent. The duties of the receiving department are to unpack, count, and inspect the goods. The quantity received is compared with the quantity shown on the receiving department's copy of the purchase order. If there is no discrepancy, the purchase order is stamped "OK— Receiving Dept." and forwarded to the accounts payable section of the accounting department. Any discrepancies in quantity or variations from specifications are called to the attention of the buyer by returning the purchase order with an explanation of the circumstances. No records are maintained in the receiving department, and no reports originate there.

As soon as goods have been inspected and counted in the receiving department, they are sent to the factory production area and stored alongside the machines in which they are to be processed. Finished goods are moved from the assembly line to a storeroom in the custody of a stock clerk, who maintains a perpetual inventory record in terms of physical units, but not in dollars.

What weaknesses, if any, do you see in the internal control over inventories?

15-32  Select the best answer for each of the following and explain fully the reason for your selection.

a.  Instead of taking a physical inventory count on the balance sheet date the client may take physical counts prior to the year-end if internal control structure policies and procedures are adequate and:

(1)  Computerized records of perpetual inventory are maintained.

(2)  Inventory is slow-moving.

(3)  EDP error reports are generated for missing prenumbered inventory tickets.

(4)  Obsolete inventory items are segregated and excluded.

b.  The auditor's analytical procedures will be facilitated if the client:

(1)  Uses a standard cost system that produces variance reports.

(2)  Segregates obsolete inventory before the physical inventory count.

      (3)   Corrects material weaknesses in internal control before the beginning of the audit.

      (4)   Reduces inventory balances to the lower of cost or market.

*c.*   When perpetual inventory records are maintained in quantities and in dollars, and internal control over inventory is weak, the auditor would probably:

      (1)   Want the client to schedule the physical inventory count at the end of the year.

      (2)   Insist that the client perform physical counts of inventory items several times during the year.

      (3)   Increase the extent of tests for unrecorded liabilities at the end of the year.

      (4)   Have to disclaim an opinion on the income statement for that year.

*d.*   Which of the following is the best audit procedure for the discovery of damaged merchandise in a client's ending inventory?

      (1)   Compare the physical quantities of slow-moving items with corresponding quantities of the prior year.

      (2)   Observe merchandise and raw materials during the client's physical inventory taking.

      (3)   Review the management's inventory representations letter for accuracy.

      (4)   Test overall fairness of inventory values by comparing the company's turnover ratio with the industry average.

*e.*   McPherson Corp. does not make an annual physical count of year-end inventories, but instead makes weekly test counts on the basis of a statistical plan. During the year, Sara Mullins, CPA, observes such counts as she deems necessary and is able to satisfy herself as to the reliability of the client's procedures. In reporting on the results of her audit, Mullins:

      (1)   Can issue an unqualified opinion without disclosing that she did not observe year-end inventories.

      (2)   Must comment in the scope paragraph as to her inability to observe year-end inventories, but can nevertheless issue an unqualified opinion.

      (3)   Is required, if the inventories were material, to disclaim an opinion on the financial statements taken as a whole.

      (4)   Must, if the inventories were material, qualify her opinion.

*f.*   The primary objective of a CPA's observation of a client's physical inventory count is to:

      (1)   Discover whether a client has counted a particular inventory item or group of items.

      (2)   Obtain direct knowledge that the inventory exists and has been properly counted.

      (3)   Provide an appraisal of the quality of the merchandise on hand on the day of the physical count.

      (4)   Allow the auditor to supervise the conduct of the count so as to obtain assurance that inventory quantities are reasonably accurate.

                                                                  (AICPA, adapted)

# ◆ GROUP III: PROBLEMS

15-33   You have been engaged by the management of Alden, Inc. to review its internal controls over the purchase, receipt, storage, and issue of raw materials. You have prepared the following comments, which describe Alden's procedures.

      (1)   Raw materials, which consist mainly of high-cost electronic components, are kept in a locked storeroom. Storeroom personnel include a supervisor and four clerks. All are well trained, competent, and adequately bonded. Raw materials are removed from the storeroom only upon written or oral authorization of one of the production first-line supervisors.

      (2)   There are no perpetual inventory records; hence, the storeroom clerks do not keep records of goods received or issued. To compensate for the lack of perpetual records, a physical

inventory count is taken monthly by the storeroom clerks, who are well supervised. Appropriate procedures are followed in making the inventory count.

(3) After the physical count, the storeroom supervisor matches quantities counted against a predetermined reorder level. If the count for a given part is below the reorder level, the supervisor enters the part number on a materials requisition list and sends this list to the accounts payable clerk. The accounts payable clerk prepares a purchase order for a predetermined reorder quantity for each part and mails the purchase order to the vendor from whom the part was last purchased.

(4) When ordered materials arrive at Alden, they are received by the storeroom clerks. The clerks count the merchandise and agree the counts to the carrier's bill of lading. All bills of lading are initialed, dated, and filed in the storeroom to serve as receiving reports.

*Required:*  Describe the weaknesses in internal control and recommend improvements of Alden's procedures for the purchase, receipt, storage, and issuance of raw materials. Organize your answer sheet as follows:

| *Weaknesses* | *Recommended Improvements* |
| --- | --- |
|  |  |

(AICPA, adapted)

15-34   The following are typical questions that might appear on an internal control questionnaire for inventory:

1.  Are written procedures prepared by the client for the taking of the physical inventory?
2.  Do the client's inventory-taking procedures include a requirement to identify damaged inventory items?
3.  Does the client maintain perpetual inventory records?

*Required:*  *a.*  Describe the purpose of each of the above internal control procedures.

*b.*  Describe the manner in which each of the above procedures might be tested.

*c.*  Assuming that the operating effectiveness of each of the above procedures is found to be inadequate, describe how the auditors might alter their substantive tests to compensate for the increased level of control risk.

15-35   David Anderson, CPA, is engaged in the audit of the financial statements of Redondo Manufacturing Corporation for the year ended June 30, 199X. Redondo's inventories at year-end include finished merchandise on consignment with consignees and finished merchandise stored in public warehouses. The merchandise in public warehouses is pledged as collateral for outstanding debt.

*Required:*  Normal inventory and notes payable auditing procedures have been satisfactorily completed. Describe the specific additional auditing procedures that Anderson should undertake with respect to:

*a.*  Consignments out.

*b.*  Finished merchandise in public warehouses pledged as collateral for outstanding debt.

(AICPA, adapted)

15-36   You are an audit manager of the rapidly growing CPA firm of Raye and Coye. You have been placed in charge of three new audit clients, which have the following inventory features:

1.  Canyon Cattle Co., which maintains 15,000 head of cattle on a 1,000 square mile ranch, mostly unfenced, near the south rim of the Grand Canyon in Arizona.

2. Rhoads Mfg. Co., which has raw materials inventories consisting principally of pig iron loaded on gondola freight cars on a siding at the company's plant.

3. Strawser Company, which is in production around the clock on three shifts, and which cannot shut down production during the physical inventory.

*Required:* What problems do you anticipate in the observation of physical inventories of the three new clients, and how would you deal with the problems?

15-37   Royal Meat Processing Company buys and processes livestock for sale to supermarkets. In connection with the audit of the company's financial statements, you have prepared the following notes based on your review of inventory procedures:

1. Each livestock buyer submits a daily report of his or her purchases to the plant superintendent. This report shows the dates of purchase and expected delivery, the vendor and the number, and weights and type of livestock purchased. As shipments are received, any available plant employee counts the number of each type received and places a check mark beside this quantity on the buyer's report. When all shipments listed on the report have been received, the report is returned to the buyer.

2. Vendors' invoices, after a clerical review, are sent to the appropriate buyer for approval and returned to the accounting department. A disbursement voucher and a check for the approved amount are prepared in the accounting department. Checks are forwarded to the treasurer for signature. The treasurer's office sends signed checks directly to the buyer for delivery to the vendor.

3. Livestock carcasses are processed by lots. Each lot is assigned a number. At the end of each day a tally sheet reporting the lots processed, the number and type of animals in each lot, and the carcass weight is sent to the accounting department, where a perpetual inventory record of processed carcasses and their weights is maintained.

4. Processed carcasses are stored in a refrigerated cooler located in a small building adjacent to the employee parking lot. The cooler is locked when the plant is not open, and a company guard is on duty when the employees report for work and leave at the end of their shifts. Supermarket truck drivers wishing to pick up their orders have been instructed to contact someone in the plant if no one is in the cooler.

5. Substantial quantities of by-products are produced and stored, either in the cooler or elsewhere in the plant. By-products are initially accounted for as they are sold. At this time the sales manager prepares a two-part form: one copy serves as authorization to transfer the goods to the customer, and the other becomes the basis for billing the customer.

*Required:* For each of the numbered notes 1 to 5 above, state the weaknesses, if any, in the present inventory procedures and your suggestions, if any, for improvement.

(AICPA, adapted)

15-38   Payne Press Company is engaged in the manufacture of large presses under specific contracts and in accordance with customers' specifications. Customers are required to advance 25 percent of the contract price. The company records sales on a shipment basis and accumulates costs by job orders. The normal profit margin over the past few years has been approximately 5 percent of sales, after provision for selling and administrative expenses of about 10 percent of sales. Inventories are valued at the lower of cost or market.

Among the jobs you are reviewing in the course of your annual audit of the company's December 31 financial statements is Job No. 2357, calling for delivery of a three-color press at a firm contract price of $50,000. Costs accumulated for the job at the year-end aggregated $30,250. The company's engineers estimated that the job was approximately 55 percent complete at December 31. Your audit procedures have been as follows:

1. Examined all contracts, noting pertinent provisions.

2. Observed physical inventory of jobs in process and reconciled details to job order accounts.

3. Tested controls over input of labor, material, and overhead charges into the various jobs to determine that such charges were authentic and had been posted correctly.
4. Confirmed customers' advances at year-end.
5. Reconciled goods in process job ledger with control account.

*Required:* With respect to Job No. 2357:

    *a.* State what additional audit procedures, if any, you would follow and explain the purpose of the procedures.

    *b.* Indicate the manner and the amount at which you would include Job No. 2357 in the balance sheet.

(AICPA, adapted)

15-39 Late in December, your CPA firm accepted an audit engagement at Nash Jewelers, Inc., a corporation that deals largely in diamonds. The corporation has retail jewelry stores in several eastern cities and a diamond wholesale store in New York City. The wholesale store also sets the diamonds in rings and other quality jewelry.

The retail stores place orders for diamond jewelry with the wholesale store in New York City. A buyer employed by the wholesale store purchases diamonds in the New York diamond market; the wholesale store then fills orders from the retail stores and from independent customers and maintains a substantial inventory of diamonds. The corporation values its inventory by the specific identification cost method.

*Required:* Assume that at the inventory date you are satisfied that Nash Jewelers, Inc. has no items left by customers for repair or sale on consignment and that no inventory owned by the corporation is in the possession of outsiders.

    *a.* Discuss the problems the auditors should anticipate in planning for the observation of the physical inventory on this engagement because of the:

        (1) Different locations of inventories.

        (2) Nature of the inventory.

    *b.* Assume that a shipment of diamond rings was in transit by corporation messenger from the wholesale store to a retail store on the inventory date. What additional audit steps would you take to satisfy yourself as to the gems that were in transit from the wholesale store on the inventory date?

(AICPA, adapted)

15-40 Smith is the partner in charge of the audit of Blue Distributing Corporation, a wholesaler that owns one warehouse containing 80 percent of its inventory. Smith is reviewing the working papers that were prepared to support the firm's opinion on Blue's financial statements, and Smith wants to be certain essential audit records are well documented.

*Required:* What substantive tests should Smith expect to find in the working papers to document management's assertion about completeness as it relates to the inventory quantities at the end of the year?

(AICPA, adapted)

15-41 The following are typical questions that might appear on an internal control questionnaire for payroll procedures:

1. Is there adequate separation of duties between employees who maintain personnel records and employees who approve payroll disbursements?
2. Is there adequate separation of duties between personnel who maintain timekeeping or attendance records for employees and employers who distribute payroll checks?

*Required:* *a.* Describe the purpose of each of the above internal control procedures.

    *b.* Describe the manner in which each of the above procedures might be tested.

    *c.*   Assuming that the operating effectiveness of each of the above procedures is found to be inadequate, describe how the auditors might alter their substantive tests to compensate for the increased level of control risk.

15-42   In connection with an audit of the financial statements of Olympia Company, the auditors are reviewing procedures for accumulating direct labor-hours. They learn that all production is by job order and that all employees are paid hourly wages, with time and a half for overtime hours.

       Olympia's direct labor-hour input process for payroll and job-cost determination is summarized in the flowchart that is illustrated below. Steps A and C are performed in timekeeping, step B in the factory operating departments, step D in payroll audit and control, step E in data input, and step F in computer operations.

*Required:*   For each input processing step A through F:
    *a.*   List the possible errors or discrepancies that may occur.
    *b.*   Cite the corresponding control procedure that should be in effect for each error or discrepancy.
    *Note:* Your discussion of Olympia's procedures should be limited to the input for direct labor-hours, as shown in steps A through F in the flowchart. Do not discuss personnel procedures for hiring, promotion, termination, and pay-rate authorization. In step F do not discuss equipment, computer program, and general computer operational controls.

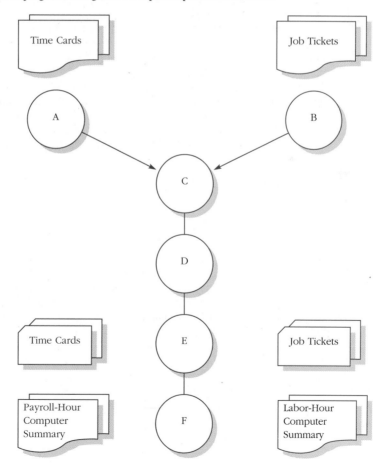

Organize your answer for each input-processing step as follows:

| Step | Possible Errors or Discrepancies | Control Procedures |
| --- | --- | --- |
| A | | |

(AICPA, adapted)

15-43  Rowe Manufacturing Company has about 50 production employees and uses the following payroll procedures.

The factory supervisor interviews applicants and on the basis of the interview either hires or rejects the applicants. After being employed, the applicant prepares a W-4 form (Employee's Withholding Exemption Certificate) and gives it to the supervisor. The supervisor writes the hourly rate of pay for the new employee in the corner of the W-4 form and then gives the form to a payroll clerk as notice that the applicant has been employed. The supervisor verbally advises the payroll department of pay-rate adjustments.

A supply of blank time cards is kept in a box near the entrance to the factory. Each employee takes a time card on Monday morning, signs it, and notes in pencil on the time card the daily arrival and departure times. At the end of the week, the employees drop the time cards in a box near the door to the factory.

The completed time cards are taken from the box on Monday morning by a payroll clerk. Two payroll clerks divide the cards alphabetically between them, one taking the A to L section of the payroll, and the other taking the M to Z section. Each clerk is fully responsible for one section of the payroll. The payroll clerks compute the gross pay, deductions, and net pay; post the details to the employees' earnings records; and prepare and number the payroll checks. Employees are automatically removed from the payroll when they fail to turn in time cards.

The payroll checks are manually signed by the chief accountant and given to the supervisor, who distributes the checks to the employees in the factory and arranges for the delivery of the checks to the employees who are absent. The payroll bank account is reconciled by the chief accountant, who also prepares the various quarterly and annual payroll tax reports.

*Required:*  List your suggestions for improving Rowe Manufacturing Company's system of internal control for factory hiring practices *and* payroll procedures.

(AICPA, adapted)

15-44  City Loan Company has 100 branch loan offices. Each office has a manager and four or five employees who are hired by the manager. Branch managers prepare the weekly payroll, including their own salaries, and pay employees from cash on hand. The employees sign the payroll sheet signifying receipt of their salary. Hours worked by hourly personnel are inserted in the payroll sheet from time reports prepared by the employees and approved by the manager.

The weekly payroll sheets are sent to the home office, along with other accounting statements and reports. The home office compiles employee earnings records and prepares all federal and state payroll tax returns from the weekly payroll sheets.

Salaries are established by home office job-evaluation schedules. Salary adjustments, promotions, and transfers of full-time employees are approved by a home office salary committee based upon the recommendations of branch managers and area supervisors. Branch managers advise the salary committee of new full-time employees and terminations. Part-time and temporary employees are hired without referral to the salary committee.

*Required:*  *a.*  How might funds for payroll be diverted in the above system?

*b.*  Prepare a payroll internal audit program to be used in the home office to audit the branch office payrolls of City Loan Company.

(AICPA, adapted)

15-45  The following "conditions" are excerpts from a report of an operational audit of a company's personnel department:

**Condition I:** The company's payroll is prepared by the personnel department.

**Condition II:** The firm's personnel manager is the proprietor's son, who has one year of experience in the personnel field.

**Condition III:** The distribution of payroll checks is made by the personnel department.

**Condition IV:** The personnel department makes a quarterly test of all personnel records to be assured that all required documentation is present.

**Condition V:** Personnel hiring is initiated by the personnel department only upon the receipt of a request from the user department. The request must be signed by the user department manager or assistant manager.

**Condition VI:** When documentation supporting a particular personnel action is received by the personnel department, a personnel clerk is assigned the task of making the appropriate changes on the file(s) affected. No one, at any time, is assigned the task of verifying that the entries are correctly transcribed.

The internal auditor is preparing a "recommendations" section for the report. The following controls are to be used: (1) competence and integrity of personnel, (2) segregation of incompatible functions, (3) execution of activities, (4) proper recording of events, (5) appropriate limitation of access to assets, and (6) comparison of existing records with records required. The internal auditor notes that one of the controls is addressed by each of the six conditions identified.

*Required:*  *a.*  Identify the control most directly addressed, using one policy or procedure per condition with no repeats.
*b.*  State whether or not that control is violated by the condition.
*c.*  If the control is violated, describe the possible consequences of any such violation.
*d.*  If the control is violated, prescribe one corrective action for any such violation.
Use the format shown below:

| Condition | a.<br>Control (1)–(6) | b.<br>Violated? | c.<br>Possible<br>Consequences | d.<br>Corrective<br>Action Needed |
|---|---|---|---|---|
| I | | | | |
| II | | | | |
| III | | | | |
| IV | | | | |
| V | | | | |
| VI | | | | |

(CIA, adapted)

---

## ◆ GROUP IV: RESEARCH AND DISCUSSION CASE

15-46  Western Trading Company is a sole proprietorship engaged in the grain brokerage business. At December 31, 199X, the entire grain inventory of the company was stored in outside bonded warehouses. The company's procedure of pricing inventories in these warehouses includes comparing the actual cost of each commodity in inventory with the market price as reported for transactions on the commodity exchanges at December 31. A write-down is made on commodities for which cost is in excess of market. During the course of the 199X audit, the auditors verified the company's computations. In addition to this, they compared the book value of the inventory with market prices at February 15, 199Y, the last day of field work. The auditors noted that the market price of several of the commodities had declined sharply subsequent to year-end, until their market price was significantly below the commodities' book values.

The inventory was repriced by the auditors on the basis of the new market price, and the book value of the inventory was found to be in excess of market value on February 15 by approximately $21,000. The auditors proposed that the inventories be written down by $17,000 to this new market value, net of gains on the subsequent sales. The management protested this suggestion, stating that in their opinion the market decline was only temporary and that prices would recover in the near future. They refused to allow the write-down to be made. Accordingly, the auditors qualified their audit opinion for a departure from generally accepted accounting principles.

*Required:*   *a.*   Were the auditors justified in issuing a qualified opinion in this situation? Discuss fully, including alternative courses of action.

       *b.*   State your opinion as to the course of action that was appropriate in this situation.

---

## ◆ SUGGESTED REFERENCES

AICPA, *Professional Standards, Volume 1,* Commerce Clearing House, *Statements on Auditing Standards 1,* Sections 560.01–.09.

FASB, *Professional Standards,* Commerce Clearing House, *Statements on Financial Accounting Standards,* Sections 4311.09–.19 and 5121.08–.10.

# 16

# AUDITING THE FINANCING CYCLE

## CHAPTER OBJECTIVES

After studying this chapter, you should be able to:

- Explain the nature of debt and equity transactions in the financing cycle.
- Identify and explain the fundamental internal control policies and procedures for debt and equity transactions.
- Describe the nature of debt and equity accounts.
- Identify the audit objectives for substantive tests of debt and equity accounts.
- Describe the nature of appropriate substantive audit procedures to accomplish the objectives for the audit of debt and equity accounts.

This chapter presents information on the financing cycle. Business corporations obtain substantial amounts of their financial resources by incurring interest-bearing debt and by issuing capital stock. The acquisition and repayment of capital is often referred to as the *financing cycle*. The financing cycle includes the sequence of procedures for authorizing, executing, and recording transactions that involve bank loans, mortgages, bonds payable, and capital stock, as well as the payment of interest and dividends. This chapter presents information on internal control, the auditor's consideration of internal control, and substantive tests first for the debt transactions and then for the equity transactions of the financing cycle.

# AUDITING DEBT TRANSACTIONS

## Internal Control over Interest-Bearing Debt

Essential for interest-bearing debt are controls over authorization, issuance, payment of interest, and repayment of the debt.

### Authorization by the Board of Directors.

Effective internal control over interest-bearing debt begins with proper authorization. The bylaws of a corporation usually require that borrowing be approved by the board of directors. The treasurer of the corporation will prepare a report on any proposed financing, explaining the need for funds, the estimated effect of borrowing upon future earnings, the estimated financial position of the company in comparison with others in the industry both before and after the borrowing, and alternative methods of raising the amount desired. Authorization by the board of directors will include review and approval of such matters as the choice of a bank or trustee, the type of security, registration with the SEC, agreements with investment bankers, compliance with requirements of the state of incorporation, and listing of bonds on a securities exchange. After the issuance of long-term debt, the board of directors should receive a report stating the net amount received and its disposition, as, for example, acquisition of plant assets, addition to working capital, or other purposes.

### Use of an Independent Trustee.

Bond issues are always for large amounts—usually many millions of dollars. Therefore, only relatively large companies issue bonds; small companies obtain long-term capital through mortgage loans or other sources. Any company large enough to issue bonds and able to find a ready market for the securities will almost always utilize the services of a large bank as an independent trustee.

The trustee is charged with the protection of the creditors' interests and must monitor the issuing company's compliance with the provisions of the indenture. The trustee also maintains detailed records of the names and addresses of the registered owners of the bonds, cancels old bond certificates and issues new ones when bonds change ownership, follows procedures to prevent overissuance of bond certificates, distributes interest payments, and distributes principal payments when the bonds mature. Use of an independent trustee largely solves the problem of internal control over bonds payable. Internal control is strengthened by the lack of trustee access to the issuing company's assets or accounting records, and by the financial institution's legal responsibility for its actions.

Interest Payments on Bonds and Notes Payable.   Many corporations assign the entire task of paying interest to the trustee for either *bearer bonds* or *registered bonds*. Highly effective control is then achieved, since the company will issue a single check for the full amount of the semiannual interest payment on the entire bond issue. In the case of bearer bonds (coupon bonds), upon receipt of this check the trustee will make payment for coupons presented, cancel the coupons, and file them numerically. A second count of the coupons is made at a later date; the coupons then are destroyed and a cremation certificate is delivered to the issuing company. The trustee does not attempt to maintain a list of the holders of coupon bonds, since these securities are transferable by the mere act of delivery. If certain coupons are not presented for payment, the trustee will hold the funds corresponding to such coupons for the length of time prescribed by statute. In the case of registered bonds, the trustee will maintain a current list of holders and will remit interest checks to them in the same manner as dividend checks are distributed to stockholders.

For a note payable, there generally is only one recipient of interest. Companies control that disbursement in the same manner as other cash disbursements, often not using a trustee.

## Obtaining and Documenting an Understanding of the Internal Control Structure for Debt Transactions

As for the other cycles, the auditor's understanding of the internal control structure of the financing cycle will include analysis of the control environment, the accounting system, and the control procedures. Because of the limited number of transactions involved, and the existence of third parties in the transactions, the auditors' documentation of the internal control structure will frequently be limited to a written description, as well as an internal control questionnaire. For both debt and equity transactions the working papers will document the client's procedures for authorizing, executing, and recording transactions.

The internal control questionnaire for interest-bearing debt will typically include questions such as the following: Are amounts of new interest-bearing debt authorized by appropriate management? Is an independent trustee used for all bond issues? Does a company official monitor compliance with debt provisions?

## Testing Controls and Assessing Control Risk for Debt Transactions

Interest-bearing debt accounts are often affected by a small number of large dollar entries during each year. As a result, auditors often choose to assess control risk at or near the maximum level, and perform substantive tests on the transactions. In the infrequent circumstance in which an adequate number of transactions occurs to justify tests of controls, the nature of the transactions and the controls involved will determine the types of tests to be performed. For example, the auditors might test the client's controls for monitoring compliance with debt convenants.

## Designing Substantive Tests of Interest-Bearing Debt

Long-term debt usually is substantial in amount and often extends for periods of 10 years or more. **Debentures,** secured bonds, and notes payable (sometimes secured by mortgages or trust deeds) are the principal types of long-term debt. Debentures are backed only by the general credit of the issuing corporation and not by liens on specific assets. Since in most respects debentures have the characteristics of other corporate bonds, we shall use the term *bonds* to include both *debentures* and secured bonds payable.

The formal document creating bond indebtedness is called the **indenture** or **trust indenture.** When creditors supply capital on a long-term basis, they often insist upon placing certain restrictions on the borrowing company. For example, the indenture often includes a restrictive covenant that prohibits the company from declaring dividends unless the amount of working capital is maintained above a specified amount. The acquisition of plant and equipment, or the increasing of managerial salaries, may be permitted only if the current ratio is maintained at a specified level and if net income reaches a designated amount. If these restrictions are violated, the indenture may provide that the entire debt is due on demand. Another device for protecting the long-term creditor is the requirement of a **sinking fund** or redemption fund to be held by a trustee.

## Objectives of Substantive Tests of Interest-Bearing Debt

The audit *objectives* for substantive tests of interest-bearing debt are to:

1. Determine the *existence* of recorded interest-bearing debt.
2. Establish the *completeness* of recorded interest-bearing debt.
3. Determine that the client has *obligations* to pay the recorded interest-bearing debt.
4. Establish the *clerical accuracy* of schedules of interest-bearing debt.
5. Determine that the *valuation* of interest-bearing debt is in accordance with generally accepted accounting principles.
6. Determine that the *presentation* and *disclosure* of interest-bearing debt are appropriate, including disclosure of the major provisions of loan agreements.

In conjunction with the audit of interest-bearing debt, the auditors will also obtain evidence about interest expense, interest payable, and bond discount and premium.

Many of the principles related to accounts payable also apply to the audit of interest-bearing debt. As is the case for accounts payable, the understatement of debt is considered to be a major potential audit problem. Related to disclosure of interest-bearing debt, the auditors must determine whether the company has met all requirements and restrictions imposed upon it by debt agreements.

## Substantive Tests for Interest-Bearing Debt

Figure 16–1 presents typical substantive tests used to meet the primary audit objectives for interest-bearing debt. In the following sections we describe these procedures in detail.

## Obtain Analyses of Interest-Bearing Debt and Related Accounts

| Primary Audit Objective: |
| --- |
| Clerical accuracy ☑ |

A notes payable analysis shows the beginning balance of each individual note, additional notes issued and payments on notes during the year, and the ending balance of each note. In addition, the beginning balances of interest payable or prepaid interest, interest expense, interest paid, and ending balances of interest payable or prepaid interest may be presented in the analysis working paper.

Figure 16–1   Objectives of Major Substantive Tests of Interest-Bearing
Debt Transactions and Balances

| Substantive Tests | Primary Audit Objectives |
|---|---|
| Obtain analyses of interest-bearing debt and related accounts | Clerical accuracy |
| Examine copies of notes payable and supporting documents<br><br>Confirm interest-bearing debt<br><br>Vouch borrowing and repayment transactions | Existence or occurrence; Completeness; and Obligations |
| Perform analytical procedures<br><br>Test computations of interest expense, interest payable, and amortization of discount and premium | Existence or occurrence; Completeness; Obligations; and Valuation |
| Evaluate whether debt provisions have been met<br><br>Verify authority for issuance of debt to corporate minutes<br><br>Review notes payable paid or renewed after the balance sheet date<br><br>Perform procedures to identify notes payable to related parties<br><br>Send confirmation letters about financing arrangements<br><br>Evaluate financial statement presentation and disclosure | Presentation and disclosure |

An analysis of the Notes Payable account will serve a number of purposes: *(a)* the payment or other disposition of notes listed as outstanding in the previous year's audit can be verified, *(b)* the propriety of individual debits and credits can be established, and *(c)* the amount of the year-end balance of the account is proved through the step-by-step examination of all changes in the account during the year.

In the first audit of a client, the auditors will analyze the ledger accounts for Bonds Payable, Bond Issue Costs, and Bond Discount (or Bond Premium) for the years since the bonds were issued. The working paper is placed in the auditors' permanent file; in later audits, any further entries in these accounts may be added to the analysis.

## Examine Copies of Notes Payable

Primary Audit
Objectives:

| | |
|---|---|
| Existence | ☑ |
| Completeness | ☑ |
| Obligations | ☑ |

The auditors should examine the client's copies of notes payable and supporting documents such as mortgages and trust deeds. The original documents will be in the possession of the payees, but the auditors should make certain that the client has retained copies of the debt instruments and that their details correspond to the analyses described in the first procedure of this audit program.

## Confirm Interest-Bearing Debt

| Primary Audit Objectives: |
| --- |
| Existence  ☑ |
| Completeness  ☑ |
| Obligations  ☑ |

Notes payable to financial institutions are confirmed as part of the confirmation of cash deposit balances. The standard confirmation form illustrated in Chapter 13 includes a request that the financial institution confirm all borrowings by the depositor. As indicated in that chapter, these confirmations are generally sent to all financial institutions doing business with the client to test the completeness of recorded liabilities. The auditors will also review the minutes of board of directors' meetings to identify debt authorized during the year that should be selected for confirmation.

Confirmation requests for notes payable to payees other than financial institutions should be drafted on the client's letterhead stationery, signed by the controller or other appropriate executive, and mailed by the auditors. Payees should be requested to confirm dates of origin, due dates, unpaid balances of notes, interest rates, dates to which interest has been paid, and collateral for the notes.

The auditors may also substantiate the existence and amount of a mortgage liability outstanding by direct confirmation with the mortgagee. The information received should be compared with the client's records and the audit working papers. When no change in the liability account has occurred in the period under audit, the only major procedure necessary will be this confirmation with the creditor. At the same time that the mortgagee is asked to confirm the debt, it may be asked for an indication of the company's compliance with the mortgage or trust deed agreement.

Bond transactions usually can be confirmed directly with the trustee. The trustee's reply should include an exact description of the bonds, including maturity dates and interest rates; bonds retired, purchased for the treasury, or converted into stock during the year; bonds outstanding at the balance sheet date; and *sinking fund* transactions and balances.

## Vouch Borrowing and Repayment Transactions

| Primary Audit Objectives: |
| --- |
| Existence  ☑ |
| Completeness  ☑ |
| Obligations  ☑ |

The auditors must obtain evidence that transactions in interest-bearing debt accounts were valid. To accomplish this objective, the auditors trace the cash received from the issuance of notes, bonds, or mortgages to the validated copy of the bank deposit slip and to the bank statement. Any remittance advices supporting these cash receipts are also examined. The auditors can find further support for the net proceeds of a bond issue by referring to the underwriting contract and to the prospectus filed with the SEC.

Debits to a Notes Payable or a Mortgages Payable account generally represent payments in full or in installments. The auditors should examine paid checks for these payments; in so doing, they also will account for payments of accrued interest. The propriety of installment payments should be verified by reference to the repayment schedule set forth in the note or mortgage copy in the client's possession.

A comparison of canceled notes payable with the debit entries in the Notes Payable account provides further assurance that notes indicated as paid during the year have, in fact, been retired. The auditors' inspection of these notes should include a comparison of the maturity date of the note with the date of cash disbursement. Failure to pay notes promptly at maturity is suggestive of financial weakness.

There is seldom any justification for a paid note to be missing from the files; a receipt for payment from the payee of the note is not a satisfactory substitute. If, for any reason, a paid note is not available for inspection, the auditors should review the request for a check or other vouchers supporting the disbursement and should discuss the transaction with an appropriate official.

In examining the canceled notes, the auditors should also trace the disposition of any collateral used to secure these notes. A convenient opportunity for diversion of pledged securities or other assets to an unauthorized use may be created at the time these assets are regained from a secured creditor.

## Perform Analytical Procedures

| Primary Audit Objectives: |
|---|
| Existence ☑ |
| Completeness ☑ |
| Obligations ☑ |
| Valuation ☑ |

One of the most effective ways to determine the overall reasonableness of interest-bearing debt is to examine the relationship between recorded interest expense and the average principal amount of debt outstanding during the year. If the client is paying interest on debt that is not recorded, this relationship will not be in line with the interest rate at which the client company should be able to borrow. Therefore, the auditors can use these procedures as a test of the *completeness* of recorded interest-bearing debt.

The auditors also compare the year-end amount of interest-bearing debt with the amount in the prior year's balance sheet. A similar comparison is made of interest expense for the current year and the preceding year.

## Test Computations

| Primary Audit Objectives: |
|---|
| Existence ☑ |
| Completeness ☑ |
| Obligations ☑ |
| Valuation ☑ |

The auditors may test the accuracy of the client's computations of interest expense and interest payable. In addition, they may examine paid checks supporting interest payments and review the confirmation responses received from payees to verify the dates on which interest on each note or mortgage has been paid. A close study of interest payments is another means of bringing to light any unrecorded interest-bearing liabilities.

The total bond interest expense for the period usually reflects not only the interest actually paid and accrued, but also amortization of bond premium or discount. The auditors may also test the amounts amortized by independent computations.

## Evaluate Compliance with Debt Provisions

| Primary Audit Objective: |
|---|
| Presentation ☑ |

In the first audit of a client or upon the issuance of a new bond issue, the auditors will obtain a copy of the bond indenture for the permanent file. The indenture should be carefully studied, with particular attention to such points as the amount of bonds authorized, interest rates and dates, maturity dates, descriptions of property pledged as collateral, provisions for retirement or conversion, duties and responsibilities of the trustee, and any restrictions imposed on the borrowing company.

The indenture provisions may require maintenance of a sinking fund, maintenance of stipulated minimum levels of working capital, and insurance of pledged property. The indenture also may restrict dividends to a specified proportion of earnings, limit management compensation, and prohibit additional long-term borrowing, except under stipulated conditions. The auditors will perform tests to evaluate whether the company is in compliance with these provisions. For example, the auditors will examine evidence of insurance coverage, vouch payments to the sinking fund, and compare the amounts of management compensation and dividends paid to amounts allowed by the agreements.

If the auditors discover that the company has not complied fully with the requirements, the auditors should inform the client of the violation. In some cases of violation, the entire bond issue may become due and payable on demand, and hence a current liability. When the client is in violation of an indenture provision and the penalty is to make the debt become payable upon demand, the client usually will be able to obtain a waiver of compliance with the provision. In other words, creditors often choose not to enforce contract terms fully. To enable the liability to be presented as long term, the waiver must waive compliance for a period of at least one year from the balance sheet date. Even if an appropriate waiver of compliance is obtained, the matter should be disclosed in the notes to the client's financial statements.

---

### ◆ ILLUSTRATIVE CASE ◆

In the audit of a large construction company, the auditors found the client's working capital to be far below the minimum level stipulated in the indenture of long-term secured bonds payable. In addition, the client had allowed the required insurance coverage of pledged assets to lapse. These violations of the indenture were sufficient to cause the bond issue to become payable on demand.

Although the client agreed to reclassify the bond issue as a current liability and disclose the problem in the financial statements, the auditors were unable to satisfy themselves that the client could meet the obligation if the bondholders demanded payment. Also, if the bondholders foreclosed on the pledged assets, the ability of the client to continue as a going concern would be questionable. Thus, even after the liability was reclassified as current, the auditors had to add an explanatory paragraph to their report referring to the uncertainty regarding the company's ability to meet its obligations and remain a going concern.

---

## Verify Authority for Issuance of Interest-Bearing Debt

| Primary Audit Objective: |
| --- |
| Presentation ☑ |

The authority to issue interest-bearing debt generally lies with the board of directors. To determine that the bonds outstanding were properly authorized, the auditors should read the passages in the minutes of directors' (and stockholders') meetings concerning the issuance of debt. The minutes usually will cite the applicable sections of the corporate bylaws permitting the issuance of debt instruments and may also contain reference to the opinion of the company's counsel concerning the legality of the issue.

Auditors do not judge the legality of a bond issue; this is the responsibility of the client's attorneys. The auditors should be familiar, however, with the principal provisions of the federal Securities Act of 1933 and of the corporate blue-sky laws of the client's state of incorporation. They should ascertain that the client has obtained an attorney's opinion on the legality of the bond issuance. In doubtful cases, they should obtain representations from the client's legal counsel.

## Review Notes Paid or Renewed after Balance Sheet Date

| Primary Audit Objective: |
| --- |
| Presentation ☑ |

If any of the notes payable outstanding at the balance sheet date are paid before completion of the audit engagement, such cash payments will provide the auditors with additional evidence on the liability. Renewal of notes maturing shortly after the balance sheet date may alter the auditors' thinking as to the proper classification of these liabilities.

In the discussion of notes receivable in Chapter 13, emphasis was placed on the necessity of close scrutiny of loans to officers, directors, and affiliates because of the absence of arm's-length bargaining in these related-party transactions. Similar emphasis should be placed on the examination of notes payable to insiders or affiliates, although the opportunities for self-dealing are more limited than with receivables. The auditors should scan the notes payable records for the period between the balance sheet date and the completion of the audit so that they may be aware of any unusual transactions, such as the reestablishment of an insider note that had been paid just prior to the balance sheet date.

## Investigate Related-Party Transactions

| Primary Audit Objective: |
| --- |
| Presentation ☑ |

As has been the case in other portions of the audit, the auditors must perform procedures to determine that any related-party debt is properly disclosed. Note here that the lower number of transactions makes discovery of such transactions less difficult than in accounts with a large number of transactions such as accounts payable.

## Confirm Financing Arrangements

| Primary Audit Objective: |
| --- |
| Presentation ☑ |

Financing arrangements and transactions can be very complex, and the details of these arrangements and transactions must be adequately disclosed in the notes to the financial statements. If the auditors determine that additional evidence is needed to verify these details, they will send a *separate* confirmation letter to the financial institution. For example, confirmation letters may be used to obtain information about lines of credit, contingent liabilities, compensating balance arrangements, letters of credit, or futures contracts. These letters are signed by the client and specifically addressed to the client's loan officer or another official at the financial institution that is knowledgeable about the information. This expedites a response to the confirmation and enhances the quality of the evidence received. Figure 16–2 is an example of a letter to confirm information about lines of credit.

## Evaluate Disclosures

| Primary Audit Objective: |
| --- |
| Presentation ☑ |

Because of the interest of creditors in the current liability section of the balance sheet and the inferences that may be drawn from various uses of notes payable, adequate informative disclosure is extremely important. Classification of notes by types of payees, as well as by current or long-term maturity, is necessary. Notes payable to banks, notes payable to trade creditors, and notes payable to officers, directors, stockholders, and affiliates should be listed separately.

Secured liabilities and pledged assets should be cross-referenced to one another with an explanation in the notes to the financial statements. In the event of financial difficulties and dissolution, creditors expect to share in the assets in proportion to their respective claims; and if significant assets, such as current receivables, have been pledged to one

## Figure 16–2    Illustrative Letter for Confirmation of Lines of Credit

**W**ALLACE **M**ANUFACTURING, INC.

1400 MAIN ST. LOS ANGELES, CA 90015

January 31, 199X

Mr. Richard M. Smith
Senior Loan Officer
First United Bank
2330 Fourth Ave.
Los Angeles, CA 90010

Dear Mr. Smith:

In connection with an audit of the financial statements of Wallace Manufacturing, Inc. as of December 31, 199X and for the year then ended, we have advised our independent auditors of the information listed below, which we believe is a complete and accurate description of our line of credit from your financial institution as of the close of business on December 31, 199X. Although we do not request nor expect you to conduct a comprehensive, detailed search of your records, if during the process of completing this confirmation additional information about other lines of credit from your financial institution comes to your attention, please include such information below.

The Company has available at your financial institution a line of credit totaling $47 million. The current terms of the line of credit are contained in the letter dated May 11, 198X.

The amount of unused line of credit, subject to the terms of the related letter, at December 31, 199X was $19 million.

The interest rate at the close of business on December 31, 199X was 9.2%.

There are no requirements for compensating balances in connection with this line of credit.

Please confirm whether the information about the line of credit presented above is correct by signing below and returning this letter directly to our independent auditors, Warren & Clark, CPAs, 2100 Century Blvd., Los Angeles, CA 90053

Sincerely,
Wallace Manufacturing, Inc.

By: _____*Robert Barr*_____
            Robert Barr, Controller

- - - - - - - - - - - - - - - - - - - - - - - - - - - - - - - - - - - - - - - - - - - - - - - - - - -

Dear Warren & Clark, CPAs:

The above information regarding the line of credit agrees with the records of this financial institution. Although we have not conducted a comprehensive, detailed search of our records, no information about other lines of credit came to our attention. [Note exceptions below or in an attached letter.]

_____

_____

_____

_____

First United Bank

By:___*Richard Smith, Senior Loan Officer*___    ___2/20/9X___
              (Officer and Title)                          (Date)

creditor, the risk to unsecured creditors is increased. Current liabilities should include not only those notes maturing within a period of 12 months (or a longer operating cycle) but also any installments currently payable on long-term obligations such as mortgages.

The essential point in balance sheet presentation of long-term liabilities is that they be adequately described. Each category of long-term debt should be stated under a separate title, which describes the type of debt, amounts authorized and issued, interest rate, maturity date, and any conversion or subordination features.

Long-Term Debt Payable in the Current Period.  Long-term liabilities include all debts that will not be liquidated with the use of current assets. In other words, any bonds or notes falling due in the coming operating cycle that are to be paid from special funds or refinanced will be classified as long-term obligations regardless of maturity date. Before accepting a long-term classification for maturing obligations, auditors must satisfy themselves that the client has both the *intent* and the *ability* to refinance the obligation on a long-term basis. Intent and ability to refinance are demonstrated by the client through either (1) refinancing the obligation on a long-term basis before the issuance of the financial statements, or (2) entering into a financing agreement by that date, which clearly permits such refinancing. Any debt maturing currently and payable from current assets should be classified as a current liability.

Restrictions Imposed by Long-Term Debt Agreements.  The major restrictions imposed on the company by long-term loan agreements are significant to the company's investors and creditors. Consequently, the nature of the restrictions should be clearly set forth in a note to the financial statements.

Unamortized Bond Premium or Discount.  Unamortized premium should be added to the face amount of the bonds or debentures in the liability section of the balance sheet. Similarly, unamortized discount should be deducted from the face amount of the debt.

## Timing of Procedures for Debt

Analysis of interest-bearing debt and interest expense takes very little time in most audits because of the small number of entries. Consequently, most auditors prefer to wait until the end of the year before analyzing these accounts.

Audit procedures intended to bring to light any unrecorded liabilities cannot very well be performed in advance of the balance sheet date. Such steps as the evaluation of compliance with debt provisions, tests of interest expense, and the investigation of notes paid or renewed shortly after the balance sheet date must necessarily await the close of the period being audited. The opportunities for performing audit work in advance of the balance sheet are thus much more limited in the case of interest-bearing debt than for most of the asset groups previously discussed.

## Audit Working Papers

The permanent file of the working papers will include a copy of the loan agreement or the indenture relating to a bond issue. A listing of the restrictions placed on the company is extracted from these documents to facilitate the auditors' tests of a client's compliance with the debt provisions. Analyses of ledger accounts for notes and bonds payable, and the related accounts for interest and discount or premium, should be obtained for the working papers. A lead schedule is only beneficial when a number of different forms of debt are outstanding.

# AUDITING EQUITY ACCOUNTS

## Internal Control over Equity Transactions

Three principal elements of strong internal control over owners' equity include: (1) the proper authorization of capital stock and dividend transactions by the board of directors and corporate officers; (2) the segregation of duties in handling these transactions (preferably the use of independent agents for stock registration and transfer, and for dividend payments); and (3) the maintenance of adequate records.

### Board of Director Authorization and Control of Capital Stock Transactions.
All changes in capital stock accounts should receive formal advance approval by the board of directors. The board of directors must determine the number of shares to be issued and the price per share; if an installment plan of payment is to be used, the terms must be prescribed by the board. If plant and equipment, services, or any consideration other than cash are to be accepted in payment for shares, the board of directors must establish the valuation on the noncash assets received. Transfers from retained earnings to the Capital Stock and Paid-In Capital accounts, as in the case of stock dividends, are initiated by action of the board. Stock splits and changes in par or stated value of shares also require formal authorization by the board.

Authority for all dividend actions rests with the directors. The declaration of a dividend must specify not only the amount per share, but also the date of record and the date of payment.

### Independent Registrar and Stock Transfer Agent.
Corporations either employ the services of an independent stock registrar and a stock transfer agent, or handle their own capital stock transactions. Internal control is far stronger when the services of an independent stock registrar and a stock transfer agent are utilized because banks or trust companies acting in these capacities will have the experience, the specialized facilities, and the trained personnel to perform the work in an expert manner. Moreover, by placing the responsibility for handling capital stock certificates in separate and independent organizations, the corporation achieves to the fullest extent the internal control concept of separation of duties. The New York Stock Exchange and most other exchanges require that listed corporations utilize the services of an independent registrar.

The primary responsibility of the **stock registrar** is to avoid any overissuance of stock. The danger of overissuance is illustrated by the old story of a promoter who sold a 25 percent interest in a new corporation to each of 10 investors. To prevent such irregularities, the registrar must verify that stock certificates are issued in accordance with the articles of incorporation and the formal authorization by the board of directors. The registrar obtains copies of the documents authorizing the total shares to be issued and maintains records of total shares issued and canceled. Each new certificate must be presented to the registrar for examination and registration before it is issued to a stockholder. The dangers of fraud and accidental error relating to improper issuance of stock certificates are greatly reduced when an independent registrar is employed.

Corporations with actively traded securities also employ independent **stock transfer agents.** Although the stock transfer agent maintains a record of the total shares outstanding, its primary responsibility is maintaining detailed stockholder records (name and address of each stockholder) and carrying out transfers of stock ownership.

The Stock Certificate Book and Stockholders Ledger.   If the corporation does not utilize the services of an independent registrar and stock transfer agent, these functions usually are assigned by the board of directors to the secretary of the company. The board of directors should designate officers who are authorized to (1) sign stock certificates, (2) maintain records of stockholders, (3) maintain custody of unissued certificates, and (4) sign dividend checks. The stock certificates should be serially numbered by the printer, and from the time of delivery to the company until issuance, they should be in the exclusive custody of the designated officer. The signatures of two officers are generally required on stock certificates.

The certificates often are prepared in bound books called **stock certificate books,** with attached stubs similar to those in a checkbook. Each stub shows the certificate number and contains blank spaces for entering the number of shares represented by the certificate, the name of the stockholder, and the serial number of any previously issued certificate surrendered in exchange for the new one. Certificates should be issued in numerical sequence and not signed or countersigned until the time of issuance. When outstanding shares are transferred from one holder to another, the old certificate is surrendered to the company. The designated officer cancels the old certificate by perforating and attaching it to the corresponding stub in the certificate book.

The stock certificate book is not generally in itself an adequate record of the capital stock outstanding. The certificates appear in the book in serial number order, and a single stockholder may own several certificates listed at various places in the certificate book. A **stockholders ledger** provides a separate record for each stockholder, thus making it possible to quickly determine the total number of shares owned by any one person. This record may be used in compiling the list of dividend checks or for any other communication with shareholders.

Internal Control over Dividends.   The nature of internal control over the payment of dividends, as in the case of stock issuance, depends primarily upon whether the company performs the function of dividend payment itself or utilizes the services of an independent dividend-paying agent. If an independent dividend-paying agent is used, the corporation will provide the agent with a certified copy of the dividend declaration and with a check for the full amount of the dividend. The bank or trust company serving as stock transfer agent is usually appointed as the dividend-paying agent, since it maintains the detailed records of stockholders. The agent issues dividend checks to the individual stockholders and sends the corporation a list of the payments made. The use of an independent fiscal agent is recommended from the standpoint of internal control, for it materially reduces the possibility of fraud or error arising in connection with the distribution of dividends.

In a small corporation not utilizing the services of a dividend-paying agent, the responsibility for payment of dividends is usually lodged with the treasurer and the secretary. After declaration of a dividend by the board of directors, the secretary prepares a list of stockholders as of the date of record, the number of shares held by each, and the amount of the dividend each is to receive. The total of these individual amounts is proved by multiplying the dividend per share by the total number of outstanding shares.

Dividend checks controlled by serial numbers are drawn payable to individual stockholders in the amounts shown on the list described above. If the stockholders ledger is maintained on a computer master file, the dividend checks may be prepared by the computer directly from this record. The stockholder list and dividend checks are submitted to the treasurer for approval and signature. The checks should be reconciled by the treasurer with the total of shares outstanding and mailed without again coming under control of the officer who prepared them.

A separate dividend bank account is then opened by the deposit of a check drawn for the total amount of the dividend. As the individual dividend checks are paid from this account and returned by the bank, they should be matched with the check stubs or marked *paid* in the dividend check register. A list of outstanding checks should be prepared monthly from the open stubs or open items in the check register. This list should agree in total with the balance remaining in the dividend bank account. Companies with numerous stockholders prepare dividend checks in machine-sensible form, so that the reconciliation of outstanding checks may be done by computer.

## Obtaining and Documenting an Understanding of the Internal Control Structure for Equity Transactions

As indicated previously, the auditors' understanding of equity transactions will include a consideration of the methods used by the client to authorize, execute, and record the transactions. Typical questions that appear on an internal control questionnaire include the following. Does the company utilize the services of an independent registrar and stock transfer agent? Are a stockholders ledger and transfer records maintained? Are entries in owners' equity accounts reviewed periodically by an appropriate officer? These questions should be regarded as identifying the areas to be investigated, rather than as items requiring simple a yes or no answer.

## Testing Controls and Assessing Control Risk for Equity Transactions

As with debt accounts, the transactions in equity accounts are typically small in number but large in amount. Typically, the most efficient approach to auditing the accounts is to assess control risk at a high level and perform substantive tests of the accounts.

## Designing Substantive Tests of Equity Accounts

Most of this section is concerned with the audit of stockholders' equity accounts of corporate clients; the audit of owners' equity in partnerships and sole proprietorships is discussed briefly near the end of the chapter.

Owners' equity for corporate clients consists of capital stock accounts (preferred and common) and retained earnings. Balances in the capital stock accounts change when the corporation issues or repurchases stock. The account balances are not affected by transfer of ownership of shares from one shareholder to another. Retained earnings are normally increased by earnings and decreased by dividend payments. Additionally, a few journal entries (e.g., prior-period adjustments) may directly affect retained earnings. Often, no change will occur during the year in the capital stock accounts, and perhaps only one or two entries will be made to the retained earnings account.

## Objectives of Substantive Tests of Equity Accounts

The audit *objectives* for substantive tests of owners' equity are to:

1. Determine the *existence* of recorded owners' equity and occurrence of the related transactions.
2. Establish the *completeness* of recorded owners' equity.
3. Establish the client's *obligations* to owners of the company.
4. Establish the *clerical accuracy* of schedules of owners' equity.
5. Determine that the *valuation* of owners' equity is in accordance with generally accepted accounting principles.
6. Determine that the *presentation* and *disclosure* of owners' equity are appropriate.

In conjunction with the audit of owners' equity accounts, the auditors will also obtain evidence about the related accounts of dividends payable and capital stock discounts and premiums. Evidence is also gathered regarding the proper cutoff of cash receipts and disbursements relating to the equity accounts.

## Substantive Tests for Capital Stock

Figure 16–3 presents typical substantive tests used to meet the primary audit objectives for capital stock. In the following sections we describe these procedures in detail.

Figure 16–3   Objectives of Major Substantive Tests for Capital Stock

| Substantive Tests | Primary Audit Objectives |
|---|---|
| Obtain analyses of capital stock accounts | Clerical accuracy |
| Examine articles of incorporation, bylaws, and minutes<br>Confirm shares outstanding<br>Reconcile shares outstanding with general ledger | Existence or occurrence;<br>Completeness; and<br>Obligations |
| Account for proceeds from stock issues | Existence or occurrence;<br>Completeness; Obligations;<br>and Valuation |
| Evaluate compliance with stock option plans and with other restrictions<br>Evaluate financial statement presentation and disclosure | Presentation and disclosure |

## Obtain Analysis of Capital Stock Accounts

| Primary Audit Objective: |
| --- |
| Clerical accuracy ☑ |

In an initial audit engagement, capital stock accounts should be analyzed from the corporation's inception to provide the auditors with a complete historical picture of corporate capital. Analysis of capital stock includes an appraisal of the nature of all changes and the vouching of these changes to the supporting documents and records. All changes in capital stock should bear the authorization of the board of directors.

The analysis of capital stock accounts may be prepared in a manner that permits updating during later audits. After the initial audit, if the analyses are kept in the auditors' permanent file, all that will be necessary is to record the current period's increases and decreases and to vouch these transactions. The auditors then will have working papers showing all changes in capital stock from the inception of the corporation.

The auditors also should analyze the Treasury Stock account and prepare a list of the number of shares of **treasury stock** on hand. All certificates on hand then may be inspected. If the certificates are not on hand, they should be confirmed directly with the custodian.

In their review of treasury stock transactions, the auditors should refer to working paper copies of the minutes of directors' meetings to determine that *(a)* the acquisition or reissuance of treasury stock was authorized by directors, and *(b)* the price paid or received was in accordance with prices specified by the board.

## Examine Articles of Incorporation, Bylaws, and Minutes

| Primary Audit Objectives: |
| --- |
| Existence ☑ |
| Completeness ☑ |
| Obligations ☑ |

In a first audit, copies of the articles of incorporation and bylaws obtained for the permanent file should be read carefully. The information required by the auditors for each issue of capital stock includes the number of shares authorized and issued, the par or stated value if any, dividend rates, call and conversion provisions, stock splits, and stock options. The auditors will also review minutes of the meetings of directors and stockholders for authorization of transactions related to the company's stock. By gathering evidence on these points, the auditors will have some assurance that capital stock transactions and dividend payments have been in accordance with legal requirements and specific authorizations by stockholders and directors. Also, they will be able to judge whether the balance sheet contains all necessary information to describe adequately the various stock issues and other elements of corporate capital.

## Confirm Shares Outstanding

| Primary Audit Objectives: |
| --- |
| Existence ☑ |
| Completeness ☑ |
| Obligations ☑ |

When an independent registrar and a stock transfer agent are used, the number of shares issued and outstanding on the balance sheet date may be confirmed by direct communication. As is the case with other confirmations, the confirmation request sent to the registrar and stock transfer agent should be on the client's letterhead, but it should be mailed by the auditors and replies should be received by the auditors. All information contained in these replies should be traced to the corporate records. It is essential that the general ledger controlling accounts agree with the amount of stock issued as reported by the independent registrar and stock transfer agent. Because of the controls of the registrar and stock transfer agent, it is not customary to communicate with individual stockholders in establishing the number of shares outstanding.

As indicated earlier in the chapter, smaller audit clients often do not use the services of an independent registrar and stock transfer agent. In such circumstances auditors occasionally confirm shares outstanding directly with shareholders, in addition to reconciling shares outstanding with the general ledger.

## Reconcile Shares Outstanding with General Ledger

| Primary Audit Objectives: | |
| --- | --- |
| Existence | ☑ |
| Completeness | ☑ |
| Obligations | ☑ |

When a corporation acts as its own transfer agent and registrar, the auditors will include procedures to: *(a)* account for stock certificate numbers, *(b)* examine canceled certificates, and *(c)* reconcile the shareholder ledger and stock certificate book with the general ledger.

The audit working papers should include a record of the last certificate number issued during the year. Reference to the working papers for the preceding audit, combined with the verification of certificate numbers issued during the current period, will enable the auditors to account for all certificates by serial number.

A working paper prepared during the auditors' examination of the stock certificate book of a small, closely held corporation is designed to be utilized during several audits; it may be retained in the permanent file or forwarded to successive current files. Additionally, the auditors should inspect the unissued certificates to determine that all certificates purported to be unissued are actually on hand and blank.

Canceled certificates should be attached to the corresponding stubs in the stock certificate book and permanently preserved. Auditors, therefore, will examine all canceled stock certificates on hand, noting in particular that they have been voided.

The general ledger account for capital stock shows the total par value or stated value of all shares outstanding, plus any treasury shares. The stockholders ledger includes an account for each stockholder. The stock certificate book contains unissued certificates, canceled certificates, and open stubs for outstanding certificates. These three records (general ledger control account, stockholders ledger, and stock certificate book) must be reconciled by the auditors to establish the amount of outstanding stock and to rule out the possibility of an overissuance of shares. If this verification were not made, it would be possible for a dishonest official to issue unlimited amounts of stock and to withhold the proceeds from such sales.

## Account for Proceeds from Stock Issues

| Primary Audit Objectives: | |
| --- | --- |
| Existence | ☑ |
| Completeness | ☑ |
| Obligations | ☑ |
| Valuation | ☑ |

Closely related to the analyses of Capital Stock accounts is the audit procedure of accounting for the receipt and proper disposition of all funds derived from the issuance of capital stock. The proceeds should be traced to the cash records and bank statements. SEC registration statements and contracts with underwriters may also be available as evidence of the amounts received from stock issues.

When assets other than cash are received as consideration for the issuance of capital stock, the entire transaction requires careful study. The auditors must determine that these accounting estimates made by the client result in a reasonable valuation.

## Evaluate Compliance with Stock Option Plans and with Other Restrictions

| Primary Audit Objective: |
| --- |
| Presentation ☑ |

Many corporations grant **stock options** to officers and key employees as an incentive-type compensation plan. When stock options are granted, a portion of the authorized but unissued stock must be held in reserve by the corporation so that it will be in a position to fulfill the option agreements. Similarly, corporations with convertible debentures or convertible preferred stocks outstanding must hold in reserve a sufficient number of common shares to meet the demands of preferred stockholders and debenture holders who may elect to convert their securities into common stock.

The auditors must become thoroughly familiar with the terms of any stock options and stock purchase plans and with the conversion features of debenture bonds and preferred stock, so that they can determine whether the financial statements make adequate disclosure of these agreements. The auditors must also verify the shares issued during the year through conversion or exercise of stock options and must ascertain that the number of shares held in reserve at the balance sheet date does not exceed the corporation's authorized but unissued stock.

## Evaluate Financial Statement Presentation and Disclosure

| Primary Audit Objective: |
| --- |
| Presentation ☑ |

The presentation of capital stock in the balance sheet should include a complete description of each issue. Information to be disclosed includes the title of each issue; par or stated value; dividend rate, if any; dividend preference; conversion and call provisions; number of shares authorized, issued, and in treasury; dividends in arrears, if any; and shares reserved for stock options or for conversions.

Treasury stock preferably is shown in the stockholders' equity section, at cost, as a deduction from the combined total of paid-in capital and retained earnings. In many states, an amount of retained earnings equivalent to the cost of the treasury shares must be restricted. This restriction is disclosed by a note to the financial statements.

## Retained Earnings and Dividends

Audit work on retained earnings and dividends includes three major steps: (1) the analysis of retained earnings and any appropriations of retained earnings, (2) the review of dividend procedures for both cash and stock dividends, and (3) the review of note disclosures.

On a first-year audit, the analysis of retained earnings and any appropriations of retained earnings should cover the entire history of these accounts. Such an analysis is prepared for the permanent file and is updated in each annual audit. Credits to the Retained Earnings account ordinarily represent amounts of net income transferred from the Income Summary account. Debits to the Retained Earnings account ordinarily include entries for net losses, cash, and stock dividends, and for the creation or enlargement of appropriated reserves. Appropriations of retained earnings require specific authorization by the board of directors. The only verification necessary for these entries is to ascertain that the dates and amounts correspond to the actions of the board.

In the verification of cash dividends, the auditors usually will perform the following steps:

1. Determine the dates and amounts of dividends authorized.

2. Verify the amounts paid.

3.   Determine the amount of any preferred dividends in arrears.

4.   Review the treatment of unclaimed dividend checks.

When reviewing minutes of the directors' meetings, the auditors should note the date and amount of each dividend declaration. This serves to establish the authority for dividend disbursements. The dividend payment may then be verified by multiplying the total number of shares as shown by the general ledger control account by the dividend per share.

The auditors' analysis of dividend declarations may reveal the existence of cash dividends declared but not paid. These dividends must be shown as liabilities in the balance sheet. The auditors also may review the procedures for handling unclaimed dividends and ascertain that these items are recognized as liabilities. The amount of any accumulated dividends in arrears on preferred stock should be computed. If a closely held company has irregular dividend declarations or none at all, the auditors should consider whether the federal penalty surtax on reasonably accumulated retained earnings might be assessed. In the verification of stock dividends, there is an additional responsibility of determining that the proper amounts have been transferred from retained earnings to capital stock and paid-in capital accounts for both large and small stock dividends.

In evaluating client disclosures, the auditors must be aware that changes in retained earnings during the year may be shown in a separate statement or combined with the income statement. A combined statement of income and retained earnings often is presented. In this form of presentation, the amount of retained earnings at the beginning of the year is added to the net income figure, dividends declared are subtracted from the subtotal, and the final figure represents the new balance of retained earnings.

One of the most significant points to consider in determining the presentation of retained earnings in the balance sheet is the existence of any restriction on the use of this retained income. Agreements with banks, bondholders, and other creditors commonly impose limitations on the payment of dividends. These restrictions must be fully disclosed in the notes to financial statements.

## Timing of Procedures for Owners' Equity

While few in number but material in amount, each transaction requires careful attention. Because so few transactions occur, it usually is efficient to make the analysis after the close of the period. In the first audit of a new client, however, some preliminary work can be done advantageously in obtaining and reviewing copies of the articles of incorporation and bylaws and in analyzing the capital accounts.

For a continuing client, the auditors will often find that audit time required will be small in relation to the dollars in these accounts and much less than is required for assets, liabilities, revenue, or expense. Thus, while the capital stock account often has a larger balance than the cash account, the audit work required for capital stock is usually far less.

## Audit Working Papers for Owners' Equity

In addition to the lead schedule for owners' equity accounts, an analysis of each equity account is prepared by the auditors for the permanent file. A detailed analysis is essential for all aspects of a stock option plan: options authorized, issued, and outstanding. For a closely held corporation not served by a transfer agent, the auditors will often prepare for the permanent file a list of shareholders and the number of shares owned by each.

## AUDIT OF PARTNERSHIP AND SOLE PROPRIETORSHIP CAPITAL ACCOUNTS

A most significant document underlying the partnership form of organization is the partnership contract. The auditors are particularly interested in determining that the distribution of net income has been carried out in accordance with the profit-sharing provisions of the partnership contract. Maintenance of partners' capital accounts at prescribed levels and restriction of drawings by partners to specified amounts are other points often covered by the contract; compliance with these clauses should be verified by the auditors in determining the propriety of the year's entries in the capital accounts. Partners' loan accounts also require reference to the partnership contract to determine the treatment intended by the partners.

Occasionally, auditors may find that a partnership is operating without any written agreement of partnership. This situation raises a question of whether profits have been divided in accordance with the understanding existing between the partners. The auditors may appropriately suggest that the partners develop a written partnership contract; for their own protection, the auditors may wish to obtain from each partner a written statement confirming the balance in his or her capital account and approval of the method used in dividing the year's earnings.

In general, the same principles described for the audit of corporate capital are applicable to the examination of the capital account and drawing accounts of a sole proprietorship or partnership. Analyses are made of all proprietorship accounts from the beginning of the business; the initial capital investment and any additions are traced to the cash and asset records; and the net income or loss for the period and any withdrawals are verified. In the case of a sole proprietorship, a common source of difficulty is the practice of intermingling business and personal transactions, making it necessary for the auditors to segregate personal net worth from business capital. Adjustments may also be required to transfer from expense accounts to the owner's drawing account any personal expenditures paid with company funds.

## ◆ CHAPTER SUMMARY

This chapter explained the details of the financing cycle, the auditors' consideration of the internal control for this transaction cycle, and the auditors' substantive tests of the financing cycle accounts—debt and equity. To summarize:

1. The financing cycle involves the activities of the company that are designed to obtain capital funds. It typically involves the issuance and repayment of debt and equity, as well as payment of interest and dividends. A primary concern for both of these types of transactions is proper authorization by the appropriate official in the company or by the board of directors.

2.   Control over the issuance of bonds by a company is enhanced when an independent trustee represents the interest of the bondholders. The responsibilities of the trustee include monitoring the company's compliance with the requirements of the bond agreement, and processing the payments of interest and principal to individual bondholders.

3.   Capital stock transactions are best controlled by employing a registrar/transfer agent who monitors the issuance of the company's stock and handles transfers of shares between investors. In smaller companies capital stock is controlled through the maintenance of a stock certificate book and a stockholders ledger.

4.   After the auditors obtain an understanding of the client's internal control structure policies and procedures for the financing cycle, they will often perform only limited tests of controls because of the limited number of transactions typically involved. It is usually more efficient to assess control risk at a high level and perform detailed substantive tests of transactions.

5.   In the audit of interest-bearing debt, the auditors' primary substantive procedures will include vouching selected transactions occurring during the period, examining debt agreements, confirming balances and terms, and evaluating compliance with restrictive covenants.

6.   The auditors' primary substantive procedures for equity transactions will typically include vouching the major equity transactions occurring during the period, confirming the number of shares outstanding with the registrar, and evaluating the company's compliance with stock option plan requirements and other restricting agreements.

---

## ◆ KEY TERMS INTRODUCED OR EMPHASIZED IN CHAPTER 16

**Debenture bond**   An unsecured bond, dependent upon the general credit of the issuer.

**Indenture**   The formal agreement between bondholders and the issuer as to the terms of the debt.

**Sinking fund**   Cash or other assets set aside for the retirement of a debt.

**Stock certificate book**   A book of serially numbered certificates with attached stubs. Each stub shows the corresponding certificate number and provides space for entering the number of shares represented by the certificate, name of the shareholder, and serial number of the certificate surrendered in exchange for the new one. Surrendered certificates are canceled and replaced in the certificate book.

**Stockholders ledger**   A record showing the number of shares owned by each shareholder. This is the basic record used for preparing dividend payments and other communications with shareholders.

**Stock option plan**   A formal plan granting the right to buy a specified number of shares at a stipulated price during a specified time. Stock option plans are frequently used as a form of executive compensation. The terms of such plans should be disclosed in financial statements.

**Stock registrar**   An institution charged with responsibility for avoiding overissuance of a corporation's stock. Every new certificate must be presented to the registrar for examination and registration before it is issued to a stockholder.

**Stock transfer agent**   An institution responsible for maintaining detailed records of shareholders and handling transfers of stock ownership.

**Treasury stock**   Shares of its own stock acquired by a corporation for the purpose of being retired or reissued at a later date.

## ◆ GROUP I: REVIEW QUESTIONS

16-1   Mansfield Corporation has outstanding an issue of 30-year bonds payable. There is no sinking fund for these bonds. Under what circumstances, if any, should this bond issue be classified as a current liability?

16-2   What does the trust indenture used by a corporation in creating long-term bonded indebtedness have to do with the payment of dividends on common stock?

16-3   In addition to verifying the recorded liabilities of a company, the auditors must also give consideration to the possibility that other unrecorded liabilities exist. What specific steps may be taken by the auditors to determine that all of their client's interest-bearing liabilities are recorded?

16-4   Two assistant auditors were assigned by the auditor-in-charge to the verification of long-term liabilities. Some time later, they reported to the auditor-in-charge that they had determined that all long-term liabilities were properly recorded and that all recorded long-term liabilities were genuine obligations. Does this determination constitute a sufficient examination of long-term liabilities? Explain.

16-5   Palmer Company has issued a number of notes payable during the year, and several of these notes are outstanding at the balance sheet date. What sources of information should the auditors use in preparing a working paper analysis of the notes payable?

16-6   What is the principal reason for testing the reasonableness of the Interest Expense account in conjunction with the verification of notes payable?

16-7   Is the confirmation of notes payable usually correlated with any other specific phase of the audit? Explain.

16-8   Audit programs for examination of accounts receivable and notes receivable often include investigation of selected transactions occurring after the balance sheet date as well as transactions during the year under audit. Are the auditors concerned with notes payable transactions subsequent to the balance sheet date? Explain.

16-9   Most corporations with bonds payable outstanding utilize the services of a trustee. What relation, if any, does this practice have to the maintenance of adequate internal control?

16-10   "Auditors are not qualified to pass on the legality of a bond issue; this is a question for the company's attorneys. It is therefore unnecessary for the auditors to inspect the bond indenture." Criticize the quotation.

16-11   Long-term creditors often insist upon placing certain restrictions upon the borrowing company for the term of the loan. Give three examples of such restrictions, and indicate how each restriction protects the long-term creditor.

16-12   What information should be requested by the auditors from the trustee responsible for an issue of debentures payable?

16-13   Compare the auditors' examination of owners' equity with their work on assets and current liabilities. Among other factors to be considered are the relative amounts of time involved and the character of the transactions to be reviewed.

16-14   What do you consider to be the most important internal control device a corporation can adopt with respect to capital stock transactions?

16-15    You have been retained to perform an audit of Valley Products, a small corporation which has not been audited during the previous 10 years of its existence. How will your work on the Capital Stock account in this initial audit differ from that required in a repeat engagement?

16-16    Comment on the desirability of audit work on the owners' equity accounts before the balance sheet date.

16-17    Name three situations that might place a restriction on retained earnings limiting or preventing dividend payments. Explain how the auditors might become aware of each such restricting factor.

16-18    Delta Company has issued stock options to four of its officers permitting them to purchase 5,000 shares each of common stock at a price of $25 per share at any time during the next five years. The president asks you what effect, if any, the granting of the options will have upon the balance sheet presentation of the stockholders' equity accounts.

16-19    Describe the significant features of a stock certificate book, its purpose, and the manner in which it is used.

16-20    In the audit of a small corporation not using the services of an independent stock registrar and stock transfer agent, what use is made of the stock certificate book by the auditors?

16-21    What is the primary responsibility of an independent registrar with respect to capital stock?

16-22    What errors are commonly encountered by the auditors in their examination of the capital and drawing accounts of a sole proprietor?

16-23    Corporations sometimes issue their own capital stock in exchange for services and various assets other than cash. As an auditor, what evidence would you look for to determine the propriety of the values used in recording such transactions?

16-24    In your second annual audit of a corporate client, you find a new account in the general ledger called Treasury Stock, which has a balance of $306,000. Describe the procedures you would follow to verify this item.

16-25    In auditing the financial statements of Foster Company, you observe a debit entry for $200,000 labeled as Dividends in the Retained Earnings account. Explain in detail how you would verify this entry.

16-26    Your new client, Black Angus Valley Ranch, is a small corporation with less than 100 stockholders and does not utilize the services of an independent stock registrar or transfer agent. For your first audit, you want to obtain or prepare a year-end list of stockholders showing the number of shares owned by each. From what source or record should this information be obtained? Explain.

# ◆ GROUP II: QUESTIONS REQUIRING ANALYSIS

16-27    Stan Jones, CPA, the continuing auditor of Sussex, Inc., is beginning the audit of the common stock and treasury stock accounts. Jones has decided to design substantive tests with control risk assessed at the maximum level.

Sussex has no par, no stated value common stock, and acts as its own registrar and transfer agent. During the past year Sussex both issued and reacquired shares of its own common stock, some of which the company still owned at year-end. Additional common stock transactions occurred among the shareholders during the year.

Common stock transactions can be traced to individual shareholders' accounts in a subsidiary ledger and to a stock certificate book. The company has not paid any cash or stock dividends. There are no other classes of stock, stock rights, warrants, or option plans.

*Required:* What substantive audit procedures should Jones apply in examining the common stock and treasury stock accounts?

(AICPA, adapted)

16-28    The only long-term liability of Range Corporation is a note payable for $1 million secured by a mortgage on the company's plant and equipment. You have audited the company annually for the three preceding years, during which time the principal amount of the note has remained unchanged. The maturity date is 10 years from the current balance sheet date. You are informed by the president of the company that all interest payments have been made promptly in accordance with the terms of the note. Under these circumstances, what audit work, if any, is necessary with respect to this long-term liability during your present year-end audit?

16-29    During your annual audit of Walker Distributing Co., your assistant, Jane Williams, reports to you that although a number of entries were made during the year in the general ledger account Notes Payable to Officers, she decided that it was not necessary to audit the account because it had a zero balance at year-end.

*Required:* Do you agree with your assistant's decision? Discuss.

16-30    In an audit of a corporation that has a bond issue outstanding, the trust indenture is reviewed and confirmation as to the issue is obtained from the trustee. List eight matters of importance to the auditors that might be found either in the indenture or in the confirmation obtained from the trustee. Explain briefly the reason for the auditors' interest in each of the items.

16-31    You are retained by Columbia Corporation to audit its financial statements for the fiscal year ended June 30. Your consideration of internal control indicates a fairly satisfactory condition, although there are not enough employees to permit an extensive separation of duties. The company is one of the smaller units in its industry, but has realized net income of about $500,000 in each of the last three years.

Near the end of your field work you overhear a telephone call received by the president of the company while you are discussing the audit with him. The telephone conversation indicates that on May 15 of the current year the Columbia Corporation made an accommodation endorsement of a 60-day, $430,000 note issued by a major customer, Brill Corporation, to its bank. The purpose of the telephone call from Brill was to inform your client that the note had been paid at the maturity date. You had not been aware of the existence of the note before overhearing the telephone call.

*Required:*    *a.* Do you think the auditors would be justified from an ethical standpoint in acting on information acquired in this manner?

*b.* Should the balance sheet as of June 30 disclose the contingent liability? Give reasons for your answer.

*c.* Prepare a list of auditing procedures that might have brought the contingency to light. Explain fully the likelihood of detection of the accommodation endorsement by each procedure listed.

16-32    You are engaged in the examination of the financial statements of Armada Corporation for the year ended August 31, 199X. The balance sheet, reflecting all of your audit adjustments accepted by the client to date, shows total current assets, $8,000,000; total current liabilities, $7,500,000; and stockholders' equity, $1,000,000. Included in current liabilities are two unsecured notes payable—one payable to United National Bank in the amount of $900,000 due October 31, 199X; the other payable to First State Bank in the amount of $800,000 due September 30, 199X. On September 30, the last scheduled date for your audit field work, you learn that Armada Corporation is unable to pay the $832,000 maturity value of the First State Bank note, that Armada executives are negotiating with First State Bank for an extension of the due date of the note, and that nothing definite has been decided as to the extension.

*Required:*   *a.*   Should this situation be disclosed in notes to Armada Corporation's August 31 financial statements?

*b.*   After the question of financial statement disclosure has been resolved to the auditor's satisfaction, might this situation have any effect upon the audit report?

16-33   Valley Corporation has a stock option plan designed to provide extra incentive to its officers and key employees. A note to the financial statements includes a description of the plan and lists the number of options for shares that have been authorized, the number granted, the number exercised, and the number expired. The option price and the market price per share on the grant dates and the exercise dates are also shown.

*Required:*   *a.*   In view of the fact that the information concerning the stock option plan appears in a note, rather than in the body of the financial statements, what responsibility, if any, do the independent auditors have for this information?

*b.*   List the audit procedures, if any, that you believe should be applied to the stock option plan information.

16-34   Select the best answer choice for each of the following, and justify your selection in a brief statement.

*a.*   The audit procedure of confirmation is *least* appropriate with respect to:
(1)   The trustee of an issue of bonds payable.
(2)   Holders of common stock.
(3)   Holders of notes receivable.
(4)   Holders of notes payable.

*b.*   An auditor is most likely to trace treasury stock purchase transactions to the:
(1)   Numbered stock certificates on hand.
(2)   Articles of incorporation.
(3)   Year's interest expense.
(4)   Minutes of the audit committee.

*c.*   In the audit of a manufacturing company of medium size, which of the following areas would you expect to require the least amount of audit time?
(1)   Owners' equity.
(2)   Revenue.
(3)   Assets.
(4)   Liabilities.

*d.*   The auditors can best verify a client's bond sinking fund transactions and year-end balance by:
(1)   Recomputation of interest expense, interest payable, and amortization of bond discount or premium.
(2)   Confirmation with individual holders of retired bonds.
(3)   Confirmation with the bond trustee.
(4)   Examination and count of the bonds retired during the year.

*e.*   The auditors' program for the examination of long-term debt should include steps that require the:
(1)   Verification of the existence of the bondholders.
(2)   Examination of copies of debt agreements.
(3)   Inspection of the accounts payable subsidiary ledger.
(4)   Investigation of credits to the bond interest income account.

*f.*   All corporate capital stock transactions should ultimately be traced to the:
(1)   Minutes of the board of directors.
(2)   Cash receipts journal.

(3)   Cash disbursements journal.

(4)   Numbered stock certificates.

(AICPA, adapted)

# ◆ GROUP III: PROBLEMS

16-35   In your first audit of Hydrafoil Company, a manufacturer of specially designed boats capable of transporting passengers over water at very high speeds, you find that sales are made to commercial transportation companies. The sales price per unit is $400,000, and with each unit sold, the client gives the purchasing company a certificate reading as follows:

> Hydrafoil Company promises to pay ＿＿＿＿＿＿ the sum of $24,000 when the boat designated as Serial No. ＿＿＿＿＿＿ is permanently retired from service and evidence of such retirement is submitted.

The president of Hydrafoil Company explains to you that the purpose of issuing the certificates is to ensure contact with customers when they are in the market for new equipment. You also learn that the company makes no journal entry to record a certificate when it is issued. Instead, the company charges an expense account and credits a liability account $200 per month for each outstanding certificate, based on the company's experience that its hydrafoil boats will be rendered obsolete by new, more efficient models in approximately 10 years from the date of sale.

*Required:*   Do you concur with Hydrafoil Company's accounting for the certificates? You may assume that the 10-year service life of the product (and therefore of the certificates) is an accurate determination. Explain your position clearly.

16-36   You have been retained to audit the financial statements of Midwest Products, Inc. for the year ended December 31. During the current year, Midwest had obtained a long-term loan from its bank in accordance with a financing agreement which provided that:

1.   The loan was to be secured by the company's inventory and accounts receivable.

2.   The company was to maintain a debt-to-equity ratio not to exceed two to one.

3.   The company was not to pay dividends without permission from the bank.

4.   Monthly installment payments were to commence July 1 of the next year.

   In addition, during the current year, Midwest Products, Inc. borrowed from its president on a short-term basis, including substantial amounts just prior to the year-end.

*Required:*   a.   For the purpose of your audit of the financial statements of Midwest Products, Inc., what procedures would you employ in examining the above-described items? Do not discuss internal control.

   b.   What financial statement disclosures are appropriate with respect to the loans from the president?

(AICPA, adapted)

16-37   The following covenants are extracted from the indenture of a bond issue of Case Company. The indenture provides that failure to comply with its terms in any respect automatically advances the due date of the loan to the date of noncompliance (the regular due date is 20 years hence). Give any audit procedures or reporting requirements you think should be taken or recognized in connection with each one of the following:

1. "The debtor company shall endeavor to maintain a working capital ratio of 2 to 1 at all times; and in any fiscal year following a failure to maintain said ratio, the company shall restrict compensation of officers to a total of $2,000,000. Officers for this purpose shall include chairman of the board of directors, president, all vice presidents, secretary, controller, and treasurer."

2. "The debtor company shall keep all property that is security for this debt insured against loss by fire to the extent of 100 percent of its actual value. Policies of insurance comprising this protection shall be filed with the trustee."

3. "The debtor company shall pay all taxes legally assessed against property that is security for this debt within the time provided by law for payment without penalty, and shall deposit receipted tax bills or equally acceptable evidence of payment of same with the trustee."

4. "A sinking fund shall be deposited with the trustee by semiannual payments of $900,000, from which the trustee shall, in its discretion, purchase bonds of this issue."

(AICPA, adapted)

16-38   You are engaged in the first audit of Microdent, Inc. The corporation has both a stock transfer agent and an independent registrar for its capital stock. The transfer agent maintains the record of stockholders, and the registrar determines that there is no overissue of stock. Signatures of both are required to validate stock certificates.

It has been proposed that confirmations be obtained from both the transfer agent and the registrar as to the stock outstanding at the balance sheet date. If such confirmations agree with the accounting records, no additional work is to be performed as to capital stock.

If you agree that obtaining the confirmations as suggested would be sufficient in this case, give the justification for your position. If you do not agree, state specifically all additional steps you would take and explain your reasons for taking them.

(AICPA, adapted)

16-39   You are engaged in the audit of Phoenix Corp., a new client, at the close of its first fiscal year, April 30, 19X1. The accounts had been closed before the time you began your year-end field work.

You review the following stockholders' equity accounts in the general ledger:

**Capital Stock**

|  |  |  |  |  |
|---|---|---|---|---|
|  |  | 5/1/X0 | CR1 | 500,000 |
|  |  | 4/28/X1 | J12–5 | 50,000 |

**Paid-In Capital in Excess of Stated Value**

|  |  |  |  |  |
|---|---|---|---|---|
|  |  | 5/1/X0 | CR1 | 250,000 |
|  |  | 2/2/X1 | CR10 | 2,500 |

**Retained Earnings**

| 4/28/X1 | J12–5 | 50,000 | 4/30/X1 | J12–14 | 800,000 |
|---|---|---|---|---|---|

**Treasury Stock**

| | | | | | |
|---|---|---|---|---|---|
| 9/14/X0 | CP5 | 80,000 | 2/2/X1 | CR10 | 40,000 |

**Treasury Stock**

| | | | | | |
|---|---|---|---|---|---|
| 9/14/X0 | CP5 | 80,000 | 2/2/X1 | CR10 | 40,000 |

**Income Summary**

| | | | | | |
|---|---|---|---|---|---|
| 4/30/X1 | J12–13 | 5,200,000 | 4/30/X1 | J12–12 | 6,000,000 |
| 4/30/X1 | J12–14 | 800,000 | | | |

Other information in your working papers includes the following:
1. Phoenix's articles of incorporation filed April 17, 19X0, authorized 100,000 shares of no-par-value capital stock.
2. Directors' minutes include the following resolutions:
   4/18/X0  Established $50 per share stated value for capital stock.
   4/30/X0  Authorized issue of 10,000 shares to an underwriting syndicate for $75 per share.
   9/13/X0  Authorized acquisition of 1,000 shares from a dissident holder at $80 per share.
   2/1/X1  Authorized reissue of 500 treasury shares at $85 per share.
   4/28/X1  Declared 10 percent stock dividend, payable May 18, 19X1, to stockholders of record May 4, 19X1.
3. The following costs of the May 1, 19X0, and February 2, 19X1, stock issuances were charged to the named expense accounts: Printing Expense, $2,500; Legal Fees, $17,350; Accounting Fees, $12,000; and SEC Fees, $150.
4. Market values for Phoenix Corp. capital stock on various dates were:

   9/13/X0  . . . . .  $78.50
   9/14/X0  . . . . .   79.00
   2/2/X1  . . . . .   85.00
   4/28/X1  . . . . .   90.00

5. Phoenix Corp.'s combined federal and state income tax rates total 55 percent.

*Required:*  *a.* Prepare the necessary adjusting journal entries at April 30, 19X1.
             *b.* Prepare the stockholders' equity section of Phoenix Corp.'s April 30, 19X1, balance sheet.

16-40  Robert Hopkins was the senior office employee in Griffin Equipment Company and enjoyed the complete confidence of the owner, William Barton, who devoted most of his attention to sales, engineering, and production problems. All financial and accounting matters were entrusted to Hopkins, whose title was office manager. Hopkins had two assistants, but their only experience in accounting and financial work had been gained under Hopkins' supervision. Barton had informed Hopkins that it was his responsibility to keep him (Barton) informed on financial position and operating results of the company but not to bother him with details.

The company was short of working capital and would occasionally issue notes payable in settlement of past-due open accounts to suppliers. The situations warranting issuance of notes were decided upon by Hopkins, and the notes were drawn by him for signature by Barton. Hopkins was aware of the weakness in internal control and finally devised a scheme for defrauding the company through understating the amount of notes payable outstanding. He prepared a note in the amount of $24,000 payable to a supplier to whom several invoices were past due. After securing Barton's signature on the note and mailing it to the creditor, Hopkins entered the note in the Notes Payable account of the general ledger as $4,000, with an offsetting debit of $4,000 to Accounts Payable.

Several months later when the note matured, a check for $24,000 plus interest was issued and properly recorded, including a debit of $24,000 to the Notes Payable account. Hopkins then altered the original credit in the account by changing the figure from $4,000 to $24,000. He also changed the original debit to Accounts Payable from $4,000 to $24,000. This alteration caused the Notes Payable account to have a balance in agreement with the total of other notes outstanding. To complete the fraud, Hopkins called the supplier to whom the check had been sent and explained that the check should have been for only $4,000 plus interest.

Hopkins explained to the supplier that the note of $24,000 originally had been issued in settlement of a number of past-due invoices, but that while the note was outstanding, checks had been sent in payment of all the invoices. "In other words," said Hopkins over the telephone, "we made the mistake of giving you a note for those invoices and then going ahead and sending you checks for them as soon as our cash position had improved. Then we paid the note at maturity. So please excuse our mistakes and return the overpayment." After reviewing the record of invoices and checks received, the supplier agreed he had been overpaid by $20,000 plus interest and promptly sent a refund, which Hopkins abstracted without making any entry in the accounts.

*Required:*   *a.*   Assuming that an audit by CPAs was made while the note was outstanding, do you think that the $20,000 understatement of the Notes Payable account would have been detected? Explain fully the reasoning underlying your answer.

      *b.*   If the irregularity was not discovered while the note was outstanding, do you think that an audit subsequent to the payment of the note would have disclosed the fraud? Explain.

      *c.*   What internal control procedures would you recommend for Griffin Equipment Company to avoid fraud of this type?

# AUDITING THE INVESTMENT CYCLE

## CHAPTER OBJECTIVES

After studying this chapter, you should be able to:

- Explain the nature of investment and property, plant, and equipment transactions in the investment cycle.

- Identify and explain the fundamental internal control policies and procedures for the investment cycle.

- Describe the nature of investments and property, plant, and equipment transactions.

- Identify the audit objectives for substantive tests of investments and property, plant, and equipment accounts.

- Describe the nature of appropriate substantive audit procedures to accomplish the objectives for the audit of investments and property, plant, and equipment accounts.

T he investment cycle deals with investments in debt and equity securities and purchases of property, plant, and equipment. Since both securities and property, plant, and equipment are purchased using the company's funds, this cycle relates closely to the acquisition cycle. Receipts from the sale of investments enter the cash receipts portion of the revenue cycle. Also, since those funds may be financed by issuing debt or equity, the cycle also interrelates with the financing cycle.

This chapter initially describes internal control and the auditors' considerations in examining investments in securities. Next it presents internal control and audit considerations for property, plant, and equipment accounts.

# AUDITING INVESTMENTS IN SECURITIES

## Internal Control over Investments in Securities

As indicated above, the investment cycle is integrally related to the disbursement and receipt of cash. Therefore, many of the internal controls for the acquisition and revenue cycles, as described in Chapters 12 and 14, also apply to the investment cycle. The approach in this chapter is to focus on additional policies and procedures that are essential to the control of investments in securities and property, plant, and equipment.

The major elements of adequate internal control over investments include the following:

1. Separation of duties among the individuals authorizing purchases and sales of securities, having custody of the securities, and maintaining the records of securities.

2. Registration of securities in the name of the company, if the company takes delivery from the broker.

3. Detailed records of all securities owned and the related revenue from interest and dividends.

4. Periodic physical inspection of securities by the internal auditors or an official having no responsibility for the authorization, custody, or recordkeeping for investments.

In many concerns, segregation of the custody and recordkeeping functions is achieved by the use of an independent safekeeping agent, such as a stockbroker, bank, or trust company. Since the independent agent has no direct contact with the employee responsible for maintaining accounting records for the securities, the possibilities of concealing fraud through falsification of the accounts are greatly reduced. If securities are not placed in the custody of an independent agent, they should be kept in a bank safe-deposit box under the joint control of two or more of the company's officials. *Joint control* means that neither of the two custodians may have access to the securities except in the presence of the other. A list of securities in the box should be maintained with the securities, and the deposit or withdrawal of securities should be recorded on this list along with the date and signatures of all persons present. The safe-deposit box rental should oe in the name of the company, not in the name of an officer having custody of securities.

Complete detailed records of all securities owned, and of any securities held for others, are essential to a satisfactory internal control structure. These records frequently consist of a subsidiary record for each security, with such identifying data as the exact name, face amount or par value, certificate number, number of shares, date of acquisition, name of broker, cost, and any interest or dividend payments received. The purchase and sale of securities often is entrusted to a responsible financial executive, subject to frequent review by an investment committee of the board of directors. The investment committee also reviews reports that compare actual interest and dividends received to budgeted amounts.

An internal auditor or other responsible employee should, at frequent intervals, inspect the securities on hand, compare the serial numbers of those securities with the accounting records, and reconcile the subsidiary record for securities with the control account. This procedure supplements the internal control inherent in the segregation of the functions of authorization, recordkeeping, and custodianship.

## Obtaining and Documenting an Understanding of the Internal Control Structure for Investments in Securities

The auditors' understanding of the internal control structure of the investment cycle will include analysis of the control environment, the accounting system, and the control procedures. Because of the limited number of transactions involved, the auditors' documentation of the internal control structure will frequently be a written description, as well as an internal control questionnaire. The working papers will include documentation of the client's procedures for authorizing, executing, and recording transactions.

The internal control questionnaire used by the auditors to assess internal controls relating to investments in securities will include such questions as the following: Are securities and similar instruments under the joint control of responsible officials? Are all persons with access to securities properly bonded? Is an independent safekeeping agent retained? Are all purchases and sales of securities authorized by a financial executive and reviewed by an investment committee of the board of directors?

## Testing Controls and Assessing Control Risk for Investments in Securities

For many companies, investments in securities are characterized by a small number of transactions each year. As a result, auditors often choose to assess control risk at or near the maximum level, and rely on substantive tests of the transactions to obtain the required audit evidence. On the other hand, certain types of companies, such as insurance companies and financial institutions, have many more transactions of this type. When auditing these companies, the auditors often decide to test the effectiveness of the company's internal controls over investment transactions. Tests of controls might include observation and inquiries about the segregation of duties related to purchases and sales transactions. The auditors also may inspect the reports that are prepared for review by the investment committee, and any evidence of follow-up on variances from budgeted amounts of dividend and interest revenue. If securities are kept on hand, the auditors may examine any reports of inspections performed by the internal auditors. After performing these tests of controls, control risk will be reassessed, and the nature, timing, and extent of the substantive procedures will be modified, if necessary.

# Designing Substantive Tests of Investments in Securities

Investments in securities are categorized as marketable securities and long-term investments. Investment of temporarily idle cash in selected types of marketable securities is an element of good financial management. Such holdings are regarded as a secondary cash reserve, capable of quick conversion to cash at any time, while producing a steady rate of return. Management may also choose to maintain some investments in marketable securities on a semipermanent basis. The length of time companies hold such marketable securities may be determined by current security yields and by the company's income tax position, as well as by its cash requirements. The most important group of these marketable securities, from the viewpoint of the auditors, consists of stocks and bonds because they are found more frequently and usually are of greater dollar value than other kinds of investment holdings. Commercial paper issued by corporations, mortgages, and trust deeds are other types of investments often encountered.

Securities classified as long-term investments may either be held to invest cash that is not needed for current operations or to maintain control or influence over affiliated companies. Other than investing for control or influence, most companies have few long-term investments. Exceptions, however, include financial institutions and insurance companies that typically maintain large portfolios of long-term securities.

## Objectives for Substantive Tests of Investments in Securities

The audit *objectives* for substantive tests of investments are to:

1. Determine the *existence* of recorded investments and the *occurrence* of investment transactions.
2. Establish the *completeness* of recorded investments.
3. Determine that the client has *rights* to the investments.
4. Establish the *clerical accuracy* of schedules of investments.
5. Determine that the *valuation* of investments is in accordance with the lower of cost or market method of accounting, or for certain specialized industries at market values.
6. Determine that the *presentation and disclosure* of investments, including current/noncurrent classifications, are appropriate.

In conjunction with their audit of investments, the auditors will also verify the related accounts of interest income and dividends, accrued interest revenue, and gains and losses on the sale of securities.

The liquid nature of investments makes the potential for irregularities high. Auditors must coordinate the performance of their procedures for cash and investments to detect any possible irregularities involving unauthorized substitution (e.g., sale of securities to hide a cash shortage) between the accounts. The overall audit approach is one of assessing control risk for securities, inspecting certificates, confirming securities held by third parties such as stockbrokers, and determining the appropriate valuation of the securities.

## Substantive Tests for Investments in Securities

Figure 17–1 presents typical substantive tests used to meet the primary audit objectives for investments. These procedures are described in the following section.

## Obtain an Analysis of Securities

| Primary Audit Objective: |
| --- |
| Clerical accuracy ☑ |

The analysis of investments in securities obtained or prepared by the auditors will show the beginning and ending balances for the year, purchases and sales of investments during the year, and interest and dividends earned. The auditors may verify the beginning balances of investments by reference to the prior year's audit working papers. If numerous purchases and sales of investments have occurred during the year, separate schedules of those transactions may support an overall summary schedule of investments. The auditors will make certain that totals on the schedules agree with totals recorded in the general ledger.

## Inspect Securities

| Primary Audit Objectives: |
| --- |
| Existence ☑ |
| Rights ☑ |

The auditors will count securities held by the client at year-end, verify that the securities are registered in the company's name, and record in the working papers a description of the securities, including the serial numbers. When the client's records indicate that a particular security has been held since the last audit, the auditors may compare the serial

---

**Figure 17–1**   Objectives of Major Substantive Tests for Investments

| Substantive Tests | Primary Audit Objectives |
| --- | --- |
| Obtain an analysis of securities and related accounts and reconcile to ledger | Clerical accuracy |
| Inspect securities on hand<br>Obtain confirmation of securities held by others | Existence or occurrence;<br>Rights |
| Vouch selected purchases and sales of securities during the year<br>Verify the client's cutoff of securities transactions | Existence or occurrence;<br>Rights; Completeness; and Valuation |
| Perform analytical procedures<br>Compute revenue from securities | Existence or occurrence;<br>Rights; and Completeness |
| Determine market value<br>Evaluate method of accounting for securities | Valuation; and Presentation and disclosure |
| Evaluate financial statement presentation and disclosure | Presentation and disclosure |

number of the certificate with that shown in the prior year's working papers. This will allow the auditors to detect securities that have been sold without authorization during the year and replaced before this year's audit.

While the count of securities ideally is made at the balance sheet date, concurrently with the count of cash and other negotiable instruments, this is not always possible. When not possible, if the securities are kept in a bank safe-deposit box, the client may instruct the bank in writing on the balance sheet date that no one is to have access to the box unless accompanied by the auditors. This arrangement makes it possible to count the securities at a more convenient time after the balance sheet date. Also, banks maintain records of access to safe-deposit boxes that can be examined by the auditors to determine who has had access to the box and at what dates. A representative of the client should be present when the auditors count the securities, and that individual should acknowledge in writing that the securities were returned intact.

## Confirm Securities

| Primary Audit Objectives: |   |
| --- | --- |
| Existence | ☑ |
| Rights | ☑ |

Client-owned securities will often be in the hands of brokers or banks for safekeeping. In such cases the auditors send a confirmation request, signed by the client, to the holders of the securities to verify the existence and ownership of the securities.

## Vouch Purchases and Sales of Securities and Verify Cutoff

| Primary Audit Objectives: |   |
| --- | --- |
| Existence | ☑ |
| Rights | ☑ |
| Completeness | ☑ |
| Valuation | ☑ |

To determine that securities purchased and sold during the period are recorded properly, the auditors vouch a sample of transactions by reference to **brokers' advices** and cash records. In addition, they review transactions for one or two weeks after the balance sheet date to ensure a correct cutoff of transactions. Sometimes sales occur shortly before the balance sheet date but go unrecorded until the securities are delivered to the broker early in the next period. Also, inspection and confirmation procedures will help ensure a proper cutoff of securities transactions.

## Perform Analytical Procedures and Compute Revenue

| Primary Audit Objectives: |   |
| --- | --- |
| Existence | ☑ |
| Rights | ☑ |
| Completeness | ☑ |

The auditors can use analytical procedures to test the reasonableness of the amounts of recorded dividend and interest income, or they can verify the amounts by independent computation. Dividends that should have been received and recorded can be computed by referring to **dividend record books** published by investment advisory services. These books show dividend declarations, amounts, and payment dates for all listed stocks. Interest earned on bonds and notes also can be computed independently by the auditors and compared with recorded amounts in the client's records. This provides evidence both that investment income has not been embezzled and that the client actually owns the securities recorded in the accounting records.

## Determine Market Value and Evaluate Accounting Method

| Primary Audit Objectives: |
|---|
| Valuation  ☑ |
| Presentation  ☑ |

Current market quotations for all marketable securities owned by the client can be verified by reference to financial publications, such as *The Wall Street Journal*, or by obtaining representations from securities brokers. The presentation of marketable equity securities in financial statements is guided by *FASB Statement No. 12*, "Accounting for Certain Marketable Securities," which requires use of the lower of the aggregate cost or market value. Unrealized losses in the current asset portfolio of these securities are recorded in the income statement.

Investments that management intends to hold for the indefinite future are classified as long-term investments. Depending on the type of investment, they are valued at the lower of the aggregate cost or market value, at cost (adjusted for amortized discount or premium), or by the equity method. When the cost method is used, the auditors determine the value by vouching the original purchase and recomputing the amount of any discount or premium amortization. To determine that there is no permanent decline in value, the auditors will obtain information about the current market value of the investment. If the investment is closely held with no active market, the auditors may obtain an appraisal of market value from a securities appraiser. In such cases, the auditors should refer to *SAS 11* (AU 336), "Using the Work of a Specialist," which requires that they consider the professional qualifications of the appraiser and obtain an understanding of the methods and assumptions used.

Investments in common stock that give the investor company the ability to exercise significant influence over operating and financial policies of the investee require use of the equity method of accounting. Ownership of 20 percent of the voting stock of an investee is used as a general indication of ability to exert influence in the absence of evidence to the contrary. Such factors as investor representation on the investee's board of directors and material intercompany transactions also suggest an ability to exercise influence.

When auditing an investment accounted for by the equity method, the auditors must verify that the investment was recorded properly initially. They must also obtain evidence regarding subsequent amounts of income from the investment and of other adjustments to the investment account. This evidence is usually obtained from *audited* financial statements of the investee.

If the audited financial statements of an investee are not available for the period covered by the independent auditors' report on the investor, the auditors should perform a sufficient investigation of the investee's financial statements to determine the fairness of amounts recorded by the investor. In some cases this might involve performing audit procedures at the investee's place of business.

## Evaluate Disclosures

| Primary Audit Objective: |
|---|
| Presentation  ☑ |

The auditors must determine that investments are properly separated into short-term and long-term portfolios. In addition, generally accepted accounting principles require the disclosure of the method of accounting for the securities, and aggregate market values of the various portfolios. Disclosure must also be provided about the amount of realized and unrealized gains and losses, as well as the allowance for market decline of both the current and long-term portfolios.

# AUDITING PROPERTY, PLANT, AND EQUIPMENT

The term *property, plant, and equipment* includes tangible assets with a service life of more than one year that are used in the operation of the business and are not acquired for the purpose of resale. Three major subgroups of such assets are generally recognized:

1. *Land,* such as property used in the operation of the business, has the significant characteristic of not being subject to depreciation.

2. *Buildings, machinery, equipment, and land improvements,* such as fences and parking lots, have limited service lives and are subject to depreciation.

3. *Natural resources* (wasting assets), such as oil wells, coal mines, and tracts of timber, are subject to depletion as the natural resources are extracted or removed.

Acquisitions and disposals of property, plant, and equipment are usually large in dollar amount, but concentrated in only a few transactions. Individual items of plant and equipment may remain unchanged in the accounts for many years.

## Internal Control over Plant and Equipment

The amounts invested in plant and equipment represent a large portion of the total assets of many industrial concerns. Maintenance, rearrangement, and depreciation of these assets are major expenses in the income statement. The sheer size of the amount of the asset and related expenses makes strong internal control essential to the preparation of reliable financial statements. Errors in measurement of income may be material if assets are scrapped without their cost being removed from the accounts, or if the distinction between capital and revenue expenditures is not maintained consistently. The losses that inevitably arise from uncontrolled methods of acquiring, maintaining, and retiring plant and equipment are often greater than the losses from fraud in cash handling.

In large enterprises, the auditors may expect to find an annual plant budget used to forecast and control acquisitions and retirements of plant and equipment. Many small companies also forecast expenditures for plant assets. Successful utilization of a plant budget presupposes the existence of reliable and detailed accounting records for plant and equipment. A detailed knowledge of the kinds, quantities, and condition of existing equipment is an essential basis for intelligent forecasting of the need for replacements and additions to the plant.

Other important internal controls applicable to plant and equipment are as follows:

1. A subsidiary ledger consisting of a separate record for each unit of property. An adequate plant and equipment ledger facilitates control over additions and retirements and comparison of authorizations with actual expenses.

2. A system of authorizations requiring executive approval of all plant and equipment acquisitions, whether by purchase, lease, or construction. Serially numbered capital **work orders** are a convenient means of recording authorizations.

3. A reporting procedure ensuring prompt disclosure and analysis of variances between authorized expenditures and actual costs.

4.  An authoritative written statement of company policy distinguishing between **capital expenditures** and **revenue expenditures.** A dollar minimum ordinarily will be established for capitalization, with lesser expenditures treated as charges against current revenue.

5.  A policy requiring all purchases of plant and equipment to be handled through the purchasing department and subjected to standard routines for receiving, inspection, and payment.

6.  Periodic physical inventories designed to verify the existence, location, and condition of all property listed in the accounts and to verify the completeness of recorded units.

7.  A system of retirement procedures, including serially numbered retirement work orders, stating reasons for retirement and bearing appropriate approvals. A copy of the retirement work order is sent to the accounting department, thus providing assurance that retirements will be reflected in the accounting records.

## Obtaining and Documenting an Understanding of the Internal Control Structure for Property, Plant, and Equipment

As is the case for investments in securities, the client's internal control over property, plant, and equipment is often documented with a written narrative or an internal control questionnaire. The following are typical questions. Are subsidiary ledgers regularly reconciled with general ledger controlling accounts? Are periodic physical inventories of plant assets compared with the subsidiary plant ledgers? Are variances between plant budgets and actual expenditures for plant assets subject to review and approval of executives? Does the sale, transfer, or dismantling of equipment require written executive approval on a serially numbered retirement work order? Is there a written policy for distinguishing between capital expenditures and revenue expenditures?

## Testing Controls and Assessing Control Risk for Property, Plant, and Equipment

If the auditors find that acquisitions of plant and equipment, whether by purchase or construction, are made in accordance with prior budgetary authorizations and that any necessary expenditures not provided for in the budget are made only on approval of a top-level executive, they will be able to minimize the testing of the year's acquisitions. Reference to the reports of the internal auditors is often a convenient method for the independent auditors to become familiar with the scope and dependability of the budgetary controls over plant and equipment. In addition, the auditors may test controls over purchases and sales of these assets by vouching the transactions to source documents. The documents may be examined for evidence of authorization and performance of controls to ensure accurate recording of transactions.

## Objectives for Substantive Tests of Property, Plant, and Equipment

The audit *objectives* for substantive tests of property, plant, and equipment are to:

1.  Determine the *existence* of recorded property, plant, and equipment.
2.  Establish the *completeness* of recorded property, plant, and equipment.
3.  Establish that the client has *rights* to the recorded property, plant, and equipment.

4. Establish the *clerical accuracy* of schedules of property, plant, and equipment.
5. Determine that the *valuation or allocation* of the cost of property, plant, and equipment is in accordance with generally accepted accounting principles.
6. Determine that the *presentation and disclosure* of property, plant, and equipment, including disclosure of depreciation methods, is appropriate.

## Contrast with Audit of Current Assets

In many companies, the investment in plant and equipment amounts to 50 percent or more of the total assets. However, the audit work required to verify these properties is usually a much smaller proportion of the total audit time spent on the engagement. The verification of plant and equipment is facilitated by several factors not applicable to audit work on current assets.

First, a typical unit of property or equipment has a high dollar value, but relatively few transactions. Second, there is usually little change in the property accounts from year to year. The Land account often remains unchanged for a long span of years. The durable nature of buildings and equipment also tends to hold accounting activity to a minimum for these accounts. By way of contrast, such current assets as accounts receivable and inventory may have a complete turnover several times a year.

A third point of contrast between the audit of plant assets and the audit of current assets is the effect of the year-end cutoff of transactions. In the discussion of inventories in Chapter 15, the importance of an accurate year-end cutoff of the transactions for purchases and sales of merchandise was emphasized. An error in the cutoff of a $50,000 purchase or sales transaction may cause a $50,000 error in the year's pretax net income. The possibility of such error is substantial because a large volume of merchandise transactions is normal at year-end. For plant assets, on the other hand, a year-end cutoff error in recording an acquisition or retirement ordinarily will not affect net income for the year. Moreover, for many companies, there may be no transactions in plant assets occurring at the year-end. Of course, a cutoff error relating to acquisition or retirement of plant assets could cause slight inaccuracies in depreciation or in the timing of gains or losses on disposals.

Because of these characteristics, the auditors' approach is to emphasize changes during the current year. In other words, the auditors verify the acquisitions and the retirements of the current period. The beginning balances of the plant and equipment accounts are readily determinable from the prior year's audit working papers. If the auditors are satisfied with the beginning balances and they verify fully the acquisitions and disposals of the current year, then the ending balances will have been completely audited.

## Overall Approach

The key audit working paper for property, plant, and equipment is a summary analysis such as that illustrated in Figure 17–2.

This working paper follows the approach we have previously described of *emphasizing changes during the year under audit*. The working paper shows the beginning balances for the various types of plant assets; these amounts are the ending balances shown in the prior year's working papers. Next, the working paper shows the additions and retirements during the year. These are the transactions upon which the auditors' attention will be

# Figure 17–2    Analysis of Property, Plant, and Equipment

K-1

## THE MANDVILLE CORPORATION

### Summary of Property, Plant, and Equipment and Accumulated Depreciation
### December 31, 19X2

| Account Number | Description | **Assets** Balance 12/31/X1 | Additions | Retirements | Balance 12/31/X2 | Method | Rate | **Accumulated Depreciation** Balance 12/31/X1 | Provision | Retirements | Balance 12/31/X2 |
|---|---|---|---|---|---|---|---|---|---|---|---|
| 151 | Land | 500,000 Ꙭ | 151,000 | | 651,000 | S.L. | | | | | |
| 152-3 | Land Improv. | 135,000 Ꙭ | 10,000 | | 145,000 √ | S.L. | 5% | 13,500 Ꙭ | 7,000 | | 20,500 √ |
| 154-5 | Buildings | 4,500,000 Ꙭ | 495,000 | | 4,995,000 √ | S.L. | 3% | 292,000 Ꙭ | 142,420 Ꙭ | | 434,420 √ |
| 156-7 | Equipment | 800,000 Ꙭ | 110,000 | 60,000 | 850,000 √ | S.L. | 10% | 235,000 Ꙭ | 70,600 Ꙭ | 50,400 | 255,200 √ |
| | TOTALS | 5,935,000 | 766,000 | 60,000 | 6,641,000 | | | 540,500 | 220,020 | 50,400 | 710,120 |
| | | | | | K | | | | | | K |
| | | | K-1-1 | | | | | | K-1-2 | K-1-1 | |

Ꙭ Agreed to prior year work papers.
√ Footed plant and equipment subsidiary ledger cards. No exceptions.

Conclusion:
As a result of our audit procedures for property, plant, and equipment and related depreciation, it is our opinion that the 12/31/X2 balances are fairly stated.

VMcH
1/17/X3

CMW
1/25/X3

focused. A final column shows the ending balances that must equal the beginning balances plus the additions and minus the retirements. A similar set of four columns is used to summarize the changes in the accounts for accumulated depreciation.

Among the other audit working papers for property, plant, and equipment are analyses of the year's additions and retirements, analyses of repairs and maintenance expense accounts, and tests of depreciation. The analyses of plant additions and retirements and the tests of depreciation are cross-indexed to the summary analysis, as illustrated in Figure 17−2. In the audit of larger companies, it is common practice for the client to prepare both a listing of the year's additions and a schedule of the year's disposals for the auditors.

Initial Audit Engagements. The auditing procedures listed in subsequent pages are applicable to repeat engagements and therefore concern only transactions for the current year. In the auditors' first examination of a new client that has changed auditors, the beginning balances of plant and equipment may be substantiated by reference to the predecessor firm's working papers. If previous years' audits were performed by other reputable firms of certified public accountants, it is not customary in a first audit to go beyond a general review of the history of the plant and equipment as recorded in the accounts.

In a first audit of a company that has *not* previously been audited, the ideal approach is a complete historical analysis of the property accounts. By thorough review of all major charges and credits to the property accounts since inception, the auditors can establish the validity of the beginning balances of property, plant, and equipment, and accumulated depreciation.

If the client has been in business for many years, the review of transactions in earlier years necessarily must be performed on a test basis in order to stay within reasonable time limits. However, the importance of an analysis of transactions of prior years deserves emphasis. Only by this approach can the auditors be in a position to express an opinion as to the propriety of the current period's depreciation. If repair and maintenance expenses have been capitalized, or asset additions have been recorded as operating expenses, or retirements of property have gone unrecorded, the depreciation expense will be misstated regardless of the care taken in the selection of depreciation rates. The auditors should make clear to the client that the initial examination of plant and equipment requires procedures that need not be duplicated in subsequent engagements.

## Substantive Tests for Property, Plant, and Equipment

Figure 17−3 presents typical substantive tests used to meet the primary audit objectives for property, plant, and equipment. In the following sections we describe these procedures in detail.

## Obtain Analysis of Changes in Property, Plant, and Equipment

| Primary Audit Objective: |
| --- |
| Clerical<br>  accuracy   ☑ |

The auditors may verify the beginning balances of property, plant, and equipment assets by reference to the prior year's audit working papers. In addition to beginning balances, the summary analysis will show the additions and retirements of property, plant, and equipment during the year under audit. As the audit progresses, the auditors will examine the support for a sample of these additions and retirements. The detailed working papers

Figure 17–3    Objectives of Major Substantive Tests for Investments

| Substantive Tests | Primary Audit Objectives |
|---|---|
| Obtain a summary analysis of changes in property owned and reconcile to ledgers | Clerical accuracy |
| Vouch additions during year | Existence or occurrence; Rights; and Valuation or allocation |
| Make physical inspection of major acquisitions | Existence or occurrence; Completeness |
| Analyze repair and maintenance expense accounts<br>Test the client's provision for depreciation | Valuation or allocation |
| Investigate the status of property not in current use | Valuation or allocation; Presentation |
| Investigate retirements of property during the year<br>Examine evidence of legal ownership<br>Review rental revenue | Existence or occurrence; Rights |
| Examine lease agreements<br>Perform analytical procedures | Existence or occurrence; Completeness; Rights; and Valuation or allocation |
| Evaluate financial statement presentation and disclosure | Presentation and disclosure |

showing this verification will support and be cross-indexed to the summary analysis worksheet.

Before making a detailed analysis of changes in property accounts during the year, the auditors will determine that the amounts in the subsidiary ledgers agree in total with the balances in the controlling accounts. Reconciliation of the subsidiary ledgers with the controlling accounts can be performed very quickly with the use of generalized audit software.

## Vouch Additions to Property, Plant, and Equipment

| Primary Audit Objectives: | |
|---|---|
| Existence | ☑ |
| Rights | ☑ |
| Valuation | ☑ |

The vouching of additions to the property, plant, and equipment accounts during the period under audit is one of the most important substantive tests. The extent of the vouching is dependent upon the auditors' assessment of control risk for the existence and valuation of plant and equipment. The vouching process utilizes a working paper analysis of the general ledger controlling accounts and includes the tracing of entries through the journals to original documents, such as contracts, deeds, construction work orders, invoices, canceled checks, and authorization by directors.

The specific steps to be taken in investigating the year's additions usually will include the following:

a.   Review changes during the year in construction in progress and examine supporting work orders, both incomplete and closed.

b.   Examine transfers from the Construction in Progress account to the property accounts, observing propriety of classification. Determine that all completed items have been transferred.

c.   On a test basis, vouch purchases of plant, property, and equipment to invoices, deeds, contracts, or other supporting documents. Recompute extensions, footings, and treatment of discounts. Make certain revenue expenditures (e.g., repairs and maintenance) were not improperly capitalized.

d.   Investigate all instances in which the actual cost of acquisitions substantially exceeded authorized amounts. Determine whether such excess expenditures were analyzed and approved by appropriate officials.

e.   Investigate fully any debits to property, plant, and equipment accounts not arising from acquisition of physical assets.

f.   Determine that the total cost of any plant and equipment assets purchased on the installment plan is reflected in the asset accounts and that the unpaid installments are set up as liabilities. Ascertain that all plant and equipment leases that in effect are installment purchases are capitalized. Interest charges should not be capitalized as a cost of the asset acquired.

The accounting for plant assets acquired in a trade-in or other exchange is specified by *APB Opinion No. 29,* "Accounting for Nonmonetary Transactions." No gain is recognized when a plant asset is exchanged for a similar plant asset. The asset required in the exchange is valued at the carrying amount of the asset given up plus any additional cash paid or amount financed.

Assets constructed by a company for its own use should be recorded at the cost of direct material, direct labor, and applicable overhead cost. However, auditors may apply the additional test of comparing the total cost of self-constructed equipment with bids or estimated purchase prices for similar equipment from outside suppliers; excess cost of self-constructed assets should be expensed.

Related-Party Transactions.    Assets acquired from affiliated corporations, from promoters or stockholders, or by any other type of related-party transaction not involving arm's-length bargaining between buyer and seller have sometimes been recorded at inflated amounts. The auditors should inquire into the methods by which the sales price was determined, the cost of the property to the vendor, length of ownership by the vendor, and any other available evidence that might indicate an arbitrarily determined valuation. Material related-party transactions must be disclosed in the notes to the financial statements.

## Inspect Major Acquisitions of Property, Plant, and Equipment

| Primary Audit Objectives: |
| --- |
| Existence ☑ |
| Completeness ☑ |

The auditors usually make a physical inspection of major units of plant and equipment acquired during the year under audit. This step is helpful in maintaining a good working knowledge of the client's operations and also in interpreting the accounting entries for both additions and retirements.

The audit procedure of physical inspection may flow in either direction between the plant assets and the records of plant assets. By tracing items in the plant ledger to the physical assets, the auditors prove that the assets shown in the accounting records *actually exist* and are in current use. The alternative testing procedure is to inspect selected assets in the plant and trace these assets to the detailed records. This test provides evidence that all existing assets are recorded.

The physical inspection of plant assets may be limited to major units acquired during the year or may be extended to include tests of older equipment as well. In a few situations (especially when control risk is very high), the auditors may conclude that the taking of a complete physical inventory is needed. Bear in mind, however, that a complete physical inventory of plant and equipment is a rare event. If such an inventory is required, the auditors' role is to *observe* the taking of the physical inventory.

Let us consider an example of a situation in which the auditors might conclude that a complete physical inventory of equipment is needed. Assume that a client is engaged in commercial construction work and that the client owns and operates a great many units of costly mobile equipment. Such equipment may often be scrapped or sold upon the authorization of a field supervisor. Under these circumstances, the auditors might regard a complete physical inventory of plant and equipment as essential. Similarly, in the audit of clients owning a large number of automobiles and trucks, the auditors may insist upon observing a physical count, as well as examining legal title.

Some large companies, as part of their internal control, perform occasional physical inventories of plant and equipment at certain locations or in selected departments. The *observation* of these limited counts is often carried out by the client's internal auditing staff rather than by the independent auditors.

## Analyze Repair and Maintenance Expense

| Primary Audit Objective: |
| --- |
| Valuation ☑ |

The auditors' principal objective in analyzing repair and maintenance expense accounts is to discover items that should have been capitalized. Many companies have a written policy setting the minimum expenditure to be capitalized. For example, company policy may prescribe that no expenditure for less than $300 shall be capitalized regardless of the service life of the item purchased. In such cases, the auditors will analyze the repair and maintenance accounts with a view toward determining the consistency of application of this policy as well as compliance with generally accepted accounting principles. To determine that the accounts contain only proper repair and maintenance charges, the auditors will vouch the larger expenditures to supporting documentation. The accuracy of the client's accounting for the expenditures may be verified by reference to vendors' invoices, to material requisitions, and to labor time records.

One useful means of identifying any capital expenditures that are buried in the repair and maintenance accounts is to obtain or prepare an analysis of the monthly amounts of expense with corresponding amounts listed for the preceding year. Any significant variations from month to month or between corresponding months of the two years should be fully investigated. If maintenance expense is classified by the departments serviced, the variations are especially noticeable.

## Test Depreciation Expense

| Primary Audit Objective: |
| --- |
| Valuation              ☑ |

The auditors' approach to verification of depreciation expense must recognize that the total is an *estimate*. Determining the annual depreciation expense involves two rather arbitrary decisions by the client company: first, an estimate of the useful economic lives of various groups of assets and, second, a choice among several depreciation methods.

Among the methods of computing depreciation expense most frequently encountered are the straight-line and accelerated depreciation methods. The most widely adopted type of accelerated depreciation method is the fixed percentage of declining balance method. The essential characteristic of this and other similar methods is that depreciation expense is greatest in the first year and becomes smaller in succeeding years. Far less common, although quite acceptable, are methods based on units of output or hours of service.

CPAs often encounter clients maintaining their records using federal income tax rules, such as the accelerated cost recovery system (ACRS) or the modified accelerated cost recovery system (MACRS). Although such methods are considered a systematic method of depreciating the cost of an asset, the depreciable lives of the assets are often much shorter than their useful economic lives. If the recovery periods are not reasonable, the depreciation expense may be materially misstated and the auditors would not be in a position to issue an unqualified opinion on the financial statements.

Depreciation relates most directly to the *valuation or allocation* audit objective. To meet this objective, the auditors, in examining depreciation methods and amounts, determine that *(a)* the methods in use are acceptable, *(b)* the methods are being followed consistently, and *(c)* the calculations required by the chosen methods are accurate. The approach for determining that the chosen methods are calculated properly is largely one of recalculation or performing tests of reasonableness.

## Investigate Property Not in Use

| Primary Audit Objective: |
| --- |
| Valuation              ☑ |
| Presentation           ☑ |

Land, buildings, and equipment not in current use should be investigated thoroughly to determine the prospects for their future use in operations. Plant assets that are temporarily idle need not be reclassified, and depreciation may be continued at normal rates. On the other hand, idle equipment that has been dismantled, or that for any reason appears unsuitable for future operating use, should be written down to an estimated realizable value and excluded from the plant and equipment classification. In the case of standby equipment and other property not needed at present or prospective levels of operation, the auditors should consider whether the carrying value is recoverable through future use in operations.

---

◆ ILLUSTRATIVE CASE ◆

During the 1970s, many large public utility companies began the construction of nuclear power plants which were believed to be the best source of electricity for the future. By the mid-1980s, however, a number of these projects had turned into financial nightmares. In many cases, the cost to date of a half-completed nuclear plant was several times the original estimate of total cost. Construction had ground virtually to a halt, and the prospects for getting these nuclear plants into operation were dim. Efforts of the antinuclear lobby and legal battles combined with engineering problems to raise doubts whether nuclear plants representing investments in the billions would ever become operational.

These developments created a most difficult situation for the CPA firms having "nuclear utilities" as clients. Should the costly nuclear facilities be written off even though such action would wipe out the stockholders' equity? Should the uncompleted facilities be carried at cost in the companies' financial statements despite the distinct possibility that they would never be completed? Most auditing firms felt that they must modify their audit reports to indicate that the future solvency of the client company rested on a favorable solution to the problem of the uncompleted nuclear plant.

---

## Investigate Retirements of Property, Plant, and Equipment

| Primary Audit Objectives: |   |
|---|---|
| Existence | ☑ |
| Rights | ☑ |

The principal purpose of this procedure is to determine whether any property has been replaced, sold, dismantled, or abandoned without such action being reflected in the accounting records. Nearly every thorough physical inventory of plant and equipment reveals missing units of property—units disposed of without a corresponding reduction of the accounts.

If the machine is sold for cash or traded in on a new machine, the transaction generally will involve the use of documents, such as a cash receipts form or a purchase order; the processing of these documents may bring the retirement to the attention of accounting personnel. However, plant assets may be scrapped rather than sold; consequently, there may be no paperwork to evidence the disappearance of a machine. The following measures often are effective for detecting unrecorded retirements:

a. If major additions of plant and equipment have been made during the year, ascertain whether old equipment was traded in or replaced by the new units.

b. Analyze the Miscellaneous Revenue account to locate any cash proceeds from sale of plant assets.

c. If any of the company's products have been discontinued during the year, investigate the disposition of plant facilities formerly used in manufacturing such products.

d. Inquire of executives and supervisors whether any plant assets have been retired during the year.

e. Examine retirement work orders or other source documents for authorization by the appropriate official or committee.

*f.*   Investigate any reduction of insurance coverage to determine whether this was caused by retirement of plant assets.

## Examine Legal Ownership

To determine that plant assets are the property of the client, the auditors look for such evidence as a deed, title insurance policy, property tax bills, receipts for payments to mortgagee, and fire insurance policies. Additionally, the fact that rental payments are not being made is supporting evidence of ownership.

It is sometimes suggested that the auditors may verify ownership of real property and the absence of liens by examination of public records. This step is seldom taken. Inspection of the documentary evidence listed above usually provides adequate proof of ownership. If some doubt exists as to whether the client has a clear title to property, the auditors should obtain the opinion of the client's legal counsel or request that a title search be performed by a title insurance company.

Possession of a deed is not absolute proof of present ownership because when real property is sold, a new deed is prepared and the old one is retained by the seller. This is true of title insurance policies as well. Better evidence of continuing ownership is found in property tax bills made out in the name of the client and in fire insurance policies, rent receipts from lessees, and regular payments of principal and interest to a mortgagee or trustee.

The disclosure of liens on property is considered during the examination of liabilities, but in the audit work on plant and equipment the auditors should be alert for evidence indicating the existence of liens. Purchase contracts examined in verifying the cost of property may reveal unpaid balances. Insurance policies may contain loss payable endorsements in favor of a secured party.

The ownership of automobiles and trucks can be ascertained readily by the auditors by reference to certificates of title and registration documents. The ease of transfer of title to automotive equipment, plus the fact that is is often used as collateral for loans, makes it important that the auditors examine the title to such property.

## Review Rental Revenue

In testing rental revenue from land and buildings, it is often desirable for the auditors to obtain or to sketch a map of the property and to make a physical inspection of each unit. This may disclose that premises reported as vacant are in fact occupied by lessees and are producing revenue not reflected in the accounting records. If the client's property includes an office or apartment building, the auditors should obtain a floor plan of the building as well as copies of all lease contracts. In this way, they can account for all available rental space as revenue producing or vacant and can verify reported vacancies by physical inspection at the balance sheet date. If interim audit work is being performed, vacancies should also be verified by inspection and discussion with management during the year.

Examination of leases will indicate whether tenants are responsible for the cost of electricity, water, gas, and telephone service. These provisions should be reconciled with utility expense accounts. Rental revenue accounts should be analyzed in all cases and the amount compared with lease agreements and cash records.

## Examine Lease Agreements

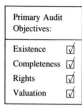

The preceding step addressed rental revenue from leases. The auditors must also be aware that generally accepted accounting principles require differing accounting treatments for operating and capital leases. The auditors should carefully examine lease agreements to determine whether the accounting for the assets involved is proper. For example, the auditors must determine whether assets leased by the client should be capitalized.

## Perform Analytical Procedures

The specific trends and ratios used in judging the overall reasonableness of recorded amounts for plant and equipment will vary with the nature of the client's operations. Among the ratios and trends often used by auditors for this purpose are the following:

*a.* Total cost of plant assets divided by annual output in dollars, pounds, or other units.

*b.* Total cost of plant assets divided by cost of goods sold.

*c.* Comparison of repairs and maintenance expense on a monthly basis and from year to year.

*d.* Comparison of acquisitions for the current year with prior years.

*e.* Comparison of retirements for the current year with prior years.

Acquisitions and retirements may vary widely from year to year; however, it is essential that the auditors be aware of these variations and judge their reasonableness in the light of trends in the client's past and present operations.

## Evaluate Disclosures

The balance sheet or accompanying notes should disclose balances of major classes of depreciable assets. Accumulated depreciation may be shown by major class or in total, and the method or methods of computing depreciation should be stated. The total amount of depreciation should be disclosed in the income statement or supporting notes.

In addition, adequate financial statement presentation and disclosure will ordinarily reflect the following principles:

*a.* The basis of valuation should be explicitly stated. Cost is the generally accepted basis of valuation for plant and equipment; property not in use should be valued at the lower of cost or estimated realizable value.

*b.* Property pledged to secure loans should be clearly identified.

*c.* Property not in current use should be segregated in the balance sheet.

## Timing of Audit Procedures

Most of the audit work on plant and equipment can be performed in advance of the balance sheet date. For the initial audit of a new client, the time-consuming task of reviewing the records of prior years and establishing the beginning balances in the plant accounts for the current period may be completed before the year-end.

In repeat engagements, as well as in first audits, many auditing firms lighten their year-end work loads by performing interim work during October and November, including the analysis of the plant and equipment ledger accounts for the first 9 or 10 months of the year. After the balance sheet date, the work necessary on property accounts is then limited to examination of the transactions for the final two or three months.

## Examination of Natural Resources

In the audit of companies operating properties subject to depletion (mines, oil and gas deposits, timberlands, and other natural resources), the auditors follow a pattern similar to that used in evaluating the provision for depreciation expense and accumulated depreciation. They determine whether depletion has been recorded consistently and in accordance with generally accepted accounting principles, and they test the mathematical accuracy of the client's computations.

The depletion of timberlands is usually based on physical quantities established by cruising. (The term **cruising** means the inspection of a tract of forestland for the purpose of estimating the total lumber yield.) The determination of physical quantities to use as a basis for depletion is more difficult in many mining ventures and for oil and gas deposits. The auditors often rely upon the opinions of such specialists as mining engineers and geologists about the reasonableness of the depletion rates being used for such resources. Under these circumstances, the auditors must comply with the provisions of *SAS 11* (AU 336), "Using the Work of a Specialist," as discussed in Chapter 6.

If the number of tons of ore in a mining property could be accurately determined in advance, an exact depletion cost per ton could be computed by dividing the cost of the mine by the number of tons available for extraction. In reality, the contents of the mine can only be estimated, and the estimates may require significant revision as mining operations progress.

The auditors investigate the ownership and the cost of mining properties by examining deeds, leases, tax bills, vouchers, paid checks, and other records in the same manner that they verify the plant and equipment of a manufacturing or trading concern. The costs of exploration and development work in a mine customarily are capitalized until such time as commercial production begins. After that date additional development work generally is treated as expense. The large oil companies capitalize the costs of drilling oil wells only if they are found to be productive. Under this "successful efforts" policy, the costs of drilling wells which prove not to be productive are immediately written off. However, some smaller companies follow an alternative "full-cost" policy, under which all drilling costs are capitalized and amortized over future years.

## Examination of Intangible Assets

The balance sheet caption "Intangible Assets" includes a variety of assets. All intangible assets are characterized by a lack of physical substance. Furthermore, they do not qualify as current assets, and they are nonmonetary—that is, they do not represent fixed claims to cash.

Among the more prominent intangible assets are goodwill, patents, trademarks, franchises, and leaseholds. Since intangible assets are lacking in physical substance, their value lies in the rights or economic advantages afforded in their ownership. Because of their intangible nature, these assets may be more difficult to identify than units of plant and equipment. When a client treats an expenditure as creating an intangible asset, the auditors must look for objective evidence that a genuine asset has come into existence.

The auditors' substantiation of intangible assets may begin with an analysis of the ledger accounts for these assets. Debits to the accounts should be traced to evidence of payment having been made and to documentary evidence of the rights or benefits acquired. Credits to the accounts should be reconciled with the client's program of amortization or traced to appropriate authorization for the write-off of the asset.

One intangible asset that may be large in amount yet of questionable future economic benefit is *goodwill*. Goodwill arises in accounting for business combinations in which the price paid to acquire another company exceeds the fair value of the identifiable net assets acquired. When business combinations result in the recording of goodwill, the auditors should review the allocation of the lump-sum acquisition cost among tangible assets, identifiable intangible assets, and goodwill.

As part of an analysis of intangible asset accounts, the auditors should review the reasonableness of the client's amortization program. Amortization is ordinarily computed by the straight-line method over the years estimated to be benefitted, but not in excess of 40 years.

## ◆ CHAPTER SUMMARY

This chapter described the details of the investment cycle, including summary comments about the auditors' consideration of the internal controls for this transaction cycle and the auditors' substantive tests of investment cycle accounts—investments in securities and property, plant, and equipment. To summarize:

1. Many of the controls present in the acquisition and revenue cycles impact the investment cycle.

2. The high value and liquid nature of many investments makes the separation of the authorization, custody, and recordkeeping functions especially important. In addition, securities should be registered in the name of the company; complete, detailed records of securities should be maintained; and securities should be physically inspected periodically.

3. After the auditors obtain an understanding of the client's internal control policies and procedures for the investment cycle, the limited number of transactions generally involved will often lead to a decision by the auditors to assess control risk at a relatively high level and to perform detailed substantive tests.

4. Auditors often vouch security transactions during the year and inspect securities on hand at year-end. The liquid nature of many investments in securities makes cutoff tests especially important. Tests of market values will be performed in conjunction with determining the proper valuation of investments.

5. Key internal controls over property, plant, and equipment should include proper authorization of acquisitions, adequate records for the various units of property, periodic physical inspection of property, and the use of serially numbered retirement work orders.

6.  In the audit of property, plant, and equipment for a continuing client, the emphasis of the testing is on transactions that occurred during the year, as contrasted to an emphasis on ending balances. Depreciation expense is often tested by recomputation or through the use of analytical procedures.

# ◆ KEY TERMS INTRODUCED OR EMPHASIZED IN CHAPTER 17

**Broker's advice**   A notification sent by a stockbrokerage firm to a customer reporting the terms of a purchase or sale of securities.

**Capital expenditure**   An expenditure for property, plant, and equipment that is properly charged to an asset account.

**Cruising**   The inspection of a tract of forestland for the purpose of estimating the total lumber yield.

**Dividend record book**   A reference book published monthly by investment advisory services reporting detailed information concerning all listed and many unlisted securities; includes dividend dates and amounts, current prices of securities, and other condensed financial data.

**Revenue expenditure**   An expenditure for property, plant, and equipment that is properly charged to an expense account.

**Work order**   A serially numbered accounting document authorizing the acquisition of plant assets. A separate series of retirement work orders may be used to authorize the retirement or disposal of plant assets, and a third variety consists of documents authorizing repair or maintenance of plant assets.

# ◆ GROUP I: REVIEW QUESTIONS

17-1   What documents should be examined in verifying the purchases and sales of securities made during the year under audit?

17-2   How can the auditors determine that all dividends applicable to marketable securities owned by the client have been received and recorded?

17-3   What information should be noted by the auditors during their inspection of securities on hand?

17-4   Assume that it is not possible for you to be present on the balance sheet date to inspect the securities owned by the client. What variation in audit procedures is appropriate if the inspection is not made until two weeks after the balance sheet date?

17-5   A well-financed audit client of your CPA firm invests large amounts in marketable securities. As part of its internal control, the company uses a monthly report of securities transactions. The report is prepared by the controller and presented to the investment committee of the board of directors. What information should this report contain?

17-6   An audit client that has never before invested in securities recently acquired more than a million dollars in cash from the sale of real estate no longer used in operations. The president intends to invest this money in marketable securities until such time as the opportunity arises for advantageous acquisition of a new plant site. He asks you to enumerate the principal factors you would recommend to create strong internal control over marketable securities.

17-7   Identify at least three elements of strong internal control for property, plant, and equipment.

17-8    What documentary evidence is usually available to the auditors in the client's office to substantiate the legal ownership of property, plant, and equipment?

17-9    Moultrie Company discovered recently that a number of its property and equipment assets had been retired from use several years ago without any entries being made in the accounting records. The company asks you to suggest procedures that will prevent unrecorded retirement of assets.

17-10    Does a failure to record the retirement of machinery affect net income? Explain.

17-11    The auditors' verification of plant and equipment is facilitated by several factors not applicable to audit work on current assets. What are these factors?

17-12    Do the auditors question the service lives adopted by the client for plant assets, or do they accept the service lives without investigation? Explain.

17-13    Should the independent auditors observe a physical inventory of property and equipment in every audit engagement? Discuss.

17-14    Hamlin Metals Company has sales representatives covering several states and provides automobiles for them and for its executives. Describe any substantive tests you would consider appropriate for the company's fleet of more than 100 automobiles, other than the verification procedures generally applicable to all property and equipment.

17-15    Explain the use of a system of authorizations for additions to plant and equipment.

17-16    What is a principal objective of the auditors in analyzing a Maintenance and Repairs expense account?

17-17    In response to threats from a terrorist organization, Technology International installed protective measures consisting of chainlink fences, concrete road barriers, electronic gates, and underground parking at its manufacturing facilities. The costs of these installations were debited to the Land account. Indicate with reasons your approval or disapproval of this accounting treatment.

17-18    Gibson Manufacturing Company acquired new factory machinery this year and ceased using the old machinery. The old equipment was retained, however, and is capable of being used if the demand for the company's products warrants additional production. How should the old machinery be handled in the accounting records and on the financial statements?

17-19    What are the objectives of establishing internal control policies and procedures for plant and equipment?

17-20    Explain how the existence of lease agreements may result in understated plant and equipment.

17-21    The auditors' verification of current assets such as cash, securities, and inventories emphasizes observation, inspection, and confirmation to determine the physical existence of these assets. Should the auditors take a similar approach to establish the existence of the recorded plant assets? Explain fully.

17-22    K-J Corporation has current assets of $5 million and approximately the same amount of plant and equipment. Should the two groups of assets require about the same amount of audit time? Give reasons.

17-23    You are conducting your first audit of Clarke Manufacturing Company. Plant and equipment represent a very substantial portion of the total assets. What verification, if any, will you make of the balances of the ledger accounts for Plant and Equipment as of the beginning of the period under audit?

17-24    List three substantive tests the auditors could use to detect unrecorded retirements of property, plant, and equipment.

17-25   Should the auditors examine public records to determine the legal title of property apparently owned by the client?

17-26   Mellon, Inc. wants to use the same depreciation methods for financial statement purposes that the corporation uses for tax purposes. Is this appropriate? Explain.

# ◆ GROUP II: QUESTIONS REQUIRING ANALYSIS

17-27   Give the purposes of each of the following procedures that may be included in an internal control structure, and explain how each procedure contributes to strong internal control:
   a.   Forecasting of expenditures for property, plant, and equipment.
   b.   Maintaining a plant ledger for property, plant, and equipment.

(AICPA, adapted)

17-28   Kadex Corporation, a small manufacturing company, did not use the services of independent auditors during the first two years of its existence. Near the end of the third year, Kadex retained Jones & Scranton, CPAs, to perform an audit for the year ended December 31. Officials of the company requested that the CPA firm perform only the audit work necessary to provide an audit report on the financial statements for the current year.

During the first two years of its operation, Kadex had erroneously treated some material acquisitions of plant and equipment as revenue expenditures. No such errors occurred in the third year.

Required:   a.   Under these circumstances, would Jones & Scranton, CPAs, be likely to learn of the transactions erroneously treated as revenue expenditures in Years 1 and 2? Explain.
   b.   Would the income statement and balance sheet prepared at the end of Year 3 be affected by the above accounting errors made in Years 1 and 2? If so, identify the specific items. Explain fully.

17-29   List and state the purpose of all audit procedures that might reasonably be applied by the auditors to determine that all property and equipment retirements have been recorded in the accounting records.

17-30   Your new client, Ross Products, Inc., completed its first fiscal year March 31, Year 10. During the course of your audit you discover the following entry in the general journal, dated April 1, Year 9.

| | | |
|---|---|---|
| Building . . . . . . . . . . . . . . . . . . . . . . . . . . . . . . . . . . | 2,400,000 | |
|    Mortgage Note Payable . . . . . . . . . . . . . . . . . . . . . . | | 1,400,000 |
|    Common Stock . . . . . . . . . . . . . . . . . . . . . . . . . . | | 1,000,000 |

   To record (1) acquisition of building constructed by J. A. Ross Construction Co. (a sole proprietorship); (2) assumption of Ross Construction Co. mortgage loan for construction of the building; and (3) issuance of entire authorized common stock (10,000 shares, $100 par value) to J. A. Ross.

Under these circumstances, what steps should the auditors take to verify the $2,400,000 recorded cost of the building? Explain fully.

17-31   An executive of a manufacturing company informs you that no formal procedures have been followed to control the retirement of machinery and equipment. A physical inventory of plant assets has just been completed. It revealed that 25 percent of the assets carried in the ledger were not on hand and had presumably been scrapped. The accounting records have been adjusted to agree with the physical inventory. Outline internal control practices to govern future retirements.

17-32   Allen Fraser was president of three corporations: Missouri Metals Corporation, Kansas Metals Corporation, and Iowa Metals Corporation. Each of the three corporations owned land and buildings acquired for approximately $500,000. An appraiser retained by Fraser in 19X1 estimated the current value of the land and buildings in each corporation at approximately $3,000,000. The appraisals were recorded in the accounts. A new corporation, called Midwest Corporation, was then formed, and Fraser became its president. The new corporation purchased the assets of the three predecessor corporations, making payment in capital stock. The balance sheet of Midwest Corporation shows land and buildings "valued at cost" in the amount of $9,000,000, the carrying values to the vendor companies at the time of transfer to Midwest Corporation. Do you consider this treatment acceptable? Explain.

17-33   Shortly after you were retained to audit the financial statements of Case Corporation, you learned from a preliminary discussion with management that the corporation had recently acquired a competing business, the Mall Company. In your study of the terms of the acquisition, you find that the total purchase price was paid in cash and that the transaction was authorized by the board of directors and fully described in the minutes of the directors' meetings. The only aspect of the acquisition of the Mall Company that raises any doubts in your mind is the allocation of the total purchase price among the several kinds of assets acquired. The allocation, which had been specifically approved by the board of directors of Case Corporation, placed very high values on the tangible assets acquired and allowed nothing for goodwill.

    You are inclined to believe that the allocation of the lump-sum price to the several types of assets was somewhat unreasonable because the total price for the business was as much or more than the current replacement cost of the tangible assets acquired. However, as an auditor, you do not claim to be an expert in property values. Would you question the propriety of the directors' allocation of the lump-sum purchase price? Explain fully.

17-34   In your first audit of the financial statements of Willman Company, you discover that the company has included in the Miscellaneous Revenue account a $10,000 commission from Bradley Realtors, Inc. Your investigation discloses that Bradley negotiated Willman's purchase for $500,000 of a tract of land from Payne Company, and that Payne had paid Bradley's commission of $50,000 on the sale.

    Would you take exception to Willman Company's accounting for the commission received from Bradley Realtors, Inc.? Explain.

17-35   Select the best answer for each of the questions below and explain fully the reason for your selection.
    a.  With respect to an internal control measure that will ensure accountability for fixed asset retirements, management should implement an internal control structure that includes:
        (1)  Continuous analysis of miscellaneous revenue to locate any cash proceeds from sale of plant assets.
        (2)  Periodic inquiry of plant executives by internal auditors as to whether any plant assets have been retired.
        (3)  Utilization of serially numbered retirement work orders.
        (4)  Periodic observation of plant assets by the internal auditors.
    b.  The auditors may conclude that depreciation charges are insufficient by noting:
        (1)  Insured values greatly in excess of book values.
        (2)  Large amounts of fully depreciated assets.
        (3)  Continuous trade-ins of relatively new assets.
        (4)  Excessive recurring losses on assets retired.

    *c.*  Which of the following is an internal control weakness related to factory equipment?

        (1)  Checks issued in payment of purchases of equipment are not signed by the controller.

        (2)  All purchases of factory equipment are required to be made by the department in need of the equipment.

        (3)  Factory equipment replacements are generally made when estimated useful lives, as indicated in depreciation schedules, have expired.

        (4)  Proceeds from sales of fully depreciated equipment are credited to other income.

    *d.*  Which of the following accounts should be reviewed by the auditors to gain reasonable assurance that additions to property, plant, and equipment are *not* understated?

        (1)  Depreciation.

        (2)  Accounts payable.

        (3)  Cash.

        (4)  Repairs.

    *e.*  In order to guard against the misappropriation of company-owned marketable securities, which of the following is the *best* course of action that can be taken by a company with a large portfolio of marketable securities?

        (1)  Require that one trustworthy and bonded employee be responsible for access to the safekeeping area where securities are kept.

        (2)  Require that employees who enter and leave the safekeeping area sign and record in a log the exact reason for their access.

        (3)  Require that employees involved in the safekeeping function maintain a subsidiary control ledger for securities on a current basis.

        (4)  Require that the safekeeping function for securities be assigned to a bank or stockbroker that will act as a custodial agent.

    *f.*  Hall Company had large amounts of funds to invest on a temporary basis. The board of directors decided to purchase marketable securities and assigned the future purchase and sale decisions to a responsible financial executive. The best person(s) to make periodic reviews of the investment activity would be:

        (1)  An investment committee of the board of directors.

        (2)  The chief operating officer.

        (3)  The corporate controller.

        (4)  The treasurer.

## ◆ GROUP III: PROBLEMS

**17-36**  You are in charge of the audit of the financial statements of Hawk Corporation for the year ended December 31. The corporation has had the policy of investing its surplus cash in marketable securities. Its stock and bond certificates are kept in a safe-deposit box in a local bank. Only the president or the treasurer of the corporation has access to the box.

    You were unable to obtain access to the safe-deposit box on December 31 because neither the president nor the treasurer was available. Arrangements were made for your staff assistant to accompany the treasurer to the bank on January 11 to examine the securities. Your assistant has never examined securities that were being kept in a safe-deposit box and requires instructions. To inspect all the securities on hand should not require more than one hour.

*Required:*  *a.*  List the instructions that you would give to your assistant regarding the examination of the stock and bond certificates kept in the safe-deposit box. Include in your instructions the details of the securities to be examined and the reasons for examining these details.

b.   Upon returning from the bank, your assistant reported that the treasurer had entered the box on January 4. The treasurer stated that the purpose of the January 4 visit to the safe-deposit box had been to remove an old photograph of the corporation's original building. The photograph was reportedly loaned to the local chamber of commerce for display purposes. List the additional audit procedures that are required because of the treasurer's action.

(AICPA, adapted)

17-37   The following are typical questions that might appear on an internal control questionnaire relating to plant and equipment:
1.   Has a dollar minimum been established for expenditures to be capitalized?
2.   Are subsidiary ledgers for plant and equipment regularly reconciled with general ledger controlling accounts?

*Required:*   a.   State the purpose of each of the above internal control procedures.
b.   Describe the manner in which each of the above procedures might be tested.
c.   Assuming that the operating effectiveness of each of the above procedures is found to be inadequate, describe how the auditors might alter their substantive tests to compensate for the increased level of control risk.

17-38   Chem-Lite, Inc. maintains its accounts on the basis of a fiscal year ending March 31. At March 31, 19X1, the Equipment account in the general ledger appeared as shown below. The company uses straight-line depreciation, 10-year life, and 10 percent salvage value for all its equipment. It is the company's policy to take a full year's depreciation on all additions to equipment occurring during the fiscal year, and you may treat this policy as a satisfactory one for the purpose of this problem. The company has recorded depreciation for the fiscal year ended March 31, 19X1.

*Equipment Account*

| | |
|---|---|
| 4/1/X0 Bal. forward | 100,000 |
| 12/1/X0 | 10,500 |
| 1/2/X1 | 1,015 |
| 2/1/X1 | 1,015 |
| 3/1/X1 | 1,015 |

Upon further investigation, you find the following contract dated December 1, 19X0, covering the acquisition of equipment:

| | |
|---|---|
| List price | $30,000 |
| 5% sales tax | 1,500 |
| Total | 31,500 |
| Down payment | 10,500 |
| Balance | 21,000 |
| 8% interest, 24 months | 3,360 |
| Contract amount | $24,360 |

*Required:*

Prepare in good form, including full explanations, the adjusting entry (entries) you would propose as auditor of Chem-Lite, Inc. with respect to the equipment and related depreciation accounts at March 31, 19X1. (Assume that all amounts given are material.)

(AICPA, adapted)

17-39   Nova Land Development Corporation is a closely held corporation engaged in purchasing large tracts of land, subdividing the tracts, and installing paved streets and utilities. The corporation does not construct buildings for the buyers of the land and does not have any affiliated construction companies. Undeveloped land usually is leased for farming until the corporation is ready to begin developing it.

The corporation finances its land acquisitions by mortgages; the mortgagees require audited financial statements. This is your first audit of the company, and you have now begun the audit of the financial statements for the year ended December 31.

*Required:* The corporation has three tracts of land in various stages of development. List the audit procedures to be employed in the verification of the physical existence and title to the corporation's three landholdings.

(AICPA, adapted)

17-40 J. Barnes, CPA, has been retained to audit a manufacturing company with a balance sheet that includes the caption Property, Plant, and Equipment. Barnes has been asked by the company's management if audit adjustments or reclassifications are required for the following material items that have been included or excluded from Property, Plant, and Equipment.

1. A tract of land was acquired during the year. The land is the future site of the client's new headquarters, which will be constructed in the following year. Commissions were paid to the real estate agent used to acquire the land, and expenditures were made to relocate the previous owner's equipment. These commissions and expenditures were expensed and are excluded from Property, Plant, and Equipment.

2. Clearing costs were incurred to make the land ready for construction. These costs were included in Property, Plant, and Equipment.

3. During the land-clearing process, timber and gravel were recovered and sold. The proceeds from the sale were recorded as other income and are excluded from Property, Plant, and Equipment.

4. A group of machines was purchased under a royalty agreement, which provides royalty payments based on units of production from the machines. The cost of the machines, freight costs, unloading charges, and royalty payments were capitalized and are included in Property, Plant, and Equipment.

*Required:* a. Describe the general characteristics of assets, such as land, buildings, improvements, machinery, equipment, and fixtures that should normally be classified as Property, Plant, and Equipment, and identify audit objectives in connection with the examination of Property, Plant, and Equipment. *Do not discuss specific audit procedures.*

b. Indicate whether each of the above items numbered 1 to 4 requires one or more audit adjustments or reclassifications, and explain why such adjustments or reclassifications are required or not required. Organize your answer as follows:

| Item Number | Is Audit Adjustment or Reclassification Required? Yes or No | Reasons Audit Adjustment or Reclassification Is Required or Not Required |
|---|---|---|
|  |  |  |

(AICPA, adapted)

17-41 You are engaged in the audit of the financial statements of Holman Corporation for the year ended December 31, 19X2. The accompanying analyses of the Property, Plant, and Equipment, and related accumulated depreciation accounts, have been prepared by the chief account-ant of the client. You have traced the beginning balances to your prior year's audit working papers.

---

**HOLMAN CORPORATION**
**Analysis of Property, Plant, and Equipment, and**
**Related Accumulated Depreciation Accounts**
**Year Ended December 31, 1993**

| Description | Final 12/31/92 | Assets Additions | Assets Retirements | Per Ledger 12/31/93 |
|---|---|---|---|---|
| Land . . . . . . . . . . . . . . . . . . | $422,500 | $ 5,000 | | $427,500 |
| Buildings . . . . . . . . . . . . . . . | 120,000 | 17,500 | | 137,500 |
| Machinery and equipment . . . . . . . . | 385,000 | 40,400 | $26,000 | 399,400 |
| | $927,500 | $62,900 | $26,000 | $964,400 |

| Description | Final 12/31/92 | Accumulated Depreciation Additions* | Accumulated Depreciation Retirements | Per Ledger 12/31/93 |
|---|---|---|---|---|
| Buildings . . . . . . . . . . . . . . . | $ 60,000 | $ 5,150 | | $ 65,150 |
| Machinery and equipment . . . . . . . . | 173,250 | 39,220 | | 212,470 |
| | $233,250 | $44,370 | | $277,620 |

*Depreciation expense for the year.

---

All plant assets are depreciated on the straight-line basis (no residual value taken into con-sideration) based on the following estimated service lives: building, 25 years; and all other items, 10 years. The company's policy is to take one half-year's depreciation on all asset additions and disposals during the year.

Your examination revealed the following information:

1.  On April 1, the company entered into a 10-year lease contract for a die casting machine, with annual rentals of $5,000 payable in advance every April 1. The lease is cancelable by either party (60 days' written notice is required), and there is no option to renew the lease or buy the equipment at the end of the lease. The estimated service life of the machine is 10 years with no residual value. The company recorded the die casting machine in the Machinery and Equipment account at $40,400, the present value at the date of the lease, and $2,020 applicable to the machine has been included in depreciation expense for the year.

2.  The company completed the construction of a wing on the plant building on June 30. The service life of the building was not extended by this addition. The lowest construction bid received was $17,500, the amount recorded in the Buildings account. Company personnel constructed the addition at a cost of $16,000 (materials, $7,500; labor, $5,500; and over-head, $3,000).

3. On August 18, $5,000 was paid for paving and fencing a portion of land owned by the company and used as a parking lot for employees. The expenditure was charged to the Land account.

4. The amount shown in the machinery and equipment asset retirement column represents cash received on September 5 upon disposal of a machine purchased in July 1989 for $48,000. The chief accountant recorded depreciation expense of $3,500 on this machine in 1993.

5. Harbor City donated land and building appraised at $100,000 and $400,000, respectively, to Holman Corporation for a plant. On September 1, the company began operating the plant. Since no costs were involved, the chief accountant made no entry for the above transaction.

*Required:* Prepare the adjusting journal entries that you would propose at December 31, 1993, to adjust the accounts for the above transactions. Disregard income tax implications. The accounts have not been closed. Computations should be rounded off to the nearest dollar. Use a separate adjusting journal entry for each of the above five paragraphs.

(AICPA, adapted)

17-42   You are the senior accountant in the audit of Granger Grain Corporation, whose business primarily involves the purchase, storage, and sale of grain products. The corporation owns several elevators located along navigable water routes and transports its grain by barge and rail. Your staff assistant submitted the following working paper analysis for your review:

---

**GRANGER GRAIN CORPORATION**
**Advances Paid on Barges under Construction—a/c 210**
**December 31, 19X1**

Advances made:

| | |
|---|---:|
| 1/15/X1—Ck. No. 3463—Jones Barge Construction Co. . . . . . . . . . | $100,000* |
| 4/13/X1—Ck. No. 4129—Jones Barge Construction Co. . . . . . . . . . | 25,000* |
| 6/19/X1—Ck. No. 5396—Jones Barge Construction Co. . . . . . . . . . | 63,000* |
| Total payments . . . . . . . . . . . . . . . . . . . . . . . . . . | 188,000 |
| Deduct cash received 9/1/X1 from City Life Insurance Co. . . . . . . . . . | 188,000† |
| Balance per general ledger—12/31/X1 . . . . . . . . . . . . . . . . . . | $ –0– |

---

*Examined approved check request and paid check and traced to cash disbursements journal.
†Traced to cash receipts journal and to duplicate deposit ticket.

*Required:*   a. In what respects is this brief analysis incomplete for audit purposes? (Do not include any discussion of specific auditing procedures.)

b. What two different types of contractual arrangements may be inferred from your assistant's analysis?

c. What additional auditing procedures would you suggest that your staff assistant perform before you accept the working paper as being complete?

(AICPA, adapted)

# AUDITING OPERATIONS AND COMPLETING THE AUDIT

## CHAPTER OBJECTIVES

After studying this chapter, you should be able to:

- Identify the audit objectives for substantive tests of revenue and expense accounts.

- Describe the nature of appropriate substantive audit procedures to accomplish the objectives for the audit of revenue and expense accounts.

- Explain the types of procedures that are necessary to complete the audit.

- Discuss the nature of the auditors' responsibilities for loss contingencies.

- Describe the auditors' responsibilities for the detection and evaluation of various types of subsequent events.

- Explain the steps involved in evaluating audit findings.

- Identify the steps involved in the final review stage of the audit.

- Discuss the auditors' postaudit responsibilities.

T his chapter presents information about the manner in which auditors examine the client's income statement accounts, and the procedures and considerations involved in completing the audit engagement. These procedures and judgments, completed at or near the last day of field work, are important in determining the nature and content of the auditors' report.

# AUDITING OPERATIONS

Today, with great emphasis being placed upon corporate earnings as an indicator of the health and well-being of corporations as well as of the overall economy, the income statement is of fundamental importance to management, stockholders, creditors, employees, and government. The relative level of corporate earnings is often a key factor in the determination of such issues as wage negotiations, income tax rates, subsidies, and government fiscal policies. In fact, accountants generally agree that the measurement of income is the most important single function of accounting. While this text has emphasized the relationships of revenues and expenses to various balance sheet accounts, this section presents additional details on the auditing of operations.

## The Auditors' Approach to Examining Operations

The doctrine of **conservatism** is a powerful force influencing decisions on revenues and expenses. The concept remains important in large part due to the subjectivity involved with many accounting estimates (as for expected future credit losses on receivables, lives of assets, and the warranty liability for products sold). Conservatism in the valuation of assets means that when two (or more) reasonable alternative values are indicated, the accountant will choose the lower amount. For valuation of liabilities, the higher amount is chosen. Therefore, when applied to the income statement, the conservatism concept results in a low or "conservative" income figure.

Most auditors have a considerable respect for the doctrine of conservatism. In part, this attitude springs from the concept of legal liability to third parties. Financial statements that *understate* financial position and operating results almost never lead to legal action against the auditors involved. Nevertheless, auditors must recognize that overemphasis on conservatism in financial reporting is a narrow and shortsighted approach to meeting the needs of our society. To be of greatest value, financial statements should present fairly, rather than understate, financial position and operating results.

Auditors obtain evidence about many income statement accounts concurrently with related balance sheet accounts. Depreciation expense, for example, is most conveniently verified along with the plant and equipment accounts. Once the existence and cost of depreciable assets are established, the verification of depreciation expense is merely an additional step. On the other hand, to verify depreciation expense without first establishing the nature and amount of assets owned and subject to depreciation would obviously be a cart-before-the-horse approach. The same line of reasoning suggests that the auditors' work on inventories, especially in determining that inventory transactions were accurately cut off at the end of the period, is a major step toward the verification of the income statement figures for sales and cost of goods sold.

The auditors' examination of operations should, however, be much more than an incidental by-product of the examination of assets and liabilities. They use a combination of cross-referencing, analytical procedures, and analysis of specific transactions to bring to light errors, omissions, and inconsistencies not disclosed in the examination of balance sheet accounts.

Specifically, the audit *objectives* for substantive tests of revenues and expenses are to:

1. Determine the *occurrence* of recorded revenue and expense transactions.
2. Establish the *completeness* of recorded revenue and expense transactions.
3. Establish the *clerical accuracy* of schedules of revenues and expenses.
4. Determine that the *valuation* of revenue and expense transactions is in accordance with generally accepted accounting principles.
5. Determine that the *presentation* and *disclosure* of revenue and expense accounts are appropriate.

# REVENUE

The auditors' review of sales activities was considered in connection with accounts receivable in Chapters 12 and 13. In this section we consider (1) the relationship of revenue to various balance sheet accounts and (2) the miscellaneous revenue account.

## Relationship of Revenue to Balance Sheet Accounts

As pointed out previously, most revenue accounts are verified by the auditors in conjunction with the audit of a related asset or liability. The following list summarizes the revenue verified in this manner:

| Balance Sheet Item | Revenue |
|---|---|
| Accounts receivable | Sales |
| Notes receivable | Interest |
| Securities and other investments | Interest, dividends, gains on sales, share of investee's income |
| Property, plant, and equipment | Rent, gains on sale |
| Intangible assets | Royalties |

## Miscellaneous Revenue

Miscellaneous revenue, by its very nature, is a mixture of minor items, some nonrecurring and others likely to be received at irregular intervals. If the client's personnel receive a cash payment and are not sure of the source, it is likely that it will be recorded as miscellaneous revenue. Because of the nature of items often recorded in the Miscellaneous Revenue account, the auditors will obtain an analysis of the account. Among the items the auditors might find improperly included as miscellaneous revenue are the following:

1.  Collections on previously written-off accounts or notes receivable.
2.  Write-offs of old outstanding checks or unclaimed wages. In many states, unclaimed properties revert to the state after statutory periods; in such circumstances, these write-offs should be credited to a liability account rather than to miscellaneous revenue.
3.  Proceeds from sales of scrap. Scrap sale proceeds should generally be applied to reduce cost of goods sold, under by-product cost accounting principles.
4.  Rebates or refunds of insurance premiums. These refunds should be offset against the related expense or unexpired insurance.
5.  Proceeds from sales of plant assets. These proceeds should be accounted for in the determination of the gain or loss on the assets sold.

The auditors should propose adjusting journal entries to classify correctly any material items of the types described above that have been included in miscellaneous revenue by the client. Before concluding the work on revenue, the auditors should perform analytical procedures and investigate unusual fluctuations. Material amounts of unrecorded revenue, as well as significant misclassifications affecting revenue accounts, may be discovered by these procedures.

# EXPENSES

The auditors' work relating to purchases and cost of goods sold was covered in Chapters 14 and 15. We are now concerned with audit procedures for other types of expenses.

## Relationship of Expenses to Balance Sheet Accounts

Let us consider for a moment the expense accounts for which we have already outlined audit procedures in the chapters dealing with balance sheet topics:

| Balance Sheet Item | Expenses (and Costs) |
| --- | --- |
| Accounts and notes receivable | Uncollectible accounts and notes expense |
| Inventories | Purchases, cost of goods sold, and payroll |
| Property, plant, and equipment | Depreciation, repairs and maintenance, and depletion |
| Prepaid expenses and deferred charges | Various related expenses, such as rent, property taxes, advertising, postage, and others |
| Intangible assets | Amortization |
| Accrued liabilities | Commissions, fees, bonuses, product warranty expenses, and others |
| Interest-bearing debt | Interest |

In the following sections, we shall complete our review of expenses by considering additional audit objectives and procedures for selling, general, and administrative expenses, other than those listed above.

## Substantive Tests for Selling, General, and Administrative Expenses

For other expenses not verified in the audit of balance sheet accounts, the following substantive tests are appropriate:

1. Perform analytical procedures related to the accounts.
    a. Develop an expectation of the account balance.
    b. Determine the amount of difference from the expectation that can be accepted without investigation.
    c. Compare the company's account balance with the expected account balance.
    d. Investigate significant deviations from the expected account balance.
2. Obtain or prepare analyses of selected expense accounts.
3. Obtain or prepare analyses of critical expenses in income tax returns.

1. Perform analytical procedures related to the accounts.

   a. Develop an expectation of the account balance.   Auditors develop an expectation of the account balance by considering factors such as budgeted levels, the prior-year audited balances, industry averages, relationships among financial data, and relevant nonfinancial data.

   An effective budgeting program will reduce control risk since budgets provide management with information as to expected amounts. The existence of these expected expense amounts increases the likelihood that errors will be detected by management, since any significant discrepancy between budgeted and actual amounts receives timely attention.

   The existence of a good budgeting program also helps the auditors in their audit of expense accounts. When the control over budgeting has been found to be effective, the budgeted amounts often provide the auditors with very good expected amounts for their analytical procedures.

   One of the previously described audit objectives was to determine whether expenses had been correctly classified. The issue of classification is most important as between manufacturing overhead costs, on the one hand, and selling, general, and administrative expenses on the other. Manufacturing overhead costs may properly be carried forward as part of inventory cost, whereas the expenses of selling, general, and administrative functions usually are deducted from revenue in the period incurred. Consequently, an error in classification may cause an error in the net income for the period. The auditors' review of the propriety of classification of expenses can be linked conveniently with the comparison of amounts of the various expenses. Comparison of yearly totals is accomplished by inclusion of amounts for the preceding year on the auditors' lead schedules or working trial balance, but this procedure may be supplemented by comparison of expenses on a month-by-month basis.

   Comparison of expense (as well as revenue) accounts with industry and nonfinancial data is another means of bringing to light circumstances that require investigation. The auditors may also examine relationships between financial and nonfinancial information, such as between production records stated in gallons or pounds and the dollar amounts of sales.

*b.*  Determine the amount of difference from the expectation that can be accepted without investigation.  The auditors use their estimates of materiality to arrive at which differences are to be investigated and which might be expected to occur by chance. However, the extent of the assurance desired from the analytical procedure must also be considered.

*c.*  Compare the company's account balance with the expected account balance. Comparisons of the revenue and expense accounts with expected amounts may reveal significant differences that warrant investigation. Figure 18–1 illustrates a working

---

Figure 18–1    Comparative Income Statement

CHEVIOT CORPORATION
Comparative Income Statement                                   R-1-4
Year Ended December 31, 19X3

|  | 19X2 | | 19X3 | | Industry |
|---|---|---|---|---|---|
|  | Amount | Percentage | Amount | Percentage | Percentage |
| Sales | $5,487,842✓ | 100% | $6,107,401ᴹ ▽ | 100% | 100% |
| Cost of goods sold | 3,746,583✓ | 68 | 4,030,701ᴹ ⊘ | 66 | 65 |
| Gross profit | 1,741,259 | 32 | 2,076,700⊘ | 34 | 35 |
| Selling expenses | 554,841✓ | 10 | 856,540ᴹ △ | 14 | 15 |
| General and administrative expenses | 796,347✓ | 15 | 875,570ᴹ ⊘ | 14 | 12 |
| Income before taxes | 390,071 | 7 | 344,590⊘ | 6 | 8 |
| Taxes | 128,732✓ | 2 | 68,693ᴹ ✗ | 1 | 3 |
| Net income | 261,339 ∧ | 5 | 275,897⊘ ∧ | 5 | 5 |

∧   *Footed.*
ᴹ   *Agreed to the general ledger.*
✓   *Agreed to the prior year working papers.*
⊘   *Amount is reasonable in relation to prior year results and industry statistics.*
▽   *See audit procedures performed on sales, R-1-2.*
△   *Large increase in selling expenses is due to the addition of a salesman to the sales staff. Based on a review of the payroll records the increase in the account appears reasonable.*
✗   *Decrease in tax rate is due to the realization of several thousand dollars in tax credits. See tax accrual working paper, 0-3.*
*Conclusion:*
*The comparative analysis revealed no unusual fluctuations that could not be adequately explained.*

*V.M.H.*            *Concur*
*2/21/X4*           *C.M.*
                    *2/25/X4*

paper that compares major income statement categories for the year under audit with the prior year amounts and industry averages.

*d.*   Investigate significant deviations from the expected account balance.   The starting point for investigating significant variations in expenses generally is inquiry of management. The auditors substantiate management's explanations for significant variations by various means, including analyses of accounts.

2.   Obtain or prepare analyses of selected expense accounts.   As a result of the above procedure, the auditors will have chosen certain expense accounts for further verification. The client should be requested to furnish analyses of the accounts selected, together with related vouchers and other supporting documents, for the auditors' review.

Which expense accounts are most important for the auditors to analyze? The AICPA has suggested investigation of (1) advertising, (2) research and development, (3) legal expenses and other professional fees, (4) maintenance and repairs, and (5) rents and royalties.[1]

The analyses of legal and other professional fees may disclose legal and audit fees properly chargeable to costs of issuing stock or debt instruments, or to costs of business combinations. Also, the analysis of professional fees expense furnishes the names of attorneys to whom letters should be sent requesting information as to pending litigation and other loss contingencies. Figure 18–2 illustrates an analysis of the professional fees expense account.

3.   Obtain or prepare analyses of critical expenses in income tax returns.   Income tax returns generally require schedules for officers' salaries, directors' fees, taxes, travel and entertainment, contributions, and casualty losses. In addition to these, officers' expense account allowances are presented in the analysis of officers' salaries. Accordingly, the auditors should obtain or prepare analyses of any of these expenses that were not analyzed when performing other audit steps. The auditors should bear in mind that details of these expenses will probably be closely scrutinized when the state or federal revenue agents examine the client's tax returns.

## COMPLETING THE AUDIT

The auditors' opinion on the financial statements is based on all evidence gathered by the auditors up to the last day of field work, and any other information that comes to their attention between that date and the issuance of the financial statements. To be effective, certain audit procedures described in previous chapters cannot be completed before the end of the audit. Among those procedures are the following:

1.   Search for unrecorded liabilities.
2.   Review the minutes of meetings.
3.   Perform final analytical procedures.
4.   Perform procedures to identify loss contingencies.

---

[1]See AICPA, *Audit and Accounting Manual* (New York, 1993), par. AAM 5400.170.

Figure 18–2  Professional Fees Analysis

CHEVIOT CORPORATION

Acct. No. 547                    Professional Fees Expense                                R-3-7
                                 Year Ended December 31, 19X3

| Date | Reference | Payee | Description | Amount |
|------|-----------|-------|-------------|--------|
| Various | Various | Hale and Hale | Monthly retainer for legal services_12 × $1000 | $12,000 |
| Mar. 5, X3 | CD 411 | Jay & Wall, CPAs | Fee for the audit | 22,000ᵞ |
| May 2, X3 | CD 602 | Hale and Hale | Fee for legal services relating to acquisition of real property adjoining Vancouver plant | 6,000ᵞ |
| Sept. 18, X3 | CD 1018 | Hale and Hale | Fee for legal services relating to modification of installment sales contract forms | 800ᵞ |
| Dec. 31, X3 | | | Balance per Ledger | $40,800 |
| Dec. 31, X3 | AJE 41 | | To capitalize May 2, X3 disbursement as part of cost of land   K-1 | 6,000 |
| Dec. 31, X3 | Adjusted balance | | | $34,800 ∧ |
| | | | | to R-3 |

AJE 41
Land                                       6,000
   Professional Fees                                  6,000
To capitalize legal fees
for acquiring land

∧  Footed and agreed to general ledger balance.
ᵞ  Examined billing and copy of client's check in payment thereof.
Conclusion:
   Professional fees expense is fairly presented
   in the adjusted amount of $34,800.              KGL
                                                   2/15/X4
                                                   CMM
                                                   2/20/X4

5.  Perform the review for subsequent events.
6.  Obtain the representation letter.

## Search for Unrecorded Liabilities

As discussed in Chapter 14, the search for unrecorded liabilities includes procedures performed through the last day of field work, such as examining subsequent cash disbursements. These procedures are designed to detect liabilities that existed at year-end but were omitted from the liabilities recorded in the client's financial statements.

## Review the Minutes of Meetings

The corporate **minutes book** is an official record of the actions taken at meetings of directors and stockholders. Typical of the actions taken at meetings of stockholders is the extension of authority to management to acquire or dispose of subsidiaries and to adopt or modify pension or profit-sharing plans for officers and employees. The stockholders also customarily approve the selection of a firm of independent auditors. Representatives of the auditing firm attend the stockholders' meeting for the purpose of answering questions that may arise concerning internal control and the financial operations of the business.

Minutes of the directors' meetings usually contain authorizations for important transactions and contractual arrangements, such as the establishment of bank accounts, setting of officers' salaries, declaration of dividends, and formation of long-term agreements with vendors, customers, and lessors. In addition, the minutes may document discussions by the board of pending litigation, investigations by regulatory agencies, or other loss contingencies. Therefore, the auditors should read the minutes of meetings held through the last day of field work.

In large corporations, the board of directors often works through committees appointed to deal with special phases of operations. Common examples include an audit committee and an investment committee. As discussed in Chapters 7 and 8, the audit committee maintains close contact with both the independent CPAs and the company's internal auditors and may be involved in discussions of weaknesses in internal control, accounting policies, and possible illegal or fraudulent acts by management. The investment committee periodically reviews and approves the investment activities of management. Minutes of the meetings of such committees are just as essential to the auditors' investigation as the minutes covering the meetings of the entire board.

### Procedure for Review of Minutes.

In the first audit of a client, it may be necessary to review minutes recorded in prior years. Copies of these minutes will be preserved in the permanent file; as succeeding annual audits are made, the file will be appropriately expanded.

The auditors will obtain from the secretary or other corporate officer copies of all minutes, including those of board committees, directors, and stockholders, for both regular and special meetings. These copies should be certified by a corporate officer and should be compared with the official minutes book to an extent sufficient to establish their completeness and authenticity.

In reviewing the minutes, the auditors will (1) note the date of the meeting and whether a quorum was present and (2) underscore or highlight such actions and decisions that in their judgment should influence the conduct of the audit. Nonessential material can be scanned rapidly, and highlighting can be limited to issues that warrant investigation during the course of the audit. For this phase of the audit work, there is no substitute for breadth of experience and maturity of judgment; the minutes include a wide range of information from matters of real importance to the audit to those that may safely be passed by.

Major decisions in the minutes, such as declaration of dividends or authorization for borrowing, usually result in actions that need to be recorded in the accounting records. As the audit progresses, the auditors should trace authorized events from the minutes into the accounting records and cross-reference their copies of the minutes to the underlying account analyses. Similarly, events recorded in the accounting records that normally require authorization by directors should be traced and cross-referenced to the auditors' copies of the minutes.

Determining that All Minutes Are Made Available.    How do the auditors know that copies of all minutes have been made available to them? First, they can review their permanent file to determine the identities of the board's committees and the scheduled date for regular meetings. Next, a typical practice at board and committee meetings is to approve the minutes of the preceding meeting. This practice enables the auditors to work backward from the most recent minutes to the oldest, noting the date of the previous minutes approved in the later meeting. Also, the auditors should obtain from management a letter representing that all minutes have been made available. The client's refusal to provide the auditors with copies of all minutes is a serious limitation of the scope of the auditors' examination. As indicated in Chapter 3, *SAS 58* (AU 508), "Reports on Audited Financial Statements," advises auditors to issue a disclaimer of opinion on the financial statements when significant scope limitations are imposed by the client.

Relationship of Corporate Minutes to Audit Objectives.    The nature of the information to be highlighted in the minutes and the usefulness of this information to the auditors can be made clear by a few examples. Figure 18–3 shows several audit objectives and indicates for each objective certain relevant events that are likely to be documented in the minutes of the board and its committees.

## Perform Final Analytical Procedures

The discussion of **analytical procedures** in Chapter 7 pointed out that they must be performed in planning as well as for overall review purposes at the completion of the audit. Analytical procedures performed as a part of the overall review assist the auditors in assessing the validity of the conclusions reached, including the opinion to be issued. This final review may identify areas that need to be examined further as well as provide a consideration of the adequacy of data gathered in response to unusual or unexpected relationships identified during the audit.

## Perform Procedures to Identify Loss Contingencies

A **loss contingency** may be defined as a *possible* loss, stemming from past events, that will be resolved as to existence and amount by some future event. Central to the concept of a contingent loss is the idea of uncertainty—uncertainty both as to the amount of loss and whether, in fact, any loss has been incurred. This uncertainty is resolved when some future event occurs or fails to occur.

Figure 18–3    Relationship of Minutes to Audit Objectives

| Audit Objectives | Relevant Information Likely to Be Included in Minutes of the Board and Its Committees |
|---|---|
| 1. Establishing the completeness of cash balances. | 1. The opening and closing of bank accounts require authorization by the board of directors. |
| 2. Financial statement presentation and disclosure of marketable securities. | 2. Pledging of securities as collateral for a loan requires approval of the investment committee of the board. |
| 3. Establishing the completeness of liabilities. | 3a. The obtaining of bank loans requires advance approval by the board. <br> b. Authority for the declaration of dividends payable rests with the board. <br> c. The issuance of bonds payable or other long-term debt requires approval by the board. |
| 4. Financial statement presentation and disclosure of loss contingencies. | 4a. Such issues as pending litigation, income tax disputes, accommodation endorsements, and other loss contingencies discussed by the board are documented in the minutes. <br> b. Unusual purchase commitments and sales commitments may be submitted to the board for approval. <br> c. The selection of legal counsel, who in turn may have information regarding pending litigation or other loss contingencies, is approved by the board. |

Most loss contingencies may also appropriately be called **contingent liabilities.** Loss contingencies, however, is a broader term, encompassing the possible impairment of assets as well as the possible existence of liabilities. The audit problem with respect to loss contingencies is twofold. First, the auditors must determine the existence of the loss contingencies. Because of the uncertainty factor, most loss contingencies do not appear in the accounting records, and a systematic search is required if the auditors are to have reasonable assurance that no important loss contingencies have been overlooked. Second, the auditors must appraise the probability that a loss has been incurred. This is made difficult both by the uncertainty factor and also by the tendency of the client management to maintain at least an outward appearance of optimism.

In *FASB Statement No. 5,* "Accounting for Contingencies," the Financial Accounting Standards Board set forth the criteria for accounting for loss contingencies. Such losses should be reflected in the accounting records when both of the following conditions are met: (1) information available prior to the issuance of the financial statements indicates that it is *probable* that a loss had been sustained before the balance sheet date, *and* (2) the amount of the loss can be *reasonably estimated*. Recognition of the loss may involve either recognition of a liability or reduction of an asset. When a loss contingency has been accrued in the accounts, it is usually desirable to explain the nature of the contingency in a note to the financial statements and to disclose any exposure to loss in excess of the amount accrued.

Loss contingencies that do not meet both of the above criteria should still be disclosed in a note to the financial statements when there is at least a *reasonable possibility* that a loss has been incurred. This disclosure should describe the nature of the contingency and, if possible, provide an estimate of the possible loss. If the amount of possible loss cannot be reasonably estimated, the disclosure should include either a range of loss or a statement that an estimate cannot be made.

Certain contingent liabilities traditionally have been disclosed in financial statement notes even though the possibility that a loss has occurred is remote. Such items include notes receivable discounted and guarantee endorsements. With the exception of those items for which disclosure is traditional, disclosure need not be made of loss contingencies when the possibility of loss is remote.

The procedures undertaken by auditors to ascertain the existence of loss contingencies and to assess the probability of loss vary with the nature of the contingent item. Regardless of the procedures performed, it is important that they be extended to near the last day of fieldwork, so that the auditors have the latest available information to evaluate the financial statement presentation and disclosure of loss contingencies. To illustrate these types of procedures, we will discuss several of the more frequent types of contingencies warranting financial statement disclosure.

Litigation.   Perhaps the most common loss contingency appearing in financial statements is that stemming from pending or threatened litigation. A **letter of inquiry** (or **lawyer's letter**) to the client's legal counsel is the auditors' primary means of obtaining evidence regarding pending and threatened litigation, as well as **unasserted claims** for which no potential claimant has yet demonstrated the intent to initiate legal action.

*SAS 12* (AU 337), "Inquiry of a Client's Lawyer Concerning Litigation, Claims, and Assessments," indicates that the auditors should generally obtain from management a list describing and evaluating threatened or pending litigation. The auditors then ask management to request the client's lawyers to comment on those areas where their views differ from those of management. The lawyers also are requested to identify any pending claims, litigation, and assessments that have been omitted from management's list. If management does not wish to prepare a list of pending litigation for review by the lawyers, the lawyers may be requested to provide an independent description of all pending claims, litigation, and assessments that they are handling.

Auditors must also inquire of the lawyers regarding the possibility of unasserted claims, on which individuals have not yet taken legal action. An unasserted claim should be disclosed if it is (1) *probable* that a claim will be asserted and (2) *reasonably possible* that a loss will result. If management prepares a list of matters for review by the lawyers, it should include such unasserted claims. The lawyers will provide any relevant additional information related to those listed unasserted claims. However, if management fails to list the unasserted claim in the letter of inquiry, the lawyer is *not* required to describe the claim in the reply to the auditors; the lawyer is, however, generally required to inform the client of the omission and to consider resignation if the client fails to inform the auditors of the unasserted claim. For this reason, auditors must always consider carefully the reasons for any lawyer's resignation.

Illustration of Disclosure.    The following note to the financial statements of an aircraft manufacturer illustrates the disclosure of the contingent liability associated with pending litigation.

> A number of suits are pending against the Company as the result of accidents in prior years involving airplanes manufactured by the Company. It is believed that insurance carried by the Company is sufficient to protect it against loss by reason of suits involving the lives of passengers and damage to aircraft. Other litigation pending against the Company involves no substantial amount or is covered by insurance.

The note of another large corporation contained the following note concerning such contingent liabilities:

> The Company is a party to a number of lawsuits and claims (some of which are for substantial amounts) arising out of the conduct of its business, including those relating to commercial transactions, product liability, and environmental, safety and health matters. While the ultimate results of lawsuits or other proceedings against the Company cannot be predicted with certainty, management does not expect that these matters will have a material adverse effect on the consolidated financial position or results of operations of the Company.

A refusal by a lawyer to furnish the information requested in the auditors' letter of inquiry would be a limitation of the scope of the auditors' examination and would necessitate qualification of the audit report. Even when all of the requested information is provided to the auditors and adequately disclosed in the financial statements, the uncertainty of the outcome of litigation may require the auditors to add an explanatory paragraph to their report referring to the uncertainty.

Income Tax Disputes.    The necessity of estimating the income tax liability applicable to the year under audit was discussed in Chapter 14. In addition to the taxes relating to the current year's income, uncertainty often exists concerning the amount ultimately payable for prior years. A lag of two or three years often exists between the filing of income tax returns and the final settlement after review by the Internal Revenue Service. Disputes between the taxpayer and the IRS may create contingent liabilities not settled for several more years. The auditors should determine whether internal revenue agents have examined any returns of the client since the preceding audit and, if so, whether any additional taxes have been assessed. In addition, the auditors should review any correspondence with the IRS and any other regulatory agencies.

Accommodation Endorsements and Other Guarantees of Indebtedness.  The endorsement of notes of other concerns or individuals is very seldom recorded in the accounts, but may be reflected in the minutes of directors' meetings. The practice is more common among small concerns—particularly when one person has a proprietary interest in several companies. Officers, partners, and sole proprietors of small organizations should be questioned as to the existence of any contingent liability from this source. Inquiry should also be made as to whether any collateral has been received to protect the company. The auditors may also decide to confirm written or oral guarantees or other contingent liabilities with appropriate financial institutions, using a specially designed confirmation letter.

Accounts Receivable Sold or Assigned with Recourse.  When accounts receivable are sold or assigned *with recourse,* a guarantee of collectibility is given. Authorization of such a transaction should be revealed during the auditors' reading of the minutes, and evidence of such agreements also may be found during the examination of transactions and correspondence with financial institutions. Confirmation by direct communication with the purchaser or assignee is necessary for any receivables sold or assigned.

Commitments.  Closely related to contingent liabilities are obligations termed **commitments.** The auditors may discover during their audit any of the following commitments: inventory purchase commitments, commitments to sell merchandise at specified prices, contracts for the construction of plant and equipment, pension or profit-sharing plans, long-term operating leases of plant and equipment, employee stock option plans, and employment contracts with key officers. A common characteristic of these commitments is the contractual obligation to enter into transactions *in the future*.

To illustrate the relationship of a commitment to a loss contingency, assume that a manufacturer commits to sell a substantial part of its output at a fixed price over the next three years. At the time of forming the agreement, the manufacturer, of course, believes the arrangement to be advantageous. However, it is possible that rising price levels could transform the fixed price sales agreement into an unprofitable one, requiring sales to be made at prices below manufacturing cost. Such circumstances could warrant recognition of a loss in the financial statements.

All classes of material commitments may be described in a single note to financial statements, or they may be included in a ''Contingencies and Commitments'' note.

General Risk Contingencies.  In addition to loss contingencies and commitments, all business face the risk of loss from numerous factors called **general risk contingencies.** A general risk contingency represents a loss that *might occur in the future,* as opposed to a loss contingency that *might have occurred in the past*. Examples of general risk contingencies are threat of a strike or consumer boycott, risk of price increases in essential raw materials, and risk of a natural catastrophe.

Since the events that might produce a loss actually have not occurred and they are part of the general business environment, general risk contingencies *need not be disclosed* in financial statements. The lack of insurance coverage is a general risk contingency. Neither the adequacy nor the lack of insurance coverage is required to be presented in financial statements.

The Auditors' Procedures for Loss Contingencies—A Summary.   A summary of the auditors' procedures to detect and evaluate loss contingencies is described below.

1. Review the minutes of directors' meetings to the date of completion of field work. Important contracts, lawsuits, and dealings with subsidiaries are typical of matters discussed in board meetings that may involve loss contingencies.

2. Send a letter of inquiry to the client's lawyer requesting:

   a. A description (or evaluation of management's description) of the nature of pending and threatened litigation and of tax disputes.

   b. An evaluation of the likelihood of an unfavorable outcome in the matters described.

   c. An estimate of the probable loss or range of loss, or a statement that an estimate cannot be made.

   d. An evaluation of management's description of any unasserted claims that, if asserted, have a reasonable possibility of an adverse outcome.

   e. A statement of the amount of any unbilled legal fees.

3. Send confirmation letters to financial institutions to request information on contingent liabilities of the company.

4. Review correspondence with financial institutions for evidence of accommodation endorsements, guarantees of indebtedness, or sales or assignments of accounts receivable.

5. Review reports and correspondence from regulatory agencies to identify potential assessments or fines.

6. Obtain a **representation letter** from the client indicating that all liabilities known to officers are recorded or disclosed.

## Perform the Review for Subsequent Events

Evidence not available at the close of the period under audit often becomes available before the auditors finish their field work and write their audit report. The CPA's opinion on the fairness of the financial statements may be changed considerably by these subsequent events. The term **subsequent event** refers to an event or transaction that occurs after the date of the balance sheet but prior to the completion of the audit and issuance of the audit report. Subsequent events may be classified into two broad categories: (1) those providing additional evidence about facts existing on or before the balance sheet date, and (2) those involving facts coming into existence after the balance sheet date.

Type 1 Subsequent Events.   The first type of subsequent event provides additional evidence as to *conditions that existed at the balance sheet date* and affects the estimates inherent in the process of preparing financial statements. This type of subsequent event requires that the financial statement amounts be adjusted to reflect the changes in estimates resulting from the additional evidence.

As an example, let us assume that a client's accounts receivable at December 31 included one large account and numerous small ones. The large amount due from the major customer was regarded as fully collectible at the year-end, but during the course of the audit engagement the customer entered bankruptcy. As a result of this information, the auditors found it necessary to recommend an increase in the December 31 allowance for uncollectible accounts. The bankruptcy of the customer shortly after the balance sheet date indicates that the financial strength of the customer had probably deteriorated before December 31, and the client was simply in error in believing the receivable to be fully collectible at that date. Evidence becoming available after the balance sheet date through the date of issuance of the auditors' report should be used in making judgments about the valuation of receivables.

Other examples of this first type of subsequent event include the following:

1.  Customers' checks included in the cash receipts of the last day of the year prove to be uncollectible and are charged back to the client's account by the bank. If the checks were material in amount, an adjustment of the December 31 cash balance may be necessary to exclude the checks now known to be uncollectible.

2.  A new three-year union contract signed two weeks after the balance sheet date provides evidence that the client has materially underestimated the total cost to complete a long-term construction project on which revenue is recognized by the percentage-of-completion method. The amount of income (or loss) to be recognized on the project in the current year should be recomputed using revised cost estimates.

3.  Litigation pending against the client is settled shortly after the balance sheet date, and the amount owed by the client is material. This litigation was to be disclosed in notes to the financial statements, but no liability had been accrued because at year-end no reasonable estimate could be made of the amount of the client's loss. Now that competent evidence exists as to the dollar amount of the loss, this loss contingency meets the criteria for accrual in the financial statements, rather than mere note disclosure.

Type 2 Subsequent Events.  The second type of subsequent event involves conditions *coming into existence after the balance sheet date*. These events do not require adjustment to the dollar amounts shown in the financial statements, *but they should be disclosed if the financial statements otherwise would be misleading*. To illustrate, assume that shortly after the balance sheet date a client sustains an uninsured fire loss destroying most of its plant assets. The carrying value of plant assets should not be reduced in the balance sheet because these assets were intact at year-end. However, anyone analyzing the financial statements would be misled if they were not advised that most of the plant assets are no longer in a usable condition.

What types of events occurring after the balance sheet date warrant disclosure in the financial statements? For example, assume that the following events occurred after the balance sheet date but prior to completion of the audit field work:

1.  Business combination with a competing company.

2.  Early retirement of bonds payable.

3.  Adoption of a new pension plan requiring large, near-term cash outlays.

4.  Death of the company treasurer in an airplane crash.

5.  Introduction of a new line of products.

6.  Plant closed by a labor strike.

Although these events may be significant in the future operations of the company and of interest to many who read the audited financial statements, none of these occurrences has any bearing on the results of the year under audit, and their bearing on future results is not easily determinable.

It is generally agreed that subsequent events involving business combinations, substantial casualty losses, and other significant changes in a company's financial position or financial structure should be disclosed in notes. Otherwise the financial statements might be misleading rather than informative. Consequently, the first three of the preceding examples (combination with a competing company, early retirement of bonds payable, and adoption of a new pension plan) should be disclosed in notes to the financial statements. The last three subsequent events (personnel changes, product line changes, and strikes) are nonaccounting matters and are not disclosed in notes unless particular circumstances make such information essential to the proper interpretation of the financial statements.

Pro Forma Statements as a Means of Disclosure.    Occasionally subsequent events may be so material that supplementary *pro forma financial statements* should be prepared giving effect to the events as if they had occurred as of the balance sheet date. The pro forma statements (usually a balance sheet only) may be presented in columnar form next to the audited financial statements. This form of disclosure is used only when the subsequent event has a significant effect upon the asset structure or capital structure of the business. An example would be a business combination.

Distinguishing between the Two Types of Subsequent Events.    In deciding whether a particular subsequent event should result in adjustment to the financial statements or note disclosure, the auditor should carefully consider *when the underlying conditions came into existence*. For example, assume that shortly after the balance sheet date, a major customer of the audit client declares bankruptcy, with the result that a large receivable previously considered fully collectible now appears to be uncollectible. If the customer's bankruptcy resulted from a steady deterioration in financial position, the subsequent event provides evidence that the receivable actually was uncollectible at year-end, and the allowance for doubtful accounts should be increased. On the other hand, if the customer's bankruptcy stemmed from a casualty (such as a fire) occurring after year-end, the conditions making the receivable uncollectible came into existence after the balance sheet date. In this case, the subsequent event should be disclosed in a note to the financial statements.

Audit Procedures Relating to Subsequent Events.    The period of time between the balance sheet date and the last day of field work is called the subsequent period. During this period, the auditors should determine that proper cutoffs of cash receipts and disbursements and sales and purchases have been made, and should examine data to aid in the evaluation of assets and liabilities as of the balance sheet date. In addition, the auditors should:

1. Review the latest available interim financial statements and minutes of directors, stockholders, and appropriate committee meetings.
2. Inquire about matters dealt with at meetings for which minutes are not available.

3. Inquire of appropriate client officials as to loss contingencies; changes in capital stock, debt, or working capital; changes in the current status of items estimated in the financial statements under audit, or any unusual adjustments made subsequent to the balance sheet date.

4. Obtain a letter from the client's lawyer describing as of the last day of field work any pending litigation, unasserted claims, or other loss contingencies.

5. Include in the representation letter a representation from the client concerning subsequent events.

Generally, the auditors' responsibility for performing procedures to gather evidence as to subsequent events extends only through the last day of field work. However, even after completing normal audit procedures, the auditors have the responsibility to evaluate subsequent events that come to their attention. Suppose, for example, that the auditors completed their field work for a December 31 audit on February 3 and thereafter began drafting their report. On February 11, before issuing their report, the auditors were informed by the client that a lawsuit had been settled on that day by a substantial payment by the client. In such a circumstance, generally accepted accounting principles require that the liability be established in the December 31 balance sheet. If the adjustment does not also require a note disclosure, the audit report ordinarily would continue to be dated as of the completion of field work. If a related note disclosure is necessary, auditors have two methods available for dating the audit report. They may *dual-date* their report "February 3, except for Note __, as to which the date is February 11." Alternatively, they might decide to return to the client's facilities for further review of subsequent events through the date of the subsequent event, February 11; in this case, the audit report would bear that date only.

Dual dating extends the auditors' responsibility for disclosure through the later date *only with respect to the specified item.* Using the later date for the date of the report extends the auditors' responsibility with respect to all areas of the financial statements. Finally, in the unusual circumstance in which the client did not agree to properly reflect the event, the departure from generally accepted accounting opinions could result in either a qualified or adverse opinion.

Figure 18-4 summarizes the auditors' responsibilities for subsequent events with respect to the balance sheet date, the last day of field work, and the date upon which the audit report is actually issued.

The Auditors' S-1 Review in an SEC Registration. The Securities Act of 1933 (Section 11[a]) extends the auditors' liability in connection with the registration of new securities with the SEC to the *effective date* of the registration statement—the date on which the securities may be sold to the public. In many cases, the effective date of the registration statement may be several weeks or even months later than the date the auditors completed their field work. Accordingly, on or as close as practicable to the effective date, the auditors return to the client's facilities to conduct an **S-1 review,** so-called because of the "Form S-1" title of the traditional SEC registration statement for new securities issues. In addition to completing the subsequent events review described in the preceding section, the auditors should read the entire prospectus and other pertinent portions of the registration statement. They should also inquire of officers and other key executives of the

Figure 18–4   Subsequent Events

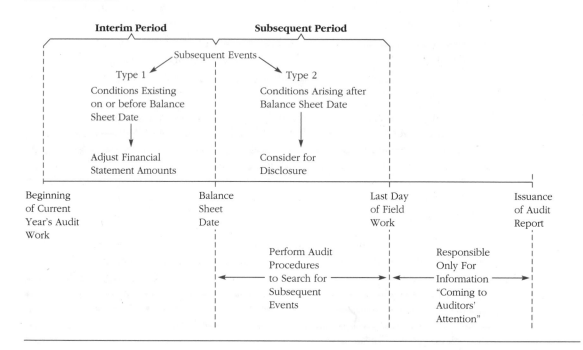

client whether any events not reported in the registration statement have occurred that require amendment of the registration statement to prevent the audited financial statements therein from being misleading.

## Obtain Representation Letter

Chapter 6 included a general description of the **representation letter** that the auditors must obtain from management. The primary purpose of the representation letter is to have the client's principal officers acknowledge that they are primarily responsible for the fairness of the financial statements. Since the financial statements must reflect all material subsequent events, the representation letter should be dated as of the last day of field work.

## EVALUATING AUDIT FINDINGS

Throughout the course of the audit, the auditors will propose adjusting entries for all *material misstatements* (errors and irregularities) that are discovered in the client's financial records. Any material misstatement that the auditors find must be corrected; otherwise, they cannot issue an unqualified opinion on the financial statements. In evaluating whether an individual misstatement is material, the auditors consider both quantitative and qualitative factors. For example, a $10,000 related-party transaction might be considered material for a particular audit, whereas a misstatement of trade accounts receivable of the same amount would not be considered material. Immaterial misstatements that are discovered by the auditors are accumulated on a working paper with a title, such as "Adjusting Entries Passed."

To issue an unqualified opinion, the auditors must conclude that there is a low level of risk of material misstatement of the financial statements. In evaluating this risk the auditors develop an estimate of the **total likely misstatement in the financial statements,** which is made up of the following three components:

1. *Known misstatements* (adjusting entries passed) include those that the client has not corrected.

2. *Projected misstatements* include those that are calculated when the auditors employ audit sampling, as described in Chapter 11. For example, if the book value of accounts receivables is $6,250,000 and the auditors, using audit sampling, estimate the audited value to be $6,100,000, the projected misstatement would be the difference of $150,000. This projected misstatement should be decreased by the amount of known misstatement used to calculate it (either included above in 1. or corrected).

3. *Other estimated misstatements* are those estimated by techniques other than audit sampling, such as analytical procedures. One significant source of these estimated misstatements is differences related to accounting estimates, such as those for inventory obsolescence, uncollectible receivables, and warranty obligations. For these items, the estimated misstatement is the difference between the client's estimate and the closest amount that the auditors consider to be reasonable. An example would be a situation in which the management estimates the company's warranty liability to be $100,000, and the auditors develop an estimate of between $120,000 and $140,000 for the account. The estimated misstatement is $20,000 ($120,000 − $100,000).

Obviously, if the auditors estimate that the total of these three misstatements (the total likely misstatement) is material to the financial statements, they would conclude that the risk of material misstatement is too high to issue an unqualified opinion on the financial statements. Even if the total likely misstatement in the financial statements is estimated to be somewhat less than a material amount, the auditors, recognizing that the actual misstatement might be greater than their estimate, may still conclude that the risk of material misstatement of the financial statements is too high. In either case, the auditors will ask management to adjust the financial statements for the known misstatements, or they will perform additional audit procedures to further reduce detection risk. The auditors should never issue an unqualified opinion on financial statements in which the risk of material misstatement is considered to be excessive.

The auditors will conclude that the risk of material misstatement is sufficiently low to issue an unqualified opinion only when *total likely misstatement is significantly less than a material amount.* The relationship between total likely misstatement and materiality is often documented in a working paper similar to that shown in Figure 18–5. As illustrated, the auditors must consider the effects of the total likely misstatement on the various components of the financial statements, such as current assets and net income. As we have emphasized throughout, whether a misstatement is material depends on its specific effect on the financial statements.

Notice that the misstatements in Figure 18–5 are adjusted for the effects of income taxes. To illustrate, consider the first misstatement, which represents an overstatement of

# Figure 18–5  Total Likely Misstatement

SOUTHMADE PRODUCTS, INC.
Total Likely Misstatement
December 31, 19X4
Overstatement (Understatement)

| W/P ref. | | Current Assets | Non-current Assets | Current Liabilities | Non-current Liabilities | Owners' Equity | Income before Taxes | Tax Expense |
|---|---|---|---|---|---|---|---|---|
| | Uncorrected Known Misstatements | | | | | | | |
| D-8 | Overstatement of prepaid expenses | $ 6,500 | | $ 2,600 | | $ 6,500 (2,600) | $ 6,500 | $ 2,600 |
| F-6 | Overstatement of prior years' depreciation | | ($10,000) | (4,000) | | (10,000) 4,000 | | |
| M-4 | Unrecorded liabilities | | | (11,215) 4,486 | | 11,215 (4,486) | 11,215 | 4,486 |
| | Projected Misstatements | | | | | | | |
| C-5 | Overstatement of accounts receivable (confirmation results) | 30,000 | | 12,000 | | 30,000 (12,000) | 30,000 | 12,000 |
| | Other Estimated Misstatements | | | | | | | |
| C-10 | Understatement of allowance for uncollectible accounts | 5,000 | | 2,000 | | 5,000 (2,000) | 5,000 | 2,000 |
| | Total Likely Misstatements | $ 41,500 | ($ 10,000) | $ 5,871 | - | $ 25,629 | $ 52,715 | $ 21,086 |
| | Amount considered material | $100,000 | $125,000 | $100,000 | $125,000 | $200,000 | $150,000 | |

*Conclusion: Total likely misstatements are small enough in amount to result in a sufficiently low level of audit risk to justify our opinion.*

2.17 X5 JW

prepaid expenses of $6,500. If that adjustment is not made, net income before taxes is overstated by that amount. However, since taxable income is also overstated by $6,500, the company's income tax expense is overstated, in this case by $2,600 (40 percent of $6,500). The 40 percent rate was used because it represents the company's marginal tax rate.

## Reviewing the Engagement

*SAS 22* (AU 311), "Planning and Supervision," states that "the work performed by each assistant should be reviewed to determine whether it was adequately performed and to evaluate whether the results are consistent with the conclusions to be presented in the auditors' report." This review of the work of the audit staff is primarily accomplished through a review of the audit working papers. The seniors on audit engagements typically perform their review of the audit working papers as the papers are completed. While audit partners and managers will generally communicate with seniors and other staff members throughout the audit, their review of the working papers generally is not completed until near (or after) completion of field work. The audit partner and manager will devote special attention to those accounts that have a higher risk of material misstatement, such as the significant accounting estimates of inventory obsolescence and warranty obligations. If a second partner review is required by the CPA firm's quality control policies, this review is usually performed just prior to issuance of the audit report.

### Reviewing the Financial Statement Disclosures.

The continuing proliferation of accounting standards makes it difficult for the auditors to evaluate the adequacy of financial statement disclosures. It is not effective to rely on the auditors' memories to evaluate the adequacy of disclosures, and it is not efficient for them to research the required disclosures each time they review a set of financial statements. Thus, many CPA firms use **disclosure checklists** that list all specific disclosures required by the FASB, the GASB, and the SEC. The auditors complete the checklist as a part of their review of the completed financial statements.

## Responsibilities for Other Information in the Financial Report

Audited financial statements generally are included in three types of reports: (1) annual reports to shareholders, (2) reports to the SEC, and (3) auditor-submitted financial reports. These documents may include a considerable amount of information in addition to the audited financial statements. In completing the audit engagement, the auditors must fulfill certain responsibilities regarding this other information. The auditors' responsibility for specific information depends on the type of report and the nature of the information.

### FASB- and GASB-required Supplementary Information.

The auditors have a responsibility to perform review procedures on supplementary information that is required by the FASB or the GASB. These procedures, as set forth in *SAS 52* (AU 558), "Required Supplementary Information," include inquiries of management regarding the appropriate presentation of the supplementary information and comparisons of the information with audited and other data known to the auditors.

If required supplementary information is omitted or not appropriately presented, or the auditors are not able to complete their limited procedures, these facts should be described in an additional paragraph in the auditors' report. Since the information is not required for fair presentation of the financial statements, the inclusion of the additional paragraph does not constitute a qualification of the auditors' opinion.

### Other Information in Client-Prepared Documents.

Audit reports on the financial statements of large companies usually are included in an annual report to shareholders and in reports to the SEC. These annual reports contain information other than audited financial statements and required supplementary information, as, for example, a discussion of the company's plans and prospects for the future. In *SAS 8* (AU 550), "Other Information in Documents Containing Audited Financial Statements," the AICPA set forth guidelines for the independent auditors with respect to such information. The auditors should read the other information and consider whether it is materially inconsistent with information appearing in the audited financial statements or notes. If the other information is inconsistent and the auditors conclude that neither the audited financial statements nor the audit report requires revision, they should request the client to revise the other information. If the client refuses to do so, the auditors should consider such alternatives as (1) revising the audit report to describe the inconsistency, (2) withholding use of their audit report by the client, or (3) withdrawing from the engagement. The auditors should also be alert for, and discuss with the client, any other types of material misstatements included in the other information.

### Information Accompanying Financial Statements in Auditor-Submitted Documents.

The auditors often process and reproduce financial reports for their clients, particularly for small companies with few shareholders. These documents may contain information in addition to the audited financial statements and the auditors' report. This *accompanying information* generally supplements or analyzes the basic financial statements, but is not necessary for the presentation of the statements in accordance with generally accepted accounting principles. When the auditors submit a document that contains audited financial statements and accompanying information to their clients or others, they should report on all the information. If the auditors have audited the information, they should express an opinion on whether it is fairly stated in all material respects in relation to the financial statements taken as a whole. Otherwise, the auditors should provide a disclaimer of opinion on the information.

## Communicating with the Client

*SAS 60*[2] and *SAS 61*[3] require the auditors to communicate certain matters to those who have responsibility for oversight of the financial reporting process, generally the client's audit committee. Recall from our discussion in Chapter 8 that the auditors must commu-

---

[2]AICPA, *Statement on Auditing Standards 60* (AU 325), "Communication of Internal Control Structure Related Matters Noted in an Audit" (New York, 1988).

[3]AICPA, *Statement on Auditing Standards 61* (AU 380), "Communication with Audit Committees" (New York, 1988).

nicate to the audit committee any significant deficiencies in internal control, known as "reportable conditions." In addition, *SAS 61* requires the communication of certain other information on audits of SEC clients, as well as on audits of other entities with active audit committees or boards of directors. Auditing matters to be communicated to the audit committee include the auditors' responsibilities for the audit and other information included with the financial statements, and any significant audit adjustments proposed by the auditors.

Regarding accounting matters, the auditors are required to communicate information on the client's selection of significant accounting policies, as well as information on significant accounting estimates made by management. Finally, the auditors will discuss any disagreements with management or other difficulties encountered in performing the audit. If management contacted other auditors concerning an accounting or auditing matter, the auditors will present their viewpoint to the audit committee. The purpose of communicating these matters is to aid the audit committee in its oversight role over senior management of the company.

# POST-AUDIT RESPONSIBILITIES

## The Auditors' Subsequent Discovery of Facts Existing at the Date of Their Report

After the issuance of its audit report, a CPA firm may encounter evidence indicating that the client's financial statements were materially misstated or lacked required disclosures. The auditors must investigate immediately such subsequently discovered facts. If the auditors ascertain that the facts are significant and existed at the date of the audit report, they should advise the client to make appropriate disclosure of the facts to anyone actually or likely to be relying upon the audit report and the related financial statements. If the client refuses to make appropriate disclosure, the CPAs should inform each member of the client's board of directors of such refusal. They should also notify regulatory agencies having jurisdiction over the client, and, if practicable, each person known to be relying upon the audited financial statements, that the CPAs' report can no longer be relied upon.

## Subsequent Discovery of Omitted Audit Procedures

What actions should the auditors take if after issuing an audit report they find that they failed to perform certain significant audit procedures? The omission of appropriate audit procedures in a particular engagement might be discovered during a peer review or other subsequent review of the auditors' working papers. Unlike the situation described in the previous section, the auditors do not have information indicating that the financial statements are in error. Instead, the subsequent review has revealed that they may have issued their audit report without having gathered sufficient evidential matter. In addressing this sensitive problem *SAS 46* (AU 390), "Consideration of Omitted Procedures after the Report Date," states that the auditors should assess the importance of the omitted procedures to their previously issued opinion. If they believe that the omitted procedures impair their ability to express the opinion, and their report is still being relied upon by third parties, they should attempt to perform the omitted procedures or appropriate alternative procedures. Because of the legal implications of these situations, the auditors should consider consulting their legal counsel.

## ◆ CHAPTER SUMMARY

This chapter explained examination of operations and the considerations and procedures involved in completing the audit. To summarize:

1. The analysis of the various transaction cycles has emphasized the need to consider revenue and expense accounts in conjunction with the audit of asset and liability accounts. However, vouching and other substantive procedures are generally necessary for revenue and expense accounts that are less directly associated with transaction cycles such as miscellaneous revenue and selling, general, and administrative expenses.

2. Because of their objectives, certain audit procedures cannot be completed before the end of the audit. These procedures include: *(a)* search for unrecorded liabilities, *(b)* review the minutes of meetings, *(c)* perform final analytical procedures, *(d)* perform procedures to identify loss contingencies, *(e)* perform the review for subsequent events, and *(f)* obtain the representation letter.

3. The auditors must perform audit procedures to determine that loss contingencies have been properly presented and disclosed in conformity with *FASB Statement No. 5*. To identify loss contingencies, auditors perform various procedures, such as reviewing minutes of directors' meetings, inquiring of the client's lawyer, reviewing correspondence with financial institutions and regulatory agencies, sending confirmations to financial institutions, and obtaining a representation letter from officers of the company.

4. Subsequent events may be classified into two broad categories: *(a)* those providing additional evidence about facts existing on or before the balance sheet date (which may require adjusting entries), and *(b)* those involving facts coming into existence after the balance sheet date (which may require note disclosures). Many of these subsequent events relate to loss contingencies, and the audit procedures involved are similar to those for auditing those items.

5. Another important part of completing the audit is the procedures performed to evaluate audit findings and review the audit work. In evaluating audit findings, the auditors accumulate known misstatements, projected misstatements, and other estimated misstatements to determine if the aggregate results of their procedures support the fairness of the financial statements.

6. Auditors also have certain postaudit responsibilities. When auditors find, subsequent to the issuance of their audit report, that the financial statements are materially misleading, they should take steps to prevent continued reliance on their report. In some cases this might involve notification of regulatory agencies.

## ◆ KEY TERMS INTRODUCED OR EMPHASIZED IN CHAPTER 18

**Analytical procedures**   Evaluations of financial information made by a study of plausible relationships between financial and nonfinancial information.

**Commitment**   A contractual obligation to carry out a transaction at specified terms in the future. Material commitments should be disclosed in the financial statements.

**Conservatism**   An accounting doctrine for asset valuation in which the lower of two alternative acceptable asset valuations is chosen.

**Contingent liability**   A possible liability, stemming from past events, that will be resolved as to existence and amount by some future event.

**Disclosure checklist**   A list of specific disclosures required by the FASB, GASB, and the SEC that is used to evaluate the adequacy of the disclosures in a set of financial statements.

**General risk contingency**   An element of the business environment that involves some risk of a future loss. Examples include the risk of accident, strike, price fluctuations, or natural catastrophe. General risk contingencies should not be disclosed in financial statements.

**Lawyer's letter**   A letter of inquiry sent by auditors to a client's legal counsel requesting a description and evaluation of pending or threatened litigation, unasserted claims, and other loss contingencies.

**Loss contingency**   A possible loss, stemming from past events, that will be resolved as to existence and amount by some future event. Loss contingencies should be disclosed in notes to the financial statements if there is a reasonable possibility that a loss has been incurred. When loss contingencies are considered probable and can be reasonably estimated, they should be accrued in the accounts.

**Minutes book**   A formal record of the issues discussed and actions taken in meetings of stockholders and of the board of directors.

**Representation letter**   A single letter or separate letters prepared by officers of the client company at the auditors' request setting forth certain representations about the company's financial position or operations.

**S-1 review**   Procedures carried out by auditors at the client company's facilities on or as close as practicable to the effective date of a registration statement filed under the Securities Act of 1933.

**Subsequent event**   An event occurring after the date of the balance sheet but prior to completion of the audit and issuance of the audit report.

**Total likely misstatement in the financial statements**   Total misstatement in the financial statements that is estimated by the auditors based on the results of audit procedures. For example, the projected misstatement from an audit sample is an estimate of the likely misstatement in the audit population.

**Unasserted claim**   A possible legal claim of which no potential claimant has exhibited an awareness.

---

## ◆ GROUP I: REVIEW QUESTIONS

18-1   Identify three revenue accounts that are verified during the audit of balance sheet accounts; also, identify the related balance sheet accounts.

18-2   Identify three expense accounts that are verified during the audit of balance sheet accounts; also, identify the related balance sheet accounts.

18-3   How are analytical procedures used in the verification of revenue?

18-4   Identify three items often misclassified as miscellaneous revenue.

18-5   For which expense accounts should the auditors obtain or prepare analyses to be used in preparation of the client's income tax returns?

18-6   When you are first retained to audit the financial statements of Wabash Company, you inquire whether a budget is used to control costs and expenses. The controller, James Lowe, replies that he personally prepares such a budget each year, but that he regards it as a highly confidential document. He states that you may refer to it if necessary, but he wants you to make sure that no employee of the firm sees any of the budget data. Comment on this use of a budget.

18-7    What auditing procedure can you suggest for determining the reasonableness of selling, general, and administrative expenses?

18-8    Describe how the auditors use analytical procedures in the examination of selling, general, and administrative expenses.

18-9    In connection with an annual audit of a corporation engaged in manufacturing operations, the auditors have regularly reviewed the minutes of the meetings of stockholders and of the board of directors. Name 10 important items that might be found in the minutes of the meetings held during the period under review that would be of interest and significance to the auditors.

18-10   What should be the scope of the auditors' review of the corporate minutes book during the first audit of a client? During a repeat engagement?

18-11   Should the auditors make a complete review of all correspondence in the client's files? Explain.

18-12   What are *subsequent events?*

18-13   What is the meaning of the term *commitment?* Give examples. Do commitments appear in financial statements? Explain.

18-14   What are *general risk contingencies?* Do such items require disclosure in the financial statements?

18-15   What is the usual procedure followed by the CPA in obtaining evidence regarding pending and threatened litigation against the client?

18-16   What are *loss contingencies?* How are such items presented in the financial statements? Explain.

18-17   Explain how a loss contingency exists with respect to an *unasserted* claim. Should unasserted claims be disclosed in the financial statements?

18-18   If the federal income tax returns for prior years have not as yet been reviewed by federal tax authorities, would you consider it necessary for the client to disclose this situation in a note to the financial statements? Explain.

18-19   List the audit procedures that must be completed near the end of audit field work.

18-20   Describe a disclosure checklist. What is its purpose?

18-21   Describe the manner in which the auditors evaluate their audit findings.

18-22   What is the independent auditors' obligation with respect to information in client-prepared annual reports to shareholders, other than the audited financial statements?

18-23   When auditors submit documents to their clients that contain audited financial statements, what are their responsibilities concerning information that accompanies the financial statements?

---

# ◆ GROUP II: QUESTIONS REQUIRING ANALYSIS

18-24   In a recent court case, the presiding judge criticized the work of a senior in charge of an audit in approximately the following language: "As to minutes, the senior read only what the secretary (of the company) gave him, which consisted only of the board of directors' minutes. He did not read such minutes as there were of the executive committee of the board. He did not know that there was an executive committee, hence he did not discover that the treasurer had notes of executive committee minutes which had not been written up."

How can the independent auditors be certain the client has provided them with minutes of all meetings of the board and committees thereof? Explain.

18-25 In your audit of the financial statements of Wolfe Company for the year ended April 30, you find that a material account receivable is due from a company in reorganization under Chapter 11 of the Bankruptcy Act. You also learn that on May 28 several former members of the bankrupt company's management formed a new company and that the new company had issued a note to Wolfe Company that would pay off the bankrupt customer's account receivable over a four-year period. What presentation, if any, should be made of this situation in the financial statements of Wolfe Company for the year ended April 30? Explain.

18-26 The auditor's opinion on the fairness of financial statements may be affected by subsequent events.

Required: a. Define what is commonly referred to in auditing as a subsequent event, and describe the two general types of subsequent events.
b. Identify those auditing procedures that the auditor should apply at or near the completion of field work to disclose significant subsequent events.

18-27 On July 27, 199X, Arthur Ward, CPA, issued an unqualified audit report on the financial statements of Dexter Company for the year ended June 30, 199X. Two weeks later, Dexter Company mailed annual reports, including the June 30 financial statements and Ward's audit report, to 150 stockholders and to several creditors of Dexter Company. Dexter Company's stock is not actively traded on national exchanges or over the counter.

On September 5, the controller of Dexter Company informed Ward that an account payable for consulting services in the amount of $170,000 had inadvertently been omitted from Dexter's June 30 balance sheet. As a consequence, net income for the year ended June 30 was overstated by $90,500, net of applicable federal and state income taxes. Both Ward and Dexter's controller agreed that the misstatement was material to Dexter's financial position at June 30, 199X, and operating results for the year then ended.

What should Arthur Ward's course of action be in this matter? Discuss.

18-28 Current pronouncements of the FASB require that under certain circumstances loss contingencies be accrued in the financial statements. Under other circumstances, loss contingencies may require disclosure only in notes to the financial statements or may be omitted entirely from the financial statements and accompanying notes. Provide three separate examples of a loss contingency, one for each of these three categories.

18-29 You are the audit manager in the audit of the financial statements of Midwest Grain Storage, Inc., a new client. The company's records show that as of the balance sheet date, approximately 15 million bushels of various grains are in storage for the Commodity Credit Corporation, an agency of the U.S. government.

In your review of the audit senior's working papers, you ascertain the following facts:
a. All grain is stored under a Uniform Grain Storage Agreement, which holds Midwest responsible for the quantity and quality of the grain.
b. Losses due to shrinkage, spoilage, and so forth are inherent in the storage of grain. Midwest's losses, however, have been negligible due to the excellence of its storage facilities.
c. Midwest carries a warehouseman's bond covering approximately 20 percent of the value of the stored grain.

In the loss contingencies section of the working papers, the senior auditor has made the following notation: "I propose recommending to Midwest's controller that the contingent liability for grain spoilage and shrinkage be disclosed in a note to the financial statements."

Do you concur with the senior's proposal? Explain.

18-30   Linda Reeves, CPA, receives a telephone call from her client, Lane Company. The company's controller states that the board of directors of Lane has entered into two contractual arrangements with Ted Forbes, the company's former president, who has recently retired. Under one agreement, Lane Company will pay the ex-president $7,000 per month for five years if he does not compete with the company during that time in a rival business. Under the other agreement, the company will pay the ex-president $5,000 per month for five years for such advisory services as the company may request from the ex-president.

     Lane's controller asks Reeves whether the balance sheet as of the date the two agreements were signed should show $144,000 in current liabilities and $576,000 in long-term liabilities, or whether the two agreements should be disclosed in a contingencies note to the financial statements.

     How should Linda Reeves reply to the controller's questions? Explain.

18-31   During an audit engagement, Robert Wong, CPA, has satisfactorily completed an examination of accounts payable and other liabilities and now plans to determine whether there are any loss contingencies arising from litigation, claims, or assessments.

     What are the audit procedures Wong should follow with respect to the existence of loss contingencies arising from litigation, claims, or assessments? Do not discuss reporting requirements.

18-32   Select the best answer for each of the following and give reasons for your choice:

    *a.*   An auditor should examine the minutes of board of directors' meetings:
      (1)   Through the date of the financial statements.
      (2)   Through the date of the audit report.
      (3)   On a test basis.
      (4)   Only at the beginning of the audit.

    *b.*   As a result of analytical procedures, the independent auditors determine that the gross profit percentage has declined from 30 percent in the preceding year to 20 percent in the current year. The auditors should:
      (1)   Express an opinion that is qualified due to the inability of the client company to continue as a going concern.
      (2)   Evaluate management's performance in causing this decline.
      (3)   Require note disclosure.
      (4)   Consider the possibility of a misstatement in the financial statements.

    *c.*   An auditor accepted an engagement to audit the 19X8 financial statements of EFG Corporation and began the field work on September 30, 19X8. EFG gave the auditor the 19X8 financial statements on January 17, 19X9. The auditor completed the field work on February 10, 19X9, and delivered the report on February 16, 19X9. The client's representation letter normally would be dated:
      (1)   December 31, 19X8.
      (2)   January 17, 19X9.
      (3)   February 10, 19X9.
      (4)   February 16, 19X9.

    *d.*   Which of the following procedures is most likely to be included in the final review stage of an audit?
      (1)   Obtain an understanding of internal control.
      (2)   Confirmation of receivables.
      (3)   Observation of inventory.
      (4)   Perform analytical procedures.

    *e.*   Subsequent to the issuance of the auditor's report, the auditor became aware of facts existing at the report date that would have affected the report had the auditor then been aware of such facts. After determining that the information is reliable, the auditor should next:

      (1)    Notify the board of directors that the auditor's report must no longer be associated with the financial statements.

      (2)    Determine whether there are persons relying or likely to rely on the financial statements who would attach importance to the information.

      (3)    Request that management disclose the effects of the newly discovered information by adding a footnote to subsequently issued financial statements.

      (4)    Issue revised pro forma financial statements taking into consideration the newly discovered information.

    *f.*    Which of the following events occurring on January 5 of 19X2 is most likely to result in an adjusting entry to the 19X1 financial statements?

      (1)    A business combination.

      (2)    Early retirement of bonds payable.

      (3)    Settlement of litigation.

      (4)    Plant closure due to a strike.

# ◆ GROUP III: PROBLEMS

**18-33**    Rita King, your staff assistant on the April 30, 19X2, audit of Maxwell Company, was transferred to another assignment before she could prepare a proposed adjusting journal entry for Maxwell's Miscellaneous Revenue account, which she had analyzed per the working paper on the following page. You have reviewed the working paper and are satisfied with King's procedures. You are convinced that all the Miscellaneous Revenue items should be transferred to other accounts. Maxwell Company's state of incorporation has an Unclaimed Properties Law.

*Required:*    Draft a proposed adjusting journal entry at April 30, 19X2, for Maxwell Company's Miscellaneous Revenue account.

**18-34**    Your client is a shopping center with 30 store tenants. All leases with the store tenants provide for a fixed rent plus a percentage of sales, net of sales taxes, in excess of a fixed dollar amount computed on an annual basis. Each lease also provides that the lessor may engage CPAs to audit all records of the tenant for assurance that sales are being properly reported to the lessor.

    You have been requested by your client to audit the records of Traders Restaurant to determine that the sales totaling $390,000 for the year ended December 31, 19X2, have been properly reported to the lessor. The restaurant and the shopping center entered into a five-year lease on January 1, 19X1. Traders Restaurant offers only table service; no liquor is served. During meal times there are four or five waiters and waitresses in attendance who prepare handwritten prenumbered restaurant checks for the customers. Payment is made at a cash register, operated by the proprietor, as the customer leaves. All sales are for cash. The proprietor also is the accountatt. Complete files are kept of restaurant checks and cash register tapes. A daily sales journal and general ledger are also maintained.

*Required:*    List the auditing procedures that you would employ to verify the total annual sales of Traders Restaurant.

                                                                    (AICPA, adapted)

**18-35**    Kenneth J. Bryan, secretary of Jensen Corporation, has given you the minutes of the meetings of the board of directors. Summarize, in good form for the audit working papers, those contents of the minutes on pages 645–46 that you consider to be of significance in the conduct of an annual audit.

**18-36**    A normal procedure in the audit of a corporate client consists of a careful reading of the minutes of meetings of the board of directors. One of the CPAs' objectives in reading the minutes is to determine whether the transactions recorded in the accounting records are in agreement with actions approved by the board of directors.

```
                            Maxwell Company
Acct. No. 430            Miscellaneous Revenue                          Q-2
                        Year Ended April 30, 19X2
                                                    C.M.
                                                    May 19, X2

Date            Description                      Reference      Amount

May 8, 19X1     Proceeds of sale of scrap from   Various CR     5,843 Y
through         manufacturing process (total of
April 7, 19X2   12 monthly sales)


July 18, 19X1   Write-off of old outstanding checks;
                nos. 118-$500; 214-$400; 407-$200   GJ 7-4      1,100 Y

Sept. 22, 19X1  Recovery of previously written off
                account receivable from Wilson
                Company                             CR 9-1      4,381 Y

Feb. 6, 19X2    Cash proceeds from sale of machine.
                Cost of $10,000 and accumulated
                depreciation of $8,000 as of Feb. 6,
                X2 not removed from accounts.        CR 2-1      3,500 Y

April 28, 19X2  Refund of premium overcharge on
                fire insurance policy no. 1856,
                for period April 1, 19X2-Mar. 31, 19X3  CR 4-1    600 Y

April 30, 19X2  Balance per ledger                            15,424
```

Y — Traced to cash receipts journal or general journal;
vouched to appropriate supporting documents.

R.A.K.
May 18, X2

Required: a. What is the reasoning underlying this objective of reconciling transactions in the corporate accounting records with actions approved by the board of directors? Describe fully how the CPAs achieve the stated objective after they have read the minutes of directors' meetings.

b. Discuss the effect each of the following situations would have on specific audit steps in the CPAs' audit and on their opinion:
   (1) The minutes book does not show approval for the sale of an important manufacturing division that was consummated during the year.
   (2) Some details of a contract negotiated during the year with the labor union are different from the outline of the contract included in the minutes of the board of directors.

(continued on page 647)

**Meeting of February 15, 19X2**

The meeting was called to order at 2:15 P.M. by H. R. Jensen, chairman of the board. The following directors were present:

| | |
|---|---|
| John J. Savage | Ruth Andrews |
| Helen R. King | Dale H. Lindberg |
| Lee McCormick | Ralph Barker |
| H. R. Coleman | H. R. Jensen |
| George Anderson | Kenneth J. Bryan |
| Harold Bruce Smith | |

Absent was Director J. B. Adams, who was in New York City on company business in connection with the opening of a sales office.

The minutes of the preceding meeting, December 15, 19X1, were read by the secretary and duly approved as read.

Upon a motion by Ms. King, seconded by Mr. Savage, and unanimously carried, the secretary was instructed to notify the firm of Black, Bryson & MacDougal, Certified Public Accountants, of its selection to conduct an annual audit of the company's financial statements as of March 31, 19X2.

President John J. Savage outlined the current status of negotiations leading toward the acquisition of a new factory site in San Diego, California, and recommended to the board the purchase of said property at a price not to exceed $600,000.

Ms. King offered the following resolution, which was seconded by Mr. Smith, and unanimously carried:

Resolved: That Mr. Savage hereby is authorized to acquire on behalf of the company the factory site located at Exmont and Donaldson Avenues, San Diego, California, at a price not in excess of $600,000, to be paid for in cash from the general funds of the corporation.

Upon a motion by Mr. Savage, seconded by Ms. King and carried unanimously, the secretary was instructed to arrange for the purchase from the estate of J. B. Williams, former director, 100 shares of the company's own stock at a price not in excess of $110 per share.

Mr. Savage, after discussing the progress of the company in recent months and its current financial condition, submitted the following resolution, which was seconded by Mr. Coleman and unanimously passed:

Resolved: That the following cash dividends are hereby declared, payable April 10, 19X2, to stockholders of record on March 31, 19X2.

a. The regular quarterly dividend of $1 per share of capital stock.

b. A special dividend of 50 cents per share of capital stock.

There being no further business brought before the meeting, the meeting was adjourned at 4 P.M.

**Kenneth J. Bryan**
Secretary

**Meeting of March 15, 19X2**

The meeting was called to order at 2:15 P.M. by H. R. Jensen, chairman of the board. The following directors were present:

| | |
|---|---|
| John J. Savage | Ruth Andrews |
| Helen R. King | Dale H. Lindberg |
| Lee McCormick | J. B. Adams |
| H. R. Coleman | H. R. Jensen |
| George Anderson | Kenneth J. Bryan |
| Harold Bruce Smith | |

Absent was Director Ralph Barker.

The minutes of the preceding meeting, February 15, 19X2, were read by the secretary and duly approved as read.

Chairman H. R. Jensen stated that nominations for the coming year were in order for the positions of president, vice president in charge of sales, vice president in charge of manufacturing, treasurer, controller, and secretary.

The following nominations were made by Ms. King, and there being no further nominations the nominations were declared closed:

| | |
|---|---|
| President | John J. Savage |
| Vice president—sales | Otis Widener |
| Vice president—manufacturing | Henry Pendleton |
| Treasurer | Ruth Andrews |
| Controller | Roger Dunn |
| Secretary | Kenneth J. Bryan |

The above nominees were duly elected.

Mr. McCormick then offered the following resolution, which was seconded by Mr. Coleman and unanimously carried:

Resolved: That the salaries of all officers be continued for the next year at the same rates currently in effect. These rates are as follows:

| | |
|---|---|
| John J. Savage—president | $150,000 |
| Otis Widener—vice president—sales | 70,000 |
| Henry Pendleton—vice president—manufacturing | 70,000 |
| Ruth Andrews—treasurer | 70,000 |
| Roger Dunn—controller | 70,000 |
| Kenneth J. Bryan—secretary | 50,000 |

Mr. Bryan offered the following resolution, which was seconded by Mrs. Andrews and unanimously carried:

Resolved: That the company establish a bank account at the United National Bank, San Diego, California, to be subject to check by either John J. Savage or Ruth Andrews.

There being no further business to come before the meeting, the meeting was adjourned at 4 P.M.

**Kenneth J. Bryan**
Secretary

(3)   The minutes of a meeting of directors held after the balance sheet date have not yet been written, but the corporation's secretary shows the CPAs notes from which the minutes are to be prepared when the secretary has time.

*c.*   What corporate actions should be approved by stockholders and recorded in the minutes of the stockholders' meetings?

(AICPA, adapted)

18-37   Robertson Company had accounts receivable of $200,000 at December 31, 199X, and had provided an allowance for uncollectible accounts of $6,000. After performing all normal auditing procedures relating to the receivables and to the valuation allowance, the independent auditors were satisfied that this asset was fairly stated and that the allowance for uncollectible accounts was adequate. Just before completion of the audit field work late in February, however, the auditors learned that the entire plant of Thompson Corporation, a major customer, had been destroyed by a flood early in February and that as a result Thompson Corporation was hopelessly insolvent.

The account receivable from Thompson Corporation in the amount of $44,000 originated on December 28; terms of payment were net 60 days. The receivable had been regarded as entirely collectible at December 31, and the auditors had so considered it in reaching their conclusion as to the adequacy of the allowance for uncollectible accounts. In discussing the news concerning the flood, the controller of Robertson Company emphasized to the auditors that the probable loss of $44,000 should be regarded as a loss of the following year, and not of 199X, the year under audit.

What action, if any, should the auditors recommend with respect to the receivable from Thompson Corporation?

18-38   In connection with your audit of the financial statements of Hollis Mfg. Corporation for the year ended December 31, 19X3, your review of subsequent events disclosed the following items:

*a.*   January 7, 19X4: The mineral content of a shipment of ore en route to Hollis Mfg. Corporation on December 31, 19X3, was determined to be 72 percent. The shipment was recorded at year-end at an estimated content of 50 percent by a debit to Raw Materials Inventory and a credit to Accounts Payable in the amount of $82,400. The final liability to the vendor is based on the actual mineral content of the shipment.

*b.*   January 15, 19X4: Culminating a series of personal disagreements between Ray Hollis, the president, and his brother-in-law, the treasurer, the latter resigned, effective immediately, under an agreement whereby the corporation would purchase his 10 percent stock ownership at book value as of December 31, 19X3. Payment is to be made in two equal amounts in cash on April 1 and October 1, 19X4. In December, the treasurer had obtained a divorce from his wife, who is Ray Hollis's sister.

*c.*   January 31, 19X4: As a result of reduced sales, production was curtailed in mid-January and some workers were laid off. On February 5, 19X4, all the remaining workers went on strike. To date the strike is unsettled.

*Required:*   Assume that the above items came to your attention before completion of your audit field work recommend for the item, listing all details that you would suggest should be disclosed. Indicate those items or details, if any, that should not be disclosed. Give your reasons for recommending or not recommending disclosure of the items or details.

(AICPA, adapted)

18-39   In connection with her audit of the financial statements of Flowmeter, Inc. for the year ended December 31, 19X3, Joan Hirsch, CPA, is aware that certain events and transactions that took place after December 31, 19X3, but before she issues her report dated February 28, 19X4, may affect the company's financial statements.

The following material events or transactions have come to her attention:

a.  On January 3, 19X4, Flowmeter, Inc. received a shipment of raw materials from Canada. The materials had been ordered in October 19X3 and shipped FOB shipping point in December 1993.

b.  On January 15, 19X4, the company settled and paid a personal injury claim of a former employee as the result of an accident that had occurred in March 19X3. The company had not previously recorded a liability for the claim.

c.  On January 25, 19X4, the company agreed to purchase for cash the outstanding stock of Porter Electrical Co. The business combination is likely to double the sales volume of Flowmeter, Inc.

d.  On February 1, 19X4, a plant owned by Flowmeter, Inc. was damaged by a flood, resulting in an uninsured loss of inventory.

e.  On February 5, 19X4, Flowmeter, Inc. issued to an underwriting syndicate $2 million in convertible bonds.

*Required:*  For each of the above items, indicate how the event or transaction should be reflected in Flowmeter's financial statements and explain the reasons for selecting this method of disclosure.

(AICPA, adapted)

---

## ◆ GROUP IV: RESEARCH AND DISCUSSION CASE

18-40   Marshall and Wyatt, CPAs, have been the independent auditors of Interstate Land Development Corporation for several years. During these years, Interstate prepared and filed its own annual income tax returns.

During 1993, Interstate requested Marshall and Wyatt to audit all the necessary financial statements of the corporation to be submitted to the Securities and Exchange Commission (SEC) in connection with a multistate public offering of 1 million shares of Interstate common stock. This public offering came under the provisions of the Securities Act of 1933. The audit was performed carefully and the financial statements were fairly presented for the respective periods. These financial statements were included in the registration statement filed with the SEC.

While the registration statement was being processed by the SEC, but before the effective date, the Internal Revenue Service (IRS) obtained a federal court subpoena directing Marshall and Wyatt to turn over all of its working papers relating to Interstate for the years 1989–92. Marshall and Wyatt initially refused to comply for two reasons. First, Marshall and Wyatt did not prepare Interstate's tax returns. Second, Marshall and Wyatt claimed that the working papers were confidential matters subject to the privileged communications rule. Subsequently, however, Marshall and Wyatt did relinquish the subpoenaed working papers.

Upon receiving the subpoena, Wyatt called Dunkirk, the chairman of Interstate's board of directors, and asked him about the IRS investigation. Dunkirk responded, "I'm sure the IRS people are on a fishing expedition and that they will not find any material deficiencies."

A few days later Dunkirk received a written memorandum from the IRS stating that it was contending Interstate had underpaid its taxes during the period under review. The memorandum revealed that Interstate was being assessed $800,000, including penalties and interest for the three years. Dunkirk forwarded a copy of this memorandum to Marshall and Wyatt.

This $800,000 assessment was material relative to the financial statements as of December 31, 1993. The amount for each year individually, exclusive of penalty and interest, was not material relative to each respective year.

*Required:* *a.* In general terms, discuss the extent to which a CPA firm's potential liability to third parties is increased in an SEC registration audit.

*b.* Discuss the implications of the IRS investigation, if any, relative to Marshall and Wyatt's examination of Interstate's 1993 financial statements. Discuss any additional investigative procedures that the auditors should undertake or any audit judgments that should be made as a result of this investigation.

*c.* Can Marshall and Wyatt validly refuse to surrender the subpoenaed working papers to the IRS? Explain.

(AICPA, adapted)

## ♦ SUGGESTED REFERENCES

Part *a:*

This textbook, pp. 129–30.

Part *b:*

This textbook, pp. 628–32.

AICPA, *Professional Standards, Volume I, Commerce Clearing House, Statement on Auditing Standards* I, Section 560.

*FASB Statement 5,* "Accounting for Contingencies."

Part *c:*

This textbook, pp. 105–6 and 171–72.

## ♦ GROUP V: AUDIT CASE EXERCISE

18-41 The audit staff of Adams, Barnes & Co. (ABC), CPAs, reported the following audit findings in their audit of Keystone Computers & Networks (KCN), Inc.:

1. Unrecorded liabilities in the amount of $6,440 for purchases of inventory. These inventory items were counted and included in the year-end total.

2. Projected misstatement from confirmation of accounts receivable in the amount of $2,042 overstatement.

3. Projected misstatement from price tests of inventory of $9,510 overstatement.

4. The staff of ABC believes that the amount of KCN's allowance for uncollectible accounts should be increased by $5,000.

In addition, the audit staff has decided that for evaluating a material misstatement of the financial statements the following guidelines should be used:

Current assets—$50,000

Noncurrent assets—$75,000

Current liabilities—$50,000

Noncurrent liabilities—$75,000

Total owners' equity—$100,000

Net income before taxes—$65,000

*Required:* *a.* Prepare a schedule modeled after the one on page 634 to be used to evaluate the above audit findings, assuming that KCN's marginal tax rate is 25 percent.

*b.* Decide whether the results indicate that there is a sufficiently low risk of material misstatement to justify ABC's audit opinion.

PART

V

♦

# OTHER RESPONSIBILITIES

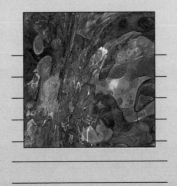

CHAPTER

19

♦

# OTHER ATTESTATION AND ACCOUNTING SERVICES

## CHAPTER OBJECTIVES

After studying this chapter, you should be able to:

- ♦ Distinguish between attestation and accounting services.
- ♦ Identify the types of special reports that auditors issue.
- ♦ Distinguish between accounting and review services.
- ♦ Discuss the issuance of letters for underwriters.
- ♦ Describe the nature of accountants' reports on prospective financial information.
- ♦ Explain the nature of management reports on internal control.
- ♦ Discuss reports by CPAs on management's assertions about internal control.

I n the preceding chapters, we emphasized the CPAs' principal type of attestation engagement—audits of a company's financial statements prepared in accordance with generally accepted accounting principles. However, CPAs perform numerous types of attestation, accounting, and other services.[1]

How do attestation and accounting services differ? When performing **attestation** engagements the CPA's role is one of expressing a written report on the reliability of a written assertion made by another party. In short, CPAs are hired to *provide assurance* as to whether information is presented in accordance with some appropriate criteria. In addition to audits of historical financial statements, the attest function is currently applied to information as diverse as prospective financial information, internal control, evaluation of controls in computer software, and evaluation of corporate codes of conduct.

---

◆ ILLUSTRATIVE CASE ◆

The United States' major defense contractors have made a commitment to adopt and implement a number of principles of business ethics and conduct. One requirement is that each firm annually complete the defense industry *Questionnaire on Business Ethics and Conduct.* Included are questions such as whether the corporation's Code of Ethics addresses standards that govern employee conduct in their dealings with suppliers, consultants, and customers.

The contractors agreed that each company would have its independent CPAs or a similar independent organization report upon the questionnaire. As a result, the public accounting profession developed standards for attesting to such information. The opinion paragraph of a report on the examination of the information appears below:

In our opinion, the affirmative responses in the Questionnaire accompanying the *Statement of Responses to the Defense Industry Questionnaire on Business Ethics and Conduct for the period from January 1, 19X1 to December 31, 19X1* referred to above are appropriately presented in conformity with the criteria set forth in the *Defense Industry Initiatives on Business Ethics and Conduct,* including the Questionnaire.

---

When performing accounting services, CPAs provide no explicit assurance as to whether the information follows the appropriate criteria. The role is one of assisting the client, and not one of providing assurance to third parties about the information. An example of an accounting service is assisting the client in preparing or *compiling* its financial information.

At this point it is helpful to distinguish between the manner in which the terms auditor and accountant are used. The term *auditor* is most frequently used when discussing a CPA's role of providing an opinion on the fairness of historical financial statements. The term *accountant,* on the other hand, refers to CPAs when they are performing other attestation services and accounting services.

This chapter describes other attestation and accounting services. Our discussion of attestation services first presents an overall description of these types of services, and then explains in separate sections attestation to historical financial information and attestation

---

[1]Other services are not discussed in this chapter but include, for example, consulting and tax services.

to other information. In the final section of the chapter we discuss various accounting services.

# THE ATTESTATION FUNCTION

The generally accepted auditing standards were adopted by the accounting profession to provide guidance for the performance of audits of historical financial statements. Expansion of the attest function has led the accounting profession to develop a more general set of *attestation standards*. Both the generally accepted auditing standards and the attestation standards were presented in Chapter 2. Essential to the attest function are both the existence of reasonable criteria (such as generally accepted accounting principles) and a written assertion (the information).

Currently, attestation standards provide guidance for three types of engagements— *examinations, reviews,* and *agreed-upon procedures*. These engagements all result in reports which provide some level of assurance about whether the information being presented is in accordance with the specified criteria.

Examinations, referred to as audits when historical financial statements are involved, are designed to provide the highest level of assurance. When performing an examination, accountants select from all available procedures to gather sufficient evidence to allow the issuance of a report with a positive opinion on whether the information follows some established or stated criteria.

Reviews consist of performing limited procedures, such as inquiries and analytical procedures. Accordingly, the resulting report provides only limited assurance that the information is fairly presented. **Limited assurance** is also referred to as **negative assurance** because the accountants' report disclaims an opinion on the reviewed information, but includes a statement such as ''We are not aware of any material modifications that should be made'' in order for the information to be in conformity with the appropriate criteria. Of course, when uncorrected material departures from the criteria are noted, the report must so indicate.

Finally, companies and specific (''specified'') users of the information may engage accountants to perform agreed-upon procedures. These reports result in a report that provides limited assurance, a summary of findings, or both. Because the nature of the agreed-upon procedures has been determined by a specified user, the reports for these engagements are intended only for that party. Reports on agreed-upon procedures are referred to as ''limited use'' (limited distribution) reports, as contrasted to ''general use'' reports, such as those on examinations and reviews. General use reports usually are appropriate for distribution to any third party. Only when the criteria have been agreed-upon by the user and the CPA, and such criteria are not deemed ''reasonable'' for general distribution must an examination or review report distribution be limited.

# ATTESTATION ENGAGEMENTS—HISTORICAL FINANCIAL INFORMATION

Throughout the text, we have concentrated our discussion on audits of financial statements presented in accordance with generally accepted accounting principles. However, CPAs attest to a variety of other types of historical financial information. In this section, we discuss special reports, audits of financial statements prepared for use in other countries, audits of personal financial statements, reviews of historical information, "comfort letters," and condensed financial statements.

## Special Reports

Auditors use the term **special reports** to describe auditors' reports issued on any of the following:

1.  Financial statements prepared in accordance with a comprehensive basis of accounting *other than* generally accepted accounting principles. (Example: cash-basis financial statements.)
2.  Specified elements, accounts, or items of financial statements. (Examples: amount of net sales or accounts receivable.)
3.  Compliance with aspects of contractual agreements or regulatory requirements *related to audited financial statements*. (Example: client's compliance with a bond indenture contract.)
4.  Special-purpose financial presentations to comply with contractual agreements or regulatory provisions (Example: financial information presented on the basis of accounting prescribed by a purchase agreement.)
5.  Audited financial information presented in prescribed forms or schedules that require a prescribed form of auditors' report. (Example: filings with a regulatory agency.)

Although the term *special reports* seems general, its use in the auditing literature is restricted to the five situations listed above. *SAS 62* (AU 623), "Special Reports," provides guidance to auditors in the issuance of these reports. In all special reports, the auditors must describe the scope of their engagements and clearly report their findings.

### 1.   Other comprehensive bases of accounting.

Auditors are sometimes requested to audit financial statements that are prepared on a comprehensive basis of accounting *other than* generally accepted accounting principles. What qualifies as another comprehensive basis of accounting? Examples of acceptable other comprehensive bases of accounting include *(a)* the requirements of a governmental regulatory agency, *(b)* the income tax basis, *(c)* the cash basis, and *(d)* a definite set of criteria having substantial support, such as price level adjustment.

Reports on financial statements on other comprehensive bases depart from the standard form in several ways. Most importantly, the report must describe the basis of accounting being used or refer to a financial statement note that provides such a description. Next, consider the first generally accepted auditing standard of reporting; that standard requires the auditors to state in their report *whether* the financial statements are presented in accordance with GAAP. Thus, if the statements are prepared using another comprehensive basis, the auditors' report must state that the financial statements follow a comprehensive basis of accounting other than GAAP.

Finally, the auditors should be cautious about the titles given to the financial statements. Titles such as "balance sheet," "income statement," and "statement of cash flows" are generally associated with financial statements presented in accordance with GAAP. Consequently, the professional standards require more descriptive titles for statements that are presented on some other basis. For example, a cash basis "balance sheet" is more appropriately titled, "statement of assets and liabilities arising from cash transactions.'' Perhaps the most common type of financial statements prepared on a basis other than GAAP is cash basis statements. An unqualified special report on cash-basis statements is shown below. The distinctive wording has been emphasized.

---

We have audited the accompanying *statement of assets and liabilities arising from cash transactions* of XYZ Company as of December 31, 19X1, and the related *statement of revenue collected and expenses paid* for the year then ended. These financial statements are the responsibility of the Company's management. Our responsibility is to express an opinion on these financial statements based on our audit.

We conducted our audit in accordance with generally accepted auditing standards. Those standards require that we plan and perform the audit to obtain reasonable assurance about whether the financial statements are free of material misstatement. An audit includes examining, on a test basis, evidence supporting the amounts and disclosures in the financial statements. An audit also includes assessing the accounting principles used and significant estimates made by management, as well as evaluating the overall financial statement presentation. We believe that our audit provides a reasonable basis for our opinion.

*As described in Note 1, these financial statements were prepared on the basis of cash receipts and disbursements, which is a comprehensive basis of accounting other than generally accepted accounting principles.*

In our opinion, the financial statements referred to above present fairly, in all material respects, the *assets and liabilities arising from cash transactions* of XYZ Company as of December 31, 19X1, and the *revenue collected and expenses paid* during the year then ended, *on the basis of accounting described in Note 1.*

---

The essence of this special report is the expression of an opinion as to whether the statements fairly present what they purport to present. The wording of the note mentioned in the report will vary from case to case in order to give an accurate indication of the content of the statements.

**2.   Specified elements, accounts, or items of financial statements.**   Auditors may be engaged to attest to specified elements, accounts, or items of a financial statement. For example, auditors may be requested by a lessee to provide reports on only the amount of the lessee's revenue. Such reports are commonly required by the provisions of lease agreements and may be relied upon to compute lease payments that are contingent on the lessee's revenue. These engagements may be either examinations—referred to as ''expressing an opinion''—or agreed-upon procedures engagements.

When the CPAs are engaged to *express an opinion* on specified elements or accounts, they modify their report to indicate the information examined, the basis of accounting used, and whether the information is presented fairly on that basis. It should be noted that materiality for such engagements is determined *in relation to the information presented* (e.g., the specific account); this is generally *less* than would be used in an audit of the complete financial statements.

On occasion, the client may request that the CPAs *not* apply sufficient procedures to express an opinion, but perform only limited *agreed-upon procedures* on the elements of financial statements. For example, the landlord of a shopping center may request that the

CPAs substantiate the revenue reported by tenants merely by agreeing the figures with the tenants' internal financial statements and state sales tax returns. The reason for limiting the CPAs' investigation procedures usually is to reduce the cost of the services.

*SAS 35* (AU 622), "Special Reports—Applying Agreed-Upon Procedures to Specified Elements, Accounts, or Items of a Financial Statement," provides guidance to CPAs who are engaged to report on the application of agreed-upon procedures to specified elements of financial statements. CPAs may accept such engagements if *(a)* the parties involved have a clear understanding of the procedures to be performed and *(b)* distribution of the report is limited to those informed parties.

The accountants' report on agreed-upon procedures disclaims an opinion on the information but may provide *negative assurance* when the accountants' procedures do not reveal the need for any adjustments to the information. Overall, the accountants' report should *(a)* state the information to which the procedures were applied, *(b)* indicate the intended limited distribution of the report, *(c)* enumerate the procedures performed, *(d)* state the accountants' findings, *(e)* disclaim an opinion on the information, and *(f)* state that the report does not extend to the financial statements viewed as a whole. Following is an example of the final paragraph of such a report in which the accountants state their findings, disclaim an opinion, and indicate that the report does not extend to the financial statements as a whole. The language of the report that provides the negative assurance has been emphasized.

---

Because the above procedures do not constitute an audit made in accordance with generally accepted auditing standards, we do not express an opinion on the revenues balance for the year ended December 31, 19X1. In connection with the procedures referred to above, *no matters came to our attention* that caused us to believe that the revenues balance might require adjustment. Had we performed additional procedures or had we made an audit of the financial statements in accordance with generally accepted auditing standards, other matters might have come to our attention that would have been reported to you. This report relates only to the account specified above and does not extend to any financial statements of XYZ Company, taken as a whole.

---

3. **Compliance reports.**   Regulatory requirements and debt agreements often require companies to provide compliance reports prepared by their independent auditors, which is the third type of special report. A common example of such reports is one prepared for bond trustees as evidence of the company's compliance with restrictions contained in the bond indenture. For example, the auditors may provide assurance that the client has complied with indenture provisions relating to the maintenance of certain financial ratios and restrictions on the payment of dividends.

This type of service, while similar to an agreed-upon procedures engagement, does not fit precisely into any of the three general types of attest engagements. For example, to provide the service the auditors must *first have performed an audit* of the related financial statements. The report issued includes an introductory paragraph summarizing the audit report on the financial statements, a paragraph providing negative assurance with respect to compliance, and a paragraph limiting distribution of the report to the client and the appropriate third party. The paragraph providing negative assurance as to compliance is illustrated below:

> In connection with our audit, nothing came to our attention that caused us to believe that the Company was not in compliance with any of the terms, covenants, provisions, or conditions of Sections 8 to 15, inclusive, of the Indenture dated July 21, 19X1, with AAA Bank. However, our audit was not directed primarily toward obtaining knowledge of such non-compliance.

4.   Special-purpose financial presentations.   The fourth type of special report is essentially an audit form of service for financial statements prepared to comply with either a contractual agreement or regulatory provisions. These presentations are typically prepared for the parties that have entered into the agreement, or for filing with the regulatory agency and they must be restricted accordingly. The statements may be prepared following either *(a)* GAAP or another comprehensive basis, or *(b)* a prescribed basis of accounting. When such statements follow GAAP or another comprehensive basis of accounting, the information required by the agreement or the regulatory provision is generally less complete than that required by GAAP, but more substantial than specified elements. For example, assume that a company is selling a portion of its assets to another company. A statement of net assets sold may be prepared following GAAP. The report issued on the statement by the CPA should include standard introductory and scope paragraphs modified only to refer to the special-purpose presentation. The remainder of the report is illustrated below:

> *The accompanying statement was prepared to present the net assets of ABC Company sold to XYZ Corporation pursuant to the purchase agreement described in Note Y, and is not intended to be a complete presentation of ABC Company's assets and liabilities.*
>
> In our opinion, the accompanying *statement of net assets sold* presents fairly, in all material respects, the net assets of ABC Company as of June 8, 19X1 sold pursuant to the purchase agreement referred to in Note Y, in conformity with generally accepted accounting principles.
>
> *This report is intended solely for the information and use of the boards of directors and managements of ABC Company and XYZ Corporation and should not be used for any other purpose.*

5.   Financial information presented in prescribed forms or schedules.   CPAs also may audit the fairness of information supplied by a client on a prescribed form, such as a loan application or a form filed with a regulatory agency. However, the language of some forms may call for the auditors to issue reports that do not conform to the applicable professional standards. For example, a loan application may require an audit report on balance sheet information presented on a form in preestablished categories that are not in

conformity with generally accepted accounting principles. In such cases, the auditors should reword the form of the report to comply with generally accepted auditing standards. Alternatively, many CPAs suggest to the client that the form simply be marked "see attached," with the attachment being the company's audited financial statements and audit report.

## Financial Statements Prepared for Use in Other Countries

A U.S.-based organization may prepare financial statements for use in other countries. For example, the organization may have a subsidiary in Germany and may prepare financial statements for that subsidiary as part of an effort to raise capital in Germany. *SAS 51* (AU 534), "Reporting on Financial Statements Prepared for Use in Other Countries," addresses the auditors' responsibility in this situation. The auditors need to be familiar with both the accounting and auditing standards used in the foreign country. They also need to obtain the client's written representations concerning the intended purpose and use of the financial statements.

When auditing the information, the auditors should follow the general and field work standards of the AICPA to the extent the standards are appropriate. In addition, the auditors may apply the other country's auditing standards and indicate so in their report.

The report issued depends upon whether it is for use primarily outside the United States (most frequently the case) or within the United States. If it is for use outside the United States the auditors may issue *(a)* a U.S. report, modified to reflect the accounting principles of the other country, or *(b)* the report form of the other country, if the auditors understand the responsibilities relating to issuance of that report. In circumstances in which the report is for general use in the United States, the auditors should use the U.S. standard report, modifying it for any departures from U.S. generally accepted accounting principles. Frequently, two sets of financial statements and audit reports are prepared—one following generally accepted accounting principles for distribution in the United States, and the other following the principles of the foreign country for distribution outside the United States.

## Audits of Personal Financial Statements

In recent years, a number of politicians have had their personal financial statements audited and made them public. Audited personal financial statements also may be required with large loan applications, or when an individual seeks to purchase a business using his or her personal credit.

Generally accepted accounting principles applied to personal financial statements are quite different from those applicable to business entities. In personal financial statements, assets are shown at their *estimated current values* and liabilities are presented at their *estimated current amounts*. Thus, auditors must apply audit procedures that will substantiate these estimates, rather than substantiating historical costs. On occasion, the auditors may need to rely upon appraisers, following the guidelines set forth in *SAS 11* (AU 336), "Using the Work of a Specialist."

The "balance sheet" for an individual is termed a *statement of financial condition*. This statement shows the individual's *net worth* in lieu of "owners' equity" and includes a liability for income taxes on the differences between the estimated current values of assets and liabilities and their income tax bases. The "income statement" for an individual is called the *statement of changes in net worth*. In addition to showing revenue and expenses, this statement includes the changes in the estimated current values of assets and in the estimated amounts of liabilities during the period.

The accounting principles for personal financial statements are described in *Statement of Position 82-1,* issued by the Accounting Standards Division of the AICPA.[2] In addition, the AICPA has issued the *Guide for Personal Financial Statements* to provide auditors with guidelines for auditing personal financial statements.[3] The reports issued on personal financial statements are standard in form, modified only for the change in financial statement names.

### Completeness—A Special Problem in Personal Financial Statements.

One of the assertions that a client makes regarding its financial statements is that the statements are complete—that is, that they reflect all of the client's assets, liabilities, and transactions for the period. Determining the completeness of financial statements may be especially difficult in the audit of personal financial statements for several reasons. First, there is generally poor internal control—all aspects of each transaction usually are under the control of the individual. Second, some individuals may seek to omit assets and income from their personal financial statements. The motivation to conceal earnings or assets may stem from income tax or estate tax considerations, anticipation of a divorce, or illegal sources of income.

The omission of assets and income from financial statements is far more difficult for auditors to detect than is the overstatement of assets and income. Thus, in deciding whether to accept a personal financial statements audit engagement, auditors should assess the risk that an individual may be concealing assets. If auditors conclude during an engagement that the individual is concealing assets, it is doubtful that they can ever develop confidence that their audit procedures have located all of the concealed assets. Therefore, they should withdraw from the engagement.

Most engagements involving personal financial statements are *not* audits, because individuals seldom need audited financial statements. The approaches described for reviews and compilations later in this chapter are more commonly applied to personal financial statements.

## Reviews of the Interim Information of Public Companies

**Public companies** are required to file interim (quarterly) financial information with the SEC on Form 10-Q. Unlike annual financial statements filed with the SEC, this interim information is not required to be audited. This does not mean that the SEC is not concerned about its reliability. Public companies are encouraged to have the interim financial information reviewed by independent accountants.

The procedures applied in a review of interim financial statements consist primarily of inquiries and analytical procedures. The accountants use their knowledge of the com-

---

[2] AICPA, *Statement of Position 82-1,* "Accounting and Financial Reporting for Personal Financial Statements" (New York, 1982).

[3] AICPA, *Guide for Personal Financial Statements* (New York, 1993).

pany's internal control structure to select the appropriate procedures to be performed. Generally, these procedures consist of inquiries of management concerning changes in the internal control structure; analytical procedures applied to the interim financial data by reference to prior interim information, budgets, and other data; reading minutes of meetings of stockholders, the board of directors, and committees of the board; inquiries regarding changes in operations and the consistent application of GAAP; and obtaining written representations from management regarding the presentation and completeness of the interim data.

To review the interim financial information of a public company, the accountants must possess a high level of knowledge of the client's internal control structure and its accounting and financial practices. This knowledge provides the basis for making intelligent inquiries and for interpreting the results of the analytical procedures. Generally, the accountants already possess this knowledge as a result of having audited the financial statements of the company for the prior year. If the accountants have not previously audited the client, this knowledge must be obtained prior to completing the review.

The accountants' review procedures provide them with a basis for expressing *limited* assurance that the information contained in the interim statements is in accordance with generally accepted accounting principles (GAAP). *SAS 71* (AU 722), ''Interim Financial Information,'' suggests the following format for the CPAs' report (emphasis added):

---

### INDEPENDENT ACCOUNTANTS' REPORT

We have *reviewed* the balance sheet and related statements of income, retained earnings, and cash flows of ABC Company and consolidated subsidiaries as of September 30, 19X1, and for the three-month and nine-month periods then ended. These financial statements are the responsibility of the company's management.

We conducted our review in accordance with *standards established by the American Institute of Certified Public Accountants*. A review of interim financial information consists principally of applying *analytical procedures* to financial data and making *inquiries* of persons responsible for financial and accounting matters. It is *substantially less in scope than an audit* conducted in accordance with generally accepted auditing standards, the objective of which is the expression of an opinion regarding the financial statements taken as a whole. Accordingly, *we do not express such an opinion.*

Based on our review, *we are not aware of any material modifications* that should be made to the accompanying financial statements for them to be in conformity with generally accepted accounting principles.

---

Since review reports by CPAs are not required, most public companies do not engage their accountants to issue these reports.

The assurance provided by a review report is necessarily limited because of the limited scope of the accountant's procedures. Although these procedures may bring to the CPAs' attention significant departures from GAAP, they do not guarantee that the CPAs will become aware of all of the significant matters that would be discovered in an audit. A review is not sufficient to enable the accountants to express an opinion on the fairness of the financial statements. Therefore, the middle paragraph of the accountants' report concludes with a statement that the accountants do not express such an opinion. The report will be modified, however, to describe any departure from GAAP that comes to light during the review. In addition, the date of the report should be the date that the accountants completed the review procedures and each page of the interim financial data should be marked as "unaudited."

---

◆ ILLUSTRATIVE CASE ◆

The difference between CPAs' responsibilities when performing audits and reviews of financial statements was dramatically illustrated by the ZZZZ Best case. ZZZZ Best, Inc. was a company engaged in the business of carpet cleaning and restoring fire and flood-damaged buildings. The company, which was founded by sixteen-year-old Barry Minkow, reported operating results that were almost wholly fictitious.

In the review of the financial statements of the ZZZZ Best, the partner-in-charge of the engagement insisted upon observing two major restoration jobs, a finished job, and a carpet warehouse. However, these locations were cleverly faked by Minkow and other officers of the company. As a result, the observations did not result in detection of the fraud, and the CPA firm also agreed not to make follow-up contacts with the insurance companies and building owners involved.

The court ruled that the accounting firm was not liable for failing to detect the misstatements of the financial statements. The court noted that the accountants' review report specifically disclaimed an opinion on ZZZZ Best's financial statements.

---

SEC regulations require certain large public companies to disclose summarized interim financial data in their annual reports, either as supplementary information or as an "unaudited" note to the annual financial statements. These regulations also require the information to be reviewed, either on a timely basis as it is filed in Form 10-Q or at year-end when the CPAs audit the annual financial statements. Even with these requirements, many of these companies do not engage their CPAs to issue review reports on the information. If the CPAs discover that the interim financial data are materially misstated when they are not engaged to report on them, they will modify their audit report on the annual financial statements to describe the situation. Since the interim information is not considered to be part of the annual financial statements, the modified report is still considered to be an unqualified opinion.

Communication about Interim Financial Information.    When performing procedures on a public company's interim financial information, the auditors may obtain information that indicates that interim financial information filed or to be filed by the company with certain regulatory agencies (e.g., the SEC) is materially misstated. In these situations the auditors should communicate the problem to management and the audit committee of the board of directors. If the company does not take appropriate action, such as filing revised information, the CPAs should consider resigning as the company's accountants.

*SAS 71* includes certain other communication responsibilities when CPAs perform a review of the financial statements of public companies. For example, the CPAs should consider whether there are matters as described in *SAS 61* (AU 380), "Communication with Audit Committees,'' that should be reported to the audit committee, such as the nature of the CPAs' responsibilities or significant adjustments discovered in reviewing the financial statements. *SAS 61* is discussed in detail in Chapter 18. The CPAs also should make sure that the audit committee is informed about any irregularities or illegal acts that come to their attention, as well as any reportable conditions related to the internal control structure of the company.

## Review Services for Nonpublic Companies

For small companies, the cost of an audit may exceed the benefits derived. Consider the example of a small company applying for a $20,000 bank loan. If the bank were to require the company to supply annual audited financial statements as a condition of the loan, the company's annual audit fees might well exceed its annual interest expense for the loan. Audits should not be performed unless the benefits are expected to exceed the cost. Therefore, companies that do not offer their securities for sale to the public (**nonpublic companies**) are not required to have annual audits. These companies are free to engage CPAs only for those services that the company wants and can afford.

The needs of nonpublic companies may differ significantly from those of public companies. Whereas public companies have large accounting departments that can prepare financial statements internally, a small nonpublic company might not even employ a full-time accountant. Therefore, the nonpublic company may turn to a CPA firm for the preparation of its financial statements. Whereas public companies may need annual audits and quarterly reviews, nonpublic companies may only occasionally need CPAs to add credibility to their financial statements. On these occasions, a review may meet the company's needs at a far lower cost than an audit.

Serving the needs of small business represents a sizable part of the practice of most CPA firms. For a smaller CPA firm, especially one with only a single office, nonpublic clients may represent the firm's entire practice. To provide CPAs with guidance in meeting the accounting needs of these nonpublic clients, the AICPA has established the Accounting and Review Services Committee. This committee was given authority to set professional standards for CPAs associated with the *unaudited* financial statements of nonpublic companies. These standards are published in a sequentially numbered series called *Statements on Standards for Accounting and Review Services,* or *SSARS*.

Rule 202 of the AICPA *Code of Professional Conduct* requires members to comply with the standards set forth in the *SSARS*. Thus, the Accounting and Review Services Committee has authority comparable to that of the Auditing Standards Board and the FASB.

*SSARS 1* established standards for two types of engagements involving unaudited financial statements of nonpublic companies: (1) **compilations,** which involve the preparation of financial statements with no attempt to verify the fairness of the presentation; and (2) **reviews,** which are limited investigations of much narrower scope than an audit, undertaken for the purpose of providing limited (moderate) assurance that the statements are presented in accordance with GAAP.[4] The following considerations regarding screen-

---

[4]AICPA, *Statement on Standards for Accounting and Review Services 1,* "Compilation and Review of Financial Statements'' (New York, 1978), AR 100.

ing of clients and engagement letters apply to both compilation and review services. Compilation services are accounting services that will be described in detail in the final section of this chapter.

### Screening Clients.

One of the basic elements of quality control in a CPA firm relates to the acceptance and continuance of clients. The purpose of policies and procedures in this area is to minimize the risk of association with a client whose management lacks integrity. One means of acquiring information about a prospective client is to contact the client's predecessor CPAs.

*SSARS 4* provides guidelines for accountants who decide to make inquiries of the predecessor accountants before accepting a compilation or review engagement.[5] These inquiries should include questions regarding the integrity of management, disagreements over accounting principles, the willingness of management to provide or to revise information, and the reasons for the change in accountants. The decision of whether or not to contact the predecessor accountants is left to the judgment of the successor CPAs. However, if inquiries are made with the client's consent, the predecessor accountants are generally required to respond.

### Engagement Letters for Compilation and Review Services.

Compilations and reviews are quite different from audits. The need to establish a clear understanding with the client concerning the nature of such services was dramatically illustrated in the *1136 Tenants' Corporation* case discussed in Chapter 5. CPAs must avoid the implication that they are performing audits when they are engaged to perform other services. Accordingly, it is very important that the CPAs prepare an *engagement letter* clearly specifying the nature of the services to be provided and the degree of responsibility the CPAs are assuming. This letter should include a discussion of the limitations of the services and a description of the accountants' report to be issued.

### Review Procedures.

The procedures for a review of a nonpublic company's financial statements are similar to those for reviews of financial statements of public companies. However, the review of a nonpublic company's financial statements does *not involve a consideration of internal control*.

To evaluate the responses to their inquiries and the results of other review procedures, the independent accountants should develop a knowledge of the accounting principles and practice in the client's industry and a thorough understanding of the client's business. The CPAs' understanding of the client's business should include a general understanding of the company's organization, its methods of operations, and the nature of its financial statement accounts.

The procedures for a review of the financial statements of nonpublic companies include inquiries of officers and other executives; analytical procedures applied to the financial data by reference to prior financial statements, budgets, and other operating data; and inquiries concerning the actions taken in meetings of stockholders, the board of directors,

---

[5]AICPA, *Statement on Standards for Accounting and Review Services 4,* "Communication between Predecessor and Successor Accountants" (New York, 1981), AR 400.

and committees of the board. In addition, the auditors must obtain a representation letter from management of the company about the presentation and completeness of the data.[6] The CPAs' inquiries should focus on whether the financial statements are in accordance with generally accepted accounting principles, and also on changes in business activities and significant subsequent events. Additional procedures should be performed if the accountants become aware that information may be incorrect, incomplete, or otherwise unsatisfactory. The CPAs should perform these procedures to the extent considered necessary to provide limited assurance that there are no material modifications that should be made to the statements.

Review Reports.   A review provides the accountants with a basis for expressing *limited assurance* that there are no required material modifications to the financial statements. The accountants' standard report on a review of a nonpublic company's financial statements reads as follows (emphasis added):

---

We have *reviewed* the accompanying balance sheet of XYZ Company as of December 31, 19XX, and the related statements of income, retained earnings, and cash flows for the year then ended, in accordance with *Statements on Standards for Accounting and Review Services issued by the American Institute of Certified Public Accountants.* All information included in these financial statements is the representation of the management of XYZ Company.

A review consists principally of *inquiries* of company personnel *and analytical procedures* applied to financial data. *It is substantially less in scope than an audit in accordance with generally accepted auditing standards,* the objective of which is the expression of an opinion regarding the financial statements taken as a whole. *Accordingly, we do not express such an opinion.*

Based on our review, *we are not aware of any material modifications* that should be made to the accompanying financial statements in order for them to be in conformity with generally accepted accounting principles.

---

The date of completion of the review procedures should be used as the date of the report, and each page of the financial statements should include the caption, "See Accountants' Review Report."

To provide any degree of assurance about the fairness of information requires that the CPAs be independent. Thus, the accountants performing a review must be independent of the client.

Departures from Generally Accepted Accounting Principles.   Review reports are not altered in cases involving a lack of consistent application of generally accepted accounting principles or the existence of major uncertainties. However, a modification of the report is required when the accountants are aware of a material departure from generally accepted accounting principles (or some other comprehensive basis of accounting). The

---

[6]AICPA, *Statement on Standards for Accounting and Review Services 7,* "Omnibus Statement on Standards for Accounting and Review Services—1992" (New York, 1992), AR 700.

departure is referred to in the report's third paragraph (e.g., "with the exception of the matter described in the following paragraph, we are not aware of any material modifications") and described in a separate paragraph of the review report. The following is an example of a report paragraph that discusses a departure from generally accepted accounting principles:

> As disclosed in Note 5 to the financial statements, generally accepted accounting principles require that land be stated at cost. Management has informed us that the Company has stated its land at appraised value and that, if generally accepted accounting principles had been followed, the land account and stockholders' equity would have been decreased by $500,000.

## Accountants' Reports on Comparative Statements

As with audited financial statements, accountants who have reviewed comparative financial statements presented with those of the current period should report on both years. *SSARS 2* provides guidance on the format of the accountants' reports on comparative financial statements.[7] If the accountants have reviewed both sets of financial statements, they will merely update their review report on the prior year by issuing one review report covering both years. The report will be dated as of the completion of the current year's review procedures.

In certain situations, the accountants may be engaged to perform a lower level of service on the current year's financial statements than they performed on the prior year's financial statements (e.g., a review this year and an audit last year or a compilation this year and a review last year). In these situations, the CPAs should not update the prior year's report. This would imply that they have performed those types of services to the date of the current year's report. Instead, the CPAs should either reissue their prior year report bearing its original date and present it with the current year's report, or include a reference to the prior year's report in the current year's report. For example, the following paragraph could be added to a compilation report on the current year's financial statements to refer to a review of the comparative financial statements for the prior year.

> The accompanying 19X1 financial statements of XYZ Company were previously reviewed by us, and our report dated March 1, 19X2, stated that we were not aware of any material modifications that should be made to those statements in order for them to be in conformity with generally accepted accounting principles. We have not performed any procedures in connection with that review engagement after the date of our report on the 19X1 financial statements.

---

[7]AICPA, *Statement on Standards for Accounting and Review Services 2*, "Reporting on Comparative Financial Statements" (New York, 1979), AR 200.

A reference similar to the one above should also be included in the current report when another CPA firm, whose report is not presented, reviewed the comparative financial statements.

## Letters for Underwriters

Investment banking firms that underwrite a securities issue often request independent auditors who audited the financial statements and schedules in the registration statement to issue a letter for the underwriters. This letter is commonly called a **comfort letter,** and *SAS 72,* "Letters for Underwriters and Certain Other Requesting Parties," provides guidance on its content. *SAS 72* indicates that a comfort letter may include the following subjects:

1. The independence of the auditors.
2. Whether the audited financial statements and financial statement schedules included in the registration statement comply with the accounting requirements of the Securities Act of 1933 and related regulations.
3. Unaudited financial statements, condensed interim financial information, pro forma financial information, financial forecasts. The auditors can provide negative assurance on the historical financial information only if it has been reviewed in accordance with *SAS 71.*
4. Changes in selected financial statement items during a period subsequent to the date and period of the latest financial statements included in the registration statement.
5. Tables, statistics, and other financial information included in the registration statement.
6. Negative assurance as to whether certain nonfinancial statement information included in the registration statement complies with SEC regulations.

Comfort letters help the underwriters in fulfilling their obligation to perform a reasonable investigation of the securities registration statement. No definitive criteria exist for the underwriters' "reasonable investigation." Therefore, the underwriters should approve the adequacy of the CPAs' procedures serving as a basis for the comfort letter.

## Condensed Financial Statements

Occasionally, a client-prepared document will include *condensed financial statements* developed from audited basic financial statements. These statements typically include considerably less detail than the complete financial statements. The CPAs who have issued an audit report on the basic financial statements may be asked to report on the condensed statements. In these circumstances, the auditors should issue a report indicating they have audited the basic financial statements, the date and type of opinion expressed, and whether the condensed information is fairly stated in all material respects in relation to the basic financial statements. *SAS 42* (AU 552), "Reporting on Condensed Financial Statements and Selected Financial Data," provides guidance for these types of reports.

---

♦ ILLUSTRATIVE CASE ♦

A number of corporations have experimented with issuing summary annual reports which were distributed to shareholders. These reports generally include condensed financial statements and refer shareholders desiring more detailed information to the annual report filed with the SEC (Form 10-K). The auditors of these companies, following *SAS 42*, issue a report on the condensed information which refers to the report included with the Form 10-K.

---

# ATTESTATION ENGAGEMENTS—OTHER INFORMATION

As the needs of society have changed over the years, CPAs have been asked to attest to a variety of information. In this section we describe CPA involvement with prospective financial statements and internal control.

## Prospective Financial Statements

Securities analysts and loan officers give considerable attention to prospective financial statements. Although such statements may be presented in various forms, accountants most frequently are involved with **financial forecasts** and **financial projections.** A financial forecast presents information about the entity's *expected* financial position, results of operations, and cash flows. On the other hand, a financial projection presents expected results, given one or more hypothetical assumptions. For example, a projection might present expected results assuming the company expanded its plant. While a forecast may be issued for general distribution, a projection's distribution should be limited to the party with whom the company is negotiating, for example, a bank considering loaning funds to the company to expand the plant. Both forecasts and projections must include certain minimum **prospective financial statement** items, background information, and a list of the major assumptions and accounting policies.[8]

Users of forecasts and projections often request assurances that this forward-looking information is properly presented and based upon reasonable assumptions. To provide such assurances, CPAs may be engaged to examine prospective statements, or they may get a request to perform certain agreed-upon procedures;[9] CPAs are not allowed to review prospective financial information.

Examinations.    In an examination of prospective financial statements, the accountants gather evidence relating to the client's procedures for preparation of the statements, evaluate the underlying assumptions, obtain a written representation letter from the client, and evaluate whether the statements are presented in conformity with AICPA guidelines.

---

[8]Details of required disclosures are presented in the AICPA's *Guide for Prospective Financial Information* (New York, 1993).

[9]Standards for providing these services are contained in the AICPA's *Statement on Standards for Accountants' Services on Prospective Financial Information* (New York, 1986).

The report issued states whether, in the accountants' opinion, the statements are presented in conformity with AICPA guidelines and whether the underlying assumptions provide a reasonable basis for the statements. In no circumstance is an accountant's report to vouch for the achievability of the forecast or projection.

Following is an example of an unqualified forecast examination report:

---

We have *examined* the accompanying forecasted balance sheet, statements of income, retained earnings, and cash flows of XYZ Company as of December 31, 19X1, and for the year then ending. Our *examination was made in accordance with standards for an examination of a forecast established by the American Institute of Certified Public Accountants* and, accordingly, included such procedures as we considered necessary to evaluate both the assumptions used by management and the preparation and presentation of the forecast.

In our opinion, the accompanying forecast is *presented in conformity with guidelines for presentation of a forecast established by the American Institute of Certified Public Accountants,* and *the underlying assumptions provide a reasonable basis for management's forecast.* However, there will usually be differences between the forecasted and actual results, because events and circumstances frequently do not occur as expected, and those differences may be material. We have no responsibility to update this report for events and circumstances occurring after the date of this report.

---

A projection report is similar, but a paragraph is added prior to the opinion paragraph indicating that the use of the report should be limited to the specified user, and the opinion paragraph explicitly states the hypothetical assumptions.

Agreed-Upon Procedures.   Specific users may request the accountants to perform certain agreed-upon procedures on prospective financial statements. In such circumstances the accountants may perform the procedures and provide negative assurance on the statements. For example, the report might state that "no matters came to our attention that caused us to believe that the statements should be adjusted or that the forecast is mathematically incorrect." As is the case with all engagements involving agreed-upon procedures, the report should indicate that its use is restricted to the specified users.

## Reporting on a Company's Internal Control Structure

A number of widely publicized incidences of fraudulent financial reporting in the 1970s and 1980s led to demands by the investing public and the SEC for improved internal controls for U.S. businesses. Chapter 8 described the reaction by the accounting profession to these demands for increased internal controls, in the form of *Internal Control— Integrated Framework* issued by the Committee of Sponsoring Organizations of the Treadway Commission (COSO).

The SEC has even proposed regulations that would require management of all public companies to issue reports on the effectiveness of their companies' internal controls that would be attested to by CPAs. While these proposals have not been adopted, Congress has passed legislation that requires such reports for large financial institutions.

---

◆ ILLUSTRATIVE CASE ◆

The Federal Deposit Insurance Corporation Improvement Act of 1991, which applies to financial institutions with total assets of $500 million or more, mandates an annual report by management that includes an assessment of the institution's internal controls over financial reporting. The law also includes a requirement for a report by the institution's auditors attesting to management's assertion about internal controls.

---

To present a report on internal control effectiveness, management evaluates the company's internal control structure using some reasonable criteria. These reasonable criteria, referred to as **control criteria,** may be issued by various bodies, such as the AICPA and regulatory agencies. COSO's *Internal Control—Integrated Framework* is an example of a reasonable criterion that may be used by management to report on a company's internal control structure. It also includes the following suggested report for management that decides to present a written assertion (**management report on internal control**) about the company's internal controls over financial reporting:

---

**MANAGEMENT REPORT ON INTERNAL CONTROL**

Winstad Company maintains an internal control structure over financial reporting, which is designed to provide reasonable assurance to the Company's management and board of directors regarding the preparation of reliable published financial statements. The structure contains self-monitoring mechanisms, and actions are taken to correct deficiencies as they are identified. Even an effective internal control structure, no matter how well designed, has inherent limitations—including the possibility of the circumvention or overriding of controls—and therefore can provide only reasonable assurance with respect to financial statement preparation. Further, because of changes in conditions, internal control structure effectiveness may vary over time.

The Company assessed its internal control structure as of December 31, 19X5, in relation to criteria for effective internal control over financial reporting described in *Internal Control—Integrated Framework* issued by the Committee of Sponsoring Organizations of the Treadway Commission. Based on this assessment, the Company believes that, as of December 31, 19X5, its internal control structure over financial reporting met those criteria.

Winstad Company

by _Will Jones_____
Chief Executive Officer

January 20, 19X6

by _Linda Beck_____
Chief Financial Officer

In accordance with the attestation standards, CPAs may be engaged to examine or perform agreed-upon procedures on management's reports on internal controls. However, review of this type of information is not permitted. Specific guidance on attesting to internal controls is contained in *Statement on Standards for Attestation Engagements,* "Reporting on Entity's Internal Control Structure over Financial Reporting."

When examining management's assertion about the effectiveness of an entity's internal control structure, the CPAs should (1) plan the engagement, (2) obtain an understanding of the internal control structure, (3) evaluate the design and operating effectiveness of the internal control structure, and (4) form an opinion about the fairness of management's assertion. Although these steps are similar to those used in the auditors' consideration of internal control for audit purposes, the purpose and scope of the study differ. The purpose of an examination of management's assertion on an entity's internal control structure is to express an opinion about whether management's assertion about internal control is fairly stated in all material respects, based on the control criteria. The CPAs' consideration of internal control in an audit is designed to enable them to plan the audit and to determine the nature, timing, and extent of tests to be performed—the CPAs may decide that it is not efficient to test particular internal controls. Consequently, the auditors' consideration of internal control for audit purposes is seldom adequate to express an opinion on the effectiveness of the company's internal control over financial reporting.

The following is an unqualified opinion on a company's internal control structure that may be issued when management's assertion about internal control is included in a separate report, such as the one presented on page 670:

---

**INDEPENDENT ACCOUNTANTS' REPORT**

We have examined management's assertion that Winstad Company has maintained an effective internal control structure over financial reporting as of December 31, 19X5, included in the accompanying Management Report on Internal Control.

Our examination was made in accordance with standards established by the American Institute of Certified Public Accountants and, accordingly, included obtaining an understanding of the internal control structure over financial reporting, testing and evaluating the design and operating effectiveness of the internal control structure, and such other procedures as we considered necessary in the circumstances. We believe that our examination provides a reasonable basis for our opinion.

Because of inherent limitations in any internal control structure, errors or irregularities may occur and not be detected. Also, projections of any evaluation of the internal control structure over financial reporting to future periods are subject to the risk that the internal control structure may become inadequate because of changes in conditions, or that the degree of compliance with the policies or procedures may deteriorate.

In our opinion, management's assertion that Winstad Company has maintained an effective internal control structure over financial reporting as of December 31, 19X5, is fairly stated, in all material respects, based upon criteria established in *Internal Control—Integrated Framework* issued by the Sponsoring Organizations of the Treadway Commission.

February 15, 19X6                                                    *C. Owen & Co., CPAs*

This unqualified opinion on management's assertions about internal control is not appropriate in all circumstances. The accountants may also issue the following types of reports:

1. *Qualified report.* This type of report is issued when the scope of the accountant's procedures has been restricted by the circumstances.

2. *Disclaimer of opinion.* This type of opinion is issued when the scope of the accountant's procedures has been restricted by the client, or severely restricted by the circumstances.

3. *Adverse opinion.* This type of report is issued when the accountants become aware of a material weakness that is not acknowledged in management's report.

4. *Modified report.* This type of report is issued when the accountants become aware of a material weakness that is acknowledged in management's report. The accountants also refer to the weakness in their report.

Restricted Reports on Internal Control.    CPAs might also be engaged to issue a report on internal control that is not appropriate for general use, for example, if the control criteria being used are those of a regulatory agency that has not followed "due process" of exposing the criteria for public comment before adoption. Then, distribution of the accountants' report should be limited to use by management, the board of directors, and the regulatory agency.

The accountants' report based upon agreed-upon procedures is also restricted to the specified user who agreed on the nature and extent of the accountants' procedures. Agreed-upon procedure engagements result in a report presenting a description of the procedures performed and a summary of the CPAs' findings.

# ACCOUNTING SERVICES

Many clients request CPAs to perform accounting services either in addition to or instead of attestation services. Reports resulting from accounting services provide no explicit assurance that the information constitutes a fair presentation. Because no explicit assurance is provided, accountants performing such services need *not* be independent of their client, although a lack of independence must be indicated in their report. In this section we will discuss compilations of financial statements of nonpublic companies, "association" with the financial statements of public companies, and compilations of prospective financial information.

## Compilation Engagements for Financial Statements of Nonpublic Companies

A *compilation* involves the *preparation* of financial statements from the accounting records and other representations of the client. The purpose of a compilation is to organize the client's representations into the format of financial statements. If the accountants submit financial statements that they have generated, or materially altered, to their client or another party, they are required, at a minimum, to compile and report on the financial statements.

Prior to performing a compilation, *SSARS 1* requires the accountants to have knowledge of the accounting principles and practices used within the client's industry and a general understanding of the client's business transactions and accounting records. The CPAs must evaluate the client's representations in light of this knowledge.

At a minimum, the accountants must read the compiled statements for appropriate format and obvious material misstatement. CPAs performing a compilation must not accept patently unreasonable information. If the client's information appears to be incorrect, incomplete, or otherwise unsatisfactory, the CPAs should insist upon revised information. If the client refuses to provide revised information, the CPAs should withdraw from the engagement. Beyond these basic requirements, CPAs have no responsibility to perform any investigative procedures to substantiate the client's representations.

Since a compilation does not enable the CPAs to form an opinion as to the fairness of the statements, their *accountants' report* should include a disclaimer of opinion. The recommended wording for an accountants' report on the compilation of financial statements is shown below (emphasis added):

---

We have *compiled* the accompanying balance sheet of XYZ Company as of December 31, 19XX, and the related statements of income, retained earnings, and cash flows for the year then ended, in accordance with *Statements on Standards for Accounting and Review Services issued by the American Institute of Certified Public Accountants.*

A compilation is limited to presenting in the form of financial statements information *that is the representation of management. We have not audited or reviewed the accompanying financial statements and, accordingly, do not express an opinion or any other form of assurance on them.*

---

Each page of the unaudited financial statements should be marked "See Accountants' Compilation Report," and the accountants' report should be dated as of the completion of the compilation.

Accountants may issue a compilation report on one or more individual financial statements, without compiling a complete set of statements. Also, financial statements may be compiled on a comprehensive basis of accounting *other than* generally accepted accounting principles. In this case, the basis of accounting used must be disclosed either in the statements or in the accountants' report.

Departures from Generally Accepted Accounting Principles.   Treatment of departures from generally accepted accounting principles parallels that for reviews of financial statements. A departure from generally accepted accounting principles requires the accountants to discuss the departure in a separate paragraph in the compilation report. A lack of consistency of application of generally accepted accounting principles or the existence of major uncertainties does not lead to modification of the report.

Compilations That Omit Substantially All Disclosures.   The numerous disclosures required by generally accepted accounting principles may not be particularly useful in the financial statements of a nonpublic business, especially when the statements are intended for internal use by management. Therefore, a nonpublic client may request CPAs to compile financial statements that omit substantially all of the disclosures required by GAAP. CPAs may compile such statements, provided that the omission is clearly indicated in the accountants' report. In such situations, the accountants should add the following last paragraph to their report:

> Management has elected to omit substantially all of the disclosures (and the statement of cash flows) required by generally accepted accounting principles. If the omitted disclosures were included in the financial statements, they might influence the user's conclusions about the company's financial position, results of operations, and cash flows. Accordingly, these financial statements are not designed for those who are not informed about such matters.

If the client wishes to include only some of the disclosures required by GAAP, these disclosures should be labeled "Selected Information—Substantially All Disclosures Required by Generally Accepted Accounting Principles Are Not Included."

**Compilations of Information in Prescribed Forms.**    Prescribed forms refer to standard, preprinted forms designed or adopted by the institution or agency to which the form is to be submitted. An example is a bank loan application. Since these prescribed forms often require financial statement items to be presented on a basis other than generally accepted accounting principles, accountants compiling the forms under *SSARS 1* would have to point out all the GAAP departures in their reports. This would seem to be unnecessary because it can be presumed that the information requested by a prescribed form meets the needs of the institution that designed the form. Accordingly, *SSARS 3*[10] allows the accountants to use the following alternative compilation report when a prescribed form calls for departures from GAAP:

> We have compiled the (identification of financial statements, including period covered and name of entity) included in the accompanying prescribed form in accordance with *Statements on Standards for Accounting and Review Services issued by the American Institute of Certified Public Accountants*.
>
> Our compilation was limited to presenting in the form prescribed by (name of body) information that is the representation of management. We have not audited or reviewed the financial statements referred to above and, accordingly, do not express an opinion or any other form of assurance on them.
>
> These financial statements (including related disclosures) are presented in accordance with the requirements of (name of body), which differ from generally accepted accounting principles. Accordingly, these financial statements are not designed for those who are not informed about such differences.

---

[10]AICPA, *Statement on Standards for Accounting and Review Services 3,* "Compilation Reports on Financial Statements Included in Certain Prescribed Forms" (New York, 1981), AR 300.03.

The accountants should modify this report to point out material departures from the requirements of the prescribed form, or other GAAP departures not required by the form.

Compilations When the CPAs Are Not Independent.    Since compilations are accounting and not attestation services, CPAs may perform them even when they are not independent of the client. The accountants should indicate their lack of independence by adding the following last paragraph to their compilation report:

> We are not independent with respect to XYZ Company.

## Other "Association" with the Financial Statements of Public Companies

CPAs also may become "associated" with the financial statements of a public company by assisting the company in preparing those statements or submitting the statements to the client or another third party. In such cases, the CPAs have no responsibility for performing investigative procedures, except to read the statements for obvious material errors. When CPAs are associated with the statements of a public company, but have neither audited nor reviewed those statements, they should determine that each page of the statements is marked as "unaudited" and issue the following disclaimer of opinion:

> The accompanying balance sheet of XYZ Corporation as of December 31, 19XX, and the related statements of income, retained earnings, and cash flows for the year then ended were not audited by us and, accordingly, we do not express an opinion on them.

If the CPAs know that unaudited financial statements are not in accordance with generally accepted accounting principles, or do not contain adequate informative disclosures, they should insist upon appropriate revision or should state their reservations in the disclaimer of opinion. If necessary, the CPAs should withdraw from the engagement and refuse to be associated with the financial statements.

CPA Firm Not Independent.    A CPA firm that is not independent of a public company may be associated with *unaudited* financial statements of that company. In such cases, the CPAs must issue a special disclaimer of opinion, which discloses the lack of independence. The AICPA has suggested the following language for this report.

> We are not independent with respect to XYZ Company, and the accompanying balance sheet as of December 31, 19X1, and the related statements of income, retained earnings, and cash flows for the year then ended were not audited by us and, accordingly, we do not express an opinion on them.

Notice that the accountants' report does not explain *why* the CPA firm is not independent of the client. The Auditing Standards Board believes it would be confusing to users of the report if these reasons were spelled out.

Figure 19–1    Services Performed by CPAs

| | Compilation | Agreed-Upon Procedures | Review | Examination |
|---|---|---|---|---|
| Type of service | Accounting | Attest | Attest | Attest |
| Explicit assurance | None | State findings or negative assurance | Limited (negative) assurance | Opinion |
| Distribution of report | General | Limited to specified parties | General, unless based on agreed-upon criteria | General, unless based on agreed-upon criteria |
| Minimum procedures | Read statements | Agreed-upon procedures | Limited procedures, such as inquiry and analytical procedures | Collection of sufficient evidence to support opinion |
| Comments | Referred to as "unaudited statements" for public companies | | | Referred to as "audits" for financial statements |

## Compilations of Prospective Financial Statements

In addition to examining prospective statements, accountants may assist their clients in compiling the forward-looking data. A compilation consists of assembling, to the extent necessary, the prospective financial information, performing various inquiry procedures, considering whether there are obvious inconsistencies in assumptions or mathematical errors, and obtaining a representations letter from the client. Because this is an accounting service and not an attestation service, the report issued provides no explicit assurance with respect to the presentation of the statements or the reasonableness of the underlying assumptions.

## SUMMARY OF REPORTING

At this point you might feel overwhelmed by what might seem to be a bewildering array of services performed by CPAs. The role of accountants has changed significantly over the years to meet society's demands for new types of services. Future modifications of accountants' responsibility might be expected to be built around the compilation, agreed-upon procedures, review, and examination distinctions discussed in this chapter. Figure 19–1 summarizes the key aspects of each of these forms of services.

---

## ◆ CHAPTER SUMMARY

This chapter described accounting and attestation services other than audits of financial statements in accordance with generally accepted accounting principles. To summarize:

1.  The attestation standards provide for three distinct types of engagements—examinations, reviews, and agreed-upon procedures.

2.  Special reports by auditors refer to those on: *(a)* financial statements prepared in accordance with some other comprehensive basis of accounting; *(b)* specified elements, accounts, or items of financial statements; *(c)* compliance with contractual or regulatory requirements; *(d)* special-purpose financial presentations; and *(e)* financial information presented in prescribed forms or schedules.

3.  There are several major differences between personal financial statements and those of other types of organizations. For example, assets and liabilities on personal financial statements are presented at their estimated current values and amounts. Accountants may audit, review, or compile personal financial statements.

4.  Management of a public company may engage CPAs to review the company's interim financial statements. If they are also engaged to issue a report, it will provide limited assurance that the financial statements contain no material departures from GAAP. The procedures performed in a review engagement consist of performing analytical procedures, making inquiries of management, reviewing minutes, and obtaining written representations from management. The accountants will adjust the specific procedures based on their knowledge of the client's internal control structure and business.

5.  Nonpublic companies may engage CPAs to review their annual or interim financial statements. The procedures involved are similar to those for the review of a public company, although the accountants are not required to obtain an understanding of the internal control structure of a nonpublic company.

6.  Letters for underwriters (comfort letters) provide assurance about various information contained in registration statements used for the sale of securities. They are designed to help the underwriters establish their due diligence requirement in investigating the fairness of the registration statement.

7.  Auditors may perform examinations, compilations, or agreed-upon procedures on prospective financial statements. The examination report includes an opinion that provides a conclusion on whether the underlying assumptions provide a reasonable basis for management's forecast or projection.

8.  Auditors are being asked to provide assurance about management's representations about the effectiveness of internal control. Such reports are based on control criteria, such as those contained in *Internal Control—Integrated Framework* developed by the Committee of Sponsoring Organizations of the Treadway Commission.

9. When accountants perform compilations of financial statements or other information, the report provides no explicit assurance. Therefore, compilations may be performed by CPAs who are not independent.

## ◆ KEY TERMS INTRODUCED OR EMPHASIZED IN CHAPTER 19

**Attestation**    To provide assurance as to whether information is presented in accordance with appropriate criteria. That is, to bear witness as to its reliability and fairness.

**Comfort letter**    A letter issued by the independent auditors to the underwriters of securities registered with the SEC under the Securities Act of 1933. Comfort letters deal with such matters as the auditors' independence and the compliance of unaudited data with requirements of the SEC.

**Compilation**    An accounting service that involves the preparation of information from client records. No assurance is provided in a compilation.

**Control criteria**    The reasonable criteria required to be followed by a company requesting a CPA's report on the effectiveness of its internal control structure.

**Financial forecast**    Prospective financial statements that present an entity's expected financial position, results of operations, and cash flows for one or more future periods.

**Financial projection**    Prospective financial statements that present expected results, given one or more hypothetical assumptions.

**Limited assurance (negative assurance)**    Assurance provided by CPAs who have performed an attestation service of a lesser scope than an examination (e.g., a review). Provides substantially less assurance than is provided by an examination.

**Management report on internal control**    A report by management that includes an assertion about the effectiveness of the company's internal control structure in meeting some established control criteria.

**Negative assurance**    An assertion by CPAs that after applying limited investigative techniques to certain information, they are not aware of the need to modify the presentation of the information. Equivalent to limited or moderate assurance.

**Nonpublic company**    A company other than one whose securities are traded on a public market or that makes a filing with a regulatory agency in preparation for sale of securities on a public market.

**Prospective financial statements**    Either financial forecasts or financial projections, including the summaries of significant assumptions and accounting policies.

**Public company**    A company whose stock is traded on a public market or a company in the process of registering its stock for public sale.

**Report on internal control**    This type of report may be either based on an examination of internal control or based on the performance of agreed-upon procedures.

**Review**    A form of attestation based on limited procedures, such as inquiry and analytical procedures applied for the purpose of expressing limited assurance that information is presented in accordance with appropriate criteria.

**Special report**    An auditors' report issued on any of the following: (1) financial statements prepared on a comprehensive basis of accounting other than GAAP, (2) elements of financial statements, (3) compliance with regulatory or contractual requirements, (4) financial presentations to comply with contractual agreements or regulatory provisions, or (5) audited information presented in prescribed forms.

# ◆ GROUP I: REVIEW QUESTIONS

19-1   Evaluate this statement: All companies should be audited annually.

19-2   Evaluate this statement: Auditors perform attestation services and accountants perform accounting services.

19-3   List the three types of attestation engagements outlined in the attestation standards.

19-4   The attest function is applied to numerous types of information other than historical financial statements. List three of these types of information.

19-5   Distinguish among forms of attestation that are for ''general'' versus ''limited'' use or distribution.

19-6   When the auditors are performing an audit of financial statements, do the attestation standards apply? Explain.

19-7   Can auditors express an unqualified opinion on financial statements that are not presented on the basis of generally accepted accounting principles? Explain.

19-8   In communications with clients, should CPAs refer to themselves as auditors or as accountants? Explain.

19-9   Does the issuance of a special report based on agreed-upon procedures indicate an audit engagement or an accounting service? Why?

19-10   What form of opinion will the auditors normally issue with respect to *condensed financial statements* that the client has developed from the audited financial statements.

19-11   Jane Wilson has prepared personal financial statements in which her assets are valued at her historical cost, less appropriate depreciation. Is this presentation in conformity with generally accepted accounting principles? Can a CPA firm audit these statements and issue an unqualified opinion?

19-12   What procedures are required when a CPA performs a compilation of financial statements?

19-13   What are the procedures performed during a review of the quarterly financial statements of a public company?

19-14   Discuss the possible forms of audit reports for a U.S.-based client that is issuing a report for use primarily outside the United States.

19-15   What types of services may be performed by CPAs with respect to the financial statements of nonpublic companies?

19-16   How does a review of the financial statements of a nonpublic company differ from an audit?

19-17   What are the types of procedures performed during the review of the financial statements of a nonpublic company?

19-18   Are engagement letters needed for accounting and review services? Explain.

19-19   Can the CPAs report on a nonpublic client's financial statements that omit substantially all disclosures required by generally accepted accounting principles? Explain.

19-20   What should the accountants do if they discover that the financial statements they are compiling contain a material departure from generally accepted accounting principles?

19-21   What is the purpose of a comfort letter? Discuss.

19-22    What is the objective of an examination of a financial forecast?

19-23    Can CPAs typically attest to management's assertion about a company's internal control structure as the result of their consideration of internal control performed during an audit? Explain.

19-24    CPAs may issue several types of reports on management's assertions about a company's internal control (e.g., unqualified, qualified, disclaimer, modified, and adverse). Describe the circumstances in which each of these types of reports is appropriate.

## ◆ GROUP II: QUESTIONS REQUIRING ANALYSIS

19-25    An accountants' report was appended to the financial statements of Worthmore, Inc., a public company. The statements consisted of a balance sheet as of November 30 and statements of income and retained earnings for the year then ended. The first three paragraphs of the report contained the wording of the standard unqualified report, and a fourth paragraph read as follows:

> The wives of two partners of our firm owned a material investment in the outstanding common stock of Worthmore, Inc. during the fiscal year ending November 30. The aforementioned individuals disposed of their holdings of Worthmore, Inc. on December 3 in a transaction that did not result in a profit or a loss. This information is included in our report in order to comply with certain disclosure requirements of the *Code of Professional Conduct* of the American Institute of Certified Public Accountants.
>
> Bell & Davis
> Certified Public Accountants

*Required:*    *a.*    Was the CPA firm of Bell & Davis independent with respect to the audit of Worthmore, Inc.'s financial statements? Explain.

*b.*    Do you find Bell & Davis' report satisfactory? Explain.

(AICPA, adapted)

19-26    Occasionally, CPA firms are engaged to report on specified elements, accounts, and items of financial statements.

*Required:*    *a.*    Discuss the two types of reports that may be provided for specified elements, accounts, and items of financial statements.

*b.*    Why should reports on the application of agreed-upon procedures to information be restricted as to their distribution?

19-27    You have been engaged by the management of Pippin, Inc., a nonpublic company, to review the company's financial statements for the year ended December 31, 19XX. To prepare for the engagement you consult the *Statements on Standards for Accounting and Review Services.*

*Required:*    *a.*    Discuss the procedures required for the performance of a review of financial statements.

*b.*    Explain the content of the report on a review of financial statements.

*c.*    Discuss your responsibilities if you find that the financial statements contain a material departure from generally accepted accounting principles.

19-28    "When performing accounting services, accountants provide no assurance in their reports. These reports may therefore be considered *special reports.*"

*Required:*   *a.*   Do you agree or disagree with the above statement? Explain.
             *b.*   Discuss the major types of special reports.
             *c.*   Provide an example of an accounting service.

19-29   The attestation standards present three basic types of engagements.

*Required:*   *a.*   List these three types of engagements.
             *b.*   Discuss the type of assurance provided by each of these types of engagements.

19-30   Rose & Co., CPAs, has satisfactorily completed the audit of the financial statements of Dale, Booster & Co., a partnership, for the year ended December 31, 19XX. The financial statements that were prepared on the entity's income tax (cash) basis include notes that indicate that the partnership was involved in continuing litigation of material amounts relating to alleged infringement of a competitor's patent. The amount of damages, if any, resulting from this litigation could not be determined at the time of completion of the engagement. The prior years' financial statements were not presented.

*Required:*   Prepare an auditors' unqualified special report on the financial statements of Dale, Booster & Co. Your report should include two "explanatory paragraphs": one to mention the basis of accounting used, and another to emphasize the matter of the pending litigation. Address your report to Dale, Booster & Co.

(AICPA, adapted)

19-31   You have been asked by Ambassador Hardware Co., a small nonpublic company, to submit a proposal for the audit of the company. After performing an investigation of the company, including its management and accounting system, you advise the president of Ambassador that the audit fee will be approximately $10,000. Ambassador's president was somewhat surprised at the fee, and after discussions with members of the board of directors, he concluded that the company could not afford an audit at this time.

*Required:*   *a.*   Discuss management's alternatives to having their company's financial statements audited in accordance with generally accepted auditing standards.
             *b.*   What should Ambassador's management consider when selecting the type of service that you should provide? Explain.

19-32   Andrew Wilson, CPA, has assembled the financial statements of Texas Mirror Co., a small public company. He has not performed an audit of the financial statements in accordance with generally accepted auditing standards. Wilson is confused about the standards applicable to this type of engagement.

*Required:*   *a.*   Explain where Wilson should look for guidance concerning this engagement.
             *b.*   Discuss the concept of association with financial statements.
             *c.*   Explain Wilson's responsibilities with respect to a preparation of unaudited financial statements.

19-33   In connection with a public offering of first-mortgage bonds by Guizzetti Corporation, the bond underwriter has asked Guizzetti's CPAs to furnish them with a comfort letter giving as much assurance as possible on Guizzetti's unaudited financial statements for the three months ended March 31. The CPAs had expressed an unqualified opinion on Guizzetti's financial statements for the year ended December 31, the preceding year; they also performed a review of Guizzetti's financial statements for the three months ended March 31. Nothing has come to their attention that would indicate that the March 31 statements are not properly presented.

*Required:*   *a.*   Explain what can be stated about the unaudited financial statements in the letter.
             *b.*   Discuss other matters that are typically included in comfort letters.

19-34    The management of Williams Co. is considering issuing corporate debentures. To enhance the marketability of the bond issue, management has decided to include a financial forecast in the prospectus. Williams' management has requested that your CPA firm examine the financial forecast to add credibility to the prospective information.

*Required:*    *a.*    Explain what is involved in an examination of a financial forecast.

*b.*    Discuss the content of the report on an examination of a financial forecast. (Do not write a report.)

19-35    Select the best answer for each of the following and explain fully the reason for your selection.

*a.*    Which of the following is *not* typically performed when the auditors are performing a review of client financial statements?

(1)    Analytical procedures applied to financial data.

(2)    Inquiries about significant subsequent events.

(3)    Inquiries directed to the client's legal counsel.

(4)    Obtaining an understanding of accounting principles followed in the client's industry.

*b.*    Which of the following forms of accountant association leads to a limited distribution report?

(1)    Compilation.

(2)    Review.

(3)    Examination.

(4)    Agreed-upon procedures.

*c.*    Which assertion is generally most difficult to attest to with respect to personal financial statements?

(1)    Existence and occurrence.

(2)    Rights and obligations.

(3)    Completeness.

(4)    Valuation.

*d.*    Special reports are appropriate for:

(1)    Reviews of interim statements.

(2)    Compliance with regulatory requirements related to audited financial statements.

(3)    Forecasts.

(4)    Projections.

*e.*    In which of the following reports should a CPA *not* express negative (limited) assurance?

(1)    A standard compilation report on financial statements of a nonpublic entity.

(2)    A standard review report on interim financial statements of a public entity.

(3)    A standard review report on financial statements of a nonpublic entity.

(4)    A comfort letter on financial information included in a registration statement filed with the Securities and Exchange Commission.

*f.*    Comfort letters to underwriters are normally signed by the:

(1)    Independent auditor.

(2)    Underwriter.

(3)    Client's lawyer.

(4)    Chief executive officer.

---

♦ GROUP III: PROBLEMS

19-36    The following report on the basic financial statements was drafted by a staff assistant at the completion of the review engagement of Delano Company, a continuing client for the year ended September 30, 19X8.

**To the Board of Directors of Delano Company:**

We have reviewed the accompanying balance sheet of Delano Company as of September 30, 19X8, and the related statements of income and retained earnings for the year then ended, in accordance with generally accepted auditing standards. Our review included such tests of the accounting records as we considered necessary in the circumstances.

A review consists principally of inquiries of company personnel. It is substantially less in scope than an audit, but more in scope than a compilation. Accordingly, we express only limited assurance on the accompanying financial statements.

Based on our review, we are not aware of any material modifications that should be made to the accompanying financial statements in order for them to be in conformity with generally accepted accounting principles applied on a consistent basis.

Anston & Co., CPAs

November 2, 19X8

*Required:* Identify the deficiencies in the draft of the proposed report on the comparative financial statements. Group the deficiencies by paragraph.

19-37   Norman Lewis, an inexperienced member of your staff, has compiled the financial statements of Williams Grocery. He has submitted the following report for your review:

The accompanying financial statements have been compiled by us. A compilation is an accounting service, but we also applied certain analytical procedures to the financial data.

As explained in Note 3, the Company changed accounting principles for accounting for its inventories. We have not audited or reviewed the accompanying financial statements, but nothing came to our attention to indicate that they are in error.

*Required:* Describe the deficiencies in the report, give reasons why they are deficiencies, and briefly discuss how the report should be corrected. Do not discuss the addressee, signature, and date. Organize your answer sheet as follows:

| *Deficiency* | *Reason* | *Correction* |
| --- | --- | --- |
| | | |

19-38   On March 12, 19X5, Brown & Brown, CPAs, completed the audit engagement of the financial statements of Modern Museum, Inc. for the year ended December 31, 19X4. Modern Museum presents comparative financial statements on a modified cash basis. Assets, liabilities, fund balances, support, revenues, and expenses are recognized when cash is received or disbursed, except that Modern includes a provision for depreciation of buildings and equipment. Brown & Brown believes that Modern's three financial statements, prepared in accordance with a comprehensive basis of accounting other than generally accepted accounting principles, are adequate for Modern's needs and wishes to issue an auditors' special report on the financial statements. Brown & Brown has gathered sufficient competent evidential matter in order to be satisfied that the financial statements are fairly presented according to the modified cash basis. Brown & Brown audited Modern's 19X3 financial statements and issued the auditors' special report expressing an unqualified opinion.

*Required:*   Draft the auditors' report to accompany Modern's comparative financial statements.

(AICPA, adapted)

19-39   Jiffy Clerical Services is a company that furnishes temporary office help to its customers. The company maintains its accounting records on a basis of cash receipts and cash disbursements. You have audited the company for the year ended December 31, 19X4, and have concluded that the company's financial statements represent a fair presentation on the basis of accounting described above.

*Required:*   a.  Draft the unqualified auditors' report you would issue covering the financial statements (a statement of assets and liabilities and the related statement of revenue collected and expenses paid) for the year ended December 31, 19X4.

b.  Briefly discuss and justify your modifications of the conventional standard auditors' report on GAAP financial statements.

19-40   The limitations on the CPAs' professional responsibilities when they are associated with unaudited financial statements are often misunderstood. These misunderstandings can be substantially reduced if the CPAs follow professional pronouncements in the course of their work and take other appropriate measures.

*Required:*   The following list describes seven situations CPAs may encounter, or contentions they may have to deal with, in their association with and preparation of *unaudited* financial statements. Briefly discuss the extent of the CPAs' responsibilities and, if appropriate, the actions they should take to minimize any misunderstandings. Mark your answers to correspond with the letters in the following list.

a.  The CPAs were engaged by telephone to perform write-up work including the compilation of financial statements. The client believes that the CPAs have been engaged to audit the financial statements and examine the records accordingly.

b.  A group of investors who own a farm that is managed by an independent agent engage CPAs to compile quarterly unaudited financial statements for them. The CPAs prepare the financial statements from information given to them by the independent agent. Subsequently, the investors find the statements were inaccurate because their independent agent was embezzling funds. They refuse to pay the CPAs' fee and blame them for allowing the situation to go undetected, contending that the CPAs should not have relied on representations from the independent agent.

c.  In comparing the trial balance with the general ledger, the CPAs find an account labeled Audit Fees in which the client has accumulated the CPAs' quarterly billings for accounting services including the compilation of quarterly unaudited financial statements.

d.  Unaudited financial statements for a public company were accompanied by the following letter of transmittal from the CPAs:

> We are enclosing your company's balance sheet as of June 30, 19X9, and the related statements of income and retained earnings and cash flows for the six months then ended to which we have performed certain auditing procedures.

    *e.* To determine appropriate account classification, the CPAs examined a number of the client's invoices. They noted in their working papers that some invoices were missing, but did nothing further because it was felt that the invoices did not affect the unaudited financial statements they were compiling. When the client subsequently discovered that invoices were missing, he contended that the CPAs should not have ignored the missing invoices when compiling the financial statements and had a responsibility to at least inform him that they were missing.

    *f.* The CPAs compiled a draft of unaudited financial statements from the client's records. While reviewing this draft with their client, the CPAs learned that the land and building were recorded at appraisal value.

    *g.* The CPAs are engaged to compile the financial statements of a nonpublic company. During the engagement, the CPAs learn of several items for which generally accepted accounting principles would require adjustments of the statements and note disclosure. The controller agrees to make the recommended adjustments to the statements, but says that she is not going to add the notes because the statements are unaudited.

(AICPA, adapted)

19-41  Loman, CPA, who has audited the financial statements of the Broadwall Corporation, a publicly held company, for the year ended December 31, 19X6, was asked to perform a review of the financial statements of Broadwall Corporation for the period ending March 31, 19X7. The engagement letter stated that a review does not provide a basis for the expression of an opinion.

*Required:*  *a.* Explain why Loman's review will *not* provide a basis for the expression of an opinion.

    *b.* What are the review procedures Loman should perform, and what is the purpose of each procedure? Structure your response as follows:

| *Procedure* | *Purpose of Procedure* |
| --- | --- |
| | |

(AICPA, adapted)

19-42  Brown, CPA, received a telephone call from Calhoun, the sole owner and manager of a small corporation. Calhoun asked Brown to compile the financial statements for the corporation and emphasized that the statements were needed in two weeks for external financing purposes. Calhoun was vague when Brown inquired about the intended use of the statements. Brown was convinced that Calhoun thought Brown's work would constitute an audit. To avoid confusion, Brown decided not to explain to Calhoun that the engagement would be to compile the financial statements only. Brown, with the understanding that a substantial fee would be paid if the work was completed in two weeks, accepted the engagement and started the work at once.

    During the course of the work, Brown discovered an accrued expense account labeled Professional Fees and learned that the balance in the account represented an accrual for the cost of Brown's services. Brown suggested to Calhoun's bookkeeper that the account name be changed to Fees for Limited Audit Engagement. Brown also reviewed several invoices to determine whether accounts were being properly classified. Some of the invoices were missing. Brown listed the missing invoice numbers in the working papers with a note indicating that there should be a follow-up on the next engagement. Brown also discovered that the available records included the fixed asset values at estimated current replacement costs. Based on the records available, Brown compiled a balance sheet, income statement, and statement of stockholders' equity. In addition, Brown drafted the notes, but he decided that any mention of the replacement costs would only confuse the readers. Brown suggested to Calhoun that readers of the financial statements would be better informed if they received a separate letter from Calhoun explaining the meaning and effect of the estimated replacement costs of the fixed assets. Brown mailed the financial statements and notes to Calhoun with the following note included on each page:

> The accompanying financial statements are submitted to you without complete audit verification.

*Required:*   Identify the inappropriate actions of Brown, and indicate what Brown should have done to avoid each inappropriate action.

Organize your answer sheet as follows:

| *Inappropriate Action* | *What Brown Should Have Done to Avoid Inappropriate Action* |
| --- | --- |
| | |

(AICPA, adapted)

# ◆ GROUP IV: RESEARCH AND DISCUSSION CASE

19-43    You are a young CPA just starting your own practice in Hollywood, California, after five years' experience with a ''Big 6'' firm. You have several connections in the entertainment industry and hope to develop a practice rendering income tax, auditing, and accounting services to celebrities and other wealthy clients.

One of your first engagements is arranged by John Forbes, a long-established business manager for a number of celebrities and a personal friend of yours. You are engaged to audit the personal statement of financial condition (balance sheet) of Dallas McBain, one of Forbes' clients. McBain is a popular rock star, with a net worth of approximately $10 million. However, the star also has a reputation as an extreme recluse who is never seen in public except at performances.

Forbes handles all of McBain's business affairs, and all of your communications with McBain are through Forbes. You have never met McBain personally and have no means of contacting the star directly. All of McBain's business records are maintained at Forbes' office. Forbes also issues checks for many of McBain's personal expenses, using a check-signing machine and a facsimile plate of McBain's signature.

During the audit, you notice that during the year numerous checks totaling approximately $240,000 have been issued payable to Cash. In addition, the proceeds of a $125,000 sale of marketable securities was never deposited in any of McBain's bank accounts. In the accounting records, all of these amounts have been charged to the account entitled ''Personal Living Expenses.'' There is no further documentation of these disbursements.

When you bring these items to Forbes' attention, he explains that celebrities such as McBain often spend a lot of cash supporting various ''hangers-on,'' whom they don't want identified by name. He also states, ''Off the record, some of these people also have some very expensive habits.'' He points out, however, that you are auditing only the statement of assets and liabilities, not McBain's revenue or expenses. Furthermore, the amount of these transactions is not material in relation to McBain's net worth.

*Required:*   *a.*   Discuss whether or not the undocumented disbursements and the missing securities' proceeds should be of concern to you in a balance sheet-only audit.

b.   Identify the various courses of action that you might at least consider under these circumstances. Explain briefly the arguments supporting each course of action.

c.   Explain what you would do and justify your decision.

d.   Assume that you are a long-established CPA, independently wealthy, and that the McBain account represents less than 5 percent of the annual revenue of your practice. Would this change in circumstances affect your conclusion in part *c*? Discuss.

## ◆ SUGGESTED REFERENCES

This textbook, discussion of *1136 Tenants Corporation* case, pp 136–38; "Audit of Sole Proprietorships and Partnerships," p. 574; and "Audits of Personal Financial Statements," pp. 659–60.

AICPA, *Personal Financial Statements Guide* (New York, 1983), pp. 12–13 and 25–26.

*Statement on Auditing Standards 60,* "Communication of Internal Control Structure Related Matters Noted in an Audit" (New York, 1988) *AU* 326.

# 20

# INTERNAL, OPERATIONAL, AND COMPLIANCE AUDITING

## CHAPTER OBJECTIVES

After studying this chapter, you should be able to:

- Distinguish among internal, operational, and compliance auditing.

- Describe the functions performed by internal auditors.

- Identify the standards for the professional practice of internal auditing.

- Explain the nature and the purpose of an operational audit.

- Distinguish among the various types of compliance audits.

- Describe the auditing and reporting requirements of *Government Auditing Standards* and the Single Audit Act.

T o this point in the text we have focused primarily on audits of financial statements by independent public accountants. This chapter describes several other types of auditing: internal, operational, and compliance auditing.

# INTERNAL AUDITING

Virtually every large corporation in the United States today maintains an internal auditing staff. This staff function has developed extremely rapidly; prior to 1940 internal auditing departments were found in relatively few entities. In 1941 the **Institute of Internal Auditors (IIA)** was founded with only 25 members. Now the Institute is a worldwide organization with over 30,000 members and local chapters in principal cities throughout much of the world. The growth of IIA has paralleled the recognition of internal auditing as an essential control function in all types of organizations.

## What Is the Purpose of Internal Auditing?

The Institute of Internal Auditors (IIA) defines **internal auditing** as:

> an independent appraisal activity established within an organization to examine and evaluate its activities as a service to the organization.

The objective of the internal auditors is to assist members of an organization in the effective discharge of their responsibilities by furnishing them analyses, appraisals, recommendations, and counsel. In performing these functions, internal auditors can be thought of as a part of the organization's internal control structure. They represent a high-level control that functions by measuring and evaluating the effectiveness of other internal control policies and procedures. *SAS 55* (AU 319), "Consideration of the Internal Control Structure in a Financial Statement Audit," states that one aspect of an organization's control environment is "management's control methods for monitoring and following up on performance, including internal auditing."

Internal auditors are not merely concerned with the organization's financial controls. Their work encompasses the entire internal control structure of the organization. They evaluate and test the effectiveness of internal control policies and procedures designed to help the organization meet all of its objectives.

## Evolution of Internal Auditing

Internal auditing has evolved to meet the needs of business and governmental and non-profit organizations. Originally, a demand for internal auditing arose when managers of early large corporations recognized that annual audits of financial statements by CPAs were not sufficient. A need existed for timely employee involvement beyond that of the certified public accountants to ensure accurate and timely financial records and to prevent fraud. These original internal auditors focused their efforts on financial and accounting matters.

Subsequently, the role of internal auditors expanded as a result of demands by the major stock exchanges and the Securities and Exchange Commission for more management responsibility for the reliability of published financial statements. These demands resulted in expanded internal auditor responsibilities to include more detailed analysis of internal control systems, as well as testing of interim and other accounting information not considered in annual audits performed by certified public accountants.

Gradually, the role of internal auditors expanded to encompass overall operational policies and procedures. Companies in the defense industry were among the first to demand such services. These companies recognized the need for reliable operating reports which were used extensively by management to make decisions. The reports often were expressed not in dollars, but in terms of operating factors, such as quantities of parts in short supply, adherence to schedules, and quality of the product. Work by the internal auditors devoted to ensuring dependability of these operating reports was better spent than additional audit effort devoted to financial and accounting matters.

As organizations became larger and more complex, they encountered additional operational problems that lent themselves to solutions by internal auditing. The internal auditors' role of determining whether operating units in the organization follow authorized accounting and financial policies was readily extended to include the determination of whether they follow all of the organization's operating policies, and whether the established policies provide sound and effective control over all operations. The extension of internal auditing into these operational activities required internal auditors with specialized knowledge in other disciplines such as economics, law, finance, statistics, electronic data processing, engineering, and taxation.

Several recent events have been important to the evolution of the internal auditing profession. The first was the enactment of the Foreign Corrupt Practices Act of 1977. The accounting provisions of that act require public companies to establish and maintain effective internal accounting control. To ensure compliance with these provisions, many companies established or augmented their internal auditing departments.

Another event that affected the internal auditing profession was the issuance in 1987 of the *Report of the National Commission on Fraudulent Financial Reporting*. This report contains the commission's findings and recommendations about preventing fraudulent financial reporting by public companies. Among its recommendations was a suggestion that public companies establish an internal auditing function staffed with appropriately qualified personnel and fully supported by top management. The commission also recommended that the companies help ensure the internal auditing function's objectivity by positioning it suitably within the organization, maintaining a director of internal auditing with appropriate stature, and establishing effective reporting relationships between the director of internal auditing and the audit committee of the board of directors.

The current scope of internal auditing is summarized in the IIA's *Statement of Responsibilities of Internal Auditing,* which states that "the scope of internal auditing encompasses the examination and evaluation of the adequacy and effectiveness of the organization's system of internal control and the quality of performance in carrying out assigned responsibilities." Specifically, the scope includes:

1. Reviewing the reliability and integrity of financial and operating information and the means used to identify, measure, classify, and report such information.

2. Reviewing the systems established to ensure compliance with those policies, plans, procedures, laws, and regulations which could have a significant impact on operations and reports, and determining whether the organization is in compliance.

3.  Reviewing the means of safeguarding assets and, as appropriate, verifying the existence of such assets.

4.  Appraising the economy and efficiency with which resources are employed.

5.  Reviewing operations or programs to ascertain whether results are consistent with established objectives and goals and whether the operations or programs are being carried out as planned.[1]

## Professional Standards of Internal Auditing

A relatively new development in the internal auditing profession is the issuance of the IIA's *Standards for the Professional Practice of Internal Auditing*. These standards set forth the criteria by which the operations of an internal auditing department should be evaluated and measured. They cover the various aspects of auditing within an organization and are divided into five general sections:

1.  Independence.

2.  Professional proficiency.

3.  Scope of work.

4.  Performance of audit work.

5.  Management of the internal auditing department.

These general standards and the specific standards that support them are summarized in Figure 20–1.

To provide interpretations of the *Standards for the Professional Practice of Internal Auditing,* the IIA also issues *Statements on Internal Auditing Standards.* To date, statements have been issued covering a variety of topics, such as control concepts and responsibilities, preventing and investigating fraud, quality assurance, audit working papers, relationships with independent auditors, communication with the board of directors, risk assessment, and assignment planning.

Independence.  The first category of *Standards for the Professional Practice of Internal Auditing* deals with independence. Since internal auditors are employees of the organization, they cannot have the perceived independence of external auditors. However, independence is still very important to internal auditors. The IIA's standards point out that independence is enhanced when the director of internal audit reports to a level of management of sufficient stature to ensure broad audit coverage and adequate consideration and implementation of the auditors' recommendations. Ideally, the director should report directly to the audit committee of the board of directors. Independence is also enhanced when potential conflicts of interest are considered in assigning staff to audit assignments. For example, it would be a conflict of interest for an internal auditor to audit an area in which that individual was recently employed. It is difficult, if not impossible, to remain objective in evaluating one's own operating decisions.

---

[1]*Statement of Responsibilities of Internal Auditing* (Altamonte Springs, Fla.: Institute of Internal Auditors, 1990), pp. 1–2.

Figure 20–1    Summary of Standards for the Professional Practice of Internal Auditing

100 INDEPENDENCE. Internal auditors should be independent of the activities they audit.

110 *Organizational Status*. The organizational status of the internal auditing department should be sufficient to permit the accomplishment of its audit responsibilities.

120 *Objectivity*. Internal auditors should be objective in performing audits.

200 PROFESSIONAL PROFICIENCY. Internal audits should be performed with proficiency and due professional care.

### The Internal Auditing Department

210 *Staffing*. The internal auditing department should provide assurance that the technical proficiency and educational background of internal auditors are appropriate for the audits to be performed.

220 *Knowledge, Skills, and Disciplines*. The internal auditing department should possess or should obtain the knowledge, skills, and disciplines needed to carry out its audit responsibilities.

230 *Supervision*. The internal auditing department should provide assurance that internal audits are properly supervised.

### The Internal Auditor

240 *Compliance with Standards of Conduct*. Internal auditors should comply with professional standards of conduct.

250 *Knowledge, Skills, and Disciplines*. Internal auditors should possess the knowledge, skills, and disciplines essential to the performance of internal audits.

260 *Human Relations and Communications*. Internal auditors should be skilled in dealing with people and in communicating effectively.

270 *Continuing Education*. Internal auditors should maintain their technical competence through continuing education.

280 *Due Professional Care*. Internal auditors should exercise due professional care in performing internal audits.

300 SCOPE OF WORK. The scope of the internal audit should encompass the examination and evaluation of the adequacy and effectiveness of the organization's system of internal control and the quality of performance in carrying out assigned responsibilities.

310 *Reliability and Integrity of Information*. Internal auditors should review the reliability and integrity of financial and operating information and the means used to identify, measure, classify, and report such information.

320 *Compliance with Policies, Plans, Procedures, Laws, and Regulations*. Internal auditors should review the systems established to ensure compliance with those policies, plans, procedures, laws, and regulations which could have a significant impact on operations and reports and should determine whether the organization is in compliance.

330 *Safeguarding of Assets*. Internal auditors should review the means of safeguarding assets and, as appropriate, verify the existence of such assets.

340 *Economical and Efficient Use of Resources*. Internal auditors should appraise the economy and efficiency with which resources are employed.

350 *Accomplishment of Established Objectives and Goals for Operations or Programs*. Internal auditors should review operations or programs to ascertain whether results are consistent with established objectives and goals and whether the operations or programs are being carried out as planned.

*(continued)*

400 PERFORMANCE OF AUDIT WORK. Audit work should include planning the audit, examining and evaluating information, communicating results, and following up.

410 *Planning the Audit.* Internal auditors should plan each audit.

420 *Examining and Evaluating Information.* Internal auditors should collect, analyze, interpret, and document information to support audit results.

430 *Communicating Results.* Internal auditors should report the results of their audit work.

440 *Following Up.* Internal auditors should follow up to ascertain that appropriate action is taken on reported audit findings.

500 MANAGEMENT OF THE INTERNAL AUDITING DEPARTMENT. The director of internal auditing should properly manage the internal auditing department.

510 *Purpose, Authority, and Responsibility.* The director of internal auditing should have a statement of purpose, authority, and responsibility for the internal auditing department.

520 *Planning.* The director of internal auditing should establish plans to carry out responsibilities of the internal auditing department.

530 *Policies and Procedures.* The director of internal auditing should provide written policies and procedures to guide the audit staff.

540 *Personnel Management and Development.* The director of internal auditing should establish a program for selecting and developing the human resources of the internal auditing department.

550 *External Auditors.* The director of internal auditing should coordinate internal and external audit efforts.

560 *Quality Assurance.* The director of internal auditing should establish and maintain a quality assurance program to evaluate the operations of the internal auditing department.

---

Source: *Standards for the Professional Practice of Internal Auditing* (Altamonte Springs, Fla.: Institute of Internal Auditors, 1978), pp. 5–8.

Professional Proficiency.   An internal auditing department should establish policies and procedures that provide assurance that staff members are competent to fulfill their assignments with professional proficiency. Ideally, the internal auditing department collectively should possess the skills and knowledge necessary to fulfill all the audit requirements of the organization. These skills and knowledge may be acquired through effective employment practices and continuing education programs.

Professional proficiency is also enhanced by establishing appropriate staffing and supervisory policies and procedures. An internal auditing department should establish policies for assigning staff members to audit areas so that the auditors will be competent to successfully complete those assignments. Once assigned to a task, the work of staff members should be adequately supervised and reviewed.

Scope of Work.   As described above, the scope of the internal auditors' work should extend beyond accounting and financial controls to include compliance with all types of internal control structure policies and procedures and operational auditing. The IIA's standards in this general section provide more detailed guidance about the appropriate scope of internal auditors' work.

Performance of Audit Work.   The IIA's standards in this category recognize that if audit work is to be effective it must be adequately planned. Guidance is also provided for the internal auditors in collecting and evaluating evidence, communicating the results of the audit, and following up to ascertain that appropriate action is taken on reported audit findings.

Management of the Internal Auditing Department.   This group of standards provides guidance for the director of internal auditing in managing the internal auditing function. The director of internal auditing is responsible for properly managing the department to help assure that (1) the audit work is performed in accordance with professional standards and fulfills the general purposes and responsibilities developed by management of the organization, and (2) the resources of the internal auditing department are efficiently and effectively employed.

## Certification of Internal Auditors

Since 1974, the IIA has administered the **Certified Internal Auditor (CIA)** program. To become certified, a candidate must hold a bachelor's degree from an accredited college, and successfully complete a two-day examination that is offered semiannually in principal cities throughout the world. The examination consists of four parts: internal audit process, internal audit skills, management control and information technology, and the audit environment. Another requirement of certification is at least two years of work experience in internal auditing or its equivalent, although an advanced academic degree may be substituted for one year of work experience in meeting this requirement. Once internal auditors become certified, they must meet requirements for continuing professional education. More information on internal auditing and the CIA examination is available from the Institute of Internal Auditors, 249 Maitland Avenue, Altamonte Springs, Florida 32701.

# OPERATIONAL AUDITING

The term **operational audit** refers to a comprehensive examination of an operating unit or a complete organization to evaluate its performance, as measured by management's objectives. Whereas a *financial audit* focuses on measurement of financial position, results of operations, and cash flows of an entity, an operational audit focuses on the *efficiency, effectiveness,* and *economy* of operations. The operational auditor appraises management's operating controls over such varied activities as purchasing, data processing, receiving, shipping, office services, advertising, and engineering.

## Objectives of Operational Audits

Operational audits often are performed by internal auditors for their organizations. The major users of operational audit reports are managers at various levels, including the board of directors. Top management needs assurances that every component of an organization is working to attain the organization's goals. For example, management needs the following:

1. Assessments of the unit's performance in relation to management's objectives or other appropriate criteria.
2. Assurance that its plans (as set forth in statements of objectives, programs, budgets, and directives) are comprehensive, consistent, and understood at the operating levels.
3. Objective information on how well its plans and policies are being carried out in all areas of operations and on opportunities for improvement in effectiveness, efficiency, and economy.
4. Information on weaknesses in operating controls, particularly as to possible sources of waste.
5. Reassurance that all operating reports can be relied on as a basis for action.

Governmental auditors, such as those employed by the General Accounting Office (GAO), perform operational audits of governmental programs that are administered by both governmental and nongovernmental organizations. Operational auditing is especially applicable to governmental programs where the effectiveness of the programs cannot be evaluated in terms of profits; they must be evaluated by measuring such elements as the number of families relocated, the number of individuals rehabilitated, or the extent of the improvement in environmental conditions. In addition to internal and governmental auditors, CPA firms perform operational audits for clients through their consulting services departments.

## General Approach to Operational Audits

In many respects the auditor's work in performing an operational audit is similar to that of a financial statement audit, but there are some significant differences. The steps may be set forth as: (1) definition of purpose, (2) familiarization, (3) preliminary survey, (4) program development, (5) field work, (6) reporting the findings, and (7) follow-up. The operational audit process is illustrated by Figure 20–2.

### Definition of Purpose.
The broad statement of purpose of an operational audit usually includes the intention to appraise the performance of a particular organization, function, or group of activities. However, this broad statement must be expanded to specify precisely the scope of the audit and the nature of the report. The auditors must determine specifically which policies and procedures are to be appraised and how they relate to the specific objectives of the organization.

### Familiarization.
Before starting an operational audit, the auditors must obtain a comprehensive knowledge of the objectives, organizational structure, and operating characteristics of the unit being audited. This familiarization process might begin with a study of organizational charts, statements of the functions and responsibilities assigned, management policies and directives, and operating policies and procedures. At this stage, the auditors may read some of the published material available on the subject to acquaint

Figure 20–2    The Operational Audit

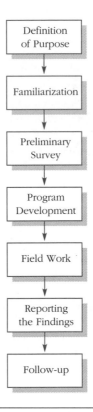

themselves as fully as possible with the functions performed. This background information equips the auditor to visit the organization's facilities and interview supervisory personnel to determine their specific objectives, the standards used to measure accomplishment of these objectives, and the principal problems encountered in achieving these objectives. During these visits, the auditors will also observe the operations and inspect the available records and reports.

In summary, the auditors attempt to familiarize themselves as thoroughly as possible with the function being performed, particularly from the standpoint of administrative responsibility and control. The auditors' understanding of the organization is documented with questionnaires, flowcharts, and written narratives.

Preliminary Survey.   The auditors' preliminary conclusions about the critical aspects of the operations and potential problem areas are summarized as the auditors' preliminary survey. This survey serves as a guide for the development of the audit program.

Program Development.   The operational audit program is tailor-made to the particular engagement. It contains all the tests and analyses the auditors believe are necessary to evaluate the organization's operations. Based on the nature and difficulty of the audit work, appropriate personnel will be assigned to the engagement, and the work will be scheduled.

Field Work.   The field work phase involves executing the operational audit program. The auditors select the items to be reviewed to determine the adequacy of the procedures and how well they are followed. Just as in financial statement audits, the auditors will frequently select representative samples of the transactions from the records and inspect them to determine whether proper procedures have been followed and to discover the nature and extent of the problems encountered. In other cases they may resort to inquiry or direct observation to satisfy themselves that the employees understand their instructions and are carrying out their work as intended.

Analysis is another important part of field work. Actual performance by the organization is compared with various criteria, such as budgets, productivity goals, or performance by similar units. This analysis provides a basis for auditors' recommendations for improvements in effectiveness, efficiency, and economy.

As each phase of the field work is completed, the auditors summarize the results and evaluate the material gathered. Deficiencies which appear to be significant are discussed with the supervisor involved. Frequently, corrective action may be taken at this time, although the primary purpose of this on-the-spot discussion is to make sure that all the relevant facts have been obtained.

Reporting the Findings.   On final completion of the field work, the auditors should summarize their findings related to the basic purposes of the audit. The report will include suggested improvements in the operational policies and procedures of the unit, and a list of situations in which compliance with existing policies and procedures is less than adequate. After they have completed the draft report, they should arrange an exit conference to review the findings with all persons directly concerned with the operations audited. The conference ensures that the auditors have a true and complete story; if there is a question about the facts, further investigation will be made until any doubt is resolved. If a serious disagreement on the interpretation of the facts remains, it is usually best to disclose both interpretations in the report. The conference also provides an opportunity for the affected management to consider and take timely action on the problems disclosed. A formal report, such as the one illustrated by Figure 20–3, is then issued to top management.

Follow-Up.   The final stage in the operational auditors' work is the follow-up action to ensure that any deficiencies disclosed in the audit report are satisfactorily handled. This follow-up responsibility may be given to a line organization or staff group, but most frequently is held to be a responsibility of the audit staff. In some instances, the auditors

Figure 20-3    Introductory Language for an Operational Audit Report

Neal McGregor
Vice President—Operations
Baxter Corporation
Kansas City, Missouri

Dear Mr. McGregor:

In September 19X1 we concluded an operational audit of the data processing operations.

**Objectives, Scope, and Approach**

The general objectives of this engagement, which were more specifically outlined in our letter dated June 30, 19X1, were as follows:

* To document, analyze, and report on the status of current operations
* To identify areas that require attention
* To make recommendations for corrective action or improvements

Our operational audit encompassed the centralized data processing facilities and the on-site computer operations of the company's retailing division. Our evaluations included both the financial and operational conditions of the units. Financial data consulted in the course of our analyses were not audited or reviewed by us, and, accordingly, we do not express an opinion or any other form of assurance on them.

The operational audit involved interviews with management personnel and selected operations personnel in each of the units studied. We also evaluated selected documents, files, reports, systems, procedures, and policies as we considered appropriate. After analyzing the data, we developed recommendations for improvements. We then discussed our findings and recommendations with appropriate unit management personnel, and with you, prior to submitting this written report.

**Findings and Recommendations**

All significant findings are included in this report for your consideration. The recommendations in this report represent, in our judgment, those most likely to bring about improvements to the operations of the organization. The recommendations differ in such aspects as difficulty of implementation, urgency, visibility of benefits, required investment in facilities and equipment or additional personnel. The varying nature of the recommendations, their implementation costs, and their potential impact on operations should be considered in reaching your decisions on courses of action.

(Specific Findings and Recommendations)

---

find it desirable to make brief reexaminations after a reasonable lapse of time to ensure that all significant recommendations have been implemented.

## COMPLIANCE AUDITING

Society has always been concerned with compliance with laws and regulations by all types of organizations. As a result, compliance auditing has evolved to become an important part of the work of both external and internal auditors. **Compliance auditing** involves testing and reporting on whether an organization has complied with the requirements of various laws, regulations, and agreements. Congress and various regulators are adopting compliance auditing requirements for a wide variety of business, governmental, and nonprofit organizations. To provide guidance for these types of engagements, the AICPA has developed an Attestation Standard titled *Compliance Attestation*. This standard provides guidance for the CPAs in performing examinations of an organization's compliance with laws and regulations and in applying agreed-upon procedures to test for compliance. Reviews of compliance with laws and regulations are not permitted.

---

**♦ ILLUSTRATIVE CASE ♦**

The Environmental Protection Agency has issued guidelines for Oxygenated Gasoline Credit Programs under the Clean Air Act, which requires CPAs (or internal auditors) to perform agreed-upon procedures regarding a company's compliance with an EPA regulation that requires the gasoline to contain at least 2 percent oxygen.

---

## Compliance Auditing of Federal Financial Assistance Programs

A major impetus for the demands for increased *compliance auditing* comes from the more than $100 billion that the federal government provides annually in financial assistance through various federal programs. This federal assistance has strings attached; it must be spent in accordance with the programs' requirements. Compliance auditing provides assurances that these requirements have been met.

Federal assistance is primarily given to state and local governmental units, such as cities, counties, states, and school districts. But certain nonprofit and business organizations may also receive federal assistance directly, in the form of grants or awards of cash or other assets. An example is a private university that receives federal education grants from the U.S. Department of Education. A nonprofit or business organization might also be a **subrecipient** of federal assistance *passed through* from a **primary recipient** that receives the assistance directly. For example, a child care facility might be the subrecipient of federal assistance for low-income families from the U.S. Department of Health and Human Services through a program that is administered by a state government agency.

The objectives of compliance auditing procedures are (1) to determine whether there have been violations of laws and regulations that may have a material effect on the organization's financial statements, and (2) to provide a basis for additional reports on compliance.

When performing compliance audits the auditors perform tests of compliance with laws and regulations to determine that violations do not have a *direct* and *material* effect on line-item financial statement amounts. These tests of compliance ("compliance procedures") are *substantive tests*, usually accomplished by examining supporting documents. The scope of these procedures may also be extended to test compliance with other laws and regulations, thereby allowing the auditors to provide additional reports specifically on compliance with laws and regulations.

*SAS 68* (AU 801), "Compliance Auditing Applicable to Governmental Entities and Other Recipients of Governmental Financial Assistance," provides guidance on performing tests of compliance in the following types of audits:

1. Audits of the financial statements of entities receiving federal financial assistance in accordance with generally accepted auditing standards.
2. Audits conducted in accordance with *Government Auditing Standards*.
3. Audits conducted in accordance with the federal Single Audit Act of 1984.

## Audits in Accordance with Generally Accepted Auditing Standards

As discussed in Chapter 2, auditors have a responsibility to design all audits to provide reasonable assurance of detecting material misstatements resulting from violations of laws and regulations that have a *direct and material effect* on line-item amounts in the financial statements. Governmental organizations are subject to a variety of laws and regulations that affect their financial statements—many more than typical business enterprises. An important aspect of generally accepted accounting principles for governmental organizations is the recognition of various legal and contractual requirements. These requirements are reflected in their bases of accounting, fund structure, and other accounting principles. Therefore, in performing an audit of a governmental organization's financial statements, the auditors are more likely to encounter laws and regulations that have a direct and material effect on the amounts in the organization's financial statements.

Governmental organizations receive funds from various sources, including taxes, special assessments, and bond issues. Laws and regulations often dictate the way the funds may be spent. While certain funds may be used for general purposes, others are restricted to specific purposes, such as schools, libraries, or highways. The funds may be restricted even further. For example, a housing program may restrict the disbursement of funds to individuals meeting certain eligibility requirements.

A governmental organization also may receive financial assistance from other governmental organizations in the form of grants, shared revenues, or loans. This financial assistance often is provided only if certain requirements are met. For example, a federal agency may provide financial assistance, but only to the extent that the funds are matched with local funds. These restrictions apply not only to governmental organizations; they may be important considerations in the audit of the financial statements of nonprofit organizations and business enterprises that receive financial assistance.

The auditors perform a number of procedures to identify the laws and regulations that have a direct effect on an organization's financial statements, including (1) discussing laws and regulations with management, program and grant administrators, and government auditors, (2) reviewing relevant grant and loan agreements, and (3) reviewing minutes of the legislative body of the governmental organization. The auditors also obtain written representations from management about the completeness of the laws and regulations identified and an acknowledgment of management's responsibility for compliance with them.

Once the auditors have an understanding of the important laws and regulations, they assess the risks that financial statement amounts might be materially misstated by violations. In making these assessments, the auditors consider the internal control policies and procedures designed to prevent violations, such as policies regarding acceptable operating practices, codes of conduct, and assignment of responsibility for complying with regulatory requirements. These risk assessments are then used to design the nature, timing, and extent of the auditors' substantive tests of compliance.

## Audits in Accordance with Government Auditing Standards

A governmental or nongovernmental organization may engage the auditors to audit its financial statements in accordance with **Government Auditing Standards.** These standards were developed by the General Accounting Office (GAO), and an audit under them is often referred as an audit in accordance with generally accepted governmental auditing standards (GAGAS) or, more commonly, the ''Yellow Book.'' These types of audits are required by law, regulation, or agreement for certain organizations that receive federal financial assistance.

In performing an audit in accordance with *Government Auditing Standards,* the auditors provide two additional reports: one on compliance with laws and regulations, and the other on the organization's internal control structure. To provide these additional reports, the auditors are *not* required to perform audit procedures beyond those required by generally accepted auditing standards. Therefore, in performing an audit in accordance with *Government Auditing Standards,* the auditors perform an audit in accordance with generally accepted auditing standards and issue three reports—an opinion on the organization's financial statements, a report on compliance with applicable laws and regulations, and a report on the organization's internal control structure.

**Reporting on Compliance with Laws and Regulations.**   The compliance report required by *Government Auditing Standards* is based on the auditors' tests of compliance with laws and regulations that have a direct and material effect on the amounts in the financial statements—tests that are required by generally accepted auditing standards. The report expresses positive assurance of compliance with laws and regulations that were tested. On items not tested, the report expresses negative assurance that nothing came to the auditors' attention that caused them to believe that the organization had not complied, in all material respects, with certain provisions of laws, regulations, contracts, and grants. A typical report on compliance with applicable laws and regulations when the auditors' procedures disclose no material violations is illustrated below:

---

The Honorable Mayor and Members of the City Council
City of Rosebud, New Jersey

We have audited the financial statements of the City of Rosebud, New Jersey, as of and for the year ended June 30, 19X1, and have issued our report thereon dated August 15, 19X1.

We conducted our audit in accordance with generally accepted auditing standards and *Government Auditing Standards,* issued by the Comptroller General of the United States. Those standards require that we plan and perform the audit to obtain reasonable assurance about whether the financial statements are free of material misstatement.

Compliance with laws, regulations, contracts, and grants applicable to the City of Rosebud, New Jersey, is the responsibility of the City's management. As part of obtaining reasonable assurance about whether the financial statements are free of material misstatement, we performed tests of the City's compliance with certain provisions of laws, regulations, contracts, and grants. However, the objective of our audit of the financial statements

*(continued)*

---

was not to provide an opinion on overall compliance with such provisions. Accordingly, we do not express such an opinion.

The results of our tests indicate that, with respect to the items tested, the City of Rosebud, New Jersey, complied, in all material respects, with the provisions referred to in the preceding paragraph. With respect to items not tested, nothing came to our attention that caused us to believe that the City of Rosebud, New Jersey, had not complied, in all material respects, with those provisions.

This report is intended for the information of the audit committee, management, and the Office of Federal Revenue Sharing and any other federal or state agencies. However, this report is a matter of public record and its distribution is not limited.

Weldon & Weston, CPAs
August 15, 19X1

The auditors may discover violations of provisions of laws, regulations, contracts, or grants that result in what they estimate to be a material misstatement of the organization's financial statements. Such violations are known as material instances of **noncompliance.** In these circumstances, the auditors must consider the effect on their opinion issued on the financial statements. The resulting misstatement, if left uncorrected, would normally require the auditors to issue a qualified or adverse opinion. Of course, management will usually decide to correct the financial statements, allowing the auditors to issue an unqualified opinion. Even though the financial statements are corrected, the auditors must still modify their report on compliance with laws and regulations and include a description of the material instances of noncompliance.

The auditors should also report a description of any indications of illegal acts that could result in criminal prosecution. Although these violations of laws and regulations may be included in the auditor's report on compliance with laws and regulations, the auditors may instead discharge this responsibility by promptly reporting the illegal act in a separate written report to the organization's audit committee or legislative oversight body. When the illegal act involves funds received from another governmental organization and management does not take appropriate action, the auditors may be required to report the matter to the officials of the other organization.

Reporting on Internal Control Structure.   In an audit in accordance with generally accepted auditing standards, the auditors are required to communicate, orally or in writing, reportable conditions noted during an audit. As discussed in Chapter 8, *reportable conditions* are significant deficiencies in the design or operation of the internal control structure that could adversely affect the organization's ability to report appropriate financial data. When performing an audit in accordance with *Government Auditing Standards,* this report becomes the third required report, and it must be prepared in writing.

There are other differences between the two types of communications. The report under *Government Auditing Standards* includes an identification and discussion of the implications of those reportable conditions that are considered to be *material weaknesses.* It also includes an identification of the categories of the organization's internal control structure. For federal agencies, for example, the internal controls over the disbursements cycle might be subdivided into categories such as grants, loans, payroll, and property and equipment. Other items in the report include (1) an indication that management is responsible for establishing and maintaining the internal control structure, (2) a description of the scope of the auditors' work in obtaining an understanding of the internal control structure and in assessing control risk, and (3) a description of deficiencies in the internal control structure not significant enough to be reportable conditions, or a reference to a separate letter to management that reported these conditions. An example of a report on internal control required by *Government Auditing Standards* is presented below:

---

The Honorable Mayor and Members of the City Council
City of Rosebud, New Jersey

We have audited the financial statements of the City of Rosebud, New Jersey, as of and for the year ended June 30, 19X1, and have issued our report thereon dated August 15, 19X1.

We conducted our audit in accordance with generally accepted auditing standards and *Government Auditing Standards,* issued by the Comptroller General of the United States. Those standards require that we plan and perform the audit to obtain reasonable assurance about whether the financial statements are free of material misstatement.

In planning and performing our audit of the financial statements of the City of Rosebud, New Jersey, for the year ended June 30, 19X1, we considered its internal control structure in order to determine our auditing procedures for the purpose of expressing our opinion on the financial statements and not to provide assurance on the internal control structure.

The management of the City of Rosebud, New Jersey, is responsible for establishing and maintaining an internal control structure. In fulfilling this responsibility, estimates and judgments by management are required to assess the expected benefits and related costs of internal control structure policies and procedures. The objectives of an internal control structure are to provide management with reasonable, but not absolute, assurance that assets are safeguarded against loss from unauthorized use or disposition, and that transactions are executed in accordance with management's authorization and recorded properly to permit the preparation of financial statements in accordance with generally accepted accounting principles. Because of inherent limitations in any internal control structure, errors or irregularities may nevertheless occur and not be detected. Also, projection of any evaluation of the structure to future periods is subject to the risk that procedures may become inadequate because of changes in conditions or that the effectiveness of the design and operation of policies and procedures may deteriorate.

For the purpose of this report, we have classified the significant internal control structure policies and procedures in the following categories: revenue/receipts, purchases/disbursements, and payroll.

For all of the internal control structure categories listed above, we obtained an understanding of the design of relevant policies and procedures and whether they have been placed in operation, and we assessed control risk.

We noted certain matters involving the internal control structure and its operation that we consider to be reportable conditions under standards established by the American Institute of Certified Public Accountants. Reportable conditions involve matters coming to our attention relating to significant deficiencies in the design or operation of the internal control structure

*(continued)*

that, in our judgment, could adversely affect the entity's ability to record, process, summarize, and report financial data consistent with the assertions of management in the financial statements.

1. Although temporary loans between funds are now being reconciled, they are not reconciled on a timely basis. We suggest that the accounting manager reconcile the funds' loans monthly.

2. The computer-prepared revenue, expenditure, and vouchers payable reports are not always reconciled to the general ledger accounts on a timely basis. We recommend that the chief accountant reconcile these reports monthly.

A material weakness is a reportable condition in which the design or operation of the specific internal control structure elements does not reduce to a relatively low level the risk that errors or irregularities in amounts that would be material in relation to the financial statements being audited may occur and not be detected within a timely period by employees in the normal course of performing their assigned functions.

Our consideration of the internal control structure would not necessarily disclose all matters in the internal control structure that might be reportable conditions and, accordingly, would not necessarily disclose all reportable conditions that are also considered to be material weaknesses as defined above. However, we believe none of the reportable conditions described above is a material weakness.

We also noted other matters involving the internal control structure and its operation that we have reported to the management of the City of Rosebud, New Jersey, in a separate letter dated August 15, 19X1.

This report is intended for the information of the audit committee, management, and the Office of Federal Revenue Sharing and any other federal or state agencies. However, it is a matter of public record and its distribution is not limited.

Weldon & Weston, CPAs
August 15, 19X1

## Audits in Accordance with the Single Audit Act

Audits in accordance with the **Single Audit Act of 1984** are specifically designed to help ensure that the billions of dollars in federal financial assistance are appropriately spent. These audits are more extensive than audits of an organization's financial statements in accordance with generally accepted auditing standards. Additional tests of controls and compliance procedures are performed. State or local governments receiving $100,000 or more of federal financial assistance within a fiscal year must be audited in accordance with the Single Audit Act. Those receiving at least $25,000, but less than $100,000, of total federal financial assistance in a year have the option of being audited in accordance with the Single Audit Act or in accordance with federal laws and regulations governing the individual programs in which the organization participates. State or local governments receiving less than $25,000 in federal financial assistance are not required to have a single audit. To assist in implementing the requirements of the Single Audit Act, the Office of Management and Budget (OMB) issued **OMB Circular A-128,** "Audits of State and local Governments."

The Single Audit Act requires an audit of the organization's financial statements and the two additional reports required by an audit in accordance with *Government Auditing*

*Standards*—the report on compliance with laws and regulations and the report on the organization's internal control structure. The Act also requires the auditors to report on the following additional matters:

1. The supplementary schedule of federal financial assistance.
2. Compliance with the general requirements applicable to federal assistance programs.
3. Compliance with specific requirements that may have a material effect on each major federal financial assistance program.
4. Compliance with specific requirements applicable to nonmajor federal financial assistance programs.
5. The internal control structure policies and procedures relevant to federal financial assistance programs.

Reporting on the Schedule of Federal Financial Assistance.  To determine that governmental organizations appropriately account for all financial assistance received, the Single Audit Act requires each organization to submit a schedule of financial assistance program expenditures, accompanied by an auditors' report. The schedule, as illustrated by Figure 20–4, presents the total expenditures for all programs. Since this schedule is considered supplementary information to the organization's financial statements, the auditors' report includes an opinion as to whether the information is presented fairly, in all material respects, in relation to the financial statements taken as a whole.

Compliance Auditing—General Requirements of All Programs.  Under the Single Audit Act, the auditors must perform compliance procedures for the general requirements of all programs. The **general requirements,** which are presented in Figure 20–5, are those that

---

Figure 20–4   Schedule of Federal Financial Assistance

**City of Rosebud, New Jersey**
**Schedule of Federal Financial Assistance**
**For the Year Ended June 30, 19X1**

| Federal Grantor | Federal CFDA Number | Program or Award Amount | Receipts | Disbursements |
|---|---|---|---|---|
| Passed through New Jersey Department of Transportation: | | | | |
| Computer Parking Lot Program . . . . . . . . . . . . | — | $ 808,432 | $ 562,453 | $ 641,941 |
| Department of the Treasury | | | | |
| General Revenue Sharing . . . . . . . . . . . . . . | 21.300 | 483,993 | 483,993 | 483,993 |
| Environmental Protection Agency: | | | | |
| Construction Grant or Wastewater | | | | |
| Treatment Works  . . . . . . . . . . . . . . . . . | 66.418 | 158,700 | — | 30,910 |
| | | $1,451,125 | $1,046,446 | $1,156,844 |

Figure 20–5     General Compliance Requirements

*Political activity*—prohibits the use of federal funds for partisan political activity.

*Davis-Bacon Act*—requires that laborers working on federally financed construction contracts be paid a wage established by the Secretary of Labor.

*Civil rights*—prohibits violation of anyone's civil rights in a program funded by the federal government.

*Cash management*—requires recipients of federal assistance to minimize the time lapse between receipt and disbursement of that assistance.

*Relocation assistance and real property acquisition*—prescribes how real property should be acquired with federal financial assistance and how recipients must help relocate people displaced when that property is acquired.

*Federal financial reports*—prescribes federal financial reports that must be filed.

*Allowable costs/cost principles*—prescribes the direct and indirect costs allowable for federal reimbursement.

*Drug-Free Workplace Act*—prescribes that grantees must certify that they will provide a drug-free workplace.

*Administrative requirements*—prescribes administrative requirements that should be followed.

apply to all or most federal programs and involve significant national policy. While they may or may not have a direct effect on the organization's financial statements, Congress wants assurance that organizations receiving federal financial assistance are complying with these general requirements. The *Compliance Supplement for Single Audits of State and Local Governments,* published by the U.S. Office Of Management and Budget (OMB), provides various procedures for testing general requirements. For example, tests of compliance may be performed on disbursements to assess whether federal funds have been improperly used for partisan political activity. The procedures outlined in the *Compliance Supplement* are generally considered to be adequate to satisfy the requirements of the Act, but the auditors must use professional judgement to determine the extent of the procedures.

Identification of Major Programs.   An important aspect of performing an audit in accordance with the Single Audit Act is identifying the **major federal financial assistance programs.** The auditors must determine and report whether the organization has complied with laws and regulations that may have a material effect on each *major program.* Whether a program is considered major depends on the amount of that program's expenditures for the year in relation to the organization's total expenditures for all federal programs. If the organization's total expenditures for all federal programs are less than or equal to $100 million for the year, a major program is one with expenditures of the larger of $300,000 or 3 percent of the organization's total expenditures. The Single Audit Act contains a sliding scale to determine major programs for organizations with total program expenditures of more than $100 million for the year.

---

◆ ILLUSTRATIVE CASE ◆

The City of Woodruff receives funds through three federal assistance programs and made the following amounts of expenditures from the programs for this year:

| Federal Grantor | Expenditures |
|---|---|
| Department of Treasury<br>  Federal Revenue Sharing | $1,328,776 |
| Department of Transportation<br>  Urban Mass Transportation Administration<br>  Project # RY-04-5676 | 787,900 |
| Department of Housing and Urban Development<br>  Community Development Block Grant<br>  Project # B76-MJ-04-0009 | 119,000 |
| Total expenditures | $2,235,676 |

The first and second programs are major programs for the City of Woodruff this year because the amount of the expenditures for each of these programs is greater than $300,000. (Three percent of total expenditures would be only $67,070.) The third program is referred to as a nonmajor program.

---

Compliance Auditing—Specific Requirements of Major Programs.   Under the Single Audit Act, the auditors must perform compliance procedures for the specific requirements of the major programs. The **specific requirements** that must be audited are those that, if not complied with, could have a material effect on a major program. They usually specify:

1.  The types of goods or services that may be purchased with financial assistance.
2.  The characteristics of individuals or groups to whom the organization may give financial assistance (referred to as eligibility requirements).
3.  Amounts the organization should contribute from its own resources toward projects for which the financial assistance is provided (referred to as matching, level of effort, or earmarking requirements).
4.  Reports the organization must file in addition to those required by the general requirements.

The auditors also perform tests of compliance with other specific requirements for which federal agencies have determined that noncompliance could materially affect a major program. For example, a program may have a deadline for the expenditure of federal financial assistance. In those circumstances, the auditors must perform tests to see that the organization met that deadline.

Designing Compliance Procedures for Major Programs.   The auditors approach a single audit in much the same way they approach an audit in accordance with generally accepted auditing standards. But they must consider the Single Audit Act's additional auditing requirements for individual major federal assistance programs. In performing an audit in accordance with generally accepted auditing standards, the auditors are concerned with compliance with laws and regulations that could have a *direct* and *material* effect on the organization's financial statements. Under the Single Audit Act, the auditors also are concerned with compliance with laws and regulations that could have a *material* effect on each major federal assistance program. Because it must be considered on a program-by-program basis, materiality for planning the compliance procedures will typically be much less. An amount that is material to one major federal assistance program may not be material to a major program of a different size or nature. This lower level of planning materiality results in an increase in the extent of the compliance auditing procedures.

In designing the compliance procedures, the auditors first assess the risk of material noncompliance with laws and regulations applicable to each major program by considering various factors, such as the amount of the program expenditures and any changes made in the program. The auditors then assess the *control risk* related to the organization's administration of the programs. The Single Audit Act requires a review of the internal control systems used in managing federal assistance programs. As a part of this review, *the auditors must test whether the system is functioning as it is designed* and examine the organization's procedures for monitoring expenditures made by any subrecipients.

Based on the auditors' assessments of the risks of material noncompliance and the related levels of control risk, the auditors design sufficient substantive procedures to test each major program for compliance with applicable laws and regulations. To assist the auditors in designing these procedures, the **Compliance Supplement** specifies requirements and suggested audit procedures for a large number of federal assistance programs. For those programs not included in the *Compliance Supplement,* the auditors may determine the significant specific requirements to be tested by (1) considering knowledge obtained from prior years' audits, (2) discussing laws and regulations with management, lawyers, program administrators, or federal, state, and local auditors, or (3) reviewing grant and loan agreements.

Evaluating the Results of Compliance Procedures of Major Programs.   In evaluating whether an entity's noncompliance is material to a major program, the auditors should consider the frequency of noncompliance, and whether it results in a material amount of questioned costs. A **questioned cost** is an expenditure that is not allowed by the requirements of the program, not adequately supported with documentation, unnecessary, or unreasonable. An example of a questioned cost is an expenditure of financial assistance to an individual who does not meet the eligibility requirements of the program. In evaluating the effect of the questioned cost on their reports, the auditors not only consider the actual amount, but also develop an estimate of the total amount of the questioned costs. Thus, when the auditors use audit sampling to select expenditures for testing, they consider the *projected amount* of questioned costs from the sample, as discussed in Chapters 10 and 11.

Regardless of whether this estimated total questioned cost is material enough to affect the auditors' opinion on compliance, the Single Audit Act requires the auditors to report any instances of noncompliance found and the resulting amounts of questioned costs. The auditors report these in a Schedule of Findings and Questioned Costs, such as the example in Figure 20–6.

Compliance Auditing—Specific Requirements of Nonmajor Programs.   The auditors are not specifically required to select transactions from **nonmajor federal financial assistance programs** for compliance testing. However, in connection with the audit of the financial statements or the testing of internal controls over major programs, the auditors will often select transactions from nonmajor programs. In a single audit, the auditors must test those selected transactions for compliance with the specific requirements applicable to the transactions, such as the allowability of the expenditure or the eligibility of the individuals or groups given the assistance. For example, when the auditors are testing the internal controls over disbursements for assistance given by a legal aid society, they may select a disbursement made under a nonmajor assistance program. In addition to the normal tests of controls, the auditors should also test whether the individual given the assistance meets the eligibility requirements of the nonmajor program.

Reporting on Compliance.   In a single audit, the auditors issue three additional compliance reports—one on general requirements, one on specific requirements of major programs, and one on specific requirements of nonmajor programs.

---

Figure 20–6   Schedule of Findings and Questioned Costs

**City of Waxville, Washington**
**Schedule of Findings and Questioned Costs**
**April 30, 19X1**

| Program | Finding/Noncompliance | Questioned Cost |
|---|---|---|
| Community Development Block Grant—Small Cities Program | | |
| 1. Grant No. 85-C-7061 Project No. C-1 CFDA No. 14.219 | Approximately $1,800 was expended for the payment of individual homeowners' property taxes and fire insurance. These are not allowable costs. The City intends to repay HUD for these costs. | $ 1,800 |
| 2. Grant No. 85-C-7071 Project No. C-1 CFDA No. 14.219 | A request for reimbursement of funds was in excess of the actual documented expenditures. The City intends to repay HUD for these costs. | 41,060 |
| | | $42,860 |

**Reporting on Compliance with General Requirements.**   As described above, the Single Audit Act requires the auditors to perform compliance procedures for the general requirements included in Figure 20–5. The auditors' report on compliance with the general requirements expresses positive assurance on items tested and negative assurance on the items not tested.

**Reporting on Compliance with Specific Requirements.**   The report on compliance with the specific requirements applicable to the major programs expresses an opinion as to whether the entity complied, in all material respects, with the specific requirements that are material to those programs. The auditors express an unqualified compliance report only if they are able to apply all the compliance procedures considered necessary in the circumstances. Restrictions on the scope of the audit may require the auditors to qualify their opinion or to disclaim an opinion. In such circumstances, the reasons for the qualification or disclaimer of opinion should be described in the report.

When the auditors detect noncompliance with specific requirements that have a material effect on a major federal financial assistance program, they should express a qualified or adverse opinion. The auditors should describe in their report the reasons for the qualified or adverse opinion.

**Reporting on Nonmajor Programs.**   The auditors' report on compliance with laws and regulations applicable to the nonmajor programs is based on the compliance tests of transactions selected for other purposes. As indicated above, the auditors are not required to select transactions specifically to test compliance with the requirements applicable to nonmajor programs. Accordingly, the auditors' report includes a statement of positive assurance that, with respect to the items tested, the results of their procedures disclosed no material instances of noncompliance with the specific requirements identified. It also includes a statement of negative assurance that, with respect to items not tested, nothing came to the auditors' attention that caused them to believe that the organization had not complied, in all material respects, with the specific requirements identified.

**Reporting on Internal Controls Relevant to Federal Financial Assistance Programs.**   The Single Audit Act requires the auditors to determine and report whether the organization has internal control systems that provide reasonable assurance that it is managing federal financial assistance programs in accordance with applicable laws and regulations. To meet this requirement the auditors must (1) obtain an understanding of the internal control systems used to administer the programs, and (2) perform tests of controls to determine whether the systems are operating effectively. If the organization passes a significant amount of the financial assistance through to subrecipients, the auditors must include in their evaluation the organization's internal controls for monitoring subrecipients and obtaining and acting on subrecipient audit reports.

The report on internal control relevant to federal financial assistance programs does not include an opinion on the internal control systems. It is similar to the internal control report required under *Government Auditing Standards* that is illustrated on pages 703–4. In fact, the two reports are often combined by adding to that report an indication of the additional tests performed on the internal controls relevant to federal financial assistance programs and the related findings.

## Compliance Auditing of Nonprofit Organizations

As discussed above, nonprofit organizations may be required by law, regulation, or agreement to have an audit in accordance with generally accepted auditing standards or *Government Auditing Standards*. In 1990, the Office of Management and Budget issued **OMB Circular A-133,** "Audits of Institutions of Higher Education and Other Nonprofit Institutions." It provides guidance for implementing a single audit concept for nonprofit organizations that receive federal financial assistance. The requirements of *Circular A-133* are similar to those for single audits of state and local governments as described above. Currently, many nonprofit organizations are required to have a single audit in accordance with this circular.

## Compliance Auditing—A Summary

The auditors' compliance auditing and reporting requirements are summarized in Figure 20–7. Notice that the requirements build on each other. An audit in accordance with *Government Auditing Standards* includes the requirements of generally accepted auditing standards, and a single audit includes the requirements of both of the other two types of audits.

## ◆ CHAPTER SUMMARY

This chapter described internal, operational, and compliance auditing. To summarize:

1. Internal auditing has been defined by the Institute of Internal Auditors (IIA) as an appraisal activity established within an organization as a service to the organization. It is a managerial control, which functions by measuring and evaluating the effectiveness of other controls. The IIA's professional standards encompass internal auditor independence, professional proficiency, appropriate scope of services, performance of audit work, and the management of the internal auditing department.

2. An operational audit is the examination of an operating unit or a complete organization to evaluate its performance, as measured by management's objectives. The stages of an operational audit might be summarized as definition of purpose, familiarization, preliminary survey, program development, field work, reporting the findings, and follow-up.

3. The objectives of compliance auditing are *(a)* to determine whether there have been violations of laws and regulations that may have a material effect on the organization's financial statements, and *(b)* to provide a basis for additional reports on compliance. Compliance auditing is involved in *(a)* audits of the financial statements in accordance with generally accepted auditing standards, *(b)* audits conducted in accordance with *Government Auditing Standards,* and *(c)* audits conducted in accordance with the federal Single Audit Act of 1984 or *OMB Circular A-133.*

4. Audits of governmental organizations in accordance with generally accepted auditing standards must reflect the fact that such organizations are subject to a variety of laws and regulations that may have a direct and material effect on the amounts in the organization's financial statements.

Figure 20–7    Auditing and Reporting on Compliance with Laws and Regulations—A Summary

**Audit in Accordance with GAAS**

**Procedures Performed**
* Audit procedures required by GAAS, including tests of compliance with laws and regulations having a direct and material effect on line-item amounts in the financial statements

**Report Issued**
* Opinion on financial statements

**Audit in Accordance with Government Auditing Standards**

**Procedures Performed**
* Same as GAAS

**Reports Issued**
* Opinion on financial statements
* Report on compliance with applicable laws and regulations, including a description of material instances of noncompliance found and all illegal acts that could result in criminal prosecution
* Report on the organization's internal control structure

**Audit in Accordance with the Single Audit Act**

**Procedures Performed**
* Same as GAAS, plus:
    * Tests of compliance with the general requirements, the specific requirements applicable to major federal financial programs, and the specific requirements for transactions from nonmajor programs selected for other audit tests
    * Tests of the internal control systems used in administering federal assistance programs

**Reports Issued**
* Same as *Government Auditing Standards,* plus:
    * Report on schedule of financial assistance received
    * Report on compliance with the general requirements applicable to federal programs
    * Report on compliance applicable to major federal programs
    * Report on compliance applicable to nonmajor federal program transactions tested
    * Report of findings and questioned costs
    * Report on internal control systems used in administering federal assistance programs

5.  Audits in accordance with government auditing standards result in a report on the financial statements, a report on compliance with laws and regulations, and a report on the internal control structure.

6.  Audits in conformity with the Single Audit Act of 1984 or *OMB Circular A-133* are specifically designed to help ensure that the billions of dollars in federal financial assistance are appropriately spent. The focus of these audits is on organizations receiving $100,000 or more in federal assistance in a year. The auditors are required to report on general and specific requirements of programs for which federal assistance has been received.

# ◆ KEY TERMS INTRODUCED OR EMPHASIZED IN CHAPTER 20

**Certified Internal Auditor**   An individual who has passed an examination administered by the IIA and has met the experience requirements necessary to be certified.

**Compliance auditing**   Performing procedures to test compliance with laws and regulations.

**Compliance Supplements**   Publications of the U.S. Office of Management and Budget that specify audit procedures for federal financial assistance programs. There is a compliance supplement for state and local governments and one for institutions of higher education and other nonprofit institutions.

**General requirements**   Requirements involving significant national policy that apply to all or most federal financial assistance programs.

**Government Auditing Standards**   Standards issued by the U.S. General Accounting Office as the *Standards for Audit of Governmental Organizations, Programs, Activities, and Functions*, commonly referred to as the "Yellow Book."

**Institute of Internal Auditors (IIA)**   The international professional organization of internal auditors.

**Internal auditing**   An independent appraisal activity established within an organization as a service to the organization. It is a control that functions by examining and evaluating the adequacy and effectiveness of other controls.

**Major federal financial assistance program (award)**   Any program or award with expenditures in excess of the amounts specified by the Single Audit Act for governmental organizations, or by *OMB Circular A-133* for colleges, universities, and other nonprofit institutions.

**Noncompliance**   The failure to act in accordance with laws or regulations.

**Nonmajor federal financial assistance program (award)**   Any program or award that does not meet the criteria to be classified as a major program or award.

**OMB Circular A-128**   A publication of the U.S. Office of Management and Budget, titled "Audits of State and Local Governments," that provides guidance in implementing the Single Audit Act of 1984.

**OMB Circular A-133**   A publication of the U.S. Office of Management and Budget, titled "Audits of Institutions of Higher Education and Other Nonprofit Institutions," that establishes audit requirements for these organizations that are similar to those required for governmental organizations under the Single Audit Act of 1984.

**Operational auditing**   The process of reviewing a department or other unit of a business, governmental, or nonprofit organization to measure the effectiveness, efficiency, and economy of operations.

**Primary recipient**   An organization receiving federal financial assistance directly from the federal agency administering the program.

**Questioned costs**   Those costs paid with federal assistance that appear to be in violation of a law or regulation, inadequately documented, unnecessary, or unreasonable in amount.

**Single Audit Act of 1984**   Legislation passed by U.S. Congress that establishes uniform requirements for audits of federal financial assistance provided to state and local governments.

**Specific requirements**   Requirements that are specific to particular federal financial assistance programs and have a material effect on those programs. These requirements generally pertain to types of services allowed, eligibility, matching, reporting, and other special tests and provisions.

**Subrecipient**   An organization receiving federal financial assistance passed through from another organization.

# ◆ GROUP I: REVIEW QUESTIONS

20-1   Describe the objectives of an internal auditing function.

20-2   Define internal auditing.

20-3   "The principal distinction between public accounting and internal auditing is that the latter activity is carried on by an organization's own salaried employees rather than by independent professional auditors." Criticize this quotation.

20-4   Describe the requirements for becoming a Certified Internal Auditor.

20-5   Evaluate this statement: "Internal auditors cannot be independent of the activities that they audit."

20-6   Describe how the organizational status of the internal audit department affects its independence.

20-7   Identify the knowledge and skills that are necessary to the performance of modern internal auditing.

20-8   Identify the five general categories of the IIA's *Standards for the Professional Practice of Internal Auditing*.

20-9   Briefly describe the factors that are important to the management of an internal auditing department.

20-10   Nearly every large corporation now maintains an internal auditing department, but 50 years ago relatively few companies carried on a formal program of internal auditing. What have been the principal factors responsible for this rapid expansion?

20-11   Compare the objectives of internal auditors with those of external auditors.

20-12   Differentiate between financial statement audits and operational audits.

20-13   Describe the purpose of an operational audit.

20-14   Should the internal auditors generally disclose their findings to operating personnel of the department involved before transmitting the report to top management? Explain.

20-15   Explain the auditors' responsibility for testing compliance with laws and regulations in an audit in accordance with generally accepted auditing standards.

20-16   Identify the three types of audits that a governmental organization might obtain.

20-17   "In an audit in accordance with *Government Auditing Standards* the auditors must perform tests of compliance with all laws and regulations." Criticize this quotation.

20-18   Contrast the requirements of an audit in accordance with *Government Auditing Standards* with the requirements of an audit in accordance with generally accepted auditing standards.

20-19   Explain why compliance with laws and regulations is so important in the audit of governmental organizations.

20-20   What is the purpose of the Single Audit Act of 1984?

20-21   When is a governmental organization required to have an audit in accordance with the Single Audit Act of 1984?

20-22   Distinguish between general and specific requirements of federal financial assistance programs.

20-23   Explain how major federal financial assistance programs are identified.

20-24   Describe what is meant by a *questioned cost*.

20-25   Distinguish between a subrecipient and a primary recipient. Provide an example of each.

20-26   Identify the nine general requirements that are applicable to most federal financial assistance programs.

20-27   Explain why tests of compliance with laws and regulations are considered to be substantive tests.

20-28   Describe the two additional audit reports required by *Government Auditing Standards*.

20-29   The auditors' responsibility for reporting violations of laws and regulations under *Government Auditing Standards* differs from their responsibility under generally accepted auditing standards. Compare these responsibilities.

## ◆ GROUP II: QUESTIONS REQUIRING ANALYSIS

20-30   In order to function effectively, the internal auditor must often educate auditees and other parties about the nature and purpose of internal auditing.

*Required:*   *a.*   Define internal auditing.
              *b.*   Briefly describe three possible benefits of an internal audit department's program to educate auditees and other parties about the nature and purpose of internal auditing.

(CIA, adapted)

20-31   Steve Ankenbrandt, president of Beeb Corp., has been discussing the company's internal operations with the presidents of several other multidivision companies. Ankenbrandt discovered that most of them have an internal audit staff. The activities of the staffs at other companies include financial audits, operational audits, and sometimes compliance audits.

*Required:*   Describe the meaning of the following terms as they relate to the internal auditing function:
              *a.*   Financial auditing.
              *b.*   Operational auditing.
              *c.*   Compliance auditing.

(CIA, adapted)

20-32   Throughout this book emphasis has been placed on the concept of independence as the most significant single element underlying the development of the public accounting profession. The term "independent auditor" is sometimes used to distinguish the public accountant from an internal auditor. Nevertheless, the Institute of Internal Auditors points to the factor of independence as essential to an effective program of internal auditing. Distinguish between the meaning of *independence* as used by the American Institute of Certified Public Accountants in describing the function of the certified public accountant and the meaning of *independence* as used by the Institute of Internal Auditors to describe the work of the internal auditor.

20-33   You are conducting the first audit of the marketing activities of your organization. Your preliminary survey has disclosed indications of deficient conditions of a serious nature. You expect your audit work to document the need for substantial corrective action. You feel certain that your audit report will contain descriptions of a number of serious defects.

Your preliminary meeting with the director of the marketing division and the principal subordinates gave you reason to believe that they will be defensive, that your audit report will receive a chilly reception, that your stated facts are likely to be challenged, and that any deficient conditions reported will be denied or minimized.

*Required:*   *a.*   Identify those aspects of the *Standards for the Professional Practice of Internal Auditing* that apply to the problems described above.

*b.*   Describe four techniques that you might use to improve the chances that your report will be well received and that appropriate corrective action will be taken.

(CIA, adapted)

20-34   Carol Warren, CPA, is performing an audit of the City of Ryan in accordance with generally accepted auditing standards.

*Required:*   *a.*   Must Carol be concerned with the city's compliance with laws and regulations? Explain.

*b.*   How should Carol decide on the nature and extent of the tests of compliance that should be performed in the audit?

20-35   Wixon & Co., CPAs, are performing an audit of the City of Brummet for the year ended June 30, 199X, in accordance with *Government Auditing Standards*. During the course of the audit Gerald Yarnell, a senior auditor, discovers violations of laws and regulations that constitute material instances of noncompliance.

*Required:*   *a.*   Explain how these violations may affect the auditors' reports.

*b.*   How would your answer to *a* change if management elected to correct the financial statements for the violations?

20-36   North County School District received $1,450,000 in federal financial assistance this year.

*Required:*   *a.*   Is North County School District required to have an audit in accordance with the Single Audit Act? Explain.

*b.*   What are the requirements of an audit in accordance with the Single Audit Act?

20-37   The City of Westmore is confused about the type of audit that it should obtain: an audit in accordance with generally accepted auditing standards, an audit in accordance with *Government Auditing Standards,* or an audit in accordance with the Single Audit Act.

*Required:*   *a.*   Explain the differences between the three types of audits.

*b.*   How should the City of Westmore decide which type of audit they are required to obtain?

20-38   Select the best answer for each of the following questions. Explain the reasons for your selection.

*a.*   Internal auditing can best be described as:

(1)   An accounting function.

(2)   A compliance function.

(3)   An activity primarily to detect fraud.

(4)   A control function.

(CIA, adapted)

*b.*   The independence of the internal auditing department will most likely be assured if it reports to the:

    (1)   Audit committee of the board of directors.

    (2)   President.

    (3)   Controller.

    (4)   Treasurer.

(CIA, adapted)

*c.*  When performing an operational audit, the purpose of a preliminary survey is to:

    (1)   Determine the objective of the activity to be audited.

    (2)   Determine the scope of the audit.

    (3)   Identify areas that should be included in the audit program.

    (4)   All of the above.

(CIA, adapted)

*d.*  Operational auditing is primarily oriented toward:

    (1)   Future improvements to accomplish the goals of management.

    (2)   Ensuring the accuracy of the data in management's financial reports.

    (3)   Determination of the fairness of the entity's financial statements.

    (4)   Compliance with laws and regulations.

*e.*  Which of the following bodies promulgates standards for audits of federal financial assistance programs?

    (1)   Governmental Accounting Standards Board.

    (2)   Financial Accounting Standards Board.

    (3)   General Accounting Office.

    (4)   Governmental Auditing Standards Board.

(AICPA, adapted)

*f.*  As compared to an audit in accordance with GAAS, an audit in accordance with *Government Auditing Standards* requires the auditors to:

    (1)   Perform additional compliance auditing procedures.

    (2)   Perform additional tests of the internal control structure.

    (3)   Issue additional reports on compliance with laws and regulations and the internal control structure.

    (4)   Fulfill all of the above requirements.

## ◆ GROUP III: PROBLEMS

20-39   You are the director of internal auditing of a large municipal hospital. You receive monthly financial reports prepared by the accounting department, and your review of them has shown that total accounts receivable from patients have steadily and rapidly increased over the past eight months.

    Other information in the reports shows the following conditions:

1.   The number of available hospital beds has not changed.

2.   The bed occupancy rate has not changed.

3.   Hospital billing rates have not changed significantly.

4.   The hospitalization insurance contracts have not changed since the last modification 12 months ago.

    Your internal audit department performed a financial and operational audit of the accounts receivable accounting function ten months ago. The working paper file for that assignment contains financial information, a record of the preliminary survey, documentation of the study, evaluation of internal controls, documentation of the procedures used to produce evidence about the validity and collectibility of the accounts, and a copy of your report that commented favorably on the controls and collectibility of the receivables.

However, the current increase in receivables has alerted you to the need for another audit. You remember news stories last year about the manager of the city water system who got into big trouble because his accounting department double-billed all the residential customers for three months. You plan to perform a preliminary survey of the problem, if indeed a problem exists.

*Required:*  a.  Write a memo to your senior auditor listing at least eight questions that should be used to guide and direct the preliminary survey. (Hint: The categories of questions used in the last preliminary survey were these: "Who does the accounts receivable accounting?" "What data processing procedures and policies are in effect?" and "How is the accounts receivable accounting done?" This time, you will use these categories and add a fourth category of questions: "What financial or economic events have occurred in the past 10 months?")

b.  Describe the phases of the audit that would be performed after the preliminary survey is completed.

(CIA, adapted)

20-40  In performing an audit in accordance with *Government Auditing Standards,* the auditors are required to issue two additional reports, one on compliance with laws and regulations and one on internal control.

*Required:*  a.  Describe the nature of the procedures that the auditors must perform beyond those required by generally accepted auditing standards to provide a basis for these reports.

b.  Describe the specific contents of the auditors' compliance report.

c.  Describe the specific contents of the auditors' report on internal control.

20-41  In performing an audit in accordance with both generally accepted auditing standards and *Government Auditing Standards,* the auditors are required to communicate information about weaknesses in the organization's internal control structure policies and procedures. However, the requirements are different.

*Required:*  a.  Describe the differences between these requirements.

b.  Describe the major aspects of the report on internal control structure required by *Government Auditing Standards.*

20-42  In an audit in accordance with the Single Audit Act, the auditors must test compliance with both specific and general requirements of federal assistance programs.

*Required:*  a.  Describe the nature of the specific requirements of federal financial assistance programs.

b.  Describe the general requirements that must be tested for compliance.

c.  Explain the difference between the auditors' report on compliance with specific requirements and their report on compliance with general requirements.

20-43  Robert Myers, CPA, has been engaged to audit the City of Mystic in accordance with the Single Audit Act. Robert is aware that the Single Audit Act requires additional tests of major federal financial assistance programs, and he is trying to identify those programs for this audit. The City of Mystic participates in four federal financial assistance programs with the following amounts of expenditures for the year.

| **Grant Program** | **Expenditures** |
|---|---|
| Office of Federal Revenue Sharing 199X Entitlement | $ 2,370,000 |
| Environmental Protection Agency Ford Creek Modification | 6,780,000 |
| Department of Housing and Urban Development | |
|     Project # C94-MC-08-0009 | 5,500,000 |
|     Project # C94-MC-08-0010 | 350,000 |
| Total Grant Awards | $15,000,000 |

*Required:*   *a.*   Identify the major federal assistance programs.

*b.*   Describe the compliance testing requirements for major federal financial assistance programs under the Single Audit Act.

20-44   You have been engaged by the County of Rancho Costa to perform an audit in accordance with *Government Auditing Standards*. Randall Young, a new assistant, has drafted the following report on compliance with laws and regulations.

---

The Honorable Ronald Myran, Chairman
Board of County Commissioners
Rancho Costa County

We have audited the financial statements of Rancho Costa County, as of and for the year ended June 30, 19X1, and have issued our report thereon dated August 21, 19X1.

We conducted our audit in accordance with generally accepted auditing standards and *Government Auditing Standards* issued by the Controller General of the United States. Those standards require that we plan and perform the audit to obtain reasonable assurance that the county has not violated significant laws and regulations.

The results of our tests indicate that Rancho Costa County complied with all significant laws and regulations.

---

*Required:*   List and explain the deficiencies and omissions in the report and explain how it might be corrected. Organize your answer as follows:

| *Deficiency or Omission* | *Correction* |
| --- | --- |
| | |

# INDEX

◆